THE DEVELOPME
OF THE
ANGLICAN LITUR
1662–1980

Also by R C D Jasper

Companion to the Alternative Service Book
(with Paul E Bradshaw)

The Development of the Anglican Liturgy

——1662–1980——

R C D JASPER

SPCK

First published in Great Britain 1989
SPCK
Holy Trinity Church
Marylebone Road
London NW1 4DU

British Library Cataloguing in Publication Data

Jasper, Ronald C. D. (Ronald Claud Dudley), *1917–*
The development of the Anglican liturgy, 1662–1980.
1. Church of England. Public worship
I. Title
264′.03

ISBN 0-281-04441-4

Typeset by Pioneer Associates, Perthshire
Printed in Great Britain at
University Press, Cambridge

Contents

Introduction

This book is like Topsy – it has 'just growed'. My original intention was to put together, simply for the record, a personal account of the two decades of liturgical revision in this country, in the hope that it might prove useful and interesting. Friends and colleagues suggested that I should do so, because I had been more closely involved in the operation than anyone else. I had been a foundation member of the Liturgical Commission and the only one to remain until the appearance of the Alternative Service Book in 1980, serving as its chairman for the last fifteen years. Indeed, throughout the whole twenty-five years I missed only one meeting of the Commission – and that was because I had an accident while actually on my way to it. Furthermore I also had a large hand in creating and running two other associated bodies, the Joint Liturgical Group and the International Consultation on English Texts. Mine had therefore been quite a unique experience.

But once I began to sort out my thoughts, I realized the need to put these years of revision into context. This led me back, first to the abortive revision of 1927–8, and then to the nineteenth century, an era which had always interested me greatly. Finally I decided to go back even further and take a broad look at the whole period 1662 to 1980, tracing events and pressures which led from the uniformity of the Book of Common Prayer to the relative flexibility of the Alternative Service Book. In doing this I have divided the book into two parts. The first eight chapters deal with events up to the creation of the Liturgical Commission in 1955. The remaining seven chapters, which bring the study down to 1980 are autobiographical, because that seemed to me to be the most convenient way of writing them. I must emphasize, it is my personal view of events. Others may see them rather differently. If that be the case, I hope that what I have written may provoke or inspire them into recording their own impressions. This will certainly help some future historian or liturgist to produce a much more objective account of this massive and complicated operation.

Quite a lot of material already exists in print. Apart from the Reports and Proceedings of the Convocations, the Church Assembly and the General Synod, together with a sizeable number of booklets and articles, Colin Buchanan, former Bishop of Aston, has produced three books on Anglican Eucharistic Liturgies, innumerable Grove Liturgical Studies and his regular *News of Liturgy*. His industry has been truly amazing and I am greatly indebted to his writings. Geoffrey Cuming was also of great help, not least by his addition of a further chapter in the second edition of his *A History of Anglican Liturgy*, bringing the story down to 1980. Only in 1987 he and I discussed the possibilities of doing another joint piece of work on the twentieth century: but his sudden lamented death put paid to these hopes. I would like to record here how much I valued his help and friendship over the years, both as Vice-Chairman of the Commission and as my colleague in the laborious and exacting job of putting the text of the Alternative Service Book together and seeing it through the press. We were very much on the same wavelength, we enjoyed one another's company and I can only say that now I miss him very much. It would, however, be invidious not to pay tribute to all the members of the Liturgical Commission. They were a delightful team; they taught me a great deal; and I was grateful for all their help and friendship. Nor must I forget the secretarial staff – particularly Barbara Ebdale and Pamela Aldwinckle, without whose prodigious and immaculate typing the Alternative Service Book would never have been published on time.

In the more immediate task of deciphering my handwriting and typing the manuscript of this book I would like to thank two ladies, Marie Carrington and Gillian Steer. The publishing staff of SPCK have been patience and kindness itself. Two other factors have also been a great asset during the years of writing – cheerfulness and love – and both of these came in abundance from my wife.

R C D Jasper
Ripon, 1989

PART ONE

1662–1955

1

1662 AND THE EIGHTEENTH CENTURY

I

The 1662 Book of Common Prayer was a compromise fulfilling neither Laudian nor Presbyterian expectations. So its Preface states: 'Our general aim . . . was not to gratify this or that party in any of their unreasonable demands; but to do that which . . . might most tend to the preservation of peace and unity in the Church.' What then were the demands made by 'this or that party', and how far were they considered 'unreasonable'?

The Restoration indicated that for the great mass of English people the Puritan way of life had been tried and found wanting. Charles II returned, not as the result of a royalist coup, but at the invitation of Parliament, which was substantially Presbyterian. Caution was therefore necessary; and Charles' intentions, as expressed in the Declaration of Breda (4 April 1660), were reassuring. There was to be, among other things, indemnity for the past and toleration for the future; and he would agree to whatever Parliament should propose on these matters.[1] His actions after returning to this country were equally reassuring. While displaced clergy were repossessed of their livings, leading Presbyterians were appointed as royal chaplains and some were invited to preach at Court. Furthermore his Worcester House Declaration concerning Ecclesiastical Affairs of 25 October 1660, with its concessions to Puritanism and its recognition of Calvinistic principles, suggested a possible future broadly-based Church, comprehending moderate Anglicans, Presbyterians and even some Independents. The Declaration went on to say that while he considered the Prayer Book liturgy 'the best we have seen', because exception was taken to certain things in it, he would appoint an equal number of divines of both persuasions to review it and make such additions and alterations as were thought necessary. Meanwhile, although some ministers might dislike some elements, it was his wish that they should not totally lay aside the Prayer Book, but use such parts against which there could be no exception; and kneeling for communion, the use of the cross in baptism, bowing at the name of Jesus, and the use of the surplice would not be regarded as compulsory.[2] In conformity with this Declaration, the King appointed on 25 March 1661 twelve bishops and twelve Puritan divines with nine assessors on each side to meet at the Master's lodgings in the Savoy to examine the Book of Common Prayer: 'and if occasion be, to make such reasonable and necessary alterations, corrections, and amendments therein as by and between you . . . shall be agreed upon to be needful or expedient; . . . but avoiding, as much as may be, all unnecessary abbreviations of the forms and liturgy, wherewith the people are already acquainted and have so long received in the Church of England.'[3]

The personnel of the two groups was interesting. The bishops were for the most part moderate in outlook, desiring a return to the 1604 Prayer Book with a minimum of change. Their nominal leader was Accepted Frewen, Archbishop of York, a veteran of the pre-Commonwealth episcopal bench; but on account of his great age, the lead was effectively taken by Gilbert Sheldon, Bishop of London. He was a staunch supporter of Clarendon, believing that the interests of the established Church and the state coincided; but their well-being was to be secured, not by concessions to the Puritans but by ensuring that they fell into line. He had little interest in liturgy and his theological outlook was latitudinarian; supported by Morley of Worcester, Sanderson of Lincoln, Henchman of Salisbury, Nicholson of Gloucester, Skinner of Oxford and Warner of Rochester, he commanded a safe majority among the bishops. Liturgical interests, represented by John Cosin, the Laudian Bishop of Durham, were in a decided minority. The Presbyterians were led by Edward Reynolds, a former member of the Westminster Assembly and the first Puritan Vice-Chancellor of the University of Oxford: he was a conformist who was ready for reconciliation with the Anglicans and had in fact already accepted the see of Norwich. He was strongly supported by Edmund Calamy and Richard Baxter. Calamy was also prepared to come to terms with the Anglicans, although he had refused the see of Lichfield. Baxter too was a champion of moderation, who had worked for the return of the king, but who felt unable to accept the see of Hereford: he was certainly the most able liturgist among the Presbyterians.

The Laudian pattern for revision was set out in *The Durham Book*, a folio copy of the Prayer Book printed in 1619 with notes and amendments inserted by Cosin and his chaplain, William Sancroft, in 1660–1. These were clearly influenced by the Scottish Liturgy of 1637[4] and indicated a desire to move towards the first Prayer Book of 1549. The most distinctive features were:

A. The Communion Service

1. The inclusion of a rubric providing for an oblation of the elements at the offertory.
2. The Prayer for the Church described the congregation as 'here assembled in thy Name to celebrate the Commemoration of the most precious death and sacrifice of thy Son and our Saviour Jesus Christ': and it included a commemoration of the faithful departed and the saints.
3. The Prayer of Consecration added a reference to the sacrifice of Christ — 'a perpetual memory of that his precious death and sacrifice': it included an epiclesis before the Institution Narrative: and it concluded with the 1549 Prayer of Oblation, followed by the Lord's Prayer.
4. The Prayer of Humble Access was inserted before Communion, and Agnus Dei was to be sung during Communion.

5. In the final prayers, the memorial of Christ's passion, resurrection and ascension were 'now represented' to God.
6. Rubrics provided for the veiling of the elements, a form of reconsecration, and the permissive use of wafer bread.

B. The Baptism Service
Provision was made for the blessing of the water.

C. The Catechism
The duty towards God included 'to honour and worship him with the outward reverence of my body' — a reference to bowing to the altar, a practice to which the Puritans took grave exception.

D. The Confirmation Service
A rubric directed Confirmation to be administered at the Lord's Table.[5]

The Puritan views were expressed in two documents. The first was *Exceptions against the Book of Common Prayer*, presented to the Savoy Conference on 4 May at the request of Bishop Sheldon. These Exceptions were arranged in two groups — the first containing eighteen general objections to principles and characteristics of the Prayer Book, and the second containing over seventy criticisms of particular details. Their aim was a comprehensive, scriptural liturgy, doctrinally acceptable to all Protestants, and sufficiently flexible to give ministers freedom in the conduct of worship and the leading of prayer. They preferred a single continuous prayer to a series of collects, which were too short and abrupt; and since the minister was the mouthpiece of the people, the vocal contribution of the latter should be confined to 'Amen'. They also objected to the observance of Lent and Saints' Days and the use of the Apocrypha. Obsolete words should disappear, many of the prayers in the Liturgy needed revision, and a new translation of the Bible and a new Psalter were required; 'Minister' should also be substituted for 'Priest', and 'Lord's Day' for 'Sunday'. Only the Lord's Supper itself was to be rehearsed at the Lord's Table: there was to be no restoration of godparents, no reference to regeneration in the Baptism and Burial services, and a stricter discipline on admission to baptism and communion. Finally, they objected to the surplice, the sign of the cross in baptism, the ring in matrimony, and kneeling for Holy Communion.[6] The second document was Richard Baxter's *Reformed* or *Savoy Liturgy*, a new service book combining both Anglican and Genevan elements. Compiled in a mere fortnight, it nevertheless represented the fruits of his experience as pastor at Kidderminster with *The Westminster Directory*. But he had no thought of rejecting the Prayer Book: rather his 'alterations' and 'additions' were designed to 'be inserted into the several respective places in the [Anglican] liturgy to which they do belong, and left to the minister's choice to use the one or the other'.[7] It therefore provided an alternative form. The Sunday service was a compilation of elements from Morning or Evening Prayer and the Ante-Communion service shorn of repetitions, redundancies and other 'unmeet' liturgicalia. While following a set form, provision was made for flexibility at the discretion of the minister. The rite of Holy Communion was a brief form following the normal Sunday service, and comprising an exhortation, a brief prayer of consecration, preceded or followed by the Institution Narrative from 1 Corinthians 11, a prayer for forgiveness and nourishment, fraction, libation, communion, thanksgiving, an exhortation, a psalm or hymn, and a blessing. Here again there was provision for flexibility. The bread and wine could be consecrated separately or together, while communicants could sit, stand or kneel. In many respects it was an admirable piece of liturgy, making creative use of Reformed liturgical ideas in an attempt to harmonize the Genevan liturgical family with that of the Prayer Book; and it compared favourably with Cranmer's work in 1552.[8]

The deliberations of the Savoy Conference and the subsequent work of the Convocations and Parliament need not detain us here.[9] What is important is to note the extent to which the Laudian and the Presbyterian proposals found their way into the 1662 Prayer Book. The Preface of that book, probably written by Bishop Sanderson of Lincoln, made it clear that the primary concern was to restore rather than to revise, and to revise only where directions or language could be made clear: as for any additions, they were necessities. The whole operation was politically restricted. The House of Commons was satisfied with the Prayer Book of 1604,[10] and the dominant Latitudinarian bishops had little sympathy for radical change. Dr. Cuming has wisely commented, 'Sheldon had a more accurate sense of the nation's religious temper than either Cosin or Baxter.'[11]

Laudian influence in 1662 was modest, with less than a dozen changes of any significance.

1. The substitution of 'priest' for 'minister' in the rubrics introducing the absolution at Morning and Evening Prayer, and 'bishops, priests, and deacons' for 'bishops, pastors, and ministers' in the Litany.
2. The Communion Service
   a. The people were directed to stand for the Gospel and the Creed.
   b. A watered-down version of the Offertory was included.
   c. A modified thanksgiving for the faithful departed was added to the Prayer for the Church.
   d. The manual acts were restored in the Prayer of Consecration.
   e. Provision was made for the consecration of additional bread and wine.
   f. The consecrated elements remaining after Communion were ordered to be veiled, and then consumed.
3. Baptism

   Provision was made for the blessing of the water.
4. The Ordinal

   The formulae for ordaining priests and consecrating bishops were reworded to indicate clearly the orders of ministry intended.

Concessions on the Puritan side were equally modest. Baxter's Liturgy was virtually ignored, and of *The Exceptions* approximately one in three were accepted, although none were of major importance.

1. The Communion Service
   a. The use of the 1611 Bible for the Epistles and Gospels.
   b. A rubric was included requiring intending communicants to give notice – at least the day before.
   c. The manual acts were restored in the Prayer of Consecration.
   d. The restoration of a modified form of the 1552 Declaration on kneeling; although the words 'corporal presence' were substituted for 'real and essential presence', so becoming a defence of the real presence instead of a denial of it.
2. Confirmation
   a. A rubric was included requiring the curate's formal consent to the confirmation of a parishioner.
   b. A modification of the final rubric permitting communion not only to those who were confirmed but also to those 'ready and desirous to be confirmed'.

Despite some six hundred changes, there was no striking departure from the 1604 Book. Neither Laudians nor Puritans could claim any major concessions in their favour: yet neither could complain that they had been totally ignored. An administration which would have preferred to reprint the old book intact nevertheless had to make some changes; but they were minimal. Horton Davies has described the outcome admirably: 'There was to be no rocking of the ark of the Church of England, whether by Laudian pushing or by Presbyterian pulling, though their combined efforts had at least taken the Prayer Book out of the harbour of 1604 . . . This was a conservative, middle-of-the-way, safe, prudential, logical, lucid, moderate, and modest revision.'[12] Nevertheless, there was an element of steel in the outcome. The Church of England opted for uniformity rather than inclusiveness. The Act of Uniformity, which received the Royal Assent on 19 May 1662, made the use of the revised Prayer Book compulsory, insisted that all ministers should be episcopally ordained, and demanded that they take the canonical oath of obedience, repudiate the Solemn League and Covenant, and abjure the lawfulness of armed rebellion against the monarchy. The operative date was St Bartholomew's Day, 24 August 1662.[13]

As a result, some 1760 ministers and 149 clerical dons and schoolmasters, finding themselves unable to conform, lost their livings and posts.[14] Furthermore, many of these ministers were supported by a considerable body of lay people, who not only approved of their action but also wished for a continuance of their ministry with forms of worship they all preferred. But their lot was not improved by the restrictive legislation of the Clarendon Code.[15] Until 1689 they were denied the right of forming their own churches, and of conducting their own forms of worship: and here was the source and origin of organized Dissent, which became a notable factor in English religious life. Those who preferred ejection to conformity acted from a variety of motives. Some were not prepared to accept reordination at the hands of the bishops: some were not prepared to repudiate the oaths they had already taken; others were not prepared to use certain rites – or parts of certain rites – in the Prayer Book. Many who were ejected were not only sincere and high-minded men, but also scholars and pastors of ability and distinction. Their going was a sad loss to the Church of England. It was, of course, not to be expected that Baxter and those who thought with him would regard the revised Book of 1662 as any substantial improvement on the unrevised. But something more than mere adjustments was necessary: and if the substantial elements of their programme had been accepted, there is no doubt that the character and ethos of Anglican worship would have changed significantly.

Nevertheless it would be wrong to suggest that Sheldon and his fellow-bishops regarded the Act of Uniformity as a welcome means of ridding the Church of an undesirable Puritan element. Years before even Laud had accepted the ideal of a comprehensive national Church, requiring assent only to the Creeds and the Scriptures; and this had never been seriously challenged by those who followed him. What had been regarded as vital, however, were authorized common forms of worship and the maintenance of a certain standard of ceremonial. 'Unity cannot long continue in the Church when uniformity (of worship) is shut out at the church-door.'[16] Once Anglicanism was restored, many of the bishops – and not surprisingly Edward Reynolds of Norwich – behaved in a conciliatory manner, and a number of moderate and inoffensive Puritan incumbents were quietly allowed to remain in their livings, although they never actually conformed.[17] Furthermore, some bishops had made efforts to persuade Puritan clergy to conform and remain within the Church of England before the fateful Feast of St Bartholomew. Sheldon himself held a special ordination for Presbyterian ministers just before the day, and other bishops followed his example.[18] A. G. Matthews concluded from his survey of the evidence that the treatment of the dispossessed ministers was mild indeed when compared with the sufferings of the royalist clergy during the Commonwealth.[19] Clearly, a number of bishops felt that the ejection of so many good men was a matter of regret, and if some modus vivendi could be found, their comprehension within the Church was desirable. Nevertheless, an eagle eye was kept on the situation; and by the end of 1664 there were few ministers left who were not episcopally ordained and of unimpeachable orthodoxy.

On the other side the Laudians were equally disappointed in their hopes, although they all remained within the Church of England – at least for the time being. It must be admitted, however, that despite their ability and influence, they were probably never more than a minority among the clergy.

It has been argued that a more thoroughgoing revision in their direction might have made the Prayer Book a more adequate medium for public worship, with greater variety and enrichment and more corporate participation.[20] Indeed, in some respects both Laudians and Presbyterians were theologically and liturgically in advance of 1662: and the idealists on both sides were sacrificed by the compromise which won the day.[21] It is not altogether surprising, therefore, that their ideals did not go away, and in the final analysis, ultimately won recognition.

II

There is no doubt that the Church of England contained a sizeable body of opinion willing to come to terms with the Presbyterians. The latter, unlike the Independents, the Baptists and the Quakers, had no desire to remain apart, and in fact were prepared to accept the principle of a national Church with a proper liturgy and some form of episcopacy. Indeed it was a mutual dislike of Roman Catholicism which generally encouraged the idea of comprehension. In 1667, when Clarendon fell from power, and again in 1668, a Comprehension Bill was mooted; but both attempts came to nothing. The Commons still harboured suspicions of both Roman Catholics and Dissenters, and memories of the Civil War had by no means disappeared.[22] Nevertheless, the principle of comprehension continued to be kept alive during the next decade, notably by people like Baxter on the one side, and by Tillotson, Dean of Canterbury, and Stillingfleet, Bishop of Worcester, on the other.

On 6 February 1685 James II, an avowed Roman Catholic, succeeded to the throne on the death of his brother Charles. Clearly he wished not merely to alleviate the condition of his fellow Catholics, but also to increase their influence. This he could not do, however, without pursuing a policy of toleration which also included Dissenters. In the event, his attempt to do this by Royal Prerogative failed lamentably. In April 1687, and again in April 1688, he issued almost identical Declarations of Indulgence, suspending all penal laws against both Roman Catholics and Dissenters.[23] The second was accompanied by an order requiring bishops to see that it was read in their dioceses. Refusal to comply led to the famous imprisonment of Archbishop Sancroft and six other bishops in the Tower of London, and their trial for disobedience to the royal command.[24] On 30 June they were declared 'Not guilty' and released amid popular rejoicing. But during their short stay in the Tower, they had been visited by ten Dissenting ministers, who began further talks on comprehension involving a review of the Liturgy.[25] As a result, an influential committee under Archbishop Sancroft himself was set up to discuss the matter; and a complete set of proposals were prepared, although not published. An introduction by Tenison (then Vicar of St Martin-in-the-Fields) stated that the principles on which they were based were *The Exceptions*. For the moment, however, nothing came of these proposals; for political events overtook any negotiations towards comprehension. Nevertheless they did form the basis of further activity in the following year.[26]

In July 1688 a formal invitation was sent to William of Orange and his wife Mary to come to England. He landed at Torbay on 5 November and entered London before Christmas. James II fled the country, but did not abdicate: and although Parliament declared the throne vacant before offering it to William and Mary, many clergy believed that by Divine Right James was still King. Some eight bishops and four hundred clergy, led by Archbishop Sancroft, felt unable to take the oath of allegiance to the new rulers and ultimately were suspended. Among these Non-Jurors were the direct descendants of the Laudian High Churchmen, many of whom were keenly interested in liturgical matters and helped to keep alive the kind of proposals set out by Cosin and Wren. Nor did the fact that the new King was a Dutch Calvinist help matters. But William was wise enough to realize that some resolution of religious questions was necessary for the well-being of the country. One significant step was taken on 24 May 1689, when the Toleration Act became law with little difficulty: and while it did not remove the civil disabilities of Dissenters, it did give most of the latter freedom to conduct their own forms of worship in their own buildings.[27] But the question of comprehension still persisted; and on 17 September 1689 William agreed to the appointment of a wide-ranging Commission to consider changes in the Liturgy, Canons, and Ecclesiastical Courts, with a view to a 'reconciling as much as is possible of all differences'.[28]

The Commission was broadly based and fell into three main groups. First there was a strong Latitudinarian group in favour of comprehension, including Burnet (Bishop of Salisbury), Tillotson (Dean of Canterbury), and Tenison. Secondly there was a strong Tory High Church group opposed to any revision of the Prayer Book, including Lamplugh (Archbishop of York), Trelawney (Bishop of Exeter) and Jane (Regius Professor of Divinity at Oxford). Thirdly there was a middle group which on the whole favoured comprehension and revision, including Compton (Bishop of London), Patrick (Bishop of Chichester), Sharp (Dean of Norwich) and Beveridge (Archdeacon of Colchester). Tenison acted as secretary. They did not start *de novo* but had before them the 1688 scheme prepared by Sancroft and his colleagues, together with a list of all the objections to the Prayer Book from before the Civil War down to the present drawn up by Tenison. Despite the fact that William and Mary and their advisers hoped for proposals which would be acceptable to both Dissenters and Non-Jurors,[29] the Commission did face problems. Minimal changes would have little impact on the Dissenters, while the Non-Jurors would regard any changes at all as uncanonical. Archbishop Sancroft's friends on the Commission were also in a quandary: either they must refuse to continue with a project which he himself had led, or they must complete it knowing that there was growing hostility to the idea of Convocation having the right to deal with liturgical changes in his absence. In the event about half the High Church members of the Commission boycotted the proceedings; and while the remainder continued to co-operate, further obstacles to progress appeared. On 21 November, when Convocation met, the Lower House by a two-thirds majority elected as its Prolocutor the anti-revisionist Jane in preference to Tillotson. Then there were problems over procedure, due to the absence of the Archbishop. Finally the Upper and Lower Houses quarrelled over the address to the Crown. By the time Convocation adjourned for the recess on 13 December, comprehension and liturgical revision had never been discussed. By 24 January 1690, when the recess ended, a dissolution of Parliament had already been decided, carrying with it the dissolution of Convocation. The latter dispersed on 13 February without further debate. The revision of the liturgy therefore died of neglect. The Commission never completed its recommendations and produced no report. The proposals can, however, be reconstructed from entries in an interleaved Prayer Book in Lambeth Palace Library, and from the copy of a private diary kept by Dr John Williams, a canon of St Paul's and a member of the Commission.[30]

Clearly they tried to meet the demands of all parties. The High Church element would have been expected to find the following proposals acceptable:

1. The provision of the Beatitudes as an alternative to the Decalogue in the Communion service — a proposal made by Jeremy Taylor in his *Collection of Offices*.
2. The inclusion of a specific group of Offertory Sentences, taken from *The Durham Book*.
3. The inclusion of references to 'the sacrifice' of Christ's Body and Blood in the Prayer of Humble Access and the Catechism.[31]
4. A rubric encouraging not only regular but frequent communion.
5. An improved form for the further consecration of the eucharistic elements.
6. A greater emphasis on Ember Weeks, and a provision of propers for Rogation Sunday and a proper preface for Good Friday.
7. The inclusion of a specific renewal of Baptismal Vows in Confirmation, taken from *The Durham Book*.

On the Dissenters' side too the Commission tried to be accommodating, and some sixty per cent of *The Exceptions* were met. The most significant were:

1. The retention of the surplice, the sign of the cross in baptism, the ring in marriage, and kneeling at communion — but on an optional basis. The Ornaments Rubric was also removed.
2. The criticism of a too easy assumption of regeneration in the Baptism and Burial Offices was acknowledged and the phraseology was modified.
3. In the Visitation of the Sick, 'I pronounce thee absolved' was substituted for 'I absolve thee'. The reference to private confession and absolution in

the first Exhortation of the Communion service was also modified, and the words 'benefit of absolution' were omitted.

4. In Baptism parents were allowed to be 'sureties': and the title 'godparents', which was objected to in *The Exceptions*, was removed.
5. All Black Letter Days were removed from the Calendar.
6. Apocryphal passages were omitted: the Benedicite and the Nunc Dimittis were replaced by psalms: a psalm was permitted as an alternative to or an addition to the Magnificat:[32] a psalm was alternative to the Te Deum: and the Benedictus became an alternative to the Jubilate.
7. Dissenting ministers were allowed conditional ordination, leaving them 'the freedom of their own thoughts concerning their former ordination', and the deacon's ordination formula was considered sufficient to admit continental Protestant ministers.

A third group of proposed alterations were uncontroversial and would have been equally acceptable to all parties:

1. Provision was made for the use of the Litany and the ante-Communion as a separate service.
2. In the Burial service the substitution of a shorter lesson from 1 Thessalonians 4 was permitted 'in colder or later seasons'.
3. 'Lord's Day' replaced 'Sunday', and 'presbyter' or 'minister' replaced 'priest' at a number of points; but there was no consistent policy in either case.
4. Weekday offices were encouraged but were no longer obligatory.
5. The number of occasions on which the Athanasian Creed was to be used was reduced from thirteen to five.
6. A revision of the collects, originally undertaken by Patrick, was overseen by Burnet, Stillingfleet and Tenison. Many were lengthened; and in a number of cases quotations from the Epistle or Gospel of the day were added to give them greater coherence with the readings.

One other feature is worthy of note. The proposals involved a great many verbal changes which could not be regarded as of party or theological significance, but were an attempt to make prayers more intelligible or applicable to life of the day. Many of these changes might not be acceptable to present thinking. Nevertheless, the Commission had commendably grasped the important principle that a liturgy should be flexible and should relate to the age in which it is used. The principle was well expressed by Humphrey Prideaux, later Dean of Norwich and a staunch supporter of revision, in a pamphlet entitled 'Letter to a friend'.

> As to the liturgy of our Church I freely acknowledge and I think no man can contradict me herein, that it is the best which was ever yet used in any Christian Church, but that it therefore be so perfect as not to be capable of amendments or alterations for the better doth by no means follow. For

> nothing of human composure can be such, especially in a thing of this nature, where process of time and alteration of circumstances frequently produce a necessity for correction, as most certainly in our liturgy they very often do. For the language in which it is wrote being constantly in flux, as all other living languages are, in every age some words that were in use in the former grow obsolete, and some phrases and expressions formerly in grace and fashion through disuse become uncouth and ridiculous, and always to continue these in our liturgy without correction would be to bring a disparagement upon the whole, and expose to contempt the worship of God among us. Besides there are several things which in one age may conduce to devotion, which through variation in times and circumstances may not be born in another; several things which may be proper of Prayer at one time which may not be so in another, and all those things call for alterations and amendments whenever they happen . . . I think it absolutely necessary from the above-mentioned particulars that it be always at least once in thirty years brought to a review for this purpose.[33]

III

Although the group which had been primarily responsible for the abortive attempt at revision in 1689 held positions of high office in the Church of England, they did not pursue their efforts further. Quite apart from the fact that Dissenters were content with the relative freedom granted under the Toleration Act, the bishops had no desire to reintroduce proposals which had already provoked strong opposition. Indeed the demise of the 1689 proposals was followed not merely by a spate of books and pamphlets defending the Prayer Book:[34] it was followed also by a brief religious revival which found in the Prayer Book its main source of inspiration. The official book of public prayer also became the basis for a great deal of private devotion:[35] and a serious effort was made to help the nation appreciate the spiritual riches it possessed. This was a period remarkable for its Prayer Book commentaries. The pioneer work, Anthony Sparrow's *A Rationale upon the Book of Common Prayer*, had in fact been written as early as 1657. This brief but learned attempt to set the Prayer Book against the background of Scripture and the early liturgies also included aids to make it more devotionally effective; and it proved to be an authoritative source from which later writers drew. Other notable works soon followed: Hamon L'Estrange's *The Alliance of the Divine Office* in 1658; John Durel's *The Liturgy of the Church of England* in 1662; Thomas Comber's *A Companion to the Temple and the Closet* in four parts between 1672 and 1677; William Beveridge's *The Excellency and Usefulness of the Common Prayer* in 1681; William Nicholl's *Comment on the Book of Common Prayer and the Administration of the Sacraments* in 1710; and finally Charles Wheatly's *A Rational Illustration upon the Book of Common Prayer* in the same year, summing up most of what had been written in the previous half-century and remaining the standard commentary until well into the nineteenth century. Two other notable works on the Calendar and Lectionary also appeared: Robert Nelson's *Companion to the Festivals and Fasts of the Church of England* in 1704, reputed by Dr Johnson to have had the greatest sale of any book ever printed in England other than the Bible;[36] and George Stanhope's *Paraphrase upon the Epistles and Gospels*, appearing in three parts between 1705 and 1708.

Nevertheless, this enthusiasm for the Book of Common Prayer did not deter individual scholars from pressing for liturgical change and in so doing drawing increasing attention to the liturgies of the early Church. One such enthusiast was the Reverend Edward Stephens of Gloucester. Trained as a lawyer before ordination, he had been influenced by the work of earlier liturgical scholars such as Thorndike, Hamon L'Estrange, and in particular Sparrow; and he believed that a return to both the forms and the practices of the early Church was desirable. He strongly advocated daily communion and for some years worshipped daily in London at 5 a.m. with a group of like-minded people, using privately the rites which he produced between 1696 and 1705. In this he was following the example of Bishop Jeremy Taylor, who in 1658 had produced his *Collection of Offices, or Forms of Prayer* for private use by groups of staunch Anglicans during the Commonwealth. This *Collection* had included a eucharistic rite quite different from that in the 1604 Prayer Book, making use of such knowledge of the early liturgies as was then available. Stephens was strongly influenced by the so-called Clementine liturgy in Book 8 of *The Apostolic Constitutions* and by the Liturgy of St James, while of the later rites 1549 and the Scottish rite of 1637 were his favourites; 1552 he disliked.[37]

His first rite, *The Liturgy of the Ancients represented, as near as well may be, in English Forms*, was for public use. Although longwinded, particularly in the liturgy of the catechumens (there were seven collects), it was nevertheless a polished piece of liturgical writing, based primarily on material from 1549, 1662 and the Scottish rite of 1637. The second rite, *The Second Service, or Office of the Faithful enlarged, according to Ancient Forms*, was for private use. Based on the Clementine Liturgy and the Liturgy of St James, it contained, as the title indicated, only the liturgy of the faithful. With its long and turgid set of Thanksgivings, it was little more than a museum piece and would have proved impracticable for regular congregational use. The third rite, *A Compleat Form of Liturgy, or Divine Service, according to the Usage of the Most Ancient Christians*, was a revised form of the second. Rather less exotic, and containing more 1662 material, it was nevertheless still unsuitable for public use. While Stephens was undoubtedly well versed in liturgical forms, he was not a constructive liturgist and as a craftsman was inferior to Jeremy Taylor. His contemporaries paid little heed to him and most would have regarded him as a crank. Nevertheless, his work was important for two reasons. In the first place he cut through what

Grisbrooke calls 'English liturgical insularity'[38] directing attention to the riches and insights of the Eastern rites. Secondly he paved the way not only for the Non-Jurors but also for other High Church liturgists of the future.

Another man with a high regard for *The Apostolic Constitutions* was William Whiston, Isaac Newton's successor as the Lucasian Professor of Mathematics at Cambridge. He declared them to be 'no other than the original laws and doctrines of the Gospel, . . . equal in authority to the four Gospels themselves . . . ; some parts of them being our Saviour's own original laws delivered to the apostles'.[39] Unfortunately, he combined this enthusiasm with an unorthodox theology, believing that the idea of a Trinity of persons in the Godhead was an invention of Athanasius, who had been forced into this position during his debates with the Arians: it was the latter who were the true guardians of apostolic doctrine. While not denying that the Son was worshipped by the early Christians, Whiston argued that such worship was different from and inferior to that of the Father, and the Holy Spirit was inferior to both Father and Son. For these views, all expressed in *Primitive Christianity Reviv'd*, he was deprived of his Professorship in 1710 and subsequently condemned by Convocation.

Four of his writings are directly concerned with liturgical proposals: *Essay on the Apostolic Constitutions* 1711, *Primitive Infant Baptism Reviv'd* 1712, *The Primitive Eucharist Reviv'd* 1736, and *The Liturgy of the Church of England, reduced nearer to the Primitive Standard* 1713 (2nd edition 1750).[40] It was his aim to purge the liturgy of what he regarded as faulty Athanasian doctrine, and to restore it to primitive standards in conformity with *The Apostolic Constitutions*. Unlike Stephens, who confined his attentions to the Eucharist, he produced proposals for the entire Prayer Book. Throughout his Unitarian stance was obvious; all creeds and doxologies were modified, and all prayer was addressed to the Father. Some of his suggestions had quite a modern look – the provision of daily alternatives to the office canticles, the use of only the first seven verses of the Venite, and the elimination of repetitions of the Lord's Prayer. What was remarkable, however, was his conservative approach to the revision of the Eucharist. The Prayer for the Church, which preceded the eucharistic prayer, was an expanded form of material from 1549 and 1637: the eucharistic prayer was the same pattern as that of 1637: and the Lord's Prayer followed communion. He did, however, provide an alternative prayer based almost exclusively on that of the Clementine Liturgy. He had hopes, of course, that such a liturgy would secure the comprehension of at least some Dissenters and at the same time would accommodate the needs of rationalism.[41] His hopes were not fulfilled: but his subsequent influence was by no means negligible.

Another enthusiast for *The Apostolic Constitutions* who adopted Unitarian views was John Henley, described by Grisbrooke as 'Whiston run mad'.[42] An Anglican clergyman, Henley served in various parishes from 1716 to 1726 before setting up his own Oratory, first in Newport Market and then in

Lincoln's Inn Fields, where he officiated until his death in 1756. Bishop Gibson of London tried to proceed against him on the grounds of 'mangling the Book of Common Prayer and setting up new liturgies and rubrics against it, and turning religious assemblies into theatres and stages': but he was advised that Henley was contravening neither the Act of Uniformity nor the Toleration Act, and he was obliged to leave him in peace.[43] The rites he produced for use in his Oratory were entitled *The Primitive Liturgy and Eucharist*, the third edition of 1729 containing what were probably the final forms.[44] His regard for *The Apostolic Constitutions* was even more uncritical than that of Whiston – they were 'the most sacred books of the primitive New Testament' – and his rites were less conservative, though they did contain some interesting features. There were five services in all: Morning and Evening Prayer, a revised Litany, a Third Service, and the Eucharist. The Third Service was really the Liturgy of the catechumens, including the Beatitudes, the Summary of the Law, collect, epistle, gospel, psalmody and sermon. On Sundays, however, Henley envisaged an interesting combination of Morning Prayer, Litany, and Holy Communion, in which the second lesson at Morning Prayer was replaced by the epistle and gospel; the Litany was abbreviated; and the eucharistic prayer, containing extensive borrowings from the Clementine Liturgy, included an act of oblation, an epiclesis and an Intercession all following the Institution Narrative.

Of greater significance than either Whiston or Henley was Dr Samuel Clarke, a friend of Whiston, Rector of St James' Piccadilly, and one of the leading thinkers of the day. The controversy over the doctrine of the Trinity intensified with the publication in 1712 of his *The Scripture Doctrine of the Trinity*.[45] In this he denied the orthodox teaching of the Creeds: God the Father was supreme; and the Son and the Holy Ghost, although divine, were subordinate. Like Whiston, this brought him into conflict with Convocation on charges of Arianism, despite his protestations: and he undertook not to preach or write any further books upon the subject.[46] He felt it necessary, however, to revise the Prayer Book in accordance with his doctrinal views. He had, in fact, already seen Whiston's *Liturgy of the Church of England reduced* before its publication in 1713; and although impressed by it, he did not have a similar uncritical veneration of *The Apostolic Constitutions*. He was therefore inclined to something on much more conservative lines, not forsaking the general pattern of Prayer Book services but confining himself to modifications which conformed to his Arian views. His main changes were:

1. The Athanasian and Nicene Creeds were omitted, the latter being replaced by a psalm.
2. All Trinitarian formulae were rephrased, and the Preface for Trinity Sunday was omitted.
3. The Blessing of the Communion Service was replaced by the Grace from Morning and Evening Prayer.

4. All references to original sin and priestly absolution were removed or modified.
5. In Baptism the sign of the cross was made optional, and parents were permitted to be sponsors as in 1689.[47]

Clarke made his amendments in a Prayer Book of 1724; but this was never published, and the copy was subsequently presented to the British Museum by his son. Other copies were made, however, which subsequently came to light and proved influential. But Clarke himself was not without influence. He was one of the members of an intellectual coterie organized by the Princess of Wales, who clearly thought highly of him. In 1727, after she had become Queen Caroline, Clarke was willing for her to propose his nomination to a bishopric, hoping that such preferment might facilitate the revision of the Prayer Book and Articles in accordance with his own views. But the Queen was dissuaded from doing so by the Bishop of London on the grounds that, despite Clarke's learning and honesty, he had one defect – he was not an orthodox Christian. Archbishop Wake, too, opposed his views and said he would refuse to consecrate him.[48] Clarke was a sincere man, however, and in later life steadfastly refused to accept any ecclesiastical preferment involving subscription to the Thirty-Nine Articles. Peaston has suggested that but for his conscientious refusal to subscribe, he might have become Archbishop of Canterbury.[49]

In 1749 one of Clarke's leading disciples, the Reverend John Jones, Vicar of Alconbury, published a collection of pleas for reform in support of his own proposals in a volume published anonymously under the title *Free and Candid Disquisitions relating to the Church of England, and the Means of advancing Religion therein.* The book was addressed to the governing bodies of Church and State and more immediately to Convocation, suggesting that it should encourage the production of reformed liturgies, as a means of securing the comprehension of Dissenters within the Church of England: but failing any official reform, private individuals should produce their own proposals. His own proposals were quite radical:

1. The omission of everything not authorized by Scripture.
2. The omission of the Athanasian Creed.
3. The removal of unnecessary repetitions of the Lord's Prayer and the Gloria Patri in Morning and Evening Prayer.
4. An improved Lectionary, proper Psalms for every Sunday, and the inclusion of hymns and New Testament passages for singing.
5. The fusion of Mattins, Litany and Holy Communion into one service on Sundays in the interests of brevity.
6. The sign of the Cross to be made optional in Baptism, and the cessation of the use of sponsors.
7. The addition of further Occasional Prayers and Forms of Service.

As was to be expected, Convocation failed to take up the challenge — indeed it had undertaken nothing but formal business since 1717. But the book created a considerable impression, and Jones followed it up by forming a Catholic Christianity Society to further his aims.[50] It may well have been Jones' activities that Archbishop Herring of York had in mind in 1748 when the Duke of Newcastle urged him to accept promotion to Canterbury. He expressed doubts as to his ability to deal with the renewed demands for reform, particularly as he feared that they would be presented 'with determination and even peremptoriness as the united sense of some of the best of the clergy and laity in the kingdom'.[51] While no official action followed Jones' efforts, between 1751 and 1768 some half-dozen people produced their own schemes of liturgical reform, for the most part acknowledging their indebtedness to him. In varying degrees these proposals were based on those of 1689 and *The Candid Disquisitions.*[52]

Support of a different kind came, however, from his friend Francis Blackburne, Archdeacon of Cleveland.[53] Although strictly orthodox, he was anxious for a considerable measure of reform; and he believed that in the Reformed Church of England nothing should be borrowed from the creeds, liturgy and ordinances of the Church of Rome. But he also took a very strict view of the terms of subscription. He could not agree that the Articles might be subscribed to in a general sense, or even that they had been intended as 'Articles of Peace'. In 1766 he published anonymously *The Confessional*, in which he denounced the Thirty-Nine Articles as unscriptural and pleaded for a relaxation in the terms of subscription. He followed this by promoting a society with the aid of his son-in-law, Theophilus Lindsey, Vicar of Catterick, at the Feathers Tavern in the Strand, to secure the abolition of subscription in favour of an acknowledgement of belief in Holy Scripture, which clergy would be free to interpret in their own way and not be bound by creeds and formularies. Signatures for a petition to this effect were sought and some 250 were collected. It was presented to the House of Commons on 6 February 1772 but was decisively rejected by 217 votes to 71. Admittedly, if successful the petition would not have secured a revision of the liturgy; but at least it would have created a situation favourable to such an undertaking. Furthermore a principle was at stake which had induced many orthodox, and indeed intellectual and influential clergy to sign the petition.[54] It had been recognized since the Restoration that the Church of England would be continually deprived of able and good men if its basis were to remain too narrow and restricted.

It was such a consideration which prompted Beilby Porteus, Master of the Hospital of St Cross Winchester and Chaplain to the King,[55] with other influential clergy to try at the end of 1772 to

> induce the bishops to promote a review of the Liturgy and Articles in order to amend in both . . . those parts which stood in need of amendment. This plan was not in the smallest degree connected with the Petition at the

> Feathers Tavern, but on the contrary, was meant to counteract that and all similar extravagant projects; to strengthen and confirm our ecclesiastical establishment; to repel the attacks which were at that time continually made upon it by its avowed enemies; to render the 17th Article on Predestination and Election more clear and perspicuous, and less liable to be wrested by our adversaries to a Calvinistic sense, which has been so unjustly affixed to it; to improve true Christian piety amongst those of our own communion; and to diminish schism and separation by bringing over to the National Church all the moderate and well-disposed of other persuasions.

An approach was made to Archbishop Cornwallis of Canterbury, who consulted some of his fellow bishops. But on 11 February 1773 they decided that 'nothing can in prudence be done in the matter that has been submitted to our considerations'.[56]

Hopes of further progress were therefore diminished, at least for the time being: and the failure of these petitions in 1772–3 did in fact result in the very kind of action which Porteus and his supporters would have liked to avoid. Theophilus Lindsey, son-in-law of Francis Blackburne and regarded by many as a young man destined for high ecclesiastical preferment, was sufficiently disillusioned to leave the Church of England and attempt to found a Reformed Church of England with a liturgy of its own. He began by opening a chapel in Essex Street, London; and although this prospered, his expectations of founding a whole new Reformed Church were never realized. Nevertheless his liturgical influence proved to be considerable. On his departure from Catterick, he found a copy of Dr Clarke's annotated Prayer Book in the possession of his brother-in-law, the Reverend John Disney;[57] and in 1774 he published *The Book of Common Prayer Reformed according to the Plan of the late Dr Samuel Clarke*, with an enlarged edition in the following year. Although he made play of the fact that his book was based on Clarke, he was in fact only using the name; for there is little evidence of any substantial borrowing: his proposals were in fact far more radical, owing a great deal to people such as Whiston. Indeed, he disagreed profoundly with Clarke and the Arians; but he regarded them as his forebears in the sense that they stood out for the true faith of the Church, although they were unable to shake off all the imbibed traditions of their early training, especially in relation to the worship of God the Son. His opinions were based on the enlightened views of the free thought of the times, believing that 'sincerity and integrity are things final in religion; right opinions are of inferior consideration and instrumental only'.[58] Lindsey therefore went beyond the Arianism of Clarke to embrace Unitarianism. In his Prayer Book the Creeds were omitted, all Trinitarian references were expunged or amended, prayers were addressed only to the Father, and canticles such as Te Deum, Magnificat and Nunc Dimittis disappeared; while his abhorrence of sacerdotalism was indicated by the removal of all references to priestly absolution. Nevertheless some of his proposals were interesting. Clearly he objected to the length of the Sunday Service, preferring to have an arrangement whereby Mattins, Litany and Holy Communion could be used separately, but at the same time could be combined into a single Service without unnecessary repetitions. In this single Service, the Litany replaced Mattins, but was extended by the addition of a number of prayers, while the final section was replaced by a 'liturgy of the word' containing psalmody and two lessons: Communion then began at the Invitation to Confession, with the Prayer of Humble Access, the Lord's Prayer and the Prayer of Thanksgiving being omitted.

Lindsey was undoubtedly the most influential figure in the history of Unitarian liturgy. Between 1793 and 1854 there were no less than thirteen reissues of his Prayer Book, while between 1776 and 1791 five other Unitarian liturgies based on his book were published.[59] His influence also extended to the Continent and to America. Equally he and his friends derived encouragement from the emergence of the American Prayer Book in 1790 with many features which they themselves had adopted.[60]

IV

The most significant figure on the liturgical scene in the eighteenth century, however, was not Theophilus Lindsey but John Wesley. Indeed his liturgical work has been described — with justification — as 'the most important single fact in the history of English Christianity in the eighteenth century'.[61] Himself a loyal son of the Church of England, he inherited from his clerical father a love of the Caroline divines and the Non-Jurors, while from his mother came a Puritan strain; his maternal grandfather, Dr Annesley, had been one of the ejected Dissenting clergy of 1662. He was a staunch High Churchman, a regular communicant and a firm believer in the four Usages of the Non-Jurors.[62] He loved the Book of Common Prayer, believing that its forms of worship were consonant with the worship of the primitive Church. In the Preface to the 1784 Service Book which he produced for the Methodists of North America he wrote: 'There is no liturgy in the world, either in ancient or modern language, which breathes more of a solid, Scriptural, rational piety, than the Common Prayer of the Church of England.' It is not surprising, therefore, that he believed that Methodists should attend their parish churches and communicate frequently: they were exhorted to 'be at Church and at the Lord's Table every week' — a remarkable injunction when it is remembered how infrequent weekly communions were in the eighteenth-century Church of England. Indeed Anglican clergy were dumbfounded at the number of Methodists who came to communicate.[63] Unfortunately, many were not made welcome and some were even repelled. Pressures grew within the Connexion for their own services in their own buildings. These were pressures which gave Wesley little joy, and he eventually gave way with reluctance. Even then loyalty to the Prayer Book was enjoined. When the first Methodist Church was opened in 1778 in the

City Road, London, the Prayer Book offices were read there Sunday by Sunday.[64] Then it was not until 1784, when Wesley was already 81 years of age, that he produced his first Service Book – and this was for the Methodists in North America.

The Sunday Services of the Methodists in North America was basically an abridged Book of Common Prayer. In the new American republic there was no national Church with a system of parish churches, so it is not surprising that Wesley permitted himself a degree of latitude. But what is surprising to some extent is that Wesley produced such a book at all, in view of the large number of Puritans in America, many of whom were Methodists. Dr Rattenbury has commented, 'A Dissenter in Wesley's time would have destroyed the Prayer Book, not revised it.'[65] The book contained not only many similarities with Lindsey and *The Candid Disquisitions* but also with the Puritan proposals at the Savoy Conference. Apparently in 1754 Wesley had read Edmund Calamy's *Abridgment of Mr Baxter's History of His Life and Times* and had found himself in sympathy with much of the Puritan position.[66] It has been suggested that he undertook his revision with Calamy's book before him; 'His revisions were dictated by love of that "Baxterian" Church of England, which would have comprehended at least his Presbyterian and perhaps also his Congregational ancestors.'[67] Nevertheless his work was conservative, in that he confined his changes only to what he considered necessary. So he wrote (20 June 1789), 'I took particular care throughout to alter nothing for altering's sake. In religion I am for as few innovations as possible. I love the old wine best.'[68] The actual changes Wesley made were therefore minimal, and most of his revision was effected by omission and abbreviation: indeed he was a master of abridgement.[69]

His Puritan leanings were seen in substituting prayers for forgiveness for priestly absolutions, and in such omissions as the provision for almost all Holy Days together with Epiphany and Lent, all lessons from the Apocrypha, the general rubrics, and a whole range of services and material – Private Baptism, Confirmation, Churching of Women, Visitation of the Sick, the Commination, the various State and Sea Services, the Athanasian Creed, and the Occasional Prayers and Thanksgivings with the exception of the Prayer for all Sorts and Conditions of Men and the General Thanksgiving. The Thirty-Nine Articles were also reduced to Twenty-Five. Of the services in the Book, Morning and Evening Prayer were commended for use by all congregations on Sundays, the Litany was to be read only on Wednesdays and Fridays, and extempore prayer was to be used on all other days. While the general structure of the Prayer Book Offices was retained, the content was considerably abbreviated. The Exhortation, the Venite, the Benedicite, the Magnificat and the Nunc Dimittis were replaced by psalms, while many psalms were omitted or curtailed because they were considered unsuitable for Christian use. 'Bishops and Curates' in the Prayer for Clergy and People was also replaced by 'all the Ministers of thy Gospel'.

While Wesley undoubtedly loved the Offices, constantly urging their use upon his congregations,[70] it was not in fact this form of service which became popular in Methodism. The staple diet in public worship became the simpler 'Preaching Service' of two hymns, sermon and extempore prayer, a form which Wesley regarded as in itself incomplete. Despite its popularity, Methodism undoubtedly suffered some loss in no longer maintaining an ordered use of the Bible with set liturgical forms, which the Offices would undoubtedly have preserved.[71]

In the Holy Communion service most of the changes were either in the interests of brevity or in recognition of the fact that the context was no longer the parish church of the English establishment. In the first category, therefore, came the omission of the first prayer for the King, the Creed,[72] the offering of bread and wine, the long Exhortations, and the Prayer of Thanksgiving, while both Invitation and Confession were shortened. In the second category, 'elder' replaced 'minister' or 'priest', and 'ministers of thy Gospel' again replaced 'bishops and curates', the absolution and the blessing became prayers, and the omission of certain rubrics — those ordering the place of the table in the chancel, the giving of notice by intending communicants, the provision of a 'bason' by the parish, and those relating to the position of the minister. There were, however, some interesting directions given to the congregation. They were required to stand for the Comfortable Words, presumably because these were on a level with the Gospel; they were required to kneel with the minister for the Prayer of Humble Access; but they were not required to kneel for communion. But by far the two most significant changes were the introduction of hymn-singing and extempore prayer — both marked features of early Methodist communion services. The fact that Wesley specifically made no provision for the singing of parts of the service itself was not due to doctrinal or ceremonial objections, but for practical considerations arising from the nature of the services and the lack of choirs;[73] while the permissive use of extempore prayer by the elder 'if he see expedient' was a further indication of Wesley's flexibility and far-sightedness in combining free with set prayer within a fixed liturgy.

The baptismal rite was a considerably truncated form of the Prayer Book order, in which concessions to Puritan views were again very clear. All references to godparents and all references to baptismal regeneration except one in the Exhortation disappeared. The omissions were the Exhortation and Thanksgiving following the Gospel, the blessing of the water, the sign of the cross and the reception of the child. Permissive additions were sprinkling in addition to immersion and affusion, and extempore prayer. It would seem that Wesley did not regard baptism as essential to salvation and he himself rarely baptized. On the other hand many Methodists in his day had probably been baptized as Anglicans in infancy. Other signs of Puritan influence in other services were the omission of the ring in Matrimony,[74] the omission of the commendation in Burial, and the substitution of Deacons, Elders and Superintendents for Bishops, Priests and Deacons in the Ordinal.

Wesley produced an edition of *The Sunday Service* for this country in

1786; and thereafter over thirty editions appeared between then and 1910. He clearly regarded his services as simply alternatives to those in the Book of Common Prayer — a view endorsed by the Plan of Pacification in 1795 — 'Wherever Divine Service is performed in England, on the Lord's Day in Church-hours, the officiating Preacher shall read either the Service of the Established Church, our venerable father's Abridgment, or at least, the Lessons appointed by the Calendar.'[75] With the passage of time, however, the situation became more confused. *The Sunday Service* survived in North America only until 1792,[76] while in England there was a tendency outside London and the principal towns to dispense with a set liturgy. Furthermore, variations between the numerous editions of the Methodist book tended to proliferate. Evidence suggests, however, that wherever set forms continued to be used, the Book of Common Prayer was preferred to The Sunday Service.[77]

Whatever benefits Methodism may have received from the Book of Common Prayer, the Church of England also received benefit from Methodism, although the influence was indirect rather than direct. The sacramentalism of Wesley and his followers undoubtedly helped in the recovery of eucharistic worship throughout the Church of England in the nineteenth century, while the contribution of the Wesley brothers to the use of hymnody was immense. But their more flexible approach to prayer and their use of the simpler Preaching Service particularly on Sunday evenings pioneered a movement which subsequently became part of established Anglican practice by the end of the next century.

V

No survey of the eighteenth century would be complete without a brief reference to Thomas Wilson, the saintly Bishop of Sodor and Man. While serving as his uncle's curate at Newchurch Kenyon in Lancashire (1687–97), he acted as chaplain to the Earl of Derby and tutor to his son. The Earl, who was also Lord of Man, persuaded him in 1698 to accept the not particularly attractive island see. It was isolated, it carried no seat in the House of Lords, it had been vacant for five years, and the stipend was small. Wilson remained there until his death in 1755, loved and revered by Anglicans and non-Anglicans alike and raising the standards of spiritual life and pastoral efficiency in the diocese to a significant degree.

Theologically he had many affinities with the Non-Jurors: and since the Act of Uniformity did not apply to his diocese, he felt free to recommend changes in the 1662 Communion Service to his clergy. In his *Sacra Privata*, compiled for use in the diocese, he included 'Private devotions at the altar, taken out of the most ancient offices of the Church, to render our present Communion-service more agreeable to apostolic usage, and more acceptable (I hope) to God, and beneficial to all that partake thereof. Until it shall please Him to put into the hearts and power of such as ought to do it, to restore to us the First Service of Edward VI or such as shall be more conformable to the appointment of Christ and His Apostles and their successors'. Among these devotions were a Prayer of Oblation and an epiclesis to be used 'immediately after the consecration' and reminiscent of those elements in the 1718 Non-Jurors' Liturgy.[78] Admittedly such changes had no widespread influence during Wilson's lifetime. Contacts with the mainland were not close: and it was not until 1781, over a quarter of a century after his death, that the *Sacra Privata* were published by C. Cruttwell. Subsequently, however, they enjoyed a wide circulation, particularly with further editions in the nineteenth century by W. Denton and John Keble. Wilson's dissatisfaction with the Prayer Book rite therefore came to be widely known and was not lost on those desiring liturgical reform.

VI

The eighteenth century closed with the activities of a rather remarkable Liberal, Richard Watson, Bishop of Llandaff. After having been both Professor of Chemistry (1765) and Regius Professor of Divinity (1771) at Cambridge, he became Bishop of Llandaff in 1782. Most occupants of the see regarded it as a stepping stone to something more lucrative and important; and Watson was no exception. But despite showing promise as a prolific pamphleteer and a speaker in the House of Lords, the Government soon found him to be sturdily independent and unwilling to toe the official line on a number of important issues, in consequence of which he was left at Llandaff until his death in 1816. He supported Roman Catholic emancipation and the repeal of the Test Act, he opposed the Slave Trade and the American War, and in its early stages he welcomed the French Revolution. He also advocated certain radical church reforms, including the reallocation of funds to secure greater uniformity in the stipends of bishops and cathedral dignitaries, and the joint establishment of the Protestant and Roman Catholic Churches in Ireland — neither of which endeared him to the Establishment.

Theologically he was also liberal. He accepted the Church of England but set no particular store by its beliefs and practices. From a robust application of the principles of scientific enquiry to Christian doctrine, he evolved an individual creed, strongly influenced by the intellectual temper of the age. So he favoured a wide latitude over the matter of subscription and believed that professions of faith and the standards of worship should be substantiated by Scripture alone. '(Creeds) are all of human fabrication; they oblige conscience, as far as they are conformable to Scripture, and of that conformity every man must judge for himself. This liberty of private judgment is recognized by our church (notwithstanding subscription to the Thirty-nine Articles) when, in the service for the ordering of priests, it proposes this question: "Are you determined, out of the said Scriptures . . . to teach nothing, as required of necessity to eternal salvation, but that which *you shall be persuaded* may be concluded and proved by the Scriptures?"'[79] If, therefore, he had to choose, he would much prefer a profession of faith composed by divines of his own day rather than one of ancient origin. 'Was I compelled to receive a creed of *human* composition, I would more willingly in these enlightened times receive one from such men as Locke, Clarke or Tillotson, than from either Athanasius or Arius, or even from hundreds of contentious or political bishops assembled in solemn council at Nicaea, Antioch or Ariminum.'[80] Furthermore, what he believed about doctrine, he believed equally of a liturgy. 'I profess I cannot listen to the opinions which would compel Protestants of future ages to submit their understandings to the decision of Cranmer and Ridley, or Parker and Grindal, without astonishment and concern. These men, it is readily allowed, did much; but have Locke, and Clarke, and Hoadly, and Taylor done nothing?'[81]

In 1790 Watson published his *Considerations on the Expediency of revising the Liturgy and Articles of the Church of England* in support of a pamphlet published in the previous year by his friend, the Duke of Grafton (who had become a Unitarian), also urging a revision of the liturgy.[82] He believed that the 1689 proposals, Dr Clarke and Jones' *Free and Candid Disquisitions* were all efforts in the right direction; the Athanasian Creed should go; and Clarke's liturgy or one based on it would be an acceptable substitute for the Book of Common Prayer.[83] '(Were) the question concerning the propriety of Dr Clarke's amended Liturgy, or one on that plan in the place of our present Liturgy, *now* proposed, . . . my opinion is that it would be decided for Dr Clarke's amended Liturgy or one on that plan.'[84] In the same year Watson also supported the Duke of Grafton's plan to introduce into the House of Lords a bill for removing the Athanasian Creed from the Prayer Book, pledging him full personal co-operation when the matter came before the House. At this stage, however, the trend of revolutionary events caused such a revulsion of feeling throughout the country that the project had to be abandoned. Soon afterwards Watson commented, 'No fit opportunity has yet offered for resuming it (i.e. the project), nor probably will offer itself, in my time.'[85] In the early stages of the French Revolution, some Liberals, like Fox and Watson himself, had seen some justification for the movement: a great people were struggling to win their freedom. Some of the Dissenters too joined in with praise for the Revolution, and they began to urge that their religious liberty was a right which had been usurped by the government and should be returned.

But as the Revolution became more republican and violent, English people grew increasingly horrified and frightened. They came to side with Burke — this was a mad outbreak of wicked violence and on no account must it be allowed to happen in this country. An open hostility to reform in general developed and Dissenters were viewed with suspicion. In 1791 there were riots in Birmingham and the houses of Unitarians and other Dissenters were destroyed.[86] By 1793, when the French revolutionaries were crusading against all monarchies, beheaded Louis XVI, and began a programme of forcible dechristianization, a wave of patriotism swept this country. The institutions of Church and State came to be regarded with great attachment as representative of law, order and security. 'There was never much doubt in their (i.e. English churchmen's) minds, that it was the rejection of religion that had wrought disaster and tyranny to France: religion was seen as the guarantee of political freedom, and the establishment of religion by law secured that freedom for all citizens in the State.'[87] Even Bishop Watson sounded the alarm, urging no reform while the French excesses remained unchecked.[88] Change — of any kind — was, at least for the moment, out of the question.

NOTES

1. H. Gee and W. J. Hardy, *Documents Illustrative of English Church History*, 1896, pp. 587–8.
2. E. Cardwell, *A History of Conferences*, 2nd edn 1841, pp. 286–98.
3. Gee and Hardy, *Documents*, pp. 590–1.
4. For a detailed exposition see G. Donaldson, *The Making of the Scottish Prayer Book of 1637*, Edinburgh 1954. This liturgy has been described as 'the Laudian programme in full flower' (G. J. Cuming, 'The Making of the Prayer Book of 1662', in *The English Prayer Book 1549–1662*, Alcuin Club 1963, p. 88).
5. G. J. Cuming, ed., *The Durham Book*, 1961, especially pp. 146–222.
6. Cardwell, *Conferences*, pp. 303–35.
7. Bard Thompson, *Liturgies of the Western Church*, Cleveland and New York 1961, p. 381. For a study of Baxter's liturgy see pp. 375–405.
8. E. C. Ratcliff, 'The Savoy Conference and the Revision of the Book of Common Prayer', in G. F. Nuttall and Owen Chadwick, ed., *From Uniformity to Unity 1662–1962*, 1962, p. 123. See also two works by B. D. Spinks: *From the Lord, and 'the best Reformed Churches': A Study of the Eucharistic Liturgy in the English Puritan and Separatist Traditions 1550–1633*, 1985; *Freedom or Order? The Eucharistic Liturgy in English Congregationalism 1645–1980*, 1984.
9. For further treatment, see the above essay by Professor Ratcliff, and G. J. Cuming, *A History of Anglican Liturgy*, 2nd edn 1982, pp. 116–27.
10. The 1604 Prayer Book was the 1559 Book with minor amendments. For details see F. E. Brightman, *The English Rite*, 2 vols. 1915, vol. 1, p. clxxx.
11. Cuming, *History*, p. 127.
12. Horton Davies, *Worship and Theology in England 1603–1690*, Princeton 1975, p. 386.
13. Gee and Hardy, *Documents*, pp. 600–19.
14. A. G. Matthews, *Calamy Revised*, Oxford 1934, pp. xiii–xiv.
15. In addition to the Act of Uniformity, there was the Corporation Act (1661), the Conventicle Act (1664), the Five Mile Act (1661), and the Test Act (1673).
16. W. Laud, *Works*, Oxford 1847–60, vol. iv, p. 60; cf. E. C. E. Bourne, *The Anglicanism of William Laud*, 1947, pp. 99ff., 154ff.
17. Matthews, *Calamy*, p. 53.
18. R. S. Bosher, *The Making of the Restoration Settlement*, 1951, p. 273.
19. Matthews, *Calamy*, p. 54.
20. Horton Davies, *Worship and Theology*, p. 389.
21. C. Hill, *The Century of Revolution*, Edinburgh 1961, p. 188.
22. T. J. Fawcett, *The Liturgy of Comprehension 1689* (Alcuin Club Collections No. 54) 1973, pp. 6–9.

23. Gee and Hardy, pp. 641–4.
24. They requested the King to withdraw the Declaration: and when he declined to do so, they refused to publish it on the grounds that it was contrary to legislation of the previous reign, and that the dispensing power seemed to them to be illegal.
25. Fawcett, p. 18; G. Every, *The High Church Party 1688–1718*, 1955, p. 22.
26. Fawcett, pp. 20–2.
27. Gee and Hardy, pp. 654–64.
28. Fawcett, pp. 25–7; Every, p. 45.
29. Every, p. 45.
30. This material was published in 1854 by Henry Black as a Parliamentary Paper. Full details of the events and proposals may be found in Fawcett: see also Every, chapter 3.
31. On the other hand, the rewording of the relevant sentence in the prayer also went some way to meet the objection in *The Exceptions*, which claimed that greater efficacy was given to the Blood of Christ than to his Body. The rewording ran, 'that our souls and bodies may be washed and cleansed by the sacrifice of his most precious Body and Blood'.
32. The point is not entirely clear – see Fawcett, pp. 198–9.
33. Quoted in Fawcett, p. 42.
34. Dr Fawcett has compiled a list of these books and pamphlets in *The Revision of the Book of Common Prayer in the Eighteenth Century*, an unpublished Ph.D. thesis, University of London, 1970.
35. 'We hear less of prayers to be said at putting on one's clothes, when going into the street, or at the bringing in of candles; instead, devotion was to spring from attendance at the Church's services which were to be meditated over and prepared for during the rest of the day' (C. J. Stranks, *Anglican Devotion*, 1961, p. 150). For this whole subject, see Stranks, chapter 3; Horton Davies, chapter 10; G. W. O. Addleshaw, *The High Church Tradition, 1941*.
36. Stranks, p. 163.
37. For a detailed study of Stephens, see W. Jardine Grisbrooke, *Anglican Liturgies of the Seventeenth and Eighteenth Centuries* (Alcuin Club Collections No. 40) 1958, pp. 37–55, 201–20. Fawcett's thesis above is also valuable.
38. Grisbrooke, p. 52.
39. Every, p. 139.
40. For a detailed study of Whiston, see Grisbrooke, pp. 55–66, 247–61; and Fawcett's thesis.
41. Horton Davies, *Worship and Theology in England 1690–1850*, 1961, p. 80.
42. Grisbrooke, p. 66.
43. Information from Dr Fawcett.
44. For a detailed study of Henley, see Grisbrooke, pp. 66–70, 263–71; and Fawcett's thesis.
45. Whiston wrote one of the standard lives of Clarke, *Historical Memoirs of the Life and Writings of Dr Samuel Clarke*, 1730, which went through several editions: the most complete is the third, published in 1748. See also J. P. Ferguson, *Dr Samuel Clarke*, 1984.
46. N. Sykes, *William Wake, Archbishop of Canterbury 1657–1737*, 2 vols., Cambridge 1957, vol. 2, pp. 154–7.
47. For a study of Clarke and those who followed him, see A. Elliott Peaston, *The Prayer Book Reform Movement in the Eighteenth Century*, Oxford 1940; also N. Sykes, *Church and State in England in the Eighteenth Century*, Cambridge 1934, pp. 386–8.

48. Sykes, *Church and State*, pp. 384–5; Sykes, *William Wake*, vol. 2, p. 159; N. Sykes, *Edmund Gibson, Bishop of London 1669–1748*, Oxford 1926, pp. 127, 133–5.
49. Peaston, p. 6.
50. Peaston, pp. 5–7.
51. Herring to Newcastle, 12 September 1748, Add. Mss. 32716, f.213, British Museum; quoted in Sykes, *Church and State*, p. 385.
52. For a study of these proposals see Peaston, pp. 38–53.
53. At one time it was believed that Blackburne was the author of *The Candid Disquisitions*, but his sole contribution was to read the greater part of the manuscript. cf. *Dictionary of National Biography*, 1887 edn, vol. 30, p. 127.
54. The signatories included the Master and all the resident Fellows of Peterhouse, Cambridge. cf. Sykes, *Church and State*, p. 381.
55. Porteus had previously been Chaplain to Archbishop Secker, and subsequently became Bishop of Chester (1776) and Bishop of London (1787).
56. R. Hodgson, *The Life of the Rt. Rev. Beilby Porteus*, 1811, pp. 38–40.
57. John Disney married another daughter of Archdeacon Blackburne. He also left the Church of England, succeeding Lindsey as Minister of Essex Street Chapel.
58. Theophilus Lindsey, *Apology of Theophilus Lindsey M.A. on resigning the Vicarage of Catterick, Yorkshire*, 1773, p. 92.
59. Peaston, p. 18.
60. Theophilus Lindsey, *Vindicione Priestleisne: an Address to the Students of Oxford and Cambridge*, 1788, p. 21.
61. Horton Davies, p. 185.
62. ibid.
63. A. E. Peaston, *The Prayer Book Tradition in the Free Churches*, 1964, p. 39; J. C. Bowmer, *The Sacrament of the Lord's Supper in Early Methodism*, 1951, p. 62: Trevor Dearing, *Wesleyan and Tractarian Worship*, 1966, p. 12.
64. Dearing, p. 28.
65. J. E. Rattenbury, *The Conversion of the Wesleys*, 1938, p. 216.
66. Peaston, p. 52.
67. F. Hunter, *Proceedings of the Wesley Historical Society*, June 1942, quoted in Peaston, p. 53.
68. Peaston, p. 53.
69. Full details of the changes may be found in Peaston, pp. 40–51.
70. Dearing, p. 28.
71. ibid., p. 41.
72. The Creed was restored in 1864. On the other hand, it is interesting to note that while Wesley retained the Manual Acts, they were omitted in 1864.
73. Bowmer, p. 84.
74. This was restored in 1846.
75. Peaston, pp. 54–5; J. C. Bowmer, *The Lord's Supper in Methodism 1791–1960*, 1961, p. 30.
76. Peaston, p. 53.
77. Peaston, p. 55; Bowmer, *The Lord's Supper in Methodism*, p. 31.
78. The complete text may be found in T. Wilson, *Works*, (ed. J. Keble, Anglo-Catholic Library of Theology, 7 vols., 1847–63), vol. 5, pp. 73–5.
79. R. Watson, *Anecdotes of the Life of Richard Watson, Bishop of Llandaff*, 1817, pp. 244–5; cf. pp. 39, 43.
80. R. Watson, *Considerations on the Expediency of Revising the Liturgy and Articles of the Church of England, by a consistent Protestant*, 1790, p. 67.
81. ibid., p. 70.

82. Watson, *Anecdotes*, p. 240.
83. Watson, *Considerations*, p. 27.
84. ibid., p. 86.
85. Watson, *Anecdotes*, p. 242.
86. A. Lincoln, *Some Political and Social Ideas of English Dissent 1763–1800*, Cambridge 1938, pp. 7f., 22ff.
87. E. R. Norman, *Church and Society in England 1770–1970*, Oxford 1976, p. 20; cf. H. McLeod, *Religion and the People of Western Europe 1789–1970*, 1981, p. 108.
88. R. Watson, *Charge to the Clergy of Llandaff*, 1798, p. 9; cf. Watson, *Anecdotes*, pp. 302–4.

2

THE NON-JURORS AND THEIR INFLUENCE

I

Any study of liturgical change in the Anglican Church as a whole must of necessity include some mention of the Non-Jurors and their influence. They began with the parliamentary ultimatum of 1689. On 22 February the Convention Parliament resolved that after 1 March all clergy must take the oath of allegiance to William and Mary. Sancroft, Archbishop of Canterbury, promptly refused to take it, firmly believing in Divine Right and Passive Obedience. He was followed by eight other bishops and some four hundred clergy, supported by a number of eminent laymen.[1] They were suspended from office on 1 August and formally deprived on 1 February 1690. Once again the established Church lost a group of able and saintly men; and on this occasion many of them proved to be remarkably competent in the field of liturgy.

It must not be thought, however, that the Non-Jurors became a vigorous and well-disciplined 'splinter' church with widely-established congregations throughout the country, all using their own distinctive forms of worship. The activities of many groups tended to be domestic and even rather clandestine, and records of Non-Juring services are in fact sparse. Some members regarded themselves as loyal adherents to Anglican orthodoxy, and were content to use the 1662 Prayer Book, simply changing the names of the royal family. Queen Anne's conciliatory attitude also encouraged others like Henry Dodwell and Robert Nelson to conform to the Church of England. Hopes of any Stuart restoration dwindled still further when James II's son, the Old Pretender, refused to become an Anglican in 1713, while the defeat of Bonnie Prince Charlie in the Rebellion of 1745 set the final seal on any Jacobite aspirations. Pockets of Non-Jurors struggled on in dwindling numbers; and the last report of their activities in England came from the beginning of the nineteenth century, when their last bishop, Charles Booth, who ministered to a congregation of thirty in Manchester while earning his living as a clock-maker, died in 1805.

But some Non-Jurors, such as George Hickes,[2] took a very different line. In 1713, with the aid of two Scottish bishops, he consecrated Jeremy Collier, Nathaniel Spinckes and Samuel Hawes to the episcopate, and continued to express their dissatisfaction with the accepted forms of worship. Some, like Hickes, used 1549 or the Scottish rite of 1637; others changed the texts of 1662 to suit their convictions.[3] Hickes, for example, in his treatise *Of the Christian Priesthood* (1707) objected in particular to three changes which subsequent revisions of the Prayer Book had made to 1549: the omission of the word 'altar', the transposition of the Prayer of Oblation to a position after communion, and the omission of the rubric ordering the priest to set the bread and the wine on the altar at the offertory. This line was developed further by John Johnson, Rector of Cranbrook, Kent, in his great work *The Unbloody Sacrifice* (1714–18). Despite the fact that Johnson remained within the established Church and found it possible to reconcile his views with the rite of 1662, the Non-Jurors set great store by his views, quoting him frequently.[4] He was a zealous but discriminating advocate of the Clementine Liturgy (*The Apostolic Constitutions* Book 8), and from his studies of the early rites he set out six elements necessary for the celebration of a valid Eucharist:

1. The priest must place bread and wine on the Lord's table.
2. The Words of Institution must be said.
3. The bread must be broken and the wine poured.
4. The priest must offer the bread and the wine after the Words of Institution in commemoration of Christ's death, resurrection and ascension.
5. There must be an Invocation of the Holy Spirit on the bread and wine.
6. There must be intercessions for the Church.

On 26 June 1716 a petition was addressed to the Non-Juring bishops by a number of priests and laymen asking for a greater degree of uniformity in their forms of worship, and the inclusion of four items in the eucharistic liturgy: the mixed chalice, prayer for the departed, the act of oblation, and the epiclesis. A meeting called to discuss these problems on 23 July 1716 under the chairmanship of Jeremy Collier,[5] and attended by the Scottish bishops, Archibald Campbell and James Gadderar, proved stormy and eventually broke up in disarray. Those desiring no change from established custom — the Non-Usagers — were intransigent. Their opponents — the Usagers — therefore decided to break with them and schism ensued. On 19 December Collier summoned a meeting of the bishops, but only Campbell, Gadderar and Brett[6] attended. They considered themselves to be a quorum, however, and decided to draw up a new Communion service 'agreeable to the primitive liturgies, taking in as much of the present established office as might be conveniently done'. On the following day they issued an injunction, requiring priests to make six changes to the existing rite as an interim measure:

1. The substitution of the Summary of the Law for the Decalogue.
2. Water to be mixed openly with the wine at the Offertory.
3. The omission of the words 'militant here in earth' in the Prayer for the Church.
4. The inclusion of prayer for the departed in the Prayer for the Church.

5. The inclusion of an anamnesis-oblation and epiclesis after the Institution Narrative in the Consecration Prayer.
6. The 1662 Prayer of Oblation to follow the Consecration Prayer before Communion.

The new rites were eventually published on 11 March 1718 under the title *A Communion Office taken partly from Primitive Liturgies, and partly from the First English Reformed Common-Prayer-Book, together with Offices for Confirmation and Visitation of the Sick.* These were the work of several hands, and in particular of Brett, Collier and Deacon.[7] It was published in the midst of a pamphlet controversy, sparked off in the previous year by a work from Collier, *Reasons for restoring some prayers and directions as they stand in the Communion Service of the first English Reformed Liturgy.* Clearly the Usagers regarded their demands – the mixed chalice, prayer for the departed, the epiclesis and the prayer of oblation – as 'necessary' for the action of the Eucharist, whereas the Non-Usagers regarded them as merely 'desiderata'. For the Usagers the ancient liturgies were part of the tradition of the Church; and while the Clementine Liturgy was not given that slavish and uncritical devotion accorded to it by Whiston and Henley, nevertheless it was the standard by which other liturgies should be judged. Furthermore, the Greek and Eastern liturgies followed it in having an epiclesis after the Institution Narrative. Substance had also been lent to the Usagers' claims by the publication in 1716 of E. Renaudot's famous two-volume work on the Eastern liturgies, *Liturgiarum Orientalium Collectio*, still an indispensable work of reference today. Brett also defended the Usagers' position in his great work, published in 1720, *A Collection of the Principal Liturgies, Used by the Christian Church in the Celebration of the Holy Eucharist: Particularly the Ancient, viz, the Clementine, as it stands in the Book call'd The Apostolical Constitutions; the Liturgies of S. James, S. Mark, S. Chrysostom, S. Basil, etc., Translated into English by several Hands. With a Dissertation upon them, Shewing their Usefulness and Authority, and pointing out their several Corruptions and Interpolations.*

The existing Anglican liturgy of 1662 was therefore regarded as defective in virtue of the absence of the ancient Usages, and the rite to be preferred was that of 1549, not only because it contained these Usages, but because it was free from the influence of Bucer and Calvin, whom the Non-Jurors detested. However, where 1549 differed from the doctrine and practice of the early Church; or where another liturgy expressed some truth in better words, the necessary alterations were made. Its most distinctive features were as follows:

1. The Introduction was slightly different both in structure and content from 1549: Introit, Salutation, Kyries, Lord's Prayer, Collect for Purity, Summary of the Law, Collect for the King, and Collect of the Day. The Gloria came in its 1662 position before the Blessing.
2. There were three Exhortations, all from 1662.

3. At the Offertory, when the priest laid the bread and the mixed chalice upon the altar, he said a prayer abridged from the Liturgy of St Basil, asking for acceptance of this 'reasonable and unbloody Sacrifice'.
4. The Eucharistic Prayer differed from 1549. After the Sursum Corda, Preface, Sanctus and Benedictus, the tie-word 'Holy' was used to introduce a recital of the acts of creation and redemption, based on those in the Liturgy of St James. The Institution Narrative was then followed by an anamnesis-oblation and epiclesis taken almost verbatim from the Clementine Liturgy, while the Intercessions were a combination of those in 1549 and the Scottish rite of 1637.
5. There was no Agnus Dei during the Communion and no Post-communion Sentences.[8]

There is no doubt that of all the eucharistic rites produced so far, claiming to follow the pattern of the primitive liturgies and the Clementine Liturgy in particular, this Non-Juring rite of 1718 was the most practical and satisfactory. It was restrained in language, sensible in length, primitive in structure, and yet contained a great deal of familiar Prayer Book material. It is not surprising, therefore, that it was a model to which others turned, subsequently becoming a basis for a whole family of rites in the Anglican Communion.

In 1732 an attempt was made to heal the Non-Juring schism; and after lengthy negotiations an Instrument of Union was signed on 17 April. It was clearly a victory for the Non-Usagers, for the Usages were accepted as 'desideranda' but not necessary. This was regarded as a volte-face on the part of Bishop Brett, who signed the Instrument on behalf of the Usagers: but he regarded it as a sacrifice of position solely in the interests of unity, and not as expressive of any change of view on his part. Unfortunately, the Instrument of Union, far from healing the schism, only provoked further division, creating three groups rather than two. First there were those who accepted the Instrument, led by Bishop Brett: secondly there were those who persisted in remaining Non-Usagers, led by Bishop Blackburne: and thirdly there were the persistent Usagers — the greater number — led by Bishop Campbell, who ensured the perpetuation of his group by consecrating two further bishops in 1733, Roger Lawrence and Thomas Deacon, a stepson of Jeremy Collier. These Usagers continued to use the 1718 liturgy until 1748, when Deacon, now leader of the group, enjoined the use of a book of rites which he himself had compiled in 1734, *A Compleat Collection of Devotions, both Publick and Private; Taken from the Apostolical Constitutions, the Ancient Liturgies, and the Common Prayer Book of the Church of England.*

This *Collection* was a considerably revised Prayer Book, containing the Eucharist, the daily offices, a penitential office, the ordinal, and the occasional offices. The revision was based on the practice and teaching of the Church of the first four centuries, and with the Clementine Liturgy being regarded as the most free from interpolation of any kind.[9] The offices of Morning and

Evening Prayer, which were basically those of 1662, nevertheless had some interesting new features, notably the provision of the Gloria in excelsis as a canticle at Mattins and the inclusion of a litany after the collects. In Baptism Deacon restored the 1549 exorcism, the anointing with oil, the use of the passive formula ('X is baptized'), the white garment, and the draught of milk and honey.

The Eucharist in pattern resembled the rite of 1718, although with variations.[10] The Introduction, for example, omitted the Lord's Prayer and the Summary of the Law, while the eucharistic prayer, including the intercessions, was almost entirely from the Clementine Liturgy. It should be pointed out that Deacon's concern was not with this particular rite to the exclusion of all else. He was steeped in the ancient liturgies and the writings of the first four centuries, and his knowledge of this field was equalled by only Brett and Rattray.[11] His love for the primitive Church stemmed from his early years, first through his intimate relations with George Hickes at Oxford, and then through his admiration for Thomas Brett, to whom he dedicated his first book, *The Doctrine of the Church of Rome concerning Purgatory*, in 1718. Nevertheless, it was Deacon's regard for the early Church which compelled him to reject Brett's plea to come to terms with the Usages problem in 1732. Whereas Brett was born and bred within the Church of England, Deacon was never a Church of England man, having been ordained priest by his Non-Juring stepfather while still in his late teens. He considered the Church of England to be defective, not only on account of its lack of loyalty to the true sovereign, but also because of its errors in doctrine and worship. His ideal was an Orthodox Catholic Church independent of Crown and Rome and looking to the first four centuries for its norms of belief and worship.[12] But while he was not in the mainstream of Anglican thought and practice, he was not without influence in the liturgical development of Anglicanism. His influence on Rattray was considerable, and the Scottish bishops clearly set great store on his doctrinal and liturgical principles when producing the rite of 1764.

II

With the restoration of the monarchy in 1660, episcopacy was also restored to Scotland, a number of clergy being despatched to England to secure consecration as bishops. These bishops made little attempt to introduce Anglican worship into their dioceses, however. Indeed, for some years there was a freedom over forms of worship which was unique.[13] Some men, like Robert Leighton, Bishop of Dunblane and Alexander Burnet, Archbishop of Glasgow favoured 1662, and copies of both this and the Scottish book of 1637 were available in the country: but for the most part public worship was basically Presbyterian in form. Gradually, however, the use of 1662 spread; and in 1680 the Privy Council agreed to a request that it might be used privately at family worship by a number of 'persons of quality'. By the reign of Queen Anne its use was even more general. Indeed, in 1712 it came to be recognized in a Toleration Act, or, to give it its full title, 'An Act to prevent the Disturbing of those of the Episcopal Communion in that part of Great Britain called Scotland in the exercise of their Religious Worship and in the use of the Liturgy of the Church of England'. This toleration, however, applied only to those clergy prepared to take the oath of allegiance to Queen Anne and the oath of abjuration of the Stuart dynasty. They ministered to what were known as 'Qualified Congregations', where 1662 was used. Many of those belonging to such congregations were English people living in Scotland, and their chapels were commonly known as 'English Chapels'.

Over against these juring episcopalians were the Non-Juring bulk of the Scottish bishops and clergy, who led a vigorous existence until the 1745 Rebellion, after which they were subjected to repressive measures. During the reign of Queen Anne there was a marked liturgical revival: and in 1712, with considerable help from George Seton, 5th Earl of Winton, a new edition of the Scottish 1637 book was published in Edinburgh. The links between Scottish and English Non-Jurors were close; and during the Usages controversy in England, both sides were keen to secure Scottish support. In 1718 the Usagers sent the Reverend Francis Peck to Edinburgh to seek a synodical decision in their favour. He suggested that the 1637 rite should be printed by itself with two changes: the offertory rubric should make provision for a commixture, and the whole or at least the latter part of the heading of the Prayer for the Church should be omitted. Bishops Campbell, Falconar and Gadderar, supported by Dr Rattray, approved the proposal; and Gadderar undertook something on these lines in 1722 and 1724 with the publication of the 'wee bookies' — reprints of the 1637 communion rite beginning at the Offertory, and omitting the two exhortations for giving notice together with the rubrics and collects after the Blessing. His aim was to encourage the use of this rite and quietly 'engraft' upon it the two usages not already there. The other bishops, including the Primus, Fullarton, disapproved, however, and until 1724 some controversy ensued. A compromise, known as the First Concordat, was then reached on 4 July of that year, by which Gadderar made certain undertakings in respect of the Usages in the interests of peace and unity. On the commixture, he agreed to discontinue the public use of the practice and to see that others under his jurisdiction did the same: at the same time he expressed his willingness to communicate from a chalice in which the consecrated wine had not been mixed with water. He also undertook not to insist on the introduction of any ancient Usages other than those authorized in the Scottish rite of 1637 and which the Primus and other bishops had permitted.

In December 1731 a second Concordat was agreed and signed by the entire episcopate, whereby they undertook to use only the Scottish (1637) or English (1662) rites in public worship, and to ensure the peace of the Church by not introducing 'any of the ancient usages, concerning which there has been lately a difference among us'.[14] Undue friction was therefore avoided, while two of the Usages — the Oblation and the Epiclesis —

received specific sanction. This agreement seems to have been observed, although with some freedom as to the order of prayers. One text provided the following order:

1. Offertory, with 1 Chronicles 29.10–11.
2. Exhortation, 'Dearly Beloved in the Lord'.
3. Sursum Corda, Consecration Prayer (including Oblation and Invocation) and Lord's Prayer.
4. Prayer for the Church.
5. The Penitential Section.
6. Prayer of Humble Access and Communion.[15]

Subsequently this was further modified by the addition of the Salutation to the Sursum Corda and the transposition of the Lord's Prayer and the Prayer for the Church.[16] In 1735 two booksellers published the rite with this changed order as a private venture, together with two further changes for which there was no sanction: the omission of the words 'militant here in earth' in the bidding preceding the Prayer for the Church and the insertion of 'which we now offer unto thee' in the Oblation. This was reprinted in 1743; and since the unmodified 1637 rite had not been available for some time, the bishops were clearly not opposed to its use. Further editions appeared in 1752, 1759 and 1764.

Meanwhile a new figure of considerable significance had appeared. Thomas Rattray, Laird of Craighall in Perthshire, became Bishop of Brechin in 1727, Dunkeld in 1731, and Primus in 1739.[17] His liturgical studies convinced him that while the Non-Jurors' rite of 1718 followed the order of the Church's primitive liturgy, the pattern to be followed was that of the Liturgy of St James, from the Church of Jerusalem. His great work therefore was to produce the text of this liturgy and to compare it with the other known texts of the early Church – the Clementine Liturgy, the rites of St Mark, St John Chrysostom, and St Basil, together with St Cyril's account of the Jerusalem rite in Book 5 of his *Mystagogical Catecheses.* To this excellent comparative study, entitled *The Ancient Liturgy of the Church of Jerusalem*, he appended a rite adapted for current use from St James.[18]

Clearly this appendix was a fine, scholarly piece of work, although it is doubtful if it was used elsewhere than at Craighall. As Dowden says, 'It was too far removed in character from the service with which both priests and people were familiar to allow it any chance of being adopted in its own form by the Church.'[19] The rite was concerned only with the Liturgy of the Faithful, starting with the Kiss of Peace and the Offertory: but in a letter to Bishop Keith, dated 20 October 1736,[20] he suggested the use of Mattins as a form of ante-Communion, a proposal with a decidedly modern appearance, although there is little evidence of its use in Scotland. This rite followed the order: Peace, Offertory including 1 Chronicles 29.10–11, Eucharistic Prayer, Intercession, Lord's Prayer and Communion; while the Eucharistic Prayer contained an Oblation and an Epiclesis after the Institution Narrative. He clearly supported the Usages, although he did not believe that people should separate from the Church on account of them – they should observe the prudent rule of common sense.

Rattray died in 1743 before his great work could be published: but it appeared in the following year, and it was not long before discerning clergy recognized that it offered possibilities of a rite superior to that of 1637 and its adaptations. Unfortunately national events intervened to subject the Scottish Non-Jurors to over a decade of virtual persecution, providing scant opportunity for liturgical development. 1745 saw the Jacobite Rebellion ending with the defeat of Prince Charles Edward at Culloden. The Duke of Cumberland was determined to destroy the Non-Juring chapels wherever he could find them, and the punitive measures which followed made it almost impossible for clergy to exercise their ministry effectively. An Act of 1746 prohibited clergy from officiating in chapels unless they took the necessary oath of obedience to George II before 1 September. Clergy discovered officiating after that date without qualifying were liable to imprisonment or even transportation; while members of the congregations could also be punished and the meeting houses shut. Furthermore, those seeking ordination were compelled to do so from bishops in England or Ireland. Then a further Act of 1748 'disqualified' all clergy ordained by the Scottish bishops, making it impossible for them to minister except in secret.

Despite the legislation the Non-Jurors struggled on. Only five clergy attempted to comply with the 1746 Act by 'qualifying', and most continued to minister to their people in small groups in their own houses at different times. Some ordinands sought ordination in England and then returned to Scotland to minister: some lay people simply attended 'English chapels'; and the bishops managed to carry on despite the difficulties. Only after the accession of George III in 1760 did life return to normal. The new king had no desire to enforce the legislation against the Non-Jurors; and a policy of toleration permitted the clergy to minister openly once again.[21]

In the face of these problems the Primus, William Falconar of Edinburgh, contrived to produce a Communion rite in 1755 which clearly showed the influence of Rattray, following his sequence of Institution Narrative, Oblation and Epiclesis in the Eucharistic Prayer. Then in 1762–3, with assistance from Bishop Robert Forbes, he undertook a further revision which was published in 1764. Although not given formal synodical approval, it was issued under the authority of the Primus and was rapidly accepted by the whole Episcopal Church in Scotland. Much of the material came from 1637: the Offertory Sentences, the Prayer for the Church, most of the Eucharistic Prayer and the Words of Administration. But there were essential differences. In 1637 the Invocation preceded the Institution Narrative, but in 1764 it followed as in Rattray: while the general structure also followed 1718, Deacon and Rattray: Offertory, Sursum Corda, Eucharistic Prayer, Intercession (including departed), Lord's Prayer, Penitence, Humble Access and Communion. Bishop John Skinner of Aberdeen commented, 'In this favourable appearance of returning serenity it was thought proper to revise our Communion Office, and bring it, now that there was no contention or difference about it, to as exact a conformity with the ancient standards of eucharistic service as it would bear.'[22] This rite of 1764 marked a watershed in Anglican liturgical history. On the one hand it gave official recognition to a liturgy following primitive patterns, which had been studied carefully by scholars over the past century. Furthermore, the revision had been unofficial, with no synodical approval. When the bishops adopted this *textus receptus* of the 1764 rite, they were only recognizing something which had come into being by a process of experiment. On the other hand it marked the beginning of a new family of eucharistic rites in the Anglican Communion stemming from 1549 rather than 1662 in a number of significant respects, with the first development overseas taking place in America. A century later a Bishop of Connecticut was to declare, 'In giving the Consecration Prayer to us Scotland gave us a greater boon than when she gave us the episcopate':[23] and in Bishop Dowden's judgement, the person to whom both Churches owed a great debt for the most characteristic features of their respective liturgies was Thomas Rattray.[24]

III

At the time of the American Declaration of Independence in 1776 American churchmen considered themselves to be members of the Church of England, with the Bishop of London as their diocesan bishop and the 1662 Prayer Book as their liturgy. But no English bishop of that time crossed the Atlantic to fulfil an episcopal obligation. The first American State to seek a remedy for this defect was Connecticut, whose clergy elected Dr Samuel Seabury as bishop on 25 March 1783, instructing him to seek consecration in England, or if refused there, in Scotland. In the event he was consecrated in Aberdeen on 14 November 1784 by three Scottish bishops, Kilgour (the Primus), Petrie and Skinner. The 1764 rite was used at their consecration, and all four bishops signed a concordat between 'the Catholic remainder of the ancient Church of Scotland and the now rising Church in the State of Connecticut'. One of the articles of the agreement expressed the hope of the Scottish bishops that Dr Seabury would commend their eucharistic rite to his brethren and sanction its use.

In the following year a convention was held at Philadelphia (27 September to 7 October), at which representatives from seven states, New York, New Jersey, Pennsylvania, Delaware, Maryland, Virginia and South Carolina, drafted a constitution for the Protestant Episcopal Church in America and agreed to a revision of the Book of Common Prayer. The revision was largely in the hands of Dr William Smith of Maryland, and he in turn owed much to a set of proposals submitted by a group from New England. The resulting revision, largely accepted by the Convention and published in 1786, made it clear that to some extent their hearts had overruled their heads. They were greatly desirous to remove anything which might prove a stumbling-block to those people otherwise desiring to enter the Church. But this desire to ease tender consciences hardly matched their statement in the Preface of the Proposed Book: 'It is far from the intention of this Church to depart from the Church of England, any farther than local circumstances require, or to deviate in anything essential to the true meaning of the Thirty-nine Articles.'[25] What they produced was a revision on latitudinarian lines, very much in accord with the abortive English 1689 revision. Indeed, Dr Smith frankly praised this work in his sermon to the Convention: 'The greatest and most important alterations and amendments were proposed at the Revolution, that great era of liberty, when in 1689 commissioners were appointed.'[26]

The Proposed Book provoked considerable hostility. Bishop Seabury strongly attacked it, declaring 'the true doctrine is left too unguarded, and . . . the offices are, some of them, lowered to such a degree, that they will, in a great measure, lose their influence'.[27] At the same time he 'recommended' the use of a draft Communion Service of his own, largely derived from the Scottish rite of 1764, a recommendation almost universally adopted by his own clergy of Connecticut. The English episcopate, who had asked to see the proposals before agreeing to a request to consecrate further American bishops, also showed scant enthusiasm for the proposals, commenting that they 'showed less respect to our liturgy than its own excellence, and your own declared attachment to it, had led us to expect'.[28]

Not surprisingly the Proposed Book proved a dead letter. Wiser counsels prevailed, and a further attempt at revision at a General Convention in Philadelphia in October 1789 met with general approval, finally coming into being on 1 October 1790. It was quite a remarkable compilation, denoting a conscious attempt to produce a book more 'contemporary' than 1662, with fewer archaisms, significant abbreviations, a wider range of services, and a recognition of hymnody. It also drew material from a wide variety of sources, the 1662 and Scottish 1637 Prayer Books, the Scottish rite of 1764, the American Proposed Book of 1786, John Jones' *Free and Candid Disquisitions* of 1749, Ireland 1711, the SPG, and Jeremy Taylor. Its most significant features were:

1. Although Black Letter Days and vigils disappeared from the Calendar, some additional forms of service were provided for special occasions: Family Prayers, probably known through their provision by SPG missionaries; the Visitation of Prisoners, from a form drawn up in Dublin 1711; Harvest Thanksgiving; the Consecration of Churches, added 1799; and the Institution of Ministers, added 1804.
2. A selection of psalms was provided for use at any service instead of the psalms appointed.
3. In the Daily Offices, the Benedictus, Magnificat and Nunc Dimittis were replaced by psalms; while in the Apostles' Creed the phrase 'He descended into hell' could be omitted or replaced by 'He went into the place of departed spirits', and 'again' was omitted after 'He rose'.

4. A combination of Morning Prayer with Holy Communion appeared to be encouraged by the following provisions:
   a. The use of Gloria in excelsis as an alternative to Gloria Patri after the psalms, while it could be replaced by a hymn at the end of Holy Communion.
   b. The collect of the day was omitted at Morning Prayer, and the first Lord's Prayer and the Nicene Creed were omitted from Holy Communion. The Nicene Creed could also be used at Morning Prayer.
5. The Eucharistic Prayer, mainly through the efforts of Bishop Seabury, followed the pattern of the Scottish rite of 1764, with the Oblation and Epiclesis after the Institution Narrative: but the text of the Epiclesis was from the Scottish rite of 1637. Again the Intercessions and the Penitential material did not follow the Eucharistic Prayer as in 1764, but followed the Offertory as in 1637. This use of 1637 is not surprising, for many Scottish clergy in America had tended to use the 'Wee Bookies' from Scotland, and these could have been in use for some seventy-five years.

The whole Prayer Book underwent some corrections in 1793, and the latter edition came to be known as the 'Standard Text'. Between 1793 and 1892 this Standard Text was subject to further minor change on six occasions: but in all essentials it remained the same book. Clearly many of its features would have met with the approval of many English liturgical reformers of very different schools of thought during the seventeenth and eighteenth centuries. But the young American Church had good cause to regard its handiwork with a certain degree of pride.[29]

NOTES

1. One bishop, Cartwright of Chester, followed James II into exile. One Irish bishop and practically all the Scottish clergy — bishops and priests — also refused to take the oath.
2. George Hickes (1642–1715): vicar of All Hallows, Barking 1680; Dean of Worcester 1683; consecrated titular Bishop of Thetford by the Non-Jurors 1694. A learned and saintly man, he became the acknowledged head of the Non-Jurors in 1709.
3. Grisbrooke, op. cit., pp. 88–9.
4. Johnson's views may be studied in detail in Grisbrooke, pp. 71–87.
5. Jeremy Collier (1650–1726): rector of Ampton, Suffolk 1679; Lecturer of Gray's Inn 1685; consecrated Non-Juring bishop 1713.
6. Thomas Brett (1667–1743): vicar of Great Chart 1696 and other incumbencies; consecrated Non-Juring bishop 1716. An eminent liturgical scholar, he wrote *Dissertation on the Ancient Liturgies* 1720.
7. Thomas Deacon (1697–1753): ordained deacon and priest by Collier 1716; consecrated Non-Juring bishop 1733. He became the leader of the Non-Jurors.
8. The text may be found in Grisbrooke, pp. 275–96.

9. A detailed commentary on these services may be found in Deacon's great work, *A Full, True, and Comprehensive View of Christianity*, 1747. See Grisbrooke, pp. 113–35.
10. The text may be found in Grisbrooke, pp. 297–316.
11. The inscription on his tombstone in St Anne's Churchyard, Manchester, described him as 'the most primitive of bishops'.
12. H. Broxap, *A Biography of Thomas Deacon*, Manchester 1911, pp. 140, 184.
13. Liturgical developments in Scotland may be traced in greater detail in: J. Dowden, *The Scottish Communion Office of 1764*, 2nd edn, Oxford 1922; F. Goldie, *A Short History of the Episcopal Church in Scotland*, 2nd edn, Edinburgh 1976; D. Forrester and D. Murray, ed., *Studies in the History of Worship in Scotland*, Edinburgh 1984.
14. Grisbrooke, p. 152; Dowden, p. 64; Goldie, p. 52.
15. This text is now in the library of Bishop Jolly, Edinburgh Theological College. Grisbrooke, pp. 153–4; Dowden, pp. 64–5.
16. Grisbrooke, p. 154; Dowden, p. 65.
17. He was elected to the see of Edinburgh just before his death in 1743.
18. *An Office for the Sacrifice of the Holy Eucharist, being the Ancient Liturgy of the Church of Jerusalem, to which Proper Rubricks are added for Direction.* For the text and a detailed commentary, see Grisbrooke, pp. 136–49, 317–32.
19. Dowden, p. 74.
20. Quoted in Grisbrooke, pp. 146–9.
21. For this policy of repression, see Goldie, op. cit., pp. 58–63.
22. Dowden, p. 98. It was not until 1792, however, that the Penal Laws were finally repealed by Parliament.
23. Quoted in Forrester and Murray, op. cit., p. 67.
24. Dowden, p. 93.
25. W. McGarvey, *Liturgiae Americanae*, Philadelphia 1895, p. xix.
26. ibid., p. xvi.
27. ibid., pp. xxii–iii.
28. ibid., p. xxiii.
29. In addition to McGarvey's monumental work, information on the American Prayer Book can be found in Dowden, op. cit.; Massey H. Shepherd, *The Oxford American Prayer Book Commentary*, New York 1955; Marion J. Hatchett, *Commentary on the American Prayer Book*, New York 1980.

3

THE NINETEENTH CENTURY

I

Loyalty to the Establishment and to the Prayer Book was relatively short-lived. Once the war with France was over in 1815, reaction set in against Tory rule and pleas for reform both sacred and secular came to be heard on an ever-increasing scale. The Whigs adopted a policy of Peace, Retrenchment and Reform, while some significant changes took place even before they assumed office in 1830. In 1828 the Test and Corporation Acts were finally repealed, and in the following year Roman Catholics were emancipated. But episcopal opposition to reform only tended to make the Church unpopular. William Palmer, one of the early Tractarians, painted this graphic picture: 'It was then that we felt ourselves assailed by enemies from within and without. Our prelates insulted and threatened by ministers of state . . . clamours loud and long for the overthrow of the Church – Dissenters and Romanists triumphing in the prospect of its subversion, and assailing it with every epithet calculated to stimulate popular hatred.'[1]

The enemies from within were people like Peel's brother-in-law, Lord Henley, who published his popular *Plan of Church Reform* in 1832, proposing the exclusion of bishops from the House of Lords, the curtailment of pluralities, a more equitable sharing of clerical incomes, and the establishment of Ecclesiastical Commissioners. Another was Dr Thomas Arnold, with his equally popular *Principles for Church Reform.* He pleaded for a truly national Church, comprehending a wide variety of opinions: the Church could only be saved if it included Dissenters – but not Unitarians, Quakers and Roman Catholics; the Articles would therefore have to be far more comprehensive and public worship involve the use of both the Prayer Book and free forms; this would avoid the difficulties involved in a revision of the Prayer Book. Nevertheless, there were others who were not averse to liturgical change, pleading their cause with moderation. The High Church magazine *The British Critic* admitted in a number of articles that it would be wrong to assume that the Prayer Book was incapable of change or improvement and admitted that the damnatory clauses in the Athanasian Creed did trouble many consciences.[2] The Evangelical magazine *The Christian Observer* made similar points, adding that the Church, with all her faults, was well worth reforming:[3] and Connop Thirlwall, one of the great and learned liberal churchmen of the century, wrote in 1832: 'Among the things most indispensably requisite to the stability of the Church of England, I hold to be a revision of her liturgy . . . Many persons are driven out of the communion of the Church by their repugnance to its liturgical form, a repugnance springing from the purest and most enlightened conviction.'[4]

The first person to take specific action on liturgical change was Prebendary Charles Wodehouse of St Margaret's, King's Lynn, who as early as 1824 approached Archbishop Howley and a number of bishops, following this with a petition to the House of Lords through the Earl of Gosford in 1833, but all to no effect.[5] He was followed by William Winstanley Hull, a barrister, and the Ven. Edward Berens, Archdeacon of Berkshire, who published pamphlets in 1828, described by *The British Critic* as 'pilot balloons' sent up to ascertain the movement of popular feeling on the subject.[6] Reaction was apparently favourable, for they marked the beginning of a stream of pamphlets and books which developed into a flood and continued for the rest of the century.[7] The schemes produced between 1828 and 1840 largely followed a uniform pattern with the proposals having a familiar ring:

1. A revision of the lectionary, including the removal of lessons from the Apocrypha and of passages which were distasteful or unedifying.
2. An abridgement of the three morning services.
3. The omission of the Athanasian Creed, or at least of its damnatory clauses.
4. The modification of all references to baptismal regeneration and priestly absolution.
5. The revision of certain passages in the Marriage Service on the grounds of delicacy.

Such proposals received wide coverage, not least through Lord Henley's *Plan of Church Reform*, which went through numerous editions. Henley had no specific proposals of his own, but he fully approved the use of the 1689 scheme as a basis for revision, for that would help secure the return of many Dissenters to the established Church.[8] Nor were these views without episcopal support: Bishop Maltby of Chichester, Bishop Carey of St Asaph and Archbishop Whateley of Dublin all spoke out in favour of change. Whateley was also ahead of his time in urging one point of great significance. In 1840 he argued in the House of Lords that Parliament was not competent to deal with such spiritual matters: the Church should have freedom to order her own forms of worship, and this should be done by reviving Convocation or by setting up some other legislative body to deal with it.[9]

In the face of these pleas for revision, a strong defence was mounted by the Tractarians. The foundations for such a defence were laid by two men, Dr Charles Lloyd, Regius Professor of Divinity (1822–9) and Bishop of Oxford (1827–9), and William Palmer, Fellow of Magdalen College, Oxford (1832–55). In 1823 Lloyd gave a course of private lectures on Christian doctrine and the history and structure of the Prayer Book to younger dons of the University, among whom were Newman, Pusey, Froude, Oakeley, Robert and Isaac Wilberforce and Denison. Lloyd demonstrated that the sources of the Prayer Book were both primitive and medieval, and he encouraged his pupils to a sympathetic study of the medieval Breviary and Missal. He was also responsible for publishing in 1825 new editions of the relevant Reformation documents *The Bishops' Book* and *The King's Book.*[10] His work was continued and in greater depth by William Palmer, who had come to Oxford from Trinity College, Dublin. He was a man of immense learning — Newman described him as 'the only really learned man among us' — thoroughly conversant with the early liturgical texts then available and what had been written about them. In his *Origines Liturgicae*, published in 1832, he took the line adopted by Charles Wheatly more than a hundred years previously and developed it, pointing out that there were not one but four great parent rites, all of apostolic source. Origins were much richer and more diverse than many writers had imagined.[11] The Prayer Book's ancestry was therefore something of which Anglicans could be proud. 'The English Prayer-Book was not composed in a few years, nor by a few men: it has descended to us with the improvements and the approbation of many centuries; and they who truly feel the calm and sublime elevation of our hymns and prayers, participate in the spirit of primitive devotion . . . There is scarcely a portion of our Prayer Book which cannot in some way be traced to ancient offices.'[12] Palmer's book was opportune in conveying to a wider public and in greater detail what Lloyd had attempted privately. Furthermore it appeared at precisely the right moment, just before the Oxford Movement 'went public'. J. H. Overton regarded Palmer's book as 'the chief factor in the preparation for the movement which was fast approaching'.[13]

The integrity of the Prayer Book together with the doctrine of Apostolic Succession were in fact the main points which the early leaders of the Movement agreed to uphold.[14] So they pleaded for a return to its original ideals, convinced that the Church of England possessed therein a worthy foundation for all its faith and practice. Meetings were held; local defence associations were formed; and an address was presented to the Archbishop of Canterbury in February 1834 expressing 'deep-rooted attachment to that venerable Liturgy, in which she [the Church] had embodied in the language of ancient piety the Orthodox and Primitive Faith', and deprecating the restless desire for change.[15] Other addresses followed: and then came the *Tracts for the Times.* Tract 3 by Newman and Tract 4 by Keble defended the Prayer Book against change; Tracts 38 and 41 by Newman pleaded for loyalty to it: Tract 9 by Froude, Tract 43 by Thomas Keble, and Tract 75 by Newman opposed the shortening of church services: John Keble defended the Lectionary in Tract 13, the Athanasian Creed in Tract 22, and the Baptism and Marriage Services in Tract 40: while Newman defended the Burial Services in Tract 3. Other Tracts upheld the doctrines enshrined in the Prayer Book services: priestly absolution, baptismal regeneration, the real presence, and the eucharistic sacrifice. Keble also defended the Prayer Book in a series of poems which first appeared in *The British Magazine* in March 1833 and were then reproduced in *Lyra Apostolica*, a book of

Tractarian verse published in 1836. Keble's poems had a section to themselves under the title 'Let us depart hence', an utterance made by angels protesting against popular contemporary religious views. They began with 'Profanation', a general protest against the agitation for reform, followed by 'The Athanasian Creed', 'The Burial Service' and 'The Length of the Prayers', and concluding with 'The Remnant', in which the angels, although departing in the face of reform, promised not to forsake those who remained faithful to the Prayer Book.

> We go, but faithful hearts will find us near,
> Who cling beside their Mother in her woes,
> Who love the rites that erst their fathers loved,
> Nor tire of David's hymn and Jesus' prayer:
> Their quiet altars, whereso'er removed,
> Shall clear with incense sweet the unholy air;
> In persecution safe, in scorn approved,
> Angels, and He who rules them, will be there.[16]

Nevertheless, this Tractarian adherence to the Prayer Book was by no means blind and uncritical. Keble, for example, while arguing that 'in all great things the Prayer Book is really the voice of the ancient Church',[17] admitted that it had deficiencies when compared with the early liturgies — a fact which the labours of Lloyd and Palmer had brought to light. Isaac Williams made a similar point in Tract 86,[18] arguing that whereas the virtues of the Prayer Book inculcated penitence and obedience, there were also losses because it lacked certain ancient elements. There was also a high regard for the 1549 Prayer Book, Pusey, for example, seeing it in Tract 81 as the key for interpretation of the subsequent revisions of the liturgy.[19] What had to be realized was the fact that the Church of England was in a state of captivity and humiliation; and in such a state even 'the crumbs from the Apostles' table' — for such was Froude's description of the Prayer Book — should be taken and used with thankfulness; 'they are far better than we deserve'.[20] What had to be avoided at all costs were schemes for revising the Prayer Book in a latitudinarian and erastian spirit. In the Prayer Book the Church knew what it had: but if such a reform were permitted, there was no knowing what the Church might get. Deficiencies in the existing rites could be made good by the private use of liturgical material from earlier rites: and it is interesting to note than in recommending this Pusey quoted the custom of Bishop Wilson of Sodor and Man as setting a good precedent.[21]

The Tractarians were therefore concerned to defend the integrity of the Prayer Book and to plead for loyalty to it: services should not be mangled and adapted, and rubrics should not be ignored. In this they were soon to receive enthusiastic support from Cambridge. In May 1839 J. M. Neale, Edward Boyle, Benjamin Webb and others founded the Camden Society, mainly for the study of ecclesiology and for the restoration of churches on medieval lines. There was no mistaking where their sympathies lay. Their periodical, *The Ecclesiologist*, stated in 1843, 'Either we must side with Pilkington, Grindal, Coverdale, Hutchinson and Burnet, in understanding our Church formularies in the lowest sense; . . . we must set up as a pattern the laxest of times, and then, with the help of a few glosses, parings down, and distortions, we shall find ourselves not far from Geneva: or else, taking our stand on the ground held by Andrewes, Bancroft, Laud, Wren, Montague, Ken and Thorndike, we must affirm that laxity and Puritanism have been *in* the Church, but were never *of* it, that where two directions appear to differ, that which involves the more Catholic sense is to be preferred; that we are to examine how much we are encouraged, not how little we are allowed, to do: and we shall vindicate for our Church that position to which, as a branch of the Church catholick she is so well entitled.'[22]

Nevertheless, pleas for such a restoration of what was claimed to be genuine Prayer Book worship provoked cries of popery. Pamphlets and articles of protest appeared in increasing numbers, and bishops made full use of their Charges to express their opposition.[23] The arguments against the Tractarians took two main lines. In the first place, it was argued that they were fussily and needlessly reviving usages which technically and legally might be correct but with the passage of time had fallen into disuse: there was little point in attempting to revive what the Church had already found unnecessary and had abandoned. Typical of such a line was an article on Ritualism by John Wilson Croker in *The Quarterly Review*, May 1843, describing the activities of these 'rubricians', who stood for the law: first there were their 'novel usages' — such as daily services, the use of the Prayer for the Church Militant when there was no communion, preaching in a surplice and the use of credence tables; then there were their 'fooleries' — altar candles — even unlit, bowing to the east or to the altar, and the eastward position of the celebrant at Holy Communion: such practices were to be deplored. Archbishop Howley himself set a seal on such an approach when he addressed a Pastoral Letter to the Province of Canterbury in January 1845, paying lip service to obedience to the law and to rubric and yet at the same time defending those who followed customary usage rather than rubric.[24]

The second attack on the Tractarians took the line that if their beliefs and practices were in fact justified by the Prayer Book, then the Prayer Book must be revised. The ground must be cut from under their feet. It was a view taken up with particular enthusiasm from 1859 onwards by a small but noisy body called 'The Association for Promoting a Revision of the Book of Common Prayer', led by Lord Ebury and others who formed 'a fanatically earnest, energetic and most aristocratic group of Low Church Reformers'.[25] For over twenty years it disseminated literature, organized petitions and secured the introduction of a succession of revision bills — all abortive — in the House of Lords. Its general attitude was expressed in the Special Address of the General Council published in May 1869: 'But for the few relics of a Popish Age, particularly in the Ordinal, the Visitation of the Sick, the Baptismal Service, and the Catechism, semi-Romanists could never have found a resting-place within the Church of England. Once remove these fruitful causes of perversion to Rome itself, or of a masked holding of Rome's tenets, and the Prayer Book will become a manual of devotion which cannot be surpassed, and a bond of union among the Reformed Churches throughout the world.'[26] But the programme of changes required was all too familiar: the removal of references to eucharistic sacrifice, the real presence, priestly absolution, and baptismal regeneration; the omission of the Apocrypha, the Athanasian Creed and indelicacies in the Marriage Service; at least the optional use of Saints' Days; the abbreviation and increased flexibility of services; and the replacement of the Ornaments Rubric by some direction in accordance with unbroken post-Reformation usage.

Feelings ran high, and the accusations of popery were undoubtedly given substance by the steady secession of prominent Tractarians – Newman, Ward, Manning, R. Wilberforce and others – to Rome. Then fuel was added to the flames in September 1850 when Pope Pius IX created England an ecclesiastical province of the Church of Rome under an Archbishop of Westminster and twelve suffragan bishops, provoking the Prime Minister, Lord John Russell, to write his famous open letter to Bishop Maltby of Durham, laying responsibility for this papal action at the feet of the Tractarians and denouncing their 'mimicries of High Church superstition'. The Clergy Discipline Act of 1840 lay at hand to deal with such clergy. Not only did it oblige all clergy to 'assent and consent' to the Book of Common Prayer and to subscribe to the Thirty-Nine Articles, but it also became an offence for an incumbent to fail to hold the necessary services in his church or to use unauthorized ritual or ceremonial. A series of court cases on ritualism did in fact take place over a period of some thirty odd years, lasting from Westerton v Liddell in 1854 to Read v the Bishop of Lincoln (Edward King) in 1888, but they proved to be ineffective. A further attempt to restore discipline was made in 1874 with the Public Worship Regulation Act: and Archbishop Tait, when introducing the measure, admitted that the expense of time and money in litigation was ruining the true spiritual work of the Church. The Act was a sad error of judgement on his part, and it did not take long for him to realize his mistake. But it has to be admitted that both he and the bishops were under strong pressure, not least from Queen Victoria herself, to restrain liturgical innovators. Furthermore, they were anxious to prevent Parliament from legislating on what actually took place at services in church; for they knew only too well that such legislation would only be ignored and might even create schism. At least it could be said for the Act that it did not alter the law of worship but only the machinery for enforcing it, as an alternative to the Discipline Act of 1840. When, therefore, the Measure was passed, they urged moderation, appealing to the clergy to accept it in a spirit of mutual understanding. But in fact it did nothing to restrain ritualism and as a simple method of exercising discipline proved to be a failure.[27] It was one thing to bring a case to find out what the law really was: it was another to compel obedience to the law. So the Evangelical journal *The Record* had to admit in 1884: 'Ecclesiastical litigation is not only undesirable, but extremely likely to do mischief in the cause of Evangelical truth. We can hardly imagine any course more certain to prejudice public opinion against the party who pursues it, more inevitably doomed to failure so far as practical result is concerned, or more calculated to deaden spiritual vitality and promote a harsh and unchristian spirit.'[28] Nevertheless, the litigation did have long-term consequences, for the inadequacy of the law to control public worship came to be recognized by the Royal Commission on Ecclesiastical Discipline in 1906. 'The law of public worship in the Church of England is too narrow for the religious life of the present generation.'[29] The Tractarians may have begun by pleading for loyalty to the rubrics: but as the nineteenth century progressed, the demands of worship and mission began to outgrow the rubrics.

II

Meanwhile, events took place in the early 1850s which were destined to have considerable influence on the liturgical life of the Church. In 1851 Lord John Russell arranged that the official census, which was about to be taken, should be accompanied by a religious census on a voluntary basis. The ministers of every place of worship, Anglican, Roman Catholic and Free Church, were asked to record the number of people present at each service on Sunday, 30 March. The returns were commendably high – in the case of the Church of England about 80%; and where ministers made no returns, estimates were made. Estimates were also made of the number of people who were unable to attend church, either through illness, infancy, old age or work, and of the number of people who could have attended but did not. Allowance was also made for the fact that some people attended more than one service. The figures published in 1854 were therefore by no means exact; nevertheless they were sufficiently reliable to indicate general trends:

Total population of England and Wales:		17,927,609
Church attendance –	Church of England:	5,292,551
	Roman Catholic:	383,630
	Free Churches:	4,536,204
Total (after deduction for people attending more than once):		7,261,032
People who could have attended:		12,549,326
People who could have attended but did not:		5,288,294

(In the industrial North, Free Church attendance outnumbered Anglican by at least 2 to 1[30])

Two important conclusions emerged from these statistics. The first was that the rate of non-attendance was high – much higher than had been imagined. England could no longer be regarded as a 'church-going people'. Some people clearly had good reasons for not attending. Quite apart from considerations of age, health, or work, some people lacked decent clothes, some lived too far from a place of worship, and some were deterred by the system of pew-appropriation.[31] But clearly many did not attend because they had no contact with the Church, or because it meant little or nothing to them. The second conclusion was that the Church of England had ceased to have a dominating role as the national Church, particularly in the industrial north. The Church was therefore faced with a missionary problem of considerable dimensions. Clergy were often faced with an impossible task, particularly in some industrial areas. The census also posed the question: 'Do the services which the Church provides meet the needs of the people?'

At approximately the same time another event occurred in the Church of England which, though attracting less public attention, was nevertheless of considerable importance and relevant to the question. In 1853 the Convocation of Canterbury resumed its active functions for the first time since 1689, largely due to the efforts of Dr Samuel Wilberforce, Bishop of Oxford, and the banker, Henry Hoare; the Convocation of York followed suit eight years later. Then on 1 February 1854 Canterbury appointed a Joint Committee to consider whether the great increase and existing condition of the population did not render necessary some adaptation of the Church's rules in order to meet its spiritual needs. The Sunday Morning Service was a good example of the problem. Traditionally this consisted of three elements, Mattins, Litany, and Holy Communion, one following immediately after the other: indeed some people argued that it was required by the Act of Uniformity. This lengthy performance had fallen largely into disuse: but many clergy wished the use of the three elements as separate services to have some official recognition. Bishop Wilberforce himself had commented that permission for an early celebration of Holy Communion on its own — a practice which was growing — was only by tacit consent; strictly it was illegal.[32] Another example was the growing need for a second Sunday evening service, in addition to the customary Evensong on Sunday afternoons. The Joint Committee reported six months later, proposing that, while the Prayer Book itself should remain unchanged, certain modifications might be made, the most significant being:

1. The Sunday Morning Service should be permissible as three separate entities.
2. On weekdays there should be a shorter form of Morning and Evening Prayer.
3. Occasional services on weekdays should be permitted provided the materials were drawn from the Prayer Book.
4. An authoritative selection of psalms and hymns should be produced.
5. Holy Communion should be permitted as a separate weekday service.
6. Parents should be permitted to stand as sponsors for their own children in baptism.

The Upper House of Canterbury discussed the Report in February 1855 and drew up three resolutions, intended to be embodied in an Address to the

Queen: first that 'some modification of the Church's rules in regard to her services was desirable to enable her adequately to minister to the spiritual necessities of the land'; secondly that as a 'fundamental principle the Book of Common Prayer should be maintained entire and unaltered'; thirdly changes should be made such as 'the division of services and the formation of new ones by the recombination of those now existing, with such alterations as might be judged fit in the Rubrics, Psalter and Table of Lessons'.[33] Any enthusiasm for such changes soon disappeared, however: the Lower House refused to endorse the proposals, and the bishops allowed the matter to drop.[34] Two interesting points emerged from the debates, however. In the first place, no one appeared to be very clear as to the purpose of such proposals – whether they were intended to meet the criticisms of those people who already attended church but were dissatisfied with existing services, or whether they were intended to meet the needs of those 'unchurched millions' who never attended. Secondly, there was no clear idea as to how liturgical change might be effected, although many people recognized the importance of avoiding recourse to parliamentary action. So, for example, when another Joint Committee suggested in January 1860 that special lessons and prayers might be provided for such occasions as Harvest Thanksgiving, National Humiliation, and National Thanksgiving, together with a 'preaching service' composed basically of a sermon and prayers, they recommended that such forms should be issued simply by royal authority, as in the case of State services: but this idea was also rejected.[35] Then in the following year Dean Pellew of Norwich proposed the appointment of a Royal Commission to consider how the Prayer Book might be adapted to meet the spiritual needs of the Church: but this proposal was also rejected.[36]

Meanwhile one small but official change in the Prayer Book was made. In 1662 three special services had been annexed to it with approval, not from Parliament but only from Convocation and the Crown. These services, commemorating the death of Charles I on 30 January, the birth and restoration of Charles II on 29 May, and the Papists' Conspiracy on 5 November, had remained annexed to the Prayer Book by virtue of a royal mandate issued at the beginning of each reign. At the instigation of Dr Milman, Dean of St Paul's, Earl Stanhope moved an Address to the Queen in the House of Lords on 28 June 1858, praying her to take the necessary steps to remove them from the book. In view of the constant demands for improvement to the Liturgy, this provided an opportunity for a modest start to be made, and the Prayer Book would be relieved of a blot and a stain. In the ensuing debate the motion received a large measure of support and was approved.[37] The Commons then agreed to a similar Address; and the services were duly removed from the Prayer Book by Royal Warrant on 17 January 1859.[38]

But while the leaders of the Church showed no great enthusiasm for initiating any significant measure of reform, the pressures for change continued and even increased. Pamphlets and articles on liturgical revision proliferated: numerous petitions were presented to Parliament: memorials – both for and against change – were sent to the bishops: and the court cases continued, the contending parties now being supported on the Catholic side by the English Church Union, founded in 1859–60, and on the Evangelical side by the Church Association, founded in 1865.[39] Furthermore the general pattern of public worship was perceptibly changing. Services, and particularly communion services, were being held more frequently: sermons were becoming shorter, more frequent and of better quality: there was an increasing dignity and order: churches were better cared for: organs and surpliced choirs were making their way: and congregations were becoming more vocal, aided by the development of hymnody. In the middle of the century new hymnals were appearing at a rate of rather more than one a year, and in 1861 there came the crowning achievement, the first edition of *Hymns Ancient and Modern.* Feelings might well have run high in places, with disorders taking place in consequence of ritualistic 'innovations', but the Church was undeniably experiencing a Liturgical Movement. Two quotations will suffice to indicate the reality of the change. The first comes from Archbishop Tait, himself no lover of ritualism, when presiding over a meeting of the Diocesan Church Building Society at Canterbury in August 1874:

> [The laity] may remember that many things to which they were perhaps accustomed in old times are remains of an age when great apathy prevailed, and they must be prepared not only for improvements in the outward appearance of the Church, but also in the services. I suppose there is no-one of my age here but looks back with a kind of shame to the sort of sermons that were preached, the sort of clergyman that preached them, the sort of building in which they preached them, and the sort of psalmody with which the service was ushered in; and, remembering these, I am perfectly astonished that the whole of the attachment of the people to the Church did not evaporate. But if all improvements had been resisted we should not have been where we are now.[40]

The second comes from A. J. Beresford Hope MP, an influential and devout layman who was president both of the Ecclesiological Society and of the Royal Institute of British Architects. He wrote in 1874:

> The full Prayer Book is no longer the badge of party . . . Monthly communions are the least measure of the highest worship in places which put out any claim to share in the general uprising, while the frequency of weekly celebrations is an ever-increasing fact . . . Choral worship is generally acknowledged to be a matter which each church may rightfully adopt or dispense with, according to its local circumstances, while the singing . . . of the Psalms and of the Canticles is everywhere accepted as the most congruous way of dealing with these sacred poems. With the recognition of choral worship has naturally come in that of choirs . . .

With choirs and with chancels in which to dispose them, the use of the surplice as their appropriate dress has also taken place . . . The Church of England, in its corporate character, has, during a period which now runs back to days before the birth of many persons in places of high trust and honour, been engaged with her whole heart in the pious work of elevating and embellishing her worship alike to the glory of God and to the edification of man. Many temperaments have shared in the task under the widest variety of circumstances, and with little or no central control . . . It has . . . by a gradual progression, changed the external aspect of worship throughout the land.[41]

But in addition to all this, strenuous efforts were being made on a broad front to reach more and more of the so-called 'unchurched millions'. Many leaders of the Evangelical Movement – William Romaine, John Venn, David Wilson, Thomas Biddulph and others – had led the way for some years with Sunday evening services;[42] but in 1851 the whole ruridecanal Chapter of Leeds, under the inspiration of Dr W. F. Hook, approved the proposal to hold evening Communion services 'in the interests of the poor'. These began in the following year and met with considerable success: Edward Jackson, Vicar of St James' Leeds, later reported, for example, that numbers of communicants in the evenings were double those at other times and included 'vagrants, hawkers, reputed thieves, poorest Irish'.[43] This example was quickly followed by the Reverend J. C. Miller, the Evangelical Rector of Birmingham, who also broke up the Sunday morning service into three separate entities and engaged in open-air preaching in the Bull Ring. Indeed, during the fifties and sixties, influenced by evangelistic piety in the Free Churches and by the labours of interdenominational itinerant preachers from America, revivalist preaching spread in the Church of England. In 1855 a leading Evangelical, Lord Shaftesbury, succeeded in securing a modification of the law prohibiting the meeting for religious worship of more than twenty people in any building except a church or a licensed dissenting chapel. This question had been a matter of debate for some time; and as early as 1833 Bishop Sumner of Winchester had declared in a charge that he did not consider cottage readings as an infringement of the Act of Uniformity. Shaftesbury's success was followed by a remarkable experiment in evangelism. Simple Sunday evening services for non-churchgoers were held in Exeter Hall, London, in the summer of 1855; and they were attended by thousands of people, to the great delight of Dr Tait, then Bishop of London. Unfortunately, they were soon inhibited by the Vicar of St Michael's, Burleigh Street, in whose parish the hall was situated, in spite of strong protests from the Bishop and Lord Shaftesbury. The services were resumed soon afterwards, however, by Free Churchmen, while the Anglicans sought alternative accommodation elsewhere. They rented seven theatres in the poorest part of London, and the Sunday evening services in these buildings met with immediate success. An onlooker reported: 'It was a strange sight; from floor to ceiling the vast house was thronged; in boxes, stalls, pit, and gallery were costermongers, street cadgers, and labourers, women in fluttering rags, many with babies in their arms, boys in shirt-sleeves and corduroys, young men and maidens in their Sunday best. The people listened with extraordinary attention, as if they had never heard of the subject before.'[44]

This effective venture soon had repercussions elsewhere. Westminster Abbey began Sunday evening services in 1858 and St Paul's Cathedral shortly afterwards. *The Illustrated London News* actually published an engraving of one of these services in Westminster Abbey in 1861. Special lighting had to be installed, chairs had to be borrowed, and the words of hymns were written on large sheets hung from the pillars because there were no hymn books. In both places the shortcomings were painfully obvious – the buildings were cold, the acoustics were deplorable, and the choice of preachers often unfortunate – but the crowds continued to come. The popular Sunday evening service had come to stay, and indeed soon became a national institution.

Anglo-Catholic priests were equally alive to the missionary situation facing the Church and recognized the inadequacy of Prayer Book services simply by themselves. The Reverend J. E. Vaux, a member of the Society of the Holy Cross, expressed this misgiving in a contribution to the symposium *The Church and the World* published by Orby Shipley in 1868.

> Without laying ourselves open to the charge of a morbid craving after unhealthy excitement, we may venture an opinion that the repetition of 'Dearly beloved brethren', at the least 730 times each year, is calculated to become a little wearisome by the time we have reached mid-life. The 'soberness' of the Prayer Book services, of which we have all heard so much at various times, past and present, may not unfairly be regarded as a convertible term with dullness; and, unless I am mistaken, has had not a little to do with the Church's loss of influence with the masses. It is that very 'soberness' which makes our Services so uninteresting and unattractive.[45]

What the Church needed was more 'colour' in its services, more dramatic preaching, and more popular evening services.[46] Another article in the same symposium by R. F. Littledale, while having less enthusiasm for the Evangelical type of preaching, strongly endorsed the need for 'colour' in services. This was, in fact, one of the very elements the ritualists were striving to provide; it was an essential missionary element in their programme, an 'object-lesson' of religion, communicating religious truth both to the young and to the illiterate.[47] The same fact was expressed in a more homely way by one of Fr Lowder's assistant priests when describing the Sunday morning Eucharist at St Peter's, London Docks, in 1868:

> The reverence and solemnity of the whole sacred act has had a surprising influence for good on the lives and tone of mind of those who took part in

it. Indeed, this is the practical value of such a service, apart from its aspect towards God as our 'bounden duty', that it raises the hearts of the poor out of the miseries of their earthly lot into the majesty and peace of heaven. The beauty and brightness of the services, the glorious music, the solemn dignity of the ritual, all these contrast with the squalidness and nakedness of their homes, and make the church to them the very house of God, the gate of heaven.[48]

Later Fr Dolling maintained a similar view at Portsmouth. There was no converting power in the 'frigid simplicity' of unadorned Prayer Book services. 'It was Dolling's conviction, unshaken to the end, and the result of almost unique experience of religious work among those below the church- or chapel-going stratum, that the Prayer Book language is uncomprehended by the multitude, and that missionary work among them demands a flexibility and elasticity as to methods of worship wider than that which the letter of the Prayer Book can afford.'[49] It was for this reason that he introduced at St Agatha's, Portsmouth the highly unconventional yet impressive forms of extra service – 'after-meetings' as he called them – with extempore prayer and secular material (e.g. hymns sung to such tunes as 'Home, Sweet Home'), and attracting large numbers of people who were not regular church attenders.[50]

The Tractarians and their successors were also responsible for making generally available in English the devotional treasures of the Roman Church. Newman was the first in this field in 1836 with extracts from the Breviary in Tract 75. The demand for such material then increased rapidly, for in April 1840 *The British Critic* could comment:

The Liturgies of Rome and Paris till very recently were sealed books to the Protestant world. We well remember that when Bishop Lloyd began his lectures, twelve years since, it was hardly possible even to procure copies of them . . . But now Mr. Parker of Oxford finds it worth while to import a considerable number of copies both of the Roman and Parisian Breviaries every year; whence we infer . . . that the ancient Services are coming to be studied, not merely as a matter of literature, but for purposes of private devotion.[51]

A growing number of devotional books were therefore published, claiming to be complementary to the Prayer Book, and drawing heavily on materials from the Roman Missal and Breviary. *The Church Times* put the position in a nutshell:

Catholics . . . feel that it is only bad workmen who quarrel with their tools, and that the Prayer Book as it is, if not all they could wish, is sufficient for the necessities of the day . . . Its faults are all faults of omission. It may be formal, unelastic, wanting in variety, deficient in expression; but all these are matters which, without meddling with the

> Act of Uniformity, are capable, if not of absolute cure, at least of sufficient modification, to render them of comparative unimportance.[52]

Typical of these devotional books were A. H. Stanton's *Catholic Prayers for Church of England People* (1880) and Orby Shipley's *Ritual of the Altar* (1870). Stanton's title is significant, for such books often went out of their way to deny any charge of disloyalty, either to the Prayer Book or to the Church of England. Shipley stated in his Preface:

> If it were permissible for the compilers of the English use in the sixteenth century to adapt materials from the Roman Missal for public recitation, it cannot be disloyal to take advantage of the same materials for the private edification of members of the same Church in the nineteenth century . . . This manual is intended to be, as far as possible, the complement of the office as printed in the Book of Common Prayer.[53]

A similar work was P. G. Medd's *The Priest to the Altar*, which went through many editions between 1879 and 1904: but its particular interest lay in its inclusion of the 1549, the Scottish and the American eucharistic liturgies in addition to 1662.

It must not be thought, however, that Anglo-Catholics as a whole were content to use the 1662 Prayer Book with unofficial complementary material from the rites of other Churches both Anglican and non-Anglican. From time to time they produced proposals for revision, showing a concern either for a return to the pattern of the 1549 Prayer Book, or for a recovery of certain pre-Reformation elements which would have provided greater variety and richness to services. Notable among the compilers of such proposals were J. M. Neale, Warden of Sackville College, East Grinstead, a founder of the Cambridge Camden Society and a noted hymn-writer, and his friend R. F. Littledale. Both men were notable liturgical scholars, *The Guardian* describing Neale as one of those people 'who discovered that they had a mission to help the Church revival on the side where Oxford left it weakest, that of religious art, notably architecture, and of worship treated in reciprocal dependence'.[54] Neale's proposals first appeared in a series of articles in *The Ecclesiologist* in 1860 under the initials 'H.S.L.',[55] and secondly in his *Essays on Liturgiology and Church History* 1863, most of which appeared as separate articles in *The Christian Remembrancer* of 1862. Littledale's proposals appeared in 1867 in the pamphlet *Catholic Revision: a Letter to Charles Thomas, Lord Archbishop of Canterbury.* It was a timely publication, coinciding with the appointment of the Royal Commission on Ritual. He pointed out that the passive attitude of Catholics towards Prayer Book revision in the past had been misunderstood. They had been deliberately silent for two reasons. In the first place they believed that the agitation of Lord Ebury and the Prayer Book Reform Society represented the wishes of only a small minority in the Church of England. Secondly they believed the time was unsuitable for revision, partly because of the controversy caused by the ritualistic troubles, and partly because of the dearth of competent liturgical scholars. Nevertheless the terms of reference of the Ritual Commission were so wide that a recasting of the entire Prayer Book could not be ruled out. In view of this possibility, it was imperative that the Catholic party should speak. Neale and Littledale's proposals may be summed up as follows:

1. A revision of the Calendar, with the addition of a number of English Saints, and the restoration of Corpus Christi and All Souls.
2. An increased provision of special psalms, collects and lections for Holy Days.
3. The removal of the penitential opening to the daily office, and the substitution of seasonal sentences.
4. An increased provision of canticles, and prayers for special occasions.
5. A reconstruction of the eucharistic prayer on 1549 lines.
6. The restoration of oil in Baptism, Confirmation, and the Visitation of the Sick.
7. The restoration of the lighted taper and white robe in Baptism, and the blessing of the ring in Matrimony.
8. The introduction of Compline with a variable lesson as the Third Service.

Whether a Prayer Book on these lines would have met with general acceptance in the Church of England in the third quarter of the nineteenth century is doubtful. But there was nothing radically new about such a programme: almost all the elements had appeared many times since the seventeenth century; and many were being used, albeit unofficially, in an increasing number of parishes.

III

By the late sixties the pressures for some action on ritualism were considerable. Large sums were being spent on litigation, not least by the Church Union and the Church Association: and people such as the Marquis of Westmeath, Lord Ebury and Lord Shaftesbury continued to present memorials to leaders of both Church and State and introduce bills (all unsuccessful) in the House of Lords.[56] Finally, on 26 March 1867 the Prime Minister, Lord Derby, announced the appointment of a Royal Commission on Ritual. A representative but lack-lustre body dominated by Bishop Wilberforce was asked to consider the differences of practice arising 'from varying interpretations put upon the rubrics, orders and directions for regulating the course and conduct of public worship . . . and more especially with reference to the ornaments used . . . and the vestments worn'. Its first Report, dealing with vestments, was issued with commendable speed on 19 August. Holding that vestments were 'by none regarded as essential, and they give grave offence to many', it recommended unanimously that 'it is expedient to restrain . . . all variations in respect of Vesture from that which has long been the established use'.[57] It was a clever document, owing a great deal to Wilberforce.[58] Vestments were not abolished or prohibited, nor was there any hint that the Ornaments Rubric should be altered. All that was suggested was 'restraint', and the form of restraint was not defined: in any case what was to be restrained were 'variations . . . from established usage'. In other words, if vestments had long been in use in any parish with the acquiescence of clergy and people, they could continue. The direction was really directed against any attempt to impose vestments on unwilling congregations. The second Report, issued 30 April 1868 and dealing with candles and incense, made recommendations similar to those of the first Report. Candles and incense were at variance with the Church's usage of the last three hundred years, and it was expedient 'to restrain in the public services of the Church all variations from established usage'.[59] Its value was diminished however by the fact that ten of the twenty-nine members of the Commission dissented wholly or in part: and when Lord Shaftesbury tried to force the issue by presenting a Bill to the House of Lords on 23 June forbidding the use of vestments, candles and incense and giving statutory force to the Commissioners' proposals, there was such opposition, that he admitted defeat without seeking a division.[60]

The third Report, this time endorsed by all the members, and issued on 12 January 1870, dealt with the Lectionary, which was essentially that of 1549, with small amendments in 1559, 1604 and 1662. Its main proposals for Morning and Evening Prayer were as follows:

1. Many lessons were shortened and chapter divisions were diregarded. The old principle of 'one lesson, one chapter' was therefore abrogated in the interests of brevity and intelligibility.
2. The number of lessons from the Apocrypha were reduced from 132 to 44; and the New Testament was rearranged so as to be read twice a year, once in the morning and once in the evening, instead of three times a year.
3. Proper lessons on Holy Days were revised, and extended to include Ash Wednesday and Holy Week.
4. Proper Old Testament lessons were provided for every Sunday, but New Testament lessons, with six exceptions, remained those for the day of the month.
5. A second set of Old Testament lessons for Sunday evenings was provided, for use either at Evensong or at a third service. At a third service the minister could choose his own second lesson from the Gospels: and on other occasions he could substitute his own lessons with the bishop's approval.[61]

There were, admittedly, weaknesses. One was the continued limitation of the Sunday provision to the Old Testament, adherence to the civil calendar for second lessons, involving the loss of a vital opportunity for suitable seasonal material, and the necessity for consulting two tables on every occasion. Another was the undue emphasis on the history of Israel in the Sunday Old Testament lessons, to the neglect of the Minor Prophets and the Wisdom literature. Nevertheless, the whole system was a marked improvement on what already existed. The needs of the layman, who was normally a Sunday worshipper, were beginning to be recognized: the first tentative steps towards the emergence of a separate Sunday cycle of lessons had been taken; and the need for a more flexible Sunday 'Third Service' was recognized. These proposals were quickly accepted by the Convocations and then incorporated in a parliamentary Measure, which eventually became law in July 1871.[62]

The fourth and final Report of the Commission dealing with the Prayer Book rubrics appeared soon after the third, on 31 August 1870. Alterations were proposed in the interests of general uniformity and greater flexibility. 'In the alterations we have proposed, we have endeavoured to explain and amend Rubrics so as to secure general Uniformity of Practice in those matters which may be deemed essential: on other matters we have recommended alterations which may give facilities for adapting the Service of the Church to the wants and circumstances of different congregations.'[63] It was remarkable for the lack of unanimity among its members. Sir R. Phillimore and Lord Carnarvon refused to sign it at all, while every one of the other Commissioners dissented on one or more points. The Ornaments Rubric, a primary cause for the Commission, was never thoroughly discussed, and no recommendations concerning its use or amendment were made. There was also considerable disagreement over the Athanasian Creed. Seventeen Commissioners qualified their assent to it; a majority, including Archbishop Tait and Lord Shaftesbury, wished to discontinue its public use; and a proposal to let the Creed stand but with an explanatory note, 'Note that the condemnations in this Confession of Faith are to be not otherwise understood than as a solemn warning of the peril of those who wilfully reject the Catholic Faith.', was only carried by eleven votes to seven with ten abstentions. Other sources of considerable disagreement were the proposals to regard the daily service as optional, and to permit the recitation of the words of administration at Holy Communion to groups of communicants instead of to individuals.[64]

There was a tremendous upheaval over its treatment of the Athanasian Creed. There was a deluge of pamphlets; and while Archbishop Tait continued to exert pressure both in parliamentary and ecclesiastical circles to secure its omission, Bishop Wilberforce strove to persuade him to modify his position. The Divinity Professors of Oxford and Cambridge were asked for their advice, but they could not agree: then Pusey and Liddon informed the Archbishop on 3 January 1872 that they would resign their orders if the Creed were degraded or mutilated.[65] Not surprisingly the debates in Convocation were heated. The Lower House of Canterbury clearly indicated that it wanted neither the omission of the Creed nor the insertion of an explanatory note; the Upper House was less sure. Agreement was finally reached on 9 May 1873. The Creed was to be retained in use in an unmutilated form, while a Synodical Declaration was to be issued 'for the removal of doubts, and to prevent disquietude in the use of the Creed', asserting that it made no addition to the faith as contained in Holy Scripture, and that its warnings were to be understood 'no otherwise than the like warnings in Holy Scripture, for we must receive God's threatenings even as His promises': nor was the Church pronouncing judgement on any particular person. Certainly the Declaration settled nothing, nor did it ever become part of the Prayer Book. But if the decision had been otherwise, and if Liddon and Pusey had left the Church of England, others would undoubtedly have followed them: and the Church might well have suffered another loss of sanctity, scholarship and orthodoxy that it could ill afford.[66]

Another sequel to the fourth Report had more positive results, however. The Convocations of both Canterbury and York discussed its other proposals and eventually agreed on a number of items which were incorporated in an Act of Uniformity Amendment Bill, moved by Archbishop Tait in the House of Lords on 11 March 1872 and becoming law on 18 July. This Measure, known as the Shortened Services Act, did not effect any changes in the Prayer Book itself, but authorized the adaptation of services to suit particular needs. Admittedly, from a liturgical point of view, its provisions left much to be desired: but it did make some effort to meet a missionary situation and provide a degree of flexibility in the use of the services of the Prayer Book. Its first main provision was for a shortened form of Morning and Evening Prayer on weekdays, by reducing each office to a single psalm, lesson and canticle, and by omitting the Exhortation, the Venite, the second Lord's Prayer and the prayers following the Third Collect except St Chrysostom and the Grace. The value of such a provision was doubtful. Perhaps there were occasions when it gave relief to hard-pressed clergy; but there is little evidence to show that it was popular or that it encouraged the attendance of lay people. It certainly discouraged the continuous reading of Scripture, and encouraged the use of the shortest psalms and lessons to those who were so inclined. Bishop Frere has also argued that such a provision was not in fact necessary, for it fell within the liberty allowed to episcopal authority under the Acts of Uniformity, and such shortened services had been common in the seventeenth century.[67]

Four further provisions were of much greater value, authorizing much needed freedom and flexibility:

1. On special occasions a minister could use a service composed of any materials from the Bible and Prayer Book, provided it had episcopal approval.
2. Sermons could be preached apart from Divine Service.
3. On Sundays a 'Third Service' could be used, and its materials could come from any part of the Prayer Book apart from the Communion Service.

4. The three elements of the 'Morning Service' could be used as three separate entities, and the Litany could be used at Evensong after the third collect.

Over the question of a division of the Morning Service there had clearly been confusion and difference of opinion for a considerable time. The Convocation of Canterbury had discussed the matter on a number of occasions in the fifties, but no action had been taken;[68] and instances abound of clergy using the services separately. It was therefore useful for the Church to be given a clear indication of what was lawfully possible, and both Morning Prayer and Holy Communion undoubtedly benefited from this authorized freedom.

As with the Sunday Morning service, special and additional forms of service had been a cause for concern for many years, with the episcopate showing reluctance to take any initiative. For example, in 1859 Bishop Wilberforce had expressed the view that if a church were reopened after restoration, 'all we can do to meet such a case is to use the ordinary Offices of the day, it may be with lessons singularly inappropriate'. Or again, requests for a form of service of Harvest Thanksgiving in Canterbury Convocation ran into very heavy weather. The Archbishop felt in 1863 that this should not be done for Canterbury alone and proposed that the Queen should issue a royal proclamation ordering the use of such a service for the whole of England and Ireland: but in reply the Lord Chancellor doubted whether the Queen had such power and said that she should not be advised to reply. Or again, shortly afterwards, on the occasion of the first Lambeth Conference in 1867, some questions were raised at the publication of even a special prayer without government permission.[69] A report on the subject to the Lower House of Canterbury Convocation in 1870 was therefore of particular interest in view of its more adventurous tone. It expressed the view that the bishop did in fact have the power to authorize special forms of prayer: the services which the Church had used over the centuries had not been limited to those in the Prayer Book, and the Act of Uniformity applied only to these official Prayer Book services: 'The long disuse of this power of ordering special services by the Bishops and the Archbishop, unless in obedience to the commands of the Crown, may perhaps be thought to throw some doubt on the lawfulness of its exercise now.'[70] In the face of such initiative, the provisions of the Act of Uniformity Amendment Act were therefore most welcome, giving freedom for the use, not only of Harvest Thanksgiving services, but of Lenten Devotions, Compline and Special services of a wide variety. Twenty years later there came a further measure of freedom. Archbishop Temple felt that the restriction of the contents of special services to materials from the Bible and the Prayer Book was too limited: he therefore proposed in Canterbury Convocation that clergy need not consider themselves bound by the actual words of Bible and Prayer Book, provided they did not use anything which could not substantially be found therein; and Convocation was happy to endorse his proposal.[71]

A further consequence of the Royal Commission's Fourth Report was the issue of Letters of Business to the Convocations in 1872 to amend the rubrics of the Prayer Book in order to give more precise guidance to the clergy in the conduct of services. This matter occupied the Convocations for the next seven years; and in an effort to make its voice heard at the very outset, the English Church Union presented a lengthy memorial to Canterbury, deploring any tampering with the Athanasian Creed, any relaxation of the rubric requiring the Words of Administration to be said to each communicant, any suggestion to make the Daily Office optional, any prohibition of wafer bread and any abolition of Black Letter Days. On the other hand it made five positive proposals:

1. Permission to use material from ancient sources as well as from the Prayer Book in special services.
2. The provision of another Litany for special occasions.
3. The provision of additional canticles, introits and proper prefaces.
4. The reservation of the Blessed Sacrament for the sick.
5. Any changes to be in accordance with the 1549 Prayer Book.[72]

Shortly afterwards a Committee of the Lower House of Canterbury, which had been considering the rubrics since the previous year under Archdeacon Freeman, a well-known liturgical scholar, published its Report. While professing great loyalty to the Prayer Book, and suggesting no basic change to the rubrics, its suggestions were very similar to those of the English Church Union. Perhaps its most important proposal, however, was the insertion of a Vestiary Rubric, making eucharistic vestments compulsory in cathedral and collegiate churches and optional in parish churches subject to the bishop's permission.[73] On 20 February a similar Committee of the Lower House of York Convocation published a Report in substantial agreement with Canterbury and the English Church Union.

Debates on these Reports now began, and for a time the Athanasian Creed dominated all else: but it was not until discussion on the Ornaments Rubric began in 1875 that any really great stir occurred. At first the Convocations agreed that the Rubric should be left untouched, claiming that legislation was neither desirable nor practicable;[74] but the Ridsdale case in 1877 gave cause for further consideration. The Reverend C. J. Ridsdale, Vicar of St Peter's, Folkestone, had been the first person to be tried under the Public Worship Regulation Act, Lord Penzance's court declaring against him on all points. Ridsdale then appealed to the Judicial Committee of the Privy Council, which in May 1877 declared against him, allowing the eastward position but condemning the use of vestments. This virtually coincided with similar proceedings taken against the Reverend Arthur Tooth, Vicar of St James' Hatcham, for illegal ritual. Tooth refused to recognize the proceedings or to appear, subsequently suffering imprisonment for twenty-eight days.[75] Convocation now felt that something must be done:

otherwise the State was in danger of becoming the controlling authority over the Church's worship.

Long discussions took place in both Houses but they failed to agree. Finally, in 1879 the Archbishop of Canterbury called a joint Conference of both Houses and urged the Lower House to accept an amended Ornaments Rubric proposed by Dr Wordsworth, Bishop of Lincoln, laying down that the normal clerical vesture should be surplice, stole or scarf and hood, with the rider 'and no other ornament shall be at any time of his ministrations used by him contrary to the monition of the Bishop of the Diocese'. It did not explicitly exclude the use of vestments, and it even implied that in particular cases they might be introduced. There was no doubt that many people were weary of the whole question; and eventually this amended rubric was accepted by 39 votes to 24. York, however, failed to agree to the proposal, the Upper House accepting it by 4 votes to 1, but the Lower House rejecting it by 25 votes to 20.[76] The Ornaments Rubric, therefore, like the Athanasian Creed, was retained in its entirety.

Both Canterbury and York Convocations completed their work on the rubrics in 1879: but they agreed not to present any Measure to Parliament until they could be sure that some new method of dealing with matters of worship had been found; for they clearly disliked the prospect of any parliamentary interference. The Bishop of Carlisle then introduced into the House of Lords a measure originally introduced by the Bishop of London five years previously, proposing that legislation on rubrics should not be by act of Parliament: instead, schemes drawn up by the Convocations should lie on the table of both Houses of Parliament for forty days, and if within that period no objections were raised, they should become law by Orders in Council. The bill, however, met with no support,[77] so the proposals of the Convocations after seven years' discussion remained simply proposals: but in the following year they were embodied in *The Convocation Prayer Book*, a 1662 Prayer Book interleaved with tinted paper on which appeared all the alterations recommended by both Provinces or by one or other of them. The main provisions would have been:

1. The inclusion of the Shortened Services Act.
2. An increase from six to sixteen of the days on which proper psalms were appointed: an improved provision of octaves.
3. A Table of Occurrences – a praiseworthy though not entirely satisfactory attempt to deal with the coincidence of Holy Days – a subject on which the Prayer Book was silent. York objected to this.
4. The modification of the Ornaments Rubric by the addition of the clause 'until further order be taken by lawful authority'. York objected to this.
5. The Synodical Declaration of 1873 appended to the Athanasian Creed.
6. Permission for an Introit at Holy Communion.
7. The reduction of the number of sponsors at Baptism to one Godmother and one Godfather if three could not be found. Sponsors should if possible be communicants.

8. Simpler arrangements for administering communion to the sick and dying, by permitting the service to be shortened and by not requiring the presence of other communicants.[78]

Such proposals would, of course, have done little or nothing to meet the needs for which the Royal Commission on Ritual was appointed. Nevertheless, in conjunction with the Shortened Services Act they would have constituted a step – though a modest one – in the right direction towards a better presentation of and a greater flexibility in services. Undoubtedly they reflected to some degree existing practice in many parishes: and they were not without influence elsewhere.

IV

It was evident that in the closing years of the nineteenth century ritualism still continued to flourish. Indeed some practices, such as the use of cassocks, surpliced choirs and processional hymns, which had once been the cause of disturbance and riot, were by then widely regarded as normal.[79] The atmosphere had undoubtedly improved: and this was undoubtedly due in large measure to the Lincoln Judgement of November 1890. The Church Association, still believing the episcopate to be conniving at the introduction of popish practices, adopted the bold move of proceeding against one of their number on six counts. In 1888 they supported a suit brought by a solicitor and churchwarden from Cleethorpes, Ernest de Lacy Read, against the saintly Edward King, Bishop of Lincoln, to test the legality of six practices which he had used when celebrating the Eucharist at the church of St Peter-at-Gowles, Lincoln, on 4 December 1887: lighted candles on the altar, the eastward position, the commixture, the sign of the cross at the absolution and the blessing, the Agnus Dei, and ceremonial ablutions. But what was even more unique in this case was the demand that it should be heard in a new and indisputably spiritual court, that of the Archbishop of Canterbury himself.

At first Archbishop Benson demurred, claiming that he had no jurisdiction to act: but when the Privy Council assured him that this was not the case, he concurred and held the trial at Lambeth Palace with the assistance of five episcopal assessors.[80] That the ethos of the proceedings would be very different from those of a Privy Council hearing was evident at the outset, when Benson commented that, as distinct from the Privy Council, which was 'obliged to go by the merest letter of the Book of Common Prayer, as if they were printers', he 'would be expected to go to historical and theological lights and side lights, and to acquaint [himself] even with the *mens* of such a student and compiler as Cranmer'.[81]

At his judgement on 21 November 1890, the Archbishop found largely in favour of Bishop King. He forbade the sign of the cross in absolution and blessing – 'an innovation which must not be continued', together with the commixture during the service – although presumably there was nothing to prevent it being done beforehand; the other four practices he declared permissible, the only rider being that the manual acts should be visible to the people. Mr Read and his friends, having appealed to the Archbishop, were now unwilling to accept his Judgement and appealed to the Judicial Committee of the Privy Council, but the latter upheld the Archbishop, with one small exception, on 2 August 1892. Inevitably, High churchmen were delighted with the outcome, admirably summed up by Sir Walter Phillimore, the eminent lawyer and a vice-president of the English Church Union: 'The Archbishop has given you [King] all the important things, and he has reduced (as it seems to me) those things which he has not given you to even less importance.'[82] But such was the general regard for the saintly bishop, that this delight was shared by churchmen of all parties. Every ruridecanal conference in his diocese had expressed support for him, and moderate Evangelicals had urged Read not to take the case to the Privy Council.

The Judgement was significant for two reasons. In the first place Dr Benson had clearly refused to recognize the sanctity of Privy Council findings in previous ritual cases and was quite prepared to reverse them. Secondly he had based his decision on the appeal to history and ancient usage: he adjudged it perfectly permissible to interpret rubrics in this way. He appealed 'not only to Reformers like Cranmer and Tyndale, but also to Laud and Cosin, to Ambrose and Basil and Chrysostom, and to the Mozarabic and Clementine liturgies'.[83] As *The Guardian* pointed out, the Judgement recognized 'that the Church of England of the present is historically one with the Church of England of the past, that . . . she was not the creation of Henry VIII or Edward VI':[84] and significantly Lord Chancellor Halsey noted the importance of this appeal to history when rejecting Read's appeal to the Privy Council. Indeed, it even offered hope that perhaps after all the Church could address itself to ritual and liturgical matters without recourse to the State.

V

The seventy-six bishops from all parts of the Anglican Communion who attended the first Lambeth Conference of 1867 had been invited to submit topics for discussion, and a number suggested both ritualism and the revision of the Prayer Book.[85] In the event neither topic appeared on the Agenda. But the failure of the Prayer Book to meet the needs of the whole Anglican Communion was a point discussed at the Conference and included briefly in Resolution 8 of the Report. This stated that 'each Province should have the right to make such adaptations and additions to the services of the Church as its peculiar circumstances may require. *Provided*, that no change or addition be made inconsistent with the spirit and principles of the Book of Common Prayer, and that all such changes be liable to revision by any Synod of the Anglican Communion in which the said Province shall be represented.'[86] But by the time of the next Conference in 1878, events in England made it certain that liturgical matters would play a larger part in the discussions. The ritual controversies, the Public Worship Regulation Act, and the legislation emanating from the Ritual Commission made the subject a live issue: and after a somewhat heated debate the Conference finally affirmed 'the principle that no alteration from long-accustomed ritual should be made contrary to the admonition of the Bishop of the Diocese'.[87] But some valuable discussion on the Prayer Book also took place in the committee dealing with Missionary Dioceses. The importance of producing Prayer Books suitable to the needs of native congregations was recognized: but such books should be based on the principles of the Book of Common Prayer and should only be authorized for use by an Episcopal Board appointed for the purpose in England or in America.[88] By the next Lambeth Conference in 1888, however, a simpler and more flexible method of authorization was being proposed.

This Conference, under Archbishop Benson, clearly recognized the principle of Prayer Book adaptation. But since the Prayer Book was the possession of the entire Anglican Communion, no member of it should undertake revision without considering the effect on its fellow-members. There was no question of denying that the Book of Common Prayer was not capable of improvement, nor was there any wish to decry attempts to supplement prayers and services to meet particular needs; indeed, the revisions produced by America, Ireland and Scotland had indicated that there was no need for strict rigidity. But further changes in the Ordinal or the sacramental services should not be undertaken without the advice of some body representing the whole Anglican Communion. Changes in the Daily Offices or local services, however, could be left to the bishops of each province: in the case of dioceses not yet in a province the bishops should consult either the Archbishop of Canterbury or the Presiding Bishop in America. The essential principle to be maintained was that there should be no growth of 'substantial divergencies'.[89]

At the 1897 Conference, one committee devoted its whole attention to the Prayer Book in the light of Additional Services and Local Adaptations. Through its deliberations the Conference made a significant step forward. While affirming that the Prayer Book, next to the Bible itself, was still the authoritative standard of the doctrine of the Anglican Communion, it accepted that no single Book could supply every possible need of worshippers in every variety of local circumstances. The Conference therefore made the important statement:

> We therefore think it our duty to affirm the right of every Bishop, within the jurisdiction assigned to him by the Church, to set forth or to sanction additional services and prayers when he believes that God's work may be thereby furthered, or the spiritual needs of the worshippers more fully met, and to adapt the Prayers already in the Book to the special requirements of his own people.

It was careful to specify, however, that this power 'must always be subject to any limitations imposed by the provincial or other lawful authority'.[90] The committee also discussed the bishop's *ius liturgicum*. It recognized that the various Anglican Churches differed in their legal position. The Church of England, for example, was limited by the Act of Uniformity, with changes in the Prayer Book needing confirmation by Parliament. Nevertheless, the committee expressed the view that it was not at all clear that such legal enactments deprived bishops of the *ius liturgicum* and in support quoted a list of forty-four occasional forms of prayer put out in the reign of Elizabeth I. Of these only five were issued on the authority of the Queen, five were on episcopal or archepiscopal authority, and the remainder gave no indication of the authority involved. The only proper course was for the bishops to avail themselves of the *ius liturgicum*, subject to any restrictions imposed by civil or ecclesiastical authority. Where such limitations were not already in force, the Conference should advise on the appropriate limitation to be placed on the independent action of a bishop.[91]

In Scotland the nineteenth century saw no change in the text of the eucharistic liturgy but changes in its status and use. In 1811 the General Synod clearly stated the Scottish rite to be of 'primary authority', although allowing congregations the use of the English rite where it had been customary – a position endorsed by the Code of Canons of 1838.[92] Nevertheless, some twenty-five years later there was a reversal of positions, for reasons which were social and political rather than liturgical. As the century progressed preference for the English rite tended to become more pronounced in the south of the country between the Clyde and the Forth with the growth of new congregations mainly of English and Irish workers.[93] Furthermore, pressures were brought to bear to suppress the Scottish rite in the interests of uniformity with the Church of England, in order to help relieve Scottish priests of certain legal disabilities to which their Scottish ordination subjected them – for example, the acceptance of an English benefice.[94] The Scottish Church therefore expressed its willingness to sacrifice its own rite in favour of that of 1662.[95] The Canons of 1863 enacted that the English Prayer Book 'is, and shall be held to be, the Service Book of this Church to which it is applicable', and was to be used in all new congregations, unless a majority requested the use of the Scottish rite at the time of their creation.[96] This decision apparently had its desired effect, for in 1864 the Clerical Disabilities Act removed the last of the civil disabilities of clergy in Scottish orders. Many Scottish churchmen felt the price too heavy to pay, however. In 1884 Scotland's great liturgical scholar, Dr John Dowden, in his *An Historical Account of the Scottish Communion Office*, issued a call on behalf of the Scottish rite, arguing that by its action in 1863 the Scottish Episcopal Church had thrown away its most precious heritage.[97] The call did not go unheeded, and the turn of the century saw a return to a position of sturdy independence of 1662 with the creation of a Scottish Prayer Book.

In Ireland the Book of Common Prayer had been the norm since 1662 and continued to be so until the Church of Ireland was both disestablished and disendowed on 1 January 1870. Although the use of 1662 was confirmed in the following month by the General Convention, the desire for liturgical change soon made itself felt. As a minority Church in a predominantly Roman Catholic country, it harboured strong anti-Roman feelings; and these were strengthened by the reports of the activities of the ritualists in England and by the Anglican secessions to Rome. Agitation on the old familiar lines against baptismal regeneration, the real presence and priestly absolution spread, and was led by William Brooke, Master of the Court of Chancery; and at the General Convention in October 1870 he urged the appointment of a committee to consider the question. But largely at the instigation of Dr Salmon, Regius Professor of Divinity at Dublin, a committee was appointed in the following year to deal with the broader issue of a general revision of the Prayer Book with the aim, not of amending error, but of trying to improve something which was already good.[98]

Discussion in the General Synod lasted for several years; and the revised Prayer Book did not finally emerge until 1 January 1879. Its Preface disclaimed any intention of departing from the standards of the English Prayer Book, but the concluding words spoke volumes of the problems which had been encountered: 'What is imperfect, with peace, is often better than what is otherwise more excellent, without it.' Some of the old Puritan pleas for revision were met, other changes came from the abortive 1689 proposals, while others were clearly influenced by the Act of Uniformity Amendment Act and *The Convocation Prayer Book.* The most significant changes were:

1. Lessons from the Apocrypha, Black Letter Days and the Ornaments Rubric were omitted.
2. Morning and Evening Prayer could be varied or shortened on weekdays, and daily recitation was no longer obligatory.
3. The Athanasian Creed was retained but the rubric ordering its use removed; and the Preface stated that it was retained as a witness to the truths of the Christian Faith.
4. Eight new Occasional Prayers and one new Thanksgiving were added.
5. In Holy Communion the Words of Administration were no longer required to be said in full to every communicant: and worshippers were required to communicate frequently instead of three times a year.
6. In Baptism parents were allowed to be sponsors, and one sponsor was sufficient if more could not be found.
7. Four new occasional forms of service were added:
   a. The beginning of a new ministry.
   b. Harvest Thanksgiving.
   c. The Consecration of a Church.
   d. The Consecration of a Burial Ground.

Clearly any attempt to produce a radically Protestant revision had not succeeded. The most the Protestants could be said to have obtained was a certain liberty of use and interpretation: but in practice they had exercised this liberty before. Nevertheless, they did succeed in creating a definitely Protestant liturgical ethos through the Constitutions and Canons Ecclesiastical of 1871 and 1877, which were bound up with the Prayer Book. In these a number of practices were forbidden: the sign of the cross, a cross or lights on the altar, incense, wafer bread, vestments, ceremonial commixture, banners in procession, and the eastward position – the north side position being explicitly required. It was summed up in the Preamble and Declaration, adopted by the General Convention in 1870 and appended to the Prayer Book: 'The Church of Ireland, as a Reformed and Protestant Church, doth hereby re-affirm its constant witness against all those innovations in doctrine and worship, whereby the Primitive Faith had been from time to time defaced or overlaid, and which at the Reformation the Church did disown and reject.'

In America the Oxford Movement exerted its influence throughout the nineteenth century. There was, as in England, the familiar debate on theological questions, together with controversy on matters of ceremonial and the development of rival parties within the Church. An outstanding figure and a conciliating influence was the saintly Dr William A. Muhlenberg, Rector of the Church of the Holy Communion, New York, 1844–77. At the General Convention in 1853 he asked the bishops to consider whether the American Church 'with only her present canonical means and appliances, her fixed and invariable modes of public worship, and her traditional customs and usages, is competent to the work of preaching and dispensing the Gospel to all sorts and conditions of men'[99] – the same question as had occupied the mind of the Convocation of Canterbury after the 1851 Census. The bishops replied in 1856 in a Declaration with three suggestions, modest enough, but helpful, and an improvement on anything proposed by the English bishops: Morning Prayer, the Litany and Holy Communion were to be regarded as three distinct services; on special occasions the clergy could use any parts of the Prayer Book and Bible at their discretion; and the bishops were free to issue special forms of service to meet particular needs. Obviously the Declaration was insufficient to meet all the problems which Muhlenberg raised, and the debate continued. Muhlenberg died in 1877 and his mantle was assumed by Dr William Reed Huntington.[100] At the General Convention of 1880 he secured the appointment of a committee to consider a revision of the Prayer Book based on two principles: enrichment from past and present sources, and flexibility in the use of services. The revision process lasted for twelve years, resulting in a new Book, which appeared in 1892. While proving to be a conservative revision, it was loyal to Huntington's principles and it clearly owed a great deal both to the Irish book and to developments in this country.

1. Morning Prayer, the Litany and Holy Communion were accepted as three distinct services.
2. Morning and Evening Prayer
   a. Provision was made for shortening both services.
   b. Seasonal sentences and proper psalms were provided for ten additional festivals and special occasions.
   c. Twenty psalm selections were provided for use at any time in place of those appointed.
   d. The entire Benedictus, Magnificat and Nunc Dimittis were restored, with the 1789 psalms retained as alternatives.
   e. The full complement of Suffrages was restored to Evening Prayer.
   f. Additional Occasional Prayers were provided.
3. Holy Communion
   a. Additional propers were provided for Christmas Day, Easter Day, and the Transfiguration.
   b. Permission was given to substitute the Summary of the Law and the Lesser Litany for the Decalogue, provided the latter was used once every Sunday.
   c. The Nicene Creed was made compulsory on the five major festivals of the year.
   d. Additional Offertory Sentences were provided from Bishop Andrewes, including 1 Chronicles 29.11–14.
4. In Confirmation a form for the presentation of candidates was provided, together with Acts 8.14–17 as a lesson.
5. Additional prayers were provided for Burial, together with greater flexibility in the ordering of the service.

An interesting development in the use of the Prayer Book also occurred in Japan. In the middle of the century, when missionaries first entered the country, Anglican missionary work was shared by England and America. Not surprisingly this led to some difference of opinion over the use of the English and American Prayer Books – a difference finally resolved in 1896, when a Japanese Book, combining translations of elements from both the others, was agreed. The most significant feature was in the Holy Communion service, where the American consecration prayer was included as an alternative to 1662. Several forms for special occasions, such as the Emperor's birthday and the admission of catechumens, were also included.[101]

Finally, brief mention should be made of the use of the Prayer Book in Methodism. At the beginning of the nineteenth century the Methodists had both the Prayer Book and the *Sunday Service* from which to choose. There was, however, a good deal of material in both books which they never used; so in 1835 the Conference published a smaller manual, *The Order of Administration of the Sacraments and other Services.* Then in 1874 the Conference appointed a committee to revise the liturgies, in the hope not only that a single book could replace the existing alternatives, but also that the opportunity would be taken to remove 'all expressions which are fairly susceptible of a sense contrary to the principles of our Evangelical Protestantism'.[102] In a number of ways the *Book of Public Prayers and Services*, appearing in 1882, indicated the continuing influence of the Prayer Book on Methodism. In the Communion Service, for example, the Nicene Creed was restored and an abbreviated Third Exhortation was included, although the offertory sentences from Tobit and the manual acts were not retained. A slightly revised form of Morning Prayer was also included, the ring in Marriage was restored, and the terms Epiphany, Septuagesima and Lent were reinstated. On the other hand, a sturdy independent line was taken both in Baptism and the Ordinal. In Baptism, references to regeneration disappeared, the first Exhortation and the Signing with the cross were removed, and the five Mozarabic prayers were placed after instead of before the act of baptism as a 'denial of baptismal grace'. The Ordinal was based on Wesley's form for ordaining elders, no distinction being made between deacon, presbyter and superintendent. Three new forms of service were also included: the Covenant Service, the Public Recognition of New Members – replacing Confirmation, and the Setting Apart of Deaconesses.

With the passage of time Anglican influence tended to wane. This was partly due to a demand for more flexible, free, charismatic types of service: to many Methodists Prayer Book services with their rather archaic language, set patterns and formal ceremonial seemed artificial and heavy. Secondly, the Oxford Movement and a fear of its Romanizing tendencies tended to push Methodists away from Anglicanism in order to avoid any charge of being Romanists: this meant, among other things, reaction against undue emphasis on the sacraments, for which class-meetings and love-feasts were regarded as sufficient substitutes.[103] Finally, when there were few ministers left who could remember the days when Methodists were societies within the Church of England, there was an increasing concern to maintain a genuine religious pluralism in England. Methodism was hardening into a separate denomination with a tendency to emphasize services which were sectarian in character.[104]

NOTES

1. W. Palmer, *A Narrative of Events connected with the Publication of the Tracts for the Times*, Oxford 1843, pp. 2–3.
2. *The British Critic*, No. 12, pp. 303, 313; No. 23, pp. 294, 391–2; No. 25, pp. 43–5.
3. *The Christian Observer*, 1826, pp. 87, 600; 1833, p. 375.
4. J. J. S. Perowne and L. Stokes, *Letters Literary and Theological of Connop Thirlwall*, 1881, p. 104. Thirlwall was Fellow of Trinity College, Cambridge, 1818 and Bishop of St David's 1840–75.
5. C. N. Wodehouse, *The Claims of Truth*, 1861, pp. 7–8; R. C. D. Jasper, *Prayer Book Revision in England 1800–1900*, 1954, pp. 9–12.

6. *The British Critic*, No. 12, p. 305.
7. For the whole subject see Jasper, op. cit.
8. Lord Henley, *A Plan for Church Reform, with a Letter to the King*, 6th edn 1832, pp. 11–12, 14–15.
9. *The Mirror of Parliament 1840*, vol. 4, pp. 3296–7.
10. Both appeared in Lloyd's *Formularies of Faith put forth by Authority during the Reign of Henry VIII*, Oxford 1825.
11. W. Palmer, *Origines Liturgicae, or Antiquities of the English Ritual and a Dissertation on Primitive Liturgies* (2 vols.), 1832, vol. 1, pp. 6–7; cf. C. Wheatly, *A Rational Illustration upon the Book of Common Prayer*, 1710.
12. Palmer, op. cit., vol. 1, p. vi, cf. pp. 12f. It should be noted that Bishop John Dowden subsequently pointed out that Palmer was defective in his knowledge of the German Reformers. (J. Dowden, *Further Studies in the Prayer Book*, 1908, p. 26.)
13. J. H. Overton, *The Anglican Revival*, 1897, p. 23.
14. Jasper, pp. 28–9.
15. Palmer, *Narrative of Events*, p. 95.
16. H. C. Beeching, ed., *Lyra Apostolica*, 1904, p. 125.
17. J. Keble, *Sermons for the Christian Year*, 1875, vol. 1, p. 346.
18. I. Williams, *Indications of a superintending Providence in the Preservation of the Prayer Book and in the Changes which it has undergone*, Tract 86, 1840.
19. E. B. Pusey, *Catena Patrum IV*, Tract 81, 1857.
20. R. H. Froude, *Remains*, part 2 vol. 1, 1839, pp. xxiii–vii.
21. Pusey, Tract 81, pp. 55f. For a detailed examination of Tractarian attitudes towards the Prayer Book, see A. Härdelin, *The Tractarian Understanding of the Eucharist*, Uppsala 1965, especially pp. 249–66.
22. *The Ecclesiologist*, Nos. 27–8 (November 1843), p. 49.
23. Note, for example, W. S. Bricknell, *The Judgement of the Bishops upon Tractarian Theology*, a volume of 700 pages analysing episcopal Charges over a period of six years, published in 1845.
24. *Report of the Royal Commission on Ecclesiastical Discipline*, 1906, p. 346, sec. 12855; *The Churchman's Newspaper*, 17 January 1845.
25. E. Wingfield Stratford, *This was a Man*, 1949, p. 133. In 1869 the Association became the Church Reform Society, extending its activities to the Ecclesiastical Courts, the Canons, and the Act of Uniformity.
26. *Special Address of the Council of the Association for promoting a Revision of the Book of Common Prayer*, adopted at the General Meeting, 13 May 1869, pp. 4–5.
27. For the whole subject see J. Bentley, *Ritualism and Politics in Victorian Britain*, 1978; P. T. Marsh, *The Victorian Church in Decline*, 1969.
28. *The Record*, 14 November 1884.
29. *Royal Comm. on Eccl. Disc.* pp. 75–6, sec. 399.
30. Two examples: (a) Leeds: 31% went to Chapel, 15% to the C. of E.; (b) Bradford: 27% went to Chapel, 12% to the C. of E. For a convenient analysis of the census, see Owen Chadwick, *The Victorian Church*, pt. 1, 1966, pp. 363–9; J. Rogan, 'The Religious Census of 1851', *Theology* LXVI (January 1963), pp. 11–15.
31. An interesting comment on the effect of pew rents on the poor was made by Dr Tait in 1860, 'It might be very difficult to lure them in, but at present they were not lured in, but locked out'. (R. T. Davidson and W. Benham, *Life of Archibald Campbell Tait*, 2 vols. 3rd edn 1891, vol. 1, p. 264.)
32. The practice of evening communion also grew from 1852 onwards. See p. 50.

33. Quoted in *Substance of a Speech recommending certain Modifications of the Liturgy, delivered in the Lower House of Convocation 14 March 1861*, Hon. George Pellew, Dean of Norwich, 1861, p. 8.
34. *Chronicle of the Convocation of Canterbury 1847–57*, pp. 158–65, 174–8, 180–6, 196–8.
35. ibid., 1859–61, pp. 139–41, 152–65. The rejection of Harvest Thanksgiving was surprising, for it was a festival of fairly long standing; and special prayers had frequently been officially produced for specific occasions. In 1862 Canterbury Convocation produced a form of service, which, although never receiving official authorization, nevertheless remained in use for at least half a century. (*Chronicle* 1862, pp. 962f.; 1863, p. 1145.)
36. ibid., 1859–61, pp. 578–83, 615.
37. Hansard, *Parliamentary Debates*, 3rd Series, vol. 151, pp. 475–7, 492–501; *Journals of the House of Lords*, vol. 90, pp. 315, 318.
38. *Journals of the House of Commons*, vol. 113, p. 306.
39. For further study see Jasper, op. cit., especially chapter 5.
40. Quoted in A. B. J. Beresford Hope, *Worship in the Church of England*, 2nd edn, 1875, p. 7.
41. ibid., pp. 20–1, 34–5.
42. Many instances are given in G. R. Balleine, *A History of the Evangelical Party*, 1908.
43. M. Hennell, 'Evening Communion in the Church of England in the 19th Century', *Theology* LXII, no. 463 (1959), pp. 3–11.
44. E. Hodder, *The Life and Work of the Seventh Earl of Shaftesbury*, 3 vols., 1886, vol. 3, p. 102.
45. Orby Shipley, ed., *The Church and the World*, 1868, pp. 158–9.
46. ibid., pp. 160, 180.
47. ibid., pp. 34, 42.
48. Anon, *Charles Lowder*, 1882, p. 167.
49. C. E. Osborne, *The Life of Father Dolling*, 1903, p. 172.
50. ibid., pp. 108–9.
51. *The British Critic*, No. 54 (April 1840), p. 251.
52. *The Church Times*, 20 April 1867.
53. Orby Shipley, *The Ritual of the Altar*, 1870, p. xvii.
54. *The Guardian* 1885, quoted in E. Towle, *John Mason Neale D.D.*, 1906, p. 40.
55. H.S.L. were the second consonants of his two Christian names and surname, Jo*h*n Ma*s*on Nea*l*e.
56. cf. Jasper, op. cit., pp. 67–73.
57. *Royal Commission on Ritual, First Report*, 1867, p. vii.
58. H. R. Ashwell and R. G. Wilberforce, *Life of Samuel Wilberforce D.D.*, 3 vols., 1880–2, vol. 3, pp. 214–15.
59. *Royal Commission on Ritual, Second Report*, 1867, pp. 1–2.
60. Hansard, *Parliamentary Debates*, 3rd Series, vol. 192, pp. 332–3, 1921: vol. 193, pp. 868–96.
61. *Royal Commission on Ritual, Third Report*, 1870, p. 7.
62. *Journals of the House of Lords*, vol. 103, p. 523.
63. *Royal Commission on Ritual, Fourth Report*, 1870, p. vii.
64. ibid., pp. viii–xxviii.
65. H. P. Liddon, *The Life of Edward Bouverie Pusey*, 4 vols, 4th edn 1894, vol. 4, p. 240. Davidson and Benham, op. cit., vol. 2, pp. 139–40.
66. cf. Jasper, op. cit., pp. 103–4.

67. F. Procter and W. H. Frere, *A History of the Book of Common Prayer*, rev. 3rd edn 1949, p. 223.
68. W. K. Lowther Clarke and C. Harris, *Liturgy and Worship*, 1932, pp. 785–6.
69. ibid., pp. 785–6; A. G. M. Stephenson, *The First Lambeth Conference 1867*, 1967, p. 209.
70. Lowther Clarke and Harris, op. cit., pp. 704–5.
71. E. G. Sandford, ed., *Memoirs of Archbishop Temple*, 2 vols. 1906, vol. 2, pp. 160–2. Subsequently Temple's interpretation was questioned. People such as Archbishop Davidson and Sir William Harcourt disagreed with it: and G. K. A. Bell commented, 'No other bishop agreed with the theory of the Archbishop [Temple], though they might all appear to act upon it' (G. K. A. Bell, *Randall Davidson*, 2nd edn 1938, p. 329).
72. *Annual Report of the English Church Union*, 1871–2, pp. 151–3.
73. *Report of the Committee of the Lower House of Canterbury Convocation on the Rubrics of the Prayer Book*, 1872, pp. 2–37.
74. *Chronicle of Canterbury Convocation*, 1875, p. 281.
75. Bentley, op. cit., pp. 97–102, for both cases.
76. For the whole discussion see Jasper, op. cit., pp. 118–23.
77. A similar Enabling Bill proposed by Randall Davidson in 1896 met with a like fate.
78. Jasper, op. cit., pp. 123–7.
79. cf. Archbishop Davidson's comment, *Report of the Royal Commission on Ecclesiastical Discipline*, 1906, vol. 2, p. 388.
80. The Bishops of London (Temple), Rochester (Thorold), Oxford (Stubbs), Salisbury (J. Wordsworth), and Hereford (Atlay).
81. A. C. Benson, *The Life of Edward White Benson*, 2 vols., 1900, vol. 2, p. 339.
82. G. W. E. Russell, *Edward King, Sixtieth Bishop of Lincoln*, 1912, p. 183.
83. Bentley, op. cit., p. 120.
84. *The Guardian*, 26 November 1890.
85. Stephenson, op. cit., pp. 201–2.
86. R. T. Davidson, *The Six Lambeth Conferences 1867–1920*, 1920, p. 56.
87. ibid., p. 97; A. M. G. Stephenson, *Anglicanism and the Lambeth Conferences,* 1978, pp. 68 70.
88. Davidson, op. cit., pp. 89–90.
89. ibid., pp. 116–17, 121, 152, 173.
90. ibid., pp. 189–90, 207–8.
91. ibid., pp. 272–5.
92. *Code of Canons 1929*, Edinburgh 1929, pp. xii, xiv; J. Dowden, *The Scottish Communion Office of 1764*, Oxford 1922, pp. 85–6. This regulation was modified in 1828, the individual bishop then being regarded as sufficient authority for change.
93. W. G. S. Snow, *Arthur John Maclean*, Edinburgh 1950, p. 79.
94. This pressure was surprisingly encouraged by an Aberdonian, Bishop Ewing of Argyll and the Isles. He was a close friend of Dr Tait and a great Anglophile. cf. A. J. Ross, *Memoir of Bishop Ewing*, Edinburgh 1877, pp. 280–97.
95. cf. *Anglican Prayer Books: a Scottish View*, a Report for the Lambeth Conference 1958, p. 8.
96. *Code of Canons 1929*, p. xvi; Dowden, op. cit., pp. 86–7.
97. Snow, op. cit., p. 79.
98. For further detail cf. W. Sherlock, *The Story of the Revision of the Irish Prayer Book*, Dublin 1910.

99. cf. M. Shepherd, *The Oxford American Prayer Book Commentary*, New York 1955, esp. p. xxi.
100. Rector of All Saints, Worcester, Mass. 1862–83, and of Grace Church, New York 1883–1909.
101. cf. C. F. Pascoe, *Two Hundred Years of the S.P.G. 1701–1900*, 1901, esp. pp. 721–46.
102. W. F. Swift, 'Methodism and the Book of Common Prayer', *Proceedings of the Wesley Historical Society* (1949), vol. xxvii, p. 40. The hope of a single new book was not fully realized; a new edition of *The Sunday Service* appeared as late as 1910.
103. Gordon Rupp, *Thomas Jackson, Methodist Patriarch*, 1954, p. 22; Horton Davies, *Worship and Theology in England 1850–1900*, 1962, p. 259.
104. J. E. Rattenbury, *Wesley's Legacy to the World*, 1938, p. 192. Some Methodists seceded to form the Primitive Methodists (1808), the Bible Christians (1815), and the United Methodists (1857). The secessions were temporary, ending with the creation of the single Methodist Church in 1932. All their services involved wide departures from Prayer Book patterns.

4

1900–1920

I

Welcome though the Lincoln Judgement had been, it failed to provide a permanent or effective solution to the ritual problems of the Church. The ritualists themselves continued to use services and ceremonies which did not conform to what was constitutionally permissible. When confronted with the challenge that they had undertaken on oath not to use forms other than those in the Book of Common Prayer 'except so far as shall be ordered by lawful authority', they claimed that the Western Church was their 'lawful authority', and this included the Church of Rome as well as the Church of England. Roman practices and services therefore continued. In return, the anti-ritualists, faced with the failure of prosecutions and imprisonments, adopted other expedients.[1]

One such expedient was hooliganism and the disruption of services, an activity led by John Kensit, secretary of the Protestant Truth Society, who began his campaign in January 1897 with a public objection at the confirmation of Dr Mandell Creighton as Bishop of London in St Mary-le-Bow Church, on the grounds that he had worn a mitre and had given preferment to persons considered by Kensit to be unfit.[2] Kensit could command a ready ear from those members of the public who were prepared to see in the growth of ritualism the danger of a conspiracy to turn the Church of England Romewards. After all, this was only one indication. Another was the activity of Lord Halifax and the English Church Union in negotiating with the Papacy in 1894 on the validity of Anglican orders.[3] Further confirmation came in 1897 with a tendentious book by Walter Walsh, assistant editor of the Evangelical newspaper *The English Churchman*, entitled *The Secret History of the Oxford Movement*, and claiming to reveal the existence of a secret Romanizing Anglo-Catholic underworld.

A further expedient was a campaign of abuse both in the press and in Parliament, led by Sir William Harcourt, an eminent lawyer and parliamentarian, who was twice Chancellor of the Exchequer under Gladstone and leader of the Liberal Party in the House of Commons after 1894. A strong and stubborn Churchman, he was an Erastian who regarded the Church as a creation of Parliament and the Prayer Book as 'the Schedule of the Statute'. Not only did he inveigh constantly against the ritualists in Parliament, but he also penned a stream of 'prodigious polemics' in *The Times*.[4] In the face of such attacks the bishops had no desire to see Parliament assuming control over the Church without the latter having any effective say, but they knew that ritualistic clergy would never recognize legislation: indeed, Lord Halifax and the English Church Union were already breathing defiance. They knew that something needed to be done, but little notice was taken of their public pronouncements. Matters reached a critical state in May 1898 when Kensit presented a petition to Bishop Creighton, who in turn referred it to the Upper House of Canterbury Convocation, protesting against services which, it was alleged, were 'largely those in use in the Church of Rome, and taken from the Roman Missal and other books belonging to that Church'.[5] In the same year Harcourt also used the debate on the Benefices Bill in the House of Commons to attack the lawlessness of the clergy and the inaction of the Bishops. In reply, the Bishops announced two moves in January 1899: a measure to reform the Ecclesiastical Courts, and a proposal to make use of the Prayer Book provision, whereby any bishop who was in doubt as to the bearing of the Prayer Book regulations on a particular service or ceremony could seek an opinion from the Archbishop. Accordingly Archbishop Temple announced that in May he and the Archbishop of York would sit at Lambeth to hear submissions on the ceremonial use of portable lights and incense, and reservation.

On 6 May the two Archbishops opened their hearings. Four days later in the course of a debate in the Commons on a Church Discipline Bill the Government gave due warning: whilst it was not prepared to accept a measure which created new offences and ignored the authority of the bishops in maintaining the discipline of the Church, nevertheless it gave the warning that 'if the effort now being made by the Archbishops and Bishops to secure the due obedience of the clergy are not speedily effected, further legislation will be required to maintain the observance of the existing laws of Church and Realm'.[6] In July the Archbishops gave a negative decision on incense and lights: both were 'neither enjoined nor permitted'; although in the case of the former, 'we are far from saying . . . in itself [it] is an unsuitable or undesirable accompaniment to divine worship'.[7] The decision, based on a strict interpretation of the Act of Uniformity, was received with dismay by the ritualists, who promptly sent a deputation of protest representing nearly 140,000 lay communicants to the Archbishop. In reply, he pointed out that he and his fellow-archbishop did not constitute a court; they had no coercive power, but were simply stating their views; it was then up to the bishops to decide whether to adopt them or not.[8] In May 1900 came the decision on reservation. Once again it was negative, but the Archbishop indicated that he was not entirely unsympathetic towards the practice. 'I am obliged to decide that the Church of England does not at present allow Reservation in any form, and that those who think it ought to be allowed, though perfectly justified in endeavouring to get the proper authorities to alter the law, are not justified in practising Reservation until the law has been altered.'[9] In January 1901 the bishops issued a Manifesto appealing for obedience to all three decisions: but its impact was overshadowed by the death of two important figures. Dr Creighton, a prime target of the anti-Ritualists, died on 14 January: and Queen Victoria, a strong opponent of ritualism, died eight days later.

Meanwhile Sir William Harcourt continued his campaign in Parliament. Church Discipline Bills were introduced into the Commons every year between 1899 and 1903; and it was while the 1903 Bill was before the House that Randall Davidson succeeded Temple as Archbishop of Canterbury, to be confronted immediately by a deputation of over a hundred MPs wishing to discuss the Commons resolution of 10 May 1899, expressing the need for further legislation if episcopal efforts to secure clerical obedience proved unsuccessful. The Archbishop gave a reassuring reply. While the area of disobedience was in fact relatively small, there were nevertheless 'a few men defiant of episcopal authority and really reckless of the true Church of England's spirit . . . In my view of such cases, tolerance has reached, and even passed its limits . . . I desire and intend that we should now act, and act sternly.'[10] Discussions continued; and in February 1904 there was a strong move to appoint a Select Committee to enquire into ecclesiastical disorders: some members of the Prime Minister's (A. J. Balfour) own party threatening to vote against him and bring down the Government if he did not agree. But Dr Davidson was conscious that this again would involve an ominous invasion of spiritual territory by the State. He pressed upon the Prime Minister a preference for a Royal Commission, arguing that neither bishops nor clergy would be ready to give evidence to a committee appointed by Parliament: furthermore, 'the Royal Supremacy is exercised by a Royal Commission much more truly, or at all events much more obviously, than by a Parliamentary Committee.'[11] He had also discovered that the Anglo-Catholics would accept a Royal Commission, though with reluctance, but not a Select Committee. The pressure was effective, and on 8 March 1904 the Prime Minister announced the appointment of a Royal Commission with Sir Michael Hicks Beach, former Chancellor of the Exchequer, as chairman. Its membership was predominantly lay and included Sir Lewis Dibdin, the eminent lawyer, and Lord Alverstone, the Lord Chief Justice. Nevertheless, the clerical representatives were influential and able men: the Archbishop of Canterbury himself, Dr Francis Paget, Bishop of Oxford, together with two scholars well versed in liturgical matters, Dr E. C. S. Gibson, later Bishop of Gloucester, and Dr T. W. Drury, later Bishop of Ripon. In churchmanship all schools of thought were represented, although the balance was slightly on the Evangelical side. Nevertheless, it was an undoubtedly strong body and it took immense pains over its work. The Commission's terms of reference were precise and strictly confined to ritualistic problems: 'To inquire into the alleged prevalence of breaches or neglect of the Law relating to the conduct of Divine Service in the Church of England and to the ornaments and fittings of Churches; and to consider the existing powers and procedure applicable to such irregularities and to make such recommendations as may be deemed requisite for dealing with the aforesaid matters.'[12]

Beginning on 4 May 1904, there were 118 meetings; some thirty books of devotion were examined; and 164 witnesses were interviewed, including seventeen diocesan bishops and the Archbishop of Canterbury.

The Archbishop's evidence is worthy of note. It was a masterly review of the history of the ritualist movement from 1840 to 1905, not accessible in a consecutive or coherent form in any existing book or paper, and deserving publication as a separate document.[13] Three of his points deserve particular mention. In the first place, there had clearly been wide variations in the mode of conducting divine service from the days of Queen Elizabeth onwards: despite rubrics, Acts of Uniformity and episcopal injunctions, strict uniformity of practice had never prevailed. Secondly, the phrase 'except so far as shall be ordered by lawful authority' in the Declaration of Assent, which clergy were obliged to make under the Clerical Subscription Act of 1865, was significant: whatever their original intent, these words, as they stood, had given to the episcopate some larger authority than had existed before. Thirdly, the efforts of Lord Shaftesbury, and later of Sir William Harcourt and Mr Kensit, to secure parliamentary action in matters of ritual and discipline without consulting Convocation and regardless of the attitude of the episcopate, were dangerous and marked an approach which hampered the administrative authorities in their efforts to cope with the situation. The four volumes of evidence give a remarkably detailed survey of the state of Anglican public worship during the Victorian era. Indeed, the sheer size and variety of the material did not make the drafting of the Report easy. This was skilfully done, however, by Sir Lewis Dibdin, aided by the Archbishop and Bishop Paget, and was endorsed by the entire Commission. It provided an exhaustive statement of the legal situation, indicating both minor breaches of the law and those of special gravity and significance. Among the former were practices contrary to the strict requirements of the Prayer Book rubrics, such as the omission of the first and second Exhortations in the Communion Service, the taking of a collection, the giving of a blessing at Morning and Evening Prayer, and the failure to catechize at Evening Prayer. Such practices had become almost normal and doctrinally were of no great significance.[14] The more serious breaches of the law — those of special gravity and significance — were as follows:

1. The interpolation of the prayers and ceremonies belonging to the Canon of the Mass.
2. The use of the words 'Behold the Lamb', accompanied by the exhibition of a consecrated wafer or bread.
3. Reservation of the Sacrament under conditions which led to its adoration.
4. Mass of the Presanctified.
5. Corpus Christi processions with the Sacrament.
6. Benediction with the Sacrament.

7. Celebration of the Holy Eucharist with no communicants except the celebrant.
8. Hymns, prayers, and devotions involving invocation of or confession to the Blessed Virgin Mary or the Saints.
9. Observance of the festivals of the Assumption of the Blessed Virgin Mary and of the Sacred Heart.
10. The Veneration of Images and Roods.[15]

Many of these breaches involved practices regarded as 'on the Romeward side of a line of deep cleavage between the Church of England and that of Rome', including the use of vestments, ceremonial commixture, the sign of the cross, portable lights, incense, holy water and genuflexion.

One of the reasons for the failure to check irregularities was of long standing, dating from the Reformation period.

> The inclination, characteristic of the temper of the sixteenth century, to ignore all varieties of feeling and opinion existing among men of the same generation, and to make no provision for changes of feeling and opinion as one age succeeded another, is one far-reaching cause of irregularity . . . It has proved impracticable to obtain complete obedience to the Acts of Uniformity in one particular direction, partly because it is not now, and never has been, demanded in other directions.

Another reason was the refusal of the clergy to recognize the authority of the Judicial Committee of the Privy Council.

> Clergymen have claimed the liberty, and even asserted the duty, of disobedience to the decisions of a tribunal the authority of which they repudiate . . . A Court dealing with matters of conscience and religion must, above all others, rest on moral authority if its judgements are to be effective. As thousands of clergy, with strong lay support, refuse to recognise the jurisdiction of the Judicial Committee, its judgements cannot practically be enforced.[16]
>
> In consequence the Report reached two conclusions.
>
> 1. The law of public worship in the Church of England is too narrow for the religious life of the present generation. It needlessly condemns much which a great section of Church people, including many of her most devoted members, value; and modern thought and feeling are characterised by a care for ceremonial, a sense of dignity in worship, and an appreciation of the continuity of the Church, which were not similarly felt at the time when the law took its present shape. In an age which has witnessed an extraordinary revival of spiritual life and activity, the Church has had to work under regulations fitted for a different condition of things, without that power of self-adjustment which is inherent in the conception of a living Church . . .

2. The machinery for discipline has broken down. The means of enforcing the law in the Ecclesiastical Courts, even in matters which touch the Church's faith and teaching, are defective and in some respects unsuitable . . .[17]

The fact that a Royal Commission could reach the first conclusion was eloquent witness to the tremendous changes which had taken place in Anglican worship and devotion during the nineteenth century.

Finally, the Report made ten recommendations, largely the work of Randall Davidson. The first proposed that the practices of 'special gravity and significance' mentioned above 'should be promptly made to cease by the exercise of the authority belonging to the Bishops and, if necessary, by proceedings in the Ecclesiastical Courts'. The second, the fundamental recommendation, proposed the initiation of the whole process of Prayer Book revision.

> Letters of Business should be issued to the Convocations with instructions: (a) to consider the preparation of a new rubric regulating the ornaments (that is to say, the vesture) of the ministers of the Church, at the times of their ministrations, with a view to its enactment by Parliament; and (b) to frame, with a view to their enactment by Parliament, such modifications in the existing law relating to the conduct of Divine Service and to the ornaments and fittings of churches as may tend to secure the greater elasticity which a reasonable recognition of the comprehensiveness of the Church of England and of its present needs seems to demand.

Significantly the Commission saw this not as an exclusively clerical activity, but as one which should also include the laity: the Convocations should sit together and take counsel with the House of Laity. The third recommendation was also important, particularly in the light of recommendations made at the Lambeth Conference;[18] although it was given less attention than it deserved.

> In regard to the sanction to be given for the use of additional and special services, collects, and hymns, the law should be so amended as to give wider scope for the exercise of a regulative authority. This authority should be exercised within prescribed limits by the Archbishops and Bishops of both Provinces acting together for the sanction and regulation of additional and special services and collects in accordance with the teaching of the Holy Scriptures and the Book of Common Prayer, and for the forbidding of the use of hymns or anthems not in accordance with such teaching. The administrative discretion of individual Bishops within the several dioceses should be used in conformity with such sanction and regulation.

The need for services over and above those in the Prayer Book was therefore recognized, and parliamentary sanction for such services was not envisaged.

In such cases 'lawful authority' lay with the episcopate. But the Report was clear about the limits of the *ius liturgicum* in the case of statutory Prayer Book services.

> Many of their Lordships, while stating the emphatic opinion that the needs of the Church of England make it essential that the Bishops should exercise, or continue to exercise, some such power, do not claim for it any legal foundation. There cannot, in our opinion, be any doubt that the law does not recognize any right in a Bishop to override the provisions as to services rites and ceremonies contained in those Acts [of Uniformity] . . . It does not appear to us that there is any legal ground for assuming that, apart from statutory provision, the Bishop of a diocese has an inherent right to dispense the clergy from observing the provisions of those Acts.[19]

Changes in statutory services therefore clearly involved Parliament. This was a matter still to be debated for many years to come. The other recommendations were of a disciplinary nature, such as the establishment of new Ecclesiastical Courts, and were not concerned with the Prayer Book or its revision.

Letters of Business were issued to the Convocations by Royal Command on 10 November 1906 'to discuss and report upon certain recommendations contained in the Report of the Royal Commission on Ecclesiastical Discipline'.

II

During the nineteenth century the frequency of Communion services increased significantly, and in many Anglo-Catholic churches the choral Eucharist became the principal Sunday service. Unfortunately the practice of non-communicating attendance at such services also developed, owing to the insistence on fasting communion. The situation was therefore far from ideal. Admittedly there were exceptions. William Bennett introduced a choral Eucharist with communicants at 8 a.m. on Sundays at Frome in 1852; at approximately the same date William Butler began a similar service on festivals at Wantage,[20] and there were undoubtedly other clergy who did the same thing. By the end of the century the pace quickened. In 1892 Walter Frere instituted a 'parish communion' at 9.30 a.m. on Sundays at St Faith's, Stepney, while his cousin Francis Gurdon did likewise at St Anne's, Limehouse, shortly afterwards.[21] Frere was clear that what was needed was a 'celebration at which it is suitable for the people to communicate, and this must form the chief service of the day'. In *Some Principles of Liturgical Reform* he indicated how this could be done.[22] Then in 1900 Dr John Wordsworth, Bishop of Salisbury, speaking to his clergy and churchwardens at his fifth triennial Visitation, deplored non-communicating attendance and pleaded for 9 a.m. as the 'canonical hour' at which services should be held on Sundays. He himself had held his ordinations at that hour for some years, and he had not found the strain excessive for those who wished to communicate fasting.[23]

A similar line was taken by Charles Gore in *The Body of Christ*, a book which started 'an avalanche of press notices' when it was first published in 1901, achieving a very wide circulation.[24]

> It still remains for us . . . to restore the Eucharist to its central place as the chief, if not the most largely attended, act of Sunday worship . . . But also we must not be content with restoring as our chief act of worship a Eucharist at which the communion of the people does not form an important part. It cannot be said too strongly that any practice which divorces eucharistic worship and sacrifice from communion, or which rests content at the 'high service' with the communion of the priest alone, really represents a seriously defective theology.[25]

Percy Dearmer was urging the same principle at the very same time in later editions of his highly popular *The Parson's Handbook* – '"The Lord's Service on the Lord's Day" must be our watchword'[26] – while in 1905 Cosmo Gordon Lang, then Bishop of Stepney, lent his voice to the cause in his Cambridge lectures on pastoral theology, published as *The Opportunity of the Church of England.*[27]

This pattern of eucharistic worship was given further impetus by the publication of *The English Hymnal* in 1906. Originally conceived as a supplement to *Hymns Ancient and Modern*, this venture, due mainly to Percy Dearmer and Ralph Vaughan Williams, finally emerged as a book of over seven hundred hymns geared to Anglican liturgical requirements in a way unequalled by any of its contemporaries. Hymns, and in particular Office Hymns, were provided for every season and Holy Day; eucharistic propers were provided for every Sunday and Holy Day in accordance with the Prayer Book Calendar, processional hymns and litanies catered for a wide variety of occasions; and guidance was given on appropriate hymns for Morning and Evening Prayer and Holy Communion on Sundays and Holy Days throughout the year. All this, together with an insistence on congregational singing, helped to secure for hymnody recognition as an important element in public worship, and in particular in the Eucharist.

Two other books associated with Percy Dearmer also influenced Anglican worship at this time. The first was *The Parson's Handbook* – 'Practical directions both for parsons and others as to the management of the parish church and its services according to the English use as set forth in the Book of Common Prayer'. Dearmer claimed that he was only attempting to popularize the conclusions of others more expert than himself; and he acknowledged his indebtedness to Frere, Brightman, and Vernon Staley.[28] He was also expanding the theme of J. T. Micklethwaite, who had argued cogently in the first tract of the Alcuin Club published in 1897 under the title *The Ornaments of the Rubric* that the ornaments in use in the second year of Edward VI were authentically Anglican and were required by rubric:

indeed, those who did not use them were guilty of breaking the law.[29] Dearmer's approach – and the approach of many of the Alcuin Club publications – was often criticized as being needlessly fussy and archaic, earning for it the nickname, 'The British Museum rite'. Nevertheless he not only claimed loyalty to the rubrics of the Prayer Book: he argued that his book was 'like the Church of England, comprehensive'. It provided guidance for those who wanted elaborate ceremonial, for those who wanted simple ceremonial, for those who used the chasuble, and for those who used the black gown.[30] The book proved to be extremely popular, reaching its fifth edition by 1903, and Dearmer's claim of comprehensiveness was fully justified. It was used by men of differing shades of churchmanship, while many moderate High Churchmen felt their position as loyal Anglicans was strengthened by its strict adherence to the Prayer Book rubrics.

Dearmer's second book, published in 1903 in association with Frere and Canon S. M. Taylor, was *The English Liturgy*. This beautifully produced altar book differed from many of its Anglo-Catholic companions in one important respect. Whereas they contained the Prayer Book eucharistic rite supplemented and 'enriched' by material from the Roman Missal, *The English Liturgy* adhered faithfully to the Prayer Book rite, confining its additional material to propers for Black Letter Days and other occasions. Like *The Parson's Handbook* it was a volume used and appreciated by a wide variety of Churchmen. These two, together with *The English Hymnal*, and supported by the volumes of the Alcuin Club and Vernon Staley's Library of Liturgiology and Ecclesiology, formed a solid foundation for an approach to the liturgy which was High Anglican and non-Roman.

It must be admitted, however, that these activities did not go unopposed. Inevitably the Protestant element, reinforced by such a doughty champion as Dr E. A. Knox, Bishop of Manchester, would have none of them: while a group of young Anglo-Catholics, led by Knox's two sons, Ronald and Wilfred, together with Maurice Child, formed the Society of SS Peter and Paul in February 1911 to act as a counter-blast to 'British Museum religion'.[31] Their aim was not a return to the past but 'a resumption of arrested development'; in other words, a move towards what the Church might have been if the Reformation in its more destructive aspects had never occurred. They therefore encouraged 'luxuriant Baroque' and in due course published their own rivals to *The Parson's Handbook* with Martin Travers' two volumes of *Pictures of the Liturgy*, one on Low Mass and the other on High Mass, while Adrian Fortescue's *Ceremonies of the Roman Rite Described* became their authoritative guide. Many of their publications were provocative and rather amusing and not all Anglo-Catholics approved. H. W. Hill, secretary of the English Church Union, wrote to Lord Halifax in 1916, 'I wonder if there is anybody who can keep these young people in order and from making such donkeys of themselves.'[32] But the fact remains their publications attracted a good deal of attention and enjoyed a brisk sale.

It is not altogether surprising that this period also saw a flowering of

English liturgical scholarship. Both in range and in quality the output was exceptional. Textual discoveries and their accompanying studies revolutionized knowledge of the liturgical history of the early centuries. Cuthbert Turner summed it up admirably in 1917:

> After a quarter of a century's debate over thesis and counter-thesis, critical study has ended in vindicating for St Hippolytus – or in other words for Rome and for the beginning of the third century – a tract on Church Order giving us a connected account, however brief, of the administration of the sacraments of Baptism and Confirmation, of Ordination and . . . of the Eucharist . . . to which, in extent and precision, there is nothing quite parallel for another century or more.[33]

The debate involved both European and English scholars, but the contribution of the latter was outstanding.[34] There was, for example, F. E. Brightman producing a monumental part I of a revised edition of Hammond's *Liturgies Eastern and Western* in 1896, followed by his work on *The Prayer Book of Sarapion* in 1900. There was George Horner, the untiring editor of Coptic texts, producing in 1904 his *Statutes of the Apostles*, with texts and studies of the Ethiopic, Arabic and Sahidic forms of the Egyptian Church Order. There was Bishop A. J. Maclean, a reputable Syrian scholar, with his work on *Ancient Church Orders* in 1910. Then the two Roman Catholic scholars, Edmund Bishop and Dom R. H. Connolly, worked together on *The Liturgical Homilies of Narsai* in 1909, followed by the latter's famous *The So-called Egyptian Church Order and Derived Documents* in 1916. Add to these the studies of Walter Frere, W. C. Bishop, Armitage Robinson, Bishop John Wordsworth and Cuthbert Turner – it was a distinguished list.

At the same time studies on the history and development of the Roman rite went on apace. H. A. Wilson was responsible for critical editions of *The Gelasian Sacramentary* in 1894 and *The Gregorian Sacramentary* in 1915, while he assisted with *Missale Romanum Mediolani* – various editions of the Roman Missal published for the Henry Bradshaw Society (vol. 33) in 1907. C. L. Feltoe produced a critical edition of *The Leonine Sacramentary* in 1896, while Edmund Bishop produced a variety of studies on the Roman Rite, including his famous essay 'The Genius of the Roman Rite', which were published posthumously in 1918 as *Liturgica Historica*. In the same period Walter Frere produced *The Sarum Gradual and the Gregorian Antiphonale Missarium* in 1895, and his two volumes on *The Use of Sarum* in 1898–1901, while he followed the publication of Wilson's *Gregorian Sacramentary* with his own article, 'The Carolingian Gregorianum; its sections and their numberings'.[35] Two other important studies were Cuthbert Atchley's edition of *Ordo Romanus Primus* in 1905, and J. Wickham Legg's edition of *The Sarum Missal* in 1916.

Nor were studies on the Prayer Book itself neglected. Here again J. Wickham Legg was a notable figure. In 1888 he had produced the first edition of Cardinal Quignon's Breviary of 1535; in 1903 he edited *The Clerk's Book of 1549* for the Henry Bradshaw Society; in 1914 he wrote *English Church Life from the Restoration to the Tractarian Movement*; and in 1915 there appeared his *Cranmer's Liturgical Projects*, which was a full study of the way in which Cranmer had proposed to use the two editions of Quignon's Breviary. Edmund Bishop and Dom F. A. Gasquet had also produced an interesting study on *Edward VI and the Book of Common Prayer* from a Roman Catholic point of view in 1891, making use not only of the German Church Orders but also producing for the first time Cranmer's projected form of the Latin breviary. Bishop John Dowden brought together a series of learned essays on a wide variety of topics in *The Workmanship of the Prayer Book* in 1899, *Further Studies in the Prayer Book* in 1908, and *The Church Year and Kalendar* in 1911; while Dr H. Gee brought to light a good deal of new material on the revision of the Prayer Book and the working of the Ornaments Rubric in the early years of Queen Elizabeth I in *The Elizabethan Prayer Book and Ornaments* in 1902. The same year also saw the appearance of W. H. Frere's rewritten and expanded edition of Proctor's *History of the Book of Common Prayer*, a book which remained a standard work of reference for nearly half a century. Then in 1912 appeared *The Prayer Book Dictionary* by S. Harford and M. Stevenson. Finally there was F. E. Brightman's monumental two-volume work in 1915, *The English Rite*, showing more completely than any other work hitherto the sources and the development of successive Prayer Books from 1549 to 1662.

This brief catalogue suffices to indicate the wealth of liturgical material and scholarship available to the Church of England at the turn of the century. It is not surprising, therefore, that valuable discussions on liturgical revision, and in particular on the revision of the eucharistic rite, began to emerge from people of influence and authority. An early essay appeared in 1898 by the Reverend T. A. Lacey, a brilliant scholar, a friend of Dearmer, Frere and Gore, and at the time principal leader-writer for *The Church Times*. *Liturgical Interpolations* was in fact the first pamphlet on the revision of the Prayer Book to be published by the Alcuin Club, and it had a wide sale. Here Lacey castigated those Anglo-Catholics who interpolated portions of the Roman rite into the Prayer Book Communion service. It was a practice which should be rooted out; and the way to do so was to remove the 'dislocation', which was both the excuse for it and the cause of its possibility. This would involve a readjustment of the elements of the Prayer Book rite without changing a single word of either text or rubric. Such a change would not only help to remove the desire for interpolations; it would make interpolations of the worst kind impossible. The amended order he proposed was: Offertory, Sursum Corda and Preface, Prayer for the Church, Consecration Prayer, Prayer of Oblation, Lord's Prayer, Invitation, Confession, Absolution, Comfortable Words, Prayer of Humble Access, Communion, Prayer of Thanksgiving, Gloria in excelsis, Blessing. It had affinities both with the 1549 rite, and with the current American and Scottish rites; and in the coming years, with some minor modifications, it achieved a wide degree of acceptance.

Gore, for example, supported it in *The Body of Christ*, and his views on language as well as on order were of particular interest. He believed that much of what had been written on the Eucharist between the sixteenth and nineteenth centuries had been defective, either by excessive intellectual definition or by the movement of a violently negative Protestantism. By contrast, it was in the early Church that men would discover the right temper of mind with which to approach the subject.

> There is a kind of clearness of statement which suits material objects but which simply does not apply to spiritual things; and it is plain that such clearness is avoided as a danger both in the Bible and in the Fathers. Nothing is in fact more striking than the constant anxiety of the Fathers to make men feel that human language can but dimly adumbrate, and not fully or precisely define, divine mysteries. They continually appear to shrink from being too clear-cut in their explanations. In our days we seem greatly to need the reminder of Hooker . . . that 'because this divine mystery (referring to the Incarnation) is more true than plaine, divines have framed the same to their own conceits, and fancies are found in their expositions more plaine than true' . . . It is a shallow rationalism and intellectual indolence, rather than the simple faith of the poor (or poor in spirit), which crave for clearness of statement beyond the measure allowed for us who 'see through a glass, darkly' – the craving must be gratified only with great reserves.[36]

Gore received weighty support from the redoubtable Anglo-Catholic scholar Dr Darwell Stone in his two-volume *A History of the Doctrine of the Holy Eucharist* (1909), where he concluded:

> It is a reasonable conclusion that the official language and the official ceremonial of great Christian bodies call for a liberal and a considerable interpretation . . . In the mystery of the Eucharist, where human thought is so apt to go astray, and human language is so inadequate to express even human thought, the interpreter will most likely be right who is patient of a wide latitude of interpretation and gentle towards what seem to him offending expressions.[37]

In structure Gore did not consider the Prayer Book rite compared favourably with primitive patterns. Nevertheless the Prayer for the Church should remain in its existing position – introductory to the Eucharist proper – rather than in the eucharistic prayer, as in the Roman and Scottish rites. Similarly the penitential material should remain in its existing position, with the exception of the Prayer of Humble Access, which would serve better as a prayer of preparation immediately before the act of communion. As for the eucharistic prayer itself, its dominant note should be thanksgiving, introduced by the Sursum Corda; and it should include the activities of all three persons of the Trinity, culminating in the Sanctus. Then would follow the Institution Narrative, leading to a commemoration of our Lord's passion, death, resurrection, ascension and expected second coming. Next would come the offering of the representative gifts of bread and wine and the prayer for the Holy Spirit or the divine power to consecrate them to be the Body and Blood of Christ for the reception of the faithful. The eucharistic prayer would be followed by the Lord's Prayer, the Prayer of Humble Access and the Communion. On the Prayer of Oblation Gore was flexible. While he would prefer this to precede communion, nevertheless if other grave mistakes in the eucharistic prayer could be avoided, the present position of the prayer might admit of 'something more than justification' on the basis of St Augustine's argument that the culmination of sacrifice is the oblation of the faithful.[38] This was the pattern Gore would have liked to see. Nevertheless, while 1662 remained the official form for the Church of England, it should be adhered to faithfully, despite its imperfections. As a temporary expedient, however, pending the provision of a new rite, two things were possible. Either the rite of 1549 could be authorized; or some readjustment on the lines of Lacey's proposal could be adopted, allowing the Prayer of Oblation and the Lord's Prayer to follow immediately the Prayer of Consecration before communion. Neither of these expedients were ideal, however.[39]

With the passage of time this 'Gore-Lacey' line or something akin to it received increasing support in articles, books and pamphlets from a wide variety of people — Dean Beeching of Norwich, W. C. Bishop, Dearmer, Frere, Canon Randolph of Ely, Athelstan Riley and Dr W. J. Sparrow Simpson to name but a few.[40] Lord Halifax discussed the matter with groups of clergy at four conferences at Hickleton and then declared himself in favour in his Presidential Address to the English Church Union in 1916, while a committee of the ECU under Darwell Stone came to the same conclusion in 1919.[41] Support also came from other parts of the Anglican Communion. In 1918 the diocese of Zanzibar authorized a rite on similar lines, while South Africa followed suit soon afterwards.[42]

Meanwhile the Lambeth Conference of 1908 tackled the whole question of Prayer Book revision with a thoroughness which far exceeded that of its predecessors. Its conclusion was stated without equivocation in the Encyclical Letter:

> The growing experience of the Anglican Communion in different parts of the world and among different races has pointed to the necessity for the adaptation and enrichment of forms of service which have come down to us from other times. Such adaptation and enrichment are advisable, and indeed essential if our Church is to meet the real needs of living men and

women today. We have accordingly made certain practical suggestions in this direction which we commend to the attention of both clergy and laity.[43]

This conclusion was reiterated in Resolution 24, while Resolution 27 set out seven general principles to be observed in any future revision of the Prayer Book:

1. The adaptation of rubrics to customs which are generally accepted.
2. The elimination of unnecessary repetitions and redundancies.
3. The enrichment of existing services.
4. The fuller provision of alternatives in forms of worship.
5. Greater elasticity in public worship.
6. The elimination of language which was obscure or misunderstood.
7. A revision of the Calendar and Tables.[44]

The question of adaptation and enrichment was considered by a committee under the chairmanship of Dr Jayne, Bishop of Chester; and its comments on rubrics were particularly interesting. Hitherto, and particularly in the nineteenth century, these had come to be regarded as binding. But now it was recognized that many customs had developed – harmless and indeed good in themselves – for which rubrics made no provision. The responses before and after the Gospel in the Communion Service was a case in point: indeed such responses had already been authorized in America, Ireland and Scotland. Here, and in similar cases, the customs should not be regarded as illegal; rather the rubrics should be changed to bring them into line with the custom.[45] The America, Irish and Scottish books were also cited as illustrations of ways in which enrichment was possible by way of additional prayers and thanksgivings, additional suffrages in the Litany, additional canticles and additional proper prefaces. The thorny questions of the Ornaments Rubric and the Consecration Prayer were not dealt with through lack of time, but the Committee made other proposals in respect of Holy Communion: the use of the Summary of the Law as an alternative to the Decalogue, permission to omit the third Exhortation, the use of Biddings before the Prayer for the Church, and shorter words of administration when the number of communicants was large. Other proposals affecting the Daily Office were obviously influenced by what had already appeared in the American book: the abbreviation of Morning and Evening Prayer when used with another service, a greater liberty in the choice of lessons, a larger provision of special psalms for Sundays and Holy Days, and permission to use the American scheme of selected psalms for use on any occasion.

These proposals were very much in line with those put out by Dr Beeching in 1907 and W. C. Bishop in 1910.[47] But by far the most detailed programme on revision came from W. H. Frere, first in a series of articles in *The Church Quarterly Review*, secondly in a Memorandum drawn up for the Province of South Africa, and thirdly in his book, *Some Principles of Liturgical Reform.*

He pointed out that the desire for liturgical reform was world-wide, and not merely confined to the Anglican Communion. It was therefore much wider than most people imagined. Furthermore, what was needed was a long period of authorized experiment, during which not only would there be some effort to satisfy the growing desire for enrichment and greater convenience in the traditional methods of service, but also an effort to provide members of the Church with opportunities for acquiring sufficient knowledge and information on these matters to enable them to arrive at instructed judgements.[48] Revision should also be undertaken by skilled hands. As far as the Church of England was concerned,

> The serious work will only begin when the Convocations decide that it is at least as crucial a matter to revise the Prayer Book as to retranslate the Bible; and therefore are content to place the initial responsibility in the hands, not of a Committee of Convocation, which, except in the Upper House, contains few of the scholars who are most competent for the work, but a body of revisers gathered and empowered for the purpose.[49]

His principal suggestions, drawn from his various writings, were as follows:

1. A revision of the Calendar with a fixed date for Easter, together with further provision of proper Collects, Epistles and Gospels for Lesser Feasts.
2. The removal of duplicated material.
3. The arrangement of psalms and lessons to be based on the ecclesiastical and not the civil year.
4. A return to the old conception of rubrics — some directive, reminders of positive ecclesiastical laws concerning services; others suggestive and elastic, giving reminders to recall the approved customs of the Church. The provision of any necessary new laws should be by means of Canons, thereby dispensing with the problems of parliamentary endorsement.
5. *The Daily Office*
   a. A revision of the introductory sentences.
   b. Permission to omit a revised Penitential Opening.
   c. The Venite, when used as an Invitatory, to end at verse 7.
   d. Alternative Canticles.
6. *Holy Communion*
   a. The Kyries as alternative to the Decalogue.
   b. A restoration of psalmody as the gradual.
   c. Omission of the Creed and Gloria on weekdays.
   d. A new Canon was required; but as a temporary measure, permission should be given for a rearrangement of existing material: Comfortable Words, Prayer of Humble Access, Sursum Corda, Preface and Sanctus, Prayer of Consecration, Prayer of Oblation, Lord's Prayer, Communion.

7. Compline as a second and more popular Evening Service.
8. A revised order for Adult Baptism, based on primitive models.
9. Permission to use the 1549 Baptism and Burial Services as alternatives.

In the light of such a programme, it is interesting to see how the official church bodies tackled the problem of producing its answers to the Royal Letters of Business.

III

At the outset Archbishop Davidson and others in authority believed that the task facing the Church was significant, but not necessarily unduly complicated nor lengthy. Rubrics certainly needed attention: some flexibility was required, and the more liberty that could be given, the fewer would be those who broke the law. In June 1906 the Archbishop appealed to the Canterbury Convocation and the House of Laity for support

> in the endeavour which must now be made to bring to an end a situation which, for those at least who are in the front rank of administrative ability, has become well-nigh intolerable. It has become abundantly clear that to secure the exact observance, in the twentieth century, of detailed rubrics drawn up in the sixteenth and seventeenth centuries, is neither possible nor, from any point of view, desirable. Rules clear in principle and yet elastic in detail we do absolutely require, if the Church, in its manifold activities, is to be abreast of modern needs and yet loyal to ancient order.[50]

Nevertheless, small though the necessary changes might prove to be, the constitutional means whereby they must receive authorization involved the delicate matter of Church–State relations. So the Archbishop warned the Upper House:

> Have you forgotten that in the long run any change of rubric or other document which has statutory force would require Parliamentary sanction? . . . It is the very crux of our difficulties. But we have to remember this — as far as I am aware, no responsible people in public life desire that the rubrical details of the Book of Common Prayer shall be discussed in Parliament . . . The task before us ultimately will be how to find a mode of securing the Parliamentary sanction which will be necessary if, and only if, the change of any rubric is recommended — how to secure that without involving discussions which would be quite obviously and manifestly unsuited to Parliament if they necessitated discussions there upon the details either of worship or of doctrine.[51]

Clearly, therefore, Davidson approached the task of dealing with the Royal Letters of Business with some misgiving and with no particular enthusiasm.[52] He was well aware that feeling in the Church was divided: both the

Convocations of Canterbury and York were recipients of numerous petitions against change: and in 1910, after three years' work, the Lower House of Canterbury could still spend two days in debating the desirability of undertaking any revision at all.[53] The Convocations began work in February 1907. It was arranged that each of the four Houses should consider matters independently as the best preparation for ultimate agreement by the whole Convocation and the two attendant Houses of Laity:[54] nevertheless, they would confer together and share information as and when necessary. Each House then appointed committees to examine what were regarded as the two major issues — the Ornaments Rubric and the changes needed in the rubrics relating to the conduct of Divine Service.

While discussion was confined initially to a strictly limited area, before long that area began to widen. It was found difficult to discuss rubrics and the conduct of divine service without involving the actual texts of services. Furthermore, other influences were at work. The Lambeth Conference of 1908 revealed an interest in the subject which went far beyond a mere consideration of rubrics; while in a number of provinces plans for revision were in the air: Canada began work in 1908, Ireland and Scotland in 1909, and South Africa published a schedule of permitted modifications of and additions to 1662 in 1911. So the Convocations gradually extended their field of operations, proposing such modest items as additional suffrages to the Litany, additional Prayers and Thanksgivings, and modifications to the first exhortation in Holy Matrimony. Then further Committees were appointed to consider particular sections of the Prayer Book: the use of the Psalter, the text of the Psalter, the Lectionary and the Calendar. By July 1911 the situation had changed to such a degree that the Lower House of Canterbury actually debated a proposal to appoint a Joint Committee of both Houses to consider the advisability of providing an alternative rite of Holy Communion on the lines of the 1549, Scottish and American rites. The proposal was rejected, but by no means overwhelmingly — 32 votes to 47;[55] and the debate was a clear indication of the widening of horizons. By the time the four Houses began to collate their various proposals, their work had become more extensive than anything contemplated by Archbishop Davidson at the outset.

Little purpose would be served by discussing in detail the work of the Convocations during the period 1907–19. But note must be made of certain significant events. The important matter at the outset was the Ornaments Rubric: and all four Houses considered it with commendable speed. By far the most weighty document to emerge was Report 416 by the Committee of the Upper House of Canterbury under the chairmanship of Dr John Wordsworth, Bishop of Salisbury, a valuable historical survey of 120 pages, dealing with four items: the origin, development and symbolism of liturgical costume, the Ornaments Rubric itself, the ornaments of a bishop in the Church of England, and the meaning of the term 'vestment'. In introducing this Report to the Upper House on 5 February 1908, Dr Wordsworth commented on the strong feelings which had been brought to play on the subject:

> Extreme partisans on one side shrink from a ritualist as they would from a snake, or dismiss him contemptuously as possessed by the idle vanity of a peacock. Those on the other side regard Puritans as 'wild boars out of the wood', bent on rooting up all that is decent and beautiful. The worst of it is that both parties are in deadly earnest, and by their mutual provocation tend to depress one another to a lower level of grace and truth.[56]

The Report contained no recommendations as to policy, but a great deal of evidence in favour of the legality of vestments. It argued that the publication of the first Prayer Book in 1549 involved a fresh start and the directions contained therein were intended to be complete. Anything therefore which was not mentioned in the book was not permitted. The words 'shall be in use' meant 'the minister shall use', and the second year of Edward VI meant 1549.[57] Dr Wordsworth made it clear where his sympathies lay.

> We hold that the ornaments of the Church are regulated by the Prayer Book of 1549, except so far as the later books have abolished certain ceremonies which required ornaments still in use in 1549 . . . We believe that vestments have never been abolished in principle, and we wish to bring the Church to feel that their retention or abolition ought not to be a matter to excite very heated controversy . . . Our ideal ought, I think, to be that of a regulated and varied liberty suitable to the local conditions.[58]

Over three years were to elapse before the Upper House on 7 July 1911 finally declared itself in favour of Dr Wordsworth's line, recommending no change in the Ornaments Rubric, a diversity of use, and no sanction for any doctrinal change.[59]

The issue generated far more heat in the Upper House of York, however. This was due to some extent to the fact that the House was what Archbishop Lang described as 'an Evangelical preserve — seven of the nine were definite Evangelicals and all so much older than I was'.[60] Their Report, a more modest affair than that of Canterbury, clearly preferred the surplice to vestments: it was the prevailing use in practically all schools of thought in the forties and fifties of the nineteenth century, and their Lordships considered it to be far truer to the spirit of primitive antiquity than 'the ministerial attire enjoined in 1549'. Nevertheless, they were prepared to accept the permissive use of vestments, provided they were white.[61] When, however, the House debated the matter (8-9 May 1912) and Dr Jayne, Bishop of Chester, moved that 'a distinctive vesture, that is a white chasuble or cope, with a white alb plain be permitted to be worn by the chief minister at the Holy Communion', a long and quite heated debate took place. Strong feelings were aroused, and Archbishop Lang recalled, 'I have a recollection of the good wives of Bishops Moule (Durham) and Chavasse (Liverpool) leading their lords up and down the lawns at Bishopthorpe on the morning before the question of permitting white vestments was to be decided, pleading with them to be faithful to their true evangelical tradition.'[62] In the event the vote was inconclusive, four bishops voting for the proposal and four against. Archbishop Lang refused to give his casting vote, on the plea that the three other Houses of Convocation were equally involved in the matter and that they should know the real facts of the case — namely that the northern Bishops were equally divided on the issue.[63]

The Lower Houses of Canterbury and York had few doubts on the matter, however. Canterbury agreed in May 1909 that alternative vesture should be recognized under proper regulations and that eucharistic vestments could not be rightly regarded as symbolic of any distinctive Roman doctrines — a decision made with only seven dissentients.[64] York followed a similar line in July 1910.[65] By 1912, therefore, all serious discussion on the Ornaments Rubric had run its course. Despite memorials and protests, neither Convocation had shown any real desire for change, and other issues such as reservation and the eucharistic Canon now became the centre of interest.

IV

A second event of significance was the appointment of the Advisory Committee on Liturgical Questions.[66] On 5 May 1911 Archbishop Davidson suggested to the Upper House of Canterbury the need for a body of experts to edit and co-ordinate the proposals which would ultimately issue from the Convocations. The House approved and the first sixteen members, with Dr A. Robertson, Bishop of Exeter, as chairman, were appointed in February 1912. A further four members were added in November.[67] It was an impressive group, including Bishop Gibson of Gloucester, Bishop Drury of Ripon, Bishop Maclean of Moray and Ross — an unusual choice from Scotland, Professor H. B. Swete, Brightman, J. N. Dalton, Dearmer, Frere, Gee, Claude Jenkins and H. A. Wilson. Unfortunately it worked under certain disadvantages. In the first place the Convocation of York evidently had no hand in its appointment and made no use of its services. Secondly it was unable to make proposals itself: it could only 'edit' and 'co-ordinate' Convocation proposals. Thirdly its terms of reference were far from clear. Claude Jenkins, who had been appointed secretary, warned the Archbishop through his senior chaplain, the Reverend J. V. Macmillan, that there was a danger of the Committee finding itself in a difficult position.

> The position of the Advisory Committee ought to be clearly understood and it apparently is not. It is, so far as the Southern Convocation is concerned, a quasi-independent body appointed by the Archbishop to which the Lower House could send direct and without consultation with the Upper House: or is it a body in close relation to the Upper House to which the Upper House will send the Lower House suggestions as a whole when it received them?[68]

All this was very different from the kind of operation envisaged by Frere; and the limitations placed upon its activities were to have unfortunate consequences.

The Committee first met on 22 October 1912 to consider three fairly innocuous matters: the liturgical position of Evensong on Easter Eve, the division of the Litany when followed by Holy Communion, and a proposed form of service for a late Evensong; and it continued to meet regularly until January 1914. By that time all four Houses of Convocation were near the end of their separate exercises, and indeed on 20 February the Upper House of Canterbury unanimously adopted Report 481 embodying their replies to the Letters of Business. But when the question of comparison and correlation of these proposals with those of the other Houses was raised, the Bishop of Exeter requested a statement on the position and future of the Committee, indicating dissatisfaction at the way in which it had been used.

> In view of the expectations which had been raised in many minds at the time when the appointment of the Committee was publicly announced, and of the implied assurance that everything which ultimately proceeded from the House would have, to some extent, the imprimatur of a body of experts as something which at any rate they could pass, he thought that perhaps there were some outside the House who would feel that the Committee of Experts had not, so far, discharged all the functions in view of which it had been originally appointed. As the person who had been honoured by being elected Chairman, he felt obliged to ask whether it was considered by the House that the Committee should be discharged.

The Archbishop assured him, however, that the work of the Committee was by no means over and demands would be made upon it in the future.[69] He followed this with a letter of reassurance on 30 April 1915, although he also reminded Dr Robertson that the functions of the Committee were limited.

> I venture to hope that you may find it possible to invite the members of your Committee to consider whether any of the recommendations which we have thus made seem to them to call for protest as being liturgically faulty to such a degree as would make the reconsideration of the question in Convocation desirable. I am anxious, however, to make it clear that I am not inviting the Advisory Committee to take in hand a revision of all our work. This would be to constitute your Committee a new House of Convocation or even Tribunal of Appeal.[70]

Initiative was clearly to remain in the hands of Convocation; and the Bishop of Exeter, both as Chairman of the Committee and as a member of the Upper House, was placed in an embarrassing position: indeed, the whole business caused him much unhappiness. Frere also wrote to the Archbishop in blunt terms expressing support for Dr Robertson: and he revealed to H. A. Wilson (17 September 1915), 'When I wrote to express views of this kind, or even bluntly say that I thought we were being used as dust in the eyes of the public, the letter had the effect at any rate in part of our being taken off the shelf and called together for this coming meeting.'[71]

This meeting was scheduled for 19 October 1915 to discuss Report 487B containing the combined replies of both Houses of Canterbury. The Bishop of Exeter again warned members beforehand of the limitations imposed upon their operations: 'It will be out of order to make suggestions in regard to points not dealt with in the Report . . . There are few paragraphs which do not in their present form come within the scope of our reference.'[72] Yet the very subjects which were considered to be beyond the Committee's terms of reference — concerning the Service of the Church, the Recitation of the Psalter, the Lectionary, the Ornaments Rubric, the Athanasian Creed, and special Collects, Epistles and Gospels — because Convocation had not made any final decisions on them, were the very subjects on which at least some of the Committee particularly desired to express an opinion. Bishop Maclean, Wilson, Jenkins and Frere all expressed their misgivings, while Brightman was critical of the whole Report: 'The whole thing is depressing enough. I should like to amend nearly every line. It does not seem to me to be done with any real care or appreciation or knowledge of real needs.'[73] He ended up by sending in criticisms described by Jenkins as 'huge in number and covering nearly the whole ground'.

What was depressing was the general attitude of the bishops towards revision. Jenkins, who as a chaplain at Lambeth Palace, had a chance of observing them, wrote to Frere (4 October 1915):

> There is a very real danger that the things we most care about not having come off, there should go through as the product of revision — with the 'acquiescence' at any rate of our Committee — the really deplorably mediocre stuff which most of the rest is . . . So far as my opportunity of judging goes, those of the Bishops who are not utterly bored with the whole subject — which is to them even as dilapidations — are rather pleased with their work; and some of them are by no means prepared to welcome criticism on it. It was quite clear at the last meeting that some of them were inclined to be restive under some frank expressions of opinion as to their ideas of a Proper Preface.[74]

A comment by Dr Pollock, Bishop of Norwich, is also revealing. It suggests not only a patronizing attitude towards the Committee, but also a lack of awareness of the wealth of expertise available to the bishops. He regarded the Committee (5 July 1916) as 'a body which was appointed for the minor function of preventing the House (of Bishops) from making slips of diction, and so on'.[75]

When the Committee finally met on 19-23 October 1915, Frere, supported by the professional liturgists, protested that though they were a body of people who were supposed to have devoted a good deal of time and thought to liturgical questions, they were not being allowed to consider any of the matters which to liturgists constituted the main points of interest in any scheme of Prayer Book revision. They then proceeded to undertake 'a microscopic scrutiny'[76] of Report 487B, bearing striking testimony to their dissatisfaction with both the manner and the content of Convocation's attempts at revision. Their scrutiny contained some 160 points on liturgical and textual details, matters of drafting, and a list of questions upon which the Committee was willing to give advice if asked. It was this list which was significant, for it revealed the Committee's unease at the way they were being ignored on a wide range of fundamental questions:

1. Principles of Psalter recitation and Lectionary at Morning and Evening Prayer.
2. The Athanasian Creed.
3. An alternative Order of Holy Communion.
4. An alternative Order of Burial.
5. The restoration of some form of Holy Unction.
6. An alternative, briefer formula for use by a bishop at Confirmation.
7. The eucharistic Lectionary.
8. Psalmody at Holy Communion.
9. Improvements to the eucharistic Preface.
10. The restoration of 'Holy' in the Nicene Creed.
11. The use of Antiphons in the Occasional Offices.
12. A Lenten alternative to Te Deum.
13. Processionals for the Major Festivals.
14. An Order for the Consecration of Churches.[77]

This document was considered by the Joint Committee of the two Houses and its findings duly presented to the Upper House in February 1917. Only the first part was considered; over three quarters of the 160 points were accepted in whole or in part; questions of drafting were postponed to a later stage: but on the final and crucial section, all the Advisory Committee's pleas were ignored, except for the Athanasian Creed; and even this was rejected by the Lower House.

With the publication of Report 504 in 1917 and Report 515 in 1918 the Canterbury proposals for revision were completed; and the Advisory Committee was summoned no more. Its life had been brief and unhappy. Both the Archbishop and Convocation appear to have refused its expert help for two possible reasons. In the first place, there was a reluctance to allow another body of people, no matter how expert, to exercise rights which they believed to be theirs. The obvious, and indeed the most fruitful, solution — as later experience has indicated — would have been for the Advisory Committee to have prepared drafts for their consideration. A modus operandi should have been possible; but the Archbishop was either unwilling to look for it or incapable of recognizing the need for it; and without an initiative from him neither House would act. Secondly, liturgy was unfamiliar territory for most members of Convocation. Few had studied it deeply — the Convocation debates reveal this all too clearly: and many members of both

Houses were unaware of the complexities of the subject. Liturgical experts were rare birds and were therefore treated with caution. Nevertheless, despite the severe restrictions placed upon it, the Committee did eventually succeed in making some valuable contributions to the process of revision. The Table of Occurrences, the Order of Compline, the Invitatories to the Venite, the additional Proper Prefaces, the rearrangement of the Litany, the new Occasional Prayers, and the form of recitation of the Decalogue — all owed a great deal to their comment and criticism. But how much more could have been done!

V

In the first year of the War there was evidence of a renewed interest in religion: services were well attended and people made increasing use of churches for their private devotions. In 1915, therefore, Archbishop Davidson appointed a committee of twelve priests of different schools of thought under Dr Armitage Robinson to report on 'The Spiritual Call to the Nation and the Church — what is being done by the War and what should be done'. Despite the initial misgivings of some members, notably Bishop Gore and Peter Green, the committee recommended in October 1915 that the Church should undertake a National Mission of Repentance and Hope to the whole nation in October–November 1916. Some critics have dismissed the Mission as a failure, and certainly the results fell short of the Archbishop's hopes. Nevertheless, the Mission was undeniably a great act of witness; many people must have been influenced by it; and its side effects were by no means negligible. It gave impetus, for example, to the Life and Liberty Movement under William Temple.[78] The Mission was continued in a less intensive form after the autumn of 1916 with the help of a Consultative Committee and five Committees of Enquiry appointed to consider problems facing the Church: Teaching, Worship, Evangelism, Administrative Reform, and the Relation of the Gospel to Industrial Problems. Their Reports were designed to promote wider discussion and action; and they undoubtedly made a significant contribution to the post-war work of reconstruction advocated and undertaken by the Church of England.[79] It is not surprising, therefore, that the second report on 'The Worship of the Church' concerned itself with liturgical revision. The Committee had a distinguished membership both clerical and lay, representing different shades of churchmanship, and was led by Dr T. Strong, Dean of Christ Church. It included Frere and W. C. Bishop as recognized liturgical experts, Dr Walford Davies the eminent musician, F. A. Iremonger, Frances Underhill, Guy Warman, and three outstanding chaplains serving with the Expeditionary Force in France — H. K. Southwell, F. B. Macnutt and Neville Talbot.[80]

The Committee was asked 'to consider and report upon ways in which the public worship of the Church can be more directly related to the felt needs of actual life at the present time'.[81] Their Report, published in 1918, was important, not so much for its actual proposals for liturgical reform — most of these had already appeared elsewhere – but for its criticism of the Book of Common Prayer and of the Church's general approach to worship. At the outset it stated in bald terms, 'The instinct for worship has seriously diminished in the people as a whole.'[82] It then examined the reasons for this decline. The Industrial Revolution was partly to blame: the people had become more mobile and the great new industrial cities had sprung up, with the Church providing inadequate spiritual oversight. In such places the tradition of Church attendance had never even existed. Furthermore the materialism of the industrial system encouraged aggressive individualism and class warfare. The poor had been alienated, and there was little sense of fellowship in the Body of Christ, so essential to worship. It was not surprising, therefore, that public worship came to have little relevance, and the tradition of private prayer and family prayer had tended to disappear: for many people worship was quite unknown. The Committee also believed that the decline was due to the failure to give lay people any effective part in the planning and conduct of public worship. The Church in fact presented an image of being governed by and administered for comparatively small circles of well-to-do people.[83] In the face of such a situation a change of attitude towards worship and a revision of the Book of Common Prayer were both essential. The Committee was disturbed to see how the Holy Communion service had ceased to play its proper part in public worship. It should be central, and not simply regarded as an exceptional service reserved for the devout. Public worship had largely come to mean attendance at Morning or Evening Prayer, neither of which was entirely satisfactory, making too heavy a demand on the intelligence and knowledge of ordinary people.[84] The Committee had in fact already considered and approved the revision proposals before the Convocation of Canterbury in the reports on the Lectionary (501), Rubrics and Services (504), and the Psalter (510); but it believed that a more drastic revision of the Prayer Book could not be long delayed: it no longer met the needs of many people in its present form. The need for revision was also particularly acute in the Church overseas; and a lead from the Church at home was imperative.[85]

But by far the most trenchant criticisms came from the three army chaplains, who added an appendix of their own to the Report. While they frankly admitted that some soldiers were deeply attached to the existing Prayer Book and were averse to change, nevertheless there was widespread preference for services which were 'simple, real and short. And we believe it is fair to argue that a great number of men at the Front will vote that, by contrast, services at home if conducted in pre-war fashion are deficient in these qualities.'[86] Failure to reform had alienated men who were mentally and spiritually alive. They therefore pressed for bold and wise experiment. They believed that all chaplains would return home anxious to make the service of Holy Communion 'the main, corporate, family, congregational act of worship and fellowship'. With that end in view they indicated some of the ways in which the service could be improved. The service itself should be set out more simply in the Prayer Book, with the Exhortations and Prefaces printed at the end; the Summary of the Law should be permitted as a substitute for the Decalogue; the prayer for the King should be omitted; and the Prayer for the Church should be simplified and enriched. Indeed they regarded the present rite as inferior to the Scottish rite in fulness and plainness of meaning.[87] The use of the Bible in current Anglican worship also left much to be desired. The Prayer Book services were built on a view of Scripture which, though acceptable to the original compilers of the Book, were now regarded as 'untrue and offensive to any lively conscience and intelligence. No doubt Dean Paget and Dr Bright on either side of Christ Church choir could make intelligent allowances about, and find mystical meanings in, any part of the lectionary and psalter. Not so the vast majority of people'.[88] Morning and Evening Prayer therefore needed modification; and in particular they approved Frere's proposals for combining Morning Prayer and Holy Communion in his *Some Principles of Liturgical Reform.* Anglican public worship needed to become more congregational and less remote from common life; and it could learn a great deal, not only from the American Prayer Book but also from the Scottish Presbyterian Book of Common Order.[89]

This rather radical approach is not surprising in view of the fact that all three chaplains had contributed to a volume of essays published in the previous year under the title *The Church in the Furnace.* Indeed it was Canon Macnutt who had been primarily responsible for the book, bringing together seventeen distinguished service chaplains to examine different aspects of the Church's life and contrast it with life in the army.[90] The result was a powerful plea for reform. Macnutt said in his Foreword, 'One thing is certain: we can never again be content with much that we accepted as quite natural in those far away days before we came out here';[91] and Bishop Gwynne added significantly in his Preface, 'I firmly believe that the discontent to which [these Essays] give expression is not a sign of weakness, but, on the contrary, a sign that we are willing to face the facts.'[92] On this occasion Macnutt, Southwell and Talbot wrote on subjects not directly concerned with worship; although in his essay on 'Personal Religion in Church Life' Southwell made the penetrating comment that the crucial problem the Church had to face in matters of worship was that of indifference: 'Revised services will not help us much if the majority of men stand apart . . . from the public worship of the Church. Many with whom I have spoken were neither satisfied nor dissatisfied with our services in their home life, they simply had no use for them.'[93] The Committee of Enquiry had reached the same conclusion – the instinct for worship had seriously diminished in the people as a whole. How, then, was this instinct for worship to be rekindled? Three different essayists now looked at the problem: Eric Milner-White, formerly chaplain of King's College, Cambridge, and subsequently Dean of York; Canon C. S. Woodward of Southwark and subsequently Bishop of Bristol; and Father Marcell Conran of the Cowley Fathers.

Milner-White obviously loved the Prayer Book but had been made painfully aware of its inadequacies. 'Fitness for place and use has become in these days the standard by which men and things are judged; and even the Prayer Book, august and beloved ever, stands for judgement . . . It has been at best *semi-used* and *semi-usable*, and we have come to look upon it from the unfamiliar distance.'[94] So the present Burial Service had 'failed badly' in the days of death: or the Litany 'with all its amazing beauty, is too cold and severe for popular use. It has . . . the crowning defect of laying all the stress on pure petition, and of requiring a great effort of mind, rather than a play of emotion . . . It demands too much. A saint might pray it well if he had a week to do it in.'[95] Canon Woodward had the same kind of criticisms, although expressed in less picturesque style.[96] Milner-White then went on to plead for bold experiment in new forms of prayer – 'No single devotion that we possess is devoted simply to God and his Christ' – in which there was a sense of fellowship, simplicity, flexibility and devotional intimacy.[97] Father Conran had in fact experimented with such forms in France with considerable success, and he wrote about them in his own essay on 'Instruction in Prayer'. He too felt the inadequacy of the existing Anglican services. 'Certainly if we have no more to offer [the men returning from the War] than what we offer to the ordinary congregation at present, they will not find [religion]. They will feel that they do not understand our services, that there is a lack of sympathy amongst us, that we offer such men . . . nothing that can lead them to God.'[98] The present indifference to religion stemmed partly from the Reformation, when all the popular devotions of the people were swept away and replaced by Morning and Evening Prayer, which were too advanced for the common use of ordinary people. People now needed to be taught how to pray before there was any hope of their using Prayer Book services profitably. They needed – and both Milner-White and Woodward also saw this – short, simple, corporate acts of devotion. Conran therefore based his Chaplet of Prayer on the pre-Reformation method of a litany form built around the events of our Lord's earthly life taken separately and in order. In this way not only did the facts of the Creed come to life in the hearts and minds of the people who used the devotion; but it led men to God by the one and only true way of approach – through Jesus Christ himself.[99] Milner-White enthusiastically endorsed this method of prayer and included it among eight new elements which he wished to see added to the Prayer Book: a framework for intercessions, forms of preparation and thanksgiving for Holy Communion, an act of Thanksgiving and Praise, devotions on the Life of our Lord, a Litany of the Saints, a Missionary Devotion, a Litany of Labour, and an Evening Commendation, such as a simple form of Compline.[100] Indeed almost all these elements, on the whole very different from proposals being considered by the Convocations, were based on the same principle — simple, corporate acts of devotion.

What these three essays said and what the three chaplains said in their Appendix to the Report of the Committee of Enquiry was all of a piece. In the light of their experiences in France, the Prayer Book failed to meet the spiritual needs of the nation. Apart from its liturgical defects, it was too intellectual, it lacked homeliness, and it failed to express the needs of ordinary people. Radical though their views must have seemed to many in authority in the Church, they nevertheless attempted to inject a healthy element of realism into the discussions on the problems facing the post-war Church in England.

VI

The first recognition in official circles of a need to tackle the problem of the 1662 Prayer of Consecration emerged in July 1910, when Report 447 from the Lower House of Canterbury Convocation proposed 'that a Service on the lines of the Scottish Communion Office be provided as an alternative'.[101] The matter was discussed at committee level during the following months with little progress; but an attempt to come to a decision, at least in the Lower House, was made by Canon Stanton in July 1911, when he proposed that the Archbishop should be asked to consider the advisability of providing an alternative order of Holy Communion on the lines of the 1549, American and Scottish rites. This motion was defeated, but not overwhelmingly, by 32 votes to 47.[102] Nearly three years were to elapse before the matter was raised again. In February 1914 the Lower House debated a rather different proposal on Gore–Lacey lines, namely that the existing material in 1662 should be rearranged in a different order: Sursum corda, Preface, Prayer of Consecration, Prayer of Oblation prefixed by 'Wherefore', Lord's Prayer, Prayer of Humble Access, Communion. This was accepted convincingly by 79 votes to 8,[103] and the Joint Committee of both Houses, appointed to harmonize all the Canterbury proposals, subsequently included it in its recommendations (Report 487), with the proviso that it should be permissive and not mandatory.[104] The Lower House accepted this; but the Upper House raised objections: it would lay new emphasis on the idea of sacrifice; a double use would create two sets of churches; and it would not satisfy the Catholic party. Nevertheless the Bishops admitted that it was a change in accordance with ancient teaching; and if they were passing a Prayer Book for the first time, it was a form which almost all of them would be glad to adopt. The proposed form could even be used privately. The Bishops were hedging; the proposal was right but inopportune. Gore, however, urged that the only way to heal was to rectify reasonable grievances; the Reformation had left out of sight the whole ancient structure of the liturgy; let them do something. His pleas fell on deaf ears: and the Upper House rejected it (28 April) by 15 votes to 5.[105] Frere commented, 'The warnings and instructions of the Bishop of Oxford seem to have fallen on heedless ears in the Upper House — or were they too deafened for the moment by the impotent thunder of the Protestant extremists to take in what he said?'[106]

It was July 1917 before the Lower House finally considered the Upper House's decision and then they decided to adhere to their 1914 decision. Concurrence with the Bishops was rejected by 57 votes to 30.[107] The matter therefore went back to the Upper House, where there was now evidence of anxiety to come to some agreement. The Bishop of Gloucester urged that liturgical propriety demanded some change of that kind: the evidence of the ancient liturgies was strong. The Bishop of London withdrew his previous opposition, admitting change to be 'unanswerable from an historical and a liturgical point of view'. The Upper House then agreed, subject to an amendment to include the 1549 anamnesis, on 7 February 1918 by 13 votes to 7.[108] The amended form was then endorsed by both Houses.

The pattern of events in the Convocation of York was not dissimilar. The Committee of the Lower House had not only recommended the same rearrangement of the Prayer Book material as Canterbury, but had also proposed the inclusion of an invocation of the Holy Spirit; and the Lower House had accepted this, apparently without demur, in February 1912.[109] The Joint Committee then included it in their joint proposals in February 1915: but six months later, the Upper House rejected any change in the Prayer Book order by 6 votes to 1:[110] and on this position the York bishops remained intransigent.

In October 1918 a joint conference of representatives of all four Houses of Convocation reviewed all the revision proposals of both Provinces. Since the only significant area of disagreement was the rearrangement of the eucharistic prayer, the Archbishop summoned a special conference in May 1919 of some fifty clergy of different schools of thought to try and resolve the matter. Opposition to the plan was considerable: a Memorial signed by 100,000 laymen, 3,000 clergy and 9 bishops protested against any change in the Communion service.[111] Significantly, six of the episcopal protesters were from the predominantly Evangelical phalanx in the Province of York — Durham (Dr Moule), Chester (Dr Jayne), Liverpool (Dr Chavasse), Manchester (Dr Knox), Carlisle (Dr Diggle), and Sodor and Man (Dr Thornton-Duesbery) — the one notable exception being Dr T. W. Drury the Bishop of Ripon and a sound liturgical scholar. He was one of those invited to the May Conference, and from November onwards he and Frere had been in close contact, preparing the ground and reaching a substantial measure of agreement.[112] Both men were realists and knew how far they could go — a fact not lost upon the Conference.

Four points were eventually agreed by 33 votes to 5.

1. The Prayer of Humble Access should immediately follow the Comfortable Words.
2. The Institution Narrative should be followed by an act of remembrance, an act of thanksgiving and an invocation of the Holy Spirit.

3. The Lord's Prayer should follow the Prayer of Consecration and immediately precede Communion.
4. The Prayer of Oblation should not be moved.

This resulted in the following form of words to follow the Institution Narrative:

> Wherefore, O Father, we thy humble servants, having in remembrance before thee the precious death of thy dear Son, his mighty resurrection and glorious ascension, looking also for his coming again, do render unto thee most hearty thanks for the innumerable benefits which he hath procured unto us. And we pray thee of thine almighty goodness to send upon us and upon these thy gifts thy holy and blessed Spirit, who is the Sanctifier and Giver of Life, to whom with thee and thy Son Jesus Christ be ascribed by every creature in earth and heaven all blessing, honour, glory, and power, now henceforth and for evermore. Amen.
> As our Saviour Christ hath commanded and taught us we are bold to say, Our Father . . .[113]

The form was meagre compared with what liturgists like Frere would have liked, but was aptly described by Dr Drury as 'culled from the 1549 or Scottish books' and 'bringing us *somewhere* into line with the American words'.[114]

This proposal was submitted to all four Houses of Convocation in February 1920. Both Houses of Canterbury and the Lower House of York accepted it; but once again the Upper House of York proved a stumbling block. Dr Knox of Manchester's amendment to reject the proposal outright was only defeated by Archbishop Lang's casting vote: but two other amendments were successful. The first, by Dr Chavasse of Liverpool, deleted the invocation of the Holy Spirit; and the second, by Dr Wild of Newcastle, changed the doxology.[115] The two Houses of York then met again together in Full Synod on 29 April to consider the amended form. Once again Dr Knox returned to the attack, although he felt his chances of success were remote; for there had been a recent change in personnel among the bishops and his supporters were now outnumbered. Indeed, when he proposed 'No change', not a single bishop rose to second him: and it was left to the new Dean of Manchester, Dr McCormick, to come to his aid. To his great surprise, however, his amendment was accepted by three votes, 28 to 25.[116] On this crucial matter, therefore, Canterbury and York failed to agree: but this was not the end of the struggle.

VII

The 1549 Prayer Book prescribed two methods of communicating the sick. One was for the priest to celebrate the Eucharist in a sick person's house: the other was for the priest to reserve the sacrament at a Eucharist in church and then carry it to the sick person 'as soon as he conveniently may'. There is evidence, however, that the traditional method of communion from the perpetually reserved sacrament still continued, thereby making the sacrament available to people *in extremis* at any hour of the day or night.[117] In the 1552 Prayer Book all mention of reservation was omitted, although it was not expressly prohibited: indeed the directions for communicating the sick are capable of various interpretations. The Latin Prayer Book of Elizabeth in 1560 specifically restored reservation, however, in a manner similar to that of 1549. 1662 made no specific reference to reservation; but the rubric requiring the priest at the Eucharist to see that the consecrated elements remaining were consumed after the blessing and not carried out of church had been interpreted in different ways. Those who opposed reservation argued that it prohibited reservation; while those who defended reservation argued that it was a safeguard against misuse of the sacrament and had no relevance to reservation for the communion of the sick. The fact remains that after 1661, the practice of reservation was rare; although cases were to be found, particularly among Non-Jurors and Episcopalians in Scotland.[118]

Continuous reservation was revived in England in the middle of the nineteenth century, the earliest evidence being that of J. M. Neale at East Grinstead in 1855; but as the practice grew, it was no longer confined to the communion of the sick. A cultus developed, involving exposition, benediction, and other devotions focused on the reserved sacrament. Convocation discussed the matter on a number of occasions between 1868 and 1885; but nothing was done until Archbishops Temple and Maclagan held the Lambeth Hearings in 1899–1900. In May 1900 the Archbishops delivered their 'Opinion' on reservation: the Church of England did not allow it in any form, and that was how the situation should remain until the law had been altered. The whole episcopate, with the exception of the Bishop of Sodor and Man, endorsed this judgement in January 1901. Then in 1906 the Royal Commission on Ecclesiastical Discipline enumerated the practices connected with reservation which were breaches of the law of special gravity and significance: reservation of the sacrament under conditions which led to its adoration, Corpus Christi processions with the sacrament, Benediction with the sacrament, and Mass of the Presanctified. These practices should 'be promptly made to cease', if necessary by proceedings in the Ecclesiastical Courts. Nevertheless, the number of churches in which reservation was used in this way was relatively small; while there was a growing recognition that some arrangements should be made to permit reservation for the communion of the sick, and for no other purpose whatsoever.

It was not surprising therefore that in 1911 both Houses of Canterbury Convocation agreed to reservation for the Communion of the Sick 'on the same day and with as little delay as may be': if communion were not immediate, the consecrated elements should be kept 'in such a place and after such manner as the Ordinary shall direct, so that they may not be used for any other purpose whatsoever'.[119] Both Houses of York also agreed to similar provisions; but in addition the Lower House specifically stated that

Benediction should not be legalized, while the Upper House recommended that 'robes, processions, and lights' should be expressly forbidden.[120] The situation therefore appeared to be reasonably harmonious; all four Houses retained the principle of reservation in their final reports;[121] and the bishops regarded this as sufficient guidance when they were called upon to deal with cases in their diocese. So, for example, Bishop Gore informed incumbents in his diocese that he was prepared to permit perpetual reservation, provided that the sacrament was reserved and administered in both kinds, that it was kept in a locked chapel, and that sick people who desired the sacrament should be given the opportunity of a private celebration at home if they so wished.[122]

With the passage of time, however, the difficulty of adhering to such rigid regulations grew. Undoubtedly an increased emphasis on communion and the impact of the War itself both had an effect;[123] and some bishops began to have doubts on the wisdom of being too strict. The Bishop of London, Dr Winnington Ingram, took the lead in adopting a more relaxed policy. In June 1915 Gore informed the Archbishop of Canterbury that as the Bishop of London had 'surrendered' and allowed access for prayer before the reserved sacrament, and as this was also happening in the dioceses of Birmingham and Chichester, he felt he must abandon his own rigid stand, and also propose to Convocation the omission of the phrase 'for no other purpose whatsoever' in the proposed rubric. The Archbishop was alarmed, summoned the Bishops of London, Winchester, Oxford and Chichester to Lambeth to discuss the matter, and at least persuaded Gore to take no action for the rest of that year.[124]

Nevertheless, the campaign for a change in regulations was growing. The Society of SS Peter and Paul published pamphlets advocating both Exposition and Benediction; and at the end of 1916 a Memorial to the archbishops was being prepared, not only opposing the Draft Rubric but stating unequivocally that compliance with any restriction involving refusal of access to the reserved sacrament 'cannot rightly be demanded and will not be given'.[125] The Memorial, signed by some 1,000 clergy, was presented to the Upper House of Canterbury before it was due to debate on 9 February a resolution by Gore, affirming the bishops' adherence to the recommendations made in the proposed rubric, which were identical with those agreed in 1911. The Archbishop was very disturbed. He wrote (28 January 1917):

> I am awaiting with genuine alarm discussions which may take place in Convocation ten days hence about Reservation, which would give evidence of a defiance of episcopal authority on the part of many hundreds of clergy who mean to insist on the right of priests and congregations to insist on the use of the reserved sacrament for purposes of devotion (as contrasted with communion) in a way which would have been not only surprising, but repellent, to Lancelot Andrewes, or William Laud, or E. B. Pusey, or John Keble.[126]

The Archbishop had further cause for alarm when Dr Darwell Stone, who had been closely involved in drafting the memorial, published a book in its support, entitled *The Reserved Sacrament*, on the very day of the debate. He had also sent advance copies to a number of the bishops.[127]

The debate in the Upper House was dominated by three speeches. The first was by Gore, who exhorted the bishops to stand firm and continue to support the Draft Rubric. The second was by Winnington Ingram. He claimed that he had never been asked to allow reservation except for the sick, nor had he allowed it in so many words for any other purpose. Furthermore he had never allowed and never would allow Benediction or Exposition unless Convocation permitted it. Nevertheless any undertaking to permit no access whatever to the reserved sacrament had proved impossible. The plan had begun to break down before the War, and the War had finished it: 'The tide of human grief and anxiety had been too great, the longing to get as near as possible to the sacramental presence had been too urgent.' He therefore was willing to vote for Gore's resolution, but only if in so doing he did not commit himself to refusing access to the reserved sacrament where it was reserved for the sick. Finally, the Archbishop summed up, giving a masterly account of the practice of reservation over the past sixty years, expressing doubts about the 'characteristically sanguine and trustful' view of the Bishop of London, and denouncing the memorial as deplorable: it was deplorable as to the manner in which it must have been devised and framed, deplorable as to the policy which it appeared to advocate, and deplorable as to the unseemly threats which it contained. In the event Gore carried the day, the bishops voting for the resolution *nem. con.*;[128] although Winnington Ingram obviously interpreted it in a very different way from Gore.

Previous to the debate Gore had also written an article in *The English Church Review*, criticizing the theological presuppositions which made the consecrated elements a centre for extra-liturgical devotion:[129] and in the March issue of *The Oxford Diocesan Magazine* he reiterated the policy he was determined to follow – for good reason he would permit reservation, but in no case was it to be accessible for extra-liturgical worship.[130] Support for the official line also came from two Counter-memorials, one from 2,000 clergy and one from a number of infuential laymen, while in the summer of the same year the Alcuin Club published a monumental work, *The Sacrament Reserved*, by W. H. Freestone. This work, inspired by Frere, had a limited field, for it only dealt with the first twelve centuries: but its careful examination of the evidence resulted in conclusions rather different from those of Darwell Stone. It stated succinctly: 'The original purpose of official reservation was purely practical (i.e. for those who could not communicate at the Liturgy by reason of infirmity or other sufficient cause). The development of any cultus of the reserved Sacrament was the direct outcome of the acceptance of the doctrine of transubstantiation as the orthodox belief.'[131]

In July 1917 the bishops held a special meeting, at which they produced a Memorandum signed by both Archbishops. This was published in 1918, serving as a guide for episcopal action. It stated quite explicitly that the Draft Rubric did not permit *permanent* reservation. If, however, a bishop went beyond this regulation, and sanctioned permanent reservation 'owing to special conditions', his action would be 'individual and exceptional, and will lie outside what the episcopate has assented to'. Nevertheless, if such sanction were given, the reserved sacrament would be for the communion of the sick, and for no other purpose whatsoever. It was less than satisfactory: and Gore was certainly unhappy – 'Not one of the bishops is capable of saying, No!'[132] Nevertheless, there the matter rested and the Draft Rubric remained in the proposals which the Convocations embodied in their Replies to the Royal Letters of Business. But as with the Prayer of Consecration, the matter was far from settled.

VIII

The process of revision had taken much longer and had become far more extensive than had originally been envisaged. It was not until early 1914 that the two Archbishops were able to announce that all four Houses of Convocation had completed their individual tasks, and harmonization of their proposals could now begin. Joint Committees of the two Houses in both provinces produced their joint Reports in February 1915: but these joint Reports had then to be considered and approved by the individual Houses; and it was not until October 1918 that a Conference representative of all four Houses was appointed to work out a single set of proposals. Their Report then again had to be approved by all four Houses. It was early 1920 before the whole protracted business reached its final conclusion. On 29 April the two Archbishops and the two Prolocutors finally signed their Reply to the Royal Letters of Business with four appended Schedules: the Proposals for revision, a revised Table of Lessons, a revised Translation of the Psalter, and a revised Translation of the Athanasian Creed.[133]

Unfortunately even this was not the end of the matter. The Archbishop pointed out to Canterbury Convocation that if the Reply had been sent two years or even twelve months earlier, the Church's task would have been complete: and it would have rested with Parliament to decide the next step. But he had promised as long ago as 1909 that the Representative Church Council should have an opportunity of expressing its views on the Reply. Since then the Council, by virtue of the Enabling Act of December 1919, had become the National Assembly of the Church of England with legislative powers of its own, though subject to parliamentary veto. This meant that the Church could now avoid what the Archbishop had always feared – the necessity of having every single proposed liturgical change debated in Parliament. Nevertheless the National Assembly was a necessary hurdle. 'The Convocational reply to the Letters of Business will in itself, and by itself, be inoperative practically until the new National Church Assembly formulates a proposal in the shape of a Bill for which it seeks Parliamentary consent.' Technically, Parliament could ignore the National Assembly, but that was most unlikely: 'no sane member of Government, or of Parliament, would think of doing such a thing as matters now stand.' It was no surprise, therefore, when the Home Secretary, the Rt Hon. Edward Shortt, informed the Archbishop on 6 July, that in accordance with the procedure laid down in the Enabling Act, the proposals would now have to be submitted to the National Assembly.[134]

What, then, did the Convocations have to show for 13½ years of work, delayed not only by three General Elections involving three new elections to the Lower Houses, but also by the 1914–18 War? In addition to Schedules 3 and 4, the main proposals in Schedules 1 and 2 were:

1. All proposals were to be an appendix to the Book of Common Prayer, intended as alternatives for optional use and for a limited period.
2. Changes in the conduct and arrangement of services must have the approval of the Parochial Church Council, and difference of opinion referred to the bishop for a decision.
3. The Ornaments Rubric remained unchanged: but a note specifically permitted the use of vestments at Holy Communion.
4. Abbreviations were permitted when Morning Prayer, the Litany and Holy Communion followed one another.
5. *Calendar*
   a. Two new Red Letter days were appointed with propers — the Transfiguration and St Mary Magdalene.
   b. The Black Letter Days were revised and commons provided.
   c. A Table regulated transferences when Feast Days or Holy Days coincided.
6. *Morning and Evening Prayer*
   a. A revised Lectionary was based on the ecclesiastical year.
   b. Proper psalms for every Sunday and Holy Day.
   c. Alternative and shorter introductions to Morning and Evening Prayer.
   d. Seasonal invitatories to the Venite.
   e. A form of Compline.
7. *The Litany*
   a. Additional suffrages.
   b. The concluding Supplication was made a separate devotion.
8. Additional occasional *Prayers and Thanksgivings*.
9. *Holy Communion*
   a. The Summary of the Law or the Lesser Litany became alternatives to the Decalogue, provided the latter was recited once every Sunday.
   b. The Collect for the King was omitted.
   c. The Commixture was permitted at the Offertory.

d. Special biddings were permitted before the Prayer for the Church.
e. The first two Exhortations were removed to the end of the service.
f. Additional Proper Prefaces.
g. The reordering of the Eucharistic Prayer with additions (Canterbury only).
h. Permission was given to abbreviate the Words of Administration.

10. In *Baptism*, godparents were required to be baptized: but there need be only one of each sex, and parents could act for their own children, provided one other sponsor was available.
11. In *Confirmation*, a new preface was provided, including Acts 8.14–17.
12. In *Matrimony* a new Exhortation was provided.
13. In the *Communion of the Sick*, provision was made for communion from the reserved sacrament. The reserved sacrament was not to be used 'for any other purpose whatsoever'.
14. *Burial.* Additional forms were provided for a baptized child and for occasions when the Prayer Book service could not be used.

Clearly the whole exercise had developed far beyond the original purpose of examining the rubrics against a background of disciplinary problems, and the proposals provided a welcome degree of variety and flexibility into Anglican worship. Nevertheless, when considered in the light of the wealth of material available they can only be described as modest. Four provinces of the Anglican Communion had produced revisions almost within living memory – Ireland in 1879, America in 1892, Scotland in 1912, and Canada as recently as 1918. Then there were the recommendations of the Lambeth Conference of 1908 and the Archbishops' Committee on Worship following the National Mission of Repentance and Hope. Finally there were the proposals for revision coming from groups and individuals, the most comprehensive being Frere's *Some Principles of Liturgical Reform.* From this wealth of material the Convocations had drawn extensively. Indeed it would be no exaggeration to say that they were merely seeking authorization for what had already been authorized elsewhere, or was being proposed, or was actually being used unofficially. There was little that was original in the Convocations' proposals; but that is not surprising. The ideas came either from liturgical experts, or from grass-roots level, where the devotional needs of worshippers had to be met. It was the function of the Convocations to recognize these needs, together with the developments in theological and liturgical understanding, and to set them all in a coherent, workable form. Furthermore attitudes towards liturgical revision were changing, with a recognition that far more was at stake than a solution of disciplinary problems within the context of the 1662 Book of Common Prayer. Reinforcement of these new attitudes came soon after the Reply to the Letters of Business was submitted. The Lambeth Conference met again in the summer of 1920; and while liturgical matters did not occupy so much attention as in 1908 the Committee on Missionary Problems spent some time considering 'Liturgical Variations'. Frere had previously been consulted by its chairman, Bishop Westcott of Calcutta, and he had advised them that there was no need for liturgical uniformity within Anglicanism provided essential and catholic unity were preserved. History justified this; and the uniformity which had existed since the sixteenth century was an anachronism. His arguments were accepted, appearing in Resolution 36: 'While maintaining the authority of the Book of Common Prayer as the Anglican standard of doctrine and practice, we consider that liturgical uniformity should not be regarded as a necessity throughout the Churches of the Anglican Communion.' Furthermore, the Committee in their report spoke not only of 'adaptations and additions' but also of 'the adoption of other uses', provided there was a maintenance of 'Scriptural and Catholic balance of Truth' and consideration was given to 'the precedent of the early Church'. The exercise of such principles within a context of lawful authority and brotherly love gave the whole process of liturgical revision a far broader dimension. This kind of activity did demand, however, considerable liturgical expertise. The Committee therefore recommended the appointment of a permanent group of scholars who could advise Churches and dioceses engaged on revision.[135] It was a recommendation which the Conference was happy to accept; and a group was set up, centred on Lambeth, with the Archbishop's chaplain, Claude Jenkins, as its secretary and Walter Frere as one of its members.

NOTES

1. For a study of this disorder at the turn of the century, see Roger Lloyd, *The Church of England 1900-1965*, 1966, chapter 6.
2. L. Creighton, *Life and Letters of Mandell Creighton*, 2 vols. 1906, vol. 2, p. 215.
3. O. Chadwick, *The Victorian Church*, pt. 2, p. 355; J. G. Lockhart, *Charles Lindley Viscount Halifax*, 2 vols. 1936, vol. 2, chapter 4.
4. G. K. A. Bell, *Randall Davidson*, 2nd edn 1938, p. 329; cf. Creighton, op. cit., vol. 2, p. 361.
5. Bell, pp. 328–9.
6. ibid., p. 340. This bill would have made it illegal for clergymen to use the word 'Mass' or to enjoin regular private confession (*Parliamentary Papers*, 1899, vol. 1, p. 205).
7. Sandford, *Temple*, vol. 2, p. 301.
8. ibid., p. 304; Creighton, vol. 2, p. 371.
9. Bell, p. 346.
10. ibid., p. 399.
11. ibid., p. 461.
12. *Royal Commission on Ecclesiastical Discipline, Report,* 1906, p. v.
13. *RCED*, Minutes of Evidence, vol. 2, scs 12846–12962.
14. ibid., *Report* pp. 12–15, scs 50–74.
15. ibid., *Report* pp. 32–44, scs 187–262.

16. ibid., *Report* p. 64, sc 355; p. 67, sc 363.
17. ibid., *Report* pp. 75–6, scs 399–400.
18. cf. pp. 63–4.
19. *RCED, Report* pp. 76–7.
20. P. J. Jagger, *A History of the Parish and People Movement*, 1978, pp. 10–11.
21. C. S. Phillips et al., *Walter Howard Frere*, 1947, p. 34.
22. W. H. Frere, *Some Principles of Liturgical Reform*, 1911, pp. 154–62, 182–98.
23. J. Wordsworth, *The Ministry of Grace*, 1901, pp. 318–19, 337; E. W. Watson, *The Life of Bishop John Wordsworth*, 1915, pp. 300–1.
24. G. L. Prestige, *The Life of Charles Gore*, 1935, pp. 220–1. The book was reprinted four times in the first year of its life.
25. C. Gore, *The Body of Christ*, 3rd edn 1902, p. 276.
26. P. Dearmer, *The Parson's Handbook*, 4th edn 1902, pp. 176–82.
27. C. G. Lang, *The Opportunity of the Church of England*, 1905, pp. 185–6; cf. G. Stephenson, *Edward Stuart Talbot*, 1936, pp. 162–4; Jagger, pp. 14–15.
28. Dearmer, p. vi.
29. ibid., p. 2. Although Micklethwaite was the author of this tract, the Alcuin Club committee devoted seven meetings to its consideration, every sentence being carefully examined.
30. ibid., pp. viii–ix.
31. For this see Peter F. Anson, *Fashions in Church Furnishings*, 1960, pp. 316–19, 325–7; Evelyn Waugh, *Ronald Knox*, 1959, pp. 114–17. Note Waugh's amusing comment, 'The "Sarum" riddle posts which Bishop Knox was felling in Manchester were equally abhorrent to Maurice Child' (pp. 114–15).
32. Lockhart, op. cit., vol. 2, p. 249.
33. C. H. Turner, 'The Church Order of St Hippolytus', *Church Quarterly Review*, No. 169, vol. LXXXV (October 1917), pp. 75–6.
34. For further information see R. C. D. Jasper, *The Search for an Apostolic Liturgy* (Alcuin Club Pamphlet XVIII), 1963.
35. *The Journal of Theological Studies* XVIII (1917), pp. 47–55.
36. Gore, pp. 155, 217.
37. Darwell Stone, *A History of the Doctrine of The Holy Eucharist*, 2 vols. 1909, vol. 2, p. 651.
38. Gore, pp. 280–5.
39. cf. Gore's introduction to W. J. Sparrow Simpson, *The Prayer of Consecration*, 1917, pp. iii–vi.
40. From 1907 onwards articles on the subject appeared in *The Church Quarterly Review* almost every year; see also 1911, W. H. Frere, *Some Principles of Prayer Book Reform*; 1911, A. Riley, *Prayer Book Revision*; 1913, Anon (P. Dearmer), *A Prayer Book Revised* (with Preface by Gore); 1914, B. W. Randolph, *A Revised Liturgy*; 1918, W. J. Sparrow Simpson, *Revision of the Prayer of Consecration*. Dearmer is revealed as the author of *A Prayer Book Revised* in P. Hinchliff, *The South African Liturgy*, Cape Town 1959, p. 84.
41. F. L. Cross, *Darwell Stone*, 1943, pp. 168–9.
42. For a detailed discussion see Hinchliff, op. cit.
43. Davidson, p. 307.
44. ibid., pp. 322–3.
45. ibid., p. 383. Frere had expressed a similar view two years earlier, 'The rubric, which was originally the most elastic of things, has now become the most rigid,

because the lawyers interpret Prayer Book rubrics as if they were part of a Statute' (R. C. D. Jasper, *Walter Howard Frere*, 1954, p. 4).
46. ibid., pp. 382–4.
47. *CQR* (October 1907), pp. 50–66; (October 1910), pp. 97–119.
48. 'The Reconstruction of Worship', *CQR* (October 1912), pp. 140–7.
49. Frere, *Some Principles of Liturgical Reform*, p. 8.
50. Bell, op. cit., p. 650. In November 1910 he also informed the Upper House, 'No thoughtful man can fail to think that such changes as are made in the Rubrics should be reduced sternly to the smallest possible dimensions' (ibid., p. 653).
51. *Chronicle Convoc.*, 1906, pp. 336–7. He returned to this point more than once. cf. ibid., 1907, p. 9; 1910, p. 3.
52. Bell, p. 652.
53. *Chronicle Convoc.*, 1910, pp. 287–393.
54. All six Houses formed the Representative Church Council, created in 1903 as a consultative body. It could only make recommendations, and these had no legal force.
55. ibid., 1911, pp. 343–67.
56. ibid., 1908, p. 28.
57. ibid., p. 30; *Report 416*, pp. 64–71. Frere had already warned the bishops, when he was consulted, that the theory of 'omission is prohibition' was extremely questionable; but they did not accept his arguments. cf. *Report 416*, pp. 59–61; Jasper, *Frere*, pp. 13–23.
58. *Chronicle Convoc.*, 1908, p. 33.
59. ibid., 1911, pp. 438–44.
60. J. G. Lockhart, *Cosmo Gordon Lang*, 1949, p. 214.
61. *Journal of York Convocation*, 1908, Appendix pp. liv–lvi.
62. Lockhart, *Lang*, p. 215; cf. E. A. Knox, *Reminiscences of an Octogenarian*, 1934, pp. 308–10.
63. *Journal Convoc.*, 1912, pp. 129–60, 192–218.
64. *Chronicle Convoc.*, 1909, p. 193.
65. *Journal Convoc.*, 1908, Appendix p. lvii; 1910, p. 197.
66. For further information on the Committee see Jasper, *Frere*, pp. 26–55.
67. *Chronicle Convoc.*, 1911, pp. 300–1, 406–7; 1912, pp. 11–12, 501–2.
68. cf. *Journal Convoc.*, 1912, pp. 7–8; D. Gray, *Earth and Altar*, 1986, pp. 30–2.
69. *Chronicle Convoc.*, 1914, pp. 201–3.
70. Jasper, *Frere*, p. 34.
71. ibid., p. 43.
72. ibid., pp. 35–6.
73. ibid., p. 48.
74. ibid., p. 52.
75. *Chronicle Convoc.*, 1916, p. 471.
76. This was the description of one of its members, the Bishop of Gloucester; ibid., 1917, p. 19.
77. *Report of the Advisory Committee upon the Resolutions of the Joint Committee* (487B), 1915, pp. 22–3.
78. A. Wilkinson, *The Church of England and the First World War*, 1978, p. 71.
79. ibid., p. 88.
80. Henry K. Southwell, Assistant Chaplain-General, Archdeacon of Lewes; Frederick B. Macnutt, Senior Chaplain, Canon of Southwark, later Provost and Archdeacon of Leicester; Neville S. Talbot, Assistant Chaplain-General, later Bishop of Pretoria.

81. *The Worship of the Church*, Report of the Archbishops' Second Committee of Enquiry, 1918, p. 5.
82. ibid., p. 6.
83. ibid., pp. 6–14.
84. ibid., pp. 15–16.
85. ibid., p. 24.
86. ibid., p. 33.
87. ibid., pp. 35–6. The Committee was here endorsing a proposal made in 1916 in a Convocation Report on *The Spiritual Needs of Sailors and Soldiers after the War*, which urged that the Eucharist should be the principal Sunday service at an hour when the greatest number of people could be expected to communicate. The Lower House had endorsed this by 54 votes to 8 (*Chronicle Convoc.*, 1916, p. 286).
88. ibid., p. 34.
89. ibid., pp. 38–9.
90. The contributors were a remarkable group, including three DSOs and four MCs; eight became bishops, and two became deans or provosts.
91. F. C. Macnutt, ed., *The Church in the Furnace*, 1917, p. x.
92. ibid., p. xxi. Dr L. A. Gwynne, Bishop of Khartoum, and the much-loved Deputy Chaplain-General of the British Expeditionary Force.
93. ibid., p. 325.
94. ibid., p. 177.
95. ibid., pp. 179, 188–9.
96. ibid., p. 224.
97. ibid., pp. 190–4.
98. ibid., p. 266.
99. ibid., pp. 245–7. Conran had also offered his Chaplet of Prayer as a contribution to the National Mission in 1916. See his article in *CQR* (April 1916), pp. 56–64, 'The National Mission – a Suggestion'.
100. ibid., pp. 194–8.
101. Canterbury Convoc., *Report of a Committee of the Lower House on the Royal Letters of Business* (No. 447), 1910, Resolution 54a.
102. *Chronicle Convoc.*, 1911, pp. 343–67.
103. ibid., 1914, pp. 152–61; *Report 480*, 1914, pp. 2, 9–11.
104. *Joint Committee on Royal Letters of Business, Report 487*, 1915, p. 28, sc 59.
105. *Chronicle Convoc.*, 1915, pp. 271–95.
106. Jasper, *Frere*, p. 61.
107. *Chronicle Convoc.*, 1917, pp. 467–79.
108. ibid., 1918, pp. 86, 137–67.
109. York Convoc., *Report 277*, 1912, p. xxiv; *Journal Convoc.*, 1912, p. 112.
110. *Journal Convoc.*, 1915, p. 316.
111. Knox, *Reminiscences*, p. 315. Two objections of the Evangelicals were: (1) the interpretation placed by Anglo-Catholics on the phrase 'our sacrifice of praise and thanksgiving' as referring to the consecrated elements; (2) the offering of 'ourselves, our souls and bodies' before communion.
112. For details of the preparatory work, see Jasper, *Frere*, pp. 56–82.
113. *Chronicle Convoc.*, 1920, pp. 66–9; Canterbury Convoc., *Report 529*, pp. 2–4.
114. Jasper, *Frere*, p. 73.
115. *Chronicle Convoc.*, 1920, pp. 66–83, 151–62; *Journal Convoc.*, 1920, pp. 56–7.

116. Knox, *Reminiscences*, pp. 316–17; *Journal Convoc.*, 1920, pp. 213–16.
117. For further information on reservation in England see: W. Lockton, *The Remains at the Eucharist*, Cambridge 1920; Charles Harris, 'The Communion of the Sick', *Liturgy and Worship*, pp. 549–615; cf. Cross, *Darwell Stone*, pp. 121–8.
118. Legg, *English Church Life*, pp. 64–6.
119. *Chronicle Convoc.*, 1911, pp. 211–12; *Report 427*, p. 17.
120. *Journal Convoc.*, 1910, pp. 215, 226; *Report 269*, p. xx.
121. Canterbury Convoc., *Report 487*, January 1915; York Convoc., *Report 302*, February 1915.
122. Prestige, *Gore*, pp. 303, 341–2.
123. Wilkinson, op. cit., pp. 133, 147–8.
124. Bell, op. cit., pp. 808–11; Prestige, op. cit., pp. 379–80.
125. Bell, p. 811; Cross, op. cit., pp. 123–4.
126. Bell, p. 798.
127. Cross, p. 126. Stone argued in his book that he himself did not desire Benediction or Exposition: but if the demand grew, there was no reason in principle against it; it would only be a further development of the devout treatment of the sacrament which was reverent towards our Lord and his work and presence.
128. *Chronicle Convoc.*, 1917, pp. 81–91, 117–26.
129. 'The Theological Bearings of certain Extra-liturgical Uses of the Blessed Sacrament', *The English Church Review*, February 1917.
130. Cross, p. 128.
131. W. H. Freestone, *The Sacrament Reserved* (Alcuin Club Collections No. 21), 1917, pp. 265–6; cf. an article by Dr Burge, Bishop of Southwark, 'Our use of the Revised Sacrament', *CQR* (October 1917), pp. 1–20.
132. Bell, p. 814; Prestige, p. 394.
133. *Chronicle Convoc.*, 1920, pp. 419–21; Canterbury Convoc., *Report 487*; York Convoc., *Report 302*.
134. Bell, pp. 978, 1328.
135. Jasper, *Frere*, pp. 194–6; Davidson, *The Six Lambeth Conferences*, pp. 36, 87–8.

5

THE PROPOSED PRAYER BOOK OF 1927–8

I

The newly constituted National Assembly began its consideration of the Convocations' Reply to the Royal Letters of Business through a committee of all three Houses under Dr Gibson, Bishop of Gloucester, a capable veteran in liturgical matters, ably supported by Dr Drury, Bishop of Ripon, Archdeacon J. H. Srawley of Wisbech, and Frere.[1] They first dealt with the Lectionary proposals as a separate item. The Committee produced its Report (NA 24) by July 1921, and general approval was given by all three Houses in November.[2] The Convocations then gave their final approval after the minimum of discussion in June 1922. The Measure's passage through Parliament was equally swift and troublefree, receiving the Royal Assent in August; and the new Lectionary came into operation on Advent Sunday as an alternative to the Lectionary of 1871. Three features deserve mention. In the first place it was based on the ecclesiastical and not the civil year, a welcome return to pre-Reformation practice. Secondly, Sunday lessons and weekday lessons were provided as two separate systems, thereby recognizing the needs of Sunday lay worshippers: while Holy Days were given full provision together with lessons for First Evensongs. Thirdly, a bold innovation was a course of lessons from the Synoptic Gospels providing a composite life of Christ for use at Evensong on weekdays in the Trinity season: it was on the lines of Tatian's *Diatessaron*, and the compilers frankly acknowledged their indebtedness to V. Staley's *Revision of the Lectionary* (1910) and W. Herschel's *The Gospel Monogram* (1911).[3] In the light of the developments in biblical theology, the wisdom of such a course can only be said to be doubtful. Inevitably there were some objections. The increase in the number of lessons from the Apocrypha — 127 in all — was criticized in some quarters, despite the fact that all were provided with Old Testament alternatives. Then again the Sunday lessons were apparently chosen on the assumption that worshippers would normally attend both Morning and Evening Prayer, the Old Testament lessons in particular forming a single course: different courses for morning and evening would have been preferable. Finally, some of the lessons were still regarded as unduly long. Nevertheless, despite such criticisms, the lectionary was a great improvement on its predecessor, providing greater variety, flexibility and intelligibility.

To the Convocations' other revision proposals the Committee found little need for extensive change; but two features in its report, NA 60, deserve mention. The first was an attempt to resolve the problem of the eucharistic

Canon, over which the Convocations of Canterbury and York had failed to agree. The new proposal, worked out by a small group consisting of Frere, Srawley and two Evangelicals – Bishop Guy Warman of Truro and Mr A. Mitchell – was substantially a return towards the form in the Canterbury Convocation's 1918 prayer, though with no epiclesis and incorporating a great deal of the 1549 wording, and which could conceivably be regarded as uncontroversial:

> Wherefore, O Lord and heavenly Father, we thy humble servants, having in remembrance the precious death of thy dear Son, his mighty resurrection and glorious ascension, looking also for his coming again, do render unto thee most hearty thanks for the innumerable benefits which he hath procured unto us; and we entirely desire thy fatherly goodness mercifully to accept this our sacrifice . . .[4]

The second feature was an additional rubric on reservation drafted by Frere. He argued, perhaps over-optimistically, that if the ready availability of the sacrament for the dying could be established as normal practice, reservation would become more widespread and less associated with a particular ecclesiastical outlook: those who agitated for extra-liturgical devotions would then be seen to be a small minority in the Church.[5] His proposal, added to the provision for either a celebration in a sick person's house or communion from the reserved sacrament, ran:

> When the aforesaid provision is not sufficient to secure that any Communicant at his last hour should be able to receive the Holy Communion, the Curate, with the permission of the Ordinary, given in accordance with Canon, or such rules as may be from time to time made by the Archbishops and Bishops in their Convocations, may make further provision to meet the needs of the sick and dying.[6]

Unfortunately these attempts at progress were insufficient to allay criticism, even within the Committee itself. Five lay members, all Evangelicals,[7] appended a Note to Report NA 60 opposing the rubrics on reservation:

> Notwithstanding the care with which those rubrics have been settled, we do not think that it is possible adequately to safeguard the practice from abuse. We do not admit that the practice of reservation is either primitive or catholic; and we believe the teaching associated with it is not conformable to Holy Scripture.[8]

Another lay member of the Committee, Athelstan Riley, a leading Anglo-Catholic, also wrote a Minority Report criticizing NA 60 as a piece of 'log-rolling', and expressing dissent on several issues: the revision of the Calendar, the disuse of the Athanasian Creed, the expurgation of the Psalter and the Scriptures, the alternative eucharistic rite, and the provisions for reservation and the anointing of the sick.[9] The fact that his views on reservation were diametrically opposed to those of his Evangelical brethren boded ill for the future.

On 28 June 1922 the Church Assembly 'received' NA 60 and affirmed the principle that any revised forms of service should not be incorporated in the Prayer Book, but should be in a separate volume and sanctioned for optional use for a specific period.[10] The Bishops accepted the report as it stood and attached it to a Measure, NA 84. This received general approval in all three Houses in January and April 1923, after which detailed consideration of the proposals began yet again in the Houses of Clergy and Laity. But by this time they faced not merely the official proposals in NA 84 but a welter of other suggestions as well. The possibility of authorized alternatives instead of a revised Prayer Book had given impetus to the production of proposals. Among the contributions to the exercise there was, for example, a complete Prayer Book by Canon J. N. Dalton of Windsor, containing most of the NA 60 proposals, but with some modifications and additions of his own, notably a eucharistic prayer which was essentially that of 1549, and a complete daily eucharistic lectionary for Lent. But by far the most important contributions were the Green, Grey and Orange Books, so designated from the colour of their covers.

The Green Book, largely the work of Darwell Stone and N. P. Williams, was another complete Prayer Book based on a Report published by the English Church Union in October 1922. It included a eucharistic Canon described as 'an attempt to combine the best features of the 1549 and South African versions',[11] provision for permanent reservation on an unrestricted basis, a revised calendar including such feasts as Corpus Christi, the Assumption of the Blessed Virgin Mary and St Joseph, and the restoration of the chrisom and chrism in the Initiation rites. Publication of the Book coincided with the spring meeting of the Church Assembly, and it marked a significant change in policy on the part of the English Church Union. With the possibility of authorized alternatives now clearly defined, it affirmed 'the policy of the Union should be, not to resist the process of Revision, but to endeavour to guide it on right lines': which meant securing a book that was 'as satisfactory as possible . . . from the Catholic point of view'.[12]

The Grey Book was not in fact a book but a series of pamphlets published by the Life and Liberty Movement between April and June 1923, largely the work of Percy Dearmer, R. G. Parsons, F. R. Barry, Leslie Hunter, F. W. Dwelly, and Mervyn Haigh,[13] while William Temple wrote a Foreword to the whole series. He had already pleaded in the Assembly for services couched in modern idiom and relevant to the great spiritual concerns of the day;[14] and these pamphlets constituted an interesting attempt to meet that need, based, as Temple claimed, on the principles of truth, intelligibility, simplicity, uniformity and comprehensiveness. Liberal in outlook, and often rather precious in language,[15] the pamphlets were in places remarkably forward-looking (e.g. they pioneered the recitation of the Nicene Creed in the plural) and at times very imaginative. Some of the Occasional Services were precisely on the lines advocated by Conron and Milner-White in *The Church in the Furnace*. One noted Evangelical scholar, R. T. Howard, claimed, 'The majority of the Grey Book proposals satisfy the aspirations of the Evangelicals towards a better form of Common Worship . . . There are things . . . which Evangelicals find unnecessary, but taking the compilation as a whole it is a new liturgical world to breathe and grow in. There is good fresh air here.'[16] This is praise indeed; for on the whole Evangelicals were not enthusiasts for Prayer Book revision. Finally there was the Orange Book, containing the Alcuin Club's proposals, and largely the work of Frere, published in 1923–4. Its object was not so much to produce another set of revision proposals as to bring together as far as possible all that was worthy of consideration in NA 84, the Green Book and the Grey Book. The three schemes were therefore set out and explained in such a way as might facilitate discussion both inside and outside the National Assembly.[17]

For the next two years the Houses of Clergy and Laity, sitting separately, went through NA 84 and the various 'Books' and other proposals in detail. The Clergy produced their amendments in Report CA 158, and once again their proposals on the eucharistic Canon and reservation were of particular interest. They rejected the Canon in NA 84, replacing it by two alternative Canons which had been worked out at an unofficial conference in the Jerusalem Chamber in November 1923 attended by the Chairman and Vice-chairman of the House of Clergy, the six members in charge of the Measure and two representatives each of the Green, Grey and Orange Books and of the Evangelical 'No Change' group.[18] They failed to agree on a single prayer but produced two alternatives, one based on the Green and Orange Book proposals of Western type, and the other based on the Grey Book proposals of more Eastern type with an anamnesis and an epiclesis following the Institution Narrative.[19] On reservation, provision was extended significantly in line with the Green Book proposals, permitting communion from the reserved sacrament not only for the sick but also for 'others who could not be present at the celebration in Church'. This was a concession to the Anglo-Catholics, and was only passed in the House of Clergy by the narrow majority of 103 votes to 98.[20]

The amendments proposed by the House of Laity appeared in Report CA 169. On the Eucharist and reservation they clearly favoured 1662; but they were prepared to accept 'one alternative form containing provision for Vestments and Reservation for the Sick only, if in their [i.e. the Bishops'] opinion, this will promote peace and order in the Church'.[21] But by far their most important proposal was to incorporate all the proposed alternatives and deviations within the Prayer Book itself.[22] This meant that the Church would have two books, 1662 and a 'Composite Book'. Such was the situation facing the House of Bishops as they began their own work of revision in October 1925; and Dr Davidson was well aware that the Laity proposal did little to diminish their problems. He pointed out that he had already received some 800 Memorials from various bodies, including one from nine diocesan bishops, praying either for no revision at all, or at least for no revision of the Communion service.[23] Nevertheless the Bishops applied themselves to their task with a will; and a proposal to leave the revision of the Communion service until the rest of the Book had been passed was defeated by 24 votes to 9. Indeed their energy was such as to produce 'the impression that they were addressing themselves to the improvement of the Prayer Book for the first time'.[24] In a sense this was true. Since 1917 some 26 new diocesan bishops had been appointed; and nearly two-thirds of the episcopate were dealing with the subject as bishops for the first time. What was unfortunate was their lack of liturgical expertise: despite the presence of some first-rate scholars – notably Headlam, Henson, Strong and Temple – only Frere was an established authority in the subject, while veteran campaigners such as Gibson and Drury had now gone. However, during the next fifteen months they spent forty-six full days on revision, during which reservation and the alternative eucharistic Canon again proved to be the focal points of lively and sometimes heated discussion.

On 14 January 1926 when the Bishops met members of the House of Clergy to discuss the latter's amendments, the point was made that only lack of time had prevented the Jerusalem Chamber Conference of the previous year from reaching agreement on one form of eucharistic Canon. Since then a number of people had continued to work behind the scenes and further progress had been made. Dr Woods, Bishop of Winchester, and one of the leading episcopal protagonists of revision, therefore called a conference of interested parties at Farnham Castle in the hope that further discussion might bring the matter to a successful conclusion. Largely due to the efforts of R. G. Parsons, one of the Grey Book leaders, these hopes were fulfilled, and an agreed Canon was produced in time for the Bishops' meeting in June.[25] It is best described as a piece of 'expediency liturgy'. First the Bishops agreed to a single alternative Canon by 29 votes to 5. The Members-in-charge then introduced the NA 84 canon with certain amendments, including two invocations, one before and one after the Institution Narrative, but with a note that only one must be used – a proposal which was largely Frere's handiwork. Dr Woods then produced the Farnham Canon: and from the two proposals a single composite canon was evolved – basically the amended NA 84 prayer, but with the Farnham anamnesis and a single obligatory invocation after the Institution Narrative proposed by Archbishop Lang of York.[26] On reservation, too, there was a policy of expediency. The rubrics in the new Book would simply prescribe the purpose of reservation: but the method of reservation would be dealt with in a series of regulations, which would not appear in the Book and could therefore be changed more easily if circumstances required.

The Bishops presented their Draft Composite Book to the Convocations sitting together on 7 February 1927. It was a brief meeting with no debate, but statements from the two Archbishops and Dr Warman, Bishop of

Chelmsford, one of the Members-in-charge. Dr Davidson explained that the Book was in its 'provisionally final form', and the Lower Houses were being provided with a last opportunity for comment before its formal presentation in March.[27] Comment was not slow in coming. The Bishops ran into an immediate storm of criticism after the meeting, for their zeal seems to have outrun their discretion. Apart from drawing freely from the unofficial books of proposals, they had added a great deal of new material, including a form of Prime, an Ordering of Deaconesses and a Devotion for use before Holy Communion. This had been done without consultation, which was contrary to the constitution of the Church Assembly: indeed, when the Archbishop of Canterbury had given the Assembly an interim progress report on the Bishops' work in July 1926, he had given no indication that new material was under consideration or even contemplated.[28] Some of the Bishops' proposals were regarded by critics as involving significant doctrinal change, notably the omission of the reference to original sin in the preface to Baptism, and the omission of the requirement of the bride to 'obey' in Marriage. The final form of the eucharistic Canon also came under fire, to say nothing of the rubrics on reservation. The decision to permit continuous reservation was severely criticized, and in particular the unfortunate phrase 'if the Bishop shall so permit', which gave the impression that a priest could be at the mercy of an arbitrary bishop, whereas it was intended to mean that it was for the bishop to choose the churches in which reservation was to be permitted in each locality. The restriction of reservation to sick communicants was also a matter for complaint from Anglo-Catholics: while the non-appearance of the regulations governing its method did nothing to allay Evangelical fears that continuous reservation would make devotions inevitable.[29] The Archbishop deplored the controversy, but failed to grasp fully the deep feelings which it aroused. He wrote (13 February):

> I intensely dislike the wretchedness of getting these things (some of them too sacred, and some of them too petty, for public discussion) bandied about as though they were the things which absorbed the Church's interest, as, indeed, for the moment they do absorb clerical interest to the detriment of wider things. In my heart I cannot honestly say that I very greatly long for any of the changes, or that they are of supreme deep-down importance.[30]

This lack of interest and appreciation was also evident to others. Mervyn Haigh, who was then his chaplain and attended Bishops' meetings, commented: 'My Archbishop . . . had always been, and remained so lukewarm about the whole project as not only to discourage ardour in carrying it out but even to allow of his tolerating certain proposals, not because he approved them, but because they were so far beyond his range of interest that he could hardly appreciate what they really involved.'[31] In an attempt to discuss and perhaps find answers to some of the criticisms before the Lower Houses of Convocation met, the Bishop of Winchester summoned yet another conference of bishops and Anglo-Catholic clergy and laity on 18 February. It achieved little, however, apart from impressing upon the bishops the strong feelings aroused by the proposals on reservation, the epiclesis in the Canon, and the omission of the reference to original sin in Baptism.[32]

On 22 February the two Lower Houses of Convocation met separately to consider the Bishops' proposals. Constitutionally they had no power to amend the Book, but they could petition the Bishops to consider amendments. Canterbury therefore produced 67 amendments and two memoranda and York 86 amendments for episcopal consideration, the most significant being:

1. Memorandum by the Reverend E. G. Selwyn on the inadequacies of the epiclesis (Canterbury).
2. A modification of the rubric on continuous reservation to safeguard against arbitrary action by a bishop (Canterbury and York).
3. Communion from the reserved sacrament for people unable to attend a Eucharist as well as for the sick (Canterbury).
4. The publication of the Regulations for Reservation before the final sanction of the new Book (Canterbury).
5. The restoration of the reference to original sin in Baptism (Canterbury and York).[33]

The Bishops now had a month to consider the amendments, and during that period criticisms continued unabated. The Home Secretary, Sir William Joynson Hicks, a prominent Evangelical leader, had already written to Archbishop Davidson on 24 March, following this with a private interview, in his quest for a positive assurance as to how the Bishops would treat disobedient clergy, supposing the new Book became lawful. The Archbishop's reply was rather vague and unsatisfactory, merely expressing 'the earnest hope of myself and other Bishops that when the new provisions are in operation we may be able to secure much more effectively a reasonable adherence within the enlarged limits to the directions of the Church in regard to the conduct of Divine Service': nevertheless he admitted 'the inability of Bishops to make a positive declaration that the observance of ritual rules in all their details will be everywhere and uniformly enforced'. Hicks was clearly dissatisfied and pressed the Archbishop again, but Dr Davidson refused to be drawn further.[34]

At the same time Anglo-Catholic opposition to the Book began to crystallize. In early March the Federation of Catholic Priests, the English Church Union and the Confraternity of the Blessed Sacrament submitted a joint memorandum to the Bishops, advocating postponement of Prayer Book revision on two grounds: the lack of agreement in the Church on fundamental issues, and the offence to Christian sentiment likely to be caused by the controversial discussion of the matters concerned in Parliament and elsewhere. The memorandum also expressed their opposition to the alternative eucharistic rite and the rubrics on reservation. It was published in *The Times* on 24 March, and in *The Church Times* on the following day – the week-end preceding the publication of the Book in its final form.[35]

On 29 March the Bishops presented their final proposals to the Convocations, again sitting together for the occasion. They had made some significant concessions to the Clergy, adopting 'a very large number'[36] of their proposed amendments. The Ordering of Deaconesses was dropped; the reference to original sin in Baptism was restored; and the contentious rubric on reservation was modified so that a bishop could no longer act arbitrarily.[37] On the other hand, Prime and the Devotion before Holy Communion were retained; no change was made in the Canon; the reserved sacrament was still restricted to the sick only; and 'obey' was not restored to the bride's vows in Marriage. At the same time the Bishops produced their Regulations on Reservation, although they refused to print them in the Book. The reserved sacrament was to be kept under lock and key in an aumbry or some other place approved by the Bishop; and it was only to be removed for communion or renewal, which should be at least once a week. Furthermore, reservation would only be permitted if properly licensed, for which a common form of licence would be used in all dioceses – a further safeguard against arbitrary bishops.[38]

After a two-day debate, the four Houses voted on the proposal to lay the Prayer Book Measure before the National Assembly for final approval. The result was overwhelmingly in favour.

Canterbury	Upper House:	21 for	4 against
	Lower House:	168 for	22 against
York	Upper House:	Unanimous	
	Lower House:	68 for	10 against[39]

Despite this impressive vote of confidence, with a total of only 36 votes cast against the Book, opposition still continued. A devastating attack came from Dr F. E. Brightman, the Church's most eminent liturgical scholar, in an article in *The Church Quarterly Review* for July 1927, just before the National Assembly's final debate and vote. 'The New Prayer Book Examined', while appreciative of some new features, was nevertheless an immensely learned, often witty, and generally devastating indictment of the Book as a whole. 'On almost every page of it I find something irritating, something inexact or untidy or superfluous or ill-considered or unreal.' In particular he was critical of the new Canon. It was

> a gratuitous departure from our tradition . . . I can see no sufficient reason for orientalizing at the cost of abandoning what has been our tradition ever since the days of St Augustine, except for a time within the area covered by the Celtic mission; while everything that is significant in what is Eastern can be, and has been secured without departure from the Western tradition.

As he had long maintained, the Church could find its answer in the rite of 1549. 'The order of 1549 is, to say the least of it, wholly defensible, . . . it gives us all we need desire, and that without any departure from Western precedent.'[40]

The debate in the National Assembly took place on 5–6 July. Archbishop Davidson moved the final approval, devoting a great deal of his speech to the questions of discipline and doctrine. While the Bishops would require obedience to the new rules and would do their utmost to secure it, ecclesiastical discipline was distinct from the authorization of church services. Today they were concerned with the latter: but the former, in the shape of a reform of the ecclesiastical courts was already under way. Meanwhile he hoped that the adoption of the new Book would reduce to 'small and steadily increasing proportion the number of recalcitrant men'. As for doctrine, there was no change.

> I do claim for it that it is an honest endeavour to provide a Book which will unite devout minds, apt as things stand to be out of touch with one another, and further, a Book which will restrain, because it makes them needless, the vagaries of independent Christian thinkers and ministrants whose fretfulness against restrictions which they deem unfair or harmful has sometimes made liberty degenerate into licence.

He concluded by pointing out that since the proposals had taken final shape, they had been before 29 Diocesan Conferences, whose voting had indicated an 81% in favour and only 19% against the Book. Despite strong opposition, led by Darwell Stone, Sir William Joynson Hicks, Sir Thomas Inskip and the Bishop of Norwich, the Archbishop won the day.

Bishops	34 for	4 against
Clergy	253 for	37 against
Laity	230 for	92 against[41]

The total vote for the Book therefore represented a majority of 79%, which was remarkably similar to the percentage indicated at Diocesan Conferences.

II

In the five months which elapsed before the Measure was submitted to Parliament controversy continued unabated. One person in particular whose opposition to the new Book attracted considerable publicity was Dr E. W. Barnes, the mathematician and scientist who had been Bishop of Birmingham since September 1924. He had already described the Book as 'an unsuccessful compromise, doctrinally invertebrate';[42] while his repudiation of the doctrine of the real presence in derisory terms led to a public demonstration by Anglo-Catholics against his sacramental teaching in St Paul's Cathedral on 16 October just before he was due to preach. If their devotions before the reserved sacrament were called in question, why should his strange views on the Eucharist go unrebuked? Frere warned

Archbishop Davidson that if such opinions were not repudiated, the Book's chances of success could suffer. At this point Barnes published an uncompromising Open Letter to the Archbishop, accusing the Church of increasingly adhering to erroneous sacramental doctrine. It immediately drew from the Archbishop a courteous but crushing rebuke, reminding him that recent Prayer Book discussions demanded a lead from the Bishops imbued with a spirit of restraint and consideration for others. Barnes replied with a further uncompromising Open Letter, but this time it went unanswered.[43] Undaunted, he published in November, just before the debates in Parliament, a collection of sermons delivered between 1920 and 1927 under the title *Should Such a Faith Offend?*, again attempting to expose what he believed to be the doctrinal errors into which the Church was in danger of falling.

Very different in style and content was Frere's final contribution to the public debate, published at the same time, first in *The Truro Diocesan Gazette* and then in *The Church Times*. This was a commendation of the new eucharistic Canon and a reply to Brightman's criticisms. It was a mistake to regard the new Prayer with its epiclesis as merely Eastern: the earlier consecration prayers had been Trinitarian, and the Roman Canon had been the exception rather than the rule: the attempt of 1549 to remedy the defect in the Roman Canon had been unsuccessful, a fact recognized in the Scottish, American, and South African prayers: the new Canon therefore marked a return to Catholic precedent, it avoided past mistakes, and afforded a policy of peaceful reconciliation.[44]

On 12 December the House of Lords began a three-day debate on the Book. The Archbishop emphasized that it involved no change in doctrine, he reiterated the Bishops' determination to see that it would be obeyed, and he expressed the hope that it would bring peace to the Church. Speeches were of a high order, the public gallery was full, and the Lords finally passed the Book by 241 votes to 88.[45] On 15 December it went to the Commons. Here only a single day had been allotted for the debate, and there was a general feeling of cautious optimism. Unfortunately, everything went wrong. The Prime Minister, Stanley Baldwin, later confessed to Dr Garbett, 'I made a great miscalculation then: I thought the Measure would go through the Commons and be defeated in the Lords. But Willie Bridgeman made a bad opening — he didn't take it seriously enough, and Hugh Cecil was a mass of nerves.'[46] The Book was badly presented. Dr Garbett commented that he and the two Archbishops sat in the Gallery completely exasperated, not only at the lack of competent supporters to answer questions and criticisms, but at their own inability to intervene.[47] By comparison the opposition was formidable. The Home Secretary, Sir W. Joynson Hicks, aroused all the old fears of Rome and accused the Bishops of not keeping their promise to exercise decisive authority; while of Mr Rosslyn Mitchell, MP for Paisley, the Archbishop noted: 'The most effective speech of all as regards votes was,

I think, Rosslyn Mitchell's. It was simply ultra-Protestant harangue, with no real knowledge of the subject, but owing its power to a rhetorical presentment of no-Popery phrases and arguments of the sort which are to be found in *Barnaby Rudge*, when the Lord George Gordon riots set London aflame.'[48] At the end of the day the Measure was rejected by 238 votes to 205. The only consolation the supporters of the Book could draw from the voting was that the members of the English constituencies showed a clear majority in favour, while the Roman Catholic members abstained.[49] Clearly the Archbishop was disappointed, but in no mood to capitulate. Sidney Dark, a journalist and for some time editor of *The Church Times*, commented:

> He was not in the least a figure of pathos, but a strong, stubborn, stern old man, temporarily defeated, but even then determined to fight on. I have often been moved to admiration by the Archbishop, but never so much as on that December evening, when the work of years seems to have been destroyed in an outburst of ignorant protestant fanaticism within the House, while a little crowd of forty or fifty people stood in the street in the rain and sang the doxology out of tune.[50]

On 23 December the two Archbishops issued a statement on behalf of the episcopate. Admittedly it was within the rights of the House of Commons to reject the Measure, but mere acquiescence in its decision would be inconsistent with the responsibilities of the Church as a spiritual society. In any case they considered that the decision had been influenced by 'certain avoidable misunderstandings as to the character of the proposals'. Consequently they intended to reintroduce the Measure into the Church Assembly as soon as possible with such changes as would remove misapprehensions, and clarify and make more explicit its intentions and limitations.[51] Reservation and the eucharistic Canon were the main issues. Dr Davidson was under considerable pressure to remove the provisions for continuous reservation; Sir Thomas Inskip indicated that he, the Home Secretary and the Lord Chancellor would accept other things they disliked, even the alternative Communion rite, provided continuous reservation were dropped. Davidson was prepared to agree, but Lang thought otherwise: this would be surrender and an acknowledgement of the overriding power of the State on a matter of spiritual importance; there should be no placating the opposition by excluding either continuous reservation or the new Canon.[52] In the event Lang prevailed. In January 1928 the Bishops published their proposed changes in Report CA 252. The most significant were as follows:

1. One of the Prayers for the King should always be said at Morning and Evening Prayer, or at Holy Communion if it followed.
2. The 'Black Rubric' or rubric on kneeling was to be inserted at the end of the alternative Order for Holy Communion.
3. Clause 4 of the 1927 Measure, permitting the Bishops to make or rescind rules to have the force of rubrics, was omitted.

4. The Regulations governing reservation were now incorporated into the rubrics of the Book and were made more restrictive. By the removal of the words 'or in some other place approved by the Bishop', the use of a tabernacle on the altar or of a hanging pyx was definitely excluded; while reservation in the vestry was explicitly permitted.[53]

The amended Measure was given general approval by all three Houses of the Church Assembly on 8 February, after which the Houses of Clergy and Laity discussed it separately and proposed their own amendments (CA Report 257).

1. If the Parochial Church Council so desired, or if the Bishop was satisfied, the 1662 Order for Holy Communion should be celebrated at least one Sunday a month, or by arrangement to suit those concerned (Clergy and Laity).
2. When the Litany was said, the suffrages for the King, provided they were used in full, should suffice instead of the Prayers for the King (Clergy).
3. The Minister or the Parochial Church Council should have the right of objections to the granting of a licence or the giving of directions by a Bishop in the case of reservation (Clergy and Laity).
4. The form of Invocation should be changed in the alternative Canon (Clergy).
5. A rubric should be inserted declaring that the fast before Communion was both optional and unessential (Clergy and Laity).
6. A declaration on eucharistic doctrine should be inserted in the alternative Order for the Communion of the Sick (Clergy and Laity).

When the Bishops made their final decisions in the light of these proposed amendments (CA Report 252A), they agreed to Nos. 1, 2, 3 and 5, but rejected Nos. 4 and 6. Furthermore, they made two significant changes in the rubrics on reservation: permission to reserve in the vestry was omitted, and the first rubric was so worded as to make reservation appear to be the exception rather than the general rule. Despite these restrictions, the Evangelicals were clearly unhappy, for continuous reservation was still possible. On the other hand, the Anglo-Catholics were equally unhappy, for nothing had been done to modify the new Canon; they disliked the new rubric on fasting communion; and they deplored the increased restriction on reservation.

One notable person who was unhappy with the changes was one of the episcopal Members-in-Charge of the Measure who had probably made the largest single contribution to the Book over the years, Walter Frere. He felt that the amendments, far from offering a hope of settlement, would only cause further trouble. He disliked the power given to Parochial Church Councils to decide what form of service should be used, he disliked the rubric on fasting, he disliked the increased restrictions on reservation, and he deplored the lack of an alternative Canon for those who could not accept the epiclesis, though he himself favoured it. He still hoped that his earlier proposal for optional invocations in the new Canon might be revived when the Measure was presented again to the Convocations, but the Bishops decided that no further amendment was possible: the House would simply vote for acceptance or rejection. Consequently when the Convocations met on 28–29 March to consider the Measure, Frere made a short statement on his reasons for withdrawing support and then abstained from voting. The Upper Houses quickly made their decisions, Canterbury approving by twenty votes to six and York approving unanimously. The Lower Houses indulged in lengthy and vigorous debates, but the results were similar: Canterbury approved by 126 votes to 48, and York by 50 votes to 19.[54] The Measure then came before the Church Assembly on 26–27 April. There was little to say that was new, and all three Houses duly gave approval: but voting trends were significant. Compared with the previous year, there was a marginal increase in the opposition vote — a mere twenty: but the supporting vote decreased by 121. Allowing for unavoidable absentees, abstentions probably exceeded 100.

	1927		1928	
	For	Against	For	Against
Bishops	34	4	32	2
Clergy	253	37	183	59
Laity	230	92	181	92
Total votes	517	133	396	153
Grand Total	650		549	

The amended Measure was due for presentation to the House of Commons on 13 June, and the barrage of literature for and against continued unabated to the very end. The Archbishop of Canterbury made a final appeal for the Book with a fifty-page pamphlet, *The Prayer Book: Our Hope and Meaning*, published at Whitsuntide. Sir William Joynson Hicks replied with a much longer work, *The Prayer Book Crisis*, deploring the Romeward tendencies, and accusing the Deposited Book of being compiled 'in the interests of an intolerant and aggressive party'.[55] Despite an excellent introduction by the Solicitor General, Sir Boyd Merriman, who had been well primed beforehand,[56] the Book fared no better than its predecessor. The Prime Minister made an effort to save the day, but to no avail. The Commons again rejected the Book, this time by a slightly larger majority — 266 votes to 220.

III

A comparison of the proposals for revision in the Schedules appended to the Answer to the Royal Letters of Business in 1920 with what finally appeared in the 1928 Book indicates that little had been done in these years apart from the controversial work on the eucharistic Canon and reservation. It is little wonder that many people grew weary of the whole subject. What, then, were the proposed changes apart from these two subjects?

The Calendar
A small handful of Black-letter Days were added – Anskar, Thomas Aquinas and King Alfred.
Morning and Evening Prayer
1. The proposed alternative ending to Evening Prayer was removed, and the prayers transferred to the Occasional Prayers and Thanksgivings.
2. Seven prayers were added to the Occasional Prayers.
3. Psalm 51 was included as a further alternative to Te Deum.

Holy Communion
1. Congregational responses before and after the Gospel were added.
2. The Prayer for the Church was expanded.
3. Three additional Proper Prefaces were included.

Confirmation
A new Blessing was provided.
Matrimony
1. The bride was no longer required to 'obey'.
2. The bridegroom no longer 'endowed' his bride with his worldly goods, but 'shared' them with her.

Burial
New material was added: opening sentences, alternative readings from Revelation 7 and Revelation 21, and two new prayers for the departed.
Appendix
The Order for Prime, A Devotion before Holy Communion, and the Collects, Epistles and Gospels for the Lesser Feasts and Fasts were included.

Bearing in mind that most of these proposals were taken from other sources, it all amounted to very little. The most significant additions were the collects and eucharistic lessons for the Lesser Feasts and Fasts; and the daily provision for Lent with its *lectio continua* was particularly valuable.

The 1928 Book has been subjected to criticism by a number of scholars, especially F. E. Brightman in his *CQR* 1927 article, Eric Milner-White in *The Occasional Prayers of the 1928 Prayer Book Reconsidered* (1929) and by W. K. Lowther-Clarke in *The Prayer Book of 1928 Reconsidered* (1943). Much of their criticism is undoubtedly justified; nevertheless over the years the contents of the book, with the exception of the eucharistic Canon, gained increasing acceptance and their use became widespread, particularly in the case of the Occasional Offices. After fifteen years of use, Dr Lowther-Clarke's comment was interesting.

> The attitude adopted, which may appear hypercritical, is justifiable in view of the necessity of returning one day to the unsolved problem of Revision . . . Let me assure the reader that I have no desire to depreciate

> the 1928 Book as a whole. I habitually use most of it, except for the Alternative Canon, and gratefully acknowledge its superiority to 1662 in most respects.[57]

This reflected the general attitude. The Book had undoubted weaknesses: but its new material and its flexibility were welcome additions to public worship, and other parts of the Anglican Communion were glad to make use of some of its provisions.

Here is an estimate made by the Liturgical Commission in 1957, of the extent to which the Book was used in England.

1. *Widely Used*
Seasonal Sentences at Mattins and Evensong.
Proper Psalms for Sundays and Holy Days.
Many of the Occasional Prayers.
Shortening of the Litany.
The Summary of the Law or the Kyries.
Additional Proper Prefaces.
Occasional Offices (in whole or in part).
Orders for Confirmation and for the Visitation of the Sick.
Order for Compline.
Propers for Lesser Feasts and Fasts.
2. *Less Widely Used*
Alternative Exhortation to 'Dearly Beloved Brethren' at Mattins and Evensong.
Shortened Venite.
Alternative Translation of the Athanasian Creed.
Omission of bracketed verses in the Psalms.
Preparation before Holy Communion.
Alternative Epistles and Gospels.
Provision for the full Passion on Palm Sunday and Good Friday.
Prayer for the Church in Holy Communion.
Revised Communion Service.
3. *Seldom Used*
Alternative Confession at Mattins and Evensong.
Invitatories with the Venite.
Psalm 51 and 40 in place of Te Deum.
Prayer of Humble Access after Comfortable Words.
The Alternative Canon.
Order for Prime.
Exhortation for use in Advent and Lent.

IV

The reasons for the failure of the 1928 Book to secure authorization deserve brief comment, if only to help assess the Church's future approach to liturgical revision.[58] First and foremost was the undeniable fact that the motives underlying the creation of the Book were hopelessly muddled. An exercise which began as an attempt to solve problems of discipline became confused with an attempt to meet pastoral and devotional needs no longer entirely satisfactorily met by 1662. Dom Gregory Dix's comment is apt:

> The Bishops had rashly wandered into a position where they could be represented as having produced a new and different rite as their answer to Parliament's instructions to observe the old one better. It was precisely the position avoided in 1662, and the result is what it would have been in like case.[59]

The 1928 Book was in effect the answer to the Royal Letters of Business of 1906; yet its Preface never referred to discipline or to 1906; its theme was the need to meet the worshipping needs of a society which had changed substantially since the seventeenth century. Nevertheless, Archbishop Davidson was still thinking — or claiming to think — in disciplinary terms in March 1927: 'I should regard any man who deliberately flouts the directions explicitly laid down not two hundred years ago but today as a very grave offender.' Yet he failed to be explicit as to how discipline could be exercised, although he admitted, 'How an offender should be treated is a question quite separate from the rubrics.'[60] Dr Davidson certainly failed to grasp the complexities of the whole subject, and his biographer admits that he failed to give a proper lead. Two separate and distinct issues were confused, and the attempt to combine them could not hope for success. Hensley Henson saw this clearly: 'The restoration of discipline and the revision of the formularies were excellent objects, but in the actual circumstances of modern England not easily harmonized.'[61] It is also worth noting that although the Bishops claimed to be meeting the needs of a society which had changed, they did not appear to realize that change could continue. While it would be unfair to suggest that they envisaged the 1928 Book lasting as long as 1662, nevertheless there were indications that they hoped that it would last a very long time. Dr Davidson commented to Sir William Joynson Hicks, 'I should not anticipate any reopening of the matter at any early period in our future history';[62] while Dr T. Woods, Bishop of Winchester, expressed the view that they had made decisions which would 'affect the life of the Church for generations to come'.[63]

Another sign of confused thinking was the shape of the Book. It was a clumsy book, with irritating side-lines, complex rubrics, and a formidable list of variations and alternatives. Brightman had illustrated this by pointing out that 'on an ordinary Sunday there are at least 384 possible varieties of Matins if said straight through to the end: but if it is immediately followed by another service, e.g. the Litany, the number rises to 2,080!'[64] As an attempt to establish limits within which a statutory liturgy should be confined, it was not particularly successful. No one recognized this more clearly than Frere, who was heard to comment, 'You could drive a coach and horses through it in almost any direction, if you had a good lawyer.'

With such a complicated piece of revision, intended — as it seems likely — to last a very long time, it is truly astonishing that the Bishops failed to see what had happened and was still happening in other parts of the Anglican Communion. No attempt was made to introduce changes piecemeal and no provision was made for experiment. Indeed, when the House of Laity suggested experiment over a period of years in 1923, the idea was rejected. It would have been wiser if episcopal ears had been open to the laity's prayers. Frere had pleaded for experiment as early as 1912, and other provinces had followed his advice with profit. Scotland had experimented with permissive variations and additions from 1912 until 1929: Canada's authorization of a new Prayer Book in 1921–2 had been preceded by experiment from 1915 onwards; India had been experimenting since 1920 and continued to do so until authorization in 1933: and South Africa undertook revision piecemeal, beginning in 1911 with a schedule of permitted modifications, which continued until the final approval of its new rite confirmed in 1929. The value of such an approach was attested by Professor P. Hinchliff: 'Though the system was slow and cumbersome (and costly), it did allow the conservative to become familiar with the rite, it allowed it to be tested in practice, and it minimized the chances of widespread and bitter controversy.'[65] Admittedly Ireland had not experimented before authorizing its new Prayer Book in 1927, but the changes made were minimal compared with those of the 1928 Book, while the case of America was rather different. America had already authorized a new Prayer Book as recently as 1892, when, on the plea of Dr William Reed Huntington, the principle of flexibility had been accepted. Some authorized variations had therefore been in use for some thirty years before the revision of 1928, while some of the proposals for revision made in 1892 remained on the table and eventually were incorporated in the 1928 American Book. England's refusal to experiment was therefore contrary to the general pattern of revision in the Anglican Communion.

There was also some muddled thinking in the Bishops' claim that there was no change of doctrine in the 1928 Book. Archbishop Davidson had made this claim on a number of occasions. The Preface also stated clearly, 'If the minds of any be troubled because we have allowed another Order of Holy Communion as well as the old, and have made further provision for the sick, let them not think that we mean thereby any change of doctrine.' Yet it was precisely in the Eucharist that there was a change of doctrine: and it was there in the prayers for the departed. Here again Hensley Henson hit the nail on the head:

> Some change of doctrine, or, if that phrase be preferred, some change of emphasis on doctrine, is plainly implicit in the process of revising sixteenth-century formularies in order to make them adequate to twentieth-century requirements. It is precisely because the doctrine of the Church of England has changed during the last three centuries that the formularies of the Church's worship need revision.[66]

It must not be forgotten that doctrine is implied, not merely in the words and phrases of prayers, but in the structure of a rite, and in rubrics which give guidance on the performance of a rite.[67] Here again, Dom Gregory Dix grasped a significant point:

> [The Bishops] seem never to have envisaged their new rite [of Holy Communion] sufficiently as a whole; and they never succeeded in clearing their minds as to what they meant their liturgy to do, i.e. as to what that eucharistic action is which the liturgy performs. They were obviously much hampered by trying to produce something upon which they could agree among themselves while maintaining unresolved a great diversity of eucharistic theology.[68]

The new eucharistic rite, the provisions for reservation, the prayers for the departed – here were elements in the new Book which for the Evangelicals indicated a move in the direction of Rome. The publication of the report on the Anglican-Roman Conversations at Malines 1921–5 at the beginning of 1928 only strengthened the suspicion. The fear of Rome was there, irrational though much of it may have been; and people like Bishop Knox, Joynson Hicks, Inskip and Rosslyn Mitchell made the most of it. Theological niceties counted for little in the face of gut-feelings. To quote Henson again, 'Englishmen are not inevitably episcopalian as the Scots are inevitably presbyterian and the Irish inevitably papists, but *au fond* they are Erastian, Bibliolatrous, and always fiercely anti-Papal.'[69] Admittedly some Liberal Evangelicals supported the Book and even the rubrics on reservation. They were not opposed to reservation for the purpose of communion. What they rejected was any localized or materialistic conception of the presence of Christ: and provided this was recognized and safeguarded, they were willing to allow the use of the reserved sacrament. Indeed, some were prepared to go further. Note, for example, the statement by the Dean of Bristol, E. A. Burroughs, in a collection of essays entitled *Liberal Evangelicalism*.

> Evangelicals might possibly concede a certain use of the reserved sacrament 'for purposes of adoration', if it were made clear that, in such use, the consecrated elements were only serving the same purpose as (say) a crucifix might more reasonably serve, by concentrating sense and thought at once, and so making possible a more vivid realisation of the Spiritual Presence of Christ: but, believing what they do about that Presence, they could not conceive any other use of the reserved sacrament which tended to localise or materialise it in the worshipper's thought.[70]

But even this would not have been acceptable to Anglo-Catholics. They would agree that a crucifix was a sign, and as such a stimulus to Christian devotion: but the Eucharist was not merely a sign, it was a sacrament – an efficacious sign, intended not to stimulate devotion but to be the Christian's spiritual food: and there was a sense in which they believed the eucharistic presence to be 'local'. The Anglo-Catholics were equally dissatisfied with the Book: the restrictive rubrics on reservation, the new Canon, the rubric on fasting – all were unpalatable to them. As a compromise, therefore, aiming to comprehend within the Church of England widely differing views, the Book was a failure: indeed it engendered opposition from the wings. Evangelicals and Anglo-Catholics were united in opposition to the Book, but for different reasons. Well might the Bishop of Norwich describe the opposition in the Convocations and the Church Assembly as 'a mixed, motley and miscellaneous crowd . . . as we united on this issue with one another, though our motives were divergent'.[71] Comprehension had been an issue in 1662: it still remained an issue.

Dr Pollock was among a group of opponents who pleaded for splitting the revision proposals into two: asking Parliament to endorse the uncontroversial elements in the Book, and leaving the controversial elements – reservation and the alternative Order of Holy Communion – until a greater measure of agreement was achieved within the Church of England.[72] It was a suggestion which the Bishops and the Church Assembly brushed aside. But it is significant that the Book failed in the House of Commons precisely on the controversial elements, reservation and the alternative Order of Holy Communion. The uncontroversial elements, Baptism, Matrimony, and Burial, would have been accepted by the Commons without much difficulty. With the passage of time, the judgement of the House of Commons proved to be more reliable than that of the Church Assembly. For while the uncontroversial elements came to be widely accepted and used in the Church of England, the alternative Order of Holy Communion failed to secure acceptance. Much has been said about the Book being defeated by non-Anglicans from Ireland, Scotland and Wales. An analysis of the voting patterns admittedly supports such a contention.[73] But the fact is inescapable – the practice of the Church was in agreement with the judgement of the House of Commons rather than with that of the Church Assembly.

A Song of the Deposited Book

This poem, in the style of Gilbert and Sullivan, appeared in whole or in part, and often in slightly different form, in a variety of books and pamphlets during the period. Authorship was ascribed to the Reverend G. G. S. Gillett, Editorial Secretary of SPG, and formerly domestic chaplain to Lord Halifax (Lockhart, *Charles Lindley, Viscount Halifax*, vol. 2, p. 346n). It sums up, in a remarkable way, the views attributed to the three groups heading the verses.

CHORUS OF *EVANGELICALS*:–

'A put-back-the-clock New Book,
A bring-in-the-Jesuits Book,
A plainly papistical, grossly sophistical,
  Most Anti-Scriptural Book.

A turn-us-all-out New Book,
A down-with-the-Gospel Book,
A give-in-to-mummery, idols and flummery
Ruin-to-souls New Book!'

CHORUS OF *ANGLO-CATHOLICS*:—

'A bait-on-the-hook New Book,
A thank-you-for-nothing New Book,
A part sentimental, a part Oriental
And part made-in-Germany Book.
A pickle-the-rod New Book,
A put-us-in-quod New Book,
A no-comprehensiveness, full-of-offensiveness,
Anti-devotional Book.'

CHORUS OF *BISHOPS*:—
'Our noble Deposited Book,
Our Composite, copyright Book,
Our most diplomatical, anti-fanatical,
Protestant–Catholic Book.
Our twenty-years-thought New Book,
Our Prayerfully planned New Book,
Our no-change doctrinal, our quite semi-final,
Our richly enriched New Book.
Our please-be-good-boys New Book,
Our don't-make-a-noise New Book,
Our why-can't-you-risk-a-bit, trust-the-episcopate,
Save the Establishment Book.'

V

The Church of England was not alone in the Anglican Communion in undertaking a revision of the Prayer Book during the early decades of the twentieth century: and it has already been hinted that she might have been wise to have followed the example of other provinces in their approach to the whole question, bearing in mind that no one else faced the same constitutional problem of a parliamentary connection. A brief survey of what was taking place elsewhere can therefore provide interesting points of comparison.

A stimulus was undoubtedly provided by the positive approach of the 1908 Lambeth Conference towards revision. It cannot have been pure coincidence that within twelve months of the Conference Ireland, Scotland, Canada and South Africa had all appointed revision committees. America was rather later — 1913 — but this is understandable, for revision had already taken place there as recently as 1892. What was evident, however, as the various patterns emerged, was the fact that none of these Churches worked in complete isolation: material was exchanged to a considerable degree, and in this exchange the English 1928 Book played a full part. It was also evident that the limits of revision were relatively modest. All six Churches regarded 1662 or their own Books of Common Prayer as the norm; none departed from recognizable limits. The one exception was India, where a brave piece of pioneering took place with proposals for an eastern form of eucharistic liturgy.

The methods employed by the Anglican Church in Canada to produce its first Prayer Book differed significantly from those used in this country. The laity, for example, were closely involved throughout the entire operation; and it was in fact a layman, Dr Matthew Wilson KC of the Diocese of Huron, who first raised the matter in 1896.[74] Six years later the General Synod approved the idea, not of a Canadian Prayer Book, but of a Canadian Appendix to 1662; and a draft, largely the work of Dr Kingdon, Bishop of Fredericton, was submitted in 1905. Opinion was divided and the House of Bishops shelved the matter. In 1908, however, after the successful launching of the Canadian Hymn Book and the impetus of the Lambeth Conference, a new Committee under Dr Dunn, Bishop of Quebec, was appointed to reexamine the project. Its recommendation, adopted in 1911, was for a Canadian edition of the Prayer Book, provided that there was no change in doctrine, no change in the Ornaments Rubric, and that Resolution 27 of the 1908 Lambeth Conference was complied with. A Central Revision Committee of twenty-five members — bishops, clergy and laity — under Dr Williams, Bishop of Huron, directed the entire operation. They began by sending a form of enquiry covering all aspects of revision to every clergyman and lay member of the General Synod. This action, providing an opportunity for all parts of the Canadian Church to be involved in the work, aroused considerable interest and enthusiasm. The Committee worked with commendable speed; and a Draft Book was ready by September 1915. After revision, this was authorized by the House of Bishops for 'temporary or occasional use, according to the discretion of the Bishop' until the next meeting of the General Synod. By Christmas 1915 50,000 copies were available and there followed three years of widespread discussion and experiment. In 1918, the General Synod approved the Book after further amendment by a unanimous vote, the Primate, Dr Matheson, commenting that it 'anticipated and embodied . . . most of the modifications and recommendations' outlined by the English Archbishops' Committee of Enquiry on Worship following the National Mission of Repentance and Hope. It was then approved for another three years' provisional use while another committee subjected it to a final detailed examination. In October 1921 the General Synod formally authorized the new Book by massive votes of approval — the Bishops unanimously, the Clergy by 83 votes to 9, and the Laity by 58 votes to 2. Admittedly the revision was conservative: little change was made in the Communion service, which could have caused trouble: but the whole operation was thorough, involving both original

Canadian material and borrowed material from other Churches, and undertaken with little or no friction after prolonged experiment. The Book came into use on Easter Day 1922. Its main features were:

1. A new Calendar on 1928 lines, making use of Canterbury Convocation's Report 481, Wordsworth's *Ministry of Grace*, and Frere's *Some Principles of Liturgical Reform.* It contained one new Red Letter Day, the Transfiguration on 6 August.
2. A new Lectionary – the 1922 English Lectionary.
3. Provision for combining services – Morning or Evening Prayer, Holy Communion and Litany.
4. Provision for shortened Morning and Evening Prayer as in the Shortened Services Act of 1872, but extended to Sundays.
5. Sixteen selections of psalms – on American lines – for use either on the 31st day of the month, or on any other day as required with episcopal sanction.
6. Morning and Evening Prayer
   a. New seasonal sentences.
   b. Alternative anthems to the Venite.
   c. Many additional Prayers and Thanksgivings, borrowing heavily from Dr Dowden in Scotland and from America, but with some original Canadian compositions.
   d. Provision for a sermon.
7. Holy Communion remained virtually untouched as in 1662, but
   a. The Summary of the Law was alternative to the Decalogue.
   b. Responses were provided before and after the Gospel.
   c. Both post-Communion prayers could be used if required.
8. Matrimony
   a. The Preface was modified on 1928 lines.
   b. An additional prayer for the gift of children from the Irish Prayer Book.
9. Many new occasional forms of prayer were included: Dominion Day, Children, Missions, Harvest Thanksgiving, Institution and Induction, Laying a Foundation Stone, Consecration of a Church and of a Churchyard, and Family Prayers.

The Prayer Book had gone to South Africa as part of the British Administration and had been accepted by the Provincial Synod as part of the church constitution in 1870. This constitution made provision for liturgical revision, although no specific machinery to deal with it was set up at the time. Then in November 1908 an episcopal revision committee was established and in 1911 the first schedule of permitted deviations appeared, including permission to omit the Decalogue and the prayer for the King and to abbreviate the Words of Administration in the Communion service; the provision of additional collects, epistles and gospels; and the provision for a combined service of Mattins, Litany and Holy Communion.[75] This schedule was reissued in 1915 under the title *Prayers upon several Occasions*.

Meanwhile proposals for a revision of the eucharistic rite were published in 1913 by two young priests in the diocese of Grahamstown, Charles Gould and Jasper Bazeley, both keen students of liturgy. Theirs was a radical revision, clearly influenced by the writings of W. C. Bishop in *The Church Quarterly Review* for January 1907 and July 1908.[76] Thanksgiving was the essential element of the Consecration prayer, and the rite in *Apostolic Constitutions* Book 8 and the Liturgy of St James were the two chief sources for their proposals, to which were added elements from 1549, 1662, Scotland and the Nestorian liturgy. Admittedly little of their text appeared in official proposals, but their view of the proper pattern for an anaphora shaped the official policy in revision.[77] At the end of 1917, the Bishops issued *The Proposed Form* for discussion and experimental use. The first part of the rite was essentially that of 1662, with the Summary of the Law and the Kyries as alternatives to the Decalogue. Thereafter it resembled the Interim Rite with modifications. The penitential element and the Prayer of Humble Access were in their 1549 position; the anaphora began, 'All glory and thanksgiving be to thee', as in Scotland and America; and after the Institution Narrative came the Scottish anamnesis; there was also an epiclesis. The prayer was virtually identical with one proposed by Gould in a pamphlet published in 1917.[78] The Bishops sent a copy of *The Proposed Form* to Frere, who in July 1918 replied with thirteen points.[79] In the light of this and local comment, the Bishops published a Revised Proposed Form in 1919 in which all but three of Frere's points were taken up. Indeed, it could almost be regarded as 'Frere's Anaphora'; and he reviewed it favourably in *The Church Quarterly Review* in July 1920, complimenting the clarity and simplicity of its anamnesis and oblation, its form of epiclesis, and its emphasis on thanksgiving. Indeed he regarded the whole rite as providing the Anglican Communion with a valuable model.[80] He was critical, however, of the provision for a 'second consecration', which merely required the recital of the words from 'Hear us O merciful Father' to the end of the Institution Narrative. Frere did not really approve of 'second consecrations'; but if provision had to be made, either the whole prayer should be recited again, or at least the anamnesis and epiclesis should be added to what was proposed.[81] This, together with the form of the epiclesis, with the crucial phrases 'these sacred gifts and creatures of thine own' and 'that he (i.e. the Holy Spirit) may hallow this oblation' became a centre of controversy in the province. Some indication of the strength of feeling was the reaction of the Provincial Synod in November 1919: all three Houses approved the rite, but the majority in the House of Laity was only three.[82]

The opposition grew, led by a formidable figure, the Reverend Dr John Darragh. Petitions also went from Natal and Cape Town, urging the Bishops to reconsider the epiclesis. Eventually, in November 1921, the Bishops omitted the two contentious phrases in the epiclesis and amended the 'second consecration' formula to include both the anamnesis and epiclesis after the Institution Narrative. The revised rite in this form was published in 1922 and after final minor amendments was approved with only one dissentient vote by the Provincial Synod in 1924. Five years later it was approved for the second time without discussion, thereby permanently ratifying the rite as the province's official alternative to 1662. The result, after periods of experiment, was one of the most satisfactory Anglican rites, expressive of the view that there is no single moment of consecration, and that the necessary requisite is thanksgiving; 'When thanksgiving has been offered in prayerful trust that God's power will accomplish his purpose, we can then securely believe in the Presence of our Lord in the Eucharist'.[83]

Apart from the eucharistic rite, other deviations from and alternatives to 1662 were dealt with over the years in piecemeal fashion. Occasional prayers and thanksgivings, for example, were authorized in 1915: the 1922 English lectionary was authorized in 1924 as the only lectionary; then in 1926 the Occasional Offices were authorized, in forms which were substantially the English proposals of NA 84 with some modifications from the Orange book. These were slightly revised in 1930, after the English book had reached its final form; a revised Calendar, also on English lines, was added together with the Anointing of Catechumens, the Blessing of a Civil Marriage, and additional forms of Burial. It was not until 1954, however, that all the various elements were brought together in a single book.

In Scotland, in response to widespread requests, the Bishops appointed a committee in 1909 to examine the 1764 Communion rite and make what changes were thought necessary.[84] They were fortunate in being able to draw on the expertise of two outstanding liturgical scholars – Dr John Dowden, Bishop of Edinburgh, and Dr A. J. Maclean, Bishop of Moray, Ross and Caithness. Both had been members of the Prayer Book Committee at the 1908 Lambeth Conference, while the latter also became a member of the English Committee of Liturgical Experts in 1912. The Committee soon decided to extend the scope of their revision by adding a schedule of 'permissible additions to and deviations from the Book of Common Prayer' and completed the whole exercise within two years. It was authorized by the Provincial Synod in 1911 and published in 1912 in a volume entitled *Common Prayer (Scotland).* It was a modest but useful revision, owing a great deal to principles first laid down by Dowden in 1884. The recommendations of the 1908 Lambeth Conference were also influential. The Communion Rite was that of 1764 with certain amendments. It had now its own form of Ante-Communion,[85] additional proper prefaces and post-communion prayers, and the eucharistic canon was improved by an epiclesis which included both communicants as well as elements. Other additions to the Book were a Bidding Prayer, provisions for reservation for the sick, and a fine collection of 'Additional Prayers upon several Occasions', owing much to Dowden, and providing a useful quarry of material for other provinces engaged on revision.

Two other committees also prepared new Tables of Psalms and Lessons, and their work was approved for experimental use in 1914. Then in 1918 a further Committee was appointed to look at the whole field of Prayer Book revision. This work, led by Maclean, continued for almost eight years, and their proposals were finally submitted to the Provincial Synod in October 1925. By this time the English Bishops were preparing to draw up their own proposals in their final form, so the Scottish Synod decided to postpone further action until the fate of the English book had become clearer. They therefore adjourned until June 1928, by which date the English book was awaiting its second consideration by the House of Commons. By a remarkable coincidence the Synod completed consideration of the proposals on 14 June, the same day as the fate of the English book was sealed in the Commons. The proposed Scottish book passed through the Diocesan Synods with almost complete unanimity, and on 12 March 1929 it was confirmed by the Provincial Synod, to come into use at the end of the year. The 1928 Book clearly exercised more direct influence on the Scottish book than any other liturgical work, as may be seen from the rites of Baptism and Ordination, the Occasional Prayers, the invitatories to the Venite and the new translation of the Athanasian Creed. There was, however, some borrowing from other Anglican sources: the opening of the eucharistic Canon, 'All glory and thanksgiving', came from South Africa, the consignation prayer in Confirmation came from 1549, and it used Benedictus es from the American book as the alternative to the Benedicite. The Scottish book also contained some fine new material of its own: a new Litany based on that in the Liturgy of St James, a new Calendar with several Scottish saints, a new Lectionary with a three year cycle for Sundays, and the seasonal sentences for Mattins and Evensong. In view of the storms created in England over reservation and the alternative eucharistic Canon, it is interesting to note these elements in the Scottish book. Here reservation was permitted without any restrictions 'according to long-existing custom'. As for the Eucharistic Prayer, it was similar in many respects to the 1928 form, with an anamnesis and an epiclesis after the Institution Narrative, continuing with the prayer of Oblation and the Lord's Prayer: where it differed from the 1928 form was its inclusion of the Intercessions (with prayer for the departed) at the end of the prayer. The penitential material also came immediately before communion, as in 1549. The Scottish rite would undoubtedly have caused as much trouble in England as the 1928 rite — probably even more. It was therefore a remarkable achievement to have secured its acceptance just across the border with little or no demur.

The harmonious passage of the Scottish book was in marked contrast to that of the English book. This was due to a number of factors. In the first place Scotland did not experience the bitter party differences which created such a problem in the Church of England. Secondly, the two men, Dowden and Maclean, exerted considerable influence. The 1912 Book embodied a great deal that Dowden had been advocating over a period of twenty-five years; while Maclean's influence on the 1929 book was such that it was known as 'The Moray Prayer Book'.[86] But thirdly, the Scottish book was achieved by a gradual process. All the 1912 and 1914 work was built into the new book and had been tested by some fifteen years' use. By Canon 23 the English Book of Common Prayer continued to be authorized for use alongside the new Scottish Book, although the latter contained both the English (1662) and the Scottish Communion rites: but services had to be clearly from one book or the other; 'mixing' was not permitted. Furthermore, the 1764 rites could be substituted for the new 1929 rite on certain conditions; while the English 1928 rite was permitted 'if and when the Episcopal Synod is satisfied that it has been authorized in the Church of England'.

The Irish revision, which began in 1909, was not completed until 1926; and in view of its conservative nature, it can only be described as painstakingly slow. The Preface of the 1926 Book stated that the Bishops and the Revision Committee had been asked 'to report upon the best manner in which without making any modification in doctrine or in the ritual Canons, the Rubrics and Services of the Church might be adapted to the requirements of the present time'. They had also been asked to enrich the liturgy by incorporating material from both ancient and modern sources. It is not surprising, therefore, that some material from other revisions found its way into the new Irish Book. The most significant changes were:

1. *The Calendar*
   St Patrick and the Transfiguration were added, but there were still no Black Letter days included.
2. *Morning and Evening Prayer*
   a. Special psalms were provided for Sundays throughout the year.
   b. The English 1922 Lectionary was included – except the lessons from the Apocrypha.
   c. The canticle Urbs Fortitudinis and Psalm 148 were provided as additional alternatives to the Te Deum.
   d. Further additional Prayers and Thanksgivings were added, with some borrowing from Scotland.
   e. In 1933 two alternative forms for Evening Prayer were added, one being Compline and the other containing a Litany of Thanksgiving and the Gloria in excelsis.
3. *Holy Communion*
   a. The Summary of the Law was included as an alternative to the Decalogue.
   b. The Offertory Sentences were almost identical with England 1928: but a special set for the Major Festivals was added.
   c. Proper Prefaces for Whitsun (1928 and South Africa) and Trinity (America, South Africa and Scotland) were added.

d. Permission was given to use either or both the post-communion prayers.

4. *Burial*

An order for the burial of Baptized Children was included.

Another relatively conservative revision was that of America. Here there had been a revision as recently as 1892, but by 1913 the pressure for further change was sufficiently strong for revision to be undertaken again. The Revision Commission's work was completed by 1925, in consequence of which it was not able to make use of the final forms of the English and Scottish revisions which appeared more or less simultaneously.[87] Some of its proposals for increased flexibility were quite radical. Indeed, Morning and Evening Prayer could disappear altogether. Not only was permission given to use 'other devotions' in addition to the two Offices, provided the Ordinary approved; but such devotions could supersede the Offices 'when the edification of the Congregation so requires'. The psalms and lessons for Morning and Evening Prayer were also made interchangeable; while the appropriate epistle or gospel from the eucharistic lectionary could be substituted for the second lesson at either office. A further provision was the permission to omit the whole of Morning Prayer after the first lesson and canticle when Holy Communion followed, thus providing a Ministry of the Word with psalmody and both Old and New Testament readings. At some points, however, there was a danger of brevity overriding flexibility. In the Daily Offices, only one psalm was required, while at Evening Prayer one lesson and one Canticle could be omitted; at the same time some of the lessons in the new lectionary were very brief — even a single verse. The sum total of an office could therefore be minute.

Other interesting features of the American revision, finally authorized in 1928, were:

1. *Morning and Evening Prayer*
   a. Seasonal antiphons to the Venite, virtually identical with those of England 1928.
   b. Benedictus es as an additional alternative to Te Deum.
   c. Gloria in excelsis as an alternative to Gloria Patri at the end of the psalms at Evening Prayer.
2. *Holy Communion*
   a. Collects for each day in Holy Week.
   b. The Lord's Prayer and the Prayer of Humble Access followed the Prayer of Consecration before communion.
3. *Baptism*
   a. A single order was provided for both children and adults.
   b. Consignation was made obligatory.
4. *Confirmation*

   The Preface was replaced by the optional reading of Acts 8.14—17.

Many years later, in 1953, the Standing Liturgical Commission in America made this interesting comment on their 1928 revision:

> [The revisers] though they paid the utmost deference to our own 'Mother Churches' in England and Scotland, and were eager to avail themselves of the great stores of devotional learning in both countries, were not content to follow their lead slavishly in all particulars, but considered each question which they raised upon its own merits, and decided upon it according to their own judgement.[88]

Any survey of liturgical developments in the Anglican Communion during this period would be incomplete without reference to a remarkable book, published in time for consideration by the Lambeth Conference of 1920. *The Eucharist in India*, edited by the Reverend J. C. Winslow, a missionary priest in the diocese of Bombay, contained a Preface by Edwin James Palmer, Bishop of Bombay, three essays, and a draft eucharistic liturgy. It was remarkable, not only as a pioneering work in the field of liturgical revision, but also because it contained the first published work of Edward Ratcliff, destined to become the foremost Anglican liturgical scholar of his day.

It was not surprising to find Bishop Palmer associating himself with the book; for he was a fine scholar, a great character, and a leading figure in the ecumenical movement. A nephew of the first Earl of Selborne, he had a distinguished career at Oxford, becoming Bishop of Bombay while still in his thirties. He was one of the founders of the Church of South India and helped to draft the 'Appeal to all Christian People' at the Lambeth Conference of 1920. He pointed out in his Preface that although Lambeth Conferences from 1867 onwards had recognized the desirability of adapting liturgy to meet the needs of particular communities, all had assumed that the basic liturgy would be the 1662 Prayer Book. This was an assumption they were not prepared to accept: their aim was 'to encourage Indians to discover the most natural expression of their congenital instincts'.[89] But the authorization of a liturgy based on something other than 1662 raised problems. First there was the problem of church order. There was nothing in the Lambeth Conference resolutions nor in the constitution of the Indian Episcopal Synod to meet such a situation: therefore before the Indian Synod considered the matter, he wished to consult the Lambeth Conference.[90] Secondly there was the problem of uniformity within the Anglican Communion: but he argued that what mattered was not uniformity, but unity; and what was needed was not a unity of identity, but a unity which included differences. If the Roman Church allowed its Uniats to retain the use of their Eastern liturgies, why should not the Anglican Communion do something similar?[91] In any case, our Lord's symbol of unity had been an identity of actions: he had said, '*Do* this', not '*Say* this'. Finally, while there was merit in seeking guidance from ancient models, pedantic purism in following them should be avoided; the aim should be, not antiquarian correctness, but living prayer. Liturgies therefore grew through use in church, and this involved experiment before a final form could be authorized.[92]

Winslow argued the case for a new form of liturgy in greater detail. After a century of Anglican missionary work in India, the only forms of worship available were still those of 1662 accompanied by *Hymns Ancient and Modern*. The forms, the words and the music were all strange to the Indian.[93] Yet something more suitable was available on their very doorstep. In Malabar, in South India, there was the old Syrian Christian Church, a truly Indian Church which could trace its origins back to the early Christian centuries, and using as its liturgy the Eastern liturgy of St James. This had been brought to India in the seventeenth century with the trappings of another culture but by dint of use over nearly three hundred years had been largely acclimatized.[94] This was what the writers of *The Eucharist in India* had adapted and abbreviated; and in so doing they believed that they had produced a rite which gave full play to the mystic and contemplative instinct of India, but which at the same time was grounded in a personal God and the historic Jesus. It also took into account other features of Indian life which were held in high regard: the veneration of saints, the reverence for deceased ancestors, the importance of sacrifice, and the love of stately ceremonial.[95]

An analysis of the structure and contents of the proposed liturgy was left to Edward Ratcliff; and this was particularly interesting as a workmanlike piece of liturgical writing from someone who was still an undergraduate. Ratcliff had been awarded a scholarship at St John's College, Cambridge, in 1915, but elected to serve with the YMCA in India from 1916 to 1918, when health reasons compelled him to return home. At Cambridge he studied Oriental Languages, taking Part I of the Tripos in 1920. But *The Eucharist in India* had already been published before the Lambeth Conference in July 1920, so his essay was a remarkably mature piece of writing from someone who had not yet begun to study officially for the Theological Tripos. It indicated an enthusiasm for the Eastern liturgies and Syriac which remained with him for the rest of his life. So he could describe the anaphora of the Syriac Liturgy of St James as 'unequalled in order and beauty by the Eucharistic Prayer of any other liturgy . . . It is one of the most sublime prayers in Christendom.'[96] In outline this liturgy agreed with the earliest known Antiochene liturgy – the Clementine Liturgy of *The Apostolic Constitutions* Book 8 – so beloved of Edward Stephens, Whiston, the Non-Jurors and other liturgists of the eighteenth century. But within this framework, elements from other Eastern liturgies and from Western liturgies had been incorporated. There were, for example, prayers from the liturgies of St Basil and St John Chrysostom, words of administration adapted from the Ethiopic anaphora of the Apostles used by the Abyssinian Jacobites, and the hymn 'Strengthen, Lord, for service' from the old Liturgy of SS Addai and Mari used by the Nestorians. At the same time the variable collects came from the 1662 Prayer Book, while the prefaces were a combination of material from 1662, the Scottish rite and the Roman rite.[97] All this was cleverly blended, and combined with various ceremonial directions and frequent biddings by the deacon, making it suitable for less instructed congregations. The result was, to quote later Indian commentators:

> A free and greatly condensed adaptation of the Liturgy of St James . . . Its ornate and stately ceremonial does appeal very strongly to the Christians of Malabar, and by dint of use and wont it had been largely Indianized . . . [It] has to a remarkable degree succeeded in producing an effect which affiliates it with the classical liturgies of the East: it transports the participant out of time into the eternal sphere and thus corresponds with an instinct deeply rooted in Indian religion . . . concentrating the worshippers' adoration on the holiness of God revealed in His redemptive activity for mankind.[98]

Hopes of its consideration by the Lambeth Conference were fulfilled. The Committee dealing with Missionary Problems was fortunately chaired by Bishop Westcott of Calcutta, the Metropolitan of India, and he took the trouble to seek the advice of Frere before the Conference began. Frere expressed his warm approval of *The Eucharist in India* and the principles on which it was based.[99] These were reflected both in the Committee's Report and in Resolutions 36-38 of the whole Conference. The widespread demand in the Anglican Communion not only for the adaptation and enrichment of the Prayer Book rites but also for quite different forms of service was accepted and approved. It was finally authorized for experimental use by the Episcopal Synod in the diocese of Bombay in places to be selected by the bishop. Ultimately it was translated into two Indian languages, Marathi and Malayalam, and when recited to the traditional chant in Malabar with the appropriate censings and ceremonial was most impressive.[100]

The UMCA 'missionary dioceses' in Central Africa also went ahead in producing diocesan rites. Zanzibar under Bishop Frank Weston had been first in the field as early as 1919 with a eucharistic rite in Swahili which was basically that of 1549 with the addition of a number of Roman elements. Northern Rhodesia and Nyasaland then followed suit in the early twenties, submitting drafts to the Lambeth liturgical committee. Both rites were based on that of Zanzibar with their own adaptations, some of which came from the proposed South African rite. Frere, as a member of the Lambeth committee, raised the question of creating a single rite for all three dioceses and South Africa; but the Bishop of Northern Rhodesia pointed out practical difficulties, notably the impossibility of people meeting regularly for the necessary discussion; he felt in any case that it would be wiser to wait until they had achieved provincial status before attempting greater uniformity, for the CMS dioceses would also be involved. By 1923, however, the Lambeth committee decided to postpone further consideration of these rites until the proposed English Book had assumed its final form; so both dioceses put their drafts to provisional use for services in the vernacular, while for services in English they adopted the South African rite.[101]

NOTES

1. For detailed information see Jasper, *Frere*, pp. 83–94.
2. The only real objection came from a group of lay members, who disliked the increase of lessons from the Apocrypha. The voting was: Bishops 25 for 0 against; Clergy 119 for 4 against; Laity 127 for 51 against. NA *Proceedings*, 1922, vol. 3, no. 2, pp. 9–14.
3. Cant. Convoc., Report 475.
4. *NA Report 60*, pp. 62–3, sc 65.
5. Jasper, p. 86.
6. *NA 60*, p. 93, sc 145.
7. Sir Edward Clarke, Dr E. Stock, H. C. Hogan, G. A. King, A. Mitchell.
8. *NA 60*, p. 8.
9. *NA 60*a.
10. NA *Proceedings*, vol. 3, no. 2, p. 66.
11. ECU, *Report of the Committee on Prayer Book Revision*, 1922, p. 40.
12. ibid., p. 1.
13. Dearmer had become increasingly liberal and had left St Mary's, Primrose Hill, in 1916; R. G. Parsons, later Bishop of Southwark; F. R. Barry, later Bishop of Southwell; Leslie Hunter, later Bishop of Sheffield; F. W. Dwelly, later Dean of Liverpool; Mervyn Haigh, later Bishop of Coventry, then Winchester.
14. NA *Proceedings*, vol. 3, no. 2, pp. 44–5.
15. For example, the Litany for the Church prayed that 'her sons and her daughters' might 'bear turbulent witness of her beauty to the world'.
16. R. T. Howard (Principal of St Aidan's College, Birkenhead), *Evangelicals and the Grey Book*, n.a., pp. 3–4, 16.
17. The Alcuin Club, *A Survey of the Proposals for the Alternative Prayer Book*, 1923, pt. 1, p. 1.
18. Jasper, p. 97; Cross, *Stone*, p. 175.
19. CA *Report 158*, 1925, pp. 77–82, sc 18.
20. Jasper, p. 98.
21. CA *Report 169*, 1925, p. 26.
22. ibid., pp. 5–6.
23. Bell, p. 1330.
24. ibid.
25. Jasper, pp. 102–4.
26. ibid., p. 106; Bell, pp. 1332–3.
27. *Chronicle Convoc.*, 1927, pp. 3–39.
28. CA *Proceedings*, 1926, pp. 167–8.
29. Jasper, pp. 106–7; Bell, pp. 1333–4.
30. Bell, p. 1335.
31. F. R. Barry, *Mervyn Haigh*, 1964, p. 87.
32. Jasper, pp. 116–21.
33. *Chronicle Convoc.*, 1927, pp. 54–69; *Journal Convoc.*, 1927, Appendix pp. v–xii.
34. Bell, pp. 1336–9.
35. Cross, pp. 180–2.
36. Archbishop Davidson's phrase.
37. A priest could now reserve 'if licensed by the bishop so to do . . . And the bishop shall grant such licence if satisfied of the need unless in any particular case he see good reason to the contrary.'
38. Jasper, pp. 124–5.

39. *Chronicle Convoc.*, 1927, pp. 158–61.
40. 'The New Prayer Book examined', *CQR*, vol. civ (1927), pp. 219–52.
41. CA *Proceedings*, 1927, vol. viii, no. 2, pp. 98–105, 196. Darwell Stone argued that the Archbishop's figures of voting at Diocesan Conferences ignored those who abstained, and those who had reservations. In fact *The Times* of 2 July had claimed that abstentions almost equalled the support – 7,938 voted for, 7,277 abstained. In two dioceses, Bradford and Blackburn, more abstained than voted.
42. John Barnes, *Ahead of his Age: Bishop Barnes of Birmingham*, 1979, p. 166.
43. For the Barnes episode see: Barnes, op. cit., pp. 161–209; Bell, pp. 1319–24; Jasper, pp. 129–33.
44. Alcuin Club, *Walter Howard Frere* (Collections No. xxxv), 1940, pp. 173–8; Jasper, pp. 129–33.
45. Bell, pp. 1342–4.
46. Smyth, p. 407. The Rt Hon. W. C. Bridgeman, First Lord of the Admiralty. It was thought that as a popular and successful minister, he would make a favourable impression. Unfortunately he was apparently nettled by interruptions and made a very weak speech.
47. ibid.
48. Bell, p. 1346.
49. ibid., p. 1347.
50. S. Dark, *Archbishop Davidson and the English Church*, 1929, p. 230.
51. Bell, p. 1347.
52. Lockhart, p. 307.
53. CA *Report 252*, 1928, pp. 10–12.
54. *Chronicle Convoc.*, 1928, pp. 4–5, 115; *Journal Convoc.*, 1928, p. 63.
55. W. Joynson Hicks, *The Prayer Book Crisis*, 1928, p. 156.
56. Smyth, p. 407.
57. W. K. Lowther Clarke, *The Prayer Book of 1928 Reconsidered*, 1943, pp. 2–3. It is interesting to note that although Milner-White's criticisms were rather severe, Professor Ratcliff was equally critical of some of Milner-White's proposed amendments (*Liturgy and Worship*, pp. 278–9).
58. For more detailed discussion on the failure of the Book, see the biographies of people closely concerned: Davidson, Lang, Temple, Garbett, Frere, Stone. See also: H. Henson, *Retrospect of an Unimportant Life*, vol. 2; Lowther Clarke, *The Prayer Book of 1928 Reconsidered*; Horton Davies, *Worship and Theology in England*, vol. 5; C. of E. Liturgical Commission, *Prayer Book Revision in the Church of England*.
59. Gregory Dix, *The Shape of the Liturgy*, 2nd edn 1945, p. 699.
60. Bell, pp. 1336–9.
61. H. Henson, *Retrospect of an Unimportant Life*, 1943, vol. 2, p. 152.
62. Bell, p. 1337.
63. F. T. Woods, *The Prayer Book Revised*, 1927, p. 8.
64. *CQR*, civ (1927), p. 221.
65. P. Hinchliff, *The South African Rite and the 1928 Prayer Book*, 1960, pp. 18–19.
66. H. Henson, *The Book and the Vote*, 1928, pp. 89–90.
67. For further discussion see S. Sykes, *The Integrity of Anglicanism*, 1978, especially chap. 3.
68. Dix, *The Shape*, p. 698.

69. Henson, *Retrospect*, vol. 2, p. 153. Compare the longer statement on similar lines in Bell, p. 1354.
70. *Liberal Evangelicalism, an Interpretation*, by Members of the Church of England, 1923, p. 60.
71. B. Pollock, *A Twentieth Century Bishop*, n.d., p. 155.
72. Jasper, p. 164.
73. *The Times* of 17 December 1927 gave an interesting breakdown of voting patterns in the House of Commons in 1927. The pattern in 1928 was very similar.

Party	*For*	*Against*	*Paired*	*Absent Unpaired*	*Total*
Unionists	167	160	23	57	407
Labour	35	54	1	65	155
Liberals	2	23	2	14	41
Independents	3	3	0	1	7
Totals	207	240	26	137	610

Country	*For*	*Against*	*Paired For*	*Paired Against*	*Absent Unpaired*	*Total*
England	199	175	12	6	95	487
Scotland	6	36	1	5	26	74
Ireland	—	11	—	2	—	13
Wales	2	18	—	—	16	36
Totals	207	240	13	13	137	610

74. For further information see: W. J. Armitage, *The Story of the Canadian Revision of the Prayer Book*, Cambridge 1922.
75. P. Hinchliff, *The South African Liturgy*, Cape Town 1959, pp. 4–5, 9.
76. ibid., pp. 17–21; cf. W. C. Bishop, 'The Mozarabic Rite', *CQR*, lxiii, pp. 298–322; and 'The Primitive Form of Consecration of the Holy Eucharist', *CQR*, lxvi, pp. 385–404.
77. Hinchliff, op. cit., p. 32.
78. ibid., p. 49.
79. Jasper, pp. 203–9.
80. 'The New South African Liturgy', *CQR*, xc (July 1920), pp. 367–74.
81. ibid., p. 371.
82. Hinchliff, p. 69.
83. ibid., pp. 108–9.
84. For further information see: W. Perry, *The Scottish Prayer Book*, Cambridge 1929; and W. G. S. Snow, *Arthur John Maclean*, Edinburgh 1950.
85. The 1764 rite commenced at the Offertory; and the Ante-Communion had been borrowed from other rites, e.g. 1662, Scotland 1637, or the Non-Jurors.
86. Snow, op. cit., p. 88.
87. PECUSA Standing Liturgical Commission, *Prayer Book Studies I*, New York, 1950, p. v.
88. PECUSA Standing Liturgical Commission, *Prayer Book Studies IV*, New York, 1953, p. 107.
89. J. C. Winslow *et al., The Eucharist in India*, 1920, pp. xi–xiii.
90. ibid., pp. xiv–xvi.
91. ibid., pp. xix–xxiv.
92. ibid., pp. xxv–xxviii.
93. ibid., pp. 3–5.

94. ibid., pp. 8–10. W. C. Bishop had already pleaded for a revision on the lines of St James in his essay in *CQR* (July 1908), pp. 385–404.
95. ibid., pp. 10–25.
96. ibid., pp. 60, 62.
97. ibid., pp. 66–8, 113–15.
98. CIPBC, *Principles of Prayer Book Revision*, 1957, pp. 82–4.
99. Jasper, pp. 193–7.
100. CIPBC, *Principles*, p. 84.
101. For a further account of these negotiations, see Jasper, pp. 230–45; C. D. Buchanan, *Modern Anglican Liturgies 1958–1968*, 1968, pp. 42–3, 70–1; B. Wigan, *The Liturgy in English* (Alcuin Club Collections 43), 1962, pp. 145–65.

6

1928 AND ITS AFTERMATH

I

In June 1928 the House of Bishops unanimously agreed to a statement drawn up by the Archbishop of Canterbury, which he delivered to the Church Assembly on 2 July. While claiming that the significance of the Commons vote could easily be exaggerated, and that it did not indicate a claim to control the faith and worship of the Church, nevertheless he believed that the Commons had departed from the reasonable spirit in which the balanced relationship of Church and State could be carried on satisfactorily and harmoniously. He therefore wished to state:

> It is a fundamental principle that the Church — that is, the Bishops together with the Clergy and the Laity — must in the last resort, when its mind has been fully ascertained, retain its inalienable right, in loyalty to our Lord and Saviour Jesus Christ, to formulate its Faith in Him and to arrange the expression of that Holy Faith in its forms of worship . . . it is our firm hope that, when the facts have been quietly considered, some strong and capable committee of statesmen and Churchmen may be appointed to weigh afresh the provisions of the existing law in order to see whether any readjustment is required for the maintenance, in the conditions of our own age, of the principle which we have here and now re-asserted.[1]

Though not going as far as some people, such as Henson, would have liked, it was nevertheless a courageous statement for the Archbishop to make. It was also his last important statement to the Church Assembly; for the announcement of his impending retirement in November was made shortly afterwards.

Three important events followed. In the first place, at the end of the year the Privileged Presses made the 1928 Book generally available by publishing it with the proviso, 'The publication of this Book does not directly or indirectly imply that it can be regarded as authorized for use in churches.'[2] Secondly, after consulting their clergy and laity in diocesan conferences and awaiting the outcome of the General Election in May,[3] the Bishops issued a policy statement on 10 July 1929. Recognizing the impossibility of bringing back the conduct of public worship strictly within the limits of the 1662 Prayer Book, they therefore resolved to act on the following three principles:

1. 'During the present emergency and until further order be taken', they would not 'regard as inconsistent with loyalty to the principles of the

Church of England the use of such additions or deviations' as fell within the limits of the 1928 proposals.

2. 'In the exercise of that legal or administrative discretion, which belongs to each Bishop in his own Diocese', they would be guided by the 1928 proposals, and would 'endeavour to secure that the practices which are consistent neither with the Book of 1662 nor with the Book of 1928 shall cease'.
3. Permission to use the 1928 Book would be conditional on 'the goodwill of the people' as represented by the Parochial Church Council or the interested parties in the case of the Occasional Offices.

The Convocations endorsed these principles with comfortable majorities: Canterbury – Bishops 23–4; Clergy 96–54; York – Bishops nem. con.; Clergy – unanimous.[4] Thirdly, the first step towards a long term solution to the problem was made. On 5 February 1930 the Church Assembly asked the Archbishops to appoint a commission to examine existing Church-State relations and to consider how the Church's right to formulate its faith and arrange its forms of worship could be effectively applied and what legal and constitutional changes, if any, would be required.[5]

Clearly the Bishops had faced a difficult situation, with various alternatives open to them, but all involving problems. They could have accepted the decision of Parliament, rejected the 1928 Book and simply continued with 1662; but this would have involved suppressing or even regarding as inconsistent with the teaching of the Church of England rites and ceremonies which the Convocations and the Church Assembly had already endorsed; it might even have involved censuring and disciplining clergy who were not prepared to use 1662 and nothing else, despite the findings of the 1906 Royal Commission. Or they could have refused to accept the decision of Parliament and authorized the use of 1928, involving the Church in a head-on confrontation with the State and risking the consequences of disestablishment. Or they could have adopted a conciliatory line, asking Parliament to approve a measure containing the uncontroversial matter on which there was general agreement, on the grounds that at least something would have been achieved; but this would have failed to meet the very needs which had necessitated the whole process of revision. In the event they rejected all these options and temporized, quietly stating that they would still do what they would have done if Parliament had passed the Book, but at the same time indicating that they had no desire to sever the State connection. Admittedly it was far from ideal: it was not particularly welcome to extremists on both wings of the Church; and it brought upon the Bishops the criticism that they lacked straightforwardness. The new Archbishop of Canterbury, Dr Lang, confessed that it was a makeshift, leaving important questions such as that of authority unanswered.[6] But at a time when the delicate balance between Church and State had been badly jolted, and the various parties within the Church had been embittered, the policy did provide a breathing space during which tempers could cool and a calmer atmosphere prevail. Indeed, what emerged was the kind of de facto Church–State relationship roughly on the lines of that which Temple had envisaged a decade earlier — a form of spiritual autonomy within the Establishment.[7] It was, of course, inconsistent with the principles accepted in the Enabling Act, when the final decision on such matters had been entrusted to Parliament; and it was this inconsistency which helped to earn for the Bishops the reputation of being rather shifty. It was also questionable as to whether they did in fact possess the *ius liturgicum* or 'legal and administrative discretion' which they claimed. Dr Lowther Clarke argued shortly afterwards that the episcopal *ius liturgicum* was limited to the sanctioning of services additional to those in the authorized service books: and this certainly seems to have been the kind of legal discretion exercised by the Elizabethan bishops mentioned at the 1897 Lambeth Conference.[8] Much later, Dom Gregory Dix argued that the source in English law of the legal discretion of a bishop to set aside the force of a parliamentary statute would be hard to find: indeed the term *ius liturgicum* was unknown until the late nineteenth century, when it was invented by certain Anglican ecclesiologists as a means of lifting the dead hand of parliamentary statutes off Anglican worship.[9] Such a view was endorsed by Mr Justice Vaisey in the 1946 Report on Canon Law — but this was many years later. Whether the Bishops had a *ius liturgicum* or not, however, the fact remains that Parliament acquiesced in the Bishops' moves of 1929, taking no action over the non-recognition of its decision: Dix aptly described it as a policy of 'dignified ignorance'.[10]

In practice the rejection of the 1928 Book by Parliament resulted in a situation such as Frere had pleaded for in 1912. A period of liturgical experiment with services bearing some degree of authorization was now possible. It was a system already used profitably in other parts of the Anglican Communion, although the situation elsewhere was easier because of the absence of the close relationship to the State. It might even be argued that if the Book had been authorized in 1928, the Church would have been deprived of the necessary incentive to seek further changes in Church–State relations, and the Worship and Doctrine Measure of 1973 might not have come into being — or at least in its present form. At the same time the pattern of liturgical revision in the Church of England in the post-war years might have taken a different appearance.

The appointment of the Archbishops' Commission on Church and State was delayed until after the Lambeth Conference, being finally announced in November 1930. The Commission of seventeen members under the chairmanship of the former Cabinet minister, Viscount Cecil of Chelwood, was a weighty one, containing three bishops: Temple of York, Bell of Chichester, and Williams of Carlisle; two eminent historians: Sir Charles Grant Robertson and Professor E. F. Jacob; and three distinguished lawyers: Sir Lewis Dibdin, Sir Philip Baker-Wilbraham, and H. B. (later Mr Justice) Vaisey. Its Report appeared in 1935. This set out two main obstacles to spiritual freedom in the Church, the disagreement within the Church itself on certain vital matters, notably reservation and the Order of Holy Communion, and the lack of effective guarantees for the maintenance of further discipline.[11] Accordingly the first recommendation was for a Round Table Conference to secure agreement on these two controversial issues; and the legislative proposals which followed were made on the assumption that this agreement would be reached. The first of these recommended that any measure of the Church Assembly, which the two Archbishops, the Lord Chancellor and the Speaker of the House of Commons should unanimously certify to relate substantially to the spiritual concerns of the Church, i.e. in doctrine or in worship, should not be subject to parliamentary debate or veto; provided that it had been approved by both Convocations, twice approved by the diocesan conferences of not less than three-quarters of the dioceses of the two provinces, and in the opinion of the Archbishops was consonant with the fundamental doctrines and principles of the Church of England as set forth in the Thirty-nine Articles and the Book of Common Prayer. The important rider was added, however, that to try to get such a measure passed by Parliament against the wishes of a sincere and substantial minority of the Church was inadvisable.[12] Next came proposals for a reform of the ecclesiastical courts, and for a Synodical Declaration interpreting the Declaration of Assent required of the clergy. The latter stated that clergy undertook to adhere to the Book of Common Prayer 'except so far as any deviation from it may be enjoined or sanctioned by the bishop of the diocese' acting within certain requirements, the most important of these being that no deviation should be authorized unless the Convocations agreed that it was not contrary to the fundamental doctrines of the Church of England, and had the approval of or was in conformity with principles laid down by the Convocations and the Church Assembly.[13] Other proposals concerned the appointment of bishops, the rules of marriage and the revision of the Canon Law.

Much of the Report was not directly concerned with the Prayer Book and its revision, but the proposals on Parliamentary Measures and the Synodical Declaration were clearly relevant. The Convocations agreed to move on the latter, and Joint Committees of both Canterbury and York were appointed in January 1937 to examine them. These two Committees then met together and agreed to present to their respective Convocations a report on the Synodical Declaration in January 1938. The two Reports, Canterbury No. 619 and York No. 438 – both substantially the same – were accordingly presented by Bishop Bell of Chichester and Bishop Williams of Carlisle. They suggested that *lawful authority* should proclaim the right, not merely to permit services additional to the Book of Common Prayer, but to sanction variations in the text and rubrics of the Prayer Book itself. The exceptive clause in the Declaration of Assent, 'except so far as shall be ordered by *lawful authority*', should therefore be understood as applying to both categories of services: and the *lawful authority* would have to reside in the

Convocations, by whose formal acts both bishops and clergy were bound. The reports consequently recommended a Synodical Declaration, as suggested by the Commission, affirming that *lawful authority* for the priest meant the authority of the bishop acting with and subject to principles and regulations laid down by the Convocations, with the goodwill of the laity as represented in the Church Assembly. Both Convocations were happy to 'receive' the Reports, and in winding up the debate at Canterbury, Archbishop Lang expressed approval of the idea of a Declaration and promised to summon the proposed Round Table Conference.[14]

This Conference met for the first time under the chairmanship of Archbishop Temple at Lambeth Palace on 18 March 1938. Dix described it as 'of unwieldy size, representative character and diversified prejudices'.[15] Certainly with a membership of fifty-four it was too large to hold out hopes of rapid progress; and although it met several times, it failed to resolve any issues, despite a plea from Archbishop Lang not to ignore the dangers and the disastrous effects of failure.[16] The outbreak of war brought its activities to an end. With hindsight, Archbishop Garbett commented in 1947 that the 1935 Commission had committed a strange error of judgement in placing this Round Table Conference to the forefront of its proposals.

> This was a fatal proposal: at once it raised again the old controversies: it gave opportunities for those who were opposed to the other recommendations to obstruct progress by refusing this preliminary agreement, and it aroused suspicion as to the purpose of all the other proposals. This preliminary condition for agreement on the Order of Communion and Reservation doomed from the outset the Report to failure.[17]

Meanwhile during the 1930s and early forties a variety of attempts were made to produce some revision of the 1662 eucharistic rite which would find acceptance with Anglo-Catholics. Most of the 1928 Book had come into general use; but the one element which proved to be an exception was the alternative Canon. Opposition to it continued to be widespread; and while some people objected to it on theological and liturgical grounds, the dislike of others was instinctive rather than reasoned.[18] In January 1931 Dr A. Chandler, former Bishop of Bloemfontein, floated the idea of a three-point plan, involving (a) the ninefold Kyries as an alternative to the Decalogue, (b) the Prayer of Humble Access to follow the Comfortable Words, and (c) the Prayer of Oblation and the Lord's Prayer to follow the Prayer of Consecration. A little later he developed the idea further by proposing (d) the transference of the penitential material to immediately before the people's communion.[19] He suggested that if a sufficient number of clergy would undertake to be content with such a rite until an official revision of the Prayer Book, it might receive some kind of provisional approval from the Bishops: consequently proposals on these lines came to be known as the 'Interim Rite'. Although the idea received only limited support in Anglo-Catholic circles at the time,[20] nevertheless it kept reappearing. It cropped up again in *The Church Times* in 1934; while in the same year N. P. Williams, Regius Professor of Moral and Pastoral Theology and Canon of Christ Church, Oxford, made similar proposals as part of a larger projected *English Sacramentary*, containing a combination of 1662 and 1928 eucharistic material, and which had the knowledge and approval of Archbishop Lang and Bishop Strong of Oxford.[21] Then in 1940–1 Dr Kirk, Bishop of Oxford, wrote a series of articles in *The Oxford Diocesan Magazine*, suggesting an improved eucharistic Canon which lay within the 1662–1928 limits, namely (a) the 1662 Prayer of Consecration, (b) the 1928 Anamnesis, (c) the 1662 Prayer of Oblation, and (d) the Lord's Prayer. Admittedly such a prayer was not ideal, for it contained no explicit reference to the Holy Spirit; but at least it contained a specific prayer for the benefits of communion. The Bishops' Resolutions of 1929 had stated that any additions to or deviations from 1662 which fell within the limits of the 1928 proposals would not be regarded as disloyal to the principles of the Church of England; and Kirk felt that his proposals fell within these limits. Furthermore, with regard to the authority for such changes, he thought it wrong for a bishop to be asked to 'authorize' or 'sanction' a deviation from 1662; but he could be asked to say whether he regarded such a deviation as harmful, pending further order. Consequently, 'until some further order . . . be taken, it is (I believe) incumbent upon me to give at least some general indication of the types of case in which I should be moved to say "I think you are morally free to do this" or "I think you ought not to do that" respectively.'[22]

In January 1942 the whole issue came before the Convocations. Dr Parsons, Bishop of Hereford, and Dr Williams, Bishop of Carlisle, moved in the Upper Houses of Canterbury and York respectively, that Dr Kirk's proposals without the 1928 anamnesis should be authorized for permissive use with the goodwill of the parish concerned. As Dr Parsons pointed out, permission for such a variation would hopefully help to end irregularities and would have the authority of the episcopate of both provinces, rather than that of the individual bishop. Both Upper Houses agreed to the proposal: but when it was sent to the Lower Houses 'for information and counsel' before any formal resolutions were made, it was rebuffed. They regarded the moment as 'inopportune' for any consideration of the matter; and Canterbury also suggested that the views of the laity be ascertained. Dr Kirk expressed his disquiet in the Upper House of Canterbury: the reply would cause a great deal of distress to both clergy and laity throughout the country; and as for the time being 'inopportune', it did suggest either that the Lower House considered no disorders existed, or that they were not anxious that disorders should cease. He suggested that in view of the resolution passed by the Upper House by a considerable majority, any bishop who followed it and permitted the use of the Interim Rite pending further consideration, need not fear that his action would be called in question by the other members of that House. No bishop challenged him on this matter, and there the matter rested.[23] The impasse caused by the action of the Lower Houses was considered to have been due, partly to opposition by some Anglo-Catholics who were unwilling to be tied to this particular form of eucharistic Canon, and partly to a threat by some Evangelicals led by Lord Caldecote to initiate parliamentary or judicial action against the Convocations if the proposal were accepted.[24] N. P. Williams then wrote to Archbishop Temple, suggesting that the Bishops might consider a further revision of the Canon. Unlike Kirk's proposal, which was to supplement 1662 material with the 1928 anamnesis, he proposed to take the 1928 prayer as a basis, but to transfer the epiclesis to a position before the Institution Narrative and in its 1662 form, thereby bringing the prayer into line with Western views of consecration; and although the epiclesis would have been weaker in form, the prayer as a whole with its anamnesis would have been an improvement on that of the Interim Rite. He hoped that this might also be regarded as a legitimate interpretation of the Bishops' 1929 Regulations. The Archbishop acknowledged Williams' proposal and promised to take the matter up, but nothing further was heard of it.[25] This was a pity: for of all the suggestions made this might well have proved to be the most satisfactory.

There was, however, an interesting postscript. In 1945 in his *Shape of the Liturgy* Dix criticized the proposed Canon of the Interim Rite, arguing that to put the Prayer of Oblation before communion was a piece of Pelagianism, laying unfortunate emphasis on the substitution of the oblation of the sons of men for that of the Son of Man – a criticism which elicited from Dr Kirk the reply that those who used Cranmer's liturgy were not necessarily committed to his theology.[26] But Dix accompanied his criticism with a commendation of Dr Kirk's method of approach, which had pleaded, not for a formal authorization of a rite, but rather for freedom to experiment after guidance on the principles underlying the experiment: by such a method the Church could move towards a clear expression of its mind.[27] In fact the Church took its first step towards such a method shortly afterwards.

In the summer of 1939 the Archbishops had appointed a commission under Dr Garbett, Bishop of Winchester, to consider a revision of Canon Law – one of the recommendations of the Cecil Report. Despite the difficulties of the war years, it completed its work by May 1946 and published its Report in the following year. Two elements were particularly relevant to liturgical revision: a memorandum on 'Lawful Authority' by Mr Justice Vaisey and the proposed Canon XIII. The memorandum endorsed the misgivings already expressed about the *ius liturgicum*: a precise definition of 'lawful authority' was impossible. The phrase had appeared in the 'exceptive words' in the form of Declaration required of clergy at ordination or on admission to a benefice, appearing in the Clerical Subscription Act of 1865 and the revised Canon 36 of the same year.

> What was apparently recognized in 1865 . . . has been consistently overlooked since – that precise definition of 'lawful authority' is

> impossible. It is true in a sense to say that nobody can be sure what the words mean, either to himself or to anybody else, and that their effect has been to convert an obligation which was impossible to perform into one which is impossible to understand. This view, however, involves an assumption which is probably unwarranted that they were ever intended or can now be taken to have a particular as distinguished from a general significance.

Nevertheless, if it were thought advisable to mitigate the obscurity of the words, this could be done by attaching to them certain definite meanings.[28] The proposed Canon XIII then indicated how this was possible. Services could be regarded as having 'lawful authority' if they were prescribed by Royal Warrant or Proclamation, or by Acts of Parliament; or there could be lawful deviations from Prayer Book forms permitted or ordered by the Convocations; or there could be forms for special occasions sanctioned by the Ordinary.[29]

In the following year, however, the Bishops indulged in a well-meaning but insensitive act which highlighted again this vexed question of 'lawful authority'. They had commissioned a small group of their number under Dr Hunter, Bishop of Sheffield, some four years previously — only months after the rejection of the attempt to secure authorization of the Interim Rite — to prepare a *Shorter Prayer Book*. This was ready by 1947. In many ways it was a laudable piece of work, representing the kind of liturgical pattern which many people would have been happy to see authorized and containing a combination of those elements of 1662 and 1928 which were in general use. Contentious material such as an alternative to the 1662 Prayer of Consecration was avoided; and the only new material was confined to rubrics and the explanatory preface on the Christian year. The book itself was short, well set out and easy to follow. What caused concern, however, was the manner in which the Bishops had conducted the project. They kept the preparatory work highly confidential; they failed to consult either the Convocations or the Church Assembly; and they published the book with little warning, bearing a provocative title and preface. It appeared as *The Shorter Prayer Book: according to the use of the Church of England*, and claiming to have been 'commissioned' by the Archbishops and Bishops of the Provinces of Canterbury and York 'in response to a growing demand from the clergy and laity of the Church, and more recently from service chaplains'.[30] Unfortunately it also appeared at a time when copies of 1662 were in short supply; and critics were quick to assume that the Bishops and the Privileged Presses had connived at diverting precious supplies of paper away from 1662 to meet the needs of this new venture. On 27 May 1948 the Lower House of Canterbury Convocation submitted a Gravamen to the Upper House, requesting that the book be withdrawn from circulation and that the paper allocated to its production should be used for copies of 1662. Relations between the two Houses were not improved when the Bishops summarily rejected the first request, although they promised to look into the second.[31]

At the November session of the Church Assembly there was a strong attack on the book led by Dr Selwyn, Dean of Winchester, and based on a motion that the Central Board of Finance, who held the copyright of 1928, should terminate the permission given to the Privileged Presses to use passages from it in *The Shorter Prayer Book*. The pastoral value of the latter was in no way denied, although some doubt was cast on the claim that it met a 'growing demand from the clergy and laity': but the manner in which it had been prepared and published came under heavy criticism. A shortened Prayer Book was in effect a revision, and as such should have had constitutional approval; instead the proper liturgical rights and functions of the Convocations had been ignored. If this went unchallenged, who could tell what would happen next in this field? Furthermore, to use in the title the words 'according to the use of the Church of England' when the book contained material outside 1662 was improper. The book gave the impression of possessing an authority which it did not possess. In the course of the debate Dix described the Bishops' action in his own inimitable way: 'constitutional episcopacy' meant that a group of unknown people could put out a new book of worship without informing or forewarning the Church, and without its consent or knowledge. The Bishops were stung into a spirited reply from Dr Hunter (Sheffield), Dr Haigh (Winchester), and Dr Wand (London). The episcopate, singly and corporately, was fully behind the book; and despite what had recently been said about lawful authority and the proposed Canon XIII in the Report on Canon Law, they clearly believed that the *ius liturgicum* resided with them. Until a new Prayer Book with statutory authority appeared, the Bishops were the people to say what variations from 1662 might be used in their dioceses; and this was precisely what the book represented. Furthermore, since 1928 had already been approved by the Convocations, there was no need to refer to them again. They did admit, however, that phrases in the title-page and preface were misleading; but these could easily be put right. In summing up Archbishop Fisher clarified the situation on copyright. The Church Assembly did not and could not hold the copyright, as so many speakers had assumed. The owners were those actual bishops who had given the Deposited Book in 1928 its final form, and it was they who had transferred it to the Central Board of Finance: the latter therefore held it as the agents of or subject to the instructions of the Bishops and not the Assembly as a whole. Dr Selwyn's motion was defeated: but the voting was interesting, for apart from the Bishops, opinion was fairly evenly divided: Bishops Ayes 0 Noes 28; Clergy Ayes 99 Noes 84; Laity Ayes 62 Noes 86.[32]

From a strictly legal point of view the Bishops were entitled to produce and publish such a book. Indeed, anyone was free to do so, provided the necessary permissions were secured from the copyright holders of 1662 and 1928. But to have done so without any reference to the Convocations or the

Church Assembly, particularly in the light of the recent report on Canon Law, was curiously insensitive and even discourteous. Indeed Dr Fisher admitted as much when addressing the Convocation of Canterbury on 13 January 1949: the Bishops might have been wise to consult the other Houses, although he could not refrain from criticizing the tendency among some clergy to 'view with distrust and suspicion any corporate acts of the Bishops'.[33] In subsequent editions of the book the title-page was amended to read *The Shorter Prayer Book: being an abbreviated form of the Book of Common Prayer with some additional matter*, while the Preface was rewritten, omitting the reference that it had been 'commissioned' by the Archbishops and Bishops, and explaining what 'the additional matter' was. *The Shorter Prayer Book* did in fact prove to be extremely popular until the advent of Series 2 and Series 3 services, selling some tens of thousands of copies.

II

1949 marked the four-hundredth anniversary of the advent of the first Prayer Book and focused the interests of Church people — at least for the time being — on the liturgy and the possibilities of future revision. The first Sunday after Trinity was observed as a special day of thanksgiving, while on 18 May the Convocations of Canterbury and York attended services in Westminster Abbey and York Minster respectively to hear the Archbishops speak of reform in their addresses.

At Westminster Dr Fisher pointed out that the last hundred years had been a period of considerable confusion, during which presuppositions had been examined, inherited practices reconsidered, and the environment of men's thoughts and habits radically changed. But the moment was now opportune for the Church to re-establish its ordered direction of public worship in the light of that experience.

> If the period of confusion has run its course, the task of garnering its fruits lies ahead . . . The proportions of the task are becoming evident to us; the method of approach to it is becoming clear; and the first necessary steps in clearing the ground are already being taken. It will be no doubt a long and anxious process. But the movement towards it and the impulse which will carry it through begins rightly in the re-apprehension of our heritage in the Book of Common Prayer.[34]

At York Dr Garbett spoke on similar lines;[35] but earlier on the same day he had described in greater detail to the York Convocation the way in which he believed revision should be undertaken. What was needed was a procedure which would meet with the approval of both Church and State. Clearly the Church should be free to express its mind, and the Royal Supremacy should be recognized as having the right of veto over any proposals; equally clearly Parliament was no place to debate changes in public worship. These conditions could be met in two ways: first, by the creation of the machinery already outlined in the Cecil Report; and secondly, by the adoption of the proposed Canon XIII.[36]

Both Archbishops evidently envisaged a conservative revision, resulting in a modified form of 1662. Indeed *The Shorter Prayer Book* could be regarded as having established guide-lines. Dr Garbett had already indicated in his *Claims of the Church of England* the need for enrichment and greater simplicity, especially in the occasional offices;[37] and soon afterwards in *Church and State in England* he specifically referred to the authorization of those parts of 1928 which had already been widely and acceptably used for many years.

> In all probability Churchmen with the exception of small groups of irreconcilables, would reach sufficient agreement on a large number of the changes in the 1928 Book so as to obtain the Royal Assent very quickly; other more controversial matters, such as the Order of Communion, would require delay until agreement is reached; stage by stage, and not all at once, the legislation for the desired changes and additions would be carried through.[38]

Revision would therefore be a fairly lengthy process and would require the help and guidance of a permanent Liturgical Commission.[39]

It is interesting to note, however, that the old idea of linking liturgical revision with discipline – condemned in the case of 1928 – also reappeared. It was implicit in Dr Fisher's plea for the Church to 're-establish its ordered direction of public worship'. But Dr Garbett was more explicit: 'At a time when the duty of order and obedience should be taught by the Church, it is open to the charge that its bishops and clergy are themselves breaking the law. There is really desperate anxiety on the part of Church people to be free from this reproach.'[40] At approximately the same time Harold Riley, General Secretary of the Church Union and a leading Anglo Catholic spokesman, made the same kind of comment:

> The revision of the Book of Common Prayer is one of the most urgent needs of the Church of England today. It is notorious that public worship in the Church of England is in a state of grave confusion . . . There is a general breakdown of discipline, and a consequent contempt for the authority of the Church of England.

Riley also desired a return to some degree of uniformity: 'To allow a multitude of alternatives as was proposed in the Deposited Book, is to perpetuate confusion . . . It is surely better to reform the Prayer Book slowly, by agreed alterations binding on all, than to train Church people in two separate traditions.'[41] But whatever form revision might take, Dr Garbett argued that the time was ripe for action.

> Practical action should no longer be delayed. Forty years have passed since the Royal Commission on Ecclesiastical Discipline reported; twenty

years since the Prayer Book was rejected; fourteen since the Commission on Church and State reported, and nothing yet has been done to set right a position regarded by thoughtful Churchmen as profoundly unsatisfactory.[42]

But the next step forward was already in the offing. In February 1949 the Archbishops had appointed yet another Commission to examine Church–State relations, and this body, led by Sir Walter Moberly,[43] and including Dr Mortimer, Bishop of Exeter, Dr Chase, Bishop of Ripon, Professor Norman Sykes, Lord Selborne, and Mr Justice Vaisey, produced a unanimous Report in 1952. It dealt with three matters: the control of Church Courts, the appointment of bishops, and the control of worship. In dealing with the third of these, it reviewed once again the rejection of the Prayer Book Measures of 1927–8. That Parliament had acted within its legal rights was accepted; but it was the propriety of Parliament's action which was questioned – as Archbishop Davidson had commented, 'Parliament had departed lamentably from the reasonable spirit in which alone a harmonious relation was possible'. The Commission also accepted that the Church had passed the 1927–8 proposals with large majorities in the Convocations and Church Assembly: but this had been only in the teeth of 'vehement opposition' from minorities representing both extreme wings of church opinion. Furthermore, it was doubtful whether these majorities were truly representative of church feeling. 'There is an undercurrent of feeling that, though the voting in elections to Church bodies may fairly reflect the views of a majority among articulate Churchmen, these themselves are only a minority of the whole body and the balance would be different if the inarticulate were taken into account.'[44] The Commission therefore claimed that it was arguable, however paradoxically, that the House of Commons represented the mind of the inarticulate mass of laymen more closely than did the House of Laity. It was therefore still possible to agree with Archbishop Davidson, who had refused to believe that the House of Commons had arrogantly claimed to take in hand the absolute control of the belief and worship of the Church of England. 'In our view it is possible and reasonable to interpret the action of Parliament as having had the legitimate purpose of delaying change until the mind of the Church was unmistakable, and not the illegitimate purpose of permanently overruling that mind upon a spiritual issue.'[45] Nevertheless, as the 1935 Commission had pointed out, the present position was unsatisfactory. In strict law there was the 'almost unmitigated rigidity' of 1662: in practice there was a 'large measure of disorder', only tempered by the recommendation that the bishops would not interfere with clergy whose deviations from the Book of Common Prayer were within the 1928 limits. But this solved no problem. 'From the angle of the State it looks like contumacy; from the angle of the Church it looks like a weak and faintly discreditable compromise.'[46]

What then were the possible solutions? The Commission ruled out both disestablishment and assimilation to the Scottish system. It also disapproved of the 1935 proposal to authorize a special procedure for 'Spiritual' Measures: in any case the Round Table Conference — a necessary preliminary to such a proposal — had ended in failure.[47] What was needed was a process of experiment with new forms of service before authorization was sought, enabling the Church to achieve a common mind. The method proposed, therefore, was the use of the 1946 Canon XIII, but redrafted to include experimental services, which would require approval by the Convocations, with the agreement of the House of Laity. Such services should be sanctioned for optional and experimental use for a period of seven or ten years, with the option of renewal for further periods; while every sanction would require a two-thirds majority in each House. By this means of trial and error it was hoped that a generally acceptable revision of the various services in the Prayer Book might gradually be secured: these would then be presented to Parliament by a Church Assembly Measure for statutory authorization. This proposal was modest in that it included no attempt to abolish or curtail Parliament's final right of legal control. But the hope was that when a Measure for liturgical revision was put forward in such terms, its claim to represent authentically the mind of the Church would be convincing. Furthermore, since the proposed Canon XIII would itself also need authorization by a Church Assembly Measure, there would in fact be a double parliamentary control. Indeed the Commission hoped that the resultant process of liturgical experiment would ensure so large a degree of acceptance that the passing of any final revision Measure would create no problem.[48] The Church Assembly finally endorsed these important proposals after a long debate occupying nearly four days in June and November 1952.[49]

It was now clearly recognized that any attempt to repeat the 1927–8 procedure would be both undesirable and unsuccessful. What was needed was an arrangement by which liturgical revision could be a continuing process over a period of years, relying not simply on parliamentary authority but also on the general consent of the Church after lengthy experiment had enabled it to make up its mind. The next significant step took place in October 1954, when the Convocations of Canterbury and York agreed with virtually no debate to the appointment of a standing Liturgical Commission. The only note of caution came from the Dean of York, Dr Milner-White. This was rather surprising, for in 1943 he had urged the appointment of such a body. But now he regarded it as a 'counsel of despair' and he pleaded with Convocation not to abrogate its constitutional responsibilities in favour of a Congregation of Rites. One can only suspect that since he had enjoyed a leading role in liturgical matters in the Northern Convocation, particularly over the creation of the York Rite of Infant Baptism, he was now reluctant to accept the necessity of a Commission. His plea found little support, however. Dr Fisher made it clear that any such Commission would come under strict archiepiscopal control, being appointed by the Archbishops, given its tasks by them, and reporting back to them.[50] Admittedly such control could safeguard a commission from being overwhelmed by widespread and perhaps frivolous demands; but it could also have its dangers. A former body, the 1911 Advisory Committee on Liturgical Questions, had in fact come to a speedy and untimely end simply because undue restriction had been placed on its activities.

Despite the ease with which the proposal was passed, the Archbishops were in no apparent hurry to implement it; although it must be remembered that Dr Garbett was ill for the greater part of 1955 and died at the end of the year. It was not until 11 October that the appointment of a Commission of twenty-four members under the chairmanship of the Rt Revd Colin Dunlop, Dean of Lincoln, was announced.[51]

NOTES

1. *Church Assembly Proceedings*, 1928, pp. 114–19.
2. The 1928 Book remained 'unofficial' in the sense that the Archbishop never went to the stage of having it made an Act of Convocation, nor did it receive the synodical concurrence of Convocation.
3. Temple thought this delay wise; cf. Jasper, *Frere*, p. 184.
4. *Chronicle Convoc.*, 1929, pp. 14–42, 55–78, 139–57; *Journal Convoc.*, 1929, pp. 13–14, 41–57, 72–3.
5. *CA Proceedings*, 1930, pp. 60–108. The voting was: Bishops 33–1; Clergy 198–38; Laity 151–66.
6. J. G. Lockhart, *Cosmo Gordon Lang*, 1949, p. 339.
7. A. M. Ramsey, *From Gore to Temple*, 1960, pp. 154–5.
8. W. K. Lowther Clarke and C. Harris, ed., *Liturgy and Worship*, 1932, p. 4.
9. Dix, *The Shape of the Liturgy*, pp. 588, 709–10.
10. ibid.
11. *Report of the Archbishops' Commission on Church and State*, 2 vols., 1935, vol. 1, p. 57.
12. ibid., pp. 62–4, 99–100.
13. ibid., pp. 87–8, 101–2.
14. *Chronicle Convoc.*, 1938, pp. 10–24, 26–42, 85–108, 142–80, 182–208; *Journal Convoc.*, 1938, pp. 6, 23–5, 32–5, App. xvi–xxxv.
15. Dix, *The Shape*, p. 913.
16. Jasper, *George Bell*, pp. 188–9.
17. C. F. Garbett, *The Claims of the Church of England*, 1947, p. 195.
18. Note for example, Dix, *The Shape*, pp. 710–11; W. K. Lowther Clarke, *The Prayer Book of 1928 Reconsidered*, 1943, pp. 30–49, 76–87.
19. These proposals appeared in *The Church Times*, January 2, April 10, 17, 1931.
20. Cross, *Darwell Stone*, pp. 217–18.
21. E. W. Kemp, *N. P. Williams*, 1954, pp. 60–3.
22. These articles appeared in *The Oxford Diocesan Magazine* as 'The Holy Communion' in October, November 1940, January, February, March 1941. They reappeared in K. E. Kirk, *Beauty and Bands*, 1955, pp. 55–93.
23. *Chronicle Convoc.*, 1942, pp. 7–37, 188–9, 192–244; *Journal Convoc.*, 1942, pp. 6–7, 23–39; Kirk, *Beauty and Bands*, pp. 91–2.
24. Kemp, *N. P. Williams*, p. 63.

25. ibid., pp. 63–4.
26. Dix, *The Shape*, pp. 666, 731; Kirk, *Beauty and Bands*, pp. 94–100.
27. Dix, *The Shape*, pp. 720–32.
28. Report, *The Canon Law of the Church of England*, 1947, pp. 221–2.
29. ibid., pp. 112–13.
30. *The Shorter Prayer Book*, 1st edn 1947, p. iii.
31. *Chronicle Convoc.*, May 1948, pp. 264–5, 319.
32. *CA Proceedings*, 1948, vol. xxviii, no. 3, pp. 449–74.
33. *Chronicle Convoc.*, January 1949, pp. 2–6.
34. ibid., May 1949, App. pp. 3–7.
35. *Journal Convoc.*, May 1949, pp. 64–9.
36. He had already expounded his policy in *The Claims of the Church of England* (1947), and did so again in *Church and State in England* (1950). *Journal Convoc.*, May 1949, pp. 34–7; cf. *The Claims* pp. 57–8, 69–70; *Church and State*, pp. 219–26.
37. *The Claims*, pp. 69–70.
38. *Church and State*, p. 222.
39. *The Claims*, p. 63. Such a Commission had been advocated elsewhere: e.g. E. Milner-White in *Theology* XLVI (Oct. 1943), p. 221; Oscar Hardmann in *Theology* LI (Jan. 1948), pp. 20–1.
40. *Church and State*, p. 220.
41. H. Riley, *The Revision of the Psalter*, 1948, pp. 9, 11–12.
42. *Church and State*, p. 226.
43. Sir Walter Moberly, son of Canon W. C. Moberly, Christ Church Oxford, and former Vice-Chancellor of Manchester University.
44. Report CA 1023, *Church and State*, 1952, pp. 21–2.
45. ibid., pp. 23–4.
46. ibid., p. 25.
47. ibid., pp. 25–9.
48. ibid., pp. 30–2.
49. *CA Proceedings*, 1952, pp. 75–115, 166–70, 268–98, 300–7.
50. *Chronicle Convoc.*, 1954, pp. 247–51, 267–72; *Journal Convoc.*, 1954, pp. 105–11.
51. *Chronicle Convoc.*, 1955, p. 177.

7

THE MIDDLE DECADES: PRESSURES FOR CHANGE

I

In 1947 Dr Garbett described the demand for enrichment and change in the worship of the Church as 'irresistible'.[1] It was a strong word to use, but not perhaps surprising from someone who had been a diocesan bishop since 1919 and had been involved in the rejection of the Deposited Book and the activities which had followed in its wake. These activities had been largely central and constitutional, involving the Convocations and the Church Assembly: but they must also be seen in the light of pressures for change which were widespread. To at least some of these pressures consideration must now be given.

First of all there were the developments in biblical theology. Liberalism was in decay; and the 1914–18 conflict had already indicated the inadequacy of the Liberal creed to satisfy man's spiritual needs. One notable figure heralding a new approach was Sir Edwyn Hoskyns, who between 1926 and 1931 published three important pieces of work: an essay on 'The Christ in the Synoptic Gospels' in *Essays Catholic and Critical* (1926), another essay on 'Jesus the Messiah' in *Mysterium Christi* (1930), and the book *The Riddle of the New Testament* (1931) written in collaboration with Noel Davey. Of the three the first has been described as 'the most brilliant and cogent';[2] while its opening sentence stating that the two questions, 'What think ye of the Church' and 'What think ye of the Christ' were but the same question differently formulated was later said to be the most influential sentence in Anglican theology written for thirty years.[3] But it must not be forgotten that Hoskyns was also responsible for translating into English Karl Barth's famous commentary on *The Epistle to the Romans*, which appeared in 1932 and challenged theologians to look again at what the Bible had to say about God and his dealings with humanity. Hoskyns himself also stressed that the Bible should be understood as a record of revelation, speaking of God's mighty acts in history and of his unique intervention in Jesus Christ for the salvation of mankind. It was a theme taken up and developed by other theologians: C. H. Dodd in *The Apostolic Preaching and its Developments* (1936), Newton Flew in *Jesus and his Church* (1938), and Gabriel Hebert in *The Throne of David* (1941) to name but three. But Hoskyns and his fellow biblical theologians not only brought men to a new perception of Jesus Christ; they also brought men to a worthier conception of the Church and its central place in Christian faith and practice as the mystical Body of Christ. The Church had a necessary part to play in God's purpose for saving man; it was at one and the same time the saved and the saving community. Inevitably this involved consideration of the sacraments: and here again Hoskyns had something significant to say in a paper delivered to the Anglo-Catholic Congress in 1927, drawing out the connection between the gospel, the Church and the sacraments, all seen as manifestations of the revelatory and redemptive activity of God.

Such ideas were taken up by other writers, notably A. M. Ramsey in *The Gospel and the Catholic Church* (1936) and Lionel Thornton in *The Common Life in the Body of Christ* (1941). Both books — the former in much simpler language — worked out not only the implications of incorporation into the Body of Christ through baptism but also the activity of the Body of Christ in its liturgical, evangelical and corporate aspects. 'In the beginning the Church entered a baptismal life corresponding to her confession of faith. The essence of this life consists in eucharistic worship, prayer and fraternal love, grounded upon, sustained by, and manifesting, union of the divine-human priest-victim in his eternal sacrifice and in his regnant glory.'[4] Both Ramsey and Thornton also emphasized the expansion of the concept of sacrifice, pointing out that Christ's sacrifice included all his saving work from incarnation to ascension, although within this total action the cross was given a special place. His work was unrepeatable: but it was not enough to leave the matter there; his sacrifice 'for us' was to become this sacrifice 'in us'. Here lay the significance of the Eucharist. But it also had the further significance of being an eschatological sign; and this took on added importance in face of the crisis involved in the Church's situation in the world.[5]

Ramsey and Thornton wrote from the Catholic point of view. An equally important but in some ways a rather unusual book from the Evangelical side was F. W. Dillistone's *The Structure of the Divine Society* in 1951. He discerned different types of Christian community in the course of the history of the Church; and among these, two were vital and dynamic, each bearing a vital principle for the ongoing life of the Church. The first was what he called the organic type, which was essentially Catholic: it stressed the common life of Christ in the Body of Christ: just as men were born into a natural family and from their relationships in this received personal work and identity, so it was with man's life in the Christian family. The second he called the covenantal type, which was essentially Protestant: it stressed the relationships into which men entered voluntarily through their personal commitments to God and to their neighbour. Nevertheless, these concepts were not opposed to one another; rather they were complementary, and both had a place in the Church. Indeed their complementarity was aptly expressed in Dillistone's phrase 'heirs of the Covenant in one Body'.

Equally valuable were new studies on the sacraments and in particular on the Eucharist. In 1927 O. C. Quick produced *The Christian Sacraments*, perhaps the most comprehensive work on sacramental theology from an Anglican pen in this period. Aware of the differences over the Eucharist which had been highlighted by the debates on the proposed Prayer Book, he tried to establish the positive principles in the different interpretations as a contribution towards reconciliation. It was a work which had a wide circulation, requiring an annual reprint regularly for some years. Then in 1930 came *The Fullness of Sacrifice* by F. C. N. Hicks, a genuine though perhaps over-optimistic attempt to resolve the differences between Catholics and Evangelicals over the doctrine of eucharistic sacrifice, arguing that if the term 'sacrifice' were used in its New Testament meaning, the grounds of difference would largely disappear. This too had considerable influence, earning from William Temple the title 'an *eirenikon* of abiding power';[6] in the next thirty years it went through many editions and reprints and figured prominently in the discussions on the sacraments at the 1937 World Conference of Faith and Order at Edinburgh; a précis of its argument was also included in the Conference's official *Report* and in Faith and Order's later publications on *Intercommunion* and *Ways of Worship.*[7] 1930 also saw the publication of the symposium *The Evangelical Doctrine of Holy Communion*, edited by A. J. Macdonald, with a particularly valuable essay on 'Anglican Theology today' by Canon Vernon Storr, one of the most able of the Liberal Evangelical theologians. He recognized that Evangelicals had not given the Eucharist its due place in the life of the Church; but he believed eucharistic theology to be in a state of transition, with Evangelicals seeking to discover a fresh theology which would express itself in an enriched sacramental worship.[8]

As the Church moved towards the middle of the twentieth century, a new and more flexible approach to theological problems seemed to be developing among the different schools of thought; and nowhere was this approach more evident than in the work of the Archbishops' Commission on Doctrine, appointed in 1922 'with a view to investigate how it is possible to remove or diminish existing differences'.[9] The Commission, an impressive group including Temple, Quick, Rawlinson, Selwyn, Storr and Thornton, had no mandate to define the doctrine of the Church of England: but they effectively summed up the most significant trends in theology, and particularly eucharistic theology, in the Report *Doctrine in the Church of England* published in 1938. While criticized for devoting too much time to the sacraments, it was that particular section of the Report which was in fact the most valuable, reflecting as it did a contemporary concern within the Church. Its treatment of differing views on sacrifice, communion and the presence of Christ in the Eucharist was remarkably eirenic: and Quick pointed out in *Theology* immediately after its publication that the Commission had hoped and intended to show that the differences on sacramental doctrine within the Church of England were 'really much less fundamental and much more readily reconcilable than most keen church people suppose'. He then gave an example of the kind of restatement of eucharistic doctrine the Report had indicated and which he believed would be acceptable to both Catholics and Evangelicals.[10]

In the post-war years the output of theological studies on the Church and the sacraments continued. J. E. L. Oulton's *Holy Communion and Holy Spirit* in 1951 was a valuable contribution to the understanding of the Eucharist from a Liberal Evangelical point of view, its main thesis being that the Eucharist could not be isolated from life within the Spirit-filled body. But perhaps the most notable contribution was Eric Mascall's *Corpus Christi* in 1953. His great service was to introduce readers to the work of Roman Catholic scholars such as de la Taille, Vonier, Masure and Journet on the eucharistic sacrifice, pointing out that they were at pains to reject any idea of the Eucharist as being a repetition of the sacrifice of Christ or even as a supplement to it: their concern was to show it as perpetuating in the life of the Church the one sacrificial act of Christ in all its efficacy, and Mascall believed that Protestant scholars were saying the same kind of thing.[11] In the light of this comment, it is worth noting that the Edinburgh Faith and Order Conference of 1937 had reached a similar conclusion.

> If sacrifice is understood as it was by our Lord and his followers and in the early Church, it includes, not his death only, but the obedience of his earthly ministry, and his risen and ascended life . . . Such a sacrifice can never be repeated, but is proclaimed and set forth in the eucharistic action of the whole Church when we come to God in Christ at the Eucharist or Lord's Supper. For us the secret of joining in that sacrifice is both a *verbum visibile* of the divine grace, and the supreme thanksgiving (*eucharistia*) of the people of God. We are throughout in the realm of the Spirit.[12]

In fact discussions on the Church and the sacraments played a growing part in the work of the Faith and Order Movement. Edinburgh 1937 had made it clear that many, if not most, of the issues on which Christians were divided had their roots in the different conceptions of the nature of the Church: further discussion on the question was therefore imperative. But because worship was a primary function of the Church, a study of the ways of worship characteristic of the various Churches was also considered to be a profitable undertaking. This led some members of the Continuation Committee to press for a discussion of the theological principles underlying what William Temple had called in his Conference sermon 'the greatest of all scandals in the face of the world', the maintenance of barriers against completeness of union at the Lord's table.[13] Consequently in 1938–9 three international theological commissions had been appointed, to study (a) the Church, (b) Ways of Worship and (c) Intercommunion.

The documents of these three commissions were published in time for consideration at the third World Conference in Lund in 1952. The first of these contained an essay by Professor Leonard Hodgson on the Anglican doctrine of the Church, and this included a section on eucharistic sacrifice as illustrative of the dialectic existing within Anglicanism. Both Catholics and Evangelicals had their contributions to make: but it was futile to attempt to arrive at a so-called 'Anglican doctrine' by paring away what was distinctive of each and concentrating on what was common to both. Rather both should try to use genuinely scholarly methods in their search for guidance from Scripture, employing the best insights of contemporary as well as patristic and Reformation exegesis.[14] It was in accordance with such principles that Gabriel Hebert claimed to be working in a further essay on eucharistic sacrifice in the symposium on *Intercommunion.* Writing as an Anglo-Catholic he expounded a view which he believed to be scriptural, in line with the early liturgies, and at the same time fully Evangelical because it was a re-expression in liturgical terms of the truth of Justification by Faith. The key-word was 'participation': and in the Eucharist the local church met together to present its corporate life to God and unite it with the one sacrifice of the Lamb of God – to offer and be offered in union with the whole mystical Body of Christ.[15]

A constructive contribution from the Evangelical side came soon afterwards from W. F. M. Scott in his essay 'The Eucharist and the heavenly ministry of our Lord', in *Theology* (February 1953). He took issue with the view that the heavenly ministry of Christ consisted of a continual pleading and offering of his sacrifice in heaven; and he quoted Bishop Westcott to support his claim that there was no such teaching in the Epistle to the Hebrews. Nevertheless Christ did offer *something* in his heavenly ministry: he 'brought' or 'offered' mankind to God (Col. 1.22; 1 Pet. 3.18), and he gave himself to mankind in Holy Communion. Christ's relationship with God was a continuous and simultaneous process of giving and receiving, and it was Christ's offering which made ours acceptable, not we who joined with him in praying that his might be acceptable.[16] A similar line was taken in 1956 by C. F. D. Moule in *The Sacrifice of Christ.* The fact that the work of Christ was final and complete did not mean that it was static or discontinuous; and within this concept of continuation room had to be found for a movement from man to God. The Eucharist was a focal point of obedience, not only of Christ's but of ours; and ours was derived from and dependent upon Christ's. Nevertheless ours was not to be identified with his, rather it was in fellowship with his. The Eucharist was therefore an entering into what Christ had already done.[17]

There was also a further fascinating and unusual Evangelical study from F. W. Dillistone in his *Christianity and Symbolism* (1955). Having examined the place of symbols in human life and thought, he saw the fundamental symbolism of the Eucharist as that of sacrifice; and from a study of the influence of the different cultural traditions – Greek, Roman, Hebrew – in which the theology of the Eucharist had developed, he argued that there had been a wide range of meaning in the idea of sacrifice; a flexibility of approach was therefore necessary.

> It is surely one of the great tragedies of Christian history that the institution of sacrifice and sacrament of the eucharist have been so often

interpreted in narrow and limited ways . . . There is more than one sacrificial context; there is more than one way of making a memorial. Inflexible liturgies and unchanging ceremonial-patterns are not worthy settings for the Lord's own symbolic acts; inflexible dogmatic formulations and unchanging verbal definitions are not edifying interpretations of the Lord's own symbolic words. It is idle at this stage of the world's history to seek after uniformity. But the tradition which will set itself to understand the symbolic structure of another tradition and in particular to appreciate its own interpretation of the eucharistic drama will both enrich its own inner life and at the same time more adequately manifest to the world the true nature of the Divine Sacrifice.[18]

This interest shewn in eucharistic theology was matched by a similar interest in the problems of Initiation. Here the discrepancy between the ideals of the Body of Christ and the actual situation in the Church was sad to contemplate. In 1937 the Social and Industrial Commission of the Church Assembly produced a report on Church and Youth (CA 553), containing some comments on baptism by a group of young people. They pointed out that the Prayer Book service of Infant Baptism assumed that parents and sponsors were themselves baptized and practising Christians; but this was frequently not the case. The Church was therefore faced with a choice: either it must alter its service to suit the laxer conditions, or it must insist on a more rigid discipline. They then made a number of suggestions including the provision of a shorter and simpler service. In response the Convocation of Canterbury appointed a joint committee of both houses under Dr Woodward, Bishop of Bristol, to prepare a report on Baptism (Report 626), which was ready by the end of 1938.[19] This supported the principle of infant baptism but deplored the indiscriminate and haphazard way in which it was administered: the choice of sponsors left much to be desired, and the association of the baptized infant with the Church frequently ended with the service itself. The committee therefore recommended a reform in discipline and a shorter and simpler alternative rite.[20] Both Houses endorsed the Report and the Lower House also recommended that the joint committee should extend its work to include confirmation.[21] The Convocation of York followed suit with a similar joint committee in May 1942.[22]

The two joint committees worked closely together, producing their first interim report *Confirmation Today* in 1944. This was concerned primarily with the pastoral aspects of the subject; but the brief theological introduction on 'Confirmation in History and Doctrine' sparked off a lively discussion throughout the Church. A series of articles, for example, appeared in successive issues of *Theology* in 1945–6; but the most important contribution came from Dom Gregory Dix in a lecture delivered at Oxford in January 1946 and subsequently published under the title *The Theology of Confirmation in relation to Baptism.* He, like many others, saw the root of the problem in the separation of baptism from confirmation and both from first communion; and indiscriminate baptism of all infants made nonsense of the doctrine of the Church.

> The existence of this vast amorphous mass of Pelagian goodwill, at least three or four times as large as the living Body of the Church which seeks to live by grace, is what muffles the whole impact of the Gospel and the whole witness of the Church of England today. Deal with this problem, incorporate these people effectively into the life of the Church (or at least prevent their increase), and you may have some prospect of making an impression on the equally large mass of sheer paganism behind.[23]

Where Dix came into conflict with other scholars was over the question of the gift of the Holy Spirit. He set out afresh the view expounded by F. W. Puller and Canon A. J. Mason at the end of the nineteenth century, that baptism conveyed rebirth and forgiveness of sins by the agency of the Holy Spirit; but initiation was incomplete until baptism had been perfected by confirmation, when the indwelling Spirit was bestowed. Consequently, baptism was a mere preliminary stage in the course of initiation; the baptized person was not a complete member of the Church until after confirmation.[24] It was a view strongly supported by Lionel Thornton a little later in *Confirmation, its Place in the Baptismal Liturgy* (1953).

Other scholars expressed a different view. Quick, for example, had argued in *The Christian Sacraments* in 1927 that theory and practice should go together: 'A theory which declares that confirmation marks the first gift of the indwelling Spirit, and a practice which places confirmation a dozen years or so after baptism, point, when taken together, to conclusions which are intolerable.' What was needed was a union in time of the two rites. Quick believed that Baptism conferred the gift of the indwelling Spirit: if, therefore, baptism and confirmation were to remain separated in time, 'confirmation cannot be called a primary necessity of the Christian's sacramental life . . . ; it confers nothing in kind or in essential principle from what baptism has already given.'[25] In 1951 Professor G. W. H. Lampe developed this line of argument more fully in *The Seal of the Spirit*. The fulness of Christian initiation, including the gift of the Holy Spirit, was conveyed in baptism; confirmation was a rite of apostolic institution only; and though it might convey certain gifts of grace associated with the Holy Spirit, it was not an essential of Christian initiation.

Inevitably, what might be regarded as a kind of mediating position tended to appear in more official documents. The Report of the Archbishops' Commission on Doctrine in 1938 indicated this.

> The precise relation between the gift bestowed in baptism and the gift bestowed in confirmation cannot be defined . . . A clear-cut answer is impossible, since originally the two were closely conjoined. All theologians agree that in confirmation the Holy Spirit is given to strengthen the Christian. Some Anglicans have pressed the language in Acts 8.16–17

and 19.6 to mean that in the laying-on of hands the Holy Spirit is bestowed for the first time; whereas in baptism He acts, as it were, ab extra. Such spatial symbolism is precarious. The Holy Spirit is active throughout the Body of Christ and therefore in each of its members, and it is by baptism that we are made members of Christ.[26]

In October 1946 both Convocations agreed that the theological issues needed further consideration. Accordingly the Archbishops appointed a Theological Commission under Dr Parsons, Bishop of Hereford, and including Dix, Ramsey and Moule 'to advise on the relations between baptism, confirmation and holy communion'. The need for a document to be ready in time for the 1948 Lambeth Conference resulted in a relatively brief Report, *The Theology of Christian Initiation,* stating conclusions, but giving little of the evidence on which those conclusions were based: but the conclusions did indicate a significant consensus of opinion. The Commission did recognize Quick's point: theory and practice must go together. In the early Church initiation involved baptism, confirmation and first communion. In the West, however, the subsequent separation of baptism from confirmation had led to a change in doctrinal emphasis, ascribing to baptism complete initiation and the gift of the Holy Spirit, while regarding confirmation as an independent sacrament of strengthening. The Church of England had followed this change; but the Commission was clear that confirmation was more than a sacrament of strengthening; it was initiatory.[27] The Church should therefore bring together again into a single rite the baptism and confirmation of adults. This did not mean, however, that the baptism of infants was to be rejected: indeed, the baptism of children of committed Christians was quite justifiable; only indiscriminate infant baptism was to be deplored. From all this the Commission pointed out that within the threefold rite of initiation involving baptism, confirmation and first communion, the word 'confirm' could bear a wide meaning. The candidate was *confirmed*: having been baptized and having made his own declaration of faith, he received the laying-on of hands as a sign and seal of God's acceptance of him and of the gift of the Holy Spirit. Secondly, the candidate's vows were *confirmed.* Thirdly the baptism was *confirmed*, in the ancient sense of confirmation as the completion of initiation.[28] This view was endorsed by the 1948 Lambeth Conference; and its committee on baptism and confirmation commented; 'We think that the sacramental rites of Initiation were fashioned on the pattern of our Lord's baptism, in which as He came out of the water the Spirit descended upon Him'; consequently, 'the dissociation of the Holy Spirit's operation from any part of the Initiation is strongly to be deprecated, as is also the attempt to measure His operation quantatively.' The committee did recognize, however, that the theology of infant baptism had lagged far behind its practice and urged that some study of this should precede any further attempts at revising the rite.[29]

This plea came too late for the Convocations, for they had already agreed in October 1943 to set up further joint committees to prepare a simpler and more intelligible rite of Infant Baptism.[30] In the event the difficulties of the war situation, and particularly the presence of flying bombs, had prevented the Canterbury committee from functioning; and the project was confined to York. When its first draft appeared in July 1945, Dr Hunter, Bishop of Sheffield, confessed that the rite was rather different from what had originally been envisaged.

> When the committee came to grips with its task, it came to the conclusion that it would not do to have an order for this primary sacrament so simple as to be defective in theology, so stark as to be wanting in mystery, so short as to be lacking in dignity . . . Without claiming any perfection for the service which follows, we would point out that it is a little shorter than the 1928 service, that as far as may be it avoids difficult words and phrases, that by comparison both with 1662 and 1928 it has a 'psychological simplicity', and that it gives the congregation more to do.[31]

The draft now went through a wearisome period of revision lasting nearly six years, and not without some moments of tension. In October 1946, for example, the Lower House decided that 'this Committee shall not proceed further until the theology of baptism and confirmation has been studied and clarified', a decision clearly influenced by Dix's pamphlet published a few months earlier.[32] Dr Garbett clearly was not pleased, and at his instigation the Upper House agreed in May 1947 to ignore the clergy reservations and push ahead.[33] It was not until June 1951, however, that the rite reached its final form (Report 503), being approved by both Houses in September of the same year, when the Archbishop was asked to take the necessary steps to secure its experimental use.[34] Another year was to elapse before he gave a rather hesitant and not particularly enthusiastic reply. In October 1952 he gave, not a ruling, but 'his personal opinion', that the Bishops in the Northern Province should feel free to allow some of their clergy, who so wished, to use the revised service, but only for a limited period, after which they should report back; further use should then be considered after the Canon on Lawful Authority had been passed, and after Canterbury had made its own decisions.[35] The service therefore received a rather vague and temporary authorization. There was really little to show for all the long years of effort lavished upon it. It was little more than a modest revision of 1928, the major change being the transfer of the duties of the godparents from the end to a place between the Gospel and the Promises. Undeniably it had some good points: the exposition of the duties of parents and godparents, the prayer following the act of baptism, and the thanksgiving at the end. But equally it had weaknesses: the failure to restore the credal interrogations into close association with the act of baptism, and the preponderance of hortatory material. Its life was relatively short-lived; and a particularly devastating critique by Professor E. C. Ratcliff in *Theology* in 1960, amply laced with his inimitable caustic wit, did nothing to help it survive.[36]

Meanwhile the Joint Committees of both Convocations dealing with baptism and confirmation published their second interim report *Baptism Today* in 1949. This reviewed the diocesan discussions and then drew attention to some of the practical issues: the differing views on the delay or refusal of infant baptism; the problem of suitable godparents; whether godparents should make the promises for themselves, or on behalf of the infants, or both; the creation of a catechumenate; and the need for a revised rite of adult baptism. Their final report *Baptism and Confirmation today* eventually appeared in 1954. Much of it was concerned with pastoral considerations; but there was a useful section on the theology of initiation. This deprecated any tendency to distinguish between 'water baptism' and 'Spirit baptism' and stated quite clearly: 'We consider that our baptismal services can claim justification in the New Testament for the doctrine that the Spirit is bestowed in baptism.' It also accepted that Initiation involved baptism, confirmation and Holy Communion, and the process was incomplete at any stage short of the communicant life. Nevertheless, current Anglican practice, in which confirmation was normally separated from baptism by a period of years, had sufficient historical and theological justification to warrant its continuance. Attention was also drawn to the relation of baptism to our Lord's baptism: 'By re-enacting our Lord's baptism in the River Jordan, which foreshadowed and anticipated his death and resurrection, the sacrament proclaimed the Gospel of salvation; and by applying that baptism to the believer, it brought home the benefits of Christ's universal Redemption to the individual.'[37] The practical recommendations for improving the preparation for and administration of initiation involved no radical changes from what any well-conducted parish was already trying to undertake. The Report also included the York Order for Infant Baptism with a few small amendments and an Order for Adult Baptism and Confirmation, which was largely a conflation of the two 1928 Orders.

At the last minute, however, three Canterbury members – Dr Trevor Jalland, Canon O'Gorman Power, and the Reverend J. D. C. Fisher – produced a Minority Report expressing disagreement on two issues. They were dissatisfied with the discipline of Infant Baptism, suggesting that in certain cases baptism should not merely be delayed but refused; parents should then be offered admission to a catechumenate as an alternative.[38] They also preferred a theological position closer to the Mason–Dix line than that expressed in the Majority Report. Their own proposed Orders for Infant Baptism, Adult Baptism Confirmation and Communion, and the Making of a Catechumen then followed.

The two Reports came before both Convocations in October 1954, and after protracted discussions lasting some two years, the recommendations of the Majority Report were endorsed with minor changes. But the proposed new orders of service got nowhere. By this time the appointment of a standing Liturgical Commission had been accepted, and both Convocations agreed to submit all the proposed rites, both in the Majority and the Minority Reports, to this new body. York also withdrew its alternative Infant Baptism service from experimental use.[39] After nearly twenty years' work, therefore, the Convocations had little to show liturgically for all their efforts. Perhaps the most that can be said is that the Church was aware of the issues.

II

In addition to the Eucharist and Initiation, the Convocations set their hands to other pieces of liturgical reform in the decades following the advent of 1928. None met with any success; but cumulatively they served to emphasize the need not only for some comprehensive plan of reform, but also for some machinery to deal with it.

First there were the attempts to improve the Lectionary. The scheme included in 1928 was substantially that of 1922; and after some years of use this was recognized as not entirely satisfactory. Many of the lessons were too long, too difficult, or unedifying. Furthermore, many clergy regarded the two sets of Sunday lessons as providing alternative lessons rather than alternative courses, resulting in some Sunday congregations being subjected to a limited diet of Scripture dependent upon the whim of the clergyman. Consequently, in May 1939 both Convocations appointed joint committees to consider some amendment. Under the guidance of Mervyn Haigh, Bishop of Coventry, they confined their energies to the lectionary for Sundays and Holy Days. Many lessons were abbreviated, and the two optional Sunday courses were replaced by two which were mandatory and to be read in consecutive years. It was, however, a conservative revision, some four-fifths of the 1922 Sunday lessons being retained. In 1944 this Amended Lectionary was approved for experimental use for a period of four years and in 1948 and 1952 this was extended for further periods. But despite further revision in 1947, it came under increasing criticism, not least for adopting the principle of reading 'purple passages' rather than continuous reading. In the following year, Mervyn Haigh, now Bishop of Winchester, commented wryly on the difficulty of producing a lectionary which satisfied everyone.

> There are at least twenty different kinds of quality or virtue of varying importance which a good lectionary ought in some degree to possess but which are largely incompatible with one another. Many who criticise lectionaries for being deficient in certain qualities rarely have in mind other qualities which a lectionary should also exhibit. It is frankly impossible for any lectionary to be perfectly satisfactory in all ways.[40]

But whatever its faults, the Amended Lectionary did come to terms with one significant fact: with the changing patterns of churchgoing, it was no longer possible to assume that regular worshippers would attend Church more than once every Sunday, and a lectionary providing a satisfactory sweep of Scripture in a single year was simply not feasible.

By 1953 Mervyn Haigh had retired, being replaced by Faulkner Allison, Bishop of Chelmsford. He began by pointing out the futility of proceeding with further revision until the existing confused situation was resolved: instead of the four lectionaries now in use – 1871, 1922, Amended Lectionary A and Amended Lectionary B – the Church really needed a single authorized lectionary. The Convocations accepted this assessment;[41] and in the short space of two years – by October 1955 – the Joint Committees produced a unanimous Report (684), containing what came to be known as the New Lectionary with three tables:

1. A two-year Sunday lectionary based on continuous reading with independent morning and evening courses.
2. A one-year lectionary for Holy Days and Special Occasions.
3. A one-year lectionary for weekdays, based on the 1922 lectionary.

These tables were authorized for use from Advent 1956;[42] and Mervyn Haigh commended it as 'an admirable production, certainly better in most ways than any of the other lectionaries in use'. Nevertheless, he had reservations. Admittedly typology could be a craze, but the New Lectionary had fewer linked Old Testament and New Testament lessons than either of its predecessors, and it reflected little of recent biblical scholarship. The pursuit of 'tidiness' did in fact prevent some important parts of the Bible ever being heard by Sunday worshippers.[43] Dr Selwyn, Dean of Winchester, and one of the creators of the Amended Lectionary, was far more outspoken: the new Sunday Lectionary was far too complicated and the victim of its own system.

> The reconstruction of the pieces into which it [i.e. the Bible] is divided and the attempt to fit them into a mould for which the Scriptures were never written, open the way to every kind of arbitrariness, artificiality and pedantry . . . 'The Word of God is not bound', said St. Paul, but here it is, bound in every joint and limb, trussed up like a chicken and filleted like a fish, so that the original lineaments of Holy Scripture are effectively concealed.[44]

Some amendments were subsequently made, and in May 1961 the Joint Committees presented their final Report (700), which the Convocations approved for use from Advent 1962.[45] The critics were not appeased, however. Bishop Hunter published a penetrating critique just before the Prayer Book (Table of Lessons) Measure was introduced in the Church Assembly in July 1962. He believed the pattern of the New Lectionary to be out-of-date: 'It clings, with quite shocking obscurantism, to a sixteenth century pattern'; it disregarded the new insights of recent biblical scholarship; lessons were still far too long; the treatment of both prophecy and parable was unintelligent; furthermore it ignored the change in the habits of Sunday churchgoing, needing consideration as a part of a reappraisal of Sunday worship as a whole.[46] Such criticisms, cogently supported by Dr Simpson,

Dean of Christ Church, were sufficient to persuade the Church Assembly to reject the Measure;[47] and the Lectionary was simply used on a temporary and optional basis for almost another two decades, until a completely new system appeared in 1978.

The use of the Prayer Book Psalter in public worship had been a matter of debate for even longer than the Lectionary. The beauty of the Coverdale version was generally acknowledged and affection for it was deep-rooted: but studies of the Hebrew text had made it increasingly clear that as a translation it left much to be desired, while doubts were expressed as to the suitability of some of the passages for use in Christian worship. Even in the late nineteenth century at least three works had drawn attention to its shortcomings: Bishop Westcott's *The Paragraph Psalter: arranged for the use of Choirs* in 1879, the new translation in the Revised Version of the Old Testament in 1881, and Dr S. R. Driver's scholarly *The Parallel Psalter* in 1898. In 1913 Archbishop Davidson appointed a committee under Dr Jayne, Bishop of Chester, to revise passages of the Psalter in which the language was particularly obscure or misleading: but its Report, published in 1916, was very conservative, proposing no change from Coverdale 'which did not present itself to us as necessary towards intelligent devotional use of the verse or passage in question'. Despite a critical assessment of the Report by the Bishops of Gloucester and Truro (Dr E. C. S. Gibson and Dr W. Burrows) as not being sufficiently thorough, the Upper House of Canterbury Convocation approved its adoption as an instalment of Prayer Book revision and even introduced the Revised Psalter (Permissive Use) Measure in the Church Assembly in 1923. This was not proceeded with, however, mainly due to Archbishop Davidson's pledge to the House of Laity to include 1662 intact in any new Prayer Book, a pledge which would have involved printing two Psalters not strikingly different from one another in the one book. All that appeared of the 1916 Report in the Deposited Book, therefore, was the list of permissive omissions.[48]

Meanwhile two individual attempts at Psalter revision appeared. The first, in 1920, was by Canon J. N. Dalton of Windsor as part of his own proposals for the revision of the Prayer Book.[49] His translation was again conservative, relying heavily on Coverdale; but a praiseworthy feature was his attempt to indicate both the structure and the meaning of psalms by dividing them into sections and by including English headings and sub-headings. Much more important, however, was Walter Frere's *A Liturgical Psalter* in 1925.[50] His proposals, the first really radical experiment, were based on three principles:

1. The needs and limitations of Anglican chant — the most popular form of psalm-singing — demanded rhythmical changes e.g. the redistribution of verses and lines, and the changing of unrhythmical words.
2. The translation must do justice to the Hebrew original.

3. Only material edifying and acceptable to a Christian worshipper should be included.

This third principle, despite resulting in an attenuated Psalter with fourteen complete psalms and sixty-six passages from other psalms omitted, was one which Frere felt wholly justifiable.

> Continuous recitation [of the Psalter] was characteristic of monastic (or clerical) services: it was suitable to experts in devotion rather than to the average man. In the people's services the method of selection prevailed over that of recitation in course. The great exception is the English Prayer Book and nowhere else in Christendom do ordinary lay-people attempt the task.[51]

The principle of selection for Sunday congregations was certainly adopted in 1928, and the resulting table subsequently underwent periodic refinement; but it was not applied to weekdays, although some interesting proposals were made after the Second World War.

The first of these was by Professor Oscar Hardman in 1946. The Psalter proposals in his *A Prayer Book for 1949* were admirable, but unfortunately never received the attention they deserved. The revised text still adhered to Coverdale wherever possible, and recitation was still on a monthly basis; but elements of both Dalton's and Frere's schemes were incorporated. Each psalm was given an English title indicating its content, and sections were clearly marked; the principle of selection was also adopted, six complete psalms being omitted and several passages being deleted, either because they were duplicated or because they were unchristian in sentiment. Excellent though these proposals were, they were overshadowed by two closely related works which appeared soon afterwards in 1948.

The text of Harold Riley's *The Revision of the Psalter: an Essay in Liturgical Reform* was again a conservative revision of Coverdale; but in other respects his proposals were radical. He pointed out that the traditional division of the Psalter into 150 psalms was an arbitrary arrangement, for it was in fact a combination of a far greater number of bits and pieces. He therefore divided it into 270 sections, all of much more uniform length, four being allocated with the Venite to Mattins each day and five to Evensong. No passages were omitted on the grounds of unsuitability, but there was a modest rearrangement of sections to achieve better sense, while Sundays, Holy Days and Special Occasions were all given proper psalms. Riley had almost completed his work when the Religious Department of the BBC decided to produce a revised version of part of the Psalter for use in its daily services; he gladly gave them permission to use his work as a basis for their own arrangement, which emerged as yet another modified version of Coverdale.[52]

The Broadcast Psalter was used regularly in the BBC Daily Service from

January 1949 onwards and was obviously heard and used regularly by a large number of people. Intelligent participation was assisted by the use of English headings and sub-headings; and the whole work was pointed for singing to Anglican chants. Inevitably the limitations of time imposed by radio services demanded strict selection; and in all seventy psalms or sections of psalms were used. In justification of selectivity the Introduction quoted the dictum of Isaac Watts: 'Never was a piece of experimental divinity so nobly written, or so justly reverenced and admired. But it must be acknowledged still that there are a thousand lines in it which were not made for a Church in our days to assume as its own.'[53] An Old Testament scholar, Eric Heaton, speaking of the book on the BBC Third Programme, defended selectivity even more forcefully, claiming that it grappled with the difficulty of moulding a work of Hebrew scholarship for the devotional use of Everyman: 'It must communicate meaning, and not just words, from the psalmist to the worshipper: it must keep faith with both: it must be at once historical, intelligible, and persuasive. Scholarship and art must be wedded — and in church, in the face of a very diverse congregation'.[54] Other scholars accorded it high praise. Professor C. F. D. Moule described it as 'a big step in the right direction'; while Bishop Hunter pleaded that this 'scholarly and sensible piece of work' should be authorized for use in the Church of England.[55] Indeed on 18 May 1949, the very day on which the Convocations commemorated the four hundredth anniversary of the 1549 Prayer Book, Dr Trevor Jalland sang its praises in the Lower House of Canterbury and asked the Archbishop to appoint a joint committee to undertake a revision of both the Psalter and the Canticles, a proposal which the House endorsed. Unfortunately the Bishops rejected it with the time-honoured excuse, 'It would be inopportune to embark on such a task at this present time'. On the same day a similar proposal from the Provost of Wakefield in the Convocation of York had happier results, being passed by both Houses.[56] There the matter rested; but sufficient had been said and done to indicate that further consideration of the Psalter could not be delayed indefinitely.

Then there were the Services for the Sick. The 1928 Order for the Visitation of the Sick was almost entirely the work of Walter Frere, incorporating the suggestions he had made years before in his *Some Principles of Liturgical Reform.* It was a great improvement on the 1662 Order, with more flexibility and the old concept of sickness as a punishment for sin considerably modified. Its weakness was the absence of a form of unction, despite the fact that this had been approved by the committee appointed by the 1920 Lambeth Conference to consider the Ministry of Healing.[57] Spurred on by the endorsement of this committee's findings by the 1930 Lambeth Conference, Canterbury Convocation appointed a joint committee in 1932 to prepare services of Unction and the Laying-on of Hands 'for temporary use in the Province until a permanent and fully authorized form can be issued under synodical sanction'.[58] Drafting dragged on for three years: and it was not until 1935 that Convocation approved the proposals in Report 602A for provisional use subject to due diocesan sanction.[59] The provisions were comprehensive, catering for all the needs of a Ministry to the Sick; only the vexed question of reservation was avoided. The Convocation of York took similar action, approving rather simpler forms of service in 1936.[60] These provincial forms, together with private forms such as those issued by the Guild of St Raphael and the Guild of Health, served the Church for many years: and it was not until October 1953 that the Archbishops appointed a commission under Dr Harland, Bishop of Durham, to consider once again the Ministry of Healing. This body laboured for another five years, finally producing a report in 1958. But this again appeared to be wasted effort, for the Convocations once more sought refuge in referring the whole matter to the Liturgical Commission, a decision destined to leave the matter unresolved for nearly another quarter of a century.

Finally, brief mention must be made of other abortive attempts to induce both Convocations to adopt small but useful pieces of liturgical reform. In York, for example, the attempts of Bishop Hunter to provide special services of Churching and Burial for those occasions when the Prayer Book forms were unsuitable met with failure in 1946. The Upper House rejected the proposal for Burial but accepted Churching, while the Lower House rejected both. Undaunted, he again tried to secure approval for Churching in 1953–4 but still to no avail. He also pleaded for the appointment of a committee simply to look at the Prayer Book and draw up a list of the sections in the greatest need of revision, but even this was rejected.[61] In Canterbury Dr Wand, Bishop of London, raised the question of Family Prayers in 1950, referring to their absence in 1662 and asking the Archbishop to remedy the omission. In support he quoted Professor Ratcliff, who had noted a similar omission in other Anglican Prayer Books and had himself offered to provide suitable material. Dr Fisher accepted that something should be done but made it clear that any proposal involving a change in 1662 would be unacceptable.[62] Evidently he did not enthuse over the idea, and it was not until May 1952 that a joint committee was appointed.[63] Another two years elapsed before it reported, providing propers for Holy Communion, an Order of Prayer for the Family and an Order of Blessing on the Adoption of a Child. Both houses then made incredibly heavy weather of the whole affair. The Upper House suggested some amendments; but the Lower House evaded consideration of them by suggesting that the matter should be submitted to York. This the Upper House declined to do, preferring instead to suggest that this was another project which should be left to the Liturgical Commission, whose appointment was imminent.[64] Another four years' delay and fruitless discussion therefore saw the end of another venture, and in fact it never did appear on the Commission's agenda.

III

From the middle of the nineteenth century Roman Catholic, Lutheran and

Reformed Churches had, like the Church of England, experienced renewed interest in liturgy, although this interest took a variety of forms. Developments on the continent remained relatively unknown in this country until the appearance of Friedrich Heiler's *The Spirit of Worship*. This work, by a German Lutheran scholar converted from Roman Catholicism, was published in English translation in 1926 as a tribute to the Stockholm Life and Work Conference of the previous year. It was a fascinating but all too brief introduction for English readers to the work of the European leaders of the Liturgical Movement both Roman Catholic and Protestant: Guéranger, Herwegen, Casel, Otto, Monod and others. Significantly it began with a quotation from Ildefons Herwegen: 'The Liturgy . . . is in very truth the medium of a transforming life-enhancing communication of the grace of Christ in His Church.' As if to support this statement an English translation of Dom Lambert Beauduin's famous *La Pieté de l'Eglise* (1914), one of the Movement's basic texts, appeared in 1929 under the title *The Liturgy, the Life of the Church*. Then in the following year Gabriel Hebert produced an English edition of the Swedish Yngve Brilioth's *Eucharistic Faith and Practice, Evangelical and Catholic*, making available for the first time a comparative study of Anglican, Lutheran and Reformed liturgical history from the sixteenth century onwards, and expressing the hope that the day would come 'when a fuller unity of Christendom shall again reveal the great Christian sacrament in the wholeness of its many-sided glory'.[65] But the most significant English work on the Liturgical Movement was Hebert's own book *Liturgy and Society: the Function of the Church in the Modern World*, published in 1935. Here he examined the movement of contemporary society away from God: it had lost the common faith by which it had once lived, and there was danger of its social life not only losing cohesion, but of disintegrating altogether. The answer to this predicament of society lay in the doctrine of the Church as the people of God and the Body of Christ. In his analysis Hebert drew largely upon the 'mystery-theology' of Herwegen and his pupil Odo Casel, which saw the Eucharist as the re-presentation of the sacrificial work of Christ, summarizing in ritual the whole truth of Christ and his Church. Furthermore, 'if Christianity is the redemption of all life, the things done and said in church must have a direct relation to the things done and said everywhere else'.[66] Such comment raised the whole discussion of liturgy above party and academic interests; and in the light of world affairs, it was now shown to have a new sense of urgency — it was truly a 'liturgiology of crisis'.

A trilogy of books appearing in 1936 — all very different and all enjoying a wide circulation — made their own distinctive contributions to this liturgical discussion. The first was Evelyn Underhill's *Worship*, illustrating on a broad canvas — Eastern and Western, Catholic and Protestant — the ways in which Christians had responded to God the Creator in worship. Like Hebert, she recognized that 'the Christian is required to use the whole of his existence as sacramental material . . . bringing the imperfect human creature and his changing experience into direct and conscious relation with God the Perfect and reminding him of the supernatural aim of human life'.[67] The second was a symposium of essays by eminent Free Church scholars to celebrate the Jubilee of Mansfield College, Oxford. The fact that they chose *Christian Worship* as their subject was in itself significant: but the emphasis which they gave to the Eucharist was even more so.[68] The third was W. D. Maxwell's *An Outline of Christian Worship.* Written by an eminent Presbyterian scholar, it was destined to become a standard liturgical textbook for students of all denominations for over a quarter of a century, and it showed a refreshing readiness to re-examine the past, to learn from mistakes, and to try again: 'To accomplish this requires a bringing forth from the Christian treasury of things both new and old.'[69]

An attempt to do just this appeared shortly afterwards. In 1938 Walter Frere produced his last book, a study of the early liturgies in the light of the fresh evidence which had become available during the previous half-century. In some ways *The Anaphora: an eirenical study in Liturgical History* marked the end of an era, for it was the final attempt to prove that the eucharistic prayer in the *Apostolic Tradition* of Hippolytus contained the basic pattern in the primitive Church, providing the norm for a vast number of later anaphoras.[70] Dix described it as 'a skilful rearguard action, an attempt to recast the traditional theory in such a way that it should still be tenable in the face of growing critical difficulties'.[71] Frere had in fact admitted to Dix that his case was difficult: and an impressive body of scholars – Edmund Bishop, Armitage Robinson, Brightman and Srawley to name but a few – agreed in rejecting the idea of a single primitive liturgy.[72] Nevertheless there was an element of truth in the traditional theory so far as structure was concerned; and it was partly to demonstrate this that Dix wrote *The Shape of the Liturgy*, which first appeared in 1945. This was a brilliant, if untidy piece of work; and although some of his views have not withstood further examination, the book as a whole did more to stimulate an interest in liturgy in England than any other book of the period. Here Dix pointed out that Frere had been correct in attributing to eucharistic rites a single origin; but he had erred in not pursuing the problem to its roots and in realizing that if such a single origin had existed, its model must have been Jewish, not Greek. 'That action was one and fixed from the evening of the Last Supper – "Do this" – and the rite that ensured its perpetuation was one and fixed in its form as far back as we can trace.'[73] Dix was, of course, saying nothing new in pointing out the significance of the Jewish thanksgivings, but he gave it new emphasis. But his important contribution to fresh thinking on the Eucharist was his assertion that the liturgy was constructed, not around any pattern of words, but around the fourfold action or 'shape' of taking, blessing, breaking and giving, based on Jesus' own actions at the Last Supper. Here indeed was a masterly presentation of the living organism of liturgy. Dix also expressed in moving language the relationship of man to the Eucharist.

> The eucharist is not a mere symbolic mystery representing the right order of earthly life, though it is that incidentally and as a consequence. It is the represented act of a fully *redeemed* human life . . . Over against the dissatisfied 'Acquisitive Man' and his no less avid successor the dehumanized 'Mass Man' of our economically focused societies insecurely organized for time, Christianity sets the type of 'Eucharistic Man' — a man giving thanks with the produce of his labours upon the gifts of God, and daily rejoicing with his fellows in the worshipping society which is grounded in eternity. This is the man to whom it was promised on the night before Calvary that he should henceforth eat and drink at the table of God and be a King. This is not only a more joyful and humane ideal. It is the divine and only authentic conception of the meaning of all human life, and its realization in the Eucharist.[74]

The Shape of the Liturgy was largely developed from an earlier essay which Dix had written on 'The Idea of "the Church" in the primitive Liturgies' for a symposium *The Parish Communion* edited by Gabriel Hebert in 1937. The contributors, a combination of experienced parish priests and young scholars, aimed 'to set forth a conception of the nature of the Church, which appears to compel the adoption of the Parish Communion as its necessary expression in liturgy'.[75] Men like Frere, Gore and John Wordworth had already championed the cause of the Parish Communion many years before; but this gave the movement new impetus, encouraging a fresh examination of the Church and its function in a secularized world. Its writing had been prompted by a letter which Hebert had received in 1935 from Brother Edward SSF, who himself published a further symposium *Sunday Morning: the New Way*. This was a series of vivid accounts of the Parish Communion by keen practitioners; and being cheap, lively and easy to read, it provided a valuable complement to Hebert's weightier collection. Through such works, men came to realize that the Church, faced by opposing totalitarian philosophies of right and left, and certainly on the mainland of Europe struggling against hostility and persecution, was in a position similar to that of the primitive Church. It was not surprising, therefore, that when men were challenged to consider afresh the divine calling and the corporateness of the 'ecclesia' of God, they were encouraged to look, not to the Middle Ages as so many people had done in the nineteenth century, but to the primitive Church. Not only was the contemporary Church living in a 'primitive Church' situation; it came increasingly to be realized that the primitive Church might have something to say about attitudes towards the Eucharist which would help to solve theological differences between parties and Churches, and at the same time help the people of God in their actual performance of the liturgy.

Two interesting developments emerged in the immediate post-war situation. One was the Parish and People Movement under the leadership of Henry de Candole and Kenneth Packard. It stemmed from a School of

Worship held at Farnham Castle in 1946, and a series of preliminary conversations expressed a concern as to 'how initiatives and a reform movement in liturgy, pastoralia and evangelism could be drawn together upon the basis of biblical theology and a comprehensive doctrine of the Church, and in the widest perspective of the Church's predicament and opportunity today'.[76] The Movement's first conference took place in January 1949; and it continued to serve the Church for nearly a quarter of a century. With the basic assumption that the Eucharist should be the chief expression of the fellowship of the Body of Christ in a particular parish, it strove to put into practice a number of important theological insights: the active participation of the laity, a clear presentation of the four-shape action, and the unity of the Word of God in the use of both Old and New Testaments and in preaching. While the Movement was content to do its best with the eucharistic rite which the Church officially provided, nevertheless the very insights which it proclaimed highlighted the need for some liturgical revision, not least in increased flexibility in rubrical directions and a reconsideration of the structure and content of the eucharistic prayer. Admittedly the Movement had its weaknesses — Archbishop Ramsey's criticisms of its views on sacrifice, communion and fellowship received wide publicity; but these were more than offset by its considerable gains. It helped to make the Eucharist the centre of Sunday worship; it engendered peace and unity, breaking down old party differences; and it enabled the congregation to realize itself as the Christian family.[77]

The second was a venture dear to the heart of William Temple. At the outbreak of the Second World War he had written graphically, 'The world of today is one of which no Christian map can be made.' He therefore saw the challenge facing the Church in the world as that of conversion. 'Our task with this world is to convert it. Its need can be met . . . by the shattering impact upon its self-sufficiency and arrogance of the Son of God crucified, risen and ascended, pouring forth that explosive and disruptive energy which is the Holy Ghost.'[78] From this challenge there emerged in 1943 the Archbishops' Commission on Evangelism, regarded as Temple's brainchild. He died in the following year, before the Commission — a large and eminent body led by Dr Chavasse, Bishop of Rochester — was able to complete its work: but its report *Towards the Conversion of England*, published in 1945, was dedicated to his memory. In fact, it contained no coherent plan for converting the country; and like the National Mission in the First World War, its effectiveness was less than was hoped for. Nevertheless, it was read and discussed more widely than any other church document of the day, bringing home to people the fact that the nation was in danger of ceasing to be recognizably Christian. Faced with such a situation, the Church had the task of evangelism; and in the setting out of this task, the Report said a great deal which had been and was still being said by the Liturgical Movement.[79] The Church, by its fellowship, teaching and worship, was intended to be the divine agency for evangelism as the Body of Christ in the world. In discussing worship the Report claimed that, despite the failure of most people to see its relevance to life, it was nevertheless 'not an activity which stands apart from the rest of life, separate, isolated and self-contained. It is not an escape from the life of everyday into some different and more rarified spiritual air. It is the offering of the life of everyday that God may fashion it and direct it': and nowhere was the true character of Christian worship revealed more clearly than in the Eucharist.[80] Among its liturgical proposals there was an urgent plea to press on with the consideration of baptism, a matter in which the Convocations were already engaged; a proposal for a People's Prayer Book – another matter already in hand, but of which the Church at large was then unaware; and a suggestion that the Cell Movement afforded the best evangelistic agency for the times.[81]

One person who took this Cell Movement very seriously was the Reverend Ernest Southcott, Vicar of St Wilfrid's Halton, Leeds, from 1944 to 1961. A leading member of the Parish and People Movement, he had the advantage of working in close association with Henry de Candole, then Bishop of Knaresborough. His development of the House Church, which transformed the life of the Church in Halton, became widely known through his two books *Receive this Child* (1951) and *The Parish comes alive* (1956).[82] As the Commission's report envisaged, the House Church could take different forms, some meeting for discussion and prayer, others for the celebration of the Eucharist. But provided those involved recognized that it was not an end in itself but was closely related to what went on in the parish church, it became an effective expression of liturgical evangelism, bringing the lapsed and the indifferent to church, demonstrating the true relationship between sacred and secular, and providing an example of what the primitive Church had been like and how it had functioned. At the same time it highlighted the need for liturgical provision beyond that of 1662 or even 1928, so that the Eucharist could be celebrated with greater flexibility and informality. Coupled with this was the recognition that here was a useful vehicle for liturgical experiment. So John Robinson commented, 'The road to living liturgical reform leads from the bottom upwards, and that is why controlled experiment in the local worshipping community, especially at the sub-parochial or house church level, is so vital to the health of the Body of Christ.'[83]

IV

In 1948 Canon G. W. O. Addleshaw of York and Frederick Etchells, an architect with expertise in church buildings, produced *The Architectural Setting of Anglican Worship.* This was a valuable complement to Dix's *The Shape of the Liturgy*, for it drew attention to the planning and arrangement of churches at a time when war damage and the movement of population demanded considerable church building and restoration. It gave a fascinating account of the way in which churches had been used for public worship from medieval times to the present day and posed the question, 'How can the building best serve the liturgy?' 'In a building which attempts to be true to all that is best in the Anglican tradition, everything must be subordinated to this principle . . . that the altar and the officiating minister must be placed in close relationship to the people.'[84] The authors questioned whether the medieval plan with an altar at the east end of a chancel with a long choir and a screen separating priest from congregation had anything to commend it.

> Liturgical worship in the Church of England necessitates the priest being both seen and heard by his people when taking a service . . . A liturgical service is an act which is both corporate and natural. It is offered by the clergy and their people, each taking their allotted part. But it is something which is eminently natural, the act of a group of people who see each other, and through seeing each other . . . become conscious that they are a homogeneous body engaged in the work of worship.[85]

They therefore pleaded for churches in which the altar was so positioned that the people could be gathered round it. The book was a pioneering work in this country, applying the principles of the Liturgical Movement to the ordering of churches, initiating a series of searching books on the relationship of liturgy to architecture, and indicating that Anglican worship needed greater flexibility than the Book of Common Prayer could provide.[86]

Then again, with the growing recognition of the importance of the Ministry of the Word came a growing desire to proclaim it in more contemporary form. John Robinson, for example, spoke of the need for a Word 'speaking to every man in his own language, cutting through all that muffles or stifles its impact'.[87] Until the middle decades of the century the King James Bible or Authorized Version of 1611 was in common use in public worship: it was like the Coverdale Psalter, beautiful and well-loved but in the light of biblical scholarship often obscure or inaccurate. This had become obvious with the advent of the Revised Version in 1881–5, although the latter had never succeeded in supplanting it in general use; nor had the twentieth-century translations in more contemporary language, such as Weymouth (1903), Moffatt (1913–24), Goodspeed (1923), Knox (1944–54) and Rieu (1952), which were used primarily for study and private reading. The first significant change came with the appearance of *The Revised Standard Version* (NT 1946, OT 1952, Apocrypha 1957). This was a revision of the American Standard Version of 1901, itself a revision of King James, undertaken by the main Protestant Churches of the USA. Its express purpose was to 'embody the best results of modern scholarship as to the meaning of the Scriptures, and express this meaning in English diction which is designed for use in public and private worship and preserves those qualities which have given to the King James Version a supreme place in English literature'. At the same time it recognized that the Word of God 'must not be disguised in phrases that are no longer clear, or hidden under words that have changed or lost their meaning. It must stand forth in language that is direct and plain and meaningful to people today.'[88] *The*

Revised Standard Version succeeded in doing just that. It was a good translation which was dignified, not radically 'modern' and undoubtedly 'read' well; it proved to be acceptable and its use in public worship became widespread.

Another work appearing shortly afterwards and making considerable impact was J. B. Phillips' translation of the Epistles published under the title *Letters to Young Churches* in 1947 and followed by the whole *New Testament in Modern English* in 1958. This was a brilliant attempt at a translation in contemporary idiom without resorting to wordy paraphrase, and many people found it both attractive and challenging when read in public worship; to quote John Robinson once again, 'It blew away some of the cobwebs and also some sleep from the eyes at eight o'clock in the morning.'[89] Just as Phillips was completing his work on the Epistles, the Protestant Churches of the British Isles began work on *The New English Bible*, intended as an accurate translation in the light of modern scholarship and expressing in contemporary idiom what the original authors had said in theirs. The New Testament was ready by 1961: and by this time Roman Catholic scholars had started work on a similar project – to emerge as *The Jerusalem Bible* in 1966. In the same year the New Testament of *The Bible in Today's English Version* had made its appearance in America and in due course appeared in this country. In the second half of the century, therefore, the Church of England was being confronted by a variety of new Bible translations differing in style and idiom from those she was accustomed to use in public worship.

During the same period hymnody also broadened its scope. Despite its success *The English Hymnal* was considered in some quarters as being too Anglo-Catholic, and the need for another hymn book on broader and more liberal lines was indicated. As a result *Songs of Praise* had appeared in 1925, largely the work of the two men who had done so much to bring *The English Hymnal* into being, Percy Dearmer and Ralph Vaughan Williams, together with Martin Shaw. Their aim was to provide a 'national collection' of hymns together with 'spiritual songs' suitable for use not only in churches but also in schools. So encouraging was the response, especially from education authorities, that it was soon followed by an adaptation entitled *Prayers and Hymns for use in Schools* together with an enlarged edition of the book itself (1931). The original edition had contained some five hundred hymns, and the enlarged edition included a further two hundred. This proved to be a mistake; for while musical standards remained high, the literary and theological standards left much to be desired. Percy Dearmer's wife later commented, 'I think Percy allowed his desire to be comprehensive to outweigh his critical sense, and that his judgement failed him somewhat in the final choice as to what should be included.'[90] The words of some well-known hymns were changed in the interests of a more liberal theology, while others were decidedly precious and even eccentric.[91] Nevertheless, it proved to be popular, especially with young people; and from it emerged a number of other publications largely concerned with worship in schools. The main edition also followed the example of *The English Hymnal* in providing lists of suitable hymns for use at Mattins, Evensong and Holy Communion for Sundays, Holy Days and Special Occasions, a provision which encouraged the integration of hymnody into the services of the Church.

Despite the increased competition *The English Hymnal* went into a second edition in 1933, while important changes took place in *Hymns Ancient and Modern.* In the first place it avoided the trap into which *Songs of Praise* had fallen of becoming too unwieldy: in 1939 a Shortened Edition appeared, in which the number of hymns was reduced from 779 to 495, although at the same time some new tunes were introduced, including some well-known favourites from *The English Hymnal.* Secondly, it followed the example of *The English Hymnal* and *Songs of Praise* in providing classified tables of hymns for Sundays and other occasions. The Shortened Edition was then followed in 1950 by a *Revised Hymns Ancient and Modern* with 636 hymns and improving still further its liturgical use.

For many people, however, congregational singing took on a new dimension in the fifties with the advent of the Twentieth Century Light Music Group under Geoffrey Beaumont and Patrick Appleford. They argued that congregational worship should be expressed musically in a style that was essentially familiar. Their rhythmic hymns and settings with appropriate accompaniment might not be 'great' music; but it was the kind of music which was acceptable to a great number of people. The worship of the people of God should therefore find expression in it. As Geoffrey Beaumont explained, he was not looking for a *modern* idiom but for a *familiar* idiom which provided a link between people's daily life and their worship. In answer to the criticism that it was inferior material and only the best should be good enough for God, Beaumont replied, 'We are not told that the stable was the best stable, or Jordan the best water, or the Cross the best wood – until Jesus made them so by his use of them.'[92] Here then was a genuine attempt to seek the sacred in the secular; and while Beaumont's Twentieth Century Folk Mass (1956) may no longer be heard, many of the hymns and melodies produced by his Group remained deservedly popular and found their way into the Church's standard hymnbooks. They constituted yet another pressure towards change and a reconsideration of the liturgy in more contemporary terms.

Much less radical but more widely influential was the work of the Royal School of Church Music. Founded by Sir Sydney Nicholson in 1927, it was granted its Royal Charter in 1945; and by 1956 some 3,500 choirs in the provinces of Canterbury and York were affiliated to it. While working loyally within the limits of the official liturgy of the Church, it was responsible for creating tremendous interest both in the content and in the performance of church services. In so doing it probably raised the standards of public worship more effectively than any other agency. It was, moreover, a body which encouraged experiment and the production of new work, all of which was conducive to the creation of a spirit of open-mindedness within the Church. Nor must the influence of the BBC be ignored. Since the nineteen-twenties services had been broadcast, some from cathedrals and parish churches, others from the BBC itself. Because the Corporation catered for the needs of all religious denominations, its material came from a wide variety of sources. Both radio and television therefore brought to all interested people throughout the country a daily religious diet which was richer, more varied and better presented than anything they could normally expect to receive in the average parish church. The widening of men's spiritual horizons was noted by Archbishop Lang when he wrote the Foreword to the first edition of *New Every Morning* in 1936.

> Its intercessions have a singularly wide range and are themselves an education in the true scope of Christian prayer, and in the breadth of sympathy and remembrance which ought to mark the Christian mind . . . They have a wider range of thought and desire, they make a more varied appeal to the imagination, they express more intimately personal need and experience than is possible within the limits of the Collect.[93]

Many years later, when Archbishop Ramsey introduced a new edition in 1973, he not only made the same point, but took it a step further.

> The changes chiefly to be noticed are in the range of the subjects for prayer in our sad and bewildered world and in the kind of language which is used. Is prayer in contemporary English a good thing? If the language is self-consciously modern and full of jargon and cliché, No. But if the language is simple and natural, Yes. The old language of the Prayer Book which many have loved for centuries was once new and contemporary, and we need not be afraid of change.[94]

NOTES

1. *The Claims*, pp. 57–8, 70.
2. A. M. Ramsey, *From Gore to Temple*, 1960, p. 134.
3. R. Lloyd, *The Church of England 1960–65*, 1966, p. 273.
4. L. S. Thornton, *The Common Life in the Body of Christ*, 1941, p. 4.
5. ibid., pp. 349–50, 369; A. M. Ramsey, *The Gospel and the Catholic Church*, 1936, p. 114.
6. F. C. N. Hicks, *The Fullness of Sacrifice*, 3rd edn, 1946, pp. vi–vii.
7. L. Hodgson, ed, *The Second World Conference on Faith and Order, Edinburgh, 1937*, 1938, especially pp. 244–5, 325–9; cf. P. Edwall, E. Hayman, and W. D. Maxwell, ed., *Ways of Worship*, 1951; and D. Baillie and J. Marsh, ed., *Intercommunion*, 1952.
8. A. J. Macdonald, ed., *The Evangelical Doctrine of Holy Communion*, 1930, p. 312.
9. *Doctrine in the Church of England*, 1938, p. 19. The Commission was first

chaired by Dr H. M. Burge, Bishop of Oxford 1922–5, and subsequently by William Temple.

10. O. C. Quick, 'The Doctrine Report and the Sacraments', in *Theology* XXXIX (Nov. 1939), pp. 344–53.
11. This book, a development of an earlier work, *Christ, the Christian and the Church* (1946), was read widely, requiring several reprints. In 1965 a second and enlarged edition appeared containing a survey of the Second Vatican Council's *Constitution on the Sacred Liturgy.*
12. Hodgson, *Edinburgh 1937*, p. 244.
13. ibid., p. 19.
14. R. Newton Flew, ed., *The Nature of the Church*, 1952, pp. 138–9.
15. Baillie and Marsh, ed., *Intercommunion*, pp. 244, 248. Hebert claimed on p. 238 that his view was that of Hicks in *The Fullness of Sacrifice* and the Roman Catholic E. Masure in *Le Sacrifice du Chef* (1932).
16. W. F. M. Scott, 'The Eucharist and the heavenly ministry of our Lord', in *Theology* LVI (Feb. 1953), pp. 42–8.
17. C. F. D. Moule, *The Sacrifice of Christ*, 1956.
18. F. W. Dillistone, *Christianity and Symbolism*, 1955, pp. 283–4.
19. *Chronicle Convoc.*, 1937, pp. 293–301, 410–11.
20. Canterbury Convoc. Report 626, *Administration of the Sacrament of Holy Baptism*, 1938, pp. 2–3, 5.
21. *Chronicle Convoc.*, 1939, pp. 229, 391.
22. *Journal Convoc.*, May 1942, pp. 13–14.
23. G. Dix, *The Theology of Confirmation in relation to Baptism*, 1946, p. 34.
24. ibid., p. 35. The earlier works are F. W. Puller, *What is the distinctive Grace of Confirmation?*, 1880; and A. J. Mason, *The Relation of Confirmation to Baptism*, 1891. The theory came to be known as 'the Mason-Dix line'.
25. O. C. Quick, *The Christian Sacraments*, 1927, pp. 182, 184.
26. *Doctrine in the Church of England*, p. 188.
27. *The Theology of Christian Initiation*, 1949, pp. 9–15.
28. ibid., pp. 19–22.
29. *Report of the Lambeth Conference 1948*, pp. I. 50–1; II. 107, 110–11.
30. *Chronicle Convoc.*, 1943, pp. 277–81, 323; *Journal Convoc.*, Oct. 1943, pp. 52–6.
31. *Journal Convoc.*, Oct. 1945, App. pp. xix–xx, cf. p. 34.
32. ibid., Oct. 1946, pp. 45–58.
33. ibid., May 1947, pp. 82–5.
34. ibid., Sept. 1951, pp. 108–11.
35. ibid., Oct. 1952, p. 69.
36. E. C. Ratcliff, 'The York Revised Service for the Public Baptism of Infants; an Appraisement', in *Theology* LXIII (Nov. 1960), pp. 459–68. See also another unfavourable criticism by E. C. Whitaker in *Theology*, Dec. 1953.
37. *Baptism and Confirmation Today*, 1955. Majority Report, especially pp. 33, 37, 43–4. The replies of the dioceses indicated an overwhelming majority of clergy opposed to any deferment of baptism until a later age (p. 13).
38. ibid., Minority Report, especially pp. 29–31. The diocesan replies had indicated very little enthusiasm for a catechumenate (Maj. Rep. p. 14).
39. *Chronicle Convoc.*, 1954, pp. 247–51, 267–72; 1956, pp. 111–14; *Journal Convoc.*, Oct. 1954, pp. 105–11; Oct. 1955, pp. 87–8; May 1956, p. 27. The Bishop of Sheffield admitted that the York rite had not been widely used, but only in '*some* of the Northern dioceses in a *restricted* number of parishes'.

40. M. Haigh, *An Introduction to the Amended Lectionary for Sundays and certain Holy Days*, 1948, p. 12.
41. *Chronicle Convoc.*, 1953, pp. 6–11, 78–85, 104–7; *Journal Convoc.*, 1953, pp. 22–8.
42. *Chronicle Convoc.*, 1955, pp. 184–203; *Journal Convoc.*, Oct. 1955, pp. 54–73.
43. M. Haigh, 'The New Lectionary', in *Theology* LIX (April 1956), pp. 135–44.
44. E. G. Selwyn, 'The Proposed Lectionary', in *Theology* LX (April 1957), pp. 135–9.
45. *Chronicle Convoc.*, May 1961, pp. 170–6, 312–17, 332–43, 371–92.
46. L. S. Hunter, 'The Prayer Book (Table of Lessons) Measure', in *Theology* LXV (July 1962), pp. 266–9.
47. *Church Assembly Proceedings*, vol. 42, no. 2, pp. 240–61, 544–59.
48. These omissions, together with the proper psalms for Sundays, Holy Days and special occasions, and the permission to transpose Psalms 113 and 141 from Morning to Evening Prayer were the sum total of the Psalter changes in 1928. It is worth noting, however, that the 1916 Report did receive further recognition. Both Ireland and America included all its proposals in their revised Prayer Books in 1926 and 1928 respectively.
49. J. N. Dalton, *The Book of Common Prayer, an Edition containing Proposals and Suggestions*, 1920.
50. Frere had briefly indicated some principles of Psalter revision some years previously in his *Some Principles of Liturgical Reform*, 1911, pp. 88–91.
51. W. H. Frere, *A Liturgical Psalter, arranged for use in the services of the Church*, 1925, p. iii.
52. H. Riley, *A Revision of the Psalter: an Essay in Liturgical Reform*, 1948, p. v.
53. *The Broadcast Psalter*, 1948, p. ix. The longest individual psalm was 104, of 36 verses; and apart from Psalm 119 only seven psalms exceeded 20 verses.
54. Quoted in *Theology* LIX (June 1956), p. 238.
55. C. F. D. Moule, 'Understandest thou what thou singest', in *Theology* LXI (Oct. 1958), pp. 407–8; L. S. Hunter, 'Psalms in Worship', in *Theology* LXII (Jan. 1959), pp. 27–8.
56. *Chronicle Convoc.*, May 1949, pp. 237–45, 268–9; *Journal Convoc.*, May 1949, pp. 44–7.
57. Clarke and Harris, ed., *Liturgy and Worship*, 1936 edn, pp. 473–4.
58. *Chronicle Convoc.*, 1931, pp. xi, 75–81, 91–104; *Report of the Lambeth Conference 1930*, pp. 182–3.
59. *Chronicle Convoc.*, 1935, pp. 351–4, 400–1, 427–9.
60. *Journal Convoc.*, 1936, pp. 21–2, 34–5, 69–70.
61. *Journal Convoc.*, May 1946, pp. 72–5; Oct. 1946, pp. 40–4; Oct. 1952, pp. xxiv, 66–7; Oct. 1953, pp. 46–8; May 1954, pp. 53–62.
62. *Chronicle Convoc.*, 1950, pp. 12–18.
63. ibid., 1952, pp. 169–71.
64. ibid., 1954, pp. 36–9, 179–85, 297–301.
65. Y. Brilioth, *Eucharistic Faith and Practice Evangelical and Catholic*, 1930, p. 288.
66. A. G. Hebert, *Liturgy and Society: the Function of the Church in the Modern World*, 1935, p. 8.
67. E. Underhill, *Worship*, 1936, pp. 77–8.
68. N. Micklem, ed., *Christian Worship*, 1936, p. 73.
69. W. D. Maxwell, *An Outline of Christian Worship*, 1936, p. 73.

70. W. H. Frere, *The Anaphora: an eirenical Study in Liturgical History*, 1938, p. 48.
71. G. Dix, *The Shape of the Liturgy*, 1945, p. 213.
72. R. C. D. Jasper, *The Search for an Apostolic Liturgy*, 1963, pp. 18–21.
73. Dix, op. cit., pp. 236–7.
74. ibid., pp. xviii–xix.
75. A. G. Hebert, ed., *The Parish Communion*, 1937, p. vii. The contributors included: J. O. Cobham, later Principal of Queen's College, Birmingham; Austin Farrer, later Warden of Keble College, Oxford; Dix; C. P. Hankey, later Dean of Ely; H. de Candole, later Bishop of Knaresborough; W. S. Baker, later Bishop of Zanzibar; Charles Smyth, later Canon of Westminster.
76. P. J. Jagger, *A History of the Parish and People Movement*, 1978, p. 22.
77. A. M. Ramsey, *Durham Essays and Addresses*, 1957, pp. 17–20.
78. W. Temple, 'Theology Today', in *Theology* XXXIX (Nov. 1939), p. 330.
79. *Towards the Conversion of England*, 1945, scs 87, 331. The popularity of the Report was such that it needed to be reprinted five times in the first six months of its life.
80. ibid., scs 308–10.
81. ibid., scs 122, 148–55, 286, 299, 350, 355.
82. See also the following articles in *Theology*: J. A. T. Robinson, 'The House Church and the Parish Church', August 1950; E. W. Southcott, 'The House Church', May 1953; E. James, 'What is going on at Halton?', February 1957.
83. J. A. T. Robinson, *Liturgy coming to Life*, p. 15.
84. G. W. O. Addleshaw and F. Etchells, *The Architectural Setting of Anglican Worship*, 1948, p. 223.
85. ibid., pp. 229–30.
86. Some noteworthy books and articles in the fifties and early sixties were: N. Comper, *Of the Christian Altar and the Buildings which contain it*, 1950; J. G. Davies, *The Origin and Development of early Christian Architecture*, 1952; *Sixty Post-War Churches*, 1957; P. Hammond, *Towards a Church Architecture*, 1960; B. Minchin, *Outward and Visible*, 1961; G. Cope, *Making the Building serve the Liturgy*, 1962; J. G. Davies, *The Architectural Setting of Baptism*, 1962; together with the Annual Reports of the Council for the Care of Churches.
87. J. A. T. Robinson, *Liturgy coming to Life*, 1960, p. 24.
88. Preface to *The Revised Standard Version*.
89. Robinson, op. cit., p. 24.
90. Nan Dearmer, *The Life of Percy Dearmer*, 1941, p. 286.
91. As examples of 'liberal' modifications see nos. 279, 392, 480.
92. C. Northcott, *Hymns in Christian Worship*, 1964, p. 72.
93. BBC, *New Every Morning*, 1936, pp. iii–iv.
94. *New Every Morning*, new edn 1973, p. viii.

8

THE WIDER VIEW

I

The concern of the 1930 Lambeth Conference with liturgical revision was minimal. In one respect it could even be said to have taken a retrograde step, for it disbanded the Committee of Liturgical Experts and allowed its functions to be taken over by the Consultative Body, which acted as a general continuation committee.[1] Its single positive action was to reaffirm Resolutions 36 and 37 of the 1920 Conference, accepting the principle that liturgical uniformity was not necessary throughout the Anglican Communion, and affirming the right of diocesan bishops to put out liturgical forms subject to any limitations laid down by higher synodical authority.[2] These two resolutions were reaffirmed once again by the 1948 Conference; but a note of warning was also sounded. Recent liturgical developments in various parts of the world had resulted in the distinctive elements of Anglican worship not being as clear-cut as they may once have been; the time had therefore come when those 'features in the Book of Common Prayer which were essential to the safeguarding of the unity of the Anglican Communion' should be examined;[3] although it was not until the 1958 Conference that any action was taken. It was clear, however, that the momentum of liturgical change was increasing; and while there was a substantial exchange of information by provinces and dioceses, there was also no lack of a spirit of independence. In such a movement the Church of England could hardly be said to be playing a leading role.

In India the Winslow rite, originally sanctioned for limited use in the diocese of Bombay only, was in 1933 authorized for use in any diocese of the province subject to episcopal permission; and in 1942 and 1947 some amendments were made to it, bringing it more closely into line with the liturgy of St James.[4] Meanwhile in 1945 the episcopal synod decided to embark on a comprehensive revision of the Prayer Book, resulting in *A Proposed Prayer Book* in 1951, containing 1662 with additional material. In 1955, this was divided into two books, the basic proposed new Indian Prayer Book, and a supplementary volume containing optional material only; at the same time further revision took place, with borrowings from America, Ceylon, Scotland, South Africa, 1928, and private individuals such as Eric Milner-White. Of particular interest were the proposals for the Eucharist. In 1951 an alternative rite was included which, in contrast to the Winslow rite, was very Western in outlook. It was based largely on 1928 but had a consecratory epiclesis exceeding anything expressed in other Anglican rites and praying that the Holy Spirit might 'hallow this oblation of the Body and Blood of Jesus Christ our Lord'. This was modified, however, before the Prayer Book emerged in its final form in January 1960, the consecratory epiclesis being abandoned in favour of one simply praying for the fruits of a good communion, on the lines of South India and Scotland. The whole question reflected a considerable difference of opinion in the province. One group saw the epiclesis as a valuable link with the Eastern Church and expressive of the relationship of the divine presence to the physical world. Another group believed that the Holy Spirit could be invoked only on people and was in no sense consecratory. A third group was happy to have an epiclesis on both people and gifts but outside the eucharistic prayer, preferably at the Offertory. But these diverse views had deep psychological roots in the apprehension of God and his indwelling in creation and were characteristic of the Eastern and Western Churches respectively. In the end the Western view prevailed, but the province felt that the whole question needed further discussion throughout the Anglican Communion.[5] The fact that this Western type of rite finally remained in the Indian Prayer Book and the Winslow rite was relegated to the supplementary volume indicated that the hopes of the latter's compilers were never fully fulfilled. It was in fact never widely used in India;[6] but it was not without influence, and other Indian rites were glad to borrow from it – Ceylon, South India, and the Lutheran Book of Worship.

Another rite in the province of India was that of Ceylon, first published as a pamphlet in 1933 and authorized for use in the diocese of Colombo in 1938. This again followed Western rather than Eastern patterns. It began with penitence; the Gloria could come in either its 1549 or 1662 positions; the Intercessions were on 1928 lines and could be used either as a single prayer or in litany form; the Preface came from the Winslow rite, but the rest of the canon was almost entirely Scottish; and the Prayer of Humble Access immediately preceded communion. It could be described as an able evaluation of all preceding Anglican revisions with some distinctive contributions of its own.

Further East, the Anglican Church in Japan agreed to the preparation of a revised Prayer Book in 1950. Hitherto both 1662 and the American rites had been used; but now American patterns tended to be followed, which is not surprising in view of American influence in the area. The draft book was accepted for experimental use in 1956 and was authorized for permanent use in 1959. The eucharistic rite was on American-1549 lines, but with its own distinctive features. The penitential element could be used as a separate service, or at the beginning of the rite, or between the Creed and the Offertory; the offertory of alms, bread and wine was accompanied by an offertory prayer; the Intercessions were in 1662 form but omitted the prayer for rulers to avoid erroneous ideas about the divinity of the Emperor and included prayer for the departed. The eucharistic prayer was substantially that of 1549 but began with phrases from Revelation 7.12 and ended with phrases from Ephesians 3.20–1, thus clearly setting it in a context of praise and thanksgiving; the anamnesis–oblation referred to the holy Bread of Heaven and the Cup of Salvation and went on to pray that God might lift up this sacrifice of praise and thanksgiving to the heavenly altar: the offering of the consecrated elements was therefore unmistakeable.

Other far Eastern dioceses also showed a tendency to move away from 1662. Korea, for example, which had decided to produce its own liturgy as early as 1919 but did not in fact produce it until 1938, followed 1549 and added certain Roman features such as a penitential opening and an embolism after the Lord's Prayer. Hong Kong and Macao began in 1938 with a modest revision of 1662, also placing the penitential element at the beginning and including 1928 elements in the Intercessions and the eucharistic prayer. Then in 1955 more extensive changes were made, including a remodelling of the eucharistic prayer, which brought the whole rite more closely in line with 1928; and these were authorized in 1957. Singapore and Malaya also produced a Prayer Book of its own in 1956, which provided for the use of the American rite as well as that of 1662.

In the USA the Anglican Church had wisely appointed a Standing Liturgical Commission after the revision of 1928 to monitor the use of the new Prayer Book; and from 1950 onwards this body published a series of valuable Prayer Book studies, containing material for study and further proposals for revision. Study IV on the Eucharist was published in 1953 and revealed that the volume of comment and criticism submitted by dioceses and groups indicated 'a widespread and insistent demand for a general revision of the Prayer Book'.[7] In the face of this pressure, however, the proposals for the revision of the Eucharist were modest.

> Since we do not have a Basil or a Cranmer to write new prayers, nor even a Johann Burchard to devise more perspicuous rubrics, for the most part we have not attempted any innovations of our own. The most practical method we have found to be an attempt at a better utilization of existing Anglican material, duly adapted and tested in practice in the Prayer Books of other branches of our Church in full communion with our own.[8]

There was, therefore, no radical restructuring: a penitential service of preparation was permitted on the day before, the Gloria was transferred to its 1549 position, two alternatives to the Prayer for the Church were provided, and the fraction was taken out of the eucharistic prayer and followed later after the Lord's Prayer — such were the main changes envisaged. Neither Evangelicals nor Anglo-Catholics greeted it with any enthusiasm, and it was quietly dropped, being eventually superseded in 1964 by a more radical set of proposals.

Canada decided on a fresh revision of her Prayer Book in 1943 and produced its new proposals in 1955. A period of experiment followed and the new book was authorized in 1959. Just as the 1918 revision had left the main Prayer Book services unaltered, so this new revision was extremely conservative. There were no significant changes to Morning and Evening

Prayer, Baptism and Confirmation, and those to the Eucharist were minimal. The Kyries became an additional alternative to the Decalogue or the Summary of the Law; the Intercessions were expanded to include some of the 1928 material; the Prayer of Humble Access was placed before communion, thereby permitting the Preface and Sanctus to lead straight into the eucharistic prayer; and the 1662 eucharistic prayer was expanded by an anamnesis taken largely from 1928 and an epiclesis on the communicants: self-oblation, however, still followed communion. These small changes met with general acceptance.

In South Africa, a Prayer Book which had been compiled piecemeal over a number of years was finally published in its entirety in 1954. The revised rites were alternative to those of 1662, for Evangelicals still tended to use the latter; but the 1929 eucharistic rite was now given more general use, no longer having the restriction 'where allowed by the bishops'. South Africa's neighbour, Madagascar, began to revise its eucharistic rite in 1931 by including the Kyries and the Summary of the Law as alternatives to the Decalogue; then in 1938 it placed the Prayer of Humble Access at the end of the penitential material, thus permitting the Preface and Sanctus to lead straight into the eucharistic prayer; the Agnus Dei and Benedictus were added in 1945.[9]

In all these revisions some general trends are discernible. In the first place the principles enunciated at the 1908 and 1920 Lambeth Conferences were followed: all the eucharistic rites, with the possible exception of the Winslow rite, remained unmistakeably Anglican. Nevertheless there was a definite move in structure away from 1662 towards a more clear-cut four-action shape as advocated by Dix, involving a closer approximation to 1549–Scottish 1637 patterns. Three features tended to mark this: (a) there was a greater emphasis on the offertory, although it is doubtful whether there was universal agreement; (b) the Prayer of Humble Access was moved to permit the linking of the Preface and Sanctus with the eucharistic prayer and the strengthening of the note of thanksgiving; and (c) there was a growing recognition that the eucharistic prayer must not end with the Institution Narrative, as in 1662, although there was no general agreement as to the form which should be used. Two other noteworthy general trends were a decided preference for retaining the Intercessions in their 1662 position, although there was greater freedom in the form they could take, together with a conscious effort to develop the congregational element. At the same time opinion was still clearly divided on the position of the Gloria in excelsis and the act of penitence; while there was a general reluctance to increase the Ministry of the Word from two readings to three — only India specifically catered for an Old Testament reading — although most rites provided for the inclusion of psalmody.

The increasing awareness of liturgical revision in the Anglican Communion as a whole became evident at the Anglican Congress at Minneapolis in August 1954. This Congress, involving some 650 delegates, clerical and lay as well as bishops, was the first gathering of its kind since the London Pan-Anglican Congress of 1908. Worship was one of the four main topics to be considered, and the discussions were guided by two important papers, the first by Professor Massey Shepherd of the USA and the second by Colin Dunlop, Dean of Lincoln. Professor Shepherd pointed out that Anglican leaders at the Reformation had provided their own distinctive interpretation of the maxim that worship should be 'agreeable to the Word of God'. Unlike the Swiss Reformers and English Puritans, who had held this to mean that worship should involve nothing not explicitly commanded in Scripture, the Anglicans had believed that nothing should be done contrary to or forbidden by Scripture, and customs of worship developed by the Church since New Testament times could be retained. (But note the caveats in Articles XX and XXIV.) Anglican worship was therefore linked with that of the pre-Reformation Church, rooted in Judaism and inspired by the complementarity of Word and Sacrament. Nevertheless, in a comprehensive system such as Anglicanism, divergencies had arisen, both in doctrinal interpretation and in outward ceremonial expression: differences of view on the eucharistic sacrifice and the real presence were examples of this. While the Anglican Communion attempted to accommodate such differences in its various liturgies, Professor Shepherd believed that the time would come, sooner or later, when they would have to be resolved. Hope for progress towards such resolution now appeared possible in such statements as that of Gabriel Hebert on eucharistic sacrifice in *Intercommunion.*[10]

Colin Dunlop dealt with practical rather than theological matters and sounded a note of caution. He began by discussing the general trends in current Anglican worship. While it was encouraging to note the deepening of sacramental life and the enrichment of eucharistic worship through renewed study of the early liturgies, there were also some tendencies which were a matter of regret: the reduction of the use of the Psalter to a minimum, the engendering of pleasant feelings as the main purpose of worship, and the over-particularization of prayer, allowing it to become an instrument of education and even propaganda. He then went on to set out criteria for future development. Clearly he disapproved of alternative forms; they confused the laity and should be kept to the minimum; and once a new form was agreed upon, the old should be scrapped. It therefore followed that any revision should be modest, not involving the disappearance of too many familiar landmarks. Nevertheless, a rigid uniformity of words or patterns was not necessary, provided the Anglican family identity was preserved.[11]

On the basis of these papers and the subsequent discussion the Congress issued some important findings. Anglican worship was fundamentally scriptural in theology, intelligible in language, and corporate in expression. The Book of Common Prayer was also accepted as a principal bond of unity between and within the various Churches; but within that unity variety in forms of worship could exist. Revision of these forms should be accompanied by controlled experiment and wide consultation. The Liturgical Movement was also welcomed, with its emphasis on the Eucharist and corporate worship: and the need was recognized for informal services and prayer meetings in addition to official rites to meet local pastoral needs. In particular the encouragement given by the 1948 Lambeth Conference to the renewed study of Initiation was endorsed.[12] Modest though this all was, it was nevertheless encouraging; for it bore witness to the fact that liturgical renewal was no longer an activity confined to particular groups or Churches within the Anglican communion but had become world-wide in its scope.

II

Of the documents prepared for the World Conference on Faith and Order at Lund in 1952, that on *Ways of Worship* confirmed the existence of a Liturgical Movement which was affecting Catholic and Protestant Churches alike, enabling them to come closer together in their forms of worship. It also set out certain basic principles which guided these developments: the Eucharist as the central act of worship, the complementarity of Word and Sacrament, the importance of baptism, worship as a corporate action in direct relation to Jesus Christ, and the concern of liturgy with the whole of life.[13] This and its fellow documents on the Church and Intercommunion were all approved at Lund, and subsequently met with Anglican acceptance in the Convocations and Church Assembly.[14] In May 1954, for example, York Convocation stated:

> We take note of the fact that there is in many churches at present a growing Liturgical Movement, which by the attempt to recover the forms of worship of the patristic period, and by a renewed emphasis on the liturgy as the corporate worship of the Body of Christ, and on the unity of Word and Sacrament in the Sunday Eucharist, renders obsolete differences which have until now been a barrier to reunion.[15]

Such liturgical change was clearly evident in other Churches in the British Isles; and over a period of years it undoubtedly helped to facilitate dialogue with the Church of England.

Liturgical renewal had begun in the Church of Scotland in 1865 with the foundation of the Church Service Society: its purpose was a 'study of the liturgies, ancient and modern, of the Christian Church, with a view to the preparation and ultimate publication of certain forms of prayer for public worship, and services for the administration of the sacraments'. Its *Euchologion* (1867) and *Daily Offices* (1893) met with considerable success, enjoyed a long life, and prepared the ground for the Church's later service books. In the 1940 *Book of Common Order* there were five orders of Communion, the first being normative and the others either abbreviations of or alternatives to it. It was a fine rite of classical shape, with provision for three lessons and a eucharistic prayer with Sursum corda, Preface, Sanctus, Benedictus, anamnesis, epiclesis and act of oblation. The introduction to the book commented that it contained 'in due succession all the great elements which in every age had been found most helpful to the spirit as it is conducted step by step to the Church's supreme act of worship'.[16] It borrowed elements from a variety of sources including 1662 and was described by W. D. Maxwell as 'not a creation *de novo*, but a long tradition brought to its perfection'.[17] The Presbyterian Church of England also included this first Order in its new *Service Book* of 1948, while a similar Order appeared in the Congregational *Book of Public Worship* of the same year. This last book had a lengthy introduction by John Marsh, in which he pointed out that Congregational worship was founded on a structure which linked the preaching of the Word with the Lord's Supper and based its Morning and Evening Worship on a eucharistic pattern rather than on the medieval daily offices.[18]

At the same time the Church of Scotland renewed its interest in the Calendar and Lectionary. The Preface to *Prayers for the Christian Year* in 1935 pointed out that the observance of the Christian year had ceased at the Reformation; and at that time there had been cogent reasons for this departure from ancient custom; but with the disappearance of the conditions from which they derived their force, these reasons had long lost their validity; indeed 'other conditions have now emerged which make it desirable that a return should be made to the general practice of Christendom'. This return enabled the Church of Scotland to unite '*ex animo* with the Holy Church throughout all the world, in celebrating the fundamental certainties which are held in common by all believers'.[19] A two-year cycle of Sunday lessons for the whole of the Christian year appeared in the 1940 *Book of Common Order*, and in 1952 a new edition of *Prayers for the Christian Year* appeared with additional commemorations. The same pattern of developments was included in the Presbyterian Church of England's *Service Book* (1948) and in the Congregational *Book of Public Worship* and *Book of Services and Prayers for Christian Festivals* (1951). It was also a Church of Scotland scholar, Dr A. A. McArthur, who pioneered a re-examination of the Calendar and Lectionary with his two works, *The Evolution of the Christian Year* (1953) and *The Christian Year and Lectionary Reform* (1958), which eventually led to the revised Calendar and Lectionary proposals accepted over two decades later by all the main Protestant Churches in this country and by a number of others overseas.

In the Methodist Churches liturgical developments had followed in the wake of moves towards greater unity. In 1907 the United Methodist Church had come into being through a union of the New Connexion, the Bible Christians and the Free Methodists; and it had produced its own *Book of Services* six years later. In turn these United Methodists joined the Primitive Methodists and the Wesleyan Methodists in 1932 to form a single Methodist Church – a union followed by the Methodist *Book of Offices* in 1936. This contained two Orders of Communion, the first being basically that of 1662 with some slight modifications borrowed from 1928, a rite which had been in regular use by the old Wesleyan Methodists. The second was a freer composition, included mainly for the benefit of the former Primitive Methodists, who had preferred not to use a set liturgy at all; nevertheless even this indicated a willingness to return to more traditional patterns of worship. There was in fact an increasing readiness, not only in the Methodist Church but also in the other Free Churches, to accept the principle that liturgy must have a 'shape', and that a balance must be held between set prayer and the free prayer which they valued so highly. So the Preface to the Methodist *Book of Offices* stated:

> It must not be thought that there is here any attempt to disparage the practice of free prayer, which has always been one of the glories of Methodism . . . There is no real conflict between free prayer and liturgical prayer, for the most helpful prayers that ever came from the inspiration of the moment will be found to owe much in their expression to the remembrance of the language of the great liturgies, and of the hymns of Methodism.

The Preface to the Scottish *Book of Common Order* expressed precisely the same principle: free prayer and set prayer must be held in balance; while the Baptist *Orders and Prayers for Church Worship*, published a little later in 1960, stated it in rather more forceful language:

> We must avoid on the one hand the dangers taught us by history of an inflexible and fixed liturgy which leaves no room for the freedom of the Holy Spirit. On the other hand we must avoid that 'squalid sluttery' and uninspired disorder which comes from disregarding the traditional patterns and forms of Christian worship.

Indeed there was nothing to fear from a fixed liturgy if used properly: it was not to be identified with rigidity and mechanical repetition; rather it emphasized the corporateness of worship, which needed shape and form.[20] Admittedly some of these Reformed service books were private compilations, and even those that were official were simply for optional use. Nevertheless the mere fact of their existence was significant, and their use was fairly widespread, tending to increase rather than diminish.

It was equally true that these Churches had further to go than the Church of England to make the Eucharist their central and regular act of worship; but the principle of its centrality was generally accepted, and it was an ideal for which they aimed, although their rate of progress might be slow. Certainly the need for readjustment and revision in the non-Anglican Reformed Churches was clearly expressed. The Presbyterian, W. D. Maxwell, writing in 1936 of the need for a revision of the Roman rite at the time of the Reformation, nevertheless recognized that the pendulum had swung too far:

> The results of the Reformation movement, so far as the forms of worship were concerned, were imperfect . . . resulting in services excessively didactic and inadequate in structure. The most serious defect lay in the

> fact that the continental Reformers were without any profound historical knowledge of the origins and principles of worship . . . To those who inherit the Reformers' spirit the task yet remains to provide forms broad enough and deep enough for man's whole being to go out to God in adoration, praise and prayer, and for God's grace to come to man without let or hindrance. To accomplish this requires a bringing forth from the Christian treasury of things both new and old.[21]

Comments such as this can easily be multiplied; but one in particular merits quotation – that of the Baptist scholar, Neville Clark:

> What, in practice, will liturgical reformation involve; what form must it take? If we are to begin to answer such questions we must be aware of the weaknesses which beset current theory and practice . . . The unbalanced exaltation of preaching, with its familiar corollaries, the disparagement of the 'preliminaries' and the treatment of the eucharist as an infrequent addendum; the continuance of a sub-Christian individualistic temper and outlook which, however fiercely it may be repudiated on the conscious level, still governs the basic assumptions that mould our liturgical practice; the depreciation of the idea of 'making an offering' in favour of that of 'receiving a blessing'; the formal and (to a large and inevitable extent) factual divorce of worship from life, resulting from the conception of the purpose of worship as the edification of a group rather than the carrying out of a representative action on behalf of a world for which Christ died – such are among the many and varied dangers to be faced and problems to be resolved . . . If we are to advance, we must first look to the past and seek to learn from it.[22]

The Roman Catholic Church marked its official acceptance of the Liturgical Movement by the promulgation of the Encyclical *Mediator Dei* by Pope Pius XII in 1947. While expressing approval of much that had already been done, not least by the Benedictine community on the continent, it was in some respects a cautious document, warning against over-venturesomeness, expressing disapproval of unauthorized innovation and what it called liturgical archaeologisms, and stressing the need for authoritative control; nor did it specifically expound the need for a balanced Ministry of Word and Sacrament. But it endorsed a number of basic principles: the continuing work of Christ through the liturgy, the close relationship between liturgy and daily life, worship as a corporate activity, and the desirability of frequent communion.[23] The first stages of revision soon followed: a revised Liturgy for the Easter Vigil (1951–2), a simplification of the rubrics of the Breviary and Missal (1955), a revised Order for Holy Week (1955), and the establishment of evening Masses (1953, 1958). The inevitability of liturgical change was emphasized by the eminent French Oratorian, Fr Louis Bouyer, in a course of lectures delivered at Notre Dame in 1954 and published in English translation under the title *Life and Liturgy* two years later.[24] The book overlapped to some extent with Hebert's *Liturgy and Society*, but Bouyer had much more to say on the need for liturgical change. The problem facing the Roman Catholic liturgy was that of reconciling permanence with adaptation: 'There is no longer any question of considering the liturgy as something which can never be altered in any way': but what was needed, as a safeguard against deadly anarchy, was a return to the sources of tradition, not in any kind of fundamentalist way, but with the strength and suppleness of a truly living organism. The revised rite for the Easter Vigil was a striking example of what could be achieved; and there was no doubt that this and the revised rites for Holy Week exerted an influence far beyond the confines of the Roman Catholic Church and not least in the Church of England. Bouyer's aim, therefore, was to help promote a return to the sources of tradition, 'using the light of the Encyclical *Mediator Dei* and taking advantage of all the recent work of research and the accumulated experience of the past'.[25] In this respect it was interesting to note the tribute he paid to the work of Anglican scholars such as Brightman, Frere and Dix and the contributors to the Henry Bradshaw Society.[26] He also emphasized the necessity of the Ministry of the Word. The medieval layman had been unable to find in the liturgy a true source of life, because various historical causes had deprived him of the direct access to Scripture within that liturgy.

> The first necessity, therefore, for a liturgical movement which will lead to an authentic revival of the Church's own piety, is never to try to give back the liturgy to the people without at the same time giving them full and immediate access to the Bible. Only a personal meditation on the Word of God in the school of the liturgy itself will enable the Christian people truly to live in that liturgy, *to live that liturgy* again.[27]

Another Roman Catholic scholar emphasizing the need not only for change but for the right approach to change was the Jesuit, Fr Josef Jungmann of Innsbruck, whose commentary on the eucharistic rite, *Missarum Solemnia*, was published in 1948 and then appeared in English translation in two volumes in 1951 and 1955. This was a massive work of erudition, by far the most scholarly and extensive of all modern Roman Catholic liturgical text-books. Its popularity was widespread and was followed by the appearance in fairly rapid succession of English translations of his other major liturgical works: *Public Worship* (1957), *The Early Liturgy* (1959), *Pastoral Liturgy* (1962) and *The Place of Christ in Liturgical Prayer* (1965).[28] Time and time again he made the point: liturgical change was bound to come, but the right way to approach it was important – a return to the sources of tradition.

> We cannot properly evaluate or properly solve the problems of the present and the future unless and until we study the past. And the more involved and profound these problems, the more thorough must be our search into history. This is particularly true in the field of liturgy, for here history

> must help us to recognize what we actually possess as an inheritance from the past . . . History is a precious corrective of mere speculation, of subjective hypotheses. True knowledge of our present liturgy is knowledge based on the solid rock of historical facts; it is by studying the past that we can best learn how to shape the future.[29]

Sufficient has been said, hopefully, to indicate that by the middle decades of the present century there was a growing convergence of opinion in Churches – Anglican, Catholic and Reformed – on the need for liturgical revision and the direction it should take. It was admirably summed up by Charles Davis, who was then Professor of Dogmatic Theology at St Edmund's College, Ware:

> One of the results of the Liturgical Movement has been to bring Christians of different communions closer together, because the new understanding of the Liturgy is overcoming various distorting prejudices and defective ideas which all the communions of the West have inherited from the Middle Ages and which explain, in part, their divisions. In the Roman Church (and this is, of course, true of other Churches too) the movement has been strongly pastoral in character, and it is the strongest force now working for the renewal of the Christian life among ordinary people.[30]

Further evidence of this new understanding was available in two publishing ventures which started in 1957–8. The SCM Press was first in the field with *Studies in Ministry and Worship*, and the Lutterworth Press followed shortly afterwards with *Ecumenical Studies in Worship*. Obviously in a total of some forty volumes there was bound to be some unevenness: but on the whole both series were eminently successful in providing short but authoritative works by scholars of different persuasions from all over the world on the worship and mission of the Church. Under their imprints appeared such notable volumes as Professor C. F. D. Moule's *Worship in the New Testament*, Max Thurian's *Eucharistic Memorial*, and Professor J.-D. Benoit's *Liturgical Renewal*; but the preface to the SCM series as a whole was sufficiently valuable to merit yet another quotation:

> Throughout Christendom there are stirrings, questionings and experiments. Men are moved to look back on their traditions, rejecting much that they had taken for granted and finding treasures that they did not expect. They look forward and outward, seeking to discern God's will in this time of change. Some come to a fresh understanding of their own and the Church's task by the theological study of the Bible which leads to an interrogation of current church life and teaching by the standards of the Bible. Others are moved not so much by this 'biblical theology' as by the 'liturgical movement', discovering the meaning of 'being the Church' in the worship – especially the eucharistic worship – which is the centre of the Church's life, and criticizing 'going to church' and much else in the light of what they find. Others again find themselves compellingly drawn by the

search of the 'Ecumenical Movement' for the unity and wholeness of Christ's Church amidst the divisions and imperfections of the churches. Men held by one movement find themselves in sympathy with the others. The three converge. Together they are bringing about a new situation which it is scarcely an exaggeration to call the Reformation of the twentieth century.

Nothing illustrated this convergence better than the liturgy of the new Church of South India, which appeared in 1952 and was described by one of its creators, Bishop T. S. Garrett, in one of the volumes of the Lutterworth series, *Worship in the Church of South India.* This rite created such an impression on the Churches of the West — not least on the Church of England — that its origins and content merit some consideration.

III

The Church of South India, composed of Anglicans, Congregationalists, Methodists and Presbyterians, was inaugurated on 27 September 1948. Its constitution (chapter X.2) envisaged the development of 'a common form or forms of the service of Holy Communion adapted to the special needs and experience of South India', and set out the elements which such a service should contain.[31] The initial intention of the new Church, however, was to proceed with caution, relying on the continued use of the familiar denominational liturgies; but its very unity quickly overruled that intention.[32] In February 1949 the Liturgy Committee was instructed to draw up a eucharistic rite in time for the next meeting of the Synod in January 1950. Dr Marcus Ward, a member of the committee, described it as a body 'for the most part liturgically illiterate', but he was being unduly modest;[33] admittedly it contained no liturgists of international repute; but it had a gifted convener and draftsman in Leslie Brown,[34] and its end product indicated a firm grasp of liturgical principles, a genuine flair for creative writing, and a willingness to experiment. As another member, Bishop T. S. Garrett, commented, 'Our not being liturgists of profound learning may have saved us from having liturgical bees in our bonnet.'[35] Leslie Brown also revealed that the work was done on a shoe-string budget: members were widely scattered, there was no money for travelling expenses, most of the work had to be done by correspondence, and the responsibility of drafting fell almost entirely on him.[36] Everyone was agreed that something more was needed than a mere tinkering with existing inherited rites, such as an attempt to dovetail elements from the Anglican *Book of Common Prayer* with the Presbyterian *Book of Common Order.* A new rite was to be constructed, based on four principles: it must be faithful to Holy Scripture, be truly corporate, preserve features dear to people brought up in particular traditions, and include features which would be congenial to Indians. It was also important that the Liturgy of the Word could be used as a service by itself, for a scarcity of presbyters precluded the possibility of every congregation having a regular weekly celebration of the Eucharist. Despite the shortage of time the final draft was completed by December 1949 and the rite was duly authorized by the Synod in the following month for use alongside existing denominational rites. Further revision subsequently took place in 1952, 1954, 1962 and 1972; but the fundamental elements remained substantially the same.

The rite was given an ecumenical launching in an unexpected manner. Shortly after the Synod Bishop Garrett attended a preparatory meeting of Faith and Order for the forthcoming World Conference at Lund. As the representative of a united Church he was invited to celebrate the Eucharist, and he agreed to use the new rite despite the fact that it had been neither printed nor published. Copies were hurriedly duplicated and he gave a brief exposition beforehand. Its effect was remarkable. One Anglican delegate, well versed in liturgical matters, declared it to be possibly the best rite in Christendom – which drew from Bishop Garrett the remark, 'I have no wish to substantiate this passing judgement against other claims. Comparisons are odious! But it doubtless represents the impression of not a few who have come to the CSI Order for the first time, that a new star has arisen in the realm of liturgy.'[37]

Several factors contributed to make this favourable impression. Primarily it created a new eucharistic pattern, even though almost all the materials were borrowed from existing rites. For an Anglican it offered an exciting alternative to both 1549 and 1662; and it certainly destroyed the myth that evangelical churchmen were not interested in liturgical matters. Its clear four-action shape undoubtedly owed much to Dix and *The Shape of the Liturgy*, a debt the compilers were ready to acknowledge;[38] while it showed an awareness of Scripture, an awareness of tradition, and an awareness of the spiritual needs of the local community in a way that no other existing rite succeeded in doing. Fr Bouyer commented:

> There is no doubt whatever that, while it skilfully incorporates quite unexceptionable Protestant customs, still, from the point of view of even a conservative Catholic (or Orthodox) liturgist, this eucharistic liturgy seems much more satisfactory than any liturgy that emanated from the Reformation. Unquestionably, it is much superior to the Prayer Book of the Church of England on account of its traditional character and its theological soundness.[39]

Then again, the rite successfully demonstrated the Eucharist as a corporate action – in itself 'an essential element in the most ancient Indian tradition'.[40] Provision was made for the Confession and Intercessions to be led by a deacon; for the lessons to be read by one, two, or three people, lay or ordained; for the alms and the elements to be presented by lay people at the Offertory; and the whole congregation, in addition to reciting the Gloria, the Creed and the Lord's Prayer, contributed vocally to the Intercessions, the Offertory, the eucharistic prayer, the Prayer of Humble Access, and the post-communion prayers. Finally, the rite indicated a new dimension in the concept of flexibility. Hitherto flexibility had normally been limited to a choice between prayers or texts within a rigid structure; but now it involved a choice both of texts and position. The Gloria and the Lord's Prayer, for example, could be used in their 1549 or 1662 positions; while certain elements – the warrant from 1 Corinthians 11, and the Decalogue or its alternatives – could be taken out of the rite itself and used in a preparatory service. And all this was achieved, not by a wholesale creation of new material, but by a careful and unobtrusive blending of elements drawn from existing traditions.[41] The rite had a unity which made it distinctive and distinctively Indian; to quote Bishop Garrett once again:

> We cannot but admit that the liturgical forms in use in South India, whether pre-union or post-union, are for the most part imported from the West, and that even those elements in them which have had their birth in India show marked signs of Western influence. This applies as much to the Liturgy of St James, which has been our main source for the recapturing of the classical heritage, as to Protestant forms of worship, in spite of its centuries of use on South Indian soil by the Christians of St Thomas. In our borrowings from this liturgical heritage we should not delude ourselves into thinking that we are making our liturgy more indigenous . . . It would not, however, be fair to the Churches in India to say that, because their forms of worship are for the most part foreign in origin, they have therefore remained equally foreign in character after a period of use in India. Like many other Oriental countries India has a faculty of assimilating foreign elements into her culture while still remaining essentially Indian.[42]

The principles which had guided the compilers of *The Eucharist in India* some thirty years previously had now borne fruit.

In the rite itself there were four main elements, one of which was preparatory.

A. *The Preparatory Service*

The Preparatory Service, held preferably on the preceding evening, conformed to Presbyterian practice.[43] It included praise, confession of sin, and the reading and preaching of the Word, to which could be added the Warrant (1 Corinthians 11.23–9), the Decalogue or Summary of the Law, and an exhortation. The Warrant was from *The Book of Common Order*, and the exhortation, modelled on Reformation exhortations, was adapted from that in the liturgy of the United Basle Mission Church.

B. *The Preparation*

1. The solemn entry of the Bible during the opening hymn, emphasizing the importance attached to the Word.
2. The presbyter was recommended to adopt the westward position, an ancient practice followed by most Protestant Churches. Leslie Brown revealed, however, that the main reason for this recommendation was

neither historical nor ecumenical, but designed to meet Indian objections to a presbyter when facing east apparently praying to a cross hanging or standing before him; to people conditioned by their Hindu past this smacked of idol worship.[44]

3. The Collect for Purity from 1662, said by the congregation.
4. The Gloria in excelsis (either here or before the Blessing) or one of the alternatives: a hymn; or the Trisagion from the Holy *Qurbana* of the Syrian Churches of Malabar, where it was sung at the Little Entrance before the Gospel; or the Litany of the Lamb, typical of the responsive readings of the former South India United Church.
5. The Warrant and the Decalogue or one of its alternatives (if there had been no Preparatory Service).
6. The Invitation to Confession from 1662.
7. The Confession from the BCO or 'certain other forms'.
8. The Comfortable Words and the Absolution from 1662.

C. *The Ministry of the Word of God*
1. The Collect of the Day or 'another short prayer'.
2. Three readings from Scripture: Old Testament, Epistle and Gospel, with a psalm or hymn, and all introduced in the same way: 'Hear the Word of God.' Standing was recommended throughout – an ancient practice and current Lutheran use; but in deference to Anglican custom, standing for the Gospel only was permitted. The material for each occasion – collect, psalm and readings – was related to a particular theme.
3. The Sermon.
4. The Nicene or Apostles' Creed.
5. The Intercessions, led by the deacon, in one of three forms: a Litany as used in the diocese of Colombo, adapted from the 1662 Prayer for the Church; or a Litany from the Holy *Qurbana*; or extempore prayer.
6. Two concluding collects and the Grace, all from 1662.

Non-communicants were now permitted to leave.

D. *The Breaking of the Bread*
1. Offertory Sentences – Psalm 133.1; 1 Corinthians 10.17; Psalm 27.7.
2. The Peace. The suggested form was derived from the Syrian Churches of Malabar and was similar to the Indian social greeting – the Kaikasuri, literally 'the kiss with the hands'.[45]
3. The Offertory of alms, bread and wine, reminiscent of the Orthodox Great Entrance, accompanied by two prayers: a new prayer based on Hebrews 4.6, 10.19f., 1 Chronicles 29.11 and Romans 12.1, said by the presbyter; and a prayer for the presence of Christ, based on the offertory prayer from the Mozarabic rite, said by the congregation.
4. The Thanksgiving.
   a. Sursum corda, Preface, Sanctus and Benedictus. The general Preface

was adapted from that in BCO; of eleven proper prefaces, eight were from BCO and three from 1928. The form of the Benedictus was from the Holy *Qurbana*, striking an eschatological note.

b. The 1662 Prayer of Consecration, with its emphasis on the uniqueness of Christ's sacrifice on the Cross — 'as much needed in India, with its background of Hindu sacrificial ideas, as it was in the days of the Reformation, when it was used to combat a false doctrine of eucharistic sacrifice'.[46] At the Institution Narrative manual acts were confined to the presbyter taking the elements into his hand.
c. A congregational Acclamation, adapted from the Holy *Qurbana* and used in the Winslow rite.
d. The Anamnesis, referring to the death and passion, resurrection, ascension and second coming of Christ.
e. A second congregational Acclamation, adapted from the Holy *Qurbana.*
f. The Epiclesis, on both the elements and the congregation, from BCO.
g. A petition for unity, based on Ephesians 4.13, 15.
h. The Doxology.

5. The Lord's Prayer, Silence and Prayer of Humble Access, from 1662. Both prayers were said by the congregation. (The Lord's Prayer could also be said after Communion.)
6. The Fraction; with words from 1 Corinthians 10.16; or the Orthodox phrase *ta Hagia tois Hagiois*, admirably translated by Dix 'the things of God for the people of God',[47] or silence.
7. The Communion. Permission was given to follow local custom, with a choice of four alternative Words of Administration. The Methodist custom of communion 'by tables' was recommended. The wine could be administered by a spoon, following the Indian custom of pouring liquid into the mouth and so avoiding contact between vessel and lips. During the communion the congregation could sing Agnus Dei or a hymn.
8. The Post-communion Prayer. One of two forms to be said either by the presbyter or the congregation: a new prayer based on Ephesians 1.6, John 6.53–6 and Romans 12.1–2, or a combination of the two 1662 post-communion prayers. Both expressed self-offering, and both concluded with a congregational doxology.
9. The Blessing from 1662.
10. A Hymn; or part of Psalm 103; or the Nunc Dimittis.

The pattern of this rite, and in particular the use of penitential material and the Gloria in excelsis at the beginning, the inclusion of an Old Testament reading, the Creed following the Sermon, the Intercessions in litany form, the four-action shape and the congregational acclamations were features which gained acceptance in a wide variety of rites, not least in the Church of England. It would be foolish to suggest that the South Indian rite was responsible for all that took place; indeed, the first section of this chapter indicates otherwise in the Anglican communion. Nevertheless, it marked a kind of watershed in the history of liturgical revision; it coloured the thinking of would-be revisers; and its influence, whether direct or indirect, was undeniable. It is also interesting to note that the document on Prayer Book revision produced by the 1958 Lambeth Conference was largely the handiwork of Leslie Brown.

Over a period of fifteen years the Church of South India produced other rites: Initiation, Ordination, Marriage, Burial, Morning and Evening Prayer and the Covenant service. All these, together with the Eucharist, the calendar and the Lectionary, were incorporated in *The Book of Common Worship* in 1963. The whole book is worthy of study, but Morning and Evening Prayer and the Ordinal deserve particular attention. The treatment of the former broke new ground. Three Orders were provided. The First simply recognized the fact that on those days when there was no Eucharist, the first two parts of the latter – the Preparation and the Ministry of the Word – could be used. The Second, adhering closely to the contents and structure of Anglican Mattins and Evensong, nevertheless had four distinctive features:

a. The inclusion of the Syrian *Kauma* or Invocation of the Trinity as an opening act of adoration.
b. In addition to transposing Benedictus and Te Deum, the morning and evening canticles were interchangeable, recognizing the fact that Sunday worshippers tended to come in the morning and not the evening, and providing the maximum variety of material.
c. Psalmody and lessons were much briefer, the psalms being on a two-monthly basis, with some psalms and sections of psalms being omitted, and the normal order being varied.
d. Two or three lessons could be used.

The Third was a rather more flexible form of the Second, catering for those congregations which had been more accustomed to Free Church forms of worship.[48] The Ordinal, which followed primitive practice, undoubtedly exercised the widest influence elsewhere apart from the Eucharist, providing patterns for the new ordinals of many Churches, notably North India and Pakistan, America, and – via the Anglican–Methodist Ordinal – the Methodist Church and the Church of England in this country. Professor Ratcliff regarded the South Indian ordination rites as fine compositions, bearing favourable comparison with any of their historical equivalents. 'The new rites resemble the ancient in simplicity of pattern, logic of movement, and economy of prayer and ceremony . . . The hope may be expressed that any Church of the Anglican Communion proposing to revise its ordination rites will turn for guidance to the rites of South India.'[49]

NOTES

1. *Report of the 1930 Lambeth Conference*, 1930, pp. 55–6.
2. ibid., p. 162.
3. *Report of the 1948 Lambeth Conference*, 1948, part II, p. 86.
4. CIPBC, *Principles of Prayer Book Revision*, 1957, p. 84.
5. ibid., p. 72.
6. ibid., p. 84.
7. PECUSA Standing Liturgical Commission, *Prayer Book Studies IV. The Eucharistic Liturgy*, 1953, p. iv.
8. ibid., p. 133.
9. I am indebted to two books in particular for the information in this section: B. J. Wigan, *The Liturgy in English* (Alcuin Club Collections no. 43) 1962; C. O. Buchanan, *Modern Anglican Liturgies 1958-1968*, 1968.
10. P. M. Dawley, ed., *Report of the Anglican Congress, Minneapolis 1954*, 1955, pp. 68–84.
11. ibid., pp. 86–99.
12. ibid., pp. 197–9.
13. Edwall, Hayman and Maxwell, *Ways of Worship*, especially pp. 16, 20–1, 24–5, 31, 35, 38.
14. O. S. Tomkins, ed., *The Third World Conference on Faith and Order*, 1953, esp. pp. 39–59; *Church Assembly Proceedings*, Autumn 1953, vol. 33, no. 3, pp. 362–79.
15. *Journal Convoc.*, May 1954, p. 42.
16. *The Book of Common Order*, 1940, p. iv.
17. Maxwell, op. cit., p. 136.
18. *A Book of Public Worship*, 1948, p. xiii.
19. *Prayers for the Christian Year*, 1935, Preface, p. v.
20. E. A. Payne and S. Winward, *Orders and Prayers for Church Worship*, 1960, pp. xiv–xv.
21. Maxwell, op. cit., pp. 72–3.
22. Neville Clark, *Call to Worship*, 1960, pp. 12–13.
23. *Christian Worship*, Encyclical Letter *Mediator Dei* (English trans. G. D. Smith), 1947, especially scs 5, 7, 8, 17–23, 38, 63, 65–7, 123, 127.
24. L. Bouyer, *Life and Liturgy*, 1956, p. vii.
25. ibid., pp. 68–9.
26. ibid., pp. 275–6.
27. ibid., p. 254.
28. This last book had originally appeared in German as long ago as 1925.
29. J. A. Jungmann, *The Early Liturgy*, 1959, pp. 1, 8. See also, for example, *Public Worship*, chaps. 1–4; *Pastoral Liturgy*, preface, pp. 89–101; *The Place of Christ in Liturgical Prayer*, pp. xv–xvi; *The Mass of the Roman Rite* vol. 1 (1951), pp. 166–7.
30. C. H. Davis, 'Church Architecture and Liturgy', in *Towards a Church Architecture*, ed. P. Hammond, 1962, p. 112.
31. T. S. Garrett, *The Liturgy of the Church of South India*, 1954, p. xii.
32. L. W. Brown, *Relevant Liturgy*, 1965, pp. 1, 29; J. R. MacPhail, 'Worship in the Church of South India', *Scottish Journal of Theology*, 17, no. 1 (March 1964), pp. 27–9.
33. T. S. Garrett commented that Marcus Ward was 'indulging in epigrammatic exaggeration' (*Worship in the Church of South India*, 1958, p. 13).

34. Principal of Kerala United Theological Seminary 1946–52; Bishop of Uganda 1952–61; Archbishop 1961–5; Bishop of St Edmundsbury and Ipswich 1966–78.
35. Garrett, *Worship in the CSI*, p. 14.
36. L. W. Brown; *Three Worlds: One Word*, 1981, p. 76.
37. Garrett, *Worship in the CSI.*, p. 17.
38. ibid., p. 13.
39. L. Bouyer, 'A Roman Catholic View of the Church of South India', *Theology*, LIX, no. 427 (January 1956), p. 4.
40. Garrett, *The Liturgy of the CSI*, p. 16.
41. The Introduction to the rite states: 'It does not conform to the pattern of any other Liturgy, but it contains elements drawn from many traditions.'
42. Garrett, *Worship in the CSI*, pp. 8–9.
43. Details of the Presbyterian Preparatory Service and its history may be found in G. B. Burnet, *The Holy Communion in the Reformed Church of Scotland 1560-1960,* 1960.
44. Brown, *Three Worlds: One Word*, p. 68.
45. ibid., p. 77.
46. ibid., p. 77; L. W. Brown, 'The Making of a Liturgy', *Scottish Journal of Theology* 4, no. 1 (March 1951), p. 61.
47. Dix, *The Shape of the Liturgy*, pp. 134–5.
48. Garrett, *Worship in the CSI*, pp. 55–7.
49. E. C. Ratcliff, 'The Ordinal of the Church of South India', *Theology* LXIII, no. 475 (January 1960), p. 14.

PART TWO

1955–1980

9

THE LITURGICAL COMMISSION: THE FIRST TEN YEARS

I

The Liturgical Commission held its first meeting at Lambeth Palace on 12 December 1955. With twenty-one members under Colin Dunlop, Dean of Lincoln, it was a fairly academic group with considerable expertise in liturgy and doctrine laced with parochial experience, and with a broad representation of churchmanship. It was limited, however, in having no diocesan bishops or lay persons among its members; but in the climate of the mid-fifties this was probably not surprising, for its work was regarded as that of a rather specialist clerical group.[1] It was also hand-picked; for although diocesan bishops had been invited to suggest names, Colin Dunlop told me and undoubtedly others as well that the Archbishop had given him a free hand in choosing his own team.[2] It was also an asset that with few exceptions everyone already knew everyone else; after all liturgical specialists were not numerous and they tended to keep in touch with one another. In this respect it is interesting to note that in 1949 Colin Dunlop, then Bishop of Jarrow, had arranged a Clergy School at Durham to commemorate the four hundredth anniversary of the first Prayer Book, and six of the seven lecturers became foundation members of the Commission, while the creation of such a body was one of the topics which came up for discussion.[3]

At the outset Archbishop Fisher made it clear that he was in control of operations. He and his fellow-archbishop would decide what work the Commission was to do, and it was not free to plan its own activities. He agreed that this limitation was to protect us from being inundated by frivolous requests from far and wide, and he cited the production of an 'Easter Egg Service' as an illustration of such frivolity. Furthermore, completed work would be sent to the Archbishops, who 'would themselves be responsible for any further action which might be taken'.[4] It all looked so sensible and straightforward; but the controls were too tight. Dr Fisher either chose to ignore or was unaware of the unfortunate consequences of Archbishop Davidson's similar restrictive attitude towards the Advisory Committee on Liturgical Questions in 1912–16.[5] I was probably more aware of this than most people, for I had just completed preparing Walter Frere's papers for publication; and I pleaded with Colin Dunlop to try and secure from the Archbishop clearer terms of reference and better working procedures, especially where the Convocations were concerned — but all to no avail. It was not until 1958 that anything at all was attempted in this direction, and by then damage had already been done. With the passage of time I became increasingly aware — and doubtless other members of the Commission did as well — that where liturgical revision was concerned the Archbishop was really out of his depth: his interest in the subject was minimal and he had no real vision as to the end product. Nor, frankly, could one expect a very great deal from our chairman. His cautious approach had been made clear at Minneapolis. He disliked alternatives; revised services should replace existing ones; and they should be sufficiently modest to retain much of what was already there. 'I venture to say that revisions of Prayer Books should be more modest in scope and less revolutionary than they commonly are . . . Would it not be a wiser policy to exercise greater restraint in compiling new forms? This is my first criterion for future development.'[6]

The Archbishop went on to outline the Commission's first four tasks. He required:

1. A schedule of 'agreed amendments' to the Prayer Book which might be given immediate statutory authority once draft Canon 13 became law. These would be simple, non-controversial changes which would make the book 'more usable and up-to-date' and would involve minor variations which were already widely used and accepted.
2. A further schedule of more radical 'variations', which would require experimental use for a period of seven years after the promulgation of Canon 13 and would include a great many elements of the 1928 Book.
3. New services of Baptism, which would take into account all the reports and proposals which the Church had produced since 1944 and including the 'York' rite of Infant Baptism.[7]
4. A survey of the position of liturgical revision in the Church of England. This would be one of the preliminary study documents required in preparation for the Lambeth Conference of 1958, and would be needed by Easter 1957.[8]

The Commission decided to make a start by looking at Morning and Evening Prayer and their attendant material and deciding which items fell into category (1) and which fell into category (2). A schedule of agreed amendments 'ripe for statutory authority' was in fact prepared by February 1956, although it soon became evident that the dividing line between the two categories was far from clear. In the event the former ceased to be the Commission's responsibility, and the exercise developed into a conservative revision of the Offices and the allied material which proceeded at a gentle, sedate pace and was finally not completed until 1962. In this exercise I was asked to be responsible with Canon Sellers for the revision of the Occasional Prayers and Thanksgivings: but since he suffered increasingly from failing eyesight and was eventually forced to resign from the Commission in 1960, I had to do the bulk of the work myself. This involved quite a lot of discussion and correspondence with individual members of the Commission: and I must put on record that the Dean of York, Eric Milner-White, although subsequently a thorn in our flesh over the question of baptism, was on this subject kindness itself. It obviously was of considerable interest to him — indeed I wondered why he was not asked to do it; but he never tried to impose his views, nothing was too much trouble, and on one occasion he sent me an enormous memorandum of some thirty handwritten pages which must have cost him a great deal in time and energy. But these contacts also revealed that there were other members of the Commission whose concern with liturgical revision was really minimal, except perhaps in a certain antiquarian and pedantic kind of way; it gradually became more obvious and I was not alone in finding it rather irksome. Kenneth Sansbury expressed it succinctly in a letter (2 March 1959): 'You are clearly concerned with the world of 1959 and do not act as some of our brethren do, as though the Holy Spirit ceased to operate in 325 or 1662 or in the days of Bishop Gibson of Gloucester' — a reference to one particular senior member of the Commission who had a propensity for reminiscing about the halcyon days of his curacy under that particular prelate.[9] Another reactionary member of the Commission revealed his opposition, for example, to the permissive use of biddings and silent prayer, regarding this as 'a dangerous innovation. There is no provision in our Prayer Books for periods of silence, which are an abuse.'

The Commission's report for the 1958 Lambeth Conference, largely drafted by Kenneth Sansbury, was accepted by the Archbishops and published in 1957 under the title *Prayer Book Revision in the Church of England.* Beginning with a brief survey of the history of the Prayer Book since the Reformation, it went on to analyse the recent influences for change before setting out the six guiding principles for revision:

1. It should be conservative; and Colin Dunlop's Minneapolis lecture was quoted in support of this.
2. Forms of worship were within the Church's competence to settle, provided they were not repugnant to Holy Scripture — another point dealt with at Minneapolis by Massey Shepherd.
3. It should give expression to the theological and liturgical insights of the time, such as the renewed emphasis on the place of the laity in the life of the Church. Lay participation in the offertory was cited as an example.
4. It should be related to current life and thought, in that it should be (a) intelligible; (b) contemporary, although not ignoring the unchanging truths of the gospel; and (c) expressive of new knowledge.
5. It should be a joint, co-operative enterprise of all the main schools of thought in the Church.
6. It should provide the Church with an enriched, worthier and more fitting vehicle for worship, and should not be undertaken for disciplinary ends.[10]

Finally the report examined the place of the Prayer Book as a bond of unity and standard of doctrine in the Anglican Communion. Here there was a healthy note of warning.

> A survey of Lambeth utterances on the subject would seem to suggest that the Lambeth Fathers hitherto have regarded the 1662 Book as the norm of Anglican doctrine, and the Prayer Books of other parts of the Anglican Communion as merely making explicit in various ways that which is implicit in the 1662 Book. In fact, however, this supposed agreement has covered a substantial cleavage.[11]

Many Anglicans would want to argue that 1662 only represented one stream of Anglican doctrine and failed to give adequate expression to another stream emanating from 1549 and the Scottish rite of 1637 and evident in most Anglican rites outside England. 'Both approaches, we believe, have a rightful place within the Anglican tradition, but if that be so, then it would appear that both the 1549 type and the 1662 type of liturgy must be recognized as having an equally authoritative doctrinal position in the Anglican Communion.'[12] Questions should therefore be asked about the doctrinal criteria of Anglican worship. Are we committed to the exact doctrinal positions of the sixteenth- and seventeenth-century Anglican reformers? Or are we committed only to their general appeal to Scripture, to the undivided Church and to reason? The Commission did not presume to answer such questions; nevertheless it pointed out that they were never far below the surface both when the revision of the Prayer Book was under discussion, and when it was being set forth as a standard of doctrine.[13]

A similar report by the Indian Church, *Principles of Prayer Book Revision*, was rather more forthright, regarding a rigid adherence to the standards of 1662 as unacceptable and frankly pointing out that its own forms did not do so.[14] A flexibility of approach was also endorsed by the American Church. America did not produce a specific report for Lambeth 1958, but by the end of 1957 its Liturgical Commission had published nine studies on different aspects of Prayer Book revision; and that on the Eucharist (1953) clearly stated the principle of doctrinal 'comprehensiveness'.

> The general fact is that the comprehensiveness of the Church, especially in the latitude of belief about the Eucharist which is permitted by all the Anglican liturgies, is something much more than an expression of the celebrated Anglican 'genius for compromise'. It is based upon a recognition of the fact that the sacraments are exactly what the Greeks have always called them, namely 'Mysteries'. They are realities which we experience, but which are beyond the capacity of the human mind completely to comprehend.[15]

A similar view was expressed by the Scottish Report for Lambeth 1958, *Anglican Prayer Books: a Scottish View.* It pointed out that far from regarding 1662 as a bond of unity in the Anglican Communion, it could even be argued that it was almost the opposite. Frere's comment on eucharistic doctrine to Bishop Palmer of Bombay was then quoted:

> There is no need to lay down any provision as to doctrine. It would be impossible, even if it were desirable, to lay this down beforehand. It would be suicidal to set up the English rite [i.e. 1662] as the standard. Certainly it would be disastrous to create a standard negatively by prohibitions, and a broad positive definition would be very difficult in the absence of any generally agreed definition of Anglicanism itself.

Reviewing the history of the Scottish liturgy with its clear differences from 1662, the Report concluded, 'We in Scotland are not concerned to judge unfavourably the liturgies of our sister Churches which follow a different pattern . . . But we do feel bound to defend our own tradition of the last three hundred years, on the grounds of good precedent, reasonableness, and fitness in eucharistic worship.'[16]

The principle of flexibility was also enunciated in another report for Lambeth 1958 on calendrical matters, prepared by a small commission under the Dean of York, *The Commemoration of Saints and Heroes of the Faith in the Anglican Communion.* Here too most parts of the Anglican Communion in the twentieth century had forsaken 1662, enlarging and enriching their own Calendars extensively by the addition of both local worthies and post-Reformation figures. This was a practice which the Report encouraged, setting out principles and safeguards which could be followed by the various Anglican Churches.

How then did Lambeth 1958 react to all this preparatory material? It certainly devoted more time and space to liturgical matters than any of its predecessors; the subject was the sole concern of a sub-committee under the Archbishop of Dublin, Dr G. O. Simms. Leslie Brown, now Bishop of Uganda, was its secretary and the draftsman of a lengthy report, described as 'of the highest importance',[17] in which pride of place went to the Eucharist. In view of Leslie Brown's influential role, it is not surprising to find its eucharistic proposals to be a virtual endorsement of the structure of the CSI liturgy. There is, therefore, no need to repeat them here.[18] It is also worth noting that during the Conference Professor J. G. Davies of Birmingham University and two colleagues, Gilbert Cope and Donald Tytler, published their *Experimental Liturgy* and had it presented on television. The structure of their rite was also very similar to that of CSI and so further exemplified the Conference's proposals.[19]

The Report also gave considerable space to a discussion of eucharistic sacrifice. In the light of subsequent events in the Church of England, its conclusions could only be described as rather optimistic and even controversial. Referring to Massey Shepherd's Minneapolis address and bolstered by Gabriel Hebert's well-known statement from *Intercommunion*,[20] it expressed the belief that

> as a result of new knowledge gained from biblical and liturgical studies the time has come to claim that controversies about the Eucharistic

> Sacrifice can be laid aside, the tensions surrounding this doctrine transcended, and the way prepared for the making of a liturgy in God's good time which will in its essential structure win its way throughout the whole Anglican Communion.[21]

The idea of incorporation was stressed. In the Eucharist worshippers were 'identified' with Christ in his passion, death and resurrection, and the implications of this union were drawn out. 'We offer our praise and thanksgiving for Christ's sacrifice and so present it again, and ourselves to him, before the Father . . . We ourselves incorporate in the mystical body of Christ are the sacrifice we offer. Christ with us offers us in himself to God.'[22] By stressing the finished character of Christ's work and the idea of our participation in it, the Report seemed to suggest that the main points of controversy had been resolved; certainly there was no reference to any dissent or reservations within the sub-committee. Subsequently this was endorsed by the whole Conference in Resolution 73, which welcomed 'the contemporary movement towards unanimity in doctrinal and liturgical matters by those of differing traditions in the Anglican Communion'.[23] Evidently the Lambeth Fathers were at pains to present a united front to the world, in view of the fact that the concept of reconciliation was the dominant note of all their work. 'At the heart of the Christian Gospel is that thought of reconciliation which has been the keynote of our Conference . . . we have tried to see all problems as problems of reconciliation.'[24]

Further evidence of this spirit of reconciliation was seen in the sub-committee's discussion of the 1662 Prayer Book as a bond of unity in doctrine and worship in the Anglican Communion. The rigidity of earlier Lambeth Statements was now modified: 'Loyalty [to 1662] may easily be overstated . . . Now it seems clear that no Prayer Book, not even that of 1662, can be kept unchanged for ever, as a safeguard of established doctrine.' Article 34 was quoted as accepting the principle of national uses, and the Report referred to a number of new Prayer Books in which there had been a revision of eucharistic rites described as 'more or less adventurous'. 'Our unity exists because we are a federation of Provinces and Dioceses of the One, Holy, Catholic, and Apostolic Church, each being served and governed by a Catholic and Apostolic Ministry, and each believing the Catholic faith. These are the fundamental reasons for our unity.' It was only at a secondary level that the Prayer Book could be said to have given Anglican worship a distinct ecclesiastical culture from the special character and quality of its forms of worship.[25] What was now needed was a recovery of the worship of the primitive Church, a principle which Cranmer had endeavoured to follow, despite the limited knowledge at his disposal. Indeed it was the progress in such knowledge which encouraged the sub-committee to hope for a liturgy which would win its way throughout the Anglican Communion; and it urged the appointment of a committee to produce a basic eucharistic pattern for the use of Churches and Provinces undertaking revision.[26] All this was again endorsed by the whole Conference in Resolutions 74 and 76.[27]

The sub-committee, while concentrating on the Eucharist, also ranged over the whole liturgical field. It expressed the hope that the next Lambeth Conference would give detailed consideration to Initiation; meanwhile any revision should follow primitive patterns, with adult baptism, confirmation and first communion as the norm. It called for a revised translation of the Psalter, recommended the adoption of the calendrical proposals in the pre-Lambeth report *The Commemoration of Saints and Heroes*, and pleaded for further study of the vexed question of prayer for the departed. Finally it warned against rapid or revolutionary change: it could only cause widespread dismay and resentment. Endorsement of all this appeared in Conference Resolutions 75, 77–80.[28]

The recommendations of Lambeth 1958 were not unlike the Papal Encyclical *Mediator Dei*: they gave a kind of official imprimatur to a movement which was already taking place; and they certainly gave useful guide-lines to Churches and provinces with only limited expertise at their command. But the weight which the recommendations carried was really quite limited. Of the 310 bishops attending the Conference, probably few were closely involved in liturgical revision or regarded themselves as liturgical experts. Colin Buchanan has pointed out that only five of the thirty-four members of the sub-committee dealing with the subject had come from provinces engaged in eucharistic revision, and many of them were not members of their own provincial liturgical commissions.[29] Furthermore, in plenary sessions involving over three hundred people with a tight time schedule to maintain, there was little opportunity for serious, detailed discussion. It has to be admitted that in the Church of England the Conference recommendations did nothing to diminish controversy over Initiation or eucharistic sacrifice. Nor did the recommendations appear to carry too much weight with Archbishop Fisher. It was over a year later, in September 1959, when he wrote to Bishop Stephen Bayne, the Anglican executive officer, asking him to implement the proposal to appoint a Pan-Anglican committee to advise on eucharistic structure. Apparently he confessed that he had 'not discussed this Resolution with anybody' and was 'not at all sure what should be done about it'.[30] But this was a surprising statement in view of the fact that he had already written to the Liturgical Commission about this proposal soon after the end of the Conference and it had sent him suggestions about setting up the committee in January 1959.[31] Perhaps it indicated forgetfulness, or a lack of interest or a loss of administrative grip, or possibly a combination of all three. After all, he was soon to retire: and no action was taken for another four years – after the Anglican Congress at Toronto in 1963, when his successor was firmly in the saddle.

One Lambeth recommendation which was taken up almost immediately, however, was that of Psalter revision. The sub-committee had made the point that there could be no spiritual benefit in repeating archaic words and phrases; these would need attention if the Psalter were to be reinstated in the affections of both clergy and people.[32] This was accepted by both Canterbury and York Convocations in October 1958; and the Archbishops appointed a small but weighty commission before the end of the year 'to produce . . . a revision of the text of the Psalter designed to remove obscurities and serious errors of translation, yet such as to retain, as far as possible, the general character in style and rhythm of Coverdale's version and its suitability for congregational use'.[33] Its chairman was Dr Donald Coggan, Bishop of Bradford, himself no mean Old Testament scholar; and with him were two Hebraists, Bishop George Chase and Professor Winton Thomas; two English scholars, T. S. Eliot and C. S. Lewis; and two musicians, John Dykes Bower and Gerald Knight.[34] Psalms 1–41 were published in 1961 and the complete Psalter in 1963; and in October 1963 the Convocations approved it 'with a view to legislation for its permissive use'.[35] Subsequently it was authorized for use under the Versions of the Bible Measure. Essentially a conservative revision of Coverdale, with those archaisms which presented difficulty in current usage removed, and benefiting from the insights of Semitic scholarship, it was aptly described by the Commission itself as a piece of 'invisible mending'.[36] For clarity and correct translation it was undoubtedly an improvement on Coverdale; but it had its critics, some arguing that certain elements of poetry had been removed unnecessarily. As *The Church Times* reviewer remarked, 'At some point in the revision the tinkerers took over.' Professor Frost later commented that the Commission suffered from a lack of breadth in its Hebrew scholarship, being influenced too much by the late Professor Sir Godfrey Driver: while on the English side 'there was by no means invariable accord between Eliot and Lewis'.[37] Valuable exercise though it may have been, it never really captured the imagination and hearts of Anglican worshippers and certainly it never ousted Coverdale from its established position.

II

The second major task of the Liturgical Commission was to produce new rites of Initiation. They were destined to have a short, unsuccessful and rather stormy existence, but they were by no means a waste of time and energy. Much of the material was ultimately used; and the exercise in itself constituted an important element in the Commission's 'growing pains'. At its third meeting in April 1956 it agreed to take the York rite as the basis for the new infant service, while the adult service was to be given separate consideration. Responsibility for drafting the latter was given to Arthur Couratin, Principal of St Stephen's House, Oxford, who joined the Commission in June 1956 together with Julian Thornton-Duesbery, Master of St Peter's College, Oxford. Couratin's advent was something of a whirlwind, and the Commission was swept along at a great pace.[38] His introductory memorandum was ready in a matter of weeks; and it was clear that he envisaged something much more radical than the York rite, with administration within the Eucharist as the norm. This was something which I and many other members believed to be what was required. In his introductory statement Archbishop Fisher had indicated that this project was quite distinct from the schedule of agreed amendments and the variations for experimental use, and the final product might ultimately replace the existing services in the Prayer Book. It was also taken to be what the Joint Committees of 1954 had proposed in their final report *Baptism and Confirmation Today*: 'a new Service for Adult Baptism should be modelled on the primitive services, which were made for adults, and not upon an adaptation of them made for infants.'[39]

Couratin's proposals were accepted in November 1956, and by the following January his draft of *The Ministration of Baptism, Confirmation and Holy Communion to such as are of age to answer for themselves* was ready. This was discussed in detail for the rest of that year; and it became increasingly clear that at some stage the Commission would have to grasp a nettle and reconsider their earlier decision on Infant Baptism: whatever its merits, the York rite – both theologically and liturgically – did not fit in with the Couratin draft. The crunch came in January 1958. Couratin introduced a draft rite for Infant Baptism to fit his other proposals; Milner-White countered by expounding the merits of the York rite; there was a long discussion; and finally the Commission agreed *nem. con.* to rescind its earlier decision and accept instead the Couratin draft.[40] The Dean of York was understandably disappointed; but he seemed unable to accept the change, regarding it almost as a personal affront. From then onwards he was single-minded in his efforts to rescue the rite on which he had lavished so much work, even if it meant the rejection of the Commission's proposals.

It was at this stage, when the drafts were nearing completion, that I pleaded once again for a clarification of our relationships with the Convocations, setting out the issues in a memorandum; but again nothing was done, the Commission being content to leave the matter to the Archbishops.[41] Events were to prove, however, that this was a mistake, particularly in view of Milner-White's opposition in the Northern Convocation. By November 1958 the Commission had sent their report to the Archbishops, who appointed Joint Committees of their Convocations to discuss it with us at a meeting planned for June 1959 in Oxford. But already things were going wrong. At our December meeting Colin Dunlop reported that Milner-White had been in touch with the Archbishops before the Commission had submitted their work, presenting them with a minority report signed by himself and Canon Evans which dissented from the proposals for Infant Baptism and Confirmation and included a revised form of the York rite. To have done this without informing the Commission or providing it with an opportunity to examine or discuss their document was, to say the least, unconstitutional; nor was it conducive to a relaxed atmosphere. But eventually a compromise was worked out. It was agreed that in future any minority report should first be discussed with the Commission and then submitted with the majority report. Milner-White also agreed to ask the Archbishops not to publish his document but to include instead a note of dissent with the Commission's published report. Peace of a kind was therefore patched up; but it was not the end of the Dean's opposition. This December meeting was in fact the last he ever attended, although he never resigned and continued to send his apologies for absence regularly until his final illness in 1962.[42]

In March 1959 he wrote to Colin Dunlop, revealing that, far from the minority report having been withdrawn, Archbishop Fisher was now requesting further copies of it for distribution to the Convocation Liaison Committees. The Chairman was provoked, not only to remonstrate with the Dean but to write a strong letter to Lambeth, pointing out that the opposition was being conducted in a most unconstitutional manner. The Dean of York's document could in no sense be called a Minority Report because the Majority had neither seen it nor discussed it: in any case the agreement to withdraw it had been ignored: and the Archbishop appeared to be treating the Minority as a separate Commission with direct access to Lambeth. In reply Dr Fisher made the excuse that if the Liaison Committee read the note of dissent appended to the Commission's report, inevitably they would want to know what it involved; and few if any of the Canterbury Committee had ever seen or knew anything about the York rite. In the event, however, the dissenting documents were forthcoming and duly circulated before the Oxford meeting in June.[43] This passed off smoothly enough, and the demonstrations were well staged in different parish churches to indicate their adaptability; but the Liaison Committees could hardly be said to have shown any great enthusiasm; and the York contingent, led by the Bishop of Sheffield, was decidedly cool.

Further trouble followed over publication. Dr Fisher was sorely displeased when the Report appeared in a format different from that usually followed for Convocation documents (and at a higher price!): and when Colin Dunlop suggested a filmstrip or a television programme to help commend it to the Church at large, he met with a flat refusal. It was becoming increasingly clear that Dr Fisher, having asked the Commission to produce something quite new, did not like what had been done. The services, published under the title *Baptism and Confirmation*, adhered to the principles set out by Lambeth 1958, attempting to return to primitive patterns.[44] The full rite of Adult Baptism, Confirmation and Holy Communion was the archetypal service, and other services, Adult Baptism, Infant Baptism and Confirmation on their own, were adapted from it. It began with a Ministry of the Word with three lessons and psalmody, in which the Gospel was Mark 1.1—11, recounting our Lord's baptism. The Gospel at Infant Baptism was Matthew 28.18—20 rather than Mark 10.13—16, which the Commission argued had no obvious connection with the rite. The promises were placed in close association with the pouring of water; and the blessing of the water, which now preceded the promises, was eucharistic in form, setting out the fundamental elements of the biblical doctrine of baptism. The consignation became a post-baptismal ceremony and the giving of a lighted candle was permitted. Confirmation could bear both meanings of the word, strengthening and completion, which were not regarded as mutually exclusive. The rite clearly taught that the Holy Spirit was given in baptism and confirmation, while in Infant Baptism the sponsors were required to make the promises, not in the name of, but on behalf of the children. The doctrine of baptismal regeneration was clearly stated: but emphasis was now laid on invitation into the new life by death and resurrection with Christ and not on the removal of the taint of original guilt.

What then was the basis of Milner-White's strong opposition? Obviously there was affection for and loyalty to a rite in which he had been closely involved; but despite Lambeth 1958 and the Convocation Joint Committees in 1954, he believed the radical approach and the appeal to antiquity to be pastorally wrong, apart from any theological or liturgical considerations. The York Convocation's call for a revision providing a simplified, abbreviated and improved rite, *but not at the expense of abolishing the familiar*, had been absolutely right. Suddenly to confront the Church with drastic change after some four hundred years of use was unwise, and he did not believe the Church wanted it. Moreover, the Commission's proposals — especially the ante-communion form of introduction — were not only pastorally impracticable; their basic principles were mistaken. He believed that in baptism infants were 'plunged into the love of God' — a favourite phrase; and this was far more important than any theology based on the adult rite.[45]

The Commission could and did answer these criticisms.[46] Its Infant rite was in fact no longer than the York rite and substantially shorter than that of 1662. Furthermore the Church had been struggling for years to remedy an unsatisfactory pastoral situation, particularly indiscriminate baptism; this was clear from the various reports, and the proposals should now be seen against this background. Admittedly they were radical in structure, breaking long-established moulds; and long familiarity had undoubtedly endeared the old rite to conservative minds. But Cranmer's rite had never been entirely satisfactory and was based on a theology which begged too many questions. Nevertheless, all this was really relevant to the point I had unsuccessfully made. If a revision of this kind was to be undertaken successfully, a fundamental prerequisite was the support and confidence of the Church and its constitutional bodies. Proper planning was therefore essential: the operation must run smoothly; and some degree of educational work was called for. The Archbishop's ban on such activity had not been exactly helpful. Nor was the timing of the operation ideal. The Report was scheduled for presentation to the Convocations in January 1960, despite the fact that Canon 13 had not yet been promulged; even if approval were given, therefore, the services would still have to be temporarily moth-balled before experiment could begin. Equally unfortunate was the fact that although

Mervyn Stockwood had already become Bishop of Southwark, providing the Commission with its own spokesman in the Upper House of Canterbury, the responsibility for presenting the Report to Convocation was given to Oliver Tomkins, Bishop of Bristol, who could not speak from first-hand experience. To the outsider this too must have seemed a little strange. Nevertheless he acquitted himself creditably on 19 January, and he was ably supported by members of the Commission: Colin Dunlop, Douglas Harrison, Kenneth Ross and Kenneth Sansbury. On the whole the debate in full Synod went well: of some twenty speeches made, those in favour of the Report were in the ratio of approximately two to one. Archbishop Fisher, however, flatly rejected a request for a demonstration for the benefit of Convocation and resisted an attempt to drop the York rite from the proposals. Finally both Houses agreed to refer the whole matter to a joint committee for further consideration.[47] The Upper House then discussed the Report on their own, and here the question of relationships between the Commission and the Convocations was again raised; but the Archbishop refused to be bothered with such matters, claiming that things would sort themselves out. 'I feel there need be no worry about how the Joint Committee and the Liturgical Commission will co-ordinate their respective functions. In the end something will emerge which is commended.'[48]

The York debate went less smoothly. Despite an able presentation of the Report by Canon Addleshaw and Archdeacon Cobham, they had to meet a formidable attack not only from Milner-White and Bishop Leslie Hunter but from Archbishop Ramsey himself, who argued that the Commission's rites were theologically overweighted. The attack continued from speaker after speaker, relieved only by a comment from Dr Dillistone, Dean of Liverpool, that many of the criticisms appeared to be about peripheral matters rather than about essentials. The debate was eventually adjourned until the May session, when both Houses agreed to follow Canterbury in referring the matter to a joint committee but insisted on expressing their preference for the York infant rite.[49] In November Professor Ratcliff published his biting attack on the York rite in *Theology*. He made no attempt to compare it with the Commission's work and indeed made no reference to the latter: but he judged it simply on its own merits and as the sole alternative to 1662, and in his view it was sadly wanting.

> It would be interesting to know in what respects the historic liturgies may be supposed to have contributed materially to the making of York. Their traces have been well concealed . . . If York's compilers possessed the knowledge, they made no expert use of it. York, considered as a liturgy, cannot be counted other than a miscarriage . . . Those who know and cherish the baptismal tradition and liturgy of the Church will receive York without welcome, and not without dismay.[50]

Unfortunately it was too late to have any influence on events, and it apparently carried no weight with the final judgements of the York joint committee.

The two joint committees did not report until October 1961, but before then an important change had taken place in the Commission itself. At its meeting on 28-9 September 1960 Colin Dunlop announced his resignation as chairman and his succession by Dr Coggan, Bishop of Bradford. He explained that increasing deafness made it difficult for him to be an effective chairman; and this was undoubtedly true. Meetings had tended to become a little unruly, with private conversations going on during sessions, of which he seemed to be unaware and which he certainly made no attempt to stop. At times this could be embarrassing. Admittedly the Commission was not an easy body to handle; but a chairman should be tough and not hesitate to administer rebuke when necessary. Secondly, he had clearly found the Archbishop a difficult person to deal with. While Dr Fisher was determined to exercise control over the Commission and its activities, liturgical revision was a subject about which he knew little and in which he had no real interest. There was little sympathy with what the Commission was trying to do; and Colin Dunlop was too gentle and sensitive to stand up to him. Thirdly the rather ruthless opposition of the Dean of York and the support which it gained in the Northern Convocation disappointed and even upset him. So he resigned; but happily he continued as a member of the Commission until it was reconstituted in 1962.

The Report of the joint committees, which had met together under the Bishop of Bristol, eventually appeared in October 1961.[51] It held little joy for the Commission. Admittedly the combined rite of Adult Baptism, Confirmation and Holy Communion was regarded as generally acceptable; but the separate rites of Infant Baptism and Confirmation posed serious problems. It was only by a majority decision that the Commission's proposals for the former were recommended as a basis, and so many points were referred back for further consideration — mainly to include York material — that a major rewrite would clearly be required. Furthermore four of the seven York members, led by the Bishop of Sheffield, still expressed a preference for the York rite and hoped that it would be authorized for experimental use. Confirmation was also referred back for revision, although on a less drastic scale, the main criticism being that undue emphasis had been placed on the Mason–Dix line; but here again the Bishop of Sheffield raised the question whether a new rite of Confirmation was either necessary or demanded by the Church. In the event, both Houses of Canterbury Convocation approved the Report in January 1962.[52] In York, however, although the combined Adult rite was accepted, the Commission's Infant Baptism and Confirmation rites were decisively rejected — a fairly predictable result. But the Bishop of Sheffield, when presenting the Report, devoted most of his speech not to its contents but to what he regarded as the root cause of the disappointment created by the Commission's proposals. It lay, not in their work, but in the 'undue haste and certain lack of careful consideration given to the relations between that Commission and Convocation when it was set up and set going'. What was needed before Canon 13 was made effective was a policy on liturgical revision. This demanded answers to certain fundamental questions. Did the Church want a revised Prayer Book on 1928 lines or something quite new? Was the Commission to be permanent or not? Was it to be an independent body planning its own work? Or was it simply to offer advice to the Convocations when required? And what of the liturgical rights and responsibilities of the Convocations? He then made it clear where he himself stood. He wanted a conservative and not a radical revision, with the new growing out of the old. The Commission's proposals, while admirable liturgical compositions in themselves, failed to meet such a requirement.[53]

This statement, reiterating all that I had been trying to put across for some years, was important in that it was clearly directed to the President, Dr Coggan, who now found himself both Archbishop of York and Chairman of the Commission. Such comment, from one of the Church's senior leaders, could not fail to carry weight; and in summing up, the Archbishop indicated that the point had been taken.

> I assumed . . . the chairmanship of that Commission at a stage when it was an adolescent, and adolescence is always a somewhat awkward stage through which any young person has to go . . . The terms of reference under which the Liturgical Commission has been working have, I think, been vague, and that has occasioned some of our difficulty. Further, our method of liaison as between the Commission and the House of Bishops, on the one hand, and as between the Commission and the Convocations, on the other, has been, I think, a little weak and ill-defined. There again has been a source of our difficulty. And I think that the members of the Liturgical Commission, who are much older in its service than I am, would agree with that . . . I am quite sure that the wise words of the Bishop of Sheffield addressed to us as almost the main part of his initial speech this afternoon will have to be taken to heart very seriously by all of us who occupy any place on that Liturgical Commission, and I hope we shall do so very shortly.[54]

Perhaps, after all, the Commission's report had served a useful purpose, although not in the way originally intended.

III

Donald Coggan took over from Colin Dunlop in December 1960. Although making no claims to be an expert liturgist, he was an established biblical scholar and was Chairman of the Commission responsible for the Revised Psalter. Moreover, he was a first-class chairman, with a clear grasp of proceedings and a strict sense of discipline. There was work to be done; there was no wasting of time; and speakers must be treated with courtesy by other members. Everyone was quelled by the tapping of his pencil on the table and his penetrating gaze. Almost immediately afterwards his appointment to the Archbishopric of York was announced, but he quickly dispelled any fears of a summary departure, despite his increased commitments and the anomaly of a position in which he, as chairman of the Commission, would report to himself as Archbishop. Indeed, far from being a disadvantage, it strengthened the Commission's position in the Church. Obviously, he found it difficult to attend the whole of every meeting; but during his four years of office his attendance was exemplary and he was absent only twice. He clearly regarded such constitutional questions as I had been frequently raising as important; and the Convocation debates on Initiation had certainly highlighted them. It was a welcome development, therefore, when both Archbishops attended a meeting of the Commission on 31 January 1962 to announce significant changes.

In the first place there was to be closer consultation between the Archbishops and the Commission in formulating policy, so that before starting a project the latter would know more precisely what was required. In this the presence of Donald Coggan was obviously of enormous help. Secondly, the relations with the House of Bishops were to be strengthened, not only by always having two diocesans on the Commission, but also by discussing proposals with them before their presentation to the Convocations; in this way there would be some assurance of episcopal support. Thirdly, the Commission was to be more broadly based, with lay representation both male and female – even though this might involve some loss in technical scholarship, for no increase in numbers was contemplated. In view of such changes the Commission felt it only right and proper to place themselves unreservedly at the disposal of the Archbishops.[55] There was now one more meeting, in March 1962, to clear the decks and finally complete the revision of Morning and Evening Prayer and its attendant material. The result was a very conservative report, with not a tremendous lot to show for over seven years' work.[56]

The group which met in September 1962 showed considerable change. Of the original foundation members some half had disappeared. Canon Sellers had already resigned from ill-health in June 1961, and Kenneth Sansbury had left shortly afterwards on becoming Bishop of Singapore. I think it would be true to say of the other eight departures that most were fairly obvious on grounds of ill-health, age, or regular absenteeism.[57] Of the newcomers, the most notable were Ernest Southcott; Christopher Evans and Austin Farrer, both eminent biblical scholars; David Ayerst, a layman eminent in education and journalism; and Elisabeth Montefiore.[58] The chairman began by pointing out that the Commission was no longer a specialist group, undertaking specific pieces of work for the Archbishops, but a representative group working for the Church at large. He then outlined five tasks. The first three involved the Eucharist: a radical revision of the rite itself, a revision of the propers for Saints' Days, and the provision of Old

Testament lessons for all occasions. The other two were a revision of the rites of Burial and the Churching of Women. It would be for the Commission to decide on the order of priority. On the rites of Initiation there was, thankfully, a discreet silence. He then went on to indicate the way in which the Commission could serve the Church as a whole, and he evidently envisaged an educative role, first by publishing material for discussion, and secondly by providing speakers at meetings and conferences.[59]

It did not take long for the Commission to agree that top priority should be given to the revision of the Eucharist; but the discussion on the method of approach took longer, bearing a marked resemblance to a similar discussion which had taken place years before in South India. Some members favoured taking an existing rite as a starting point; and three possibilities were mooted: 1662; the Draft Liturgy for Africa, based on CSI and recently produced by Leslie Brown; and the Birmingham Experimental Rite. I pleaded, however, for starting from scratch with a 'clean sheet': it was far better to look first at principles rather than existing rites, for there was always a danger of the latter clouding issues; and once principles were settled, rites could always be used as quarries for suitable material. In the end the 'clean sheet' approach was accepted; and Arthur Couratin and Henry de Candole undertook to prepare a discussion booklet on principles and structure.[60] This document, *Reshaping the Liturgy*, eventually appeared in July 1964. While bearing the names of the authors, it was prepared after full consultation with the Commission and was published jointly with the Church's Board of Education. To some degree it could almost be described as 'a layman's guide to the Lambeth 1958 recommendations'. A chapter was devoted to each section of the rite: the Ministry of the Word, the Prayers and the Ministry of the Sacrament; and while possible lines of revision were indicated, care was taken not to create an impression that the lines were already settled. It was essentially a discussion document, with numerous questions for study; and it was exactly the right kind of material to put before the Church at this juncture. The Initiation rites might well have had a better reception if they had been introduced in a similar way. The Chairman's Foreword was also valuable for two reasons. First he reminded readers how much had happened elsewhere even since Lambeth 1958: the publication of the complete South Indian *Book of Common Worship*, the appearance of the Draft *Liturgy for Africa*, the promulgation of *The Constitution on the Sacred Liturgy* by the Second Vatican Council, to say nothing of the creation of the interdenominational Joint Liturgical Group in this country. 'Except for a few unofficial experiments here and there, the ordinary Church of England worshipper has so far shown little awareness of all this.' Here was a challenge to be up and doing. Secondly, he seemed to indicate, though rather tentatively, that this new eucharistic rite would be alternative to that in the Prayer Book and would not be substituted for it. 'This would presumably be intended not to supersede the existing service of the 1662 Prayer Book but to provide a permissive alternative.'[61] This concept of permissive alternatives expressed in the Convocation debates on Canon 13 in 1960, was to gain ground with the passage of time.

This was accompanied by a second booklet on the general subject of liturgical reform, *Why Prayer Book Revision at all?*, written by Basil Naylor, the gifted Chancellor of Liverpool Cathedral and one of the newcomers to the Commission. Its purpose was both to instil interest and to reassure. Some Anglicans would question revision simply because they were by nature conservative and reluctant to lose what was familiar; others would be worried at the prospect of a renewal of controversy such as that of 1927-8: others again would feel that the Church should be addressing itself to more pressing concerns — social, missionary and ecumenical. He tried to find an answer by surveying the Liturgical Movement, Catholic and Reformed, and indicating the breadth of the concerns in which liturgy was involved. It was a masterpiece of compression and could well be regarded as the best short survey of the whole subject to appear from an Anglican pen to date.

In June 1963 Dr Coggan announced a further extension of the Commission's activities with the creation of the Joint Liturgical Group, a project in which I was closely involved. It really started to take shape in my mind when I began to teach liturgy at King's College, London, in 1960. Not only did the students come from a variety of Churches: I also came into contact with non-Anglican scholars and clergy who had similar or allied interests. At the Methodist college in Richmond, for example, there were Marcus Ward, one of the creators of the South Indian rite, Norman Goldhawk, an authority on hymnody, and later Raymond George, an able liturgist well known in ecumenical circles. From the Congregational New College came another eminent ecumenical leader, John Huxtable, and Geoffrey Nuttall, an authority on Richard Baxter. Then from outside the University but having numerous contacts, mainly through students, were the well-known Congregationalists James Todd and Caryl Micklem and the Baptists Neville Clark and Stephen Winward. Interests in the world of publishing also brought me into close and friendly contact with other people concerned with liturgy: Gordon Wakefield, who ran the Epworth Press, J. J. von Allmen of Neuchâtel, Max Thurian of Taizé, and most important of all, Dr John Lamb, Librarian of New College, Edinburgh. This dour and shy Scot was probably the most learned liturgical scholar of his day in the Church of Scotland. I came to know him through his researches into the liturgical use of the Psalter and eventually helped him with the publication of his *The Psalms in Christian Worship*, a standard text-book on the subject. We became firm friends, and it was he who first suggested to me that talking together about liturgy was not enough: creating liturgy together would be more productive; and he firmly believed that this offered more opportunity for progress towards Christian unity than any other activity. He set out some of these ideas in a paper read to the Edinburgh Theological Club in March 1960.[62]

I took this suggestion up with Donald Coggan privately in December

1960, pleading that it was high time to explore the possibilities of an interdenominational exercise, despite the very real difficulties. There would clearly be reservations within the Commission itself; for when it had agreed to the sharing of information with other Anglican Churches, it had also decided, 'This ought not to be done for non-Anglicans; discussions with them should be on a personal basis by individual members of this Commission, who would have authority to commit nobody but themselves.'[63] But this was precisely what I did not want; something far weightier and involving a creative element was required. Yet to seek synodical authority for such an exercise could involve considerable delay and the risk of rejection; it only needed someone to trot out the well-worn argument, 'The time is not ripe', and the whole operation could be shelved indefinitely. Then again there were the British Council of Churches and the World Council of Churches to consider. Although neither body had as yet undertaken the kind of exercise I envisaged, to ignore them was to risk offending them; yet to seek their co-operation might result in the exercise taking on very different direction. Nor had we any idea what the official reaction of the other Churches in this country to such an idea might be. Fortunately Donald Coggan was wholeheartedly supportive, despite the difficulties. Without his tactful co-operation the whole operation could have ended in failure. He consulted the Archbishop of Canterbury and the House of Bishops and apparently successfully overcame any misgivings or indifferences which might have existed. He then gave me permission to take soundings and report back.

I went on talking to people, individually and in small groups, for a year. The idea also had a public airing when the Free Churches held a service to commemorate the 1662 Prayer Book at Westminster in November 1962 and one of the speakers, a Congregationalist, pleaded for liturgical co-operation between the Churches. Finally I held a meeting at King's College Hostel, London, on 20-1 March 1963 attended by a dozen hand-picked Baptists, Congregationalists, Methodists, Presbyterians and Anglicans from England and Scotland. Most of the people already mentioned had arranged to be there with the knowledge and consent of their own Church authorities. Indeed, the Primus of Scotland himself represented his own Church, while Henry de Candole and Douglas Harrison came with me from the Commission. It was highly successful; and the satisfaction of the other Church representatives was expressed by John Huxtable when he said, 'This is what we have been waiting for'. A great deal of ground was covered: information on revision programmes was shared and various questions were discussed – what kind of joint revision projects were considered practical, what kind of group should be created, what machinery should be used to bring it into being, and how it should be financed. By the end of the second day it was agreed that a Joint Liturgical Group should be formed, the Archbishop of Canterbury should be asked to help bring it into being, and if possible operations should begin in October 1963.

Both Archbishops were pleased at the outcome, and Dr Ramsey gladly agreed to write to the heads of the Churches involved, inviting them to nominate two members each. He also produced an important statement on the Group's status, which proved to be generally acceptable.

> It is clearly to be understood that any work produced by this Group will have no authority greater than that which its own members give to it by their own weight; but it will be for particular Churches, through their own customary modes of decision, to make use of the results if they are willing to do so.[64]

This was an admirable *modus vivendi*: it gave the Group maximum freedom to plan its own programme and work in its own way; the reputation of the Group would depend entirely on the value of the work it produced: and there was a suggestion or hint to the Churches concerned that they ought not to ignore what was being done, although they were under no obligation to accept it. In practice it all worked very well. The fifteen members who attended the first meeting on 10-11 October 1963 were really an impressive group, containing the Primus of Scotland, four college Principals, and seven or eight established scholars.[65] They elected Douglas Harrison, Dean of Bristol, as chairman; and it seemed to be assumed that I would be secretary and generally responsible for running the Group. While it was agreed that the first major piece of work should deal with Calendar and Lectionary matters, it was also felt that some kind of introduction to the public was desirable. A symposium of seven essays was therefore published under the title *The Renewal of Worship*, clearing up some misunderstandings which might exist about each other's worship and providing some reasons why joint creative work in the field of liturgy was now considered possible. It was a fine little piece of work, the essays by Stephen Winward on Embodied Worship, John Huxtable on Prayer — Fixed, Free and Extemporary, and Aled Davies on Liturgy and Mission being particularly valuable. One reviewer made the interesting comment that if the author's names had been erased, it would have been difficult to tell which Churches the various essays had come from. I must confess that working with this Group was exhilarating: members were keen and worked tremendously hard; there were no ecclesiastical politics to bother about; and members were stimulated by the fresh insights which the representatives of other Churches provided. We were all conscious of the lack of any Roman Catholic contribution; but this was remedied before very long.

IV

In 1960, when Canon 13 embodying the proposals in the 1952 Moberly Report for the authorization of new services came before the Convocations of Canterbury and York, it was agreed to divide it into five: it therefore became Canons B 1—5.[66] The procedure of approving these new canons and embodying them in suitable legislation was to prove rather lengthy and wearisome: but at least it was brilliantly introduced by Dr Mortimer, Bishop of Exeter, himself a member of the Moberly Church and State Commission. He reminded the Convocations that strict and exact conformity to 1662 was impossible – a fact accepted by the Royal Commission of 1906. The 1928 Book's attempt to deal with the problem had failed, for three reasons: it had been a book of the study, never tested in the common life of the Church; it had been a package deal, with no alternative to voting for or against the whole book; and its compilers had been dominated by two motives which were not fully reconcilable, to improve public worship and to restore discipline. Parliament had rightly refused to accept it. In the light of this experience they were now proposing something different, involving a slow, cautious and piecemeal revision, which would also help to resolve doubts and ease consciences on questions of legality. The proposed canons were themselves uncontroversial, simply conferring limited powers to the Church: but they were vital to its life and it was essential that they approached the Crown and Parliament with a clear and unanimous voice.[67]

To save time the legislation giving effect to these Canons – the Prayer Book (Alternative and other Services) Measure – was drafted and introduced into the Church Assembly while the Canons were still being considered.[68] This was a wise precaution; for there were occasions when the House of Laity in particular made quite heavy weather of the whole business. Happily what opposition existed tended to evaporate, and the Measure was eventually given final approval on 7 July 1964 virtually with that 'clear and unanimous' voice that Dr Mortimer had originally pleaded for.[69] It became law on 23 March 1965; and it was not until over a year later that the Church's constitutional bodies solemnly gave final approval to the relevant Canons – a strange timetable of events![70]

Under this Measure, which required the Provinces of Canterbury and York to act together, the Church could now lawfully use services alternative to those in the Prayer Book for a period of seven years with an extension if necessary to fourteen, provided all four Houses of Convocation and the House of Laity approved them by at least a two-thirds majority. A preliminary trial use of such services could also be held for two years in cathedrals or selected parishes under episcopal control.[71] At local level the consent of the Parochial Church Council was required, or in the case of the Occasional Offices that of the parties concerned. In the case of services for which the Prayer Book made no provision, these could be authorized by the Convocation of either province or by the diocesan bishop: and for special occasions of local significance the individual minister was free to produce his own rites; he was also free to make variations in any service, including those in the Prayer Book, which were 'not of substantial importance'. All services under this Measure were required to be reverent, seemly and doctrinally sound; and if guidance or advice were needed, the bishop was to be consulted; moreover, they were all deemed to have been ordered by lawful authority within the meaning of the Clerical Subscription Act of 1865.[72]

At the same time as this legislation was going through the Convocations and Church Assembly, two other Measures relevant to liturgical revision were also dealt with. In the first place the long-standing problems of the Ornaments Rubric were resolved. Under Canon B 8 vestments were declared legal, no doctrinal significance was attached to them, and the consent of the Parochial Church Council was required if a minister wished either to introduce or to discontinue them. These provisions were incorporated into the Vestures of Ministers Measure in 1962, and despite some Evangelical opposition this eventually became law two years later.[73] Secondly, the Versions of the Bible Measure was approved without difficulty in 1965. This was first prompted by the publication of the New Testament of *The New English Bible* in 1961. It was recognized that while there was nothing to prevent it being used for the lessons at Morning and Evening Prayer, it could not be used for the Epistles and Gospels of the Eucharist, where the texts themselves were set out in the Prayer Book. Then the Revised Psalter appeared in 1963 and its use required proper authorization. The Versions of the Bible Measure therefore sanctioned the use of any modern version of the Scriptures at all services after due consideration.[74]

It was in the light of these changes — all imminent — that the Archbishop of Canterbury visited the Liturgical Commission in April 1964 to give warning that a great deal of material must be ready for consideration within a matter of months. This, together with the reconstitution of membership, was to mark a new phase in the Commission's life.

NOTES

1. The members were: Colin Dunlop, Dean of Lincoln; the Rt Revd. H. de Candole, Bishop of Knaresborough; the Very Revd. E. Milner-White, Dean of York; The Very Revd. R. A. Beddoes, Provost of Derby; The Ven. J. O. Cobham, Archdeacon of Durham; the Ven. D. E. W. Harrison, Archdeacon of Sheffield; Canon G. W. O. Addleshaw; Canon Ernest Evans; Professor E. C. Ratcliff; Canon C. K. Sansbury; Canon R. V. Sellers; Canon D. R. Vicary; the Revd. C. W. J. Bowles; the Revd. D. F. Horsfield; the Revd. R. C. D. Jasper; the Revd. K. N. Ross; the Revd. A. M. Stockwood; the Revd. R. P. Symonds; the Revd. B. J. Wigan; the Revd. G. G. Willis (Secretary). Canon Eric Abbott, the Warden of Keble College Oxford, was also appointed; but he never attended a single meeting and after a year he resigned. He was replaced by the Revd. Arthur Couratin, Principal of St Stephen's House, Oxford, and the Revd. J. P. Thornton Duesbery, Master of St Peter's College, Oxford.
2. Note the comment of Bishop Leslie Hunter in *Journal Convoc.*, 1962, pp. 106–7.
3. The six were Dunlop, de Candole, Harrison, Beddoes, Addleshaw and myself. The seventh was the Dean of Chichester, the Very Revd. A. S. Duncan-Jones, who died before the Commission was appointed.

4. Liturgical Commission *Minutes* 1. 1.
5. See pp. 91–5.
6. *Minneapolis Report*, pp. 95–6.
7. See pp. 167–72.
8. *LC Minutes* 1.1.
9. This constant reminiscing only ceased when Canon Sellers, a Yorkshireman with a great sense of humour, could stand it no longer, and deliberately started to match the interminable 'When I was curate of X' with, 'But when I was Vicar of Mytholmroyd . . .'. It caused such hilarity that the reminiscing soon ceased.
10. *Prayer Book Revision in the Church of England*, 1957, pp. 29–34.
11. ibid., p. 37.
12. ibid., p. 38.
13. ibid., p. 39.
14. CIPBC, *Principles of Prayer Book Revision*, 1957, pp. 64–5.
15. American Prayer Book Studies IV, *The Eucharistic Liturgy*, 1953, pp. 140–1.
16. *Anglican Prayer Books: a Scottish View*, 1958, especially pp. 1, 6, 14.
17. *The Lambeth Conference 1958*, 1958, p. 2, 64.
18. Leslie Brown wrote subsequently, 'All these [i.e. the Lambeth Conference] suggestions had been in fact already carried out in the "Order for the Lord's Supper or Holy Eucharist" of the Church of South India' (*Relevant Liturgy*, 1965, p. 51).
19. G. Cope, J. G. Davies and D. A. Tytler, *An Experimental Liturgy* (Ecumenical Studies in Worship no. 3) 1958.
20. See p. 166.
21. *Lambeth 1958*, p. 2, 83.
22. ibid., p. 2. 84.
23. ibid., p. 1. 47.
24. Encyclical Letter, ibid., p. 1. 18.
25. ibid., pp. 2. 78–9.
26. ibid., pp. 2. 80–1.
27. ibid., pp. 1. 47–8.
28. ibid., pp. 1. 47–9; 2. 86–7, 90, 92–3, 94–8.
29. C. O. Buchanan, *Modern Anglican Liturgies 1958–1968*, 1968, p. 8.
30. S. F. Bayne, *An Anglican Turning Point*, p. 16, quoted in Buchanan, op. cit., p. 22.
31. *LC Minutes*, 15. 2; 17. 2c.
32. *Lambeth 1958*, p. 2. 90.
33. *The Revised Psalter*, 1963, p. vii; *Chronicle Convoc.*, 1958, pp. 230–44.
34. Bishop G. Chase, formerly Master of Selwyn College, Cambridge and Bishop of Ripon; Winton Thomas, Regius Professor of Hebrew, University of Cambridge; C. S. Lewis, Professor of Medieval and Renaissance Literature, University of Cambridge; J. Dykes Bower, Organist of St Paul's Cathedral; Gerald H. Knight, Director of the Royal School of Church Music.
35. *Chronicle Convoc.*, 1963, pp. 176–92.
36. *The Revised Psalter*, pp. viii–ix.
37. D. Frost, *Making the Liturgical Psalter*, (Grove Liturgical Studies 25), 1981, pp. 15–16.
38. *LC Minutes*, 3. 48.
39. *Baptism and Confirmation Today*, 1954, p. 30.
40. *LC Minutes*, 12. 2. III; 13. 5. IV.
41. ibid., 13. 3; LC Memorandum 13.

42. ibid., 16. 2b; 16. 5.
43. ibid., 18. 4; LC Memorandum 17.
44. *Baptism and Confirmation*, 1959. A Report submitted by the Church of England Liturgical Commission to the Archbishops of Canterbury and York in November 1958.
45. He eventually set this out in a Memorandum — No. 19, which the Commission discussed and answered, but to no avail.
46. LC Memorandum 20, 20a.
47. *Chronicle Convoc.*, 1960, pp. 20–54, 94–109, 115–16, 129–37, 144–5.
48. ibid., pp. 133–4.
49. *Journal Convoc.*, January 1960, pp. 37–70, 78–9, 87–104; May 1960, pp. 10–11, 71–95.
50. E. C. Ratcliff, 'The York Revised Service for the Public Baptism of Infants: An Appraisement', in *Theology* LXIII (November 1960), pp. 459–68.
51. Canterbury Convoc., Report 706; York Convoc., Report 546.
52. *Chronicle Convoc.*, January 1962, pp. 89–90, 164–84.
53. *Journal Convoc.*, January 1962, pp. 105–11.
54. ibid., p. 133. For the whole debate, pp. 105–33.
55. *LC Minutes*, 32. 7.
56. ibid., 33. 4–7.
57. The eight were: Colin Dunlop, Dean of Lincoln; Eric Milner-White, Dean of York; the Ven. J. O. Cobham; Canon Ernest Evans; Canon Douglas Vicary; the Revd. Douglas Horsfield; the Revd. Robert Symonds; and the Revd. Julian Thornton-Duesbery.
58. The ten new members were: the Bishops of Newcastle and Sheffield; the Very Revd. E. A. Southcott, Provost of Southwark; Canon Basil Naylor of Liverpool Cathedral; Canon Basil Smith of York; Professor Christopher Evans, Canon-Professor of Durham; Dr Austin Farrer, Warden of Keble College, Oxford; David Ayerst; Elisabeth Montefiore; and Miss Kate Williams, a lecturer at Cheltenham Training College and a member of the House of Laity.
59. *LC Minutes*, 34. 4, 6, 7.
60. ibid., 34. 11; 35. 6.
61. H. de Candole and A. Couratin, *Reshaping the Liturgy*, 1964, p. iii.
62. J. A. Lamb, 'Liturgy and Unity', in *The Annual of the Church Service Society*, 1960, pp. 27–39. Some of this subsequently reappeared in his essay in the symposium, *The Renewal of Worship*, 1965.
63. *LC Minutes*, 29. 2.
64. R. C. D. Jasper, ed., *The Renewal of Worship*, 1965, p. vii. This statement was inserted at the beginning of all the JLG Reports.
65. The foundation members were: C. of E.: the Dean of Bristol, the Bishop of Knaresborough; C. of Scotland: Dr J. A. Lamb, F. N. Davidson Kelly; Baptist Union: the Revd. Neville Clark, the Revd. Stephen Winward; Congregational Union: the Revd. James Todd, the Revd. John Huxtable; Episcopal Church in Scotland: the Primus (Francis Moncrieff), Canon Donald Nicholson; Methodist Church: the Revd. Rupert Davies, the Revd. Raymond George; Presbyterian C. of E.: the Revd. Aled Davies, Dr R. D. Whitehorn. John Huxtable left in the first year on being appointed General Secretary of the Congregational Union, and was replaced by the Revd. Winfred Evans.
66. *Chronicle Convoc.*, 1960, pp. 166–7.
67. ibid., 1960, pp. 150–5.
68. ibid., 1962, pp. 310–12; *CA Proceedings*, 1962, vol. XLII, pp. 262–71, 275–6.

69. The voting was: Bishops — 30 for, 0 against; Clergy — 200 for, 1 against; Laity — 203 for, 11 against. *CA Proceedings*, 1964, vol. XLIV, pp. 238–48.
70. cf. ibid., 1966, vol. XLVI, pp. 453–6.
71. In practice this provision for preliminary trial was never used.
72. Details of the Canons and legislation may be found in convenient form in Cuming, *History of Anglican Liturgy*, pp. 328–9; and C. O. Buchanan, *Recent Liturgical Revision in the Church of England* (Grove Booklet 14), 1973, pp. 6–7, 35.
73. The voting at the final approval stage was interesting: Bishops 31–0; Clergy 214–30; Laity 182–68. *CA Proceedings*, 1964, vol. XLIV, pp. 62–93.
74. Here final approval was given almost 'on the nod': Bishops 15–0; Clergy 202–6; Laity 168–6. ibid., 1965, vol. XLV, pp. 377–8.

10

REVISION BEGINS: SERIES ONE

I

The Report of Lambeth 1958 marked the beginning of intense liturgical activity throughout the Anglican Communion. A new Prayer Book appeared in Canada in 1959 after sixteen years' preparation; while India, Pakistan, Burma and Ceylon, after nine years with a provisional Book, produced a definitive version in 1960. New eucharistic liturgies appeared in Japan and the West Indies in 1959; and between 1964 and 1967 sixteen other new rites appeared elsewhere in the Anglican Communion.[1] All this work justified the view expressed in 1958 that the Prayer Book of 1662 could no longer be regarded as a bond of unity; nevertheless, a desire for some kind of unity, at least in the eucharistic structure, became evident. It was seen, for example, in the proposal to produce a Liturgy for Africa. In April 1961 the African archbishops decided to try and create a new eucharistic rite which might form a bond of unity between Anglicans throughout the continent. The operation was again in the hands of Leslie Brown, who had left South India to become Bishop (1952) and then Archbishop (1961) of Uganda: but this time he faced a more difficult task; for whereas all the Churches involved in South India had been evangelical in theological outlook, in Africa's five provinces every shade of opinion was represented, to say nothing of racial differences. 'Different rites were used, sometimes different rites by different races.'[2] Four members of our own Commission (Donald Coggan, Bowles, Couratin and Ratcliff) had some hand in the preliminary work, for they were among the experts invited to comment on the initial drafts.[3] Bishop Stephen Bayne also sent copies to all Anglican metropolitans: and the general response was sufficiently encouraging for Leslie Brown to press ahead. Following a pan-African conference at Kampala in May 1963, the first 'official draft' emerged in time to be discussed at the Liturgical Consultation after the Anglican Congress at Toronto in August. After submission to the Anglican metropolitans' meeting at Canterbury in April 1964, the text was finally published in October of that year.[4]

Intended for such experimental use as the African bishops might authorize, Leslie Brown's hand was clearly evident. It owed a great deal to the CSI rite and to the principles of Lambeth 1958, and it made use of much more Anglican material. It was designed for use as the principal Sunday service, with or without communion: hence the permissive use of the Venite as an introit and of the Prayer Book morning canticles between the lessons. The Intercessions were in the form of a new litany, which could be replaced on weekdays by the Prayer for All Sorts and Conditions of Men with the addition of the final petition from the 1662 Prayer for the Church. The eucharistic prayer had two distinctive features: a developed trinitarian preface which served all occasions, and an anamnesis which attempted a Catholic–Evangelical compromise, 'We do this as thy Son commanded, offering to thee, with this holy Bread and Cup, our praise and thanksgiving for his one sacrifice once offered upon the cross, for his mighty resurrection and glorious ascension.' The rite's oddity was the isolation of the Prayer of Humble Access between the Intercessions and the Peace, possibly reflecting a tension between the desire to retain a well-loved prayer and the inability to find an ideal place for it. Roger Beckwith, reviewing the Liturgy in *The Church of England Newspaper*, indicated two elements which he considered made it unacceptable to Evangelicals, and both of which subsequently proved to be contentious in the Church of England: the prayer for the departed in the Litany and the anamnesis in the eucharistic prayer: in the latter the words 'Bread' and 'Cup' were given capitals and he commented, 'This puts it beyond doubt that it is the *consecrated* bread and wine that are being offered to God, and the overtones of the sacrifice of the mass are unmistakable.' His final judgement was that Anglo-Catholics would not want to use the rite, and Evangelicals ought not to use it.[5]

In fact the rite never fulfilled the hopes of its proponents, possibly because it was too Anglican. 'It has not become a living tradition of worship in the mainstream of the church's life . . . It has little that is demonstrably African and is indeed in cultural terms far more akin to the Western European tradition than to that of any part of Africa.'[6] Nevertheless it was by no means a complete failure. With small modifications it was authorized for use in Australia; both the New Zealand rite and the United Liturgy for East Africa made extensive use of it; and it had some influence on the Pan-Anglican document emerging from the Liturgical Consultation at Toronto.

This Consultation, held on August 23—5, was attended by representatives of fourteen Anglican Churches or provinces, including the Archbishop of York, Donald Coggan. Consideration of the Liturgy for Africa served as an introduction to an important discussion on Unity in Liturgy. It was now accepted that recent liturgical revision in the Anglican Communion had shown greater diversity, a feature which owed something to both the Liturgical and the Ecumenical Movements. It was also accepted that while local culture should be reflected in liturgy, Western culture was in fact becoming a world-wide phenomenon, and the two needed to be reconciled. How far then should diversity go? Was it necessary for every new revision exercise to examine the basic principles — in itself a worthy exercise but involving a great deal of work that had already been done many times over? Furthermore, mutual consultation was no longer possible on an exclusively Anglican basis. The most that the Anglican Communion could hope for was to set out a basic pattern of eucharistic liturgy in accordance with Resolution 76 of Lambeth 1958.[8] Steps were therefore taken to implement this. It has already been noted that despite being asked to take the initiative in this matter by Lambeth 1958, Archbishop Fisher had in fact done nothing beyond consulting our own Commission and then apparently forgetting about it. Bishop Stephen Bayne, as Executive Officer of the Anglican Communion, had therefore undertaken to do something himself. Certain important preliminary steps had already been taken: the creation of a list of liturgical consultants throughout the Anglican Communion, the widespread discussion of the Liturgy for Africa, and the planning of the Toronto Liturgical Consultation. The Consultation itself now appointed a small group of four to deal with the matter: Archbishop Clarke of Canada, Archbishop Brown of Uganda, Bishop Kenneth Sansbury of Singapore and Professor Massey Shepherd of the USA.[9]

Once again Leslie Brown did the drafting, the others commenting by correspondence. The document, 'The Structure and Contents of the Eucharistic Liturgy', was completed by July 1964 and eventually circulated to metropolitans and liturgical consultants by Bishop Bayne in March 1965. Embodying the essential recommendations of Lambeth 1958, it set out five 'phases' of the rite, with the caveat that flexibility was necessary in order to meet local needs.

1. The Preparation, which could include Confession and Absolution, together with a psalm or hymn of praise, such as Gloria in excelsis or Te Deum.
2. The Service of the Word of God, beginning with a collect and concluding with the Creed.
3. The Great Intercession, normally in litany form and including petitions for both Church and world.
4. The Service of the Lord's Supper, with a four-action shape and the eucharistic prayer concluding with the Lord's Prayer.
5. The Dismissal, including a corporate expression of praise, and an act of dismissal but no blessing.[10]

It is difficult to assess the influence of this document on Anglican revision as a whole, for metropolitans and liturgical consultants were left free to use it or ignore it as they wished. It was certainly not followed slavishly; and I must confess it never loomed large in our own Commission's discussions. Possibly its value lay in the sheer fact of its existence as a kind of semi-official recognition that the Anglican Communion no longer paid lip-service to 1662 as a bond of unity. As Bishop Bayne himself stated at Toronto, 'The time may not be too far off, I believe, when, like "Full Communion", "Prayer Book" is going to be too loose and perplexing a concept to be of much use in distinguishing ourselves from other Christians.'[11]

A second important document emerging from the same period was the Report of the Fourth World Conference on Faith and Order which met at Montreal just before the Toronto Congress. One of its major topics was 'Worship and the Oneness of Christ's Church' and Professor Edward Hardy wisely commented:

> As one looks over the whole period, it does become clear that the topic of worship, very much on the fringe of Lausanne (1927) and almost absentmindedly introduced, has come to occupy (by Montreal) a central position in Faith and Order discussions. This does not mean that it is a dominant topic, but rather that the life of the worshipping community can be seen as the centre to which our faith leads us, for the sake of which the Order of the Church exists, and from which our life of service to the world radiates.[12]

The Report on Worship was a weighty declaration agreed on by the representatives of the two hundred member Churches, recognizing the need for relevance to daily life, and also the need for its transformation; at the same time worship was a participation in Christ's own self-offering and as such was an act formative of the Christian community and essentially corporate.[13] The central act of worship was the Eucharist; and while its structure and content were not worked out in detail, its general pattern was in line with that of the Pan-Anglican document: there should be reading and preaching of the Word, intercession for the Church and for the World, and the four-shape sacramental action; it should be celebrated frequently, involve active participation of the laity, and use language and imagery intelligible to the modern mind.[14] It also agreed with Toronto that there had been an increasing development of a 'world civilization'; and this had been responsible, for example, in Asian life being increasingly influenced by Western culture. But here two interesting points had to be borne in mind: first, there was often resistance to the use of indigenous symbols in Asian culture, simply because these had non-Christian associations; and second, indigenization should not be used merely as a human contrivance, but should be seen as part of a divine activity: 'We ought not to be so much concerned with adapting worship to the local culture that we forget that the culture itself is to be transformed . . . converted and transfigured by the redemption that is in Christ.'[15] Finally, there was a fine statement on the meaning of the Eucharist, which was of particular interest in view of the impending controversy over the subject in the Church of England:

> In the Holy Eucharist or Lord's Supper, constantly repeated and always including both Word and Sacrament, we proclaim and celebrate a memorial of the saving acts of God . . . The events are unique; they cannot be repeated or extended or continued. Yet in this memorial we do not only recall past events: God makes them present through the Holy Spirit . . . thus making us participants in Christ . . . [It is] a gift of God to his Church, a sacrament of the presence of the crucified and glorified Christ until He come, a means whereby the sacrifice of the Cross, which we proclaim, is operative within the Church . . . By Him, with Him, and in Him who is our great High Priest and Intercessor we offer to the Father in the power of the Holy Spirit our praise, thanksgiving and intercession.

With contrite hearts we offer ourselves as a living and holy sacrifice, a sacrifice which must be expressed in the whole of our daily lives.[16]

A third important document appeared before the end of the year, *The Constitution on the Sacred Liturgy*, promulged by the Second Vatican Council on 4 December. Unlike Montreal, which was a joint declaration of a limited kind by representatives of a large number of Churches differing widely in outlook, the *Constitution* was the official statement of a single world-wide Church, providing the basis for the 'aggiornamento' of its liturgy. What was most remarkable was the change of ethos. Since the Council of Trent the liturgy had been regarded as part of Rome's legal regulations; while theologically based, its practical discharge was a matter of compliance with specific rubrics. But now a new-found biblio-patristic theology made possible a new understanding of the liturgy, far more pastoral in outlook and recognizing the need for meeting local needs and situations. In all this the *Constitution* had a great deal in common both with Montreal and with Lambeth 1958, showing once again the remarkable convergence of liturgical thinking among the Christian Churches.

It saw the liturgy as central to the whole life and mission of the Church, for Christ's saving work for mankind was effected through it.[17] Obviously some elements were divine and immutable; but others were subject to change, needing adaptation to local tradition and culture — as, for example, in the use of the vernacular.[18] In making such changes, certain general principles were to be followed:

(a) elements which, with the passage of time, had been duplicated or added 'with but little advantage' were to be discarded.
(b) elements which 'through accidents of history' had suffered injury were to be restored 'to the vigour which they had in the days of the holy Fathers'.[19]

This restoration of early simplicity should be seen in a variety of ways. There was a recognition of the primacy of Scripture and the importance of preaching: 'In the liturgy God speaks to his people, and Christ is still proclaiming his gospel.'[20] Furthermore rites should be simple, clear and comprehensible.[21] Then again, they should be truly corporate, involving the full, conscious and active participation of the laity: it was their right as well as their duty, for services were not private functions, but an activity of the whole body of Christ.[22] All this applied in particular to the Eucharist, in which the 'Community prayer' or 'Prayer of the Faithful' was to include not only the Church but the whole world.[23] None of this would have created any problems in Anglican circles, nor would its description of the Eucharist as 'a memorial of Christ's death and resurrection, a sacrament of love, a sign of unity, a bond of charity, a paschal banquet in which Christ is eaten, the mind is filled with grace and a pledge of future glory given to us'.[24] There would have been Anglican problems, however, when it went on to speak of the Eucharist as 'perpetuating the sacrifice of the Cross throughout the centuries' or of Christ's followers 'offering the immaculate victim'.[25] Indeed, phrases far more modest than these were destined to raise considerable difficulties as the constitutional bodies of the Church of England set about a revision of the Eucharist within the next two or three years.

II

In late September 1964, just before the Liturgical Commission's autumn meeting, Donald Coggan summoned me to the Athenaeum for a talk. He told me that he proposed giving up the chairmanship; his other commitments made it impossible for him to give the necessary time to it, and soon there would be the added burden of piloting new services through the Convocations. He and the Archbishop of Canterbury were keen that I should take over, and if possible straight away. This was quite unexpected; and I remember temporizing by asking how long I would be expected to cope. He replied, 'Until the whole job is done.' But I think neither of us then realized that this would take over sixteen years, bringing me almost to the end of my active working life. My feelings were mixed. Obviously I was gratified to be asked; but the job would make considerable demands on my time and energy, and at that precise moment I was not at all sure that this was what I wanted to do or ought to do. I enjoyed working with the Commission; but I was wedded to university teaching, and I had almost finished the biography of Bishop Bell with other possibilities of a great deal more writing already in the offing. I was, in fact, doing the very things in life I had always wanted to do; and to take on the Commission would not only involve a serious disruption, it would also mean an end to further writing for a very long time. Nor could I raise any great enthusiasm at the prospect of being involved with the Convocations and the Church Assembly, a world I had hitherto studiously avoided.[26] One part of me therefore protested violently, and my first inclination was to say 'No'.

On the other hand, I could not really ignore the challenge presented by both Archbishops, and here there were strong ties of both respect and friendship, particularly with Michael Ramsey. We had known each other for some twenty-five years and in my Durham days I owed him an enormous debt, with help and encouragement in a variety of ways. I knew I could get on with him and I was not afraid to argue or disagree with him. On reflection, I also realized that my long study of Walter Frere's papers had given me an almost unique insight into the whole process of liturgical revision in the twentieth century, for at that time the papers at Lambeth Palace were not yet open to scholars. Then again, almost without realizing it, I had become increasingly involved in the Commission's work since 1960. I was now sharing with Arthur Couratin the bulk of the preparatory work on the new eucharistic rite, I had brought the Joint Liturgical Group into being, I had made the initial liturgical contacts with the Roman Catholics, and – at the Archbishops' request – I had chaired the small independent group which had revised the list of Black Letter Days in the Calendar.[27] I was being increasingly 'hooked'. After further talks with both Archbishops, I finally agreed to take over from Donald Coggan – not without some misgivings – and on 30 September he personally presented me to the Commission as his successor. I think most of them were surprised, for I was still one of the youngest members, but on the whole they took it very well.

It was at this meeting that Colin Buchanan, then a young lecturer at the London College of Divinity, joined the Commission. He came with a reputation of being a very able scholar of decidedly Conservative Evangelical views: and at first he was clearly conscious of his position as a rather lonely representative of a particular party line. But it did not take him long to lose his nervousness or whatever prickles he may have had; and we all came to appreciate his cheery and uncompromising presence. At the outset his stand over things such as prayer for the departed and the eucharistic prayer undoubtedly created problems: but they were problems capable of ultimate resolution, and his contribution here was by no means negligible. Over the years he gave a very great deal to the Commission.

One or two things were clear to me from the outset. The first was that little benefit would derive from the 'conservative' approach clearly favoured by Archbishop Fisher and even by Colin Dunlop. Simply to tinker with 1662, replacing it with something probably not very different from 1928 was not the way to go on. 1662 had had a long history; and many generations of worshippers had found it a source of inspiration and spiritual enrichment. Clearly it still had many devotees and it could continue to serve the Church for a long time to come. But to put it to death and drive it out of existence by some legal fiat would be both unkind and unnecessary. If it were to die, it must die a natural death, simply because people did not want it any longer. What was needed was a series of alternative services to place beside it. Public worship would then ultimately find its own level; and whatever survived would do so because that was what met people's needs; and new services would have to win their way on their own merits.

Secondly, new services involved some sort of sales exercise, in which they could be explained and commended and the Commission itself could create a caring image, infecting people with their own convictions and enthusiasms. It was not a body of high and dry academics living up in the clouds, but a group of sensible people, concerned for the spiritual welfare of others. A great deal could, of course, be achieved with the pen; but even more important was personal contact. Individual members should be ready to go out and talk to people; and it was incumbent upon me to set a good example. On the whole the Commission backed me up marvellously in this, stumping the country for well over a decade; and I visited every diocese in both provinces, while I made it a golden rule that no letter or enquiry was to be left unanswered.[28]

Thirdly, it was important to commend the principle of 'live and let live'. The Church of England was a comprehensive Church, and since 1662 whenever that principle had been ignored it had clearly suffered. What was needed, therefore, was the creation of services expressed in sufficiently broad terms to meet with general acceptance. This principle had been in evidence in the worship of the early Church, and three eminent modern bishops who had pointed this out were Walter Frere, Charles Gore and Arthur Headlam (to say nothing of such scholars as Darwell Stone and Oliver Quick).[29] Both the Lord's Prayer and the Apostles' Creed were in fact classic examples of this principle. Unfortunately some people argued that it involved a deliberate attempt to mislead, by saying one thing and meaning another. But nothing could be further from the truth.

Creating new services, dealing with the Convocations, planning what I have called the 'sales campaign', fostering inter-church relations and helping other Churches at home and abroad with comment and advice — all this meant a considerable extension of the Commission's original activities, requiring a great deal of administrative and secretarial help. To imagine that the Secretary, Geoffrey Willis, indefatigable though he was, but living out in the country some fifty miles from London, with all the commitments of a parish priest — to say nothing of his work as editor of the Canterbury *Convocation Chronicle* and assistant secretary of Canterbury Convocation — could or even should shoulder this burden which was increasing weekly, was pure nonsense. In any case some kind of central office which people could refer to or even visit was becoming a necessity. The Archbishops and Sir John Guillum Scott[30] were quick to appreciate the situation; and by March 1965 an office was established in Church House. The Archbishop suggested to Geoffrey Willis that he should hand over the secretarial duties to a lay person and devote his energies to being a full-time member of the Commission. Unfortunately this was something he refused to do and he resigned. The parting was not easy but was achieved without undue friction. In any case Geoffrey had little sympathy with the way events were taking shape and his departure was almost inevitable. Unfortunately his sight began to fail, ultimately ending in total blindness. It was a sad end for a very fine scholar. Sir John was fortunate to find Daphne Fraser to take his place: as a graduate in theology and a former Church House secretary, she was well qualified for the job.

This was by no means the only problem which had to be dealt with during my first few months as chairman. Almost immediately after taking over I discovered that plans were already afoot for the Archbishops to set up another new commission under the Dean of Christ Church to undertake a further revision of the Lectionary. I was furious, reminding Michael Ramsey that it was less than a year since he had expressed his warm approval of the Joint Liturgical Group undertaking the very same thing: they had almost completed the first and most important part of their task and to be faced by apparent Anglican disregard at this juncture was both embarrassing and discourteous. The Archbishop replied immediately, confessing that the work of the Group had slipped his memory and promising that no further action over the new commission would be taken until the JLG lectionary had appeared. It was, in fact, the last that was heard of such a commission, and future lectionary revision was done co-operatively by the Liturgical Commission and the JLG.

A second problem involved the composition of the Commission. For some strange reason a rumour began to circulate that there were to be changes and a number of the existing members were to be 'axed'. Once again I approached the Archbishop, strongly deprecating change at this stage, and suggesting that members should be appointed for a fixed term — say three years — but open to renewal. This would then permit changes to be made, or members to leave if they so wished, without feelings being ruffled. I think the rumour was without foundation; but the idea of a triennial review was entirely acceptable, and late 1965 — roughly three years since the last batch of appointments — was fixed as a suitable time for the first review. This permitted the recruitment of five new members, all of whom brought valuable specialist expertise to the work of the Commission: Dr Stella Brook, of the University of Manchester, had just published an important study on *The Language of the Book of Common Prayer*, and was the Commission's first acknowledged expert on language; Charles Whitaker, a country parish priest with a reputation as an expert on Initiation, and Geoffrey Cuming, an acknowledged scholar on Prayer Book history, proved to be absolutely indispensable and became leading draughtsmen of *The Alternative Service Book*; John Wilkinson, the editorial secretary of the SPG, brought expertise both in typography and consumer research; and Allan Wicks, organist of Canterbury Cathedral, proved a valuable corresponding member on musical matters. A little later the Archbishop himself raised the question of representation of the House of Laity on the Commission, a suggestion which I welcomed. I already had regular sessions with the Dean of Arches, Walter Wigglesworth, who was generally responsible for introducing liturgical matters in the House, briefing him as thoroughly as I could; but it was an additional asset to have members who could be closely involved in the working of the Commission. In the event Jean Mayland and Tom Horan were appointed, both of whom gave sterling service. The former was a clergyman's wife who had studied liturgy at Oxford; the latter, the brother of a bishop, was a rumbustious and articulate industrialist with an incisive mind, who was ideal at expressing the view of 'the man in the pew'.

III

In December 1959 Archbishop Fisher had paid the Commission his last official visit before retirement, mainly to inform us that the drafting of the Schedule of Agreed Amendments, needed immediately Canon 13 became law, would no longer be our responsibility; it would now be in the hands of the Bishops, although our advice would still be sought. We could therefore devote our energies to preparing the more radical pieces of revision, although he felt that the boundaries between the two types of material might sometimes be difficult to define, and some of the latter might even be considered for inclusion with the former. The whole revision pattern was therefore seen as something rather conservative. On the delicate matter of the Initiation services there was a discreet silence.[31] This meeting was followed by a letter, indicating that the Archbishop himself had drawn up a Schedule of Agreed Amendments, on which he now sought the Commission's views (14 January 1960). Basically it was the 1928 Prayer Book; but his proposals for the Communion Service were of particular interest. Here he suggested two eucharistic prayers: the 1928 canon, despite the fact that it was very rarely used, and the Interim Rite canon i.e. the 1662 prayer of consecration, the 1662 Prayer of Oblation and the Lord's Prayer.

The Commission's reply was confined almost entirely to these two proposals. It doubted the wisdom of including the 1928 canon. Parliament could well complain that the Church was now attempting to secure authorization through the back door of material it had previously failed to secure through the front. Furthermore it took little account of what Lambeth 1958 had said or what had been done elsewhere in the Anglican Communion. Nor was the Commission convinced of the wisdom of including the Interim Rite canon, for this too could arouse controversy. It therefore proposed a compromise canon of the 1662 Prayer of Consecration, the 1928 anamnesis and the first half of the 1662 Prayer of Oblation, thereby avoiding any reference to offering, while the second half of the Prayer of Oblation could still be used as an alternative to the Prayer of Thanksgiving after communion. Admittedly it was not an ideal solution, but it was certainly not a contentious one. To avoid further controversy, the Commission suggested omitting the 1928 provisions for the communion of the sick, which might arouse all the old antagonisms over reservation and might even endanger the entire Schedule. Finally the Archbishop's attention was drawn to the lists of 1928 material which the Commission had included in its Report for Lambeth 1958, set out in the three categories — widely used, less widely used and seldom used.[32]

Soon after receiving this Archbishop Fisher retired; and for some time the Commission heard no more of the Schedule; although in December 1960 his successor, Archbishop Ramsey, appointed a small joint committee of bishops and Commission members to be responsible for any further work required on it.[33] It was in fact not until April 1964 that the Archbishop gave further warning that the Church Assembly was about to complete its consideration of the Prayer Book (Alternative and Other Services) Measure. Approval was duly given on 7 July, and after an easy passage through Parliament, it received the Royal Assent on 23 March 1965. Thirty-seven years after the final rejection of the Deposited Book, therefore, the first important legal step towards achieving a new liturgy and liturgical freedom was secured.[34]

Archbishop Ramsey was keen that new services should secure the necessary authorization with the minimum of delay, avoiding if possible the lengthy and tedious debates which had accompanied the revision of Canon Law. He wrote (21 January 1965):

> From your presence at Convocation yesterday you will have experienced how repetitive and frustrating the procedures can be, and when we realise that for all we know York may have been making decisions different from those which we made, the tale of repetitive frustration is beyond belief. That is why I am pleading for Joint Sessions of the two Convocations for purposes of Prayer Book Revision, and I hope you will back this up.[35]

Joint Sessions were in fact achieved in 1966 and proved a great boon. Another device which proved a great asset in the early years of revision was the introduction of 'Liturgical Conferences'. The constitutional position was such – as the earlier debacle over Initiation has indicated – that the Commission itself was unable to present its proposals to the legislative bodies of the Church. It would obviously be an advantage for the Commission to be able to state its own case and share in initial discussion. Informed joint meetings would also provide an opportunity to assess early reactions to proposals and even allow for last-minute adjustments. Thirdly, such meetings would provide an opportunity for the laity to share in discussion with the Convocations – an opportunity which at the moment did not exist. The Province of Wales had already planned such a Liturgical Conference for the spring of 1965, and I threw out the suggestion of a similar gathering for the Church of England. The two Archbishops and other Church leaders accepted the idea with enthusiasm, pointing out that there were no great difficulties in arranging such gatherings. All that was needed was an extension of a meeting of the Church Assembly and a suspension of the normal standing orders. The first of such conferences was then planned for February 1966, in readiness for the Convocations to begin official discussions at their May sessions.

If, however, proposals were to be available in print in good time for such a conference, a tight schedule was involved. SPCK gave warning that for copies to be ready by Christmas, all material would have to be complete, and approved by the Bishops, by the summer. Responsibility for arranging this was at this time in the hands of the Archbishops' Copyright Committee, centred at Lambeth. Inevitably I found myself drawn into this, and it was an aspect of the work I enjoyed. In a variety of ways I had been involved with printers and publishers for some years; I could speak their language and found their company congenial. The decision was now made to publish two volumes, the first containing the Schedule of Agreed Amendments, which came to be known as Series One, and the second containing the Commission's own proposals, which came to be known as Series Two. It was at this stage that Walter Wigglesworth, an absolute tower of strength on the legal aspects of liturgical revision, pointed out that under the terms of the Alternative Services Measure, the publication of a simple Schedule was not enough: the actual texts of all Series One services, together with the relevant lectionaries, were required down to the last detail. This involved a major piece of drafting work, mostly of the scissors and paste variety, which had to be done at speed. It was done largely by Michael Nott, the Archbishop's chaplain,[36] and me, with help at the proof stage from Bernard Wigan and the Commission's secretary, Daphne Fraser. By a superhuman effort the material for both volumes was sent to SPCK by 14 July.

The Series One volume contained seven sets of services: Morning and Evening Prayer, including the Litany and Athanasian Creed but no Occasional Prayers and Thanksgivings; Holy Communion, together with the collects and biblical references to the epistles and gospels and the Old Testament lessons from the 1960 Indian Prayer Book; Baptism, both Infant and Adult but not Private; Confirmation; Matrimony; Burial; and a Commination. All these were essentially the 1928 rites except in the case of Holy Communion, which included three forms of the eucharistic prayer: that of 1662, that of the Interim Rite, and that proposed by the Commission. The Communion of the Sick was omitted as being too controversial, although up to the last minute there had been some hope of including some provision:[37] and there was no Churching of Women, no Ordinal and no Catechism. To all intents and purposes, the volume was not unlike *The Shorter Prayer Book* of 1947.

At the Liturgical Conference on 17–18 February 1966 Archbishop Ramsey introduced the Series One services, emphasizing that they were not to be regarded as a work of revision so much as a work of current authorization, and expressing the hope that they could be approved by the Convocations in May, in readiness for consideration by the House of Laity in June. He appealed for speed, in contrast to the discussions on Canon Law; and I think he genuinely believed at this stage that all Series One services would be approved 'on the nod' and be available for use by midsummer. He ended by suggesting that if any members of the Conference wished to suggest any improvements to these services, they should contact the secretary of the Liturgical Commission.[38]

The debate augured well, being brief and uncontroversial; but the invitation for suggested improvements had embarrassing results. The number of proposals submitted exceeded all expectations and indicated two differing views on the Series One services. Some people saw them as setting out the reasonable limits beyond which current practice should not go; but others saw them as a heaven-sent opportunity to secure authorization for every conceivable current practice. I was given the task of producing some kind of order from this welter of proposals, and a paper entitled 'Guidelines with Addenda and Corrigenda' was duly presented to the Steering Committee on 3 March. Here I followed the Archbishops' line, pleading that experiment should not be delayed unduly at this stage by consideration of detailed amendments; far better to make provision within the experimental period for the collection of comment and criticism and plan for future modification; rites could then develop in the light of experience. Happily good sense prevailed and the Steering Committee kept the amendments to reasonable proportions.

The Convocations of Canterbury and York, sitting for this occasion separately, also heeded archiepiscopal pleas for speed and restraint, passing all the services with their amendments with the necessary two-thirds majorities on 9–10 May.[39] Such expedition was not matched, however, by the House of Laity on 10 June. Sir Kenneth Grubb, the chairman, and Walter Wigglesworth, responsible for piloting the services through, exercised considerable patience and wisdom. Morning and Evening Prayer, Infant and Adult Baptism and Matrimony were eventually passed with the necessary two-thirds majorities. Confirmation fell, however (129—79), mainly on the grounds that the phrase referring to a special gift of the Holy Spirit being bestowed through the imposition of hands with prayer was an unwarranted inference from Acts 8. Until the authorization of the Series Two Confirmation rite, therefore, the Bishops were thrown back on the exclusive use of 1662. Consideration of the other two rites had to be postponed, prayer for the departed and the eucharistic prayer both proving to be controversial. Burial was eventually passed in September but only narrowly, 184–76; and Holy Communion followed suit in November by an even narrower margin, 174–79.[40] It did mean, however, that by the end of 1966, for the first time in just over three hundred years, the Church of England had a solid core, if not a complete range, of services available for public use, alternative to those of 1662 and possessing lawful authority. Furthermore, at a number of points there was an improvement on what had been proposed in 1928. Most of these services were published rapidly in separate booklets, a format which subsequently proved to be an inexpensive and very popular method of providing congregations with orders of service. The most significant features, distinct from those of 1928, were as follows:

Morning and Evening Prayer

The invitatories were omitted: a new table of psalms for Sundays and Holy Days produced by the Commission in 1959 was included; and the 1961 Lectionary was permitted as an alternative to those of 1871 and 1922.

Holy Communion

The 1928 rite was considerably modified and improved, even at the expense of a large number of alternatives; but by a judicious use of the latter, it was possible to produce a structure very similar to that of the Series Two rite.

a. The Gloria in excelsis was permitted in its 1549 or 1662 position.
b. Old Testament lessons were provided; and only biblical references were given, permitting a choice of Bible versions.
c. The Sermon could follow either the Gospel or the Creed.

d. The Offertory could precede either the Intercessions or the Sursum corda, with the optional use of 1 Chronicles 29. 11, 14.
e. The Intercessions could be used in litany form.
f. The Prayer of Humble Access could be used in its 1662 or 1928 position.
g. There were three eucharistic prayers: 1662, the Interim Rite form, and the form produced by the Commission.
h. The Lord's Prayer could be used in its 1662 or 1928 position.
i. There were four alternatives for the post-communion: 1662 Prayer of Thanksgiving, 1662 Prayer of Oblation, and the second half of the Prayer of Oblation with or without the Prayer of Thanksgiving.
j. The Black Rubric was omitted.

Matrimony
The 1662 and 1928 prefaces and vows were provided and these were interchangeable: a blessing of the ring was provided.

Burial
The lesson from 1 Corinthians 15 was abbreviated; the Committal followed the Prayers.

NOTES

1. Buchanan, *Modern Anglican Liturgies 1958–68*, p. 3.
2. Brown, *Relevant Liturgy*, pp. 52–3.
3. Buchanan, p. 49.
4. ibid., p. 55.
5. C. Beckwith, 'The Liturgy for Africa', *Church of England Newspaper*, January 1965.
6. Buchanan, p. 55.
7. ibid., pp. 56, 73–7, 324–5.
8. cf. pp. 216–17.
9. Report of the Liturgical Consultation, Toronto, 23–5 August 1963; S. F. Bayne, *An Anglican Turning Point*, Austin, Texas, 1964, pp. 16, 19–20.
10. The text may be conveniently found in Buchanan, pp. 31–2.
11. Bayne, *An Anglican Turning Point*, p. 125. For further discussion of this document see Buchanan, pp. 22–31.
12. E. R. Hardy, 'The Place of Worship in Faith and Order Discussions', in *Studia Liturgica*, 1965, vol. IV, no. 2, p. 80.
13. 'Worship and the Oneness of Christ's Church: report of Section IV of the Montreal Conference', in *Studia Liturgica*, 1963, vol. II, no. 4, pp. 243–4, 256.
14. ibid., pp. 248–9.
15. ibid., pp. 252–3, 255.
16. ibid., pp. 247–8. For the official text see P. C. Rodger and L. Vischer, ed., *The Fourth World Conference on Faith and Order, Montreal 1963*, 1964, pp. 69–76.

17. *Constitution on the Sacred Liturgy* (translation of Clifford Howell), 1963, sc 7.
18. ibid., scs 21, 36, 38.
19. ibid., sc 50.
20. ibid., scs 33, 35.
21. ibid., sc 34.
22. ibid., scs 14, 26.
23. ibid., scs 48, 53.
24. ibid., sc 47.
25. ibid., scs 47–8.
26. In fact I became Proctor for the University of London in December 1964, and soon found myself landed with membership of the Steering Committee for Liturgical Matters.
27. The group consisted of Dr Kemp and Canon Max Warren, members of the group which had prepared the report on the Calendar for Lambeth 1958; Canon Basil Smith of the Liturgical Commission; and myself. At this time, the Archbishops apparently still regarded the Calendar and Lectionary as subjects which did not really concern the Commission.
28. I excepted 'fan mail' from people who deliberately set out to be vindictive or offensive. It was incredible how cruel some so-called Christians could be.
29. cf. Chap. 4 for Gore; Jasper, *Walter Howard Frere*, pp. 250–1; Jasper, *Arthur Cayley Headlam*, 1960, pp. 143–4.
30. Secretary-general of the Church Assembly.
31. *LC Minutes* 21. 7.
32. cf. p. 127 (Chap. 5. sc 3); *LC Minutes* 23. 4; LC Memorandum 28.
33. The Bishops of Chichester, Exeter, Wakefield and Worcester; Canon Addleshaw, Canon Bowles, Arthur Couratin and Geoffrey Willis (*LC Minutes* 26. 2).
34. It was in fact only one of a parcel of Parliamentary Measures passed during the sixties which affected the worship of the Church. The Alternative Service Measure applied only to actual services; other measures, covering such items as calendar matters, vesture, the use of lay ministers, and the versions of the Bible were covered by the Holy Table Measure (1964), the Vestures of Ministers Measure (1964), the Prayer Book (Versions of the Bible) Measure (1965), the Prayer Book (Miscellaneous Provisions) Measure (1965), and the Prayer Book (Further Provisions) Measure (1968). In this way a large number of the new Canons Ecclesiastical became law.
35. cf. *Chronicle Convoc.*, 1965, pp. 39–41.
36. Subsequently Archdeacon of Maidstone, Archdeacon of Canterbury and Provost of Portsmouth.
37. The volume contained a final page with the heading, 'An Order for the Communion of the Sick', and a note, 'A form of service and rubrics are under consideration'; but the rest of the page was left blank. Discussions at Lambeth, chaired by the Bishop of London, failed to reach any acceptable conclusions.
38. *The Liturgical Conference 1966*, Report of Proceedings, pp. 1–4, 45–7.
39. *Chronicle Convoc.*, 1966, pp. 121–44; *Journal Convoc.*, 1966, pp. 24–79, 93–131.
40. CA *Proceedings*, 1966, pp. 732–816. The Burial of a Child was passed separately and again by a narrow margin 187–76.

11

SERIES TWO

I

A final concession from Archbishop Fisher before his retirement in 1960 was permission to work on an interim report on the Shape of the Eucharist, a task which the Commission tackled with considerable enthusiasm. Indeed, it was not long before the project developed, with archiepiscopal blessing, into the production of an actual rite. Donald Coggan devised a pattern of working in which Arthur Couratin and I seemed to do most of the drafting, subsequently helped by Ronnie Beddoes in the Intercessions and Douglas Harrison in the eucharistic prayer. In the early stages we leaned a great deal on the advice of Edward Ratcliff; and normally he ran a critical eye over drafts before they were submitted to the Commission. His comments were often delightful and he was not upset if we decided not to accept them. There was, for example, his plea for the inclusion of the word 'joyful' at the end of the Preface – 'with all the joyful company of heaven' – a suggestion which was not accepted. He commented, 'The joy of the court of heaven was not to be found in the court of Edward VI, so Cranmer overlooked it. But it belongs to a true picture of heaven (Rome, *socia exsultatione concelebrant* – cf. Job 38.7).' Drafting also could have its problems in the Commission as a whole. Couratin and I decided, for example, to give the Intercessions a new pattern, based roughly on the old Roman *orationes solemnes* of Good Friday; but when we showed the initial drafts to the Commission, they were rejected rather peremptorily. We refused to be beaten, however; and with help from Ronnie Beddoes, we finally persuaded everyone to think again and finally won the day. In view of the subsequent widespread acceptance of this pattern, I sometimes wonder what would have ultimately happened if we had just meekly given way to these first impressions.

By the time I took over as chairman good progress had been made, with the prospect of completion within a couple of years. The decision to print the Series One and Series Two books of services in preparation for the Liturgical Conference of February 1966 precipitated matters, however. Members of the Commission were worried that if the forms of the Interim Rite now to appear in the Series One services were authorized, many people would feel that their needs had been met and lose all interest in anything different. There was need, therefore, to get something into print without delay. An Interim Report on the Eucharist was in consequence included as an appendix to the Series Two services, comprising the rite in its unfinished state and an introduction, in which I drew attention to its incompleteness:

> It must be emphasized that this draft is essentially an interim report. The Commission is well aware that certain sections of it still require

> considerable discussion and possibly amendment. Certainly at this stage we do not consider ourselves, either individually or corporately, irrevocably committed to all its details. But it does provide the Church with some indication of the lines on which we have been working during the past few years.[1]

The principal contents of the Series Two book were Morning and Evening Prayer, with Intercessions and Thanksgivings, completed as long ago as 1962, and Thanksgiving after Childbirth and Burial of the Dead, completed in 1964. After the fate of the Baptism and Confirmation services in 1958–9, many of the Commission awaited their reception at the Liturgical Conference on 17–18 February 1966 with some trepidation. I remember Arthur Couratin writing to me in despondent mood (27 January): 'I hope it is not going to break your heart, but pretty obviously the Convocations are going to butcher us . . . We have been through it all before with the Baptism/Confirmation stuff. We can only pray for the gifts of humility and good humour.' But we need not have worried. The Conference proved to be a great success exceeding our wildest hopes. Far from being butchered, the new rites, and particularly the draft Eucharist, were received with considerable enthusiasm. Inevitably there were criticisms – on prayer for the departed and on the second part of the eucharistic prayer – but at this stage they were fairly muted. At the end of the discussions, the chairman, Dr Stopford, Bishop of London, revealed that over the two days some 105 members had spoken – a sizeable cross-section of the Convocations and House of Laity.[2] Two points received particular emphasis. First there was a general desire for the use of more modern language – a problem which I realized the Commission must tackle far more seriously than it had done hitherto. Secondly, the enthusiasm for the draft Eucharist was so great that demands were made for its authorization forthwith, despite the fact that it was unfinished. Indeed, enthusiasm for the Eucharist exceeded the desire for modern language most emphatically; and Michael Ramsey himself urged us to regard its rapid completion as our most urgent task (25 February).

It was now clear to everyone that the original plan to introduce the new rite to the Church by limited experiment for the first two years was quite impractical; demand for its general use was far too great – indeed any attempt to limit its use would probably have been ignored. The Commission also decided that little purpose would be served in spending time on further polishing. Except for a few minor adjustments the rite was therefore prepared for submission to the Convocations in May 1966. The honeymoon period, however, was short-lived.

II

The optimism expressed by Lambeth 1958 over the doctrine of the eucharistic sacrifice had not been shared by Conservative Evangelicals. Such was their unease that it became the subject of the Conference of Evangelical

Churchmen at Oxford in September 1961. The lectures were subsequently published under the title *Eucharistic Sacrifice* (1962) and Dr J. I. Packer's introduction was forthright in accusing the Bishops of using 'familiar theological language in an unfamiliar way', describing their statement as 'this episcopal experiment in double-talk', which was a departure both from Scripture and Anglican teaching.[3] 'The Lambeth Fathers are inviting us all' to believe that 'the Anglican understanding of the Gospel itself was fundamentally deficient for three centuries after the Reformation.'[4] While accepting that they had been attempting to make a reconciling statement and had certainly avoided expounding the Roman doctrine of the Mass, nevertheless they had capitulated to Anglo-Catholicism, assimilating the two sacrifices, Christ's and ours, which older Anglican divines had laboured so hard to keep distinct.[5] He concluded:

> The Bible tells us that we share in the benefits secured by Christ's sacrifice, but where does it suggest that we share in the offering of it? The Bible exhorts us to offer ourselves to God through Christ, but where does it tell us that our sacrifice is incorporated into His?[6]

The protest against the Lambeth approach was also expressed by A. M. Stibbs in *Sacrament, Sacrifice and Eucharist* (1961): and even the Jesuit, Francis Clark, in his massive *Eucharistic Sacrifice and the Reformation* (1960), had commented that this 'new comprehensive language about eucharistic sacrifice now recommended to Anglicans may cover, but it does not resolve, the basic doctrinal tensions . . . in the Reformation century'.[7]

Mascall attempted to conciliate, arguing that much of the conflict between Catholic and Protestant theologians during the Reformation period and later was due to their common inheritance from late medieval theology of false or unbalanced assumptions which made fruitful discussion difficult and agreement impossible.[8] (This was a line also taken by C. W. Dugmore in *The Mass and the English Reformers*, 1958.) Mascall argued that the deadlock could be broken by recognizing the idea of *sacramental signification*, by which the Eucharist neither commemorated nor repeated the sacrifice of Christ, but made it sacramentally present: it was not a different *offering* of the same Victim, but a different *re-presentation* of the same *offering*. Furthermore, concepts should be seen in their entirety: the Body of Christ was one, both the Head, which is Christ, and its members, by their baptismal incorporation into his Body. In the Eucharist this unity of Christ and his Body should be maintained. He went on to quote Brightman's statement on the 1549 canon as depicting the eucharistic sacrifice as threefold: a commemoration of our Lord's historical self-oblation in his death on the cross, a sacrifice of praise and thanksgiving for the benefits of redemption so secured, and the offering of the Church — ourselves, our souls and bodies.[10]

> Is it not clear that these three very different offerings — so different, indeed, that left to themselves they would almost seem to make the

> eucharist into three sacrifices rather than one — are drawn into a real unity and supplement one another if we see them all as subsumed into the offering of the Whole Christ by the Whole Christ, that *totus Christus* which, as St Augustine tells us, *caput est et corpus*.

This all-inclusive view contained the fundamental truth of the Eucharist, and he was content to leave the matter there. Conservative Evangelicals, however, could not agree: they wished to keep our Lord's sacrifice in a category distinct from ours; and ours should be expressed in the post-communion if it were not to fall into the danger of Pelagianism; and here they could quote Dom Gregory Dix in their support.[12]

It was here that the Commission ran into trouble in the new eucharistic prayer. Couratin had pleaded earnestly for the use of the phrase 'we offer this bread and this cup' in the anamnesis, arguing that the bald offering of bread and cup without the addition of any adjectives, seen in the context of the undeveloped theology of the early Church, could win general acceptance. This was the line he adopted when introducing the draft Eucharist to the Liturgical Conference in February 1966:

> In the Prayer of Consecration we offer the Bread and the Cup to the Father. This need mean no more than we put the Bread and the Cup at God's disposal so that he may use it to feed those who receive with faith. It can, of course, be interpreted to mean something else, but it does not assert the fully developed doctrine of the Eucharistic Sacrifice. It confines itself to the simple language of the first two centuries. This is the way in which Hippolytus and Iranaeus and Justin talked, and it is a way of talking which goes back into New Testament times; for Clement used this way of talking too. It is going to be very difficult to maintain the Anglican appeal to antiquity if we are not prepared to talk like this, if we are not prepared to offer the Bread and the Cup to the Father. Each can use the phrase with his own interpretation, and no one need try to force his own interpretation on other people.[13]

Such an approach met with the approval of all the Commission, including the Liberal Evangelicals Cyril Bowles and Douglas Harrison, except one — our Conservative Evangelical, Colin Buchanan, who insisted on including a Note of Dissent in the Commission's subsequent report to the Archbishops[14] and expounded it in a pamphlet *The New Communion Service — Reasons for Dissent.*[15] His objections were twofold: the phrase 'we offer this bread and this cup', and the prayer for the departed in the intercessions. On the former he argued that offering was not one of the instituted acts of Christ, and to quote Hippolytus was unacceptable: 'Hippolytus obviously used the words as innocent of all offence (as the ante-Nicenes did in their sub-Trinitarian statements about God), but that does not mean in either case that we can. The innocence is lost when they are imported into our present context.'[16] On the latter, while admittedly the prayer was optional, similar petitions occurred in other services coming up for authorization: Holy

Communion Series One and Burial; once such texts were authorized, they would be part of Anglican doctrine; and neither the New Testament nor Anglican doctrine enjoined such prayer.[17]

The fact that the Commission had decided not to include a lengthy explanatory introduction in its report placed it at a disadvantage. On 31 March I therefore consulted Ratcliff and the Archbishop (Cantuar), to see whether we should get someone to put out a defence under his own name. Ratcliff commiserated – 'What a bed of nails you lie on'; but advised silence: 'I am sure that public controversy should be kept away from the Commission and its work as far and as long as may be. I hope devoutly that the counsel of silence will prevail.' It was a sentiment endorsed by the Archbishop: but the ensuing weeks saw an increase in controversy and a hardening of attitudes. When I presented the service to the Convocations on 10 May, it was clear that the original enthusiasm expressed at the Conference was now tempered by reservations over the eucharistic prayer. Despite the declared support of the Church Union for the Commission's wording, some people on the Catholic side also shared the unhappiness of the Conservative Evangelicals; and the Archbishop finally adjourned the debate until October, hoping that in the meantime some independent group might find a more acceptable form of words.[18]

The Steering Committee quickly chose a well-balanced and scholarly group: on the Catholic side were two distinguished scholars, the Bishop of Oxford, Dr H. J. Carpenter, and Canon E. W. Kemp; on the Evangelical side the Reverend Peter Johnston, Vicar of St Mary's Islington, and the Reverend Leo Stephens-Hodge, an able liturgical scholar who had already been largely responsible for the publication of *A Conservative-Evangelical Liturgy*;[19] finally there was Bishop Leslie Brown, recently returned from Uganda to become Bishop of St Edmundsbury and Ipswich.[20] They worked with commendable speed, and their compromise formula was presented at the next meeting of the Steering Committee (8 July). The text ran:

> Wherefore, O Lord, having in remembrance his perfect and sufficient sacrifice once offered upon the Cross, his resurrection from the dead, and his glorious ascension into heaven, and looking for the coming of his Kingdom, we do this in obedience to his command. Accept, we pray thee, this our duty and service which we with all thy holy people offer unto thee, and grant that we who eat the bread and drink the cup may be united by thy Spirit and filled with heavenly grace.

The Steering Committee grasped it with alacrity, agreeing to commend it to the Convocations in the place of 'We offer' in October, but their enthusiasm for it was not matched elsewhere. Colin Buchanan was not very happy with it, although he would accept it for the sake of unity and peace. I regarded it as a clumsy piece of liturgical writing, offering little or no improvement on what the Commission had produced, while the Archbishop plainly had no enthusiasm for it. He regarded it as 'obviously a mere makeshift', a combination of various phrases intended to please various people, and poor as a prayer. During the summer he and I had a number of discussions on the best course to adopt. It was in fact he who first suggested at one of our talks that some phrase based on 'we make the memorial' might offer a hope of a solution, and this was something with which I had considerable sympathy. He even considered the possibility of a compulsory part of the prayer down to the Institution Narrative followed by an optional part, on the lines of what had recently been authorized in the Series One service; although this would be a last resort and one he would be reluctant to adopt. In the end his inclination was to wait and see; and if nothing better emerged, to stick to the Commission's text, expound it as well as possible, and hope for the best.

A veritable spate of literature on the subject appeared before the resumed Convocation debate, by far the most interesting being a series of four studies on 'We offer this bread and this cup' in the October issue of *Theology*. Three were in favour of the phrase, and of these two were by members of the Commission. Arthur Couratin surveyed the biblical and early patristic evidence, concluding with the plea that it should be accepted as a fair compromise, especially as 1662 was still available to those who could not use it.[21] Michael Moreton, a lecturer at Exeter University, examined the early liturgies, deducing that eucharistic offering had been both central to the eucharistic prayer and to have prevailed universally.[22] Geoffrey Cuming then dealt with the Anglican evidence of the sixteenth and seventeenth centuries, showing that the idea of offering the bread and cup as a representative memorial had been accepted in the Anglican Communion, if not *semper*, *ubique*, or *ab omnibus*, at any rate for most of the time, in many places and by very many people: 'The mother Church finds herself almost alone in maintaining the posture of 1552.'[23] The critical study, however, was by Leslie Houlden, an Oxford biblical scholar, who pointed out that it was not simply Conservative Evangelicals who disliked the phrase; many Catholics disliked it too. Granted the weight of historical evidence for it, nevertheless it did not say what he wanted to say about the Eucharist now. To regard it with the old God-ward–man-ward distinction was crude and inadequate. Accepted that the initiative was God's: but man responded and God was his goal; there was therefore a two-way action. The one who offered was Christ — he offered himself; and man by grace through faith participated. The Eucharist was the means by which all this was 'earthed'; but it was the whole Eucharist, its total setting and symbolism, which effected this, not any single part of it. While liturgy admittedly had to produce a kind of shorthand to express all this, 'we offer this bread and this cup' was manifestly inadequate in doing so.[24]

These articles appeared just a few days before the Bishops met on 10 October to see whether they could make any progress before the Convocations resumed their debate. At Michael Ramsey's request I submitted a paper to help their discussions. I began by pointing out that while 'we offer' had had a long history and had been acceptable to both Catholic and

Reformed Churches, it had to be recognized, however, that it was now unacceptable to many, both Evangelicals and Catholics. Nor did I think it acceptable to suggest that opponents of the phrase were free to use 1662. There were three possible solutions to the difficulty:

1. Provide alternative forms at this point in the prayer.
2. End the prayer after the Institution Narrative but permit 'other devotions' by rubric.
3. Seek an agreed formula, and here I tentatively suggested the possibility of using 'memorial' as the definite concept.

I pointed out, however, that to seek alternatives *before* having made any decision on the original proposal was most unfortunate; for it gave the impression that it had been condemned without a vote. Here the Catholics had cause for complaint, and they were now saying that they were tired of being pushed around in this way. The Bishops saw the point of this, and notwithstanding the existence of the Bishop of Oxford's 'compromise formula', decided that they would still support the Commission's original text as providing the best opportunity for a breathing space during the experimental period.[25]

On the following day in the Convocations I made it quite clear that I could not support the Oxford formula, which had all the appearance of a political compromise, warned against the dangers of frantically scrambling around for words, and pleaded for 'we offer' as a working compromise, with the reminder that no vote had yet been taken on it.[26] In the course of the long debate, covering two days, Dr Ramsey stoutly defended the Commission's proposals, describing it as 'not a particularly High Church rite, and a rather strikingly non-medieval rite', loyal to the Lambeth Conference call 'to state things in primitive simplicity': and he also condemned the Oxford formula as a poor piece of liturgical writing because it was so obviously a conflation.[27] In the event some progress was made before the Convocations were prorogued, despite the fact that no decision was taken on the rite as a whole: the Oxford formula was rejected and 'we offer' was retained, with 'we give thanks unto thee over this bread and this cup' included as an optional alternative.[28] The Archbishop was pleased with the outcome: alternatives were at least an honest solution and they would provide the necessary breathing space for further consideration.

The House of Laity began its consideration of the Eucharist on 17 February 1967 and after five hours of debate had only reached the Intercessions.[29] Towards the end of the day, however, there was one notable achievement. Professor Anderson, a leading Evangelical, indicated lines on which he would be prepared to accept a compromise over prayer for the departed. In some remarkable way his proposal infected the House with a new spirit of enthusiasm and a will to succeed, which transcended party differences. His action was warmly welcomed and the House agreed to ask the Steering Committee not only to include the Eucharist on the agenda for the next Liturgical Conference, scheduled for 25 April, but to give it precedence over Initiation, which was the main item.[30] This the Steering Committee gladly agreed to do and also commissioned two papers to be prepared for the Conference, one by Douglas Harrison on the eucharistic prayer and another by the House of Laity's own Steering Committee on their proposals for prayer for the departed.

In his introductory speech to the Conference Douglas Harrison set out three possibilities for the eucharistic prayer: the Commission's text 'we offer', the Convocation proposal for alternative phrases, and thirdly the omission of both phrases, simply leaving the prayer to say, 'we pray thee to accept this our duty and service'. The latter he dismissed briefly, pointing out that there was a danger of it being regarded as inadequate; of the other two he still pleaded vigorously for 'we offer' as being one phrase possessing 'such authority as we give to the Early Church' and capable of different interpretations.[31] After a long and sometimes heated debate, the Bishop of London decided to take straw votes on the various options in an attempt to clarify the position:

1. 'We offer' as the only form of words. While passed by overwhelming majorities in the Convocations, it narrowly failed to secure the necessary two-thirds majority in the House of Laity, 101–86.
2. 'We give thanks' as the only form of words. This was defeated overwhelmingly in all Houses.
3. Inserting both phrases as alternatives. This was defeated in the House of Laity and failed to secure a two-thirds majority in the Convocations, 115–100.
4. Omitting both phrases. Although passed by a substantial majority in the House of Laity, it was defeated in the Convocations, 104–116.[32]

The Conference had therefore reached an impasse, insisting on a single phrase yet unable to find one that was acceptable. Sensing that we were heading for trouble, I had spent the later stages of the debate in doing some hurried drafting and then trying out a form of words, first on Peter Johnston as a leading Evangelical and then on Dr Trevor Jalland as a leading Catholic. Both approved, although admittedly the latter showed some reluctance. Immediately the results of the straw votes were known, I intervened, warning the Conference that we were in danger, not merely of postponing experiment indefinitely, but of killing the new rite altogether. I therefore proposed that we should adopt a solution already tentatively suggested, of making the idea of 'memorial' the main verb:

> Wherefore, O Lord, with this bread and this cup we make the memorial of his saving passion, his resurrection from the dead and his glorious ascension into heaven, and we look for the coming of his Kingdom. We pray thee to accept this our duty and service.[33]

To persist with the phrase 'we offer' was clearly no way forward: and to argue that no other phrase would do did seem to me to smack of historical fundamentalism. Furthermore 'to make the memorial' had a long Anglican history, being used both in the 1549 rite and in the Scottish 1637 rite: and at least in general terms it made clear what we were trying to 'do' with the bread and wine. It is true that it could not be understood to mean 'we offer': but the phrase by no means excluded the concept of sacrifice from the rite as a whole, and I believed that it would go at least some way to meet the requirements of people like Leslie Houlden.

Offered as a stop-gap solution, the Conference welcomed it, carrying it by substantial majorities in all Houses;[34] and then, swept on by a wave of new-found enthusiasm, accepted the compromise text on prayer for the departed proposed by the House of Laity:

> Hear us as we remember those who have died in faith and grant us with them a share in thy eternal Kingdom.[35]

On the following day the two Convocations passed the whole rite almost unanimously.[36]

This was not the end of the matter, however. On 1 June the Exeter proctors, led by Dr Jalland, who had now changed his mind, issued a statement repudiating my 'stop-gap' formula, criticizing the Intercessions, and announcing that they would use the Series One rite as a temporary refuge. The General Council of the Church Union also reaffirmed their support of 'we offer' and expressed the hope that the House of Laity would reject the Series Two rite in its revised form. A rumour had also begun to circulate that the Liturgical Commission itself might want to repudiate what I had done. When it met, therefore, on 7–9 June, I not only asked those present whether they supported me or not, but I also wrote to the absentees.[37] All replies, written and verbal, were in my favour except those of Couratin and Ratcliff. Couratin wrote very briefly to say that he could not support my action and submitted his resignation to the Archbishop immediately afterwards. It was a sad parting, for he had played a major part in the Commission's early work and had endured considerable criticism over the Initiation proposals. Ratcliff's reply was even sadder. He wrote (22 June) that 'we offer' was the '*ne plus ultra* of compromise' and 1549 was not enough; although he admitted, 'Meanings of both a catholic and protestant kind can and have been attached to the clause. Which one is right? We don't know. The clause is equivocal.' This must have been one of the last letters he ever wrote; just over a week later he died.

On the other side Evangelicals were trying hard not to appear completely negative. One such attempt was made in the book *Guidelines* written in preparation for the National Evangelical Anglican Congress at Keele in July 1967.[38] An essay on the Eucharist by E. M. B. Green, while making some predictable criticisms of Anglo-Catholic teaching on sacrifice and arguing that Jesus' eternal self-offering in love was distinct from his sacrifice on the cross,[39] nevertheless agreed that the Eucharist could be regarded as a sacrifice, apart from the presentation of ourselves, and of our praise and thanksgiving. In the first place it represented dramatically the sacrifice of the cross: 'It is normal in the sacramental language of Scripture to apply to the sign the term appropriate to the thing signified.' Secondly it could be seen as a counterpart of the Old Testament peace-offering and burnt-offering, a communion-feast shared with Christ and a pledge of our commitment to him.[40] This, claimed Green, was how the early Church spoke of the Eucharist as a sacrifice, the church's response of sacrifice of thanksgiving to her creating and redeeming Lord. But he insisted on retaining the distinction between Christ's sacrifice and ours: the only way in which we share in Christ's sacrifice was not as offerers or victims, but as beneficiaries.

This positive attitude was confirmed in the statement issued by the Congress itself.[41] It commended the services presented by the Commission as having many excellent features, and while objecting to prayer for the departed and the offering of the bread and cup in the Eucharist, it reiterated Green's point about the way in which the service could be spoken of in sacrificial terms, and went on to affirm a readiness to enter into dialogue with those who thought differently in order to secure a liturgy that was both biblical and unifying. The secretary of the Congress, the Reverend Raymond Turvey, claimed that this represented the feelings of some 3,500 clergy, a figure which, if correct, represented a far higher proportion of the Anglican total than some people imagined.[42]

Roger Beckwith and Colin Buchanan also wrote an article in the June number of *Theology*, 'This Bread and This Cup: An Evangelical Rejoinder'. Here they denied that Evangelicals were opposed to Prayer Book revision, or that they were bogged down with Reformation controversies and unable to adjust to current theological argument, or that the Eucharist was an objective means of grace. A solution to current problems could only be found, however, if 'the historical school shows a willingness to read the text of Hippolytus as less than verbally inspired'. They had written the article too early to include any detailed consideration of my 'stop-gap formula': but there was time for the inclusion of a brief postscript in which Beckwith wrote encouragingly of it: 'Though not entirely ambiguous, it may be the best on which to agree for the present.'[43]

It was against such a background that the House of Laity resumed its consideration of the rite on 7 July. Admittedly there was another fairly lengthy debate; but there was also a determination to reach a successful conclusion. A number of proposed amendments were withdrawn, and the only point of substance was Professor Anderson's proposal urging a reconsideration during the experimental period of the prayer for the departed in the Shorter Litany in the Appendix, to bring it into line with what was expressed in the rite itself.[44] Sir John Best-Shaw, a prominent Catholic layman, aptly described the attitude of the House, 'People are meeting half-way and holding out hands to each other.'[45] There was a final plea for rejection based on the Exeter proctors' statement from west country members, but it came to nothing. The rite was finally approved by a massive majority: 185 votes to 8, with 15 abstentions.[46] It was published in booklet form on 7 September, together with a popular illustrated commentary *Experiment in Worship*, an imaginative work by Michael Perry which did a great deal to commend the rite to the Church at large. This was in fact only one of a large number of guides and commentaries to appear, many of them local; and among these three were by members of the Liturgical Commission. Colin Buchanan's *A Guide to the New Communion Service*, written from an Evangelical point of view, was an enthusiastic commendation of the new rite; indeed Roger Beckwith, reviewing it in *The Church of England Newspaper* (20 October 1967) felt impelled to say, 'His approach to the new service is, in fact, so positive that he is less than fair to 1662!' John Wilkinson's *Eucharist for Experiment*, written from the Catholic point of view, was published by the Church Union, indicating a willingness on the part of that body to associate itself with the new rite, despite the reservations of at least some of its members. Then there was Charles Whitaker's *The New Services 1967: A Guide and Explanation*, which included the new initiation rites as well as the Eucharist; it was semi-official in the sense that it appeared as one of the Commission's own series of booklets and had been vetted by several of its members.

Holy Communion Series Two in general followed the patterns laid down by Lambeth 1958 and Toronto 1963. It envisaged a parish communion as its normal setting, with the time fairly evenly divided between the Ministry of the Word and the Communion itself. As with the Liturgy for Africa, provision was made for its use when there was no communion, the service ending with the Grace after the Intercessions. During its passage through the Convocations it acquired a significant amount of additional material from 1662, inserted to provide additional alternatives; but overall its linguistic approach was rather more modern than that of 1662. It is best described as 'RSV language', with God still addressed as 'thou' but people as 'you'. For the first time, the typography was radically revised in the interests of the worshipper, with the use of two-colour printing, different founts of type, the lining-out of congregational elements and the use of sub-headings. Indeed, the use of the little sixteen-page booklets became so popular that in many congregations subsequent revisions were viewed with trepidation and even reluctance. Its principal features were:

1. The Gloria in excelsis could be used in its 1549 or 1662 position, but everything before the collect of the day was optional.
2. There was provision for three lessons with psalms, canticles or hymns.
3. The Intercessions followed the pattern of the Roman Solemn Prayers for Good Friday.
4. The penitential section, now called the Preparation of the People, followed the Intercessions and concluded with the Peace.

5. The Four-Shape action was clearly set out, with the Offertory being termed the Preparation of the Bread and Wine. No Offertory Sentences were provided.
6. At the insistence of the Convocations, manual acts were mandatory at the Institution Narrative, but they confined the priest's actions to taking the elements into his hands — there was no fraction.
7. Provision was made for the optional use of the Benedictus after the Thanksgiving. This, together with the concluding reference to heavenly worship, suggested some reference to Edward Ratcliff's theory that the Hippolytean canon had ended with the Sanctus.[47]
8. The Lord's Prayer followed the Fraction before Communion.
9. The service ended with a Dismissal or the 1662 Blessing or both.
10. There was no provision for further consecration, it being tacitly assumed that at least for the time being the 1662 arrangements would stand.

III

Of the other Series Two services in the original volume, Morning and Evening Prayer presented few problems. The Steering Committee decided not to proceed with the Intercessions and Thanksgivings, not only to avoid interminable debate — particularly over the prayers for the departed, but in recognition of the fact that the numerous collections of prayers available made an official provision unnecessary. When I presented the services themselves to the Joint Convocations in October 1966, I pointed out that while the Commission was aware of widespread demands for more flexible forms, the present proposals were of necessity modest, being simply revisions of Morning and Evening Prayer under section I of the Alternative Services Measure. Three things should be borne in mind, however: the Joint Liturgical Group's briefer and more flexible proposals were almost complete, the Commission's own report on Family and Evangelistic Services was about to be presented to the Archbishops, and clergy were still free to produce their own forms of service with episcopal approval under the Act of Uniformity Amendment Act of 1872.[48] This seemed to suffice, for both services were approved with little debate by all four Houses, and by the House of Laity in February 1968.[49] Structurally the offices were similar to those of 1662, but with new introductory sentences, a new penitential section, a transposition of Benedictus and Te Deum, and the inclusion of Gloria in excelsis as an alternative to both — a feature which restored to it its original function of an office canticle and facilitated the use of the office itself as an alternative form of the Ministry of the Word at Holy Communion.

Thanksgiving after Childbirth, despite a short and unsuccessful appearance, served a useful purpose. It was a simple, brief service over which the Commission had taken a great deal of trouble, mainly through Elisabeth Montefiore and Ronnie Beddoes. They had consulted various groups, social workers, doctors, and members of the Mothers' Union, and the old idea of a rite of purification had been carefully avoided. In May 1966 York Convocation, sitting on its own, approved it;[50] but Canterbury simultaneously rejected it after offering a wealth of contradictory comment. As Ronnie Beddoes drily remarked, if the Commission had acted on the advice given, there would have been no service at all.[51] What was particularly annoying was the total lack of episcopal support in the debate. I later complained to the Archbishop, pointing out that by an arrangement of 1962,[52] no Commission report should be presented to the Convocations without endorsement from the Bishops. The Bishops of Newcastle and Southwark revealed, however, that although the service had been submitted to the Archbishops in October 1964, it had never been before the Bishops at all. The Archbishop admitted his mistake and apologized: and the agreed procedure was carefully followed in future. Indeed, the Commission itself saw to that.

The Burial Service also met with failure, not for any lack of merit in the rite itself, but over the thorny question of prayer for the departed. The initial report, submitted to the Archbishops in October 1964, owed a great deal to Bernard Wigan, with a particularly fine introduction setting out the purpose of the service and justifying the inclusion of such prayer.[53] It was the only matter which provoked real criticism at the Liturgical Conference on 18 February 1966; and all four Houses of Convocation approved the new service with little difficulty in October.[54] The House of Laity, however, had reservations; after a short debate it decided to ask the Archbishops to appoint a group to consider the prayers for the departed with their own representatives.[55] The joint committee, chaired by Leslie Brown, succeeded in agreeing a set of amendments, but the Convocations found them generally unacceptable and insisted on retaining the original forms.[56] Again, however, the House of Laity refused to be persuaded, insisting instead on suggesting that the whole matter be referred back to the Commission, who should 'take a new line'.[57] What the new line should be no one was prepared to suggest, not even the Archbishops. In January 1969 they informed the Convocations that the Liturgical Commission had been asked to draft a new Burial Service, 'it being left to the Commission to determine the width or narrowness of the word "new"'.[58] The ball was in the Commission's court, and once again it was faced with a seemingly thankless task.

After the disasters of the 1958–9 Initiation Report, the Commission did no further work on the subject during the chairmanship of Donald Coggan. By early 1965, however, the Bishops had begun to press for the early introduction of a new 'simple' service of Infant Baptism; and I realized that the time had come to grasp the nettle. It did not help matters to know that Michael Ramsey still favoured the York rite, and he took a lot of persuading to accept that it did not fit in with the Commission's ideas. We were still convinced that the 1958 proposals had been on the right lines, even if they had been a little too academic in approach. They were still used, therefore, as the basis of our discussions on the criticisms and suggestions made by the Convocations' Joint Committee of 1961.[59] Arthur Couratin continued to act as the principal draughtsman – no easy task for him, for it involved rewriting much of his own handiwork and it was clear that he frequently did not regard the new as an improvement on the old. But it was now a great help to have the benefit of Charles Whitaker's expert knowledge on the subject, which he contrived to offer with considerable patience and modesty. By the summer of 1966 the work was sufficiently advanced for me to show a draft to the Archbishop, who to our great relief expressed himself as satisfied and refrained from further pleading on behalf of the York rite. Colin Buchanan still thought the Confirmation rite came down too heavily in favour of the Mason–Dix line but on this occasion was content with a note in the introduction to the report to the effect that he 'would have desired the services more clearly to express that the work of the Spirit in sacramental initiation is complete in baptism'.[60] The report was completed by the end of the year, in time to be printed and introduced at the second Liturgical Conference on 25 April 1967.

Here there was a relatively short debate immediately following the hectic session on the Eucharist, and one wonders precisely how much of it registered. I pointed out that the Commission still stuck to the principles of its 1958 Report, but its new proposals were simpler, briefer and less academic; they could not include provision for the making of a catechumen, as some people had demanded however, as we were still operating under section I of the Alternative Services Measure. Possibly the Conference was relaxed and relieved after its successful resolution of the problems over 'we offer', but no major criticisms were offered and the rites were warmly welcomed.[61] The same euphoric atmosphere was evident on the following day in the official debate of the joint Convocations. Possibly members were too relieved and happy to argue unduly, but the services positively sailed through, the two Upper Houses passing them unanimously and the Lower Houses passing them nem. con.[62] This time the House of Laity followed suit: Confirmation was considered first in September, since there was an urgent need for an alternative rite to 1662; and the other services followed in February 1968. All secured a quick and easy passage.[63] The Commission's 1958 principles were ultimately vindicated; and what was equally important, the relations between the Commission and the Convocations, highlighted by Dr Leslie Hunter in January 1962, had been considerably clarified and improved.[64]

The combined rite of Baptism, Confirmation and Holy Communion was still regarded as the basic service; but the theology now tended to be spread throughout the various rites rather than concentrated in the opening collect and the blessing of the water. The Ministry of the Word remained essentially unchanged from 1958, with the account of our Lord's baptism retained as the Gospel. The acts of renunciation were placed in their primitive and 1662 position before the blessing of the water and embodied important new features: they now became the Decision, beginning with a positive commitment to discipleship. At first this provoked criticism on the grounds that such turning should follow and not precede repentance and renunciation. But the Commission successfully argued that the latter were consequent upon the first positive movement of turning; the verb 'turn' also had good precedent, being used in the 1662 Communion service both in the Absolution and in the preamble to the Comfortable Words.[65] The blessing of the water, still eucharistic in form, was now shorter and simpler and no longer included prayer for those to be baptized. It was followed by the profession of faith, now based on the profession in the Prayer Book Catechism, and the baptism itself. This in its turn was followed by consignation and a welcome by the congregation on behalf of the Church, an addition requested by the joint Convocation Committee of 1961. The formula of confirmation – 'Confirm, O Lord, thy servant with thy Holy Spirit' – as in 1958, accommodated the various views on the relation between baptism and confirmation: the Spirit is given fully in baptism, the Spirit is given fully in confirmation, or the Spirit is given in both. The 1662 formula, 'Defend, O Lord . . .', then followed, to be said by bishop and congregation. The use of Acts 8.14–17 and Acts 19.1–7 was carefully avoided.

The derived rite of Infant Baptism was considerably simplified. The 1958 introduction was replaced by a preface which was no part of the actual service, setting out the pastoral requirements for baptism. The lessons and psalmody were also replaced by a catena of short biblical texts, including one from the controversial Mark 10, and divided into two, each part being followed by a congregational prayer, the first a thanksgiving for baptism and the second a prayer for the baptizands. The promises were also addressed to parents and sponsors but so introduced as to apply to them or to the infants.

The Series Two services were therefore a limited operation and took much longer to be authorized than had originally been envisaged: admittedly only two years after the passing of the Alternative Services Measure, but ten years after the publication of the first proposals on baptism and confirmation. Once authorized, however, there was no doubting their popularity, particularly the rite of Holy Communion. Its booklet went out of print on the day of publication, and demand exceeded supply for some months. Some idea of this popularity can be seen from the approximate sales figures of the service booklets to the end of 1968 –

Morning and Evening Prayer	110,000
Holy Communion	1,660,000
Infant Baptism	300,000
Confirmation	535,000

The sale of the Series One booklets for Matrimony and Burial, for which no Series Two services existed, was also remarkably healthy: Matrimony 105,000, and Burial 70,000.[66] Notwithstanding this popularity, however, it had already become clear by 1968 that the demands for even more radical forms of service could not be ignored; and these new rites could only be regarded as a temporary stage in the general movement of liturgical reform.

NOTES

1. The C. of E. Liturgical Commission, *Alternative Services, Second Series,* 1965, p. 148.
2. *The Liturgical Conference 1966*, Report, p. 87.
3. J. I. Packer, ed., *Eucharistic Sacrifice*, 1962, pp. 1–2.
4. ibid., p. 3.
5. ibid., pp. 9–13.
6. ibid., p. 19.
7. F. Clark, *Eucharistic Sacrifice and the Reformation*, 1960, p. 522.
8. See his article on 'The Eucharistic Sacrifice', in *The Church Quarterly Review*, April 1961 and July 1961; and 'Eucharistic Sacrifice and the Reformation', in *Theology* LXIV (August 1961), pp. 310–16.
9. See the article in *Theology* (August 1961), pp. 312–14; cf. *Corpus Christi*, 2nd edn, 1965, p. 104.
10. F. E. Brightman, *The English Rite*, 1915, vol. 1, p. cvi.
11. Mascall, *Corpus Christi*, pp. 183, 188.
12. Dix, *The Shape of the Liturgy*, p. 666.
13. *Liturgical Conference 1966*, p. 74.
14. *An Order for Holy Communion*, a Report of the C. of E. Liturgical Commission to the Archbishops of Canterbury and York, April 1966, p. xi.
15. This was one of a series of pamphlets published by the Evangelicals on Prayer Book Reform in 1966–7: J. I. Packer, *Tomorrow's Worship*; D. D. Billings, *Services on Trial*; G. E. Duffield, *Revision and the Layman*; R. T. Beckwith, *Prayer Book Revision and Anglican Unity*. They expressed a commitment to the principle of liturgical revision, but insisted that it must be true to Scripture. Hence they were critical of the Lambeth 1958 statement on eucharistic sacrifice and were opposed to prayer for the departed and reservation.
16. C. O. Buchanan, *The New Communion Service – Reasons for Dissent*, 1966, pp. 4–5.
17. ibid., pp. 6–9.
18. *Chronicle Convoc.*, 1966, pp. 164–91.
19. cf. *Studia Liturgica*, 1964, vol. III, no. 3, pp. 175–7.
20. He had already written to me (15 March), to express his own misgivings over the phrase 'we offer this bread and this cup': 'I cannot see that this is the chief thing we want to say at this point; however rich it may be in symbolism, I don't believe it is Biblical . . . In India and Africa I know that such a conclusion of the Anaphora would have frustrated its eirenic purpose.'
21. A. H. Couratin, 'The Tradition Received' in *Theology* LXIX (October 1966), pp. 437–42. It was unwise to add this reference to 1662, for Evangelicals resented any suggestion that they need have no share in revision.
22. M. J. Moreton, 'The Early Liturgies', in *Theology*, ibid., pp. 442–7; cf. his further essay, 'The Anaphoral Prayer', in *CQR* CLXVIII (January 1967), pp. 45–52.
23. Geoffrey Cuming, 'The English Rite', in *Theology*, ibid., pp. 447–52.

24. J. L. Houlden, 'Good Liturgy or even Good Battlefield?', in *Theology*, ibid., pp. 433–7.
25. *Chronicle Convoc.*, 1966, pp. 267–8.
26. ibid., pp. 308–11.
27. ibid., pp. 325–6.
28. For the whole debate, ibid., pp. 331–68, especially pp. 359, 365.
29. *Church Assembly Proceedings*, 1967, vol. XLVII, no. 1, pp. 2–38.
30. ibid., pp. 38–58.
31. *The Liturgical Conference 1967*, Report, pp. 2–5.
32. ibid., pp. 36–7.
33. ibid., pp. 38–9.
34. ibid., pp. 39–40, 53–4.
35. ibid., p. 54.
36. *Journal Convoc.*, 1967, pp. 115, 127, 133. The voting was as follows:

Canterbury	Bishops 22–0	Clergy 130–13
York	Bishops 12–0	Clergy overwhelming majority

37. *LC Minutes*, 51. 104.
38. J. I. Packer, ed., *Guidelines: Anglican Evangelicals face the Future*, 1967.
39. ibid., pp. 111–12.
40. ibid., pp. 108–9.
41. The Keele Statement, 1967.
42. Letter to R.C.D.J., 7 August 1967.
43. R. Beckwith and C. Buchanan, 'This Bread and This Cup: An Evangelical Rejoinder', in *Theology* LXX (June 1967), pp. 265–71.
44. I think this single petition in the Scottish Shorter Litany, tucked away as it was in an Appendix, had simply been overlooked.
45. *CA Proceedings*, 1967, vol. XLVII, no. 3, pp. 525–6.
46. ibid., p. 554; for the whole debate, pp. 521–55.
47. cf. 'The Sanctus and the Pattern of the Early Anaphora', in *Journal of Ecclesiastical History* vol. 1, no. 1 (1950), pp. 29–36; vol. 1, no. 2, pp. 125–34.
48. *Journal Convoc.*, 1966, pp. 289–92.
49. ibid., pp. 292–307; *CA Proceedings*, 1968, pp. 262–86.
50. *Journal Convoc.*, 1966, pp. 57–67.
51. *Chronicle Convoc.*, 1966, pp. 153–64.
52. *LC Minutes*, 32. 7ff.
53. *Alternative Services: Second Series*, 1965, pp. 105–6.
54. *Journal Convoc.*, 1966, pp. 269–88.
55. *CA Proceedings*, 1967, vol. XLVII, pp. 945–9.
56. *Chronicle Convoc.*, 1968, pp. 7–41; *Journal Convoc.*, 1968, pp. 39–63, 125–6. The voting of the Convocations was most emphatic: Canterbury, Bishops – unanimous, Clergy 85–10, while in York only one Clergy vote was registered against.
57. *CA Proceedings*, 1968, vol. XLVIII, pp. 894–920.
58. *Journal Convoc.*, 1969, p. 13.
59. cf. pp. 223–4.
60. Report of the C. of E. Liturgical Commission, *Baptism and Confirmation*, 1966, p. 4.
61. *The Liturgical Conference*, 1967, pp. 43–52, 58–71.
62. *Journal Convoc.*, 1967, p. 161: for the whole debate pp. 133–61.
63. *CA Proceedings*, 1967, vol. XLVII, pp. 867–75; 1968, vol. XLVIII, pp. 291–303.

64. cf. p. 224.
65. Report, *Baptism and Confirmation*, 1966, p. 2. cf. E. C. Whitaker, *The New Services 1967*, pp. 25–7.
66. It is interesting to note that SPCK also printed 60,000 copies of *Experiment in Worship*, which also appeared on the day of publication of Holy Communion Series Two. By way of contrast the sales of two other Series One booklets to the end of 1968 were relatively small: Holy Communion 80,000, Baptism 25,000.

12

A LITURGICAL JIGSAW

At first sight this Chapter might appear to be a collection of oddments, a variety of unrelated events and changes. Nevertheless they are all elements in the liturgical jigsaw, some small but nevertheless significant, which must be included in order to make sense of the developments in the middle and late seventies ultimately leading to the appearance of *The Alternative Service Book*. They might equally be called 'preparatory pieces'.

I

In May 1967 Michael Ramsey asked me whether I thought it would serve any useful purpose in the Anglican Communion as a whole to include liturgy on the agenda of the 1968 Lambeth Conference. I pointed out that while the subject had been given a good airing in 1958, the process of revision had subsequently become more widespread and some Anglican Churches were conscious of their lack of liturgical expertise; in particular the question of language was exercising many minds; an opportunity for discussion might therefore be widely appreciated. The Archbishop thought this made sense and left me to make plans with Bishop Ralph Dean, who had succeeded Stephen Bayne as Anglican Executive Officer. We arranged for another Consultation similar to that of Toronto 1963 and in preparation asked the Reverend R. M. C. Jeffery of the Missionary and Ecumenical Council to produce a survey of liturgical work completed or in progress throughout the Communion.[1] This resulted in a 35-page document, by far the most comprehensive survey so far produced, covering work in 22 Anglican Churches or provinces, which indicated that the principles laid down at Lambeth 1958 were being widely followed and that ecumenical co-operation was growing.[2]

The Archbishop asked me to chair the two-day Consultation (27–8 August), attended by some thirty bishops and representatives. The English members were Leslie Brown and Henry de Candole. The latter was about to retire and I thought the invitation would be some recognition of his past labours:

> The important items on the agenda refer to Calendar and Lectionary and the Daily Office – all based on the reports of the JLG . . . Since these things have been so close to you and you have worked so hard at them, I suggested that you should be invited to help . . . It might be rather nice for you to be recognized in this way and to be given the opportunity of laying the foundations of what might be some important new development in the Anglican Communion.[3]

The agenda had a distinctly ecumenical flavour and the Consultation's reactions to it were encouraging. The JLG Calendar proposals were generally welcomed, in particular the naming of Sundays 'after Pentecost' rather than 'after Trinity' and the dropping of the three '-gesima' Sundays before Lent; the only division of opinion was on the proposed extension of the pre-Christmas season to nine Sundays. The JLG Daily Office also met with warm approval, resulting in a call for a shorter and more flexible Office more closely related to the Eucharist: Leslie Brown and I were then asked to revise the Pan-Anglican document on the contents and structure of the Eucharist to reflect this closer relationship.[4] The Consultation then went on to examine and approve the Liturgical Commission's *Modern Liturgical Texts*;[5] while the final session was spent on discussing supplementary consecration at the Eucharist: while no agreed policy on this was worked out, a number of important points emerged. There was general acceptance that the 1662 direction to repeat the Institution Narrative over further supplies of bread and wine was unsatisfactory; there was no widespread approval for taking further elements in silence; and a declaratory form appeared to be preferable to a prayer.

It took several months for Leslie Brown and me to prepare a new Pan-Anglican document; there was further delay while we submitted it to the compilers of the original statement for comment; and the two Archbishops did not approve the new form until February 1970. Although widely distributed, it was again difficult to assess its influence.[6] Three points deserve mention. The first was its recognition of the use of contemporary language and in particular the recent ICET texts.[7] The second was its justification of the closer relationship between Office and Eucharist and its guidance as to ways in which this could be done:

> Such an arrangement is desirable not only on weekdays but on Sundays in those congregations which do not have the Eucharist as their principal act of worship. In many Churches of the Anglican Communion this is the case not from choice, but from necessity, because the number of priests is inadequate.[8]

The third was its attempt to produce a brief, constructive statement on the section of the eucharistic prayer following the Institution Narrative, bearing in mind the differing and strongly held opinions on this subject. With Holy Communion Series Three now in preparation, we ourselves were in a rather delicate position.

> It is recognised that this is the most difficult section of the prayer in view of the different doctrinal emphases which are expressed and recognised within the Anglican Communion. The whole concept of anamnesis is, however, so rich in meaning that it should not be impossible to express it in such a way that the needs of everyone are met. Whatever language is

adopted should, however, avoid any idea of a propitiatory sacrifice or a repetition of Christ's sacrifice. The 'once for all' character of his work must not be obscured.[9]

This document appeared in the Anglican Consultative Council's 1972 Report *Partners in Mission*, accompanied by another survey of Anglican liturgical developments down to 1972, which I was asked to compile. This new survey, containing some twenty individual reports of varying length, revealed a number of interesting features:

1. There was a general move towards the use of contemporary language and a willingness to incorporate the ICET common texts. The Council recognized in its Report, however, that a great deal of work needed to be done in this field. 'It questions whether the problems connected with the provision of liturgies in acceptable modern English have been satisfactorily solved, and notes the difficulties involved in the translation, adaptation, and development of modern liturgies in other languages.'[10]
2. There was a general readiness to implement a closer relationship between Office and Eucharist.
3. Many Churches showed a readiness to borrow from this country's Series Two and JLG material. Apparently the Council regarded this as a mixed blessing: 'We are critical of the liturgies being produced by different Churches of the Anglican Communion as being rearrangements of 1662 and Series Two of the Church of England. We hope that consideration might be given to the possible inclusion of elements of worship from the traditional religion of the country where the Church carries on its mission.'[11] Nevertheless, it had to be remembered that many parts of the Anglican Communion were very conscious of their lack of liturgical expertise and at least in the short term were glad of help; furthermore, as the Toronto Consultation had recognized, Western culture was becoming a world-wide phenomenon and this, as well as local culture, had to be accommodated in liturgy. It was a factor which South India had clearly grasped.[12]
4. In spite of borrowings, however, the Council recognized that 'within a common eucharistic structure the present tendency is towards variety and transience'.[13]

II

From its inception in 1963 the Joint Liturgical Group had committed itself to work on the Calendar and Lectionary and the Daily Office. At the first meeting Stephen Winward (Baptist) had suggested that agreement over an ecumenical Calendar and Lectionary would stimulate their use in the Free Churches, a view endorsed unanimously by the others present; the work already done by CSI was regarded as an encouraging example, while Bishop de Candole's two recent articles in *Theology* had drawn attention to important work done on the subject by the Presbyterian scholar, Dr A. A.

McArthur, and had indicated some guide-lines for reform.[14] At the same meeting the Free Church members had also expressed a desire for some form of daily office but had made it clear that their adoption of Anglican Morning and Evening Prayer was unacceptable for two reasons – they were too long and rigid, and they contained no distinctively Free Church elements. The members of JLG fell conveniently into three geographical sections; so a Northern section under Henry de Candole worked on the Calendar, a London section under Neville Clark (Baptist) worked on the Lectionary, and a Western section under Douglas Harrison worked on the Daily Office. Revision by the whole group then followed; and the Calendar and Lectionary proposals were the first to be published in early 1967.[15]

The Calendar was simple, being based on the three foci of Christmas, Easter and Pentecost, although provision for Advent and Lent was still made if so desired. The Lectionary provided three readings for every Sunday, one of which was regarded as the controlling lesson: the Old Testament on Sundays before Christmas, the Gospel from Christmas to Pentecost and the Acts and Epistles after Pentecost. This idea resulted from a decision to begin by selecting those key passages regarded as indispensable to a rich sweep of biblical revelation over the year. Once these were chosen, allied readings were found to support them; it was then possible to arrange them in some order, from which a progression of themes emerged. This was different from arbitrarily choosing themes and then looking for passages to fit them; the themes simply indicated the thrust of the passages and in no way exercised a rigid control.[16] While these proposals marked a significant departure from 1662, JLG claimed that tradition had not been ignored.

> The Lectionary system belongs to the tradition of the Church and is a facet of her ongoing life. It has been tested, revised and proved over many centuries . . . The Lectionary cannot be treated with academic detachment or recreated *in toto* as a contemporary exercise in scholarly ingenuity. But significant insights in regard to Scripture must be allowed to find expression in lectionary terms.[17]

Work on the Daily Office, involving another complete lectionary, took rather longer; but it still appeared in time for consideration at Lambeth 1968. While owing a great deal to the Prayer Book offices, what emerged was a shorter and more flexible form. The office for each day was regarded as a single entity but in two parts, with a minimum of duplication in each part. Psalmody was used in both parts but on a reduced scale, being arranged on a quarterly rather than a monthly basis. The two-year lectionary had three readings each day, two in the morning and one in the evening, so planned that it could be used for either Office or Eucharist or both. Proper canticles were provided for each day of the week, the additional material coming from various sources, Anglican, Free Church and Roman Catholic, while hymns could also be substituted. Finally, there was a weekly scheme of intercessions and thanksgivings, theologically based on the earthly and heavenly ministry of Christ. The Office, intended for weekday use, also appeared in a single, shortened form largely for use by lay people. The proposals were prefaced by a superb essay by Stephen Winward, which came to be regarded as one of the finest apologies for the Daily Office to appear for many years.[18]

The Lectionary proposals were supplemented in 1969 by a further JLG *Additional Lectionary for use at a Second Sunday Service* based on the same principles; and the three documents subsequently provided a major contribution to the Anglican revision of the Calendar, Lectionary and Daily Office. They were widely and even enthusiastically reviewed, and *The Daily Office* was reprinted at least ten times. This was in marked contrast to the reactions of the House of Bishops. When I asked Michael Ramsey to show *The Calendar and Lectionary* to them, they clearly preferred something on 1928–Series One lines; they considered the proposals so radical that they urged no action until Lambeth 1968 had expressed an opinion.[19] I was moved to remonstrate with the Archbishop, deploring the lack of interest and enthusiasm, so different from attitudes elsewhere: the Roman Catholic *Tablet*, for example, had said, 'The evident scholarship and the fertile resourcefulness displayed suggest that it would be all to the good if their ideas were given full weight by the Concilium Liturgicum'; while *The Times Literary Supplement* had described them as an important landmark in ecumenism. He sympathized, told me not to be too depressed, and suggested that I should come to a Bishops' Meeting and expound the new proposals myself. This I agreed to do and in preparation submitted a memorandum pointing out the widespread favourable reactions, the fact that other Churches had already authorized them or were about to authorize them for use, and concluding with the comment of the New Testament scholar, Professor Christopher Evans, 'On the whole a difficult if not impossible task seems to me to have been excellently done.' This, coupled with my personal harangue at their January 1968 meeting, persuaded the Bishops to change their minds. Afterwards the Archbishop wrote:

> Thank you for participation in the Bishops' meeting. It was an immense advantage to have your exposition of Calendar and Lectionary, and I think that the wish to have a further revision of the Lectionary on the present Calendar basis is now dead. The Bishops are content to go on with the existing lectionaries until a new, thorough Calendar–Lectionary project is available.

With this approval Charles Whitaker and Henry de Candole began preparing comprehensive proposals for a revised Calendar and Lectionary, together with a Table to Regulate the Service. A considerable amount of work had already been done on the Sanctorale, including the revision of the Black-letter days in 1964;[20] and with the general approval of the Lambeth 1968 Consultation for the JLG proposals, progress was rapid. In autumn 1968 preparations for a further Liturgical Conference of the Church

Assembly in February 1969 were made with the Commission's Calendar–Lectionary proposals as the main item on the agenda. These proposals were published in January in the report *The Calendar and Lessons for the Church's Year*, containing all the lectionary material required, except for the weekday Daily Office, together with the collects. Four points merit particular notice:

1. The Temporale proposals were substantially those of JLG.
2. The Red-letter Days, now called Greater Holy Days, were those of 1662 together with the two 1928 additions, St Mary Magdalene and the Transfiguration, and were recommended for optional use.
3. The Black-letter Days, now lesser Holy Days, were substantially those recommended in 1964 and were one third fewer than those of 1662.[21]
4. The Rules permitted only one evensong for any occasion, in accordance with the arguments in the 1958 Lambeth Report.

At the last minute I suggested to the Archbishop that if possible some discussion of the JLG Daily Office might be permitted, in view of its enthusiastic reception. He readily agreed; and although the decision was made too late for it to appear on the official agenda, all members of the Conference were sent a copy, while the chairman, Dr Stopford, introduced it in the final session with his own commendation, 'Perhaps I might be allowed to become personal for a moment on the question of *The Daily Office* and say a word of deep appreciation of a good many of my own clergy and myself for the admirable introduction to that book written by Mr Winward.'[22]

The Conference on 10 February was a low-key affair. Few of the speakers attempted to deal with the principles underlying the proposed Calendar and Lectionary, a great deal of time being spent on matters of detail such as the absence of particular names in the list of Lesser Holy Days. The lack of enthusiasm was not altogether surprising, for as I pointed out, neither Calendar nor Lectionary by themselves could be authorized for use under the Alternative Services Measure, for they were not services. But since a separate parliamentary measure would be required, it was thought wise to give the proposals an airing before expending time and energy on detailed legislation.[23] The Conference brightened considerably, however, when the Daily Office was discussed. Enthusiasm for it was marked. Canon Welsby, for example, revealed that 'a considerable number of clergy are already using it, many of them with a sigh of relief . . . This will be a godsend to many, and I hope we shall soon authorize its use.'[24] The most stirring speech, really lifting the Conference at the end of the day, came from one of the Assembly's veterans, Mrs Mildred Rawlinson, widow of the late Bishop of Derby. She spoke as 'an old woman who had not missed Mattins or Evensong for thirty-five years for a single day'. Urging the need for a shorter and more definitely pointed office, she claimed that the new proposals met that need – 'They are very, very good.' She had nothing but thanksgiving for 'this valiant scheme to make the whole of our worship knit up together. I think it has been a most marvellous adventure . . . This whole scheme is conducive to interest and to devotion, and I believe it ought to be tried out.'[25] Mrs Rawlinson was a great and beloved character, and the Conference was thoroughly appreciative.

The Archbishop took little persuading that the JLG Daily Office should be authorized, and he secured the Bishops' agreement in June. It was at this juncture that the future of Series Two Morning and Evening Prayer had to be considered, for its period of experiment was due to end in early 1971. To renew this as it stood and then add the JLG Office as a further alternative to 1662 and Series One[26] would be unnecessarily confusing. I therefore suggested that we might try to dovetail the more important elements of the JLG proposals into Series Two, while the Office Lectionary might be included as part of the rite, so obviating the need for separate authorization. Furthermore, since the Anglican–Methodist Unity scheme had just foundered, an ecumenical gesture from the Church of England at this stage might not be out of place.[27] Again the Archbishop readily agreed and the process of integration, largely the work of Geoffrey Cuming, was rapidly completed. It was published as the report *Common Prayer 1970* in October 1969.

The proposal was to retain Series Two Morning and Evening Prayer, but to add as optional alternatives certain JLG material (e.g. the sentences and canticles) and to permit a number of omissions (e.g. the first morning canticle or the first evening canticle and lesson): the JLG course of psalmody and lectionary were included as alternatives, and the single shortened form of Office was added. This was clearly regarded as a holding operation pending the production of a form in contemporary language.[28] Both Convocations passed these proposals in January 1970 with virtually no dissent and with only one significant amendment: the JLG adaptations were made permissible on Sundays as well as on weekdays.[29] Completion of authorization was found to be impossible at the final session of the Church Assembly in July 1970; but the proposals were eventually set out in detail as *Morning and Evening Prayer Second Series Revised* and considered at the inaugural meeting of the General Synod in November. Once again they presented no problems, securing Final Approval in February 1971 with dissent confined to only two members of the House of Clergy.[30] These services, authorized for a period of four years, were eventually extended until 31 December 1979. The Series One forms, whose essential provisions were covered by the new rites, were allowed to lapse in February 1973.[31]

Despite their increased variability and flexibility, these revised services still failed to meet the Sunday needs of some clergy. From 1965 onwards pleas for the production of a 'Family Service', distinct from the Eucharist or Morning and Evening Prayer, were constant. Many clergy in fact produced their own forms and these varied considerably in content and structure: but in general they were envisaged as short, simple, non-eucharistic services to which parents could bring their children before confirmation. As the preface to one such service stated, there was 'a crying need for gospel services, to present the simple Good News to young people, and older people, who know hardly anything about it'.

Dr Ramsey had made specific reference to such services at the outset of the 1966 Liturgical Conference: 'It should be made clear that under the Prayer Book (Alternative and Other Services) Measure there can be lawful provision of services in various ways to meet needs and occasions for which the Prayer Book does not provide': and he went on to point out how section 6 gave a minister the right to be responsible for such services. 'It will be important for parishes, dioceses and the Convocations to review this field, and for the Archbishops to ask the Liturgical Commission to give what help is needed.'[32] Despite this clear statement, many people continued to plead for an official Family Service, which could take its place as an alternative to Morning and Evening Prayer. The Archbishop therefore asked the Commission to prepare a report on Informal Services, which would cover both Family Services and services for special occasions. As a preliminary exercise the Commission published another booklet, *Family and Evangelistic Services*, in March 1967. It was written by John Wilkinson and vetted by the Commission and was intended, not as a book of services for actual use but as a set of guide-lines, indicating how such services could be constructed and where to find the necessary material.

Three months later the Report itself was ready. It was brief — a mere five typewritten pages — setting out the thinking which lay behind the Wilkinson booklet. The Commission argued that the needs of the people who attended such services, whether regularly or on special occasions, were so diverse that they should be met, not by publishing set forms for all comers, like those of the Prayer Book, but rather by providing a selection of suitable structures and a wide choice of material. It was also pointed out that the acceptance of such services as official alternatives to those in the Prayer Book was not a matter for the Commission to decide: it was a matter for the Bishops and might even involve changes in the Canons. The Commission firmly believed that these services should be the products of local knowledge and experience, created with the approval of the bishop under section 6 of the Alternative Services Measure. Since they were likely to be ephemeral, small and adaptable collections were preferable to large and permanent books; but the whole field provided wonderful opportunities for creative liturgical work both by individuals and by local committees and groups.

Both Archbishops accepted the Report and in due course the House of Bishops did likewise, agreeing to commend it to their dioceses. Unfortunately it never became widely known, possibly because it was so short and possibly because it was never the concern of either the Convocations or the Church Assembly. The little document simply got lost in the pile of papers which descended on episcopal desks; some bishops obviously just didn't bother with it. Certainly the Commission continued to be approached by many people who had heard nothing of the Report and still wanted an official Family Service. The challenge to experiment at diocesan or local level was taken up all too rarely.

III

As early as January 1965 the Liturgical Commission began to give thought to the way in which experimental services should be evaluated. Simply to launch them on the Church and then do nothing more would not do. Professor Christopher Evans had pointed out to us that those who had produced the Revised Catechism some years previously had felt considerable frustration because no real effort had been made to discover what the Church thought about it. Furthermore the conduct of liturgical experiment on an official basis for a specific period of time was something new: we were exploring unknown territory. Fortunately one member of the Commission, David Ayerst, had had considerable experience in the educational world of conducting experiments and of collecting and analysing evidence; and he was able to guide us in formulating a policy. We believed two things to be important: the creation of liturgical committees in every diocese to provide local assistance, and the use of questionnaires. The working out of details took longer than expected, mainly because the completion and authorization of the Series Two services demanded so much time and energy; and it was not until January 1967 that I asked Michael Ramsey to discuss both local committees and questionnaires at the next Bishops' Meeting. The outcome of this was rather disappointing. While the Bishops were prepared to accept diocesan committees, they were 'vehemently opposed' to the questionnaires being given to lay people to answer.[33] This seemed incredible: I reminded the Archbishop that David Ayerst had long experience in this kind of work, and statistical experts — all lay people — had been consulted. 'While the Bishops consider this not to be the sort of document which should be presented to laypeople, nevertheless a group of laypeople after long and careful consideration feel that this *is* the sort of thing which they and their fellows have good reason to expect.'[34] He accepted the point, agreed that the project should not be abandoned, and finally asked me to speak to the Bishops myself. This I did in July 1967, and with happy results: plans for the questionnaires on Holy Communion Series Two were therefore discussed at a conference of the newly created diocesan committees in November.

The questionnaires were distributed in 1968 in two groups: the first, comprising some ten per cent of all parishes, was carefully chosen to ensure a fair representation of the various types of background and churchmanship; the second comprised everyone who wished to use the questionnaire, the sole proviso being genuine experience of the Series Two rite based on at least a dozen attendances.[35] The results, published in January 1970, were judged by experts to indicate trends which were reliable and representative. They covered all dioceses, representing five different types of parish or congregation – rural, suburban, industrial, new estates, others. The more significant figures were as follows:

Questionnaires distributed: 300,000 (85% returned)
Total 'official' replies (i.e. representative 10% of all parishes):
Canterbury: 20,000 York: 8,600
Clergy: 6% Laymen: 41% Laywomen: 53%
Age 16–20: 13% 21–40: 26% 41–65: 40% over 65: 21%
Those wishing to continue using the rite: 77% (Clergy: 90%)
Those satisfied with the RSV type of language: 76%.

Preferences for different elements in the rite:

	Yes	Don't mind	No
Collect for Purity	90%	4%	2%
Prayer of Humble Access	88%	5%	5%
Eucharistic Canon	83%	5%	10%
Post-communion Prayer	73%	7%	9%
New Intercessions	68%	5%	6%
New Confession and Absolution	67%	6%	20%
The Peace	67%	12%	15%

These figures were encouraging and, coupled with the fact that some two million copies of the rite had been sold by 1969, indicated that something on these lines was acceptable to a significant number of people in the Church of England. The comments submitted on the back page also gave valuable guidance when the time came for the Commission to undertake revision. The exercise was judged to be successful and well supported at local level. Here the diocesan committees had given valuable assistance. Obviously the steps taken by the dioceses to create these varied considerably: some did nothing or merely sent a representative to the annual conference. Fortunately these were a small minority, for most did valuable work, arranging demonstrations, disseminating information and producing special services for local use.

The response to this first questionnaire did in fact emphasize the general interest and enthusiasm for the service itself. It was in marked contrast to a less detailed enquiry made in 1971–2 on the use of Holy Communion Series One. Here again all forty-three dioceses were asked to co-operate, but only twenty-five bothered to reply, while the information received was insufficient to make any reliable estimate. For what they were worth the figures from twenty-three dioceses suggested that the rite was in use in eight to nine per cent of their parishes and in only half of those regularly. All that can be said is that the interest shown was by no means overwhelming.

IV

Two constitutional changes which materially affected the process of liturgical revision were the passing of the Synodical Government Measure in 1969 and the Worship and Doctrine Measure in 1974. The former superseded the

Enabling Act of 1919, which had marked a great step forward in self-government for the Church; although experience had proved it to be far from ideal, and particularly so when liturgical matters came up for consideration. For bishops and clergy attendance at both Convocation and Church Assembly could be time-consuming, while the laity's inability to play a full part in liturgical deliberations was frustrating. Joint sessions of the Convocations and informal Liturgical Conferences were undoubtedly a help, but they could only be regarded as temporary expedients. Negotiations on a reform of the system began in 1952, resulting in the appointment of a commission which suggested in its report *The Convocations and the Laity* in 1958 that the Church Assembly should remain as it was, but that the House of Laity should be divided into two on a provincial basis, each part being attached to its respective Convocation with the same rights as the other Houses.[36] This proposal met with little favour; and in 1962 a joint committee of the two Convocations recommended a more radical plan, integrating Convocations and Church Assembly into a single body, with the former retaining a separate existence as and when required.[37] Discussion on details occupied another seven years: and it was not until February 1969 that the Church Assembly finally approved the Synodical Government Measure.[38] Parliament accepted it without demur and it received the Royal Assent on 25 July 1969.[39] The General Synod, inaugurated by Queen Elizabeth II on 4 November 1970, contained three Houses – Bishops, Clergy and Laity – with power to make canons and pass measures; all three Houses could sit together or separately, so the handling of liturgical business was much more satisfactory.

The constitution of the Liturgical Commission now underwent some change. It ceased to be an Archbishops' Commission, becoming instead a Commission of the General Synod and answerable to it through the House of Bishops. This made sense, for in addition to funding the Commission's activities the Synod had become the legislative organ for liturgical revision; and for practical purposes, apart from a slight reduction in size, the changes to the Commission were cosmetic rather than real. The system of working through the Archbishops, which had been so effective in the past, in fact remained in being; for as presidents of the House of Bishops they still had a position of considerable influence. At that time we all expected the current round of revision to be completed by 1975–6; there seemed little sense in making radical changes to the system if we were approaching the final stage.[40] The estimates for a completion date were, of course, optimistic: there was far more to be done than we then realized.

The most important consequence of the new system was a change in the method of actually dealing with proposals. Despite having all three Houses working together, the procedure could still prove lengthy and even rather wearisome; but eventually four main stages evolved.

1. Proposals were presented to the General Synod 'for consideration'.

2. If they were accepted by a simple majority, they underwent a revision stage, during which amendments from members of the Synod were considered. This was where problems developed. It soon became clear that all amendments could not be dealt with in plenary session, nor could the Steering Committee function as a permanent Revision Committee. Separate Revision Committees were therefore appointed for each set of proposals, and even their work became increasingly burdensome.[41]
3. The revised proposals were reconsidered by the whole Synod with any final amendments, and Provisional Approval was sought requiring a simple majority.
4. The House of Bishops decided on the final form of the proposals, after which Final Approval was sought, requiring two-thirds majorities in each House. This was usually done with little or no debate.

The second constitutional change occurred with the passing of the Worship and Doctrine Measure, involving a change in Church–State relations and giving the Church freedom from parliamentary control in matters of worship and doctrine. The process began in November 1965 with the appointment of another Archbishops' Commission 'to make recommendations as to the modifications in the constitutional relationship between Church and State which are desirable and practicable and in so doing to take account of current and future steps to promote greater unity between the Churches'.[42] The Commission of seventeen under Dr Owen Chadwick, Master of Selwyn College, Cambridge, and Dixie Professor of Ecclesiastical History, had a strong Church orientation, with only one member of the legal profession, Mr Justice Cumming-Bruce, and two MPs, D. W. Coe and W. R. van Straubenzee. Their brief was wide-ranging, concerned not only with worship and doctrine, but also the appointment of bishops, clerical representation in Parliament, and the Church's organization and property; and they were required to consider, not disestablishment but modifications in existing Church–State relations. Their approach was therefore cautious: 'We have not recommended a total severing of the historic links; first, because we think such a programme to be impracticable in the present state of opinion; and second, because even if such a programme was practicable, most of us would not like it.'[43] Unfortunately, on this fundamental issue there was disagreement, for three members of the Commission, firmly believing disestablishment to be the right approach, felt unable to sign the Report.[44] Nevertheless, the majority recommended that within the Establishment the time had come for a relaxation of controls, making the General Synod the final authority in matters of worship and doctrine.[45]

The Report *Church and State* was presented to the General Synod in February 1971. Archbishop Ramsey pointed out that something needed to be done fairly soon, for when the Alternative Services Measure lapsed in 1980, the only lawful services would be those of 1662. He thought it inconceivable that the Church would want to take a revised Prayer Book to Parliament; nor did he think that the Church would be content with another Alternative Services Measure and a further round of temporary experiments. 'My guess is . . . that when the time comes we shall want a strategy whereby we shall not only have a book that we can take with us when we go to church, but that we shall also want authority for the continuance of experiments.'[46] The Report was considered by the dioceses over the next two years and received weighty support, every diocesan synod except one voting in favour of the proposed measure by majorities which were substantial and in most cases overwhelming.[47] A majority, but less substantial, was also in favour of giving the General Synod power to replace 1662 with another Prayer Book; but a strong minority expressed unease at the idea,[48] and this unease was reflected in the draft Measure presented to the General Synod in November 1972. Two versions were set out, the first requiring further recourse to Parliament if authority were needed to produce a single new Prayer Book in place of 1662, the second proposing that this authority should be given immediately. The Archbishop made it clear that he wanted 1662 to remain and that the first version of the Measure with the narrower powers should be adopted,[49] a view strongly supported by Sir Marcus Worsley MP, the Second Church Estates Commissioner,[50] and Sir Harold Kent, Dean of the Arches, who confessed that he was more or less the Measure's author.[51] The first version eventually prevailed by votes of roughly two to one in all three Houses;[52] but despite the substantial majority, the unease over insufficient safeguards for 1662 persisted through the revision stage, an unease fostered by opponents of the Measure such as the Prayer Book Action Group. When it was further debated on 6 November 1973 Professor D. R. Jones of Durham was able to quote from an article in that day's *Daily Telegraph*, which claimed that the General Synod was about to deprive the Book of Common Prayer of authority, to leave the Church without a standard, and to permit a bishop to abolish altogether the traditional forms of service in his diocese. Professor Jones roundly condemned such a statement as 'culpable misrepresentation'.[53] In the event a further safeguard was built into the Measure, which was given Final Approval by massive majorities, only ten votes being cast against it.[54] The Archbishop summed it up admirably:

> Now, after 46 years, the Church's Synod is producing . . . a proposed solution which gives to [it] control in the determining of the Church's doctrine, control in the ordering of the Church's worship, and yet doing it in partnership with the State: a proposed partnership in which the State gives to the Church a degree of power that it is wonderful to think of, while at the same time the State knows the identity of the Church with which it is in partnership, an identity guaranteed by the continuing role in doctrine and, whenever desired in use, of the Book of Common Prayer.[55]

Under this Measure the General Synod was authorized to approve, amend, continue or discontinue forms of service, in addition to the services of the Book of Common Prayer which remained permanently available. Forms of service in a parish were to be the joint decision of the incumbent and the Parochial Church Council; and if they disagreed, the services were to be those of 1662, unless in the previous four years another form had been in use for at least two years, in which case the PCC could require that form to be used. The Measure also gave the General Synod authority to provide the Declaration of Assent which clergy and others were required to make in subscribing to the doctrine of the Church of England; and it was under this clause that a new Declaration was authorized in 1975. The general terms of this had been proposed by the Doctrine Commission in 1968 in their report *Subscription and Assent to the Thirty-Nine Articles.* A shorter and simpler Formula was introduced by a Preface indicating the context in which it was to be understood. The 1662 Prayer Book with the Thirty-Nine Articles and the Ordinal were described as 'historic formularies of the Church of England' which bore witness to Christian truth, while the Formula itself stated a 'belief in the faith which is revealed in the Holy Scriptures and set forth in the catholic creeds and to which the historic formularies of the Church of England bear witness'. As the Doctrine Commission explained it:

> The Preface would make clear that the Church of England is both *reformata* and (under the Holy Spirit) *semper reformanda*; and that within a present commitment to the Church as it is, there is a guaranteed liberty to the individual to ask doctrinal questions without having his conclusions spelt out in advance.[56]

The implication was there, 1662 still had a distinctive but not exclusive role.

It now remained for the Measure to secure parliamentary approval and here there was a delay for which the Church was in no way responsible. Parliament had already been dissolved; and the minority government elected in February 1974 proved to be short-lived, preventing any progress with the Measure. It was not until 14 November, after another general election in October, that Dr Ramsey was able to introduce it into the House of Lords. For him the delay had been disappointing, for it meant that the Measure could not reach the Statute Book before he retired from the primacy; nevertheless it was still a moving occasion for him, being his seventieth birthday and his last day in office. Tracing events briefly since the Royal Commission of 1906, he argued that the Alternative Services Measure had eventually enabled the Church of England to produce forms of worship which had proved to be reconciling factors between High and Low Churchmen. What was now being asked for was long-term legislation to continue this work and at the same time safeguard 1662. No one could accuse the Church of hurrying over all this: it was 54 years since the Church Assembly had started on liturgical revision, 46 years since the deadlock of 1928, and 9 years since the Alternative Services Measure.[57] Lord Shepherd, the Lord Privy Seal, then indicated that the government's attitude was one of benevolent neutrality; and in the ensuing debate only four speeches expressed opposition. Lord Clitheroe disliked the Measure simply because he disliked the new services,[58] Baroness Berkeley deplored the passing of the Church of England as people had known it,[59] the Earl of Onslow opposed it because he thought the *Authorised Version* better than the *New English Bible*,[60] and Lord Sudeley opposed it as a staunch supporter of 1662.[61] By far the best contribution came from Dr John Habgood, Bishop of Durham, making his maiden speech in the House: he denied that the General Synod was 'hell-bent on a programme of thoughtless reform'; nothing beyond the Series Three services was contemplated, and the Measure was simply a sober and constructive attempt to enable the Church of England to retain its integrity and viability as the Church of the nation.[62] After a four-hour debate, quite a portion of which was inevitably devoted to eulogies on the Archbishop, the House agreed to the Measure without a division.[63]

The Commons debate on 4 December was a much longer and livelier affair. It was something of a baptism of fire for Mr Terry Walker, the new Second Church Estates Commissioner, who was responsible for introducing the Bill: he stuck manfully to his task of reiterating the points made by the Archbishop despite constant heckling from opponents — behaviour which brought a rebuke from the Speaker.[64] Admirable support came from Richard Wood, who attempted to keep the debate in proper perspective by wisely pointing out that it was not concerned with 'how the Church should worship or what is its doctrine. We are discussing the kind of authority which should order that worship and define that doctrine.'[65] Unfortunately most of the Bill's opponents ignored his advice, concentrating their attack on new services: typical were John Stokes — 'weak stuff and a sort of gibberish'; and David Mudd, a Methodist local preacher — 'sterile bureaucratic words of modern usage'.[66] There were, however, two notable exceptions among the critics. Eldon Griffiths thought the Church wanted the fruits of disestablishment without being disestablished and could see no reason why Parliament should not concern itself with worship and doctrine — of necessity it constantly had to concern itself with matters in which it had no particular expertise.[67] Enoch Powell likewise argued in favour of the existing system, for it gave the Church its characteristic stamp and quality; they now had to decide 'whether we are to remove that stamp and stability and replace them by the freedom of unlimited innovation in the future which this measure portends'.[68] Despite a concentrated attack in the latter part of the debate, when a succession of Tory speakers criticized the Measure solidly for over two hours, it was passed comfortably by 145 votes to 45.[69]

The Church of England (Worship and Doctrine) Act finally came into force on 1 September 1975, when some seventeen existing parliamentary measures involving worship and doctrine disappeared either wholly or in part, the most notable casualties being the Act of Uniformity of 1662, the Act of Uniformity Amendment Act of 1872 and the Prayer Book (Alternative and other Services) Act of 1965. Church legislation under the new Measure was now enshrined in Canons B1 to B5a. It was a piece of legislation which must have given Michael Ramsey considerable satisfaction, providing a fitting conclusion to his primacy. Despite his early opposition to the Commission's first proposals on Baptism and Confirmation in 1959, I have to say that during my time as chairman of the Commission he embraced the cause of liturgical revision with enthusiasm. Not long before his retirement he paid a farewell visit to the annual gathering of diocesan liturgical representatives, at which he reminded them that they were all participating in a remarkable revolution: in 1966 the Church of England had still to be content with 1662 and 1928; but by 1973 it had a wide range of fully authorized alternative services from Series I to Series 3. Furthermore it had been a 'bloodless revolution', with the Church still intact and with changing attitudes towards public worship and particularly the Eucharist; not only had the Series 2 and Series 3 forms been strong unifying influences, they had made people realize that the Eucharist was an action in which they shared rather than an observation which they witnessed. His prediction of some twenty years previously had come true: 'In the long run [the Eucharist] will be its own interpreter and teacher. For the supreme question is not what we make of the Eucharist, but what the Eucharist is making of us.'[70] I found it a great delight to work with him and in a remarkable way he had an infectious enthusiasm for the undertaking. Immediately after leaving Lambeth he wrote me a letter which I appreciated enormously (8 December 1974):

> I have in these last Lambeth years so much enjoyed the occasions of working with you, and in personal terms this is one of the things I miss. I realise that your 'Liturgy Years' have been pretty strenuous, with many frustrations and exasperations, and I think you have been wonderfully patient, reconciling and creative. I am sure that about the work of these years two things are very true. One is that any imperfections in production — and I have, as you know, felt that there be such — are due to what our Church, *being what it is*, is able to take and agree to — which is a very great deal! The other, which I feel deeply convinced about, is that in these last years of 'revision', in spite of the variety of services and pamphlets, the process has enabled our Church to experience a *new inner unity* in 'doing the liturgy'. This is something for which we can be deeply thankful.

NOTES

1. He received valuable help from Colin Buchanan, who had just completed his *Modern Anglican Liturgies 1958–1968*, and was now engaged in collecting material for his *Further Anglican Liturgies 1968–1975.*
2. *Lambeth Conference 1968: Preparatory Information*, 1968, p. 35.

3. R.C.D.J. to H. de Candole, April 15, 1968.
4. cf. p. 237.
5. cf. pp. 291–2.
6. It was officially distributed through the Anglican Executive Officer (now Bishop John Howe) to all Metropolitan and Liturgical Consultants; copies were available to the public from the Church Information Office, which reported a steady demand; it was also reproduced in PECUSA's *Prayer Book Studies no. 21* (*The Holy Eucharist*) 1970, pp. 35–41, in the Anglican Consultative Council's second Report, *Partners in Mission*, 1973, pp. 70–3, and in Colin Buchanan's *Further Anglican Liturgies 1968–75*, 1975, pp. 26–31.
7. *Partners in Mission*, 1973, p. 71.
8. ibid., pp. 70–1. The situation is now quite familiar in England.
9. ibid., p. 72.
10. ibid., p. 35.
11. ibid., p. 48.
12. cf. p. 203; note in particular Bishop Garrett's statement.
13. *Partners in Mission*, p. 35.
14. H. de Candole's two articles were, 'Can we rationalise the Christian Year?', in *Theology* LXIII (December 1960), pp. 486–90; and 'Sundays after Trinity', in *Theology* LXV (September 1962), pp. 358–64. Dr McArthur had written two books, *The Evolution of the Christian Year*, 1953; and *The Christian Year and Lectionary Reform*, 1958.
15. R. C. D. Jasper, ed., *The Calendar and Lectionary*, 1967.
16. ibid., pp. 18, 20.
17. ibid., p. 15.
18. R. C. D. Jasper, ed., *The Daily Office*, 1968, pp. 13–25.
19. Michael Cantuar to R.C.D.J., 9 June 1967.
20. cf. pp. 240–1.
21. 1662 has 66 entries; 1928 had 76; the proposed list had 44.
22. *The Liturgical Conference 1969*, p. 8.
23. ibid., p. 2.
24. ibid., p. 39.
25. ibid., p. 49.
26. The period of experiment for Series One was not due to end until June 1973.
27. R.C.D.J. to Michael Cantuar, 4 July and 15 July, 1969. The Anglican–Methodist Unity scheme failed to secure the necessary 75 per cent majorities in the Convocations on 8 July 1969.
28. *Common Prayer 1970*, p. vii.
29. *Chronicle Convoc.*, 1970, pp. 9–26, 28–47; *Journal Convoc.*, 1970, pp. 37–52.
30. *General Synod Proceedings*, 1970, vol. 1, pp. 59–70; 1971, vol. 2, pp. 19–20. The voting was: Bishops 27–0; Clergy 182–2; Laity 143–0.
31. *GS Proceedings*, 1973, vol. 4, pp. 6–8.
32. *Liturgical Conference 1966*, pp. 1–2.
33. Michael Cantuar to R.C.D.J., 2 February 1967.
34. R.C.D.J. to Michael Cantuar, 6 February 1967.
35. 87 per cent of the replies claimed to have fulfilled the attendance requirement.
36. Paul A. Welsby, *A History of the Church of England 1945–1980*, 1984, pp. 146–8.
37. *Chronicle Convoc.*, 1962, pp. 226–43, 363–467; Report 708, *Synodical Government*.

38. *CA Proceedings*, 1969, pp. 91–100, 465. Only two members of the Clergy and five of the Laity voted against it.
39. Welsby, pp. 148–9.
40. Michael Cantuar to R.C.D.J., 6 October 1971. He wrote to say that any ideas of radical change in the Commission's constitution were not contemplated. While membership was reduced to fifteen, the permission to have 'consultants' and 'corresponding members' resulted in little change in our available expertise.
41. The Revision Committees made particularly heavy demands on those members of the Commission who were on the General Synod, for Commission representatives were always appointed to them. I think I sat on every Revision Committee except two or three.
42. *CA Proceedings*, 1965, pp. 524–66; *Church and State*, Report of the Archbishops' Commission, 1970, p. ix.
43. Report, p. 65, sc 215.
44. Miss Valerie Pitt, the Revd. P. R. Cornwell, and D. W. Caroe MP. Report, pp. 68–84.
45. ibid., p. 64, sc 211.
46. *GS Proceedings*, 1971, vol. 2, pp. 68–70.
47. Report GS 161, *The Future Course of Liturgical Revision*, 1973, sc 15.
48. ibid., sc 16.
49. *GS Proceedings*, 1972, vol. 3, pp. 599–600, 620–2.
50. ibid., p. 610. He warned the Synod that the second version would be controversial and in his opinion would not get through the House of Commons.
51. ibid., p. 615.
52. ibid., p. 622. The voting was: Bishops 19–11; Clergy 134–66; Laity 128–43.
53. ibid., 1973, vol. 4, p. 669. The article was by Peter Simple in *The Daily Telegraph*, 6 November 1973. In contrast it is worth noting that in the previous July the General Synod had accepted its Standing Committee's report on *The Future Course of Liturgical Revision*, which specifically recommended the continuance of 1662 as an element in the liturgical life of the Church of England – GS 161, sc 18; *GS Proceedings*, 1973, vol. 4, pp. 354–72.
54. ibid., vol. 5, p. 100. The voting was: Bishops 34–0; Clergy 170–2; Laity 140–8.
55. ibid., p. 96.
56. Doctrine Commission, *Subscription and Assent to the Thirty-Nine Articles*, 1968, p. 73.
57. Hansard, *Parliamentary Debates*, House of Lords, 5 ser. vol. 354, pp. 867–74.
58. ibid., pp. 891–4.
59. ibid., pp. 907–10.
60. ibid., pp. 915–8.
61. ibid., pp. 928–33.
62. ibid., pp. 894–7.
63. ibid., p. 945.
64. Hansard, *Parliamentary Debates*, House of Commons, vol. 882, pp. 1567–76.
65. ibid., pp. 1577–80. Richard Wood was MP for Bridlington and a member of the Halifax family.
66. ibid., pp. 1590–4, 1681–3.
67. ibid., pp. 1628–34.
68. ibid., pp. 1666–77.
69. ibid., p. 1696. 44 of the 45 opponents were either Tories or Ulster Unionists; cf. Welsby, op. cit., p. 222.
70. A. M. Ramsey, *Durham Essays and Addresses*, 1956, p. 21.

13

QUESTIONS OF LANGUAGE

I

The Liturgical Commission had first referred to the question of language in its report for Lambeth 1958, recognizing the need to give expression to new knowledge and to be contemporary.[1] But at that time no detailed thought had been given to the subject and nothing more radical was envisaged than a replacement of words which were obsolete or had changed their meaning. Such a policy was followed for another ten years; and the changes in style both in Series I and Series II services were minimal. Nevertheless the Commission frequently nibbled at the subject without reaching any positive conclusions. In 1961 Helen Gardner was invited to speak to the Commission on 'an English style for modern liturgy'; and over the next two or three years there were several discussions on the subject, sometimes based on drafts supplied by such people as J. B. Phillips, but always with the same result: 'No conclusions were reached'.[2] It was obviously aware of a problem but had difficulty in finding a satisfactory way of tackling it. This was not altogether surprising, for there had been no systematic study of liturgical language in this country: for too long writers had been content to imitate Cranmer.[3]

The first indication of a constructive approach to the subject appeared in Basil Naylor's booklet, *Why Prayer Book Revision at all?*, in 1964, where he drew attention to recent philosophical discussions on the function of language and the meaning of words and symbols, more particularly the contemporary use of biblical myths and symbols in the rites of baptism and the Eucharist. He also pointed out that recent translations of the Bible had introduced worshippers to a new religious language which inevitably posed questions: 'Is the nature of common prayer such as to require archaic expression?', and 'Does the success of the sixteenth-century revisers mean that they provided a norm that is valid for today?'[4] An important attempt to answer such questions appeared shortly afterwards in *The Language of the Book of Common Prayer* by Dr Stella Brook, an expert philologist. This study argued that the creation of a modern English liturgical style was difficult, but not impossible. The difficulty lay in the divorce of spoken and written styles in twentieth-century English, to the detriment of both. Written style had deteriorated into a stylized and unnatural idiom, employing a vocabulary that had ceased to be a genuine part of living speech; while spoken style had also deteriorated, becoming slipshod, riddled with vague catch-words and limited in vocabulary. Such joint deterioration impeded the development of a good liturgical style; the former because liturgy needed to reach the heart and mind of the worshipper, the latter because liturgy needed to express profundities in a decorous and comely language. Possibly some people resisted current attempts at change because of an intuitive recognition of the limitations of twentieth-century English; but if there could be a vigorous cross-fertilization between written and spoken English, then a living liturgical style could well emerge again, as it had done four hundred years previously.[5]

It was as a result of this book that Dr Brook was invited to join the Liturgical Commission; and for an all too brief period we enjoyed the benefit of her expertise until ill-health forced her premature retirement. She was one of the principal speakers at the Liturgical Conference of February 1966, where she repeated the arguments of her book in a plea for a conservative approach.

> The idea of a wholly 'contemporary' liturgy – a liturgy composed exclusively in the current idiom of 1966 – seems presumptuous . . . The offering to God will be the poorer if the liturgy of a particular time has to express itself wholly in the current idiom of that particular time. Each successive century has something to contribute from its own particular idiom . . . A wholly 'contemporary' liturgy . . . will have nothing to offer to the future, when our own immediate idiom will have lost its currency: on the other hand it denies all virtue to our liturgical inheritance from the past.[6]

The Church should therefore draw on things old as well as new and should aim at a formal, hieratic language, helping to educate men in the loving and serious use of words.[7] Despite her cautious approach, speaker after speaker pleaded for a 'modern liturgy', although it is doubtful whether they would all have agreed on what this implied. The very first speaker from the floor, Tom Horan, a rumbustious but very articulate engineer, who subsequently became a valued member of the Liturgical Commission, delivered a veritable broadside. New services should have a converting value and they should be reasonably comprehensible to ordinary people; instead, some of the proposed phraseology was ecclesiastical obscurantism at its very worst, and it was dangerous because its very obscurity made it an incantation which was an insult to God and of no use to mankind.[8] These were strong words indeed; but many speakers followed the same line, though less vehemently. By the end of the debate it had become clear that language was now regarded as a matter for major concern.[9]

Such pressure, and the presence of Stella Brook, made a serious impression on the Commission; and in the summer of that year it had its first really constructive discussion on language, with an examination of sentence structure, word forms and meanings, rhythms and poetry, while Geoffrey Cuming presented his own modern versions of the canticles as a stimulus to further study. In September 1966 the decision was made to start work on rites in modern language, and as a start a small group under David Ayerst undertook to modernize the recently completed texts of the Series Two Baptism and Confirmation services.[10] This undertaking was made public in the report published shortly afterwards: 'The Commission is aware of the desire for the use of language that is alive in contemporary society and is engaged in the preparation of texts.'[11] Such an announcement was timely, for pressure for prompt action was mounting. In December 1966, for example, the Bishop of Bristol (Dr Tomkins) suggested to the Archbishop the appointment of another commission to deal exclusively with contemporary forms of worship to meet the needs of a missionary situation. But Dr Ramsey disagreed: not only was he unwilling to appoint yet another body, but he insisted that the Commission had the resources to cope with the situation. It was good to have his expression of confidence; but the warning was clear — the sooner something appeared in print the better. So the idea of another discussion booklet was born: and *Modern Liturgical Texts* duly appeared just before the Lambeth Conference of 1968. Meanwhile work was proceeding in other directions.

II

In 1964 I met Monsignor Gordon Wheeler, the Administrator of Westminster Cathedral, and we became good friends.[12] He arranged for two Roman Catholic laymen to visit the Commission in December of that year: Bernard Dunne, a director of Burns Oates and Washbourne, publishers to the Holy See, and Professor Herbert Finberg of Leicester University, the co-producer with Fr J. O'Connell of the English translation of the Roman Missal which bore their names. The primary purpose of their visit was to provide the Commission with first-hand information on recent Roman Catholic liturgical developments: but what proved to be of particular interest was Professor Finberg's account of the problems facing his Church in its attempts to produce a new liturgy in the vernacular. We agreed that a mutual objective should be the production of a set of agreed common texts and we undertook to keep in touch. Our meeting was destined to have important consequences.[13]

Soon afterwards I was invited to attend meetings of the Roman Catholic Liturgical Commission for England and Wales, then chaired by Dr Dwyer, Bishop of Leeds. One of its concerns was the preparation of texts in the vernacular: and since Dr Dwyer endorsed the hope of securing agreement on such texts as the Creeds, the Gloria and the Lord's Prayer, drafts of their proposals were sent to our Commission for discussion and comment.[14] By the autumn of 1965, however, this work became international rather than regional, for with Vatican approval the bishops of the ten English-speaking hierarchies set up the International Committee on English in the Liturgy (ICEL) under the chairmanship of the Most Reverend Gordon Gray, Archbishop of St Andrews and Edinburgh, for the purpose of creating a single set of English texts. To assist them this International Committee appointed a small Advisory Committee of eight experts, five clergy and three laymen, who did the initial drafting: among them were Professor Finberg and Fr Harold Winstone from this country, while their secretary was a remarkable American priest, Fr Gerald Sigler, a man of considerable energy, ability and charm, to whom we all subsequently owed a great deal.[15] This Advisory Committee met for the first time in Rome in November 1965 and began by drawing up a set of Principles of Translation, together with two sample translations of the Ordinary of the Roman Mass. These Principles, although concerned with translation and not with the composition of new texts, were useful in providing simple guidelines for any Church, not least ourselves, to follow, and were significant in their recognition that ecumenical considerations were important and that other Churches were more experienced than Rome in the use of liturgical English. The primary purpose was to express 'the meaning, intention and character of the original, yet allow for adaptations required by pastoral needs'. This demanded a particular vocabulary and style, suitable to the sacred character of the texts; and while technical theological words such as 'grace, absolution and salvation' were permissible, words or phrases not in living use should be avoided. Texts should be aimed 'mainly with an eye to the middle range of church-goers, rather than to the least or the most intelligent or literate'.

This document *English for the Mass* (part I), published in March 1966, invited comment from both Catholics and non-Catholics and was followed some months later by a second part with further texts and a collection of early reactions to the first part. The proposals and principles evoked strong feelings, even within the Advisory Committee itself. Its chairman, Professor Harrison, later revealed that at its first meeting the 'You–thou' debate continued over several days; and although the final decision was overwhelmingly in favour of 'You' (7—1), the single dissentient resolutely refused to abandon his opposition.[17] The initial reactions, based on over 4,000 replies, revealed 'a great and conflicting variety of strongly held, and often violently expressed, opinions', ranging from the ultra-radical to the ultra-conservative. The review also frankly recognized the difficulty of trying to produce a single set of texts for the entire English-speaking world.

> An idiom which is modern and contemporary to the liturgiologist in Chicago is very different from the idiom natural to a taxi-driver in London, a lawyer in Durban, a store-keeper in Karachi, or a bank clerk in Sydney. It follows that the final translation cannot be in any particular 'idiom'; it must aim at good, straight, simple English which brings understanding to the unlearned and delight to the literate. Such writing demands the highest kind of literary art.[18]

Undeniably praiseworthy as an ideal, it was extraordinarily difficult to achieve in reality. Gerald Sigler sent both booklets to our own Commission with a request for advice and criticism, for he was 'particularly conscious of your special qualifications in liturgy and language': but we could offer him little comfort, regarding their first attempts as sticking too close to the Latin originals.[19]

All this undoubtedly encouraged us to produce our own set of texts before the Lambeth Conference of 1968, conscious of the fact that two Anglican

Churches had already published experimental liturgies in a 'You' form. The first was New Zealand, which in April 1966 published a eucharistic rite in a language described as of RSV type, but with God addressed as 'You'.[20] Three months later the Liturgical Commission of Australia published a report on Prayer Book Revision with two eucharistic rites, the first a conservative revision of 1662 and the second a more radical 'You' form produced by a group in New South Wales. Both rites were submitted for experimental use; but the majority of the Commission expressed the view that nothing less than a radical revision in modern language was called for and was both possible and practicable.

A further input of material resulted from my appointment as an observer to the Concilium Liturgicum at the Vatican in May 1966. There were six observers: two Anglican, Professor Massey Shepherd of America and myself; two Lutheran, Dr Künneth of Germany and Dr Brand of America; one from the Reformed Churches, Frère Max Thurian of Taizé; and one from the World Council of Churches, who by happy chance was Raymond George, an English Methodist and already a member of the Joint Liturgical Group. Attendance at the Concilium involved two visits a year to the Vatican over a period of five years. At plenary sessions we literally 'observed': but there was ample opportunity for wide-ranging discussions with the 'periti' or experts at other times, and through the good offices of Dr Dwyer, now Archbishop of Birmingham, we also attended meetings of ICEL's Advisory Committee, whose sessions normally coincided with those of the Concilium. Here some of our most important work was done, including the formation of the International Consultation on English Texts (ICET). As early as February 1967 the Advisory Committee had been instructed to prepare a translation of the Canon of the Roman rite as a matter of urgency, after which they undertook a revised translation of the Ordinary of the Mass, published as *The Order of Mass* in April 1968. The driving force behind this activity was Gerald Sigler, who wanted to promote extensive ecumenical dialogue before any Church or group of Churches had completed its work of revision. The new translation was therefore intended as a discussion document both for Roman Catholic hierarchies and for the Protestant Churches.[22] Ecumenical discussion on texts had in fact already started in America at the instigation of the Lutheran Churches in March 1968.

Nevertheless we had not been idle in this country. In November 1966 I had pointed out to Dr Ramsey that in matters of Anglican–Roman Catholic liturgical co-operation, virtually all the initiatives had hitherto come from Rome. He took the point, immediately contacted Dr Dwyer, and they arranged for Fr J. D. Crichton, one of the leading Catholic liturgical scholars in this country, to attend meetings of our Commission as an observer. It was an excellent arrangement, for he was a delightful companion and readily placed his considerable learning at our disposal. I also recruited a number of people with expertise in specialist fields such as music, drama and literature to comment on our draft texts. Obviously some were more helpful than others; but we were particularly grateful to a small group of students under Pamela Barnard from the Royal Academy of Dramatic Art and to a small music group under Allan Wicks at Canterbury Cathedral. At the end of 1966 Allan Wicks and a young composer, Alan Ridout, submitted some penetrating criticisms on Geoffrey Cuming's modern translations of the canticles. They admitted that they were being hypercritical; but this was deliberate, for the canticles had to stand up to a great deal of hard wear, and it was important to aim for a high degree of stylistic purity. They argued that despite claims to the contrary, some twentieth-century writers *had* shown fineness of style, and it was not necessary for a really good practitioner to be a genius. People like David Cecil, L. P. Hartley, Richard Church, Elizabeth Jennings and Anthony Powell were cases in point. 'As far as words for music are concerned, we have yet to see better statements of what is required than in Lewis' *The Poetic Image* and *The Lyric Impulse*.' They also examined the various methods of singing psalms and canticles, coming to the conclusion that in the present situation the only viable alternative in this country to the Anglican chant was a metrical form, and this should be seriously examined.[23] These comments on C. S. Lewis and metrical forms interested me considerably. The old metrical versions of Tate and Brady, without being great poetry, had undeniably given the Church long and valuable service and some were still found in current hymn books. The possibility of modern versions was certainly worth examining; and who better to do it than C. Day Lewis, born and bred in a vicarage, a fine classical scholar, with long experience as a schoolmaster and a reputation both as a poet and a writer of popular fiction.[24] I approached him just after he became Poet Laureate in 1967, suggesting that he might experiment with writing modern metrical versions of the canticles. He readily agreed, but on one condition: a musician should be involved in the project from the beginning. This presented no problem, for Alan Ridout had worked with him before. These two eventually produced metrical forms of the canticles together with tunes, which were included in *Modern Liturgical Texts* and recorded by Allan Wicks and the Canterbury Choral Society.[25] It did not prove an easy exercise; and Day Lewis emphasized that the requirements of the metrical form inevitably demanded liberties of translation: if correct translations were regarded as essential, then the number of psalms and canticles which could be dealt with in this way was very small. Despite the rather negative conclusions, it proved a worth-while and interesting experiment; at least we were satisfied that at this particular juncture little was to be gained in pursuing this idea further.

Modern Liturgical Texts was published in August 1968 just before the Lambeth Conference. It was essentially a discussion document; and to provoke discussion alternative forms were provided for some texts. There were four sets of material:

1. Common texts: the Lord's Prayer, the Gloria in excelsis, the Nicene and

Apostles' Creeds and the four main Canticles. These were the Commission's contribution to the international and ecumenical exercise and had already benefited from comparison with other experimental texts, e.g. ICEL, Australia and New Zealand.
2. The metrical canticles and their tunes by C. Day Lewis and Alan Ridout.
3. A 'You' form of the Series Two Baptism and Confirmation services, largely but not entirely the work of David Ayerst, Elisabeth Montefiore and Stella Brook.
4. A 'You' form of the Series Two Holy Communion service, entirely the work of Geoffrey Cuming and not even discussed by the Liturgical Commission.

Two elements in the booklet deserve comment. In the first place the Commission set out six principles governing its approach to modern liturgical language. They were applicable to both translation and the creation of new texts and formed a valuable supplement to the principles set out earlier in ICEL's *English for the Mass.*

1. Translation of *sense* is prior to translation of words.
2. Modern language requires the removal of all archaic words and, in most cases, of esoteric words.
3. 'Thou' and its cognates have been eliminated.
4. Subject to the requirements of theological accuracy, Anglo-Saxon words have been preferred to Latin ones.
5. Relative and other dependent clauses have been avoided in favour of co-ordinate main clauses.
6. Self-consistency between the . . . texts has been kept in view.[26]

Secondly the section on the Lord's Prayer was the work of Austin Farrer. Usually he said little at Commission meetings, and I constantly hoped he would say more. But this was his most significant contribution to the work on texts and unfortunately it never secured the recognition it deserved. He drew particular attention to the shape of the Greek text in St Matthew's Gospel, pointing out both its symmetry and its poetry.

> The force and meaning of the prayer in this form is inseparable from the shape; if the shape is not in essentials preserved, the prayer goes to pieces. In the original Greek the prayer begins with a single antithesis (heaven—earth) within which are placed three *aspirations* in strict mutual parallel — a parallel which is emphasized in the Greek by three rhyming syllables in each of the three lines. For the first word of each line ends in *-to* . . . and each line ends in *-a sou* . . . The rest of the prayer is again triple — three petitions; the form is now most interestingly reversed. Instead of being embraced by one antithesis, the three lines contain each an antithesis within it (e.g. today–tomorrow . . .). In the second half of the prayer, as in

the first, the phrases in balance against one another are pointed with assonance or rhyme.[27]

A similar analysis of other early Greek liturgical texts, an exercise surprisingly ignored by liturgists in this country,[28] might well provide further valuable lessons and illustrations for those engaged in writing liturgical texts today. Sadly much of the heated debate over a modern translation of the Lord's Prayer has ignored the points Austin Farrer was trying to make.

III

The reception given to *Modern Liturgical Texts* by the Lambeth 1968 Liturgical Consultation was encouraging. It was accepted that 'You' forms now reflected an 'irresistible trend' and that the first group of texts constituted a basis for wider discussion. The texts of the Lord's Prayer, the Creeds and the Gloria in excelsis were therefore sent to all provinces of the Anglican Communion with a request for comments. Members of the Joint Liturgical Group also undertook to remit them to their respective Churches. This decision marked a turning point, for after 1968 'You' forms became invariable in new rites in the Anglican Communion.[29]

When the observers attended the next meeting of ICEL's Advisory Committee in Rome in October of that year, there were three sets of texts to compare: those of ICEL, the Anglican *Modern Liturgical Texts*, and the texts of the Consultation on Common Texts, an ecumenical group rather similar to JLG in America, together with all the comments which had been submitted. From these we succeeded in working out a single set of agreed forms: and Gerald Sigler suggested that these should be discussed ecumenically in different parts of the world. On my return I consulted the Archbishop on the best way to approach this in the British Isles; for while it was important at this stage to retain the freedom of informal discussion, we realized that the official bodies of the various Churches could not be left out indefinitely. On the other hand to involve them at too early a stage could result in serious delays. Dr Ramsey suggested that for the time being the Joint Liturgical Group might provide machinery, with its officially appointed membership yet its freedom to act informally. I therefore consulted Bishop Gordon Wheeler, who had taken over from Archbishop Dwyer as chairman of the English RC Liturgical Commission, and we agreed on two things. First, there should be full Catholic representation on the JLG, with two full members rather than a single observer: this he agreed to, arranging for the appointment of himself and Fr Harold Winstone, thereby giving JLG a direct link with ICEL. Secondly there should be a joint JLG—ICEL meeting as soon as possible to discuss methods of working. A preliminary meeting was held in February 1969; but an opportunity to arrange something far more ambitious then occurred rather unexpectedly.

The April meeting of the Concilium in Rome was cancelled: and Gerald Sigler promptly transferred the meeting of the Advisory Committee to London, at the same time inviting the Concilium observers, members of JLG and members of other representative bodies to attend. Some 21 people met for three days at the Strand Palace Hotel, and here the International Consultation on English Texts (ICET) came into being. It comprised the Advisory Committee of ICEL, members of JLG, Lutheran and Anglican observers to the Concilium, the Welsh and Irish Anglican observers to our own Liturgical Commission, and a representative of the America CCT. The Churches represented were Roman Catholic, Anglican, Presbyterian, Lutheran, Baptist, Methodist and Congregationalist, from seven different countries: England, Ireland, Scotland, Wales, USA, Canada and Australia. Admittedly the geographical balance was not comprehensive: there was no one from Africa or India, for example; but bearing in mind the speed with which the meeting had to be arranged and the fact that the group possessed no funds, the representation was reasonable. Some people also represented more than one body. Dr Percy Jones, for example, the Australian member of ICEL, also spoke for his country's equivalent of JLG of which he was a member; while Professor Charles Smith, who represented the American CCT, was also a leading member of PECUSA's Liturgical Commission. The group elected Harold Winstone and myself as joint chairmen – a convenient arrangement for we both lived in London; and Gerald Sigler acted as secretary. Indeed, we could not have existed without him; for he put the secretarial resources of ICEL at our disposal, shouldering all the financial and administrative responsibilities. We agreed that there should be no formal membership; assistance and representatives from any English-speaking Church would be welcome. The only restriction would be on numbers, simply to ensure efficient working, and ICEL offered to reduce its own representation if ever membership became too unwieldy. ICET was relatively short-lived, coming to an end by 1974: for the hard grind of preparatory work had already been done in the various groups and there was already significant progress towards agreement.

At the second meeting in October 1969 it was agreed to publish a progress report, and the first edition of *Prayers We have in Common* duly appeared in March 1970 with two sets of material. Set A comprised six texts on which tentative agreement had already been reached: the Lord's Prayer, the Nicene and Apostles' Creeds, the Gloria in excelsis, the Sanctus and Benedictus, and the Gloria Patri. Set B comprised three texts on which work was still being done: Sursum Corda, Agnus Dei and Te Deum: and the hope was expressed that the completed form of these together with the Gospel canticles would be published in the coming year.[30] A third meeting was held in April 1970, fitting in with what proved to be the final meeting of the Concilium Liturgicum in its existing form, with all the major Roman liturgical projects now complete. With visits to Rome now at an end, personal contacts with many members of ICEL and the Concilium observers became severely restricted. Harold Winstone and I therefore had to complete the work on the second edition of *Prayers We have in Common* by correspondence — a laborious and complicated business. We succeeded in finishing on schedule, however, and the new booklet was published both in England and in the USA in 1971.

These texts were offered to the Churches on the same basis as the reports of JLG. They bore no kind of official stamp and would have to win acceptance on their own merits. It was hoped that Churches would make use of them over a period of three or four years, after which final corrections and improvements could then be made. The speed and readiness with which Churches over a wide front adopted them for experimental use was in fact most gratifying.

IV

The transition to modern language forms had also gathered momentum in other directions. The Versions of the Bible Measure was implemented in January 1966 with the authorization of the use of the Revised Version, the Revised Standard Version, and the New Testament of the New English Bible, to which the Jerusalem Bible and the rest of the New English Bible were added in 1969–70.[31] It was generally recognized that these new versions lacked the sonority and beauty of the Authorized Version, but they had directness, clarity and force which made many passages of Scripture far more intelligible to lay people than they had been hitherto. Professor Nineham had made this important point to the Church Assembly in 1963:

> The important point was that they did not go to church primarily for an aesthetic fillip; but to worship God and to hear his Word mediated to them through the Bible; and therefore, surely the first question was whether that was as good an instrument as they could find for purveying the meaning of God's Word and allowing that Word to have its maximum impact. That was the question which should be uppermost in their minds and not questions about whether the New English Bible was as beautiful or as dignified as it could be.[32]

Hymnody also took a significant step forward in 1969 with the appearance of *100 Hymns for Today*, a supplement to *Hymns Ancient and Modern*, in which both 'Thou' and 'You' forms appeared, with the editors pointing out that there was room for both in public worship: 'A collection of hymns has to be both modern and ancient if it is genuinely to express the full mind of the people of God.'[33] Despite the difficulties, not least the danger of 'sounding bizarre, if not grotesque', there were some brave attempts to use contemporary symbols and imagery in the works of Fred Kaan, Richard Jones and Sydney Carter.[34] Then in 1968–9 changes in the membership of the Commission significantly strengthened its resources in tackling the language problem. Sadly, Dr Brook was compelled to resign because of increasing ill-health: but she was replaced by two people who proved to be a considerable asset throughout the next decade. The first was Canon Cyril Taylor, well known as a composer of fine hymn tunes[35] and an editor of *Hymns Ancient and Modern*, with years of experience at the BBC and the Royal School of Church Music. Blessed with a superb speaking voice, he had a fine ear for sound and rhythm, with a knack of finding just the right word or phrase. The second was Dr David Frost, a young English don at Cambridge with a particular interest in renaissance drama, whose drive and critical faculty combined with a real flair for liturgical writing left their mark on *The Alternative Service Book*.

Shortly afterwards the Commission began work on a 'You' form of the Eucharist in response to the Archbishops' request that any revision of the Series Two rite should have a parallel version in modern language which could accommodate the ICET texts.[36] In preparation for this David Frost produced a critical analysis of the Commission's earlier writing, arguing that there was all the difference between a Form of Words and a Liturgy. A document designed to communicate the faith to the greatest number of people, demanding simplicity of syntax and a limited vocabulary, could be good but was not necessarily beautiful: it was a Form of Words. On the other hand, 'liturgy should have some of the qualities of poetry, yielding further meanings at each repetition, exercising the hearts and minds of congregations: . . . considerations of verbal beauty, subtlety and precision would then demand a wider vocabulary and a more sophisticated syntax'. He suggested that too many of the earlier texts were in the former category. The Commission seem to have been embarrassed by imagery, tending to avoid it, while syntactical options were restricted to an unreasonable degree: phrases were too staccato and flat, there was a lack of relative clauses, and syntactical patterns were irritatingly repetitive. Such criticisms proved healthy; discussion was lively; and a new set of principles for modernization emerged, forming in some respects an interesting commentary on those in *Modern Liturgical Texts*.

1. Each item or prayer must be judged on its own merits.
2. There should be no general rule forbidding relative clauses.
3. Good syntax and rhythm must be preserved.
4. Cross-fertilization of language between daily experience and the needs of worship was necessary. While some urban and other new images were needed, the poetic and evocative were also desirable. Thus soldier and servant images were still strong, but pastoral and royal images were decreasingly viable.
5. Some technical theological words must be retained.
6. People recognized many more words than they themselves used.
7. Ancient and well-loved prayers should be retained with the minimum of change. If major change in thought or structure were required, it would be preferable to write a new prayer.[37]

Much of this appeared in the commentary published with the proposals for Holy Communion Series Three, together with a reminder that most of what was set out in prayer still derived from Scripture:

> Religious ideas and emotions must often be expressed through metaphor and image; and for most of our ideas and images we have returned to Scripture and the sayings of our Lord. Through the centuries liturgical prayer has commonly been a tissue of scriptural allusion; and the rationale of our new material and its full meaning can be seen from the scriptural texts from which it is derived.[38]

The Commission also pointed out that the texts for which it had been responsible were quite distinct from those of ICET: indeed, for the latter its approval was far from wholehearted.

> Clearly the ICET proposals differ in some respects from what we proposed in our *Modern Liturgical Texts* in 1968 and from what we ourselves would have proposed now. Nevertheless, we believe it right, in the interests of Christian unity, to use these texts experimentally in Series 3; and we would hope to add our comments to those of other Churches when they come up for review in a few years' time.[39]

The main reservations were over the Lord's Prayer and especially lines two and nine: 'Holy be your Name', and 'Do not bring us to the test'. Over line two there was in fact a difference of opinion within ICET itself, members from the United Kingdom, supported by our own Liturgical Commission, favouring 'hallowed', but the majority from overseas regarding it as archaic and preferring 'holy'. Line nine was undeniably difficult, and I think every body which discussed it, including ICET itself, could not find a suitable translation.[40] When introducing Holy Communion Series 3 to the General Synod on 10 November 1971, I pointed out these problems and the ensuing debate made it evident that reaction to this particular text was hostile.[41] No decision was then taken; but subsequent discussion and correspondence indicated that this hostility was widespread, not least within the Roman Catholic Church. Nevertheless, when ICET met in February 1972, it decided to make no change but to review the situation in two years' time; it did make the important concession, however, that both lines could have recognized variants. In July 1972, when the General Synod had to make a decision before authorizing the experimental use of the new eucharistic rite for the next four years, it made two changes: in line two 'hallowed' replaced 'holy' and in line nine 'time of trial' replaced 'test'.[42]

It was unfortunate that at its final meeting in April 1974 ICET still found it impossible to find a text for the Lord's Prayer which would meet with widespread approval. It did accept 'hallowed' for 'holy' in line two; but in line nine it decided on a form which provoked even further criticism. Whereas in the United Kingdom there was acceptance of the fact that a negative form with the use of 'but' was in line with the Greek text, preserving its antithetical structure, the overseas members of ICET succeeded in adopting a positive form followed by 'and':

Save us from the time of trial
And deliver us from evil.

It was a disappointing decision, for the remaining ICET texts were in due course accepted by all the main English-speaking Churches, either as the sole authorized texts or as authorized alternatives. But on the one prayer which should be 'common', Churches continued to use their own variations.[42] In the Church of England, all the ICET texts with this single exception ultimately appeared in *The Alternative Service Book* with only a few significant changes: in the Nicene Creed line 17, 'he suffered, died and was buried' replaced 'he suffered death and was buried'; while in the Te Deum 'abhor' was preferred to 'spurn' in line 19, and the last line was given a very different meaning, 'let us not be confounded at the last' replacing 'and we shall never hope in vain'.

ICET and its *Prayers We have in Common* was a brave ecumenical and international venture operated on a shoe-string budget. Undeniably it had its limitations, but it did have its successes and was well worth while. Not least it helped to remind Christians of facts which were so often ignored. The first was that although English may be an international language, no two communities use it in exactly the same way. Secondly, local methods of use may demand variations of texts, particularly in the case of singing canticles. Thirdly, and most important of all, words and prayers can change their meaning with the passage of centuries: this is the problem with the Lord's Prayer. Perhaps it may not be a bad thing to realize that the ideal translation is probably unattainable; at least it helps to stimulate continuing thought and discussion.

V

A further language question was that of the Psalter. All previous proposed Psalter revisions had simply been variations on Coverdale[44] — even the *Revised Psalter* of 1963. The whole issue was raised again, however, with the advent of services in contemporary language, the Liturgical Commission being first confronted with the need for psalms in 'You' form when working on the Series 3 Funeral Services in late 1969. An attempt to 'translate' the *Revised Psalter* was quickly rejected as unsuccessful;[45] so David Frost was asked to attempt something more original with help from Andrew Macintosh, a Hebrew scholar at St John's College, Cambridge, possibly making use of the draft Psalter being prepared by the American Liturgical Commission and consulting the Hebrew text. Their preliminary drafts, ready by June 1970, were considered to be so promising that I was asked to send them to the Archbishops for comment.[46] Both reacted favourably. Michael Ramsey replied that he was 'very fascinated — I would encourage you to work on a further instalment of psalms'.[47] Donald Coggan's approval was particularly welcome in view of his close involvement with the *Revised Psalter*: he suggested that we should consult Bishop Chase, who had been responsible for much of the initial drafting of that work.[48] The Bishop's reply was equally favourable; and further encouragement was soon to come from John Emerton, Regius Professor of Hebrew at Cambridge and recently elected to a fellowship at St John's. The three people destined to play a major part in the Psalter project, Emerton, Frost and Macintosh, were therefore housed under the same college roof. In the second half of 1970 the Commission became convinced that what was required was not merely a selection of psalms for inclusion in particular services but an entire Psalter. Furthermore, as Cyril Taylor insisted, it would have to be a *Liturgical* Psalter, essentially geared to public worship, capable of being sung as well as said.[49] Here again St John's College proved to be a valuable asset: for as psalms were completed, the college organist, George Guest, and his choir ensured that they could be pointed and sung to Anglican chants.

Work continued steadily throughout 1971; and an indication of what was afoot appeared in David Frost's article, 'A Dying Church or a Living Word', in the November issue of *Theology*. In a discussion of the whole field of liturgical language, he included a section on the Psalter with a draft of Psalm 50 and an exposition of the principles on which he and Andrew Macintosh were working.

> Our language sticks close to the Hebrew idiom, and though we try and avoid outdated syntax and language, we accept that the result should sound a little foreign, archaic, compared to the rest of the service. We do our best to render the Massoretic text, in the light of the ancient versions and modern scholarship, but when composing, I write with approximately seventeen English versions in front of me and steal quite shamelessly anything I can use. In a sense, then, we offer a traditional/modernist version, in the hope that the Church will find it fits the present need.[50]

Even with help from the Liturgical Commission, which vetted every draft with great care, the exercise proved a formidable undertaking for two people. There was a real danger that it would overtax their resources. Then came two interventions which eventually transformed the whole situation.

At the end of 1971 Bishop Gordon Wheeler began to take considerable interest in what was being done; and we arranged for John McHugh, a fine Roman Catholic biblical scholar from Ushaw College and Durham University, to explore with Andrew Macintosh the possibilities of ecumenical co-operation. Admittedly it was an advantage to keep the project small and informal; but it was very obvious that to expect Andrew to be entirely responsible for the Hebrew text placed an impossibly heavy load on his shoulders. Then shortly afterwards Professor Emerton warned us that, apart from the weight of work, to attempt the entire Psalter with only one Hebrew scholar left us open to severe academic criticism: a panel of Hebraists was necessary. He himself had such a panel which had been working for the British and Foreign Bible Society; it could be kept in being and with an addition such as John McHugh, it would constitute an admirable advisory body.[51] This, of course, was a marvellous offer, and I immediately consulted the Archbishops as to what should be done. They not only urged acceptance but helped to evolve a rather novel working procedure.

1. The translation of the entire Psalter was to be undertaken as a semi-official operation. The Hebrew panel and David Frost were to produce draft psalms which would then be vetted by the Liturgical Commission.
2. The copyright was to be retained by David Frost and Andrew Macintosh. Neither the General Synod nor any other body would have the right to revise or change the text without consulting them. The Psalter would therefore have the same kind of status as the various Bible translations, e.g. RSV, JB, and NEB.
3. The Hebrew panel would be regarded simply as a body of advisers. Michael Ramsey defined its status: 'The Old Testament scholars should be employed, not as a sub-committee or as a body appointed by the General Synod, but as a group of persons whom the Liturgical Commission with the approval of the Presidents choose to confer with as experts.'[52]
4. To meet the expenses of the panel I was able to make an arrangement with the publishers William Collins, whereby they became joint publishers of the Psalter with the Church Information Office and at the same time undertook to meet the expenses of translation. It was very much an act of faith on their part, for at that stage they had no guarantee that the Church of England or any other Church would authorize the Psalter for use: and we were extremely grateful for their help.

Since Coverdale was regarded with such affection, Donald Coggan advised us to 'test the temperature' by publishing a small selection of our psalms in an advance booklet. This duly appeared in March 1973 as *Twenty Five Psalms from a Modern Liturgical Psalter*. They were in fact the early psalms produced by the Frost–Macintosh duo, although subsequently they were worked over by the Hebrew panel before appearing in the final Psalter. At this stage they did not meet the complete requirements of a Liturgical Psalter, for they were not pointed for singing; but some devices were introduced to facilitate devotional use: the bracketing of verses for omission, the division of psalms into sections, the insertion of sub-headings, and the printing of refrains in italics. On the whole their reception was encouraging, while *The Church Times* was positively enthusiastic, describing the translation as clear, meaningful and of high quality, yet sensitive to the values of the old, and looking forward to the advent of the entire Psalter 'with confidence and even eagerness'. Furthermore the General Synod accepted the new psalm translations in the Series Three Funeral Services virtually without criticism: and when one member did attempt at the revision stage to substitute the 1662 and the Grail versions, he met with summary rejection.[53]

Meanwhile, as batches of psalms were translated, drafts went to a wide variety of people to assess both sayability and singability. We were grateful for the vetting by the choir of St John's College, but we were also conscious that its musical expertise was far greater than that of the average parish choir. We wanted to be absolutely sure that every psalm was capable of congregational use; and here we were particularly grateful for the help given by the Royal School of Church Music and its director, Lionel Dakers, in trying them out at parish level. In the event a small team with RSCM links was made responsible for pointing the entire Psalter for Anglican chants and this was also copyrighted, thereby avoiding the danger of an eventual wide variety of editions.[54] By 1977 the project was complete, and in September Collins and the Church Information Office published both pointed and unpointed editions of *The Psalms: a New Translation for Worship* together with a free booklet of Notes on the Text. The Introduction insisted that it was 'a literary version for public recitation and singing', and as such was not bound by the strict letter of the Hebrew text.[55] For example, to improve singability in places, one or two words were added to a half-verse, or 'God' might be substituted for 'the Lord' — or even 'O Lord our God': but these were always regarded as justifiable expansions of the meaning of the Hebrew. Since it was not envisaged for exclusive use by the Church of England, no attempt was made to follow Frere's example of 1925[56] and omit or rearrange whole psalms or portions of psalms; nor was there any division into groups for recitation in four or thirteen week cycles. All that was done at this stage in the interests of liturgical use was to bracket some 58 verses which were considered unsuitable for public worship, and to include the typographical devices used in the preliminary booklet.

The General Synod authorized it for experimental use under the Versions of the Bible Measure in 1978. Introducing it for Provisional Approval in February the Archbishop of York, Dr Blanch, commended it on four grounds: it was based on the best text available, there was no change for change's sake, it made as much sense as could possibly be made of an obscure text and an alien poetic form, and it was reasonably euphonious.[57] Spirited opposition came from the Bishop of London, Dr Ellison, who thought it unnecessary, not good enough, and conducive to confusion:[58] but it was sturdily and successfully defended by the Bishops of Winchester (Dr Taylor) and Durham (Dr Habgood) and Professor Douglas Jones of Durham.[59] A further attack by the Bishop of London at the Final Approval stage in July was equally unsuccessful, the Synod accepting it by 305 votes to 73.[60] But at this particular moment it was not prepared to accept it as an authorized text for inclusion in the proposed Alternative Service Book.[61] That had to wait until later.

Then there was the question of the eucharistic lectionary, assuming that in any new Prayer Book the readings would be set out in full. If contemporary language was to be used, only the *Jerusalem Bible* among the modern authorized versions met all the requirements. Admittedly not every reading in the lectionary involved the use of 'You' for God, but the Liturgical Commission felt that at least during the experimental period the Church should be encouraged to use all the authorized versions, while any moves towards the production of Prayer Books based exclusively on one particular version were to be resisted as divisive – a view shared by both Archbishops. The problem first arose with the appearance of the Commission's report, *The Calendar and Lessons for the Church's Year*, introduced at the Church Assembly's Liturgical Conference of February 1969.[62] At that particular stage it was envisaged that the authorization of the proposals would require another parliamentary measure at some future date; but for the moment the proposals were there for all to see and some people undoubtedly used them without authorization. Furthermore, they were ecumenical proposals and other Churches were prepared to make use of them without waiting for the Church of England. They had already been included in the new Presbyterian Service Book of 1968, they were authorized by the Methodists in October 1969, and they appeared in the new Congregational *Order of Public Worship* in early 1970. The Anglican province of South Africa also authorized them for experimental use for a period of four years in July 1969. The publishers of the *Jerusalem Bible*, Darton Longman and Todd, realizing the progress the proposals were making, took the initiative in early 1970 and published the lectionary in full as *Readings at Holy Communion*, but geared them to fit the current calendar with the new proposals in brackets; it also included the South African modifications as alternatives at various points.[63]

Meanwhile the Liturgical Commission had completed the drafts of the Series 3 Funeral Services. Here the policy of using all three authorized modern versions, RSV, NEB and JB, was followed, the readings fortunately not involving the use of 'You' for God. It was a policy which the General Synod found acceptable, and it became the norm in all future services. The eucharistic lectionary was, however, a much bigger problem. I had discussed the Report on *The Calendar and Lessons* with Walter Wigglesworth at the beginning of 1970, and we had evolved a scheme to divide its implementation into three:

1. The Rules involving occurrences and concurrences etc. should be dealt with under Section 4 of the Prayer Book Further Provisions Measure, therefore requiring no further legislation.
2. The eucharistic lectionary should be attached to Series 3 Holy Communion, but modified to fit the existing calendar. It would then be authorized with the service itself and would require no further legislation.
3. Only the Calendar would require legislation, and if necessary this would be initiated at some future date; although some other method of

> authorization might be found if Church–State relationships were modified as a result of the Chadwick Report.[64]

The Commission therefore set to work on the texts of the eucharistic lectionary, using all three modern Bible versions, while I sought agreement from their publishers. This proved to be quite a delicate and protracted operation, for the plan really did nothing to promote their own Bible sales, and effectively torpedoed any hopes they may have had of producing their own individual versions of any future Prayer Book; it also provided a formidable rival to the JB book. In the event all three sets of publishers agreed; while those of RSV were particularly co-operative, also permitting us to use 'You' for God. I then sounded out the constituent Churches of the JLG[65] and the province of South Africa, now reinforced by the Church of Ireland, and all of them welcomed the project. All these negotiations were finally concluded by October 1972, by which time the Series Three Eucharist with the lectionary had already been given Provisional Approval by the General Synod in the previous July; and Final Approval was not expected to provide any serious problem in November.

The project was then completed at speed, being published by the Church Information Office as *The Lessons for Holy Communion Series 3* in March 1973. Obviously it was not a perfect solution: what was really required was some kind of 'Liturgical Bible', translated and arranged specifically for reading aloud at public worship. But the Commission realized that this was an undertaking requiring years of work by a team of specialists, working preferably on an ecumenical basis. As a relatively short-term venture, undertaken quickly and with limited resources,[66] the volume proved to be acceptable, selling steadily over a period of time at the rate of 1,000 copies per month.

Finally, there was the question of collects. The JLG published a set of collects for the Temporale in its *Daily Office* 1968. They were in traditional language but geared to the proposed Calendar and Lectionary. Shortly afterwards the Liturgical Commission accepted them, publishing them with another set for the Sanctorale in its report *The Calendar and Lessons*. But even before they could be authorized for use they were being overtaken by events. Rites in contemporary language had begun to appear and were welcomed by the 1968 Lambeth Liturgical Consultation. The purpose and structure of collects were also discussed at a conference of the Societas Liturgica, an international society of liturgical scholars and teachers, at Glenstal Abbey, Co. Limerick, in September 1969. Must they of necessity have a connection with the Scripture readings? Would it not make more sense for such readings to be prefaced by a prayer for the worthy hearing of God's Word? If this were so, the weekly collect, if still required, would then make more sense as a post-communion prayer. Or on structure: 'The question of today is whether that structure, especially the relative clause applied to God, is suitable for our time. If the "court approach" implicit in the early Latin prayers is removed, can we continue to use the same prayer material?' The Societas finally came to the conclusion that, despite the problems, the collect in its traditional position and structure should be preserved.[67] This judgement was endorsed by the new Roman *Ordo Missae* published shortly afterwards, and then in the new Anglican rites which began to appear. In fact 1970 saw three Anglican Churches publish sets of collects in contemporary language – America, Australia and New Zealand.

Work on contemporary collects began in the Liturgical Commission in the same year and it soon developed into another ecumenical exercise between South Africa, the JLG and ourselves. All were concerned with preparing collects for the same calendar and lectionary and drafts were freely exchanged. Three sources of material were particularly useful.

1. The collects of the American Commission in its Prayer Book Studies No. 19 *The Church Year* (1970). Although producing a different lectionary system, it still continued to use a large number of 1662 collects in contemporary form.
2. The South African collects, based on the JLG lectionary and published as *Modern Collects* in 1972. Their liturgical committee sent us batches of material regularly from 1969 onwards and co-operation was close, particularly with Leonard Lanham, Professor of Linguistics and Phonetics at the University of Witwatersrand, who exercised a major influence on their work. He persuaded them to use the relative clause introduced by 'who' with a third person verb, although retaining the second person in the rest of the prayer viz. 'Almighty God, who *has* taught us . . . , give us . . .' He argued that this was a paraphrase for 'You, Almighty God, who has taught us . . .', and that 'usage, rather than traditional grammar, has influenced our choice in this case'.[68]
3. *Collects with the New Lectionary* by Peter Akehurst and Anthony Bishop and published by Grove Books in 1972. The new lectionary was authorized for use with Holy Communion Series 3 in July 1973 but without new collects, adjustments being made instead for the temporary use of 1662 material.[69] This private set therefore provided an unofficial stop-gap. The authors made no attempt to 'touch up' or modernize the 1662 collects, aiming rather to be 'as modern as possible, without becoming colloquial or trite'.[70] Frankly the Commission made no extensive borrowings; but they were useful for comparison and sometimes provided valuable insights.

The JLG and the Liturgical Commission virtually worked in tandem until early 1974, and the complete Anglican proposals were finally published in April 1975 (GS 230). These went through the General Synod with little significant change and were authorized for use from 1 February 1977. With minor variations they were used by all Churches throughout the British Isles except the Roman Catholic Church. The difficulty of the relative clause was dealt with in one of four ways:

1. The use of a different kind of relative clause — 'Almighty God, whose Son Jesus Christ fasted' (Lent I).
2. The use of the past definite tense — 'Almighty God, who anointed Jesus at his Baptism' (Epiphany I).
3. The substitution of a statement — 'Almighty God, you have knit together your elect' (All Saints).
4. The substitution of a noun in apposition — 'Lord of all power and might, the author and giver' (Pentecost 17).

The traditional form of the collect was preserved, however, and a surprising number of the old collects were used with much of the familiar wording. Some seventy of the Prayer Book collects were used in whole or in part; while a number of ancient collects which did not appear in 1662, including four from the Leonine Sacramentary, were introduced.[71] The whole collect operation had taken a long time, almost longer than any other pieces of liturgical revision: but the expenditure of time and trouble was justified. Experience might well prove them to have been one of the really significant pieces of revision.

NOTES

1. *Prayer Book Revision in the Church of England*, p. 32.
2. *LC Minutes*, 28.3d; 29.7; 30.6; 34.5; 37.9; 40.12.
3. While there is an extensive continental literature on the subject, English studies are few. Outstanding are C. S. Lewis's classic essay in *English Literature in the Sixteenth Century* (1954); and A. C. Clark's *The Cursus in Mediaeval and Vulgar Latin* (1910), heavily borrowed by later writers. New avenues were opened up by F. L. Cross's translation of Anton Baumstark's *Liturgie Comparée* (1958) and Christine Mohrmann's *Liturgical Latin* (1959). The most recent study is Stella Brook's *The Language of the Book of Common Prayer* (1965). But surely one of the finest English studies in this field — and sadly neglected — is Bishop J. B. Lightfoot's literary study of the Intercessory Prayers in 1 Clement, in *The Apostolic Fathers: St Clement of Rome* 2 vols. (1890), vol. 1, pp. 382–96.
4. B. Naylor, *Why Prayer Book Revision at all?*, 1964, esp. pp. 38–9.
5. Stella Brook, *The Language of the Book of Common Prayer*, 1965, pp. 218–19.
6. *The Liturgical Conference 1966*, Report, p. 11.
7. ibid., pp. 13–14.
8. ibid., pp. 15–16.
9. ibid., pp. 14–30. Only one speaker (a bishop) opposed the idea of a modern liturgy.
10. *LC Minutes*, 48.78, 81; *LC Memorandum* 72c.
11. *Report on Baptism and Confirmation*, 1967, p. 4.
12. At the end of 1964 he became coadjutor-bishop of Middlesbrough and in 1966 Bishop of Leeds.
13. *LC Minutes*, 41.9.
14. ibid., 44.30; Letter, Dr Dwyer to R.C.D.J., 10 July 1965.

15. There was in fact another Englishman on the Advisory Committee, Professor G. B. Harrison of Santa Fé, New Mexico, a Professor of English; but he was regarded as an American representative.
16. ICEL, *English for the Mass*, Part I, 1966, p. 7.
17. Memorandum from Prof. G. B. Harrison, December 1967.
18. *English for the Mass*, Part II, 1966, pp. 1–2.
19. *LC Minutes*, 50.100b.
20. *The Liturgy or Eucharist of the Church of the Province of New Zealand*, 1966; Buchanan, *Modern Anglican Liturgies 1958–1968*, pp. 321–39.
21. Australian Lit. Comm., *Prayer Book Revision in Australia*, Sydney 1966, p. iv; Buchanan, pp. 297–320.
22. Letter, Fr G. Sigler to R.C.D.J., December 1967. Gerald Sigler did in fact allow us in strict confidence to see these texts before publication to help promote dialogue.
23. *LC Memorandum* 73A.
24. He wrote thrillers under the pen-name Nicholas Blake.
25. *Modern Canticles for Congregational Singing*, Abbey Records FE 644.
26. Lit. Comm., *Modern Liturgical Texts*, 1968, p. 4.
27. ibid., p. 1.
28. I have referred to Bishop J. B. Lightfoot's study of the Intercessions in 1 Clement in note 3 of this Chapter.
29. C. Buchanan, 'Liturgical Revision in the Church of England in retrospect', in K. Stevenson, ed., *Liturgy Reshaped*, 1982, pp. 147, 175; cf. Buchanan, *Further Anglican Liturgies 1968–75*, 1975.
30. ICET, *Prayers We have in Common*, 1st edn 1970, p. 4.
31. Ten years later the *Jerusalem Bible* was supplemented by the authorization of another 'You' version, *Today's English Version*.
32. *CA Proceedings* 1963, vol. lxiii, p. 100.
33. *100 Hymns for Today*, 1969, preface.
34. Examples are Kaan's 'For the healing of the nations', no. 28; Jones' 'God of concrete, God of steel', no. 33; and Carter's 'No use knocking on the window', no. 67.
35. His tune 'Abbott's Leigh' must rank as one of the best and the most popular in the present generation.
36. *LC Minutes* 59.12.
37. ibid., 62.8; *LC Memorandum* 111.
38. C. of E. Lit. Comm., *A Commentary on Holy Communion Series 3*, 1971, p. 8; cf. David Frost, 'A Dying Church, or a Living World?', in *Theology* LXXIV (November 1971), pp. 499–512; and *The Language of Series 3* (Grove Booklets on Ministry and Worship 12), 1973.
39. *A Commentary on H.C. Series 3*, p. 9.
40. *LC Minutes* 58.3, cf. 57. 180. This line has created problems for translators and commentators for centuries.
41. *General Synod Proceedings* 1971, vol. 2, pp. 618–23.
42. ibid., 1972, vol. 3, p. 562.
43. I was later told by Fr Anthony Boylan, the secretary of the English RC National Liturgical Commission, that the only English-speaking part of the Roman Catholic Church to adopt the ICET text of the Lord's Prayer was the Philippines.
44. cf. pp. 174–5.
45. *LC Minutes* 61.36; *LC Memoranda* 96 D and E.
46. *LC Minutes* 63.21.
47. Michael Cantuar to R.C.D.J., 2 July 1970.

48. Donald Ebor to R.C.D.J., 10 July 1970. The other Hebrew scholar involved in the *Revised Psalter*, Professor Winton Thomas, Regius Professor of Hebrew at Cambridge, had just died. Bishop Chase died not long afterwards.
49. He and I pleaded that the proposals of Walter Frere sixty years earlier (cf. pp. 174–5) should be given careful attention.
50. This essay also appeared as chap. 1 in D. L. Frost, *The Language of Series 3* (Grove Booklets on Ministry and Worship no. 12), 1973, p. 12.
51. The panel consisted of six clergy and two laymen: The Revd Dr J. A. Emerton, Regius Professor of Hebrew, Cambridge (chairman), Anglican. The Revd A. Macintosh (Secretary), Anglican. Dr Sebastian Brock, Anglican. The Revd Dr W. Horbury, Anglican. The Revd Dr J. McHugh, Roman Catholic. The Revd A. G. MacLeod, United Reformed. The Revd Dr E. Nicholson, Anglican. John Snaith Esq., Methodist. When the panel was appointed, all its members were academics.
52. Michael Cantuar to R.C.D.J., June 1972.
53. *Report GS 147 Y*, sc 24, p. 5 (September 1974).
54. The members of the team were: Lionel Dakers, Director of RSCM; Roy Massey, Organist and Master of the Choristers at Hereford Cathedral and former Warden of RSCM; and Cyril Taylor, Precentor of Salisbury Cathedral and also a former Warden of RSCM.
55. *The Psalms: a new Translation for Worship*, 1977, p. 15.
56. cf. pp. 174–5.
57. *GS Proceedings 1978*, vol. 9, pp. 372–80.
58. ibid., pp. 380–2.
59. ibid., pp. 382–3, 383–4, 385–6.
60. ibid., pp. 448–50; 458. The voting was by Houses: Bishops 32–4; Clergy 127–36; Laity 146–33.
61. ibid., pp. 459–72. It is worth noting that the Psalter had already been accepted for inclusion in the new Australian Prayer Book in 1976, and was being used in the Churches of Ireland, South Africa and North India. For further information see D. L. Frost, *The Making of the Liturgical Psalter* (Grove Liturgical Studies 25), 1981.
62. cf. p. 273.
63. *Readings at Holy Communion*, 1970, p. viii.
64. This did in fact happen and it was authorized under the Worship and Doctrine Measure.
65. Obviously the Church of Rome had made other arrangements and was not involved.
66. Before the publication of ASB a further modern Bible version, *Today's English Version* or *The Good News Bible*, was authorized and used: cf. p. 355.
67. Societas Liturgica, Documents 8, 14, 16. 1969.
68. LC Text 48.
69. cf. p. 323.
70. P. R. Akehurst and A. J. Bishop, *Collects with the New Lectionary*, 1972, p. 6.
71. Christmas 1 (Year 1); Epiphany 2; Pentecost 16; St Peter and St Paul.

14

SERIES THREE

I

In June 1969, encouraged by the replies to the questionnaire on Holy Communion Series 2 and the discussions at the Liturgical Consultation of Lambeth 1968, the Archbishops proposed to the Liturgical Commission that any revision of the rite should be accompanied by a parallel version in modern language incorporating the ICET texts.[1] Work began in the autumn on certain questions such as the best place for the penitential section, the form of the Peace and the content of the Intercessions;[2] but the Commission was well aware that the crucial problem would undoubtedly prove to be the wording of the second half of the eucharistic prayer. The formula in Series 2, originally intended as a temporary measure, had been accepted with surprising enthusiasm; but discussions on the sacrificial nature of the Eucharist had continued on a wide front and we were encouraged to think that an improved, or at least an alternative, form of words could be found.

This optimism was to some extent a reflection of the tone of the World Council of Churches' statement on *The Eucharist in Ecumenical Thought*, published in 1968 and bringing together agreements registered at Faith and Order Conferences at Lund, Montreal, Aarhus and Bristol between 1952 and 1967. Accepting the view that the whole eucharistic action depended on the work of the Holy Spirit, and rejecting any notion of consecration being limited to a particular moment,[3] it laid particular emphasis on the concept of anamnesis and its richness of meaning.

> Christ instituted the eucharist . . . as the anamnesis of the whole of God's reconciling action in him. Christ himself with all he has accomplished for us and for all creation is present in this anamnesis as is also the foretaste of his Parousia and the fulfilment of the Kingdom . . . It is not only a calling to mind of what is past, or of its significance. It is the Church's effective proclamation of God's mighty acts.[4]

On the domestic front the same note of optimism appeared in an essay on eucharistic sacrifice by Eric Mascall and E. M. B. Green in the symposium *Growing into Union*, produced in 1970 by leading opponents of the Anglican–Methodist unity proposals attempting to bridge important Anglo-Catholic–Evangelical differences.[5] Given the traditional crux – the Catholic insistence on the sacrificial nature of the Eucharist and the evangelical denial of any sacrificial element other than one of response, the essay claimed that both points of view found a common source in the desire to do justice to the once-for-allness of the atonement and to the ongoing grace in the soul of man.[6] 'Christ offered himself on the cross in our stead and without our aid, and we certainly cannot repeat that offering' – that was agreed. But was there anything else? The essayists suggested that what was offered was more than 'the fruit of the lips' or undefined 'spiritual sacrifices'; it was 'ourselves as re-appropriated by Christ'. The Eucharist, in communicating afresh to the Church the benefits of Christ's passion also communicated to it his demands – it was re-apprehended for service. 'In the act of communicating, the Church, re-integrated and re-appropriated by the one means of grace, is made a living sacrifice to God.'[7] Communion and sacrifice belonged together; they were contemporaneous: and the fact that the Prayer of Oblation followed communion in no way expressed a time sequence, but simply a logical dependence of self-offering on God's grace. The two men frankly admitted that not all differences had been settled; but the fact that they could agree this far was a significant advance towards rapprochement. Furthermore the entire symposium suggested not so much a desire for complete doctrinal uniformity as for mutual understanding. The comprehensiveness of the Church of England was recognized.

The concept of comprehensiveness and the richness of meaning in the anamnesis were also recognized in the important Agreed Windsor Statement on Eucharistic Doctrine issued by the Anglican–Roman Catholic International Commission in 1971. This claimed to represent agreement on essentials, with room left for diversity of representation. It emphasized the uniqueness, finality and sufficiency of Christ's death on the cross and argued that the idea of memorial or anamnesis opened the way to a clearer understanding of the relationship between Christ's sacrifice and the Eucharist. Here was no mere calling to mind of a past event but a means whereby God's mighty acts were proclaimed and made effective in the life of the Church. In the Eucharist the Church, united with God and with all its members, gave thanks for his mercies, entreated the benefits of Christ's passion, and both participated in those benefits and entered into the movement of his self-offering.[8] Inevitably the Statement met with criticisms and reservations, with demands for clarification on a number of points;[9] but as Bishop McAdoo the Anglican co-chairman explained, the Statement did not seek to make definitions of how the Eucharist effected its purpose: rather it sought to go behind divisive definitions to a deeper understanding of the reality of the Eucharist consonant with biblical teaching and with the tradition of a common inheritance.[10] Shortly afterwards he and his fellow-chairman, Bishop Alan Gray, published this Statement together with three other recent documents on the Eucharist, one by an American Lutheran–Roman Catholic group, a second by the French interconfessional Les Dombes group, and the third the WCC statement just referred to, with the comment that these constituted 'a movement of shared thought and prayer producing a type of approach which has clearly cut across confessional boundaries as well as the line of past disagreements, and which opens the way for a real ecumenical advance'.[11]

It is also worth noting at this juncture that the Liturgical Commission had asked the Doctrine Commission for advice on the Eucharist. Unfortunately their help in the form of a series of essays, *Thinking about the Eucharist*, did not appear until 1972 – rather late for our immediate needs; but one of their number, Leslie Houlden, had also become a member of the Liturgical Commission in 1968, and with a foot in both camps, was able to provide valuable help in the work on the Series 3 eucharistic prayer.[12]

The climate seemed fair; and in April 1970 I discussed the anamnesis with Colin Buchanan, pointing out that since Series 2 had appeared I had been inundated with requests from both Anglo-Catholics and Evangelicals, urging changes more in keeping with their particular views, while Michael Ramsey was arguing that we should leave well alone, on the grounds that while Series 2 might not be ideal, it was at least tolerable, and anything different might only cause another furore. Colin Buchanan was keen to try again, however; and a similar positive response came from Kenneth Ross and Leslie Houlden.[13] So began a triangular correspondence between Colin Buchanan, Kenneth Ross and myself, with proposals and counter-proposals following one another in rapid succession. My role was primarily that of an honest broker, seeking to reconcile the differences of the other two, and from time to time asking the advice of Leslie Houlden. By the beginning of June a text had been produced which both Colin Buchanan and Kenneth Ross were prepared to accept unreservedly. We had admittedly taken a limited step, but definite progress had been made. Unfortunately our delight was short-lived. Two days after expressing agreement Kenneth Ross died suddenly (8 June). His loss was felt keenly. His wit, his charm and his lively mind had made him a popular and valued member of the Commission ever since 1955; and he would have been particularly useful as an advocate of the revised text in Anglo-Catholic circles, although he never regarded himself as a 'typical Anglo-Catholic'.

After consulting the whole Liturgical Commission I sent the proposed anamnesis to both Archbishops, who expressed warm approval. Michael Ramsey was particularly encouraging in view of his earlier reservations.

> The draft which you send seems to me to mark an improvement rather more than one might have hoped for. The language of offering is less jejune, and it is clearly right to mention the 'perfect sacrifice made once for all upon the cross' and also to substitute 'his coming' for 'the coming of his Kingdom'. I do not see anything in the draft which the Evangelical should object to, and indeed he should be glad of the two points just mentioned. The Catholic will find nothing very explicit about the doctrine which he holds but the general tone is a big improvement. I am sure it is worth trying out.[14]

The anamnesis ran:

> Therefore, heavenly Father, we do this in remembrance of him: with this bread and this cup we celebrate his perfect sacrifice made once for all

upon the cross; we proclaim his resurrection from the dead and his ascension into heaven; and we look for the fullness of his coming in glory.

Meanwhile proposals for improvements to the rite continued to pour in from all quarters: they came at such a rate that at the beginning of 1971 I commented to Leslie Brown that there were sufficient proposals to enable a weekly revision of the eucharistic prayer.

Meanwhile the Commission made progress with revising other elements of the rite. The original plan to have a revised form of Series 2 and a parallel version in contemporary language was soon modified, Series 2 being left as it was and the revision being confined to the contemporary language form. Structurally there was little change; but a great deal of additional material was included: seasonal sentences both introductory and post-communion, extended intercessions and penitential material, more proper prefaces, provision for further consecration, seasonal blessings, and the new eucharistic lectionary. The ICET texts were included en bloc; but the modernization of the rest of the rite was by no means easy. In January 1971, David Frost expressed his misgivings about the drafts, wondering whether they would prove acceptable and whether they were aimed at the right kind of people. I must confess I shared his misgivings; like everyone else we were working very much in the dark and had to feel our way. As for the consumer level, it seemed to me that for severely practical purposes we should be aiming to cater for the members of the General Synod, since in the first instance they were the people who would decide by two-thirds majorities what was acceptable; and on the whole they were a middle-aged, middle-class, fairly well-educated group. It was a rough and ready principle, but as good a guide as any other. Furthermore we should aim for a judicious blend of old and new, so that people would be reassured by the presence of familiar elements: it would be wise, for example, to start the rite with a virtually unchanged Collect for Purity. Series 2 had encouraged people to break with the 1662 structure while retaining the language; Series 3 must now encourage people to break with the 1662 language; and I believed this would prove to be a much more difficult and lengthy task. David Frost and I spent nearly five days going over the drafts with a toothcomb, trying to pin-point and analyse the main problems. I then encouraged him to go away and attempt some rewriting, if necessary seeking help from any literary friends and colleagues. From this we hoped to present a revised draft to the Commission in early April 1971.[15] These hopes were fulfilled and the rite as it finally emerged from the April meeting contained three important new pieces of writing from David Frost: a revision of the General Confession and additional forms of the Prayer of Humble Access and the post-communion prayer.

To our great surprise the House of Bishops seemed quite well disposed towards the proposals: no single point seemed to attract particular attention, there was a total lack of comment of the revised canon, and no one expressed a positive dislike of the rite as a whole.[16] The report was published in readiness for consideration by the General Synod in November. Three points call for particular comment. In the first place the proposals contained one element on which the Commission had been unable to come to a clear decision — that of the provision for additional consecration. Series 2 had made no such provision, it being suggested that for lack of anything else the 1662 arrangement should be used, i.e. the recital of the Institution Narrative, although this was contrary to our understanding of consecration. The matter had been discussed at Lambeth 1968, and here too, although the 1662 arrangement was disliked, no clear alternative had emerged. After seeking advice from the Doctrine Commission, we finally proposed that further supplies of bread and wine should be brought into the sacramental action by associating them with the elements already consecrated. The question then remained as to whether this should be done in silence or with a brief statement of intent. In favour of silence it could be said that it caused the least possible disruption; while in favour of a statement, it indicated what was happening. Neither we nor the Doctrine Commission could find any theological objection to either method, although there was no agreement as to which should be adopted if only one method were to be provided. Both methods were therefore included and it was left to General Synod to make a final decision.[17]

Secondly the Report was published in a new typographical format, resulting from the conviction that typography and lay-out were an important element in liturgical reform: 'Rites have to be presented in a printed form which reveals the intentions of the authors and enables congregations to understand them and to follow them easily.'[18] Since 1662 little typographical change had taken place. Apart from the use of italic, the average Prayer Book made little attempt to distinguish between different elements in a service, while pages and lines were filled with little regard to sense. Furthermore, the Church had become accustomed to accepting what the Privileged Presses provided: no financial outlay was involved; the average Prayer Book was commendably cheap, and no difficult questions were asked. In its early days the Liturgical Commission had been content to follow the traditional patterns. But a change of climate occurred in the sixties, with the arrival of Holy Communion Series 2, in which the use of two-colour printing, variations of type, lining out and spacing were all employed to assist the worshipper in following the service intelligently. This change owed a great deal to John Wilkinson, who had been brought up in the world of printing and was knowledgeable in this field. In March 1966 he raised the question of typography, arguing that presentation should go hand in hand with the revision of the text, and the Church as well as the Presses should be involved in the formulation of policy. Shortly afterwards he and I discussed these questions with representatives of the Privileged Presses, who accepted the principle of a fresh approach, evidence of which was seen in the various Series 2 services. Encouraging though this was, John was by no means satisfied. In January 1968 he gave an important lecture on 'The Visual Presentation of Services' to an interdenominational conference of publishers and booksellers, pointing out that while the lay-out of Holy Communion Series 2 was far superior to anything previously produced, the actual printing operation had highlighted a number of problems. The text was still too cramped and many of the turn-overs were unsatisfactory because the rite had been squeezed into sixteen pages, a limitation created by the fact that the printing had been done on machines which could cope with nothing bigger. This reflected poor relationships between author, editor and printer. Who, in fact, was ultimately responsible? Two people were needed: first, a designer fully conversant with printing techniques, who could understand and interpret the needs and intentions of the author (i.e. the Church); secondly, some individual from the Church, fully conversant with the text which had been produced, with authority to make decisions. Between them these two should enable the printer to express in the best way possible the requirements of the worshipper.

This was followed by a top-level meeting of all interested parties with the Archbishop of Canterbury in July 1968. John Wilkinson's analysis of the situation was accepted, and the meeting agreed to seek an independent designer who would be responsible for all new services. The choice eventually fell on Keith Murgatroyd, current President of the Society of Typographic Designers and well known on both sides of the Atlantic; he had already done work for the Church and beneath a mild exterior had a toughness which was to prove a great asset in dealing with the Presses.[19] He began with the Report on Holy Communion Series 3, in which his radical approach caused many printers of traditional outlook to shudder. But faced with a situation where worshippers were confronted with unfamiliar texts, he believed the use of strongly contrasting typefaces to be helpful; furthermore, he regarded the sense of the text to be paramount, controlling the lay-out. To the printer this could have unusual and even untidy results; but to the worshipper it made sense. Happily both Archbishops supported him. In February 1972 Michael Ramsey wrote, 'It is certainly our hope that Mr Murgatroyd's design will continue to be used, for it gives the printed services a quality of helpfulness to worshippers in church which is greatly appreciated.' Undoubtedly the typography of Series 3 services had considerable influence on liturgical printing in other Churches; but what is more important is the fact that the printed word itself was recognized as having its own unique contribution to liturgical revision.

The third distinctive feature was the supportive material which accompanied the rite. First there was a straightforward *Commentary on Holy Communion Series 3* of some 32 pages. Then there was an illustrated booklet, *The Presentation of the Eucharist*, produced by a working party appointed jointly by the Commission and the Council for the Care of Churches. Since 1966 there had been an encouraging number of comments and queries about Series 2 coming from parochial clergy; but most of these were concerned with presentation rather than text. Some people had obviously experimented imaginatively and successfully and were keen to report what they had done: others sought advice because they were faced with problems, either with conservative parishioners or with architectural difficulties; others again complained because Series 2 had proved a disaster, usually because they failed to appreciate that liturgy involved actions as well as words. I consulted the Archbishops, who gladly gave permission for the creation of a small group of clergy, architects, artists, actors and musicians to explore these questions and offer some advice on the use of Series 3. The report, described by the Archbishop of York as 'a piece of down-to-earth common sense', was accompanied by a film-strip, both indicating how the rite could be used in different kinds of churches and with different kinds of ceremonial. It was in fact this group which produced the first cassock-alb, designed by Peter Rice, whose costumes and stage sets adorned many a London theatre production at this time. Finally there was the first musical setting of Series 3. New words demanded new music: and in January 1971 at Cyril Taylor's suggestion I convened a small group of cathedral organists and the staff of the Royal School of Church Music to choose a composer. By general consent John Rutter, then a young music don at Cambridge, was the ideal person; and his setting had its first public performance at the Edington Music Festival in August 1971.

The publication of the Series 3 proposals in September aroused tremendous interest. The Report and the commentaries were a sell-out, the publishers having difficulty in keeping pace with demand. *The Church Times* warmly congratulated the Commission on its efforts, while John Gunstone in a long review in the same paper not only commended the new prayers for their richness of association and beauty of sound, but described the anamnesis as a work of considerable ingenuity: 'If Anglo-Catholics and Evangelicals object to this solution to their differences, then I for one will cease to believe that they ever intended to seek a way forward from their controversies about the Eucharist.'[20] Dr James Packer, no mean protagonist of 1662, also showed equal enthusiasm in *The Church of England Newspaper*, claiming that 'the language has acquired concreteness, weight and warmth'.[21] Two old Roman Catholic friends also had words of praise. Professor Finberg wrote in *The Tablet*: 'So much thought, experiment and consultation lie behind the new order . . . that it deserves the respectful attention of all who are interested in the problem of modernising the forms of public worship': while Fr J. B. Crichton described the rite in *Life and Worship* as 'admirably clear and unfussy' with a special word of praise for lay-out and typography.[22] On the other hand, Conservative Anglo-Catholics were still strongly critical. The Society of the Holy Cross, for example, accused the rite of leaning 'heavily to the position of the Conservative Evangelicals, while the surface decorations serve to conceal this from undiscerning Anglo-Catholics': and Michael Moreton delivered another broadside on the failure of the eucharistic prayer to express any language of offering: 'While borrowing freely from *The Apostolic Tradition*, it has destroyed its ethos by forsaking it at its crucial paragraph.'[23] Then, of course, there were the expected outcries both in the daily press and in correspondence over the language question, particularly the use of 'You' for 'God', and the substitution of 'President' for 'Priest'.

Everything pointed to a lively session when the rite was introduced to the General Synod on 10 November, and the number of amendments tabled was vast, far greater than anything experienced hitherto. I tried to assure the Synod that the Church was in no danger of suddenly being deprived of Series 2, which was deservedly popular, and of being confronted with a stark choice between 1662 and Series 3; for this was apparently what many people feared. The period of authorization for Series 2 was to be extended, enabling experiment to be conducted with both rites concurrently, with possibly a gradual transition from the one to the other. Furthermore, we hoped that the Church might have three authorized rites: 1662, Series 3, and an intermediate rite embodying the best features of Series 1 and Series 2. Finally, since the proposed rite was radically different in language, I pleaded for a measure of charity and forbearance while the Church discovered by experience whether it was acceptable or not.[24] The ensuing debate, despite an opening vitriolic attack on the language by the Dean of Guildford (the Very Revd. A. Bridge) and subsequently described by David Frost as 'a defence of Cranmerian English that would have made Cranmer weep', was clearly in favour of the proposals, and further consideration was agreed without difficulty.[25] Now began the marathon of amendments, covering three days of the Synod's time and spilling over into the February 1972 session. On the first day all went well until the debate was adjourned to deal with other scheduled business. When the debate was resumed, unfortunately without proper warning, there was an inexplicable half-hour's madness in a very thin house; some of the Commission's proposals were treated with derision and the new form of Confession and the alternative Prayer of Humble Access were swept aside without proper discussion. Almost immediately some members began to express concern at this hasty action, pleading for further consideration: but the decisions had been made in accordance with the rules, and the chairman stated quite firmly, 'What we have done, we have done, and that is not subject to revision.'[26] The incident was probably a blessing in disguise, for it emphasized the futility of dealing with large numbers of amendments on the floor of the house; and in any case no permanent harm was done.[27] It certainly attracted public attention. *The Church Times* rashly commented that in the debate 'only about a dozen of the fifty amendments were taken' — an error to which I replied in the following week, pointing out that of the fifty amendments on the notice paper, thirty-three were taken, five were accepted and the remainder were either rejected or withdrawn.[28] Despite the disappointments, the general result had in fact been quite good. David Frost, for whom liturgical debate in the Convocations or the General Synod was a new experience, was dismayed to see his work rejected so peremptorily and even contemplated resignation. But I told him not to worry unduly; this was not the first time the Commission's proposals had been given a rough passage,[29] and with patience there would still be opportunity to get things right. The important thing was to find a better way of dealing with amendments: and as I wrote to Leslie Brown (29 November), 'If this goes on with every service we produce, I wonder how soon the Synod will get fed up with liturgy?'

The Liturgical Steering Committee succeeded in settling a number of the remaining amendments in private discussions with their movers in December 1971 and January 1972, although this proved very time-consuming for those of us concerned. Clearly it would be impossible to deal with amendments to every Series 3 service in this way. The Standing Committee accepted the fact that some new system was necessary, but rightly pointed out that changes could not be made during the progress of this particular service through the Synod. We therefore had to soldier on, facing the unpalatable fact that some thirty amendments still remained to be dealt with in the February 1972 session. Fortunately that session proved to be less of a problem than we feared. The resumed debate began (9 February) with several expressions of dismay at the turn of events in November, and there seemed to be a general determination that there should now be no repeat performance.[30] Furthermore, a number of members, reassured by the promise of an eventual 'intermediate' rite, were prepared to drop their amendments. Remarkably little was changed in the rest of the service, several speakers commenting that they would prefer to experiment with Series 3 more or less as the Liturgical Commission had drafted it. On further consecration a clear decision was made in favour of a statement rather than silence;[31] but on the anamnesis there were still murmurs.[32] It was therefore decided to ask the House of Bishops to consider the theology of the rite in the light of the recently published Anglican-Roman Catholic Statement, although Dr Ramsey pointed out that there were limits to the liturgical conclusions that would necessarily follow from their advice: the Synod would still be left with the task of deciding what should be done about the shape and content of the liturgy.[33]

Another round of discussions on the anamnesis now followed, involving not only the Bishops and the Liturgical Commission but a number of interested parties, both Anglo-Catholic and Evangelical. A variety of proposals was made, which the Commission discussed in March 1972. We agreed that the minimum of change was desirable, that the cross and resurrection/ascension should not be treated in different ways with separate verbs, that the retention of the word 'memorial' was in line with the Windsor Statement, and that the use of the verb 'celebrate' as in 1 Corinthians 5.8 justified its inclusion. Accordingly we proposed to make just one significant change from our original proposal — linking the verbs 'celebrate' and 'proclaim' rather than using them separately with the cross and resurrection/ ascension.[34] The Bishops approved this change and the service had a relatively easy passage in the General Synod in July 1972, when provisional approval was given after a brief debate.[35] Final approval followed with massive majorities in November, and the rite was authorized for use for four years from 1 February 1973.[36]

The rite was a milestone in Anglican liturgical revision. It was the first authorized service in contemporary language and much of its content was the product of ecumenical co-operation. In structure it remained identical with Series 2, but in content it was considerably enriched and improved.

1. There was an increased provision for silence.
2. There was an increase in seasonal material: introductory sentences, Proper Prefaces, post-communion sentences, blessings and a two-year Lectionary.
3. The Intercessions were supplemented by thanksgivings.
4. The Confession included a specific act of repentance.
5. The Peace became mandatory.
6. The Offertory was provided with a sentence from 1 Chronicles 29.
7. The four-action shape was clearly expressed typographically.
8. The eucharistic prayer was given an improved anamnesis, an epiclesis and congregational acclamations.
9. There was provision for further consecration.
10. There was an additional optional post-communion prayer.

As with Series 2, a number of useful popular commentaries and devotional aids soon appeared,[37] together with a substantial book of essays, *The Eucharist Today*, by seven members of the Liturgical Commission and three non-members. Of particular interest was the final piece, 'Liturgy and her Companions', by Leslie Houlden, which I had encouraged him to write. It was critical, constructive and forward-looking. He argued that while liturgical study in the past century had made immense strides, it had been mostly in an historical direction; revision had been marked by a return to the past, failing to take into account developments in other directions. Some would complain that Series 3 was too modern, but from some points of view it was archaic – 'its thought forms and theological assumptions are wholly traditional'. Liturgists needed to widen their horizons and enlist support from other disciplines, biblical studies, doctrine, anthropology, psychology, sociology.[38] The essay was a valuable pointer to future lines of study, even on a long-term basis.

For the moment, however, the critics had a field day, particularly on the language question, which was to be expected. Inevitably I was the recipient of a considerable 'fan mail', much of which expressed sentiments which could hardly be called Christian, and some even expressing the hope that I would suffer an early and painful demise! This furore was delightfully described by Philip Cecil in his review of *The Eucharist Today* in *The Church Times*,

> On the day on which I received this book for review *The Times* carried a leader pouring scorn upon it [Series 3] from its usual Olympian heights: and this was followed in the course of the next week or two by letters from witty bishops, comical clergymen and some of their less amusing supporters, extolling the matchless beauties of the service in the Book of Common Prayer (which, I fancy, none of them in fact ever uses as it stands).

This kind of opposition found further expression in 1975 with the foundation of the Prayer Book Society, 'to uphold the worship and doctrine of the Church of England as enshrined in the Book of Common Prayer and to encourage the use of that book as a major element in the worshipping life of the Church of England'. The existence of such feeling was not surprising; for to many people 1662 had been the foundation stone of their devotional life. For them to see not only the appearance of a new liturgy, but its rapid acceptance over a wide area must have been very disturbing. Indeed the speed and extent of its acceptance surprised me. By the end of February — a month after authorization — a million copies of Series 3 had been sold, while John Rutter's music went through three impressions in a fortnight. It showed every promise of outshining Series 2 in popularity.

II

Before the General Synod considered any further services, a new method of procedure was introduced. The Liturgical Steering Committee was disbanded and each new service was given its own Steering Committee on which the Liturgical Commission was always represented; this committee was then included in a Revision Committee, also freshly appointed for each service with a chairman who was not a member of the Commission. Since I became chairman of the Steering Committees for all but three of the services still to be revised, and since services tended to overlap in their passage through Synod, demands on my time remained pretty constant. Indeed, when I became heavily committed to the production of the Alternative Service Book, I had to call a halt on Steering and Revision Committee work, leaving it to the other members of the Commission to cope. In any case the activities of the Revision Committees mushroomed. At first the number of amendments submitted was quite small and a committee could complete its work in a couple of sessions; but gradually the submission of amendments became almost a synodical obsession: they could number hundreds for a single service and on one occasion exceeded a thousand.[39] Some Revision Committees lasted for months, proving very expensive; and at one stage the question was raised as to whether this was an economic and useful expenditure of the Church's time and money.[40] Certainly whether this was the ideal method of creating good liturgy was a matter of debate, particularly when a great deal more time would sometimes be spent at the Provisional Approval stage, attempting to restore what had been originally proposed.

The next Series 3 services to be dealt with were the Funeral rites. They had been in the pipe-line for a very long time. After the House of Laity had returned the Series 2 proposals for further consideration in 1968, the Archbishops had asked the Liturgical Commission to draft new forms, it being left to the Commission to determine the width or narrowness of the word 'new'. It was a daunting prospect, for in the light of what had already transpired, it was difficult to imagine what differences over prayers for the departed could be solved by the word 'new'.[41] What emerged in early 1970 were drafts in contemporary language, largely the work of Geoffrey Cuming, together with the first batch of Frost–Macintosh psalms. The title was also changed from Burial to Funeral Services in view of the significant increase in the number of cremations.[42] In September I sent copies to the Archbishops to see whether they thought we were on the right lines, and on the clear understanding that we could not complete our work until the Doctrine Commission had produced its requested report on Prayer for the Departed. Both expressed their approval, regarding the proposals as a great improvement on Series 2, and in due course submitted them to the Bishops, who, while approving of them in principle, suggested one amendment which caused the Commission some embarrassment. They wished to reintroduce the prayer 'For those whom we love but see no longer', which, despite its popularity since 1928, had proved a serious bone of contention in the 1969 debates.[43] I made this point to the Archbishops, pleading that it should not be included and suggesting that if the Bishops felt so strongly about it, they could introduce it themselves as an amendment — a plea to which they finally agreed.[44]

The Doctrine Commission report *Prayer and the Departed* (GS 52), containing both a theological exposition and a set of proposed prayers, was published in 1971 and discussed by the Synod in November 1972. The fact that the debate created problems was due in some measure to an intervention by Archbishop Ramsey which, to say the least, many of us did not expect. While describing the report as a 'masterly theological analysis of the question', he was unable to commend the proposed prayers: 'I wonder whether the sort of prayer that the report suggests is really a prayer that anyone wants to say': and he then went on to express the hope that a new service would include two or three optional prayers of the very kind that the Commission had been trying to avoid, even mentioning the prayer 'Father of all'.[45] It was enough to open the floodgates to all the old arguments for and against prayer for the departed, ending with the passing of a motion to include such prayers on an optional basis in any new service, while an amendment proposing that any such prayers 'should, wherever possible, be expressed in terms acceptable to the consciences of every major section of the Church' was defeated.[46] This left the Liturgical Commission, waiting to complete its own report, in a difficult position; for the successful motion required us to do something which we honestly believed would only cause dissension. At this stage two events occurred which proved to be providential.

The first was a private negotiation between two leading Evangelical laymen, Professor Norman Anderson (Chairman of the House of Laity) and Hugh Craig, and two leading Anglo-Catholic clergy, Prebendary Harold Riley (Prolocutor of the Lower House of Canterbury) and Canon John Tinsley, to produce an amended version of 'Father of all' which they hoped would be acceptable to all parties. This they succeeded in doing, sending it to me in late December in a 'Thou' form with a plea that I should try to convert it into a 'You' form. With a few minor amendments I did this within a fortnight, producing a prayer which all four felt they could commend with enthusiasm. The Archbishops and the Liturgical Commission also found it acceptable and it was included in our Report *Funeral Services Series 3* (GS 147) published in April 1973. The second event was the delay in bringing the report to Synod, giving plenty of time for calmer thoughts to prevail. During this period the Synod was overwhelmed with business and found it quite impossible to keep to proposed timetables; liturgical matters therefore had to take their place in the queue. It was not until February 1974 that the report was considered, over three years after the main work had been completed.

The structure of the basic Funeral Service was similar to that proposed in Series 2; and this had already been found acceptable in 1966. A good deal of familiar material had also been retained, together with a considerable enrichment of material and increased flexibility of use. Hopes of a general welcome from the General Synod were justified, the introductory debate being relatively brief and uncontentious.[47] The new Revision Stage system now had its first test. Over 120 proposals from 28 members were considered by a committee of sixteen, including four from the Liturgical Commission. It was a protracted business, involving five sessions over a period of six months. Frankly there was not a great deal to show for the labour: minor changes in the choice of psalms and lessons, some readjustment of prayers, and the addition of a little new material. But the procedure did enable a number of comments and criticisms to receive a proper airing, and the result might have been very different if revision had been attempted in full Synod. Certainly the Synod appeared to be content with what had been done, for both Provisional and Final Approval were readily given, and the services were authorized for use from 1 June 1975.[48]

Compared with 1662 the new Funeral Services were similar in structure and indeed at a number of points familiar in content; but there was a wider variety of material from which to choose and the ethos had significantly changed: there was a greater note of confidence and hope and a stronger emphasis on resurrection. Furthermore there was a recognition of the fact that cremation had largely replaced burial, with increased adaptability in the use of the rite itself. Indeed, concurrently with the new rite the Commission produced a simplified form for specific use in crematorium chapels — the brainchild of Geoffrey Cuming; simple in language and structure and without psalms or responses, it was intended for use by people who had no church links but still needed a Christian service. Finally a solution had been found at long last to the vexed question of prayer for the departed both by the provision of prayers acceptable to all parties and by the inclusion of a rubric permitting a variety of choice but not specifying content.[49]

Literally minutes after the General Synod had given Provisional Approval to the Funeral Services in November 1974, I introduced the Report on *Morning and Evening Prayer Series 3* (GS 215). It was the response to a request by the Synod in February 1971 for a version of the Series 2 Revised services in contemporary language. The work had been done with minimal change and a few additions: the Confession and Absolution from Holy Communion Series 3, the State Prayers, the Litany, the Endings and an additional canticle – 'The Song of Christ's Glory'. Publication of the report was delayed to await the final meeting of ICET in April 1974,[50] but once it appeared every effort was made to secure authorization of the services in the lifetime of the existing Synod, which was due to end after the July session of 1975. They contained nothing controversial, little time was spent on debate, even the Revision Committee was only required to meet twice, and Final Approval was eventually given on schedule.[51] What emerged was a form of Morning and Evening Prayer, still recognizably following the traditional pattern but very different in use. In contrast to the rigid form of 1662 it was now variable in length and content and capable of being used for various purposes: a said office clerical or lay, a Sunday service with hymns, sermon and additional prayers, or an ante-communion service. Some of the content still had to be settled: the collects, the lectionary and the psalter recitation; but these were temporarily covered by using materials already authorized either in 1662 or in the Series 1 and Series 2 services.

On the day the Synod gave Provisional Approval to Morning and Evening Prayer the next service was introduced – *Holy Communion Series 1 and 2 Revised* (GS 217). I had realized the need for a eucharistic rite half-way between 1662 and Series 3 as early as March 1971, suggesting it in the plan for the future of liturgical revision submitted to the Archbishops.[52] By the end of that year it had also become very evident that Series 2 was widely used and very popular; and by no means everyone would want to transfer to Series 3, particularly those who preferred traditional language; furthermore, Series 1 had its adherents, while others who claimed to be 1662 loyalists were not unwilling to accept a modicum of revision. The Liturgical Commission agreed that the best solution to these various needs would be a flexible rite of Series 2 shape but containing Series 1 material.[53] I prepared a draft on these lines during 1972, receiving considerable help from Canon John Tinsley of York, who quite independently had been thinking in a similar direction, spurred on by the Commission's questionnaire on the use of Series 1.[54] He sent me a massive document in August 1972 which gave me great help in preparing my own draft.

The Commission had its proposals ready by September 1973 and submitted them to the Bishops with hopes of a quick decision, particularly in view of the Synod's endorsement of the principle of such a rite in the previous July.[55] Unfortunately the Bishops were experiencing the same problem of overloaded agendas as the Synod itself, and they were unable to approve the proposals until June 1974; while it was July 1975 before the document reached the Synod itself. The irritation of the Commission, who at one stage had hoped to complete all its revision work by the end of 1975, was understandable.

What was proposed was a rite whose structure was substantially that of Series 2, but with a choice of two forms of Intercession (Series 1 and Series 2) and two eucharistic prayers (Series 1 and Series 2), and supplemented by seasonal material drawn from Series 3. By means of notes and rubrics it was also possible to substitute the 1662 penitential material, and to use the Gloria in excelsis and the Lord's Prayer in their 1662 positions. Some people complained that it looked confusing: but the proposals were intended to serve as an umbrella for a variety of local preferences; and once a congregation had decided on its options, there need be little difficulty. As I pointed out when introducing the proposals, the Church had entered a period of flexibility and four rites were already available: 1662, Series 1, Series 2 and Series 3. The Church now had to decide (a) whether it was desirable or necessary to retain all four rites, and (b) whether the rites had something to offer one another. The function of the present proposals was to assist in the consideration of these two questions. The Synod welcomed the report;[56] but the Revision Committee had to face over 130 amendments, involving four days of interviews and a considerable correspondence. The changes it proposed were, however, very modest. The most significant were a reduction in the number of alternatives and a slight move away from Series 1 towards Series 3, in the prayers for the departed, in the position of the Peace, and in the Proper Prefaces. All these were acceptable to the General Synod in February 1976 and Provisional Approval was readily given.[57]

On this occasion, however, the Final Approval stage was not the usual formality, the House of Clergy only approving the rite by a single vote. This action may have been partly due to a lurking fear in some people's minds that the existence of the new rite side by side with Series 1 and Series 2 would cause confusion; but it was also due to a measure of disapproval of what appeared to be rather high-handed behaviour on the part of the House of Bishops. The text of the Prayer of Humble Access in the original proposals was the abbreviated form from Series 2, omitting the lines 'that our sinful bodies . . . precious blood', although a note permitted the use of the original 1662 text if so desired. Attempts had been made, both in the Revision Committee and in the Synod itself, to change the definitive text to the 1662 form, but on both occasions it had been decisively defeated.[58] Despite these clear expressions of opinion, and only by the narrowest of majorities in their own House (19–18), the Bishops had restored the 1662 lines. Disapproval of such action at this stage could only be shown by voting against the entire rite or by abstaining, and some clergy had undoubtedly taken this rather drastic action.[59] Despite its shaky start, however, the rite soon won its way. Users of Series 1 and Series 2 were quick to appreciate its advantages in flexibility and richness of material; and when the time came to include a rite in traditional language in the Alternative Service Book, it was this rite which was chosen.

Collects, about which something has already been said,[60] were another victim of the bottleneck in synodical agendas. Although completed in 1974, they were not introduced until July 1975, at the same time as Holy Communion 1 and 2 revised.[61] Once they appeared, however, the Synod welcomed them with incredible speed, remitting them to a Revision Committee after a debate of precisely nine minutes.[62] Although only seven members submitted amendments, there were over 120 separate proposals to consider, of which 88 came from Mr Oswald Clark, intent on restoring as much 1662 material as possible.[63] However, the Revision Committee's report (GS 2307) proved to be commendably restrained and constructive. More than half the proposed amendments were rejected; a number of collects were improved; only two completely new collects were introduced; and six more from 1662 were restored, two as additions to those already proposed (Good Friday and Easter Day). Out of a total of 127 collects, therefore, representing one of the Liturgical Commission's most difficult and delicate pieces of work, the proposed changes made were modest. The General Synod examined them with some care in July 1976, but made only three major changes, restoring two of the Commission's original collects and adding one more from 1662. Final Approval was given in November.[64]

III

No attempt at revision of the Marriage Service had been made in the Series 2 programme, the only alternative to 1662 being the Series 1–1928 order. Here the bride was no longer required to 'obey' her husband and the language of the preface was modified, although the reasons for marriage were retained in the same order: the procreation of children, the hallowing of sexuality and the mutual society and comfort of the two parties. Nevertheless, this lack of a new rite did not mean that the marriage question had not been discussed by the Church. In the face of the growing prevalence of divorce the Archbishop of Canterbury had appointed a commission under Dr Mortimer, Bishop of Exeter, which in 1966 had published the report *Putting Asunder*, proposing the abolition of the matrimonial offence as the ground for divorce and the substitution of the irretrievable breakdown of marriage. This met with appreciative comment in the Law Commission's report *The Field of Choice* (1966), and the Divorce Reform Act of 1969 followed, making effective what *Putting Asunder* had proposed. Admittedly this had simply involved the law in secular society; but the Church was bound to take cognizance of the change and examine its own position.[65] A motion in the

Convocation of Canterbury in October 1967 by Dr Charles-Edwards, Bishop of Worcester, for a reconsideration of the discipline of the Church of England was defeated on the grounds that such reconsideration could only follow a fresh examination of the Church's doctrine of marriage. The Archbishop therefore appointed another commission under Professor Howard Root of Southampton University to undertake this and it reported in 1971 in *Marriage, Divorce and the Church.*[66] Its unanimous decision, that the marriage of divorced persons in Church was 'compatible with reason, the word of God in Scripture, and theological tradition', inevitably aroused controversy when discussed in the General Synod, but its suggestions for a revision of the marriage rite met with warm approval.[67] It clearly believed that revision was desirable despite the presence of problems. There was, for example, the problem of language: it 'must *sound* right . . . it must be the language of symbolism, of worship, not of flat description . . . its roots must remain deep in tradition':[68] furthermore it could not ignore the fact that 1662 was deeply engrained in English life, containing 'probably the oldest and longest sequence of middle English phrases and constructions ever occurring in the lives of most people and actually spoken by them'.[69] They were not to be jettisoned lightly. The report then went on to indicate some of the features which should be included in a new rite: that marriage was a personal relationship in which the community had an interest, that it was God's gift of a new relationship, and that it was a means of grace to the Church as well as to the couple – 'They create an occasion of Christ's presence to his people.'[70] It then questioned whether 1662 set out the purposes of marriage in their true order, and whether it was still right to ask the modern wife to 'obey' or whether 'obey' was the right word.[71] Complementarity rather than subordination was the mark of a good marriage, a point of view subsequently endorsed by a survey of the Church's Board of Social Responsibility *Marriage and the Family in Britain Today* (1974) and a statement prepared for the Mothers' Union by Dr J. Dominian, *The Marriage Relationship Today* (1974).

Meanwhile the Liturgical Commission had not ignored the subject. As early as 1966 Ronnie Beddoes, the Provost of Derby, had conducted a local survey which had revealed three facts: considerable dissatisfaction with both 1662 and 1928 prefaces, a deep rooting of certain parts of the service in the English consciousness, and a need for a different emphasis due to the changed status of women.[72] From this had emerged a memorandum to the Bishops, setting out a number of questions which the Commission felt needed answering before work started on a new rite. The appointment of the Root Commission had followed shortly afterwards,[73] and there matters rested until 1971. Furnished with the recommendations in *Marriage, Divorce and the Church*, the Liturgical Commission then worked away for over two years, receiving considerable help from Helen Oppenheimer and Elisabeth Montefiore's husband, Hugh,[74] both of whom had served on the Root Commission. As expected, the new preface proved extraordinarily difficult to construct, and Elisabeth Montefiore was indefatigable in getting the wording absolutely right, seeking advice from a variety of literary people. There were also quite lengthy negotiations with the Law Commission to ensure that what was proposed met with the necessary legal requirements. It was December 1974 when the Commission was finally in a position to submit its proposals to the Bishops: and despite their rapid approval in January 1975, the report then hit the synodical bottleneck. It was not until November 1975 that *The Wedding Service Series 3* (GS 228) was submitted to the General Synod for general consideration.

The structure of the proposed rite remained identical with that of 1662, but there was increased flexibility when combined with the Eucharist: it could either precede the Eucharist in the traditional manner or it could come within the Eucharist. A great deal of traditional phraseology was also retained, particularly in the vows, for it was recognized that this had 'sunk so deeply into English life'.[75] Nevertheless the ethos of the rite had significantly changed. A shorter preface reversed the 1662 order of the purposes of marriage, putting mutual help and comfort first and the procreation and care of children third – an order incidentally which Martin Bucer had favoured as long ago as 1551 in his *Censura.*[76] The consent and the vows were still adapted versions of the old, but the husband was no longer seen as the head of the family and his wife as subordinate. Bride and bridegroom faced each other as equals; there was no obligation for the bride to be given away; and the vows of both were identical. Nevertheless, for those who preferred a more traditional view, the bride could still include 'obey' in her vows. Similarly, rings could be exchanged or the bridegroom alone could give a ring. The couple clearly married one another and they were the real ministers of the sacrament. The marriage concluded with a responsorial form of the *berakoth* used at Jewish weddings, which not only gave the families and friends a small but vocal part but added an element of joy to the proceedings. Finally the couple were encouraged to write or select their own concluding prayers in co-operation with the priest.

The initial debate in the Synod was brief;[77] but it was in the Revision Committee that problems again arose. Over 150 amendments were submitted; the correspondence was enormous; and every sentence was subjected to microscopic scrutiny. An exercise, initially expected to last a couple of days, eventually dragged on for a whole year; and the Provisional Approval stage was not taken until November 1976. While not denying that improvements were made, they were not so fundamental as to require this expenditure of time and money. It was not surprising that questions were asked in General Synod.[78]

1. The title was changed to *The Marriage Service.*
2. A reading from Scripture was made mandatory on all occasions.
3. The Preface, although modified in language, in essence remained unchanged.
4. An alternative set of Vows was included, in which the bride's

undertaking to obey was matched by the bridegroom's undertaking to worship.

5. A mistranslation in the declaration was corrected – 'That which God has joined together, let not man divide.'[79]

If the revision process had its shortcomings, so did the ensuing debate in the Synod. It was literally 'fitted in' between other items of business in three half-hour sessions, and finally had to wait until February 1977 for completion. There was no sense of continuity and there was even a protest from the floor of the house at the way the business was handled. Happily the Synod was not disposed to make further radical change, and the service received Final Approval in July, over six years after the Liturgical Commission had completed its first draft.[80]

IV

The revision of the Calendar, the Lectionaries and the Rules to Order the Service was a massive and complicated operation, undertaken piecemeal over a period of years. The first stage was to append a new office lectionary to Morning and Evening Prayer Series 2 revised and a new eucharistic lectionary to Holy Communion Series 3.[81] Both were based on the JLG proposals but modified to fit the existing Calendar. They were therefore short-term expedients, containing anomalies and inconsistencies, and creating problems for the producers of annual Church Calendars. In the face of criticism all we could do was to counsel patience until a comprehensive set of proposals appeared. The next stage, and again a temporary one, was to produce some Rules to Order the Service under Section 4 of the Prayer Book (Further Provisions Measure) in 1972. These Rules (GS 85) had first appeared in the Commission's 1969 report, *The Calendar and Lessons for the Church's Year*, setting out the guidelines governing Concurrences and Occurrences.[82] 1662 had not included such guidelines; and an attempt to remedy the omission in 1880 had failed.[83] 1928 had also provided a set of Rules, but this too had never been authorized. The Church had therefore tended to muddle along, using the 1928 provision as an unofficial basis and with Church Calendars sometimes offering conflicting advice. From a legal point of view the absence of official guidance could create some interesting problems. For example, if Palm Sunday or Easter Day fell on 25 March, either could be given second place to the feast of the Annunciation; and a bishop could not be consecrated on a Holy Day which had been unofficially transferred. The 1972 proposals in GS 85 endeavoured to establish four important principles:

1. To emphasize the importance of Sunday as a weekly memorial of our Lord's resurrection, as set out in Canon B6.
2. To ensure that Saints' Days did not fall into neglect.
3. To produce consistency in the transfer of Saints' Days from a Sunday.

4. To encourage one Evensong only for Holy Days, as set out in the Lambeth 1958 recommendations.

This was accepted, virtually without comment,[84] and was followed almost immediately by the next stage in early 1973.

Obviously nothing final could be settled about lectionaries or collects or even the Rules until the General Synod had given some indication as to whether it was prepared to endorse the rather radical JLG proposals on the Calendar. The Liturgical Commission therefore produced in January 1973 Report GS 125, *The Calendar, and Lectionary problems related to the Calendar*, proposing a pre-Christmas season of nine Sundays, eliminating the Epiphany season in favour of Sundays after Christmas and the '-gesima' pre-Lent Sundays in favour of Sundays before Easter, and substituting the title 'Pentecost' for all Sundays after Whitsun. Despite the fact that such proposals had already been authorized for use both at home and overseas by a number of Free Churches and Anglican provinces,[85] they met with spirited opposition from such traditionalists as Michael Moreton, who argued that such proposals would separate the Church of England from Rome and the Orthodox Churches and constitute a break with ancient liturgical and theological traditions.[86] Not surprisingly the Synod compromised. A plea to produce a Lectionary on the existing traditional calendar was defeated; but the Commission was asked to modify some of its proposals, notably by reconsidering those for the post-Christmas-Epiphany period and by retaining the title 'Trinity'.[87] It was a price that I for one was quite prepared to pay.

So began the massive operation of completing the Calendar, revising and integrating the lectionaries of both Office and Eucharist into one coherent system, producing appropriate courses of psalmody, revising the Rules, and drawing up tables of moveable feasts and the dates of Easter for the next fifty years. It was a complicated and tedious business, involving constant checking and cross-checking and requiring a capacity to carry an immense amount of detail in the mind. Fortunately the ideal person to do all this was available in Charles Whitaker, who had the necessary patience and diligence; although regarded as the Commission's expert on Initiation matters, he shouldered this additional burden without demur; and it was with good reason that the Commission regarded the resulting report as 'Whitaker's Almanac'. For the whole of 1974 and 1975 he beavered away, and eventually, with the endorsement of the Commission and the approval of the Bishops, GS 292, *The Calendar, Lectionary and Rules to Order the Service*, was published in June 1976. The Synod did not consider it until February 1977 but, recognizing that detailed material of this kind could be dealt with more appropriately by a committee and having already expressed its views on the general principles, wasted no time in submitting it to the Revision Committee stage.[88]

Here the members had a veritable field-day. Their report can speak for itself:

> More than 350 individual proposals for the amendment of the draft Calendar alone were received from members of the Synod . . . Very many more were received for the amendment of the draft Lectionary: indeed one member of Synod submitted 96 proposals. In addition the Committee took note of suggestions made during the debate of the General Consideration stage and by correspondents who were not members of the Synod.[89]

In all they spent some fifteen days – as long as the General Synod spent on its whole agenda for a year – dealing with nearly 1,000 proposals and it was not until December that their report was completed. Fortunately they had a first-class chairman in Dr Margaret Hewitt, who with a clear head and a firm hand dealt with the detailed business superbly. Charles Whitaker was also of tremendous value behind the scenes, making sure that proposed changes did not create more problems than they solved. What finally emerged was a series of proposals which, though involving a number of changes in detail, left the basic principles intact.

The Calendar

> The Epiphany was added to the Principal Holy Days; Whit Sunday became Pentecost with the old name retained as a subsidiary title; the dates of the Feasts of St Matthias (February 24) and St Thomas (December 21) were changed to May 14 and July 3 respectively, falling into line with the Roman Catholic Church and a number of Anglican Churches; and the two lists of Lesser Holy Days submitted for discussion by the Liturgical Commission were coalesced into one.

The Lectionary

> Here the most significant change was an accommodation of readings from Genesis and Exodus in both Office and Eucharist in the pre-Lent and Lent seasons in deference to the traditionalists.[90]

When the report was considered by the General Synod in February 1978 three further changes were made: Pentecost became the primary title for Sundays after Trinity, despite a previous decision to the contrary; the date of the Feast of the Blessed Virgin Mary was changed from 15 August (the traditional date of the Feast of the Assumption) to 8 September (the 1662 date for the Nativity of the Blessed Virgin Mary) in the hope of avoiding doctrinal problems; and four names were added to the Lesser Holy Days – Catherine of Siena, Queen Margaret of Scotland, Martin of Tours and King Edward of East Anglia. Josephine Butler was only rejected by 117 votes to 120, a decision which subsequently had interesting repercussions.[91]

When the proposals came in for Final Approval in July, the Bishops, as they were constitutionally empowered to do, restored Josephine Butler to the list of Lesser Holy Days, mainly on the grounds that she had been a clergyman's wife, and this was a small way of recognizing the devoted service of clergy wives to the Church. Nevertheless, some members of

Synod, including Dr Hewitt, objected to the Bishops overturning a synodical decision, narrow though it may have been. Moreover, there was no way in which the decision could be reversed except by rejecting the whole measure — an expedient for which there was obviously no desire. The annoyance was reflected in the unusually large number of abstentions from voting, although the majorities in favour were still comfortable; nor was the Bishops' action easily forgotten.[92] The Church of England had now acquired a Calendar and Lectionary together with various Rules, providing a richer and more flexible alternative to those already in use:

1. The Temporale was clearly based on the three foci of Christmas, Easter and Pentecost, with greater emphasis on every Sunday being a festival of our Lord.
2. The Sanctorale provided an increase of both Greater and Lesser Holy Days with a further provision for their observance on an optional basis; encouragement was also given to create diocesan observances.
3. There was a two-yearly Lectionary for both Office and Eucharist, with guidance on the interchangeability of readings. It recognized, too, that the average layperson went to church once a week — on Sundays — and while most preferred the Eucharist, for many Morning or Evening Prayer was still the staple diet.
4. Psalmody was provided for both Office and Eucharist on all occasions; in the Office it could be used on a ten-week or four-week basis, and there was a distinct provision for Sundays.
5. For the first time Rules gave clear guidance on questions of Occurrences and Concurrences and the use of collects and prefaces.

The omission in this new system was a daily eucharistic lectionary; but this did not indicate any reluctance on the part of the Liturgical Commission to provide one. We had already recognized that some people would be prepared to accept the view expressed at Lambeth 1968 that the Office could be used as an ante-communion service; while for those who wished to keep the two services distinct, the office readings for the year not in use could be used for the Eucharist. But in addition to this we had produced in 1976 a separate eucharistic lectionary, largely worked out by David Silk, one of our new members.[93] It was quite an ingenious piece of work, based on the new Roman Daily Lectionary, but geared into the system set out in GS 292. Hoping for its inclusion in GS 292 as a supplement, we submitted it to the Bishops in September 1976.[94] Unfortunately they rejected it as unnecessary, since the Roman Lectionary was already available in print, and ignored the fact that in its printed form the latter simply did not fit the lectionary system so carefully worked out in GS 292. Instead they apparently passed by 30 votes to 10 a proposal that a rubric should be inserted in GS 292 permitting the use of the Roman Lectionary on those days for which no provision was made. Apparently nothing was done about this, so the Reverend Brian Brindley put down a Private Member's motion in the

General Synod to the same effect, which finally resulted in the Commission being asked to prepare a Daily Eucharistic Lectionary for optional use from the readings in the Roman Lectionary.[95] This was, of course, more radical than the Commission's original plan, in that the Roman readings would be read on the same day in both Churches. Once again David Silk undertook the drafting, although he warned the Synod in February 1978 that it was by no mean ideal. It certainly gave the Church of England the opportunity to use a book already in print and to use the same texts on the same day; nevertheless one could not alter the fact that it was based on a different calendar and different principles, involving at times clashes between Office and Eucharist. I bitterly regretted the system by which the Bishops' rejection of the Commission's original proposals prevented the Church from ever seeing them let alone examining them; the suppression of material for the sake of convenience is not the right way to construct good liturgy. It was a small crumb of comfort to know that my regret was shared by some members of the General Synod.[96] When the new proposals were presented for General Consideration in February 1979, the timetable was already becoming tight if the material were to be included in ASB. There was therefore no Revision Committee stage, and both Provisional Approval and Final Approval were given in July and November respectively virtually without debate.[97]

V

As early as September 1967 the Liturgical Commission had examined the Draft Anglican–Methodist Ordinal and expressed its approval: 'In general the Commission expressed itself as most grateful for this rite and commended it highly. They considered that it should be acceptable to all Anglicans, and they agreed unanimously that it was a considerable improvement on the Ordinal in the Book of Common Prayer.'[98] This favourable comment was not surprising. The Draft Anglican–Methodist Ordinal had owed much to the earlier CSI Ordinal, which had won high praise from liturgical scholars, including Edward Ratcliff, who, in reviewing it in 1960, had expressed the hope that 'any Church of the Anglican Communion proposing to revise its ordination rites will turn for guidance to the rites of South India'.[99] This advice had subsequently been followed, not only by a number of Churches, but by the group which produced the A–M Ordinal. On that group the Anglican members had been Dr Eric Kemp, Dr James Packer, and three members of the Liturgical Commission: Ratcliff, Couratin and myself. Ratcliff had in fact been the principal draftsman.

There had been no Series 1 or Series 2 Ordinal; and when the Bishops asked the Commission to start work on a Series 3 rite in early 1973 I suggested to Michael Ramsey that it would really be a sensible thing to use the A–M document as our basis, particularly as it had been overwhelmingly endorsed by the Convocations in May 1969 (312 votes to 16). He readily agreed, but with one caveat: anything we did must not impair Anglican–

Roman Catholic relations.[100] There was in fact little danger of that, for the A–M Ordinal had already been sent to the English Roman Catholic authorities for an opinion in 1968, and they through Fr B. Leeming had replied, 'It seems immune from the objections which Catholics found in the 1552 Ordinal and it seems sufficient in itself to confer true ordination.'[101] I did, however, consult Bishop Gordon Wheeler and subsequently discussed the matter with the Joint Liturgical Group in September. Here three points were agreed:

1. That at the moment an ecumenical Ordinal was not a practical possibility.
2. That the A–M Ordinal provided an excellent basis for a new Ordinal.
3. That everyone, while doing their own work, should be helped by 'mutual consultation and influence'.[102]

By the autumn the Commission had sufficient material to start work. In particular there were some valuable notes which Ratcliff had produced in 1965 when working on the A–M Ordinal: 'Now is the time to finish with Anglican forms and their mistakes and to turn to simpler and older patterns which are clear as to meaning and not open to objections on the ground of "prelacy".'[103] Then there was a series of questions drawn up by Geoffrey Cuming, whom I had asked to be responsible for drafting: the relation of the imposition of hands to the ordination prayer, the real significance of the *Veni Creator*, the significance of the giving of the Bible, the place of vesting and the *porrectio instrumentorum*, and the length of the exhortation.[104] After spending the whole of 1974 in drafting, he submitted his proposals to the Commission in March 1975. Revision took another nine months; and the texts were finally ready to send to the Bishops by the end of the year. In view of their close involvement with these services and because the Ordinal was regarded as an important element in Anglican doctrine, particularly in the light of current ecumenical discussions on the Ten Propositions of the Churches' Unity Commission,[105] the Bishops decided to remit them in the first instance to a small expert committee of their own number (the Bishops of Durham, Chichester, Derby and Worcester), who would then consult with a similar small group from the Commission (Geoffrey Cuming, Cyril Taylor and myself). These two groups eventually met in May 1976, while copies were sent out to the Churches represented on the Unity Commission for comment.[106] Further discussion and revision followed; and the House of Bishops finally agreed the texts in January 1977 (GS 327, *Ordination Services Series 3*).

The Ordinal comprised four rites: the ordination of Deacons, Priests, Bishops, and Deacons and Priests together. All were based on the Anglican–Methodist Ordinal and were identical in structure, embodying the principle that the essential form and matter of ordination was prayer with the imposition of hands, preceded by the assent and prayer of the people. The Litany, omitted in the Anglican–Methodist Ordinal, was restored, in conformity with ancient tradition, to a place immediately preceding the ordination prayer. This meant that, unlike 1662, *Veni Creator* was no longer associated with the ordination prayer itself, but preceded the Litany. Another departure from 1662 and following primitive custom was the imposition of hands on all candidates during the ordination prayer, a petition for the gift of the Holy Spirit being repeated over each candidate. Ordination therefore clearly involved a prayer addressed to God and not an imperative formula addressed to the candidate. Another distinctive feature was the giving of a pastoral staff to the new bishop, not as an essential element in the conferring of orders, like the medieval *porrectio instrumentorum*, but as a supplementary ceremony, indicating the bishop's pastoral office.

On this occasion Geoffrey Cuming, as the Commission's draftsman, acted as chairman of the Steering Committee and introduced the proposals to the Synod in July. He pointed out that the Commission had been fortunate in having a wealth of material at its disposal in the shape of ecumenical statements on the ministry and several new Ordinals from other Churches; it had, moreover, consulted widely, not least with those Churches involved in the Churches' Unity Commission. In fact a draft of their Common Ordinal had just appeared, although it was still incomplete. If, therefore, the Synod felt inspired to make improvements in what the Liturgical Commission now proposed, there was still opportunity to do so in the Revision Committee.[107] The Synod's desires for change were relatively modest, however, some 150 amendments being submitted, and none of these being of major importance. Of the amendments agreed, two deserve mention:

1. The inclusion of a new opening collect common to all rites, and the addition of post-communion collects for all three orders.
2. The insertion of notes permitting the vesting of the newly ordained, and the presentation of the 'symbols of the priest's or of the bishop's office', but only if 'it is so agreed'.

The Revision Committee also decided against incorporating any elements from the proposed Common Ordinal, partly because it contained nothing which appeared to be any improvement on what the Liturgical Commission proposed, and partly because the structure of both sets of proposals was similar.[108] When the General Synod examined the revision in January 1978, two further amendments to the Notes were made. The first permitted the newly ordained 'to exercise their new ministry in the course of the service', if invited to do so by the bishop. Specifically how this should be done was not indicated; but it was clearly intended as giving priests permission to concelebrate. The second specifically mentioned the symbols of office which could be offered to priests – chalice and paten; and to bishops – the pastoral staff. The rubric originally permitting the latter was therefore removed from the rite itself. Final Approval was given by overwhelming majorities in July.[109]

The Church had therefore acquired an alternative Ordinal by a combination of the old and the new. There was considerable borrowing from the Anglican–Methodist and South Indian Ordinals, with the rites following primitive models. On the other hand, where possible familiar material was still retained: the questions to the candidates together with the declaration of the duties of the priest drew heavily from 1662, which in its turn used Bucer's *De Ordinatione Legitima*, while Cosin's version of *Veni Creator* from 1662 was also included. This judicious blend of material, together with greater freedom in the choice of readings and the conduct of the services, once again provided greater and welcome flexibility.

VI

The authorization of the Series 2 Initiation Services in 1967–8 did not end discussion on the subject. Indeed I had hinted at the possibility of future debate at the Liturgical Conference in April 1967: 'If the Church wishes to establish some new pattern of initiation, then the Church it is which will first have to make decisions on fundamental principles and perhaps even amend the canons before the Commission can get to work and produce the necessary forms.'[110] Discussions therefore continued in the Convocations and the House of Laity, resulting in the appointment of a commission under the Bishop of Ely (Dr E. Roberts) in October 1969 to consider the pastoral and theological problems concerned with Confirmation and admission to Holy Communion, while Infant Baptism was referred to the Doctrine Commission.[111] Both bodies reported in 1971, the Ely Commission in June (GS 30, *Christian Initiation: Birth and Growth in the Christian Society*); and the Doctrine Commission in October (GS 56, *Baptism Thanksgiving and Blessing*). The former made five important proposals:

1. The Church should make explicit its recognition of Baptism as the full and complete rite of Christian initiation.
2. There should be a new rite of Thanksgiving after Childbirth, with the clear understanding that it was not a substitute for baptism.
3. People could be admitted to Holy Communion after baptism, at the parish priest's discretion.
4. Confirmation should continue to be a service of commitment and commissioning for adults.
5. Those baptized as adults should not be presented for Confirmation.[112]

The Doctrine Commission agreed with these recommendations but suggested rather more for the new service of Thanksgiving; it should be a Service of Thanksgiving and Blessing, it should be available to all who asked for it, and hopefully it should be a stepping-stone to baptism.[113]

Initial reactions indicated that the proposals were regarded as controversial and would require further study, particularly at local level. Discussions continued for the next two years; and it was not until 1974 that the situation became sufficiently clear for further progress to be made. After lengthy debates in the General Synod in February and July, it became evident that the main proposal in the Ely Report — the recognition of baptism as the full and complete rite of Christian initiation — was not acceptable as the only view to be held within the Church of England. Three decisions were therefore made:

1. Infant baptism should continue to be available to the children of all parents who requested it and were willing and able to make the requisite promises.
2. The dioceses were to be consulted on the need for
   a. a Service of Thanksgiving for the Birth of a Child
   b. a Service of Blessing a Child

   on the clear understanding that these would be distinct from and not alternative to baptism.
3. The dioceses were also to be consulted on two possible alternatives, bearing in mind the divergent theological understandings of Christian initiation:
   a. That baptized persons might be admitted to Holy Communion at the discretion of the parish priest in consultation with the bishop, followed later by Confirmation at the hands of the bishop.
   b. That Baptism, accompanied by the imposition of hands and/or anointing with oil, might be followed by admission to Holy Communion at the discretion of the parish priest, with provision, where appropriate, for a later affirmation of the baptismal promises accompanied by the imposition of hands.[114]

The dioceses reported their findings in early 1976; and they were heavily weighted in favour of a policy of no change, a policy endorsed by the General Synod in July 1976. All that emerged was a decision to proceed with a new Service of Thanksgiving for the Birth of a Child, and approval for the lowering of the age of confirmation. It was little to show for five years of discussion.[115]

Meanwhile the Liturgical Commission had not been idle. As early as 1970 a useful exercise was undertaken through the diocesan liturgical committees to discover parochial reactions to the Series 2 services. It was on a modest scale; but 36 dioceses co-operated in securing a clear expression of warm approval: the rites were clear, straightforward and far preferable to those of 1662 and 1928; both Baptism and Confirmation were still normally used as separate services, but the number of occasions when they were combined with the Eucharist was increasing steadily. The Commission began work with Charles Whitaker as draftsman in the summer of 1971, just as the Ely and Doctrine Commissions' reports appeared, and by March 1973 revised texts were ready for publication.[116] The Bishops felt, however, that it would be wise to postpone further action until the Church had declared its mind on the two reports. The rites were therefore put into cold storage for some twelve months, by which time the Synod was experiencing the bottleneck in its agenda. In July 1974, on the initiative of its Policy Sub-Committee, an attempt was made to expedite matters. Since the decision had just been made to leave the Baptism of Infants generally available to the Church, thereby putting it outside the scope of the forthcoming Initiation debates, it was decided to detach it from the Commission's proposals and proceed with it independently. The Commission agreed, but with reluctance and considerable misgiving: it was putting the cart before the horse, with the danger of creating confusion and wasting even more time in the future. The proposal came to nothing, however. Although the rite was placed on the Synod's agenda in July and in November 1975, it was squeezed out on both occasions, and by early 1976 the Diocesan Replies were due to be published. The idea was therefore dropped.

In the light of the Synod's decision of 'No change' in July 1976, the Commission submitted its final proposals to the Bishops in the autumn of that year, though not without a hiccough. Some members of the Commission, and particularly Colin Buchanan, still wished to maintain the sufficiency of baptism and the non-essentiality of confirmation, even mooting the possibility of including a Note of Dissent in the Report. This I wanted to avoid at all costs: the timetable for the Alternative Service Book was already getting uncomfortably tight, and anything provoking undue debate and delay could be disastrous. Eventually, with help from Geoffrey Cuming, I produced a form of words for inclusion in the Introduction, which the entire Commission was prepared to accept:

> Recent debates on initiation did not directly touch the question of initiating adults in this two-stage manner [i.e. Baptism and then Confirmation]: and in July 1976 the General Synod voted, in a proportion of three votes to two, to keep the present practice in regard to confirmation. The Commission clearly accepts this decision; although some of its members regret it and would prefer to see baptism itself to be the liturgical climax of initiation — particularly in the case of adults. As far as confirmation for those who have been baptized in infancy is concerned, a case can certainly be made for keeping it. But problems do arise when attempting to justify the confirmation of adults who have just been baptized: and the number of such people is increasing. Some members of the Commission feel that the time has come when this issue must be faced.[117]

Unfortunately the Bishops decided to delete these very sentences, which had been the result of such delicate negotiation. I promptly sent off a pretty stiff remonstrance to the Archbishop, who happily came to the rescue, and the sentences were restored.[118] The Bishops also did not share the Commission's insistence on linking the profession of faith to the actual baptism, particularly at a service where there were both baptism and confirmation candidates and the latter might be in a different part of the church when the profession was required. This problem was solved by the insertion of a note permitting the ordering of the service to be determined by the bishop and the parish priest. The report (GS 343) was finally published on 18 August, just in time for the statutory two months' notice before consideration by the General Synod in November. It contained a far more comprehensive set of services than had appeared in Series 2. In addition to Baptism and Confirmation, there was Thanksgiving for the Birth of a Child, Thanksgiving after Adoption, Renewal of Baptismal Vows, Conditional Baptism and Emergency Baptism, and Prayers after the Death of a newly-born Child or a Stillbirth. There was also an interesting Note on the Use of Chrism, indicating a change of mind in the Church. In its 1958 report the Commission had stated that it did not consider a permissive use of oil before baptism or of chrism after baptism or confirmation would command any widespread support. The Ely report, however, had commended its use as a ceremony which would enhance the central act of baptism if carried out with skill and imagination. Here, however, the Commission, recognizing that the Church had not declared its mind, made no provision for it but held out possibilities of its future use.[119] Structurally there was little change in the main Initiation rites from those in Series 2, and the General Synod had few comments or criticisms before referring them to a Revision Committee.[120] The customary pattern then became obvious, some fifty members submitting nearly 350 amendments. Fortunately the committee again had a strong chairman in the Bishop of Southwark (Mervyn Stockwood), a former member of the Commission with a particular interest in initiation. Its work was completed in six days, although the revised rites and the accompanying report were not considered by the Synod until November 1978. Four important changes were proposed.

1. The committee decided to retain confirmation for those baptized as adults: to have done otherwise would have implied an important change in Anglican doctrine which it regarded as beyond its terms of reference.
2. It provided for the optional use of chrism. Since the services were unlikely to be revised again for some years, perhaps not before 1990, it felt that the Church should not be deprived of the opportunity of experimental use.
3. It transferred consignation from after baptism to the decision, although the former position remained an option. This was a move which Charles Whitaker had always urged, for it clearly indicated that consignation was not to be regarded as part of the sacrament.
4. It transferred the Prayers after the Death of a newly-born Child or a Stillbirth to the Funeral Services — a more appropriate place.[121]

On this occasion the Synod debate proved to be quite a lengthy and lively affair, with attempts made to overturn the changes made by the Revision Committee. These all failed, however, and both Provisional and Final approval were secured without difficulty by February 1979.[122] The Church was therefore provided with a considerably enriched and improved set of Initiation services. Despite the initial stormy reception, many of the principles set out in the Commission's 1958 report were finally vindicated. A return to primitive patterns was combined with a praiseworthy attempt to provide for the situations of twentieth-century life. There was recognition that Christian Initiation involved more than a social formality and was expected to be taken seriously. Nevertheless at the same time those people who were not prepared to undertake full Christian commitment either for themselves or for their children were not ignored but encouraged to take at least a first step towards baptism. While it was a disappointment to many that the findings of the Ely Report did not find liturgical expression, the whole pattern of Christian Initiation acquired a new ethos which gave promise of further study and possible change in the future.

The Commission had now completed the range of Series 3 services to be included in The Alternative Service Book. The operation had taken much longer than originally envisaged. At one stage we had hoped to be finished by December 1975, when the term of office of existing members came to an end; but circumstances beyond our control demanded another five years' work. As events proved, this was no bad thing. The projected publication date of November 1980 still produced an uncomfortably tight schedule; and many of the new services eventually went into the book with little or no experimental use and certainly no revision in the light of experience. In fact only one service was revised — Holy Communion. This proved to be a major operation, influencing the texts of other services throughout the book at a number of points. This final piece of revision should therefore be seen, not as an entirely self-contained project, but as part of the final work of preparation for the book as a whole.

NOTES

1. *Liturgical Commission Minutes* 59.12.
2. ibid., 61.37; *LC Memorandum* 104 B.
3. WCC, *The Eucharist in Ecumenical Thought*, 1968, para. 4.
4. ibid., para. 3.
5. C. O. Buchanan, E. L. Mascall, J. I. Packer, G. D. Leonard, *Growing into Union*, 1970.
6. ibid., p. 189.
7. ibid., p. 191.
8. A. Clark and H. R. McAdoo, *Modern Eucharistic Agreement*, 1973. The Windsor Statement, para. 5, pp. 27–8.
9. e.g. J. W. Charley, *The Anglican-Roman Catholic Agreement on the Eucharist*, 1971; articles in *Faith and Unity*, July 1972, vol. XVI, no. 3; R. J. Beckwith, *Christ's Presence and Sacrifice*, 1973.
10. Clark and McAdoo, p. 5.
11. ibid., p. 12.
12. See his valuable essay on 'Sacrifice and Eucharist', in *Thinking about the Eucharist*, 1972, pp. 81–98. This was a development of his earlier essay on 'We offer this bread and this cup', in *Theology*, October 1966.

13. Kenneth Ross had been well known as Vicar of All Saints, Margaret Street, and had recently become a Canon residentiary of Wells Cathedral.
14. Michael Cantuar to R.C.D.J., 25 July 1970.
15. Two people who were particularly helpful with comments and suggestions at this stage were Christopher Macgregor of Cambridge and Robert Cockcroft of Nottingham University.
16. On this occasion through pressure of time the Bishops were asked to send in their comments by post; and these reactions emerged from the letters we received (R.C.D.J. to Michael Cantuar, 28 May 1971). Possibly reactions might have been different if the Bishops had met and discussed the proposals as a group.
17. *LC Minutes* 58.5; 59.14. *LC Memorandum* 95 C. When I consulted the Archbishops in September 1969, both preferred a statement to silence. I think it would be true to say that the Liturgical Commission was so evenly divided on the matter that the chairman's casting vote would have been necessary for a decision. I personally favoured a statement.
18. LC, *A Commentary on Holy Communion Series Three*, 1971, p. 29.
19. He had done work for the Consumers' Council, the Post Office, and the University of Aston, and he had staged exhibitions in various American Universities and at the British Embassy in Washington. His church work included commissions for the GFS, the SPG and the Bible Reading Fellowship.
20. *The Church Times*, 17 September 1971.
21. *The Church of England Newspaper*, 17 September 1971.
22. *The Tablet*, 9 October 1971; *Life and Worship*, October 1971. I also sent copies of Series 3 to the Vatican with a request for comments. In due course two replies arrived, one from Fr J. Gelineau in Paris and the other from Professor E. J. Lengeling in Münster. The former wrote, 'Trés sincèrement je n'ai que de l'admiration pour cette réalisation. Il me semble un modèle d'anaphore christologique, dans la ligne de l'anaphore de la Tradition Apostolique, heureusement ajusté à l'usage actuel. J'y trouve tout l'essentiel de la tradition, dans la structure, l'énoncé et le genre littéraire.' The latter wrote, 'Ich bin besonders erfreut über den Gesamt-Ductus des Textes. Die Anamnese and die Annahme-bitten "Accept" freuen mich in ökumenischer Sicht.' These replies obviously gave the Commission considerable encouragement.
23. *The Catholic Standard*, December 1971; M. Moreton, 'A Liturgical Pastiche', *Theology* LXXV (February 1972), pp. 79–83.
24. *GS Proceedings*, 1971, vol. 2, pp. 618–23.
25. ibid., pp. 623–54; D. Frost, *The Language of Series 3*, 1973, p. 17.
26. *GS Proceedings*, 1971, vol. 2, pp. 697, 699.
27. In fact, both the Confession and the Prayer of Humble Access eventually found their way into the *Alternative Service Book* in 1980.
28. *The Church Times*, 19 and 26 November 1971. For further details of the debate and some lively comment on it, see *GS Proceedings*, 1971, vol. 2, pp. 653–71, 681–700; Frost, *The Language of Series 3*, pp. 17–23.
29. cf. its earlier proposals on Initiation.
30. *GS Proceedings*, 1972, vol. 3, pp. 27–31.
31. ibid., pp. 151–61.
32. ibid., pp. 31–8.
33. ibid., pp. 185–9.
34. *LC Minutes* 70.2.
35. *GS Proceedings*, 1972, vol. 3, pp. 505–12, 539–66.

36. The voting was: Bishops 27–0; Clergy 148–10; Laity 123–9; ibid., p. 580.
37. The most notable were: Michael Perry, *Sharing One Bread*; Paul Bradshaw, *In Remembrance of Me*; George Reindorp, *Holy Communion Series 3*; Peter Dale, *A Guide to Series 3* (Grove Books No. 10); and Margaret Stevens, *In Life Eternal*.
38. J. L. Houlden, 'Liturgy and her Companions: a Theological Appraisal', in R. C. D. Jasper, ed., *The Eucharist Today*, 1974, pp. 168–76. He returned to this theme again in *Patterns of Faith*, 1977, pp. 1–3.
39. On Collects one member alone submitted 88 amendments – *GS Proceedings*, 1976, vol. 7, p. 875.
40. The Revision Committee on the Marriage Service lasted for nearly a year and cost £1,200. ibid., 1976, vol. 7, pp. 1123, 1288; cf. a comment by Colin Buchanan in his *Supplement to Recent Liturgical Revision in the C. of E. 1974–6*, (Grove Booklet 14B), 1976, p. 3.
41. cf. p. 262.
42. *LC Minutes*, 61.96; 63.21–2; *Memoranda* 96, 96B.
43. cf. p. 302.
44. R.C.D.J. to Michael Cantuar, 16 July 1972.
45. *GS Proceedings*, 1972, vol. 3, p. 672.
46. In a vote by Houses, the support of the Laity was less substantial: Bishops 19–1; Clergy 149–32; Laity 90–61. For the whole debate see ibid., vol. 3, pp. 662–84.
47. ibid., 1974, vol. 5, pp. 203–27.
48. ibid., 1974, vol. 5, pp. 762–88; 1975, vol. 6, p. 131. The Final Approval vote was: Bishops 20–1; Clergy 107–11; Laity 73–7.
49. This was achieved by the simple rubric, 'Additional prayers may be said here.'
50. cf. pp. 297–8.
51. *GS Proceedings*, 1974, vol. 5, pp. 788–96; 1975, vol. 6, pp. 143–50, 286–302, 406–7. The voting was: Bishops 15–0; Clergy 134–3; Laity 91–6.
52. cf. p. 343.
53. *LC Minutes* 69.29.
54. *LC Memorandum* 157.
55. cf. p. 343.
56. GS Report 217, *Holy Communion Series 1 and 2 revised*, 1975; *GS Proceedings* 1975, vol. 6, pp. 407–16.
57. ibid., 1976, vol. 7, pp. 583–603.
58. Revision Committee 10 votes to 2; in the full Synod it lapsed through lack of support.
59. *GS Proceedings*, 1976, vol. 7, pp. 856–61. The voting was: Bishops 29–0; Clergy 105–52; Laity 115–35. In the House of Clergy the transfer of a single vote would have resulted in a failure to secure the necessary two-thirds majority.
60. cf. pp. 303–5.
61. Collects, together with Lectionaries and Tables of Rules, not being themselves services, required a new Canon, B4a, to permit their authorization and subsequent revision. This was passed quickly through the General Synod in July and November 1975, and was promulged on 25 February 1976.
62. GS Report 230, *Collects to accompany the Lectionary for Holy Communion, Series 3*, 1975. *GS Proceedings*, 1975, vol. 6, pp. 651–3.
63. ibid., 1976, vol. 7, p. 875.

64. ibid., 1976, vol. 7, pp. 1277–83. The voting was: Bishops 30–1; Clergy 151–21; Laity 136–15.
65. *Marriage, Divorce and the Church*, 1971, pp. 2–3.
66. *Chronicle Convoc.*, 1967, pp. 267–76.
67. *GS Proceedings*, 1972, vol. 3, pp. 75–115, esp. p. 90.
68. *Marriage, Divorce and the Church*, para. 103, p. 54.
69. ibid., para. 105, p. 55.
70. ibid., paras. 106–8, pp. 55–6.
71. ibid., paras, 109, 111, pp. 56–7.
72. *LC Minutes* 49.89.
73. *LC Memorandum* 76C.
74. The Rt Revd. Hugh Montefiore, then Bishop of Kingston, later Bishop of Birmingham.
75. GS 228, *The Wedding Services Series* 3, 1975, p. 7.
76. E. C. Whitaker, *Martin Bucer and the Book of Common Prayer* (Alcuin Club Collections 55), 1974, pp. 120–2.
77. *GS Proceedings*, 1975, vol. 7, pp. 178–96.
78. ibid., 1976, vol. 7, pp. 1123, 1288.
79. GS 228A, *The Marriage Service Series 3 as revised*, 1976; GS 228X, *Report of the Revision Committee*, 1976.
80. *GS Proceedings*, 1976, vol. 7, pp. 1284–91, 1323–33, 1428–34; 1977, vol. 8, pp. 181–9, 482–3. The final voting was: Bishops 21–1; Clergy 132–7; Laity 136–7.
81. cf. pp. 302–3.
82. Concurrences – occasions when two Holy Days fell on consecutive days. Occurrences – occasions when two Holy Days fell on the same day.
83. cf. p. 60.
84. *GS Proceedings*, 1972, vol. 3, pp. 623–7; 1973, vol. 4, p. 5. The final voting was: Bishops 27–0; Clergy 141–5; Laity 113–0.
85. They were already in use in the Church of Scotland, the Free Churches of this country, and the Anglican Churches of South Africa, Central Africa and Iran, and were being used permissively or were under consideration in the Anglican Churches of Scotland, Wales, Ireland and Australia. They were also similar to those of CSI; while the term Pentecost was in use in the Roman and Lutheran Churches.
86. M. Moreton, 'The Calendar and Lectionary: the Question of Principle', in *Theology* LXXVI (July 1973), pp. 369–74.
87. *GS Proceedings*, 1974, vol. 5, pp. 122–46.
88. ibid., 1977, vol. 8, pp. 189–207.
89. *Report of the Revision Committee*, GS 292X, 1977, sc 2, pp. 1–2.
90. ibid., pp. 1–19.
91. *GS Proceedings*, 1978, vol. 9, pp. 144–51, 280–91.
92. ibid., pp. 442–8. The voting was: Bishops 37–0; Clergy 147–8; Laity 127–16. Abstentions 62.
93. *LC Memoranda* 180B and E. David Silk was Rector of St George's, Beckenham, and subsequently Archdeacon of Leicester and Prolocutor of the Lower House of the Convocation of Canterbury.
94. *LC Minutes* 87.85.
95. *GS Proceedings*, 1977, vol. 8, pp. 1163, 1169; 1978, vol. 9, pp. 291–7, 361–72.

96. ibid., 1977, vol. 8, pp. 1166; 1978, vol. 9, pp. 293, 361–2; 1979, vol. 10, pp. 428–9.
97. ibid., 1979, vol. 10, pp. 408–11; 426–32; 948–9. The voting was: Bishops 27–0; Clergy 138–2; Laity 136–0.
98. *LC Minutes* 52.129.
99. E. C. Ratcliff, 'The Ordinal of the Church of South India', in *Theology* LXIII (January 1960), p. 15.
100. R.C.D.J. to Michael Cantuar, 15 February 1973; Michael Cantuar to R.C.D.J., 22 February 1973.
101. *JLG Memorandum* 83.
102. *JLG Minutes* 21.8; *Memorandum* 83.
103. *LC Memorandum* 168A.
104. *LC Memorandum* 169B.
105. The Churches' Unity Commission, representing the C. of E., the Methodist and the United Reformed Churches, the Moravians and the Churches of Christ, finally published its report in Spring 1980, *Towards Visible Unity: Proposals for a Covenant*, based on its earlier Ten Propositions and a Common Ordinal.
106. *GS Proceedings*, 1978, vol. 9, p. 98.
107. ibid., 1977, vol. 8, pp. 564–87.
108. GS 327A and Y, Reports of the Revision Committee.
109. *GS Proceedings*, 1978, vol. 9, pp. 40–85, 440–2. The final voting was: Bishops 36–0; Clergy 161–4; Laity 155–4.
110. *The Liturgical Conference*, 1967, p. 44.
111. *CA Proceedings*, 1967, vol. XLVII, pp. 869–71; *Chronicle Convoc.*, 1967, pp. 213–42; 1968, pp. 91–104, 163–71; 1969, pp. 269–70; *Journal Convoc.*, 1968, pp. 138–9; 1969, pp. 13–14.
112. GS 30, paras. 93, 105, 122, 126, 128, 154–9.
113. GS 56, pp. 5–6.
114. *GS Proceedings*, 1974, vol. 5, pp. 20–59, 252–93, 480–503, 555–60.
115. GS Misc. 34, *Christian Initiation: Reference to the Dioceses*, 1974, pp. 1–7; GS 291A, *Christian Initiation: Results of Reference to Diocesan Synods, 1974–5*; GS 291, *Christian Initiation: Follow-up of the Reference to Diocesan Synods; GS Proceedings*, 1976, vol. 7, pp. 815–55. The voting on an alternative provision for the ordering of initiation practice was: Bishops 17–27; Clergy 83–132; Laity 86–112.
116. *LC Memorandum* 158D.
117. GS 343, *Alternative Services Series 3 Initiation Services*, 1977, pp. 6–7.
118. R.C.D.J. to Donald Cantuar, 20 April 1977.
119. GS 343, p. 10.
120. *GS Proceedings*, 1977, vol. 8, pp. 939–59.
121. GS Reports 343A, 343X.
122. *GS Proceedings*, 1979, vol. 10, p. 137. The Final Voting was: Bishops 29–0; Clergy 180–3; Laity 146–10.

15

THE ALTERNATIVE SERVICE BOOK

I

In early 1971 Michael Ramsey discussed with me the need for a policy on future liturgical revision; I therefore submitted to him an eight-point document setting out the position as I saw it:

1. 1662 should remain available in its existing form.
2. The Series 1 rites should lapse with the possible exception of Holy Communion, which would need further consideration.
3. The Series 2 rites should be replaced by Series 3 rites with the addition of Marriage and Funerals.
4. The Series 3 rites should mark the end of current liturgical revision and form the nucleus of an Alternative Prayer Book.
5. This Book might appear in two forms, a short form containing simply Morning and Evening Prayer and Holy Communion, and a complete form with the Occasional Offices, a new Psalter, and the eucharistic lections set out in full.
6. A new Ordinal should be included, based on the Anglican–Methodist Ordinal.
7. The Book might be available by 1975–6, provided there were no unforeseen difficulties and the General Synod could devote considerable time to it.
8. All this could be achieved without recourse to Parliament, provided that the Worship and Doctrine Measure were passed.[1]

Shortly afterwards I added a further point: if the Worship and Doctrine Measure were to give the Church control over new services, this control should also apply to the printing and publishing of such services.

Both Archbishops approved this document, after which I discussed it with the Liturgical Commission and then with the General Synod's Liturgical Steering Committee, which at that time still existed. In due course I was also asked to discuss it with the Synod's Policy Sub-Committee, which agreed that as soon as Holy Communion Series 3 was approved, the subject should be aired in the Synod. In preparation for this Derek Pattinson, the new Secretary-General, prepared a much fuller discussion document, which was published in early 1973 as report GS 161, *The Future Course of Liturgical Revision.*

This began with a survey of liturgical revision from 1965 to 1973 under the Alternative Services Measure. By 1973 most parishes used either 1662 or one of the authorized Series 1 or Series 2 alternatives: it could therefore be said that the restoration of some kind of order had been achieved;

although it had to be recognized that the Church of England had 'a very broad base for the ordering of its public worship'.[2] This work had been undertaken with considerable enthusiasm and a sense of unity, although some people had been saddened by the movement away from 1662.[3] The report then discussed the forthcoming Worship and Doctrine Measure and its implications for liturgy, accepting the inevitability of tensions between the old and the new, and pointing out that the ecumenical factor presented the problem of making use of ecumenically acceptable material without compromising the distinctive element of Anglican witness.[4] Three basic principles were laid down for future work:

1. Services should be capable of periodic revision or supplementation.
2. Different forms of service should be available, for rigid uniformity was no longer practicable.
3. These forms of service should not be too numerous.[5]

A programme similar to that in my 1971 paper was then set out, concluding with four specific proposals for the consideration of the Synod.

1. The provision of a set of Series 3 alternatives to the 1662 services, retaining such Series 1 and Series 2 forms as were pastorally necessary.
2. The appointment of a working party to plan a People's Service Book.
3. The retention of the freedom simply to authorize new services rather than a new book.
4. The replacement of Holy Communion Series 1 and Series 2 by a single rite.

The Archbishop of Canterbury introduced the report to the Synod in July 1973, contributing substantially to its acceptance by a piece of first-class advocacy. The Church, he pointed out, must be content with limited objectives: and it was just this that the report tried to indicate.

> In undertaking and planning a still continuing big operation of liturgical revision we should bear in mind that there are limits to which a particular group can be expected to go, and, furthermore, there are limits to what may be expected at all, within a span of a few years, of really good quality. We cannot order chunks of liturgy in the kind of way that we get various items from the laundry. I say this because I believe that this essential understanding of what is a literary art as well as a theological art has been somewhat lost sight of in the way in which we have set about it in our proceedings.

He also strongly supported the proposal for a combined Series 1-2 Communion rite, not as 'a sort of X-Y-Z rite' but as 'a skilful piece of liturgical drafting whereby the options most likely to be wanted in these two rites would be within a single cover'. In a surprisingly short debate considerable enthusiasm for the proposed programme emerged; and an amendment to substitute a 'Book of Common Prayer 1980' for a 'People's

Service Book' was quickly rejected. Both Archbishops spoke against a target date of 1980, Dr Ramsey being particularly dismissive:

> I do not like the suggestion about the year 1980. The pastoral need is far more urgent than that. It is really urgent, as a number of speakers here have pointed out, to have the book in the hands of the people really soon — I would hope within two years from now, not more than that.

On this point I must confess I thought it wise to remain silent. Admittedly I had suggested a completion date of 1975–6 in my 1971 paper; but it was becoming clear that with the amount of work still to be done and the present state of progress hopes of achieving such a target were unrealistic. But this was no time to start an argument or to damp the Synod's enthusiasm: and all four proposals were accepted without difficulty.[6]

As I expected, hopes of a 1975–6 completion soon vanished. The Working Party was not appointed until February 1974; and it did not have its first meeting until May, nearly a year after the Synod's decision. It was a fairly small body of seven clergy and five laity including two members of the Liturgical Commission — David Silk and myself — and people with professional experience in the world of publishing. The chairman was Dr John Habgood, Bishop of Durham, who, despite describing himself as a 'reluctant liturgical reviser', proved to be first-class, with all the qualities needed for guiding a rather difficult and delicate venture: toughness, fairness, patience and a grasp of detail. The group met eleven times, producing its report GS 284, *An Alternative Service Book*, at the end of 1975. The range of its discussions had been extensive, including not only the contents of the proposed book but its timing, style and design, questions of finance and copyright, and the position of the Privileged Presses. Evidence both written and oral was collected from a variety of sources: the Privileged Presses, religious publishers, technical experts and other Churches engaged in publishing new service books. Opinion within the Church of England was also sought, a questionnaire being sent to a random sample of 620 parishes in the autumn of 1975.[7] On the basis of all the information received the Working Party came down decisively in favour, not of a People's Service Book, but of an Alternative Service Book, to be published in 1980 with a projected life of at least ten years and containing a full range of alternative services together with a liturgical psalter and excluding all 1662 material.[8] Such a book might be published in two versions, a complete edition including the Revised Catechism and the eucharistic lections set out in full; and a shorter edition without the Catechism and the Ordinal and with only scripture references to the lections.[9] It should also be an independent publication, the Church being free to make its own publishing arrangements, provide its own designer, retain the copyright of material, and have its own financial stake.[10] The report also included some interesting figures, indicating the extent to which the Series 2 and Series 3 eucharistic rites had been accepted by the Church: between September 1967 and June 1975, a period of 7 years 10 months, the pew edition of Series 2 had sold 2,957,000 copies; and between February 1973 and June 1975, a period of 2 years 5 months, the pew edition of Series 3 had sold 1,299,000 copies and continued to sell at double the rate of Series 2.[11] These figures took no account of the copies of both rites sold in other publications, music editions, communicants' manuals and authorized parochial booklets; the total numbers were therefore very much greater.

The General Synod accepted these proposals in February 1976, the Standing Committee being instructed 'to take such steps as it thinks fit to secure publication of the Book'.[12] It therefore appointed a small group of four, which with the Synod's Secretary-General and Financial Secretary was to be responsible for the operation from June 1976 onwards. The Bishop of Durham continued to act as chairman, supported by Humphrey Cranfield, a business man with publishing connections, who was a member of the General Synod and its Standing Committee; Robert Cross, an experienced technical expert in printing and publishing; and myself, acting as the link between the Church and the publishers and as general editorial dogsbody. Its first two tasks were to plan the collection of material needed for the book and to consider the process of publication.

The former was remitted to the recently reconstituted Commission,[13] for it was essentially a liturgical matter. The services and other contents of the book were now in the process of being authorized for use by the General Synod as separate entities and remained so in a series of booklets. But they now had to be brought together to appear as a single coherent unit. Texts appearing in more than one service had to appear in a standard form; introductory sentences, appearing in several services, had to be merged into a single group; the notes to each service had to be replanned to avoid unnecessary duplication; and punctuation and typography had to be standardized. Much of this was purely straightforward editorial work; but matters of principle were also involved, the text of the Lord's Prayer being a case in point. Geoffrey Cuming and I worked out a method of procedure which the Commission then tested by applying it to Morning and Evening Prayer Series 3.[14] This method, which came to be known as 'Adaptation' was then approved by the General Synod in February and November 1977 before being applied to every service in the proposed book.[15] These adaptations constituted a form of revision, requiring statutory approval by the Synod: but to save time a shortened procedure was devised, virtually eliminating preliminary consideration by the House of Bishops and the Revision Committee stage, and requiring each set of proposals to come before the Synod only twice. Nevertheless there was some concern lest even this abbreviated method should prove too time-consuming: if members chose to discuss individual adaptations before voting upon them — and they were constitutionally entitled to do so — the tight schedules could soon be disrupted. Fortunately when I introduced the first set dealing with Morning and Evening Prayer in July 1978, the Synod accepted them without debate.[16]

To our great relief this established a precedent and the whole process of Adaptation subsequently went through virtually on the nod.

In the second major task, the process of publication, the group was guided by three principles:

1. The control of material should remain in the hands of the Church.
2. The Book, both in pew and altar editions, should be reasonably priced.
3. The Church should benefit financially from any profit involved.

It therefore recommended that the Church should not be tied to the Privileged Presses but should be free to employ any interested and suitable publishers. Competition would ensure supplies and keep down prices. Nevertheless no widespread operation was envisaged: 'a small number of publishers — more than one, but less than (say) six, would be desirable'.[17] Control over design and pagination could be secured by the Church itself being responsible for putting the entire text on film, which all publishers would then be required to use on payment of a royalty. Variations in their editions would therefore be limited to size, paper and binding. Once these proposals were endorsed by the Synod, the group of four began negotiations with interested publishers. The going was not always easy. The fact that the Church itself dared to enter territory which hitherto publishers had regarded as very much their own preserve and insist on certain lines being followed, particularly in matters of design, was a new experience for some of those involved and at times caused the temperature to rise. But it was very evident that despite all difficulties a number of eminent publishing firms were genuinely keen to be involved in The Alternative Service Book. At the end of the day virtually all the interested parties had some share in the project. The Queen's Printers were given responsibility for the origination and the production of the film and for publishing the altar edition, while the pew edition was to be published by three groups, Hodder and Stoughton, Oxford University Press with Mowbrays, and Cambridge University Press with SPCK and William Clowes.

Meanwhile two developments took place which caused the original plan to have longer and shorter versions of the Book to be modified. The first was the decision not to include the Revised Catechism. The old Catechism Commission had been consulted on the feasibility of a new edition, but in early 1977 they advised that it should not be included in its existing form while there was insufficient time to undertake a revision before 1980.[18] The second was a decision in July 1978 not to include the Psalter, although this decision was subsequently changed. Immediately after the Synod had approved the use of the new Liturgical Psalter under the Versions of the Bible Measure by a majority of over 4 to 1,[19] the Bishop of Durham proposed that this should be the version to be included in The Alternative Service Book: but this the Synod was not prepared to accept. There was a moving plea by the Bishop of Guildford to omit the Psalter altogether, permitting people the free use of different forms of psalmody and even hymns in the interests of mission and pastoral need; and this proposal attracted not only those who supported him but opponents of the new Psalter and even opponents of the whole book.[20]

With the removal of these two items, it was thought wise to concentrate on planning a single edition for 1980, although there was a growing feeling that the Psalter decision would have to be reconsidered. When presenting a further Progress Report (GS 413) in July 1979, the Bishop of Durham admitted that it had been a mistake in the previous year to link the issue of the inclusion of a Psalter with the issue of which Psalter. But he reminded the Synod that the replies to the parochial questionnaire had been heavily in favour of the inclusion of a Psalter and he believed that 'an Anglican service book without a Psalter would be a poor truncated thing, frustratingly inadequate for the very large number of people whose devotional lives are rooted in the Psalms'. Consequently the Synod changed its mind, deciding after all to have two versions of the Book, one with a Psalter and one without.[21] The matter was finally settled in November, when despite a spirited defence of the Revised Psalter by the Bishop of London, the Synod decided to include the new Liturgical Psalter.[22] It was a sad decision for Donald Coggan, for he retired from the archbishopric on the same day (8 November): and though he had loyally supported the Liturgical Commission in undertaking the Liturgical Psalter project, his heart was really in the Revised Psalter, which had been very much his concern. In his farewell speech to the General Synod, he could not refrain from a friendly and even light-hearted reference to the decision:

> Very shortly in the Church of England when we have our new Prayer Book and the new Psalter, you will be singing with typical Anglican lustiness 'All my loins shake continuously'. I felt I had to remind you of your decision today, but only in the context of the fact that my loins have never shaken so continuously as they do tonight.[23]

So the Commission bade farewell to another staunch friend and supporter. His firm and wise leadership had counted for a great deal, particularly in those critical years 1960–4, when under his chairmanship the Commission had recovered its sense of purpose and direction and significantly broadened its horizons. Very different from Michael Ramsey both in temperament and in outlook, he made a valuable and distinctive contribution to the process of revision, not so much in matters of liturgical expertise but administratively, easing the path of progress, removing difficulties and getting things done. His strong, steadying influence was always there, his sympathetic ear was readily available, and I can only say that I missed him greatly.

II

The acceptance of Holy Communion Series 3 at parish level was far more rapid than I for one had expected, soon replacing Series 2 as the most popular alternative rite. In 1976, however, when the Synod's Standing

Committee decided that it should be revised before inclusion in the ASB,[24] another questionnaire had to be arranged. Fortunately John Wilkinson returned from St George's College, Jerusalem, just at the right moment and he immediately took responsibility for planning the operation. A ten per cent sample of all parishes which had used Series 3, approximately 1,000, was asked to participate. Each diocese chose its own sample and analysed all individual comments which were submitted; non-parochial groups – the services, prisons, hospitals, universities and religious communities – were asked to co-operate; and an invitation through the Church press invited parishes not included in diocesan samples to take part as well. A report on the returns was ready by March 1977. On the whole the returns were good: 86% of the parish sample, 60% of the non-parochial groups, and 50% of the 'voluntary' parishes. Bearing in mind that we had made clear on the questionnaire that the Commission was not contemplating any major rewriting – 'nothing like a Holy Communion Series 4 is in prospect' – there was a general acceptance of the rite. Approval was expressed by 86% of the laity and 88% of the clergy – figures also reflected in approval of individual items in the rite, the eucharistic prayer, for example, showing laity 87% and clergy 81%. The only significant differences were for the use of the Decalogue: laity 37%, clergy 56%; and the ICET Lord's Prayer: laity 47%, clergy 63%. An analysis of the diocesan reports on individual comments also showed that no particular item was singled out for widespread criticism. The report as a whole therefore seemed to suggest a policy of leaving well alone; although this was by no means reflected in some of the literature published during this period.

On the language front criticism both of the rite and of modern translations of the Bible continued unabated, fostered largely by the Prayer Book Society.[25] General inadequacies of the rite on the lines of those expressed by the critics when Series 3 first appeared also continued to be argued;[26] and it was evident that the old conflicts were by no means forgotten. Roger Beckwith, writing on 'The approaching Revision of Series Three' in *The Churchman* (November 1976), still claimed that eucharistic sacrifice, prayer for the departed and reservation were causes of division and urged Evangelicals to concentrate on these issues.[27] The Commission therefore devoted its energies mainly to the provision of supplementary material for optional use.[28]

1. The seasonal element was enriched by additional introductory and post-communion sentences and Proper Prefaces.
2. Alternatives to the Intercessions were provided by the addition of the General Intercession, portions of the Litany, or any suitable form of prayer.
3. Permission was given to use the Penitential section either at the beginning or after the Intercessions, and alternative forms were provided.

4. Five additional eucharistic prayers were included for optional use: a new JLG prayer for ecumenical occasions;[29] modern versions of the Series 1 and Series 2 prayers; and two shorter prayers, one for use with house groups and the sick, and another responsive form modelled on Roman Catholic experimental prayers for use with children.[30]

There were two other matters of particular concern. The first, almost inevitably, was the anamnesis–oblation in the original eucharistic prayer. We had still not given up hope that something even better might be produced, despite the apparent satisfaction with the existing form. Discussions between our two Anglo-Catholic members, David Hope and David Silk, and our two Evangelicals, Colin Buchanan and Hugh Craig, with assistance from Geoffrey Cuming and myself, resulted in a series of possible minor variations on the existing text, some more generally acceptable than others; and we decided to submit them all to the House of Bishops for consideration. The second problem was line 9 in the Lord's Prayer. Support for the existing text, 'Do not bring us to the time of trial', was clearly lukewarm. On the other hand, the final ICET form, 'Save us from the time of trial', had been rejected by all ICET members in the British Isles.[31] Nevertheless the Commission found it extraordinarily difficult to find an acceptable alternative despite seeking help from a number of distinguished biblical scholars. Finally we sent the Bishops a memorandum written by Leslie Houlden setting out the problems and suggesting possible solutions:

1. We could attempt a bold paraphrase such as 'Keep us in trials of faith'.
2. We could abandon any attempt at historical accuracy and leave well alone, recognizing that the prayer was a Church formulary existing in its own rite.

To this I added an appendix of my own suggesting, 'Let us not be led into temptation', which was the kind of petition most people seemed to want to say, was an English form dating back to the medieval primers, fitted the Aramaic causative form which probably lay behind the Greek, had parallels in other Jewish prayers, and was identical with the form adopted in France.

Despite the fact that the Commission's proposals were carefully vetted by a preliminary group of four bishops and four members of the Commission,[32] the outcome of the full Bishops' meeting on 21–2 February 1978 was frankly disappointing. Actually they accepted a great deal, including my proposal for the Lord's Prayer; but their decisions on the eucharistic prayers could only be described as cautious in the extreme. They rejected three of the five alternative prayers, the JLG prayer and the two short prayers, not on liturgical grounds but on grounds of expediency. Then, in the original prayer, in view of the fact that we had offered them a variety of choices rather than an agreed text for the anamnesis, they proposed that we should revert to the Series 2 form and use it in all three prayers now remaining. The Commission felt that this displayed a defeatist attitude and persuaded them to make at least one more attempt at an agreed solution. A further meeting of the joint sub-committee then produced a text on which both Bishops and Commission were prepared to agree:

> Therefore, heavenly Father, we do this in remembrance of him. We proclaim his offering of himself made once for all upon the cross, his mighty resurrection and glorious ascension; and, as we celebrate his one perfect sacrifice with this bread and this cup, we look for his coming in glory.

This again was not radically different from the 1972 text, using all the same words although in a slightly different way; but as we said in the report, 'We hope that the small amendments now proposed will be found to be eirenic.'[33]

The report *Holy Communion Series 3 Revised*, GS 364, was published in May 1978 and presented to the General Synod in July. It was introduced by Colin Buchanan, acting as chairman of the Steering Committee. He reminded the Synod of the long process by which the rite had reached its present form and made an interesting comparison of the present situation with that of fifty years before when the 1928 Book had been rejected by the House of Commons:

> Then it was the Commons which had the final say: this time we have. Then it was a simple majority which settled the issue: this time we have more careful procedures. Then it was an untried text which was being debated: this time it is a well-tried one, slightly revised in the light of use. Then the issue was basically disciplinary: this time it is liturgical and pastoral. Then there was bitter division within the Church of England over the issues: this time there has been a considerable growing together. Then even the proponents of the book had heavy hearts and had to rake around for courage: this time the Liturgical Commission and the House of Bishops together lay before the Synod a text of which we have good hope.[34]

The ensuing two-hour debate was lively but positive. There was no lack of criticism; but it seemed to be taken for granted that the rite would be referred to a Revision Committee and none of the thirteen speakers suggested its rejection.[35]

Proposals for amendment then flooded in — well over 1,000 from 96 members of the Synod and others from groups and individuals outside.[36] It was an incredible situation, particularly after the questionnaire had suggested general satisfaction with the rite in its existing form. Moreover, the timetable was extremely tight: it was imperative to complete the Revision Committee stage by February 1979 in order to get Final Approval possibly in July and at the very latest in November. So many details in the ASB were dependent on decisions in this particular rite; and the printers really wanted a completed text by October if publication was to be guaranteed on time. Fortunately the Revision Committee had a first-class chairman in Cyril Bowles, Bishop of

Derby, who knew the ropes intimately. He approved a plan to expedite matters whereby the Steering Committee drafted variants to the text incorporating the substance of a number of proposed amendments before they were considered. To quote Colin Buchanan:

> We usually drafted our own 'mainstream' text *in advance of (Revision) Committee meetings*, got it accepted as 'on the table', indicated all the variety of proposed amendments that would thus be swallowed up and fall, and, in effect, dared anyone to try then to amend *our* text: sometimes instead we produced texts in parallel columns, and worked our way in full Committee through the choices thus given to the members.[37]

In this way the operation was completed in seven meetings covering eleven days and the timetable was maintained. Whether it was the ideal way to create liturgy was, of course, another matter. But the fact remains that a great deal was achieved and the rite was improved in a variety of ways.

1. The seasonal material was again extended; and in the case of the introductory and post-communion sentences there was provision for every occasion for which there were propers.
2. The Confession was abbreviated – a great improvement; and three alternative confessions were provided in the Appendices: the original Series 3 text, the Series 2 text in 'You' form, and the 'Frost' text rejected in 1972. The 'Frost' Prayer of Humble Access was also included in the Appendices.[38]
3. The introduction to the Peace was replaced by a form from the Scottish Episcopal rite; but again the original Series 3 form was included in the Appendices together with five seasonal forms.
4. Obviously many of the proposed amendments cancelled each other out, and the Offertory provided a good example. Some people wanted a return to the 1662 pattern with no words or specific directions, while others wanted the inclusion of the new Roman 'offertory prayers'. A compromise was found by inserting a rubric, 'The president may praise God for his gifts in appropriate words', to which were added the Roman response, 'Blessed be God for ever'. There was no mistaking what the 'appropriate words' were, although their absence indicated the reservations about their theological suitability on the part of some. The Revision Committee frankly admitted that it was a compromise, although they hoped it would be acceptable in good conscience to all traditions. In any case its use was optional.[39]
5. The second part of the original eucharistic prayer was again redrafted in an attempt to produce a more eirenic form. The anamnesis now ran:

   > Therefore, heavenly Father, we remember his offering of himself made once for all upon the cross and proclaim his mighty resurrection and glorious ascension. As we look for his coming in glory, we celebrate with this bread and this cup his one perfect sacrifice.

and this was destined to survive and find its way into the ASB.

But the most important change was the inclusion in the actual text of the rite four eucharistic prayers: the original amended prayer, the Series 1 and Series 2 modernized prayers, and an entirely new prayer having affinities with both Hippolytus and the second prayer of the revised Roman rite. This new prayer was the result of an 'arrangement' – made public in November 1978 – between Brian Brindley, an Anglo-Catholic member of the Revision Committee, and Roger Beckwith, a strong critic of Series 3 and an advocate of a modernized version of 1662. Beckwith undertook to support the new prayer, so worded that it would not compromise what he considered to be the doctrinal position of the Church of England, although it was not a prayer that he himself would want to use. In return Brindley would commend a modernized form of 1662 such as Beckwith desired, although in fact such a form was already envisaged; the first part of the Series 1 prayer was essentially that of 1662, while provision was made by rubric to end the prayer after the Institution Narrative and to follow the 1662 order. But all this was now set out as a separate text.

This Third Eucharistic Prayer, as it came to be known, marked a significant step forward, for it would probably have never survived the Series 2 arguments of 1966.[40] The Revision Committee rightly pointed out that it had 'a style and phrasing refreshingly different' from the Cranmer-based models of the other prayers; and 'if a variety and choice of eucharistic prayers is being included for use in many and varied circumstances and settings, there is much to be said for inclusion of a prayer which owes its origin to a different "root" characteristic of the earliest centuries of the undivided Christian Church'.[41] The prayer came to be much appreciated and widely used.

In addition an abbreviated form of the original prayer, not entirely dissimilar from that proposed by the Liturgical Commission and rejected by the Bishops, was included in the Appendices for use with the sick.

6. Both the position and the text of the Lord's Prayer were changed. On historical, ecumenical and practical grounds the Revision Committee placed it before instead of after the Fraction: while in line 9 it was decided after all to follow the ICET text, 'Save us from the time of trial'.

Careful analysis justifies the Committee's contention that their work had largely continued the process of supplementation begun by the Liturgical Commission. Admittedly a great deal more material had been added, and a first impression was of a very different rite: but in fact very little of the existing Series 3 rite had been jettisoned.[42] Nevertheless, the extent of the Committee's supplementation and in particular their introduction of completely new eucharistic prayers raised the question: 'Precisely what constitutes revision?' It was a question raised more than once in the ensuing Synod debate and expressed succinctly by the Bishop of Durham:

> When a Revision Committee produces a very extensive revision, the Synod is then considering a matter of deep importance which has not come to it in the form presented by the House of Bishops: and the House of Bishops has had no opportunity to look at fundamentally important eucharistic prayers now before the Synod. And the House of Bishops also knows full well that if at a later stage it says, 'What about this?', it will get its head chopped off.[43]

The unease was also reflected in the large number of amendments – some two hundred – submitted for the Revision Stage in full Synod on 21–2 February 1979, many of which were attempts to restore to the text elements of the original Series 3 rite which the Committee had either omitted or relegated to the Appendices. In introducing the Committee's proposals the Bishop of Derby set them in a broad historical context. For the first four hundred years of its distinctive life the Church of England had accepted the principle of liturgical uniformity and in practice had lived by it fairly loyally; but in the last century the principle had been eroded by various influences – doctrinal, aesthetic, pastoral, missionary – and by an ignorance of the theological and devotional values of liturgical worship. There was now a need for some degree of liberty within the liturgical framework of order and words; but there had to be a balance between this uniformity and freedom, and this the Committee had attempted to find.[44]

There now followed some nineteen hours of further discussion, which unfortunately spilled over into the July session. Admittedly it was the final opportunity for an examination of details; but whether such a marathon was justified by the results is debatable. The number of amendments rejected was substantial – roughly two thirds – and no really radical decisions were made. At eight or nine points the original text of Series 3 was restored – mostly small matters, but sufficient to comfort those who wanted to retain what had already become familiar: a line in the Confession, the congregational response to the Dismissal, and, most significant of all, the final petitions in the first eucharistic prayer, which some years before had been the inspired suggestion of Colin Buchanan. An attempt to introduce the texts of the Roman Offertory prayers was defeated: and at long last a decision was made on line 9 of the Lord's Prayer, the Synod playing for safety and returning to the traditional form, 'Lead us not into temptation'.[45] Provisional Approval was given as the final item on the July agenda, on the last possible day this could take place if the ASB publishing timetable was to be kept. It was evident that the Synod had worked under pressure and the Bishop of Winchester, Dr John Taylor, voiced misgivings felt by many:

> We have just completed the last of a hurly-burly of changes and additions . . . I have felt increasingly through the whole process that this is something which I hope our Church will never do again. This is not the way to write liturgy . . . To my mind, this monstrosity of a process has

> taken place, and I think taken us all by surprise. I am not prepared at this moment to say whether I think that the net result is an improvement or not on what we set out to revise. I am just too confused to know. It is very important that the Synod, if it is to be responsible, should have enough time to look at the finished product, and then be asked to make up its mind about it.[46]

It was a misgiving echoed by Colin Buchanan, who felt the system to be 'unique on the earth's surface' and worthy of a place in the *Guinness Book of Records* for the number of hours spent, the number of amendments proposed, and the amount of verbiage expended on a particular rite. He also pointed out the unsatisfactory role of the Liturgical Commission: 'The existence of this particular procedure inhibits the Liturgical Commission. There is no incentive to it to try to do a really perfect job of work when it knows that it is going to be hacked around from start to finish when it has done it.'[47] It was a sentiment which I heartily endorsed.

In July, just before the vote on the Final Approval stage, a journal, *P.N. Review 13*,[48] was published, containing over forty articles and quotations by a variety of people – academics, poets, musicians and politicians – attacking modern versions of the Bible and modern liturgies, and pleading for the retention of the Authorised Version and the Book of Common Prayer in a central and regular place in the life of the Church. It clearly had links with the Prayer Book Society, and Professor David Martin, described as 'Guest Editor', set the tone with an aciduous article entitled 'Why spit on our luck?' in which he described the recent Revision Committee as 'composed of hard-line Anglo-Catholics and Evangelicals, set to work like scorpions in a bottle'.[49] It concluded with the texts of three petitions addressed to the General Synod. The first, signed by over six hundred academics and leaders of the arts, including practising and non-practising Christians and others claiming to have no religious belief, pleaded for the 'continued and loving use in churches as part of the mainstream of worship' of the AV and BCP. The second, signed by great public figures including former and serving members of the Government, expressed 'concern' for the AV and BCP. The third, the Saint Cecilia petition, signed by eminent musicians, pleaded for the continued use of the traditional texts and their musical settings.[50] All three were cleverly phrased and could have been signed with a good conscience by people who were also happy to accept a revision of the liturgy; indeed, many of the signatories had helped the Liturgical Commission over the years. But placed within the context of the journal a rather different impression was created, with reformers and those who supported them being shown in a bad light.

The petitions were presented to the Synod at the opening of the November session; and while there was no discussion on them at the time, a courteous reply was published in the following session in February 1980. Clearly they had little effect on the Final Approval stage, however. Despite another moving plea from the Bishop of Winchester to think again, all three Houses registered their approval in decisive manner. The misgivings of some people who had originally felt that what was proposed was too complicated and confusing were allayed; and many who had found both Series 2 and Series 3 unacceptable on theological grounds now had a rite which they were happy to use. The Bishop of Derby summed up the situation aptly in his concluding speech: the revised rite recognized a degree of uniformity and an opportunity for variety, it contained treasures still to be discovered, and it would stand the test of wear in actual use.[51]

III

With the authorization of Holy Communion Series 3 Revised the last major hurdle confronting the Liturgical Commission and the Working Group had been overcome. The process of adaptation could now be completed and the contents of what the Commission called its 'Ragbag' dealt with. This involved a handful of items, none of a radical nature but too important to be regarded as adaptations: a final revision and correction of the Calendar and Lectionary, the production of some consequential collects and a few other prayers, and the provision of a Subject Index of prayers throughout the book. These were put together in the Report GS 405, *Miscellaneous Liturgical Proposals*, and went through the General Synod on an abbreviated procedure in July and November 1979. The precise contents of the book could now be endorsed.[52] Nevertheless, a variety of details still had to be settled, making progress by no means simple and straightforward.

There was, for example, the question of the versions of the Bible to be used in the eucharistic lectionary. It had been the original intention of the Commission to produce its own versions; and a start had been made in the Wedding and Funeral Services. These had proved acceptable, while the ASB Working Party had commended the idea in its proposals in 1975.[53] When it came to dealing with the entire two-year lectionary, however, the Commission began to have second thoughts. In early 1976 David Frost, fresh from his Psalter labours, warned us that any attempt to do this within a very restricted time limit, particularly in the case of the Old Testament lessons, would place a mill-stone around our neck — a view endorsed by Anthony Boylan from his experiences with the Roman Catholic translation body ICEL.[54] The only alternative, therefore, was to revise the 1973 *Lessons for Holy Communion Series 3*, choosing from the various versions authorized under the Versions of the Bible Measure — a principle accepted by the General Synod in January 1978.[55] Later that year *The Bible in Today's English Version* (or *The Good News Bible*) was also authorized for use;[56] and although much of the selection had already been done, it was felt that it too must be given a place in the versions used. A great deal of work therefore had to be done to accommodate it. Nor was this all. Every lesson had to be edited not only to ensure that it made sense as a self-contained unit, but also to conform to the ASB typographical style. The various publishers then required us to submit all the lessons chosen from their particular version set out in the exact form that we proposed to publish them before giving their permission. This involved our tiny office staff in a massive, meticulous, typing operation to be done at speed; and our indebtedness to them was considerable.

Another question was the future of 'separates'. Over a period of twenty years the Church had grown accustomed to the use of separate booklets for the alternative services; they had proved popular, being handy, inexpensive and easily replaceable. But one consequence of their existence had been the loss by worshippers of the habit of using their own Prayer Book, to the detriment of private devotion. It was not surprising to find church leaders, Donald Coggan in particular, expressing the hope that the day of the privately owned book would soon return. All Series 3 services, once authorized for use, had been published in booklet form in accordance with the principle that all such services should be available to the public.[57] By 1977, however, the Working Group realized that the continued existence of such separates might present problems. Progress Report GS 325 pointed out that their ready availability might discourage both parishes and individuals from buying copies of the ASB, and the publishers were not slow to express their concern.[58] On the other hand, it was clear that any phasing out of separates would be extremely unpopular at parish level. Happily an acceptable compromise was worked out.

1. Booklets of the Series 3 Initiation Services were published in June 1979 in the proposed ASB format. This gave them an assured life of eighteen months and provided the Church with an opportunity to experience the format of the book.
2. A similar policy would be adopted for Holy Communion Series 3 revised.
3. Booklets of other Series 3 services in the old format would continue until stocks ran out. They would then be replaced by booklets in ASB format after an interval, probably about a year after publication of the ASB. Any non-availability would therefore only be temporary.
4. Any Series 1 or Series 2 services which continued to be authorized would remain available in their familiar booklet form.[59]

Another question was the size and cost of the ASB. The returns of the parochial questionnaire in 1975 had suggested that enthusiasm for the book was not exactly overwhelming. Admittedly there was a majority in favour of publication: 276 to 115; but on the likelihood of purchase the figures were much more evenly balanced: 222 to 165.[60] Cost would obviously be an important factor; but until size, format and printing runs were worked out, any figures were mere guesswork. The nearest guide at that time was the recently published Roman Catholic *Sunday Missal*, a book of 800 pages, which went on the market at £1.90 and sold over 100,000 copies in the first ten months of publication. When tenders for the ASB were invited from interested publishers in early 1979, we advised them that the book complete with Psalter was likely to be some 900 pages long but might rise to just over 1,000. Unfortunately this figure continued to rise, for the General Synod authorized additional material as late as November 1979, particularly in the appendices to Rite A, the mass of new sentences, and in the inclusion of the 1662 canticles. The Queen's Printers had in fact started to set material before we were able to work out the final size, 1292 pages. It was an embarrassment to have to warn the publishers of the steady increases, for the estimating of costs became extremely difficult, to say the least. In November 1977 the Financial Secretary, J. W. D. McIntyre, had hazarded a guess in the General Synod that the publishing price of the ASB would probably work out at about £3.[61] It was remarkably accurate. When the book was published in November 1980 parishes could make bulk purchases at just over £3.10 a copy, while an individual copy could be bought for £3.50. The publishers had pegged costs remarkably well in spite of inflation and the late increases in size.

The General Synod's part in the creation of the ASB ended in November 1979 with the authorization of all the contents of the book from the date of publication until 31 December 1990.[62] It was therefore clear that what was being produced was a book of authorized services and not an authorized book of services. The book itself was in effect a convenience: its contents could be changed or it could even be dismembered without affecting the authorization of the contents. Furthermore, it did not contain all the authorized rites alternative to those of 1662. For many congregations a choice between 1662 and the ASB was too stark. Some, for example, were still attached to Series 2 Holy Communion, while others preferred the 1928 or Series 1 type of services. The Commission therefore advised the Synod (Report GS 439) to retain the following:

Series 1. Matrimony and Burial.
Series 2. Holy Communion, Baptism and Confirmation.
Series 2 revised. Morning and Evening Prayer.

All these services were therefore authorized for a further period of five years in July 1980,[63] providing the Church, at least temporarily, with not two but three choices of services: 1662, Series 1 and 2 'Thou' forms in separates, and Series 3 forms in the ASB. Some rationalization of lectionaries and rules was also necessary. When the Alternative Calendar, Lectionary and Rules were authorized in October 1979, the situation was confused: there were then available five tables of lessons and three tables of psalms for Morning and Evening Prayer, and four tables of lessons for Holy Communion. Furthermore, the calendars of 1662 and the ASB were different; and some people would want to use the former but with subsequent additions and improvements. Charles Whitaker therefore proposed the following alternative scheme:

1. The 1961 Table of Lessons from Series 1 Morning and Evening Prayer.
2. The Series 1 Table of Psalms for Sundays and other days.
3. The Series 1 Table of Eucharistic Lessons and collects.
4. A modified set of Rules.
5. All other tables should lapse.

These proposals, presented in Reports GS 427 and 441, were approved by the Synod in July 1980 with the concession that the 1922 Table of Lessons should also remain available, simply because the only existing Office Book still used by many clergy employed this table.[64]

For the Liturgical Commission two tasks now remained before it completed its term of office. The first was to prepare a brief commentary on the ASB, to be published with the book. This was primarily intended as a 'stop-gap' introduction, bringing together information from the various Commission and Synod reports over the years with advice on how the services could be used. The second was to draft a series of Services for the Sick. They had first been asked for in 1959; but preliminary and informal discussions with various groups had broken down due to disagreements over reservation. Then when Michael Ramsey became Archbishop of Canterbury he postponed further consideration on two grounds:

1. It was important to try and get the Eucharist settled before tackling reservation.
2. Priority should be given to revising the public services used in parish churches.

The revision of the public services was still incomplete when he retired; but in November 1976 the House of Bishops reconsidered the policy in the light of representations from the hospital chaplains and agreed to some modification. While accepting that Services for the Sick should not be included in the ASB, they nevertheless asked the Commission to work on them with a view to their publication in a separate volume.[65]

The Commission completed its proposals in September 1980 at the final meeting of its five-year term, which also happened to be the one hundredth since it came into being in 1955. Two reports were published: *Services for the Sick*, GS 471, containing Holy Communion, the Laying on of Hands and Anointing, Prayers for use with the Sick, and a Commendation at the Time of Death; while the second, GS 472, comprised *The Blessing of the Oils* and *The Reconciliation of a Penitent*. The latter were deliberately kept separate, for they were not specifically Services for the Sick; and it was also feared that the forms of reconciliation would prove controversial. Two members of the Commission, Colin Buchanan and Hugh Craig, refused to accept them on doctrinal grounds, and in fact in due course they were rejected by the General Synod.[66] By the time the reports were considered in 1981, they were no longer our responsibility; a newly appointed Commission and a newly elected General Synod were in office. Briefly, the proposals in GS 471, some of which were already in ASB, presented few problems and they were duly authorized from 1 June 1983.[67] The vexed question of reservation was at least partially overcome in two ways: by applying the principle of Communion by Extension, and by recourse to the rubrics in Rite A and Rite B in ASB which referred to the consumption of those consecrated elements 'not required for purposes of communion'. The connection between reservation and communion was unmistakeable; but care was taken not to go into detail. There the matter rested and common sense had prevailed. These services were published in the booklet, *Ministry to the Sick*, in the same format as ASB, and were available until the end of 1990. The issue of authorized alternatives to 1662 was now complete.

The task of editing the ASB was left to a small group of five people. First there was Keith Murgatroyd, the designer. Secondly there was Philip Haynes, an expert proof-reader who checked the text at every stage; he was a clergyman who before ordination had worked professionally with the Clarendon Press. Thirdly there was Robin Brookes, seconded from SPCK to supervise timetables and costings with the publishers and printers. Fourthly there was Geoffrey Cuming, who helped me on the editorial side and was invaluable in the thankless job of cross-checking. Finally I acted as general editor, attempting to solve everyone's queries, which seemed to come in almost daily. For music and pointing we were also glad of the help of Cyril Taylor. The book was long, the text was complicated, and time was all too short. The publishers insisted on having completed camera copy by 1 April 1980 if publication were to be possible in November; and in their turn the Queen's Printers required from us the first batches of typescript not later than the previous October. It was therefore imperative that this should be as perfect as possible. Keith Murgatroyd and I worked out each page individually, setting out on each typed sheet exactly what we wanted on each printed page, simply to ensure that facing pages and turnovers made sense. This involved a great deal of experiment; and we must at times have driven the Commission's secretary, Barbara Ebdale and her successor, Pamela Aldwinckle, to distraction. For months on end they typed away, producing immaculate work dead on schedule. At times the pressures were considerable. Great credit was due both to the 'back-room' team and to the Queen's Printers that we completed the entire operation only two days behind schedule. At the end of the day, however, they had their own particular reward. The Design Council of Great Britain showed considerable interest in the ASB. They were impressed that the Church should have considered the technical aspects of design so carefully; in the world of commerce and industry this was quite unique, and they regarded the book as a piece of specialist printing and design of high order. Consequently in November 1980 the Council staged an exhibition of ASB material at the Design Centre, allowing it to share the main area with the new version of the British Leyland Mini.

Sadly, as publication day approached, the hostile campaign against the book continued unabated. The Prayer Book Society appeared to be in no way appeased either by the courteous reply to their petitions or by a constructive comment from the Bishop of Durham. He told the General Synod:

> Many rude things were said in the orange-covered book about us and about our liturgies, but I see no value in being rude or dismissive in return. It seems to me that a Christian gathering ought to listen very hard to those who speak to it out of great emotion, even if we believe that emotion is misdirected. It ought to be especially concerned with those on the very fringes of the Church's life and not dismiss them as not being allowed to have a say in our affairs.[68]

It was most unfortunate that such a bitter note was sounded at a time when others experienced a feeling of genuine excitement. There were programmes on radio and television; the publishers went to town with their advertising, hailing it as 'the major publishing event in the Church of England since 1662'; and even the new Archbishop of Canterbury, Dr Robert Runcie, was moved to claim, 'We stand at a point where the heroic age of constitutional and liturgical change is over.'[69]

The Alternative Service Book was finally published on 10 November and was used in Westminster Abbey two days later at the opening service of the newly elected General Synod in the presence of Her Majesty the Queen. Almost every diocese celebrated the occasion with some special event; and the enthusiasm which greeted its appearance exceeded expectations. The publishers had initially produced half a million copies; but reprinting had already begun before publication day. It was now time for me to depart. When Michael Ramsey and Donald Coggan had asked me in 1965 to become chairman of the Liturgical Commission and finish the job, none of us had envisaged that it would take another fifteen years. But it was a commission I was proud to undertake, despite the fact that it altered the course of my future life. Moreover, it ended with a tangible result, something which had proved so elusive in many attempts at liturgical reform since the second half of the seventeenth century.

IV

The Preface to the ASB points out that for the first time since the Act of Uniformity the balance between the old and the new in the public worship of the Church of England is officially expressed in two books rather than in one.[70] The new book has broken a mould which had survived for three and a half centuries, and it has done so by a process of supplementation. Furthermore, the inclusion of the date 1980 in its title marks it as the product of a particular period and culture, indicating that worship is an element in the life of the Church subject to change.[71] At some stage, hopefully in less than another 350 years, it will in its turn be superseded or supplemented by another revision. The form that the latter will take is anyone's guess.

Meanwhile 1662 remains; and although its use is limited, it still retains authority as a standard of Anglican doctrine, regarded with affection and gratitude by many. At the moment it is still the service book most familiar to those people on the fringes of the Church, although it may not remain so indefinitely. In June 1980 there was a Gallup Poll of 1178 people claiming to be members of the Church of England, of whom 52% said they would be 'very unhappy' or 'mildly unhappy' at the adoption of new services in their church, while 42% admitted that their churchgoing really amounted to 'at least once or twice a year'. John Whale commented in *The Sunday Times* (26 October 1980), 'In general the petitions [i.e. to the General Synod in 1979] and the poll looked like a declaration by people who seldom went to church that they expected to find things unchanged when they did.'[72] He went on to say that if the Church of England wanted to lay claim to being a national institution, she must pay attention to casual voices, even if they were partially informed. But it is not *just* the casual worshipper who must be considered. A traditional element in the Church of England must not be regarded as a freak; it is precisely what one should expect to find. Liturgy, flexible and changing though it may be, also has a tendency — a wholesome tendency — to retain features created by earlier generations. It is therefore not surprising that some worshippers find the traditional, familiar element more welcome and reassuring than anything new.

The ASB is not the answer to every spiritual need in the Church of England, nor does it claim to be: as the Preface rightly says, 'The Gospel of the living Christ is too rich in content and the spiritual needs of his people are too diverse, for a single form of worship to suffice.'[73] This, of course, is recognized by the Canons of the Church, for they provide for forms of service to meet local and special needs as well as those in the official book and booklets. It was this kind of service which the Liturgical Commission tried to promote in its report on Family and Evangelistic Services in 1967;[74] and while the official response to the proposals was fairly muted at the time, the need has been recognized again by the Archbishop of Canterbury's Commission on Urban Priority Areas. In its report *Faith in the City* (1985) it argued that in such areas something radically different from the ASB was needed. 'To give people a 1,300 page ASB is a symptom of the gulf between the Church and ordinary people in the Urban Priority Areas.'[75] For all its flexibility, the ASB was still insufficient to meet all the requirements of a Church which was, or should be, missionary minded; the needs it fulfilled were frankly limited. 'Many Churches convey an attitude of spirituality which makes prayer and worship available only to those who turn up at the right place at the right time and go through the correct motions from start to finish.' Something more was needed, something less structured and more radical; but something demanding imaginative leadership, special kinds of expertise, and careful study and training. 'We have heard calls for short functional service booklets or cards, prepared by people who will always ask if all the words are really necessary.' Nevertheless, 'worship which encourages informality and spontaneity will not dispense with care and preparation. The local UPA Church will be as concerned with the beauty of worship and its excellence as are often the local schools with their productions.'[76] The report therefore argued that in this field of informal and spontaneous acts of worship and witness, the work of liturgical reform had only just begun, and consequently urged the Liturgical Commission to give it urgent attention. Happily the General Synod has also recognized this need, and in its 1985 report, *The Worship of the Church*, suggested that the future tasks of the Commission should include not only the monitoring of the rites in the ASB but also the consideration of such questions as language and the liturgical dimensions of doctrine, discipline, ecumenism and mission.[77]

Much of such study will obviously affect the pattern and contents of any future Service Book as well as forms of service outside it. I have always regarded the ASB as a pioneering work, a catalyst, a necessary step towards the creation of something even better. It should stimulate work in a variety of directions: as Leslie Houlden had commented in 1974, liturgists should widen their horizons and enlist men of other crafts, both within the traditional frontiers of theological study and outside them, to enable God's people to express themselves wholeheartedly in worship.[78] Some years ago Joseph Gelineau expressed a similar view of the revised Roman Catholic rites: he regarded them as incomplete, simply stepping-stones towards further change, and he described the task facing his Church in graphic terms:

> Our explanatory and moralizing liturgy needs figures whose very mystery is our hope, metaphors that surprise us and lead us on (where?), poetry which 'means nothing' but makes us think and imagine (what?), music which does not give us information but which moves us (how?) and the gesture which commits us (to what and to whom?)[79]

We could be forgiven for thinking such a programme daunting. Yet we must face the fact that the liturgy is a changing element in the life of the Church, will never be absolutely perfect and will always present us with tensions. What we need is the grace of God to persevere and to hope. So says the ASB Preface:

> Words, even agreed words, are only the beginning of worship. Those who use them do well to recognize their transience and imperfection; to treat them as a ladder, not a goal; to acknowledge their power in shaping faith and kindling devotion, without claiming that they are fully adequate to the task. Only the grace of God can make up what is lacking in the faltering words of men.[80]

Thomas à Kempis, the fifteenth-century devotional writer, spoke of institutional religion or worship as having two eyes, one looking on Time and one looking on Eternity — a truth expressed more recently by Evelyn Underhill as 'perpetually bringing into a touching association the unchanging Majesty of God and the little changing insights and desires of men, with their close dependence on the life of sense'.[81] This is where the tensions come in: people are so different and their world keeps on changing, while God can only be seen through a glass darkly — anything we say about him can only be inadequate. It is not surprising that we find difficulty in keeping both eyes properly focused. But one thing is clear: different people respond to God in different ways. Conformity to a single liturgy with few alternatives — the 1662 pattern — is inadequate both for the Church of England and for the wider Anglican Communion. To say this in no way denies the great service 1662 has given to the Church over the years; it is a wonderful book and it is undeniably great literature. But Anglican worshippers now see things differently. A new concept first found expression at the 1958 Lambeth Conference[82] and has subsequently been endorsed. A group of Anglican primates, for example, meeting in Kenya in 1983, studied the question, 'How does the Anglican Communion retain its traditional sense of unity?': and while they accepted that 1662 could be recognized as one of the agencies by which the ethos of Anglicanism had been maintained in the Anglican Communion, it was nevertheless only one. Furthermore its influence had not been and was not uniform. 'We would suggest that historically 1662 and its influence upon different parts of the Anglican world has varied greatly, and the constraints imposed by 1662 forms have been set aside in different degrees and at different times without the local Churches becoming any less Anglican in ethos and outlook.' They went on to express the view that 'Anglicanism in liturgy is exemplified by an ordered freedom and a limited diversity which have produced a balance and restraint which increasingly, over the centuries, seem to conform to and express a psychological outlook, that would appear able to transcend the differences in varied racial and cultural characteristics'.[83] That certainly would appear to be the position now accepted in the Church of England and it is a position slowly learned over a long period of time.

Here, then, was the first important achievement of the ASB. Despite its imperfections it helped to broaden the basis of the worship of the Church of England, providing the main alternative to 1662. In its turn it was supplemented by other Series 1 and Series 2 material, together with the provision for meeting local and special needs. Secondly, it provided evidence of a significant development in the ecumenical movement, possibly the most important to take place for a long time. While schemes for organic unity wended their weary and often unproductive way, Churches have been ready to grow together in their worship, using each other's material and sharing each other's insights. Only a small fraction of the ASB is distinctively and peculiarly 'Church of England': and it has done a great deal to transcend the barriers of 'party' churchmanship within the Church of England. The business of praying together has now taken a great step forward; and so has the business of thinking together. We return to the old adage, 'Lex orandi – lex credendi'. There is today widespread agreement that no single approach to theology can claim absolute priority over all others; and relevant to this point was the comment of Maurice Wiles in his contribution to the Doctrine Commission's essays on *Thinking about the Eucharist* as long ago as 1972: 'We need perhaps to become less concerned with drawing boundaries of what is or is not a genuine Eucharist and more ready to ask in what varied ways we can today give expression to that rich range of religious reality which is offered to us in the whole eucharistic tradition.'[84] Thirdly the work of creating the ASB stimulated local interest in liturgical matters to a considerable degree. For a quarter of a century there was intense public discussion of the liturgy, sparked off by the almost continuous debates in the General Synod and its predecessors. It stimulated the laity, encouraging them to take a more active role in public worship. Much that is regarded as common practice today: the reading of lessons, the leading of prayers and the distribution of the consecrated elements at the Eucharist by members of the congregation, were almost unknown even as recently as 1960. This is not to say that mistakes were not made on the way; and some of the decisions made by the General Synod were to be regretted.[85] But responsible people were not slow to point out weaknesses in the system; and hopefully even better ways will be found for the future.[86] However, healthy widespread interest must be based on solid foundations. Activities such as expert training in the leading of public worship or cross-fertilization with other disciplines require in the first instance study at the highest level. Here, sadly, the Churches in this country are at a disadvantage. Few universities bother to include liturgy as a major element in their theological studies and many ignore it altogether. Any kind of Liturgical Institute with a full-time staff of scholars just does not exist. Dom Gregory Dix commented some fifty years ago that liturgy was trapped in a kind of whirlpool, with too few scholars chasing too few books around and around in a vicious never-ending circle. That situation still exists today.

But it will not do to end this study on a depressing note. Hopefully, therefore, I suggest a few ideals for the future, drawn in part from the great master himself, Thomas Cranmer. The first is that liturgy must be produced for its own time. In his Preface to the *Great Bible* in 1540 Cranmer defended the principle of fresh writing to keep language relevant and contemporary; and he criticized those people who took offence because they were presented with something new or different.

> Such is the nature of custom, that it causeth us to bear all things well and easily, wherewith we have been accustomed, and to be offended with all things thereunto contrary . . . But such as will persist in their wilfulness, I

> must needs judge, not only foolish, froward, and obstinate, but also peevish, perverse and indurate.[87]

There was no merit in reverence for what was ancient, simply because it was ancient. In dealing with the Latin Processional, he had no hesitation, when finding it 'barren . . . and little fruitful', to make changes, using more than the liberty of a translator, 'because I thought I had better matter for the purpose'.[88] A liturgist must have the strength of his own convictions and do what he believes to be right. Every generation has the right, even the duty, to make its own contribution to the Church's liturgy, however modest that contribution may be.

Then again, in his final imprisonment, Cranmer wrote to Queen Mary, deploring the reimposition of Latin and reminding her of the Pauline dictum 'that when the people be gathered together, people should use such language as the people may understand and take profit thereby'.[89] That was not merely a plea for the use of the vernacular. It was also a plea that liturgy should be comprehensible and should have purpose. It should not only communicate but should produce in worshippers the necessary response: contrition and a change of heart from the Confession, assent and commitment from the Creed, thanksgiving from the eucharistic prayer, love and action from the Intercessions. Indeed, the liturgy is much more practical and urgent than simply preserving a particular intellectual or cultural image. That in itself may not be a bad thing; but there are certainly other considerations which are more important. Which would we rather have, words which a composer finds delightful to set to music, or words which drive worshippers out to help those for whom Christ died? Hopefully some words will fulfil both functions; that would be ideal. But we do not live in an ideal world: and if we have to choose, what then? 1662 and the ASB alone are simply not enough.

Even so, liturgy should strive to be evocative, expressing in word and action, albeit inadequately, that which is really inexpressible. Here is the eye which looks on Eternity. The important element in our liturgy is God himself: it is he whom we worship, not the words or the music or the actions. Yet these are the things which we must use, daily, year in year out. They must be sufficiently durable to bear endless repetition and in so doing to become for us, through familiar patterns of sound and action, an expression of the sacred and the holy. What demands are made upon the liturgy! Small wonder that it produces tensions and that we are never satisfied with it. So we must keep our sense of proportion, never forgetting that the liturgy is the ladder, not the goal. Once again I must quote Evelyn Underhill, for she expresses it so well:

> It is for the Prayer Book to keep as close as may be to the living and growing soul of the Church; not for that living and growing soul to make a virtue of keeping close to a Static Book . . . It is part of the domestic

> apparatus of the household of faith; *a means of promoting and directing that corporate adoration of God, which is the essence of institutional religion.* At best it represents good family customs, to be respected rather than slavishly conserved . . . As the body is more than raiment, so living religion is more than the forms – even the loveliest, most venerable and most significant forms – in which it is expressed.[90]

Nor must we forget that the ladder of the liturgy must be climbed. Effort is required on the part of the worshipper. A criticism often heard of the ASB is that its language is flat, that it lacks the sense of the numinous, and that it bears no comparison with 1662. Granted that 1662 is great literature, created in an age of literary giants; and granted that the ASB is the child of an age which is not one of the golden periods of English literature, and our standard style is low-keyed. But use the ASB with love and imagination, work hard at it, and it can still attain great heights. Let the last word come from a former member of the Liturgical Commission, James Kinsley, and himself an eminent English scholar:

> It is clear, after years of experiment with the new eucharistic rite and other main services in congregations large and small, that here *is* a vehicle which is able to sustain liturgical drama of a high order – *provided* that the clergy work imaginatively with it and do not read it as though it were a shopping-list. What we have in ASB . . . is great or moving substance indeed. *But we have to create* from ASB in phrasing, emphasis, and variety, what we have been accustomed to feel in our early literature: a surge of music, of profound feeling rhythmically expressed, which carries the substance on and up to almost unbearable climaxes.[91]

As we eat and drink these holy gifts
in the presence of your divine majesty,
renew us by your Spirit,
inspire us with your love,
and unite us in the body of your Son,
Jesus Christ our Lord.

Through him, and with him, and in him,
by the power of the Holy Spirit,
with all who stand before you in earth and heaven,
we worship you, Father almighty,
in songs of everlasting praise:
Blessing and honour and glory and power
be yours for ever and ever. Amen.

NOTES

1. R.C.D.J. to Michael Cantuar, 23 March 1971.
2. GS 161, *The Future Course of Liturgical Revision*, 1973, para. 10.
3. ibid., paras. 11–13.
4. ibid., paras. 14–18, 21–2, 28.
5. ibid., paras. 31–4.
6. *GS Proceedings* 1973, vol. 4, pp. 354–72.
7. This was done with the expert advice and help of the Statistical Unit of the Central Board of Finance.
8. GS 284, *An Alternative Service Book*, 1976, paras. 7, 14, 15, 22, 26, 28.
9. ibid., para. 42.
10. ibid., paras. 61, 66, 68, 69, 71.
11. ibid., para. 48.
12. For the whole debate, *GS Proceedings* 1976, vol. 7, pp. 605–45.
13. A small handful of people had already indicated a desire to retire: notably Cyril Bowles, Bishop of Derby, on account of increased episcopal commitments; and Leo Stephens-Hodge, on account of ill-health. The former, one of the Commission's founder members, had always been a great stabilizing influence; since 1969 he had been an invaluable link with the House of Bishops and since 1971 had been vice-chairman of the Commission. The latter, a quiet, scholarly Evangelical, had since 1969 done valuable work particularly on the collects and in helping Charles Whitaker with the Lectionary – a necessary but very wearisome task. David Frost also departed on his appointment to the Chair of English at Newcastle, Australia. For new arrivals, there was the welcome return of John Wilkinson from Jerusalem; Dr David Hope, a reputable Anglo-Catholic liturgical scholar; James Kinsley, Professor of English at Nottingham University who was also a clergyman; and two able members of the General Synod, Dr Diana McClatchey and the Reverend David Silk.
14. *LC Minutes* 88.93; 89.3; *LC Memorandum* 182.
15. *GS Proceedings* 1977, vol. 8, pp. 208–22, 960–81, 1030–33.
16. ibid., 1978, vol. 9, pp. 757–63.
17. GS 325, *The Alternative Service Book, Progress Report* 1977, paras. 19–28.
18. Statement by the Archbishop of Canterbury to the General Synod, 5 July 1977. *GS Proceedings* 1977, vol. 8, p. 488.
19. cf. p. 301; ibid., vol. 9, pp. 448–58.
20. ibid., pp. 459–72. The voting was 126–195.
21. ibid., vol. 10, pp. 686–7; 710–20.
22. ibid., pp. 1149–54, 1214–30.
23. ibid., p. 1266.
24. GS 284, *An Alternative Service Book*, p. 4, para. 3.
25. See for example: Ian Robinson, *The Survival of English*, 1973; and articles in *Theology*: Richard Harries, 'Alternative Services: the Test of Practice' (LXXIX, July 1976, pp. 221–6); David Cockerell, 'Liturgical Language' (LXXX, March 1977, pp. 110–16); Derek Brewer, 'Liturgy: Need and Frustration' (LXXX, May 1977, pp. 173–7); Stephen Prickett, 'What do the Translators think they are up to?' (LXXX, Nov. 1977, pp. 403–10). The Prayer Book Society had developed from the Book of Common Prayer Action Group in 1975.
26. T. G. A. Baker, *Questioning Worship*, 1976, especially pp. 10–19.
27. R. T. Beckwith, 'The Approaching Revision of Series Three', *The Churchman*, November 1976, pp. 289–93.

28. GS 364, *Holy Communion Series 3 Revised*, 1978, report by the Liturgical Commission, p. 5.
29. The text and a brief commentary can be found in R. C. D. Jasper, ed., *The Daily Office Revised*, 1978, pp. 11–13.
30. GS 364, pp. 27–30; *LC Memoranda* 145 I and J.
31. cf. pp. 297–8.
32. The Sub-Committee were: Bishops – Chichester (chairman), Southwell, Jarrow, Kingston; Liturgical Commission – Colin Buchanan, Geoffrey Cuming, David Silk and R.C.D.J.
33. GS 364, pp. 8, 20.
34. GS *Proceedings*, 1978, vol. 9, p. 707.
35. ibid., pp. 707–37.
36. GS 364X, *Report of the Revision Committee*, 1979, paras. 2–3.
37. Colin Buchanan, *Latest Liturgical Revision in the Church of England 1978–1984* (Grove Liturgical Study No. 39), 1984, p. 9.
38. cf. p. 311.
39. GS 364X, para. 136.
40. cf. pp. 251–60.
41. ibid., para, 187.
42. ibid., para. 285.
43. GS *Proceedings*, 1979, vol. 10, pp. 158–9.
44. ibid., vol. 10, pp. 139–45.
45. ibid., vol. 10, pp. 170–239, 302–33, 432–75, 635–83, 794–832, 881–912.
46. ibid., pp. 909–10.
47. ibid., p. 911.
48. *P.N.Review* is an abbreviation for *Public Nation Review*: the figure 13 is unexplained. It was published in Manchester and claimed to have financial assistance from the Arts Council of Great Britain.
49. *P.N.Review 13*, p. 2. Compare his article of March 1979, 'Profane Habit and Sacred Usage', in *Theology*, LXXXII, pp. 83–95.
50. ibid., pp. 51–63.
51. GS *Proceedings*, 1979, vol. 10, pp. 1104–28; 1980, vol. 11, pp. 68–70. The final voting was: Bishops 33–4; Clergy 207–10; Laity 150–23.
52. ibid., vol. 10, pp. 880–1, 1128–42, 1302–3, 1303–4; *Report of the Revision Committee*, GS 405X.
53. GS 284, paras. 23–4, p. 12.
54. He felt that it should be done on an ecumenical basis as a long-term project – something which is now apparently happening.
55. GS *Proceedings*, 1978, vol. 9, pp. 65–71.
56. ibid., vol. 9, pp. 737–57, 766. This version, originally a venture of the American Bible Society, was given an English edition in 1976 with the co-operation of the British and Foreign Bible Society and the National Bible Society of Scotland.
57. The only exception was the Series 3 Ordinal. This was regarded as a special case, for there would be no great general demand for it; but every bishop was given a copy and he was free to make it available as he thought best.
58. Progress Report GS 325, para. 12.
59. Progress Report GS 413, paras. 17–20.
60. Working Party Report GS 284, para. 29.
61. GS *Proceedings*, 1977, vol. 8, p. 876.
62. ibid., 1979, vol. 10, pp. 1230–5, 1303–4. In the final vote there were only three dissentients: Bishops 13–0; Clergy 107–1; Laity 105–2.
63. ibid., 1980, vol. 11, pp. 577–98.

64. ibid., 1979, vol. 10, pp. 1142–9; 1980, vol. 11, pp. 598–600, 748–9. The final vote must have constituted a record in liturgical matters, with only one dissentient: Bishops 25–0; Clergy 123–0; Laity 134–1.
65. *LC Minutes* 88.89.
66. Report GS 472, 1980, p. 3. Information on the fate of these reports may be found in Colin Buchanan's *Later Liturgical Revision*, pp. 29–33.
67. The Communion rite was an abbreviation of the authorized rites in *ASB*, the short eucharistic prayer had been included in the Appendices of Rite A, and the propers for the Sick, the Dying and in Time of Trouble were also included.
68. GS *Proceedings*, 1979, vol. 10, p. 1232. A high point in the Prayer Book Society's literature in 1980 was a symposium of essays entitled *Ritual Murder*, edited by Brian Morris. My letter was to *The Church Times*, 13 June 1980.
69. GS *Proceedings*, 1980, vol. 11, pp. 446–7.
70. The Preface was originally drafted by the Bishop of Durham and later worked over by the Liturgical Commission and the House of Bishops.
71. *ASB*, p. 9, para. 1.
72. It will be interesting to see how long the ASB is regarded as new and strange. Its familiarity should increase with the passage of time.
73. ibid., p. 9, para. 3.
74. cf. pp. 274–5.
75. *Faith in the City*, 1985, 3.39; 6.110.
76. ibid., 6.105, 110, 112.
77. ibid., 6.110; GS 698, *The Worship of the Church*, 1985.
78. See also his *Patterns of Faith*, 1977.
79. J. Gelineau, *The Liturgy Today and Tomorrow*, 1978, p. 100.
80. *ASB*, p. 11, para. 7.
81. E. Underhill, 'The Essentials of a Prayer Book', in *The New Prayer Book*, ed. H. M. Relton, 1927, p. 50.
82. cf. pp. 215–17.
83. Quoted in C. Buchanan, *Anglican Eucharistic Liturgy 1975–1985* (Grove Liturgical Study 41), 1985, pp. 30–2, especially paras. 4 and 8.
84. M. Wiles, 'Eucharistic Theology — the Value of Diversity' in *Thinking about the Eucharist*, essays by the Doctrine Commission, 1972, p. 122.
85. Two examples will suffice: 1. The tampering with the post-communion prayer by David Frost in Rite A, thus depriving it of one of its most telling symbols — the anchor as the symbol of hope, clearly recognized in the New Testament and the early Church, and well known more recently through Wesley's hymns. 2. The introduction of oil into the Initiation rites simply by rubric and without explanation and then the subsequent refusal to authorize the Blessing of the Oils, which at least would have helped; but it remains a 'dumb' ceremony.
86. Note the Bishop of Winchester and Colin Buchanan, pp. 353–4.
87. C. S. Meyer, *Cranmer's Selected Writings*, 1961, p. 2.
88. ibid., pp. 80–1.
89. ibid., pp. 90–1.
90. E. Underhill, op. cit., pp. 48–9. The italics are mine.
91. *The ASB Commentary by the Liturgical Commission*, 1980, pp. 167–8. James Kinsley, D.Litt., FBA, and a member of the Liturgical Commission 1976–80, was both a clergyman and Professor of English Studies at the University of Nottingham. He was editor of the Oxford English Novels and an authority on 17th- and 18th-century literature. The italics are mine.

Index